D0359505

PENGUIN BOOKS
THE BIG BOOK OF BLUES

Robert Santelli is a New Jersey–based music journalist whose
articles have appeared in *Rolling Stone, CD Review, The New York
Times, New Jersey Monthly,* and *The Asbury Park Press.* He is
the author of *Aquarius Rising, Sixties Rock: A Listener's Guide,*
and, with Max Weinberg, *The Big Beat: Conversations with
Rock's Greatest Drummers.*

11
5-97   x 12 2/98 12/99

CH

SAN DIEGO PUBLIC LIBRARY

COLLEGE HEIGHTS

ALWAYS BRING YOUR
CARD WITH YOU.

3/95
(4)

JUN 24 1994   GAYLORD

THE BIG BOOK OF BLUES

COLLEGE HEIGHTS BRANCH
SAN DIEGO PUBLIC LIBRARY

A BIOGRAPHICAL ENCYCLOPEDIA

ROBERT SANTELLI

3 1336 03436 3789

PENGUIN

PENGUIN BOOKS
Published by the Penguin Group
Penguin Books USA Inc., 375 Hudson Street,
New York, New York 10014, U.S.A.
Penguin Books Ltd, 27 Wrights Lane,
London W8 5TZ, England
Penguin Books Australia Ltd, Ringwood,
Victoria, Australia
Penguin Books Canada Ltd, 10 Alcorn Avenue,
Toronto, Ontario, Canada M4V 3B2
Penguin Books (N.Z.) Ltd, 182–190 Wairau Road,
Auckland 10, New Zealand

Penguin Books Ltd, Registered Offices:
Harmondsworth, Middlesex, England

First published in Penguin Books 1993

1 3 5 7 9 10 8 6 4 2

Copyright © Robert Santelli, 1993
All rights reserved

LIBRARY OF CONGRESS CATALOGING IN PUBLICATION DATA
Santelli, Robert.
The big book of blues: a biographical encyclopedia/Robert Santelli.
p. cm.
Includes index.
ISBN 0 14 01.5939 8
1. Blues musicians—Biography.   2. Blues musicians—Discography.
I. Title.
ML400.S227   1993
781.643′092′2—dc20
[B]   93–4127

Printed in the United States of America
Set in Postscript Times Roman
Designed by Ann Gold

Except in the United States of America, this
book is sold subject to the condition that it
shall not, by way of trade or otherwise, be lent,
re-sold, hired out, or otherwise circulated
without the publisher's prior consent in any form
of binding or cover other than that in which it
is published and without a similar condition
including this condition being imposed on the
subsequent purchaser.

FOR JAKE

"The blues? It's the mother
of American music. That's what it is—
the Source."   —B.B. King
                           Red Bank, N.J.
                           1992

ACKNOWLEDGMENTS

It took a whole lot of help from a whole lot of people—blues historians, librarians, fellow journalists, musicians, managers, record company people, friends, and family—to complete *The Big Book of Blues*. I owe all of them my heartfelt thanks and sincere appreciation. I hope *The Big Book of Blues* lives up to their expectations.

From the ranks of the many record companies that cater to the blues in one form or another, my gratitude goes out to Darrell Anderson (Hightone), Bing Broderick (Smithsonian-Folkways), Jennifer Dirkes and Bob Koester (Delmark), Lindsey Ellison (Rounder), Jerry Gordon (Evidence), Terri Hinte (Fantasy), Sally King (Antone's), Randy Labbe (Deluge), Marc Lipkin and Ken Morton (Alligator), Larry Lewis (Jewel), Bob Merlis (Warner Bros.), Andrew Seidenfeld (Shanachie), Joanne Sloan (Columbia-Legacy), Chris Strachwitz (Arhoolie), Helen Urriola (Ichiban), Pat Weaver (Mobile Fidelity Sound Lab), and Heather West (Black Top).

Thanks to Dan Morgenstern and the Institute of Jazz Studies at Rutgers University in Newark, New Jersey; the Delta Blues Museum in Clarksdale, Mississippi; Jonathan Miles and the rest of the staff at the Blues Archive at the University of Mississippi at Oxford; the Blues Foundation in Memphis, Tennessee; the Rhythm & Blues Foundation in Washington, D.C.; the Chicago Public Library; *Living Blues Magazine* (Oxford, Mississippi); the Smithsonian Institution; the Jersey Shore Jazz & Blues Foundation (Ocean Grove, New Jersey); and *The Asbury Park Press* (Neptune, New Jersey).

Thanks are due to all those musicians and music makers (producers, independent record company owners, etc.) who granted me interviews and helped supply much-needed information about themselves and their music or their fellow blues musicians: Buddy Ace, Johnny Adams, Billy Boy Arnold, Lynn August, Etta Baker, Marcia Ball, Booba Barnes, Lou Ann Barton, Carey Bell, Lurrie Bell, Fred Below, Buster Benton, Elvin Bishop, Bobby "Blue" Bland, Blues Boy Willie, Roy Book Binder, Billy Branch, Lonnie Brooks, Charles Brown, Mojo Buford, R.L. Burnside, Chris Cain, John Campbell, Bobby Charles, Jimmie and Jeannie Cheatham, Francis Clay, Gary B.B. Coleman, Albert Collins, Johnny Copeland, James Cotton, Willie Dixon, Dr. John, Ronnie Earl, Archie Edwards, David "Honeyboy" Edwards, Sue Foley, Lowell Fulson, Denny Freeman, Anson Funderburgh, Paul Geremia, Adam Gussow, Buddy Guy, Phil Guy, John Hammond, Jr., Johnny Heartsman, Erwin Helfer, Wendell Holmes, John Lee Hooker, John Jackson, Etta James, Luther "Houserocker" Johnson, Casey Jones, Danny Kalb, Albert King, B.B. King, Little Jimmy King, Al Kooper, Sam Lay, Chris

Layton, Frankie Lee, Little Charlie and the Night Cats, Robert Jr. Lockwood, Taj Mahal, Bob Margolin, Johnny Mars, Tina Mayfield, Larry McCray, Lillian McMurry, Jay Miller, David Myers, Louis Myers, Mark Naftalin, Raful Neal, Tracy Nelson, the Nighthawks, Darrell Nulisch, Odie Payne, Jr., Pinetop Perkins, Rod Piazza, Greg Piccolo, Jerry Portnoy, Bobby Radcliff, Sonny Rhodes, Jimmy Rogers, Roy Rogers, Otis Rush, Saffire: The Uppity Blues Women, Omar Shariff, Johnny Shines, Corky Siegel, Barkin' Bill Smith, Dave Specter, Angela Strehli, Koko Taylor, Melvin Taylor, Jimmy Thackery, Tabby Thomas, Ron Thompson, Stevie Ray Vaughan, Robert Ward, Katie Webster, Valerie Wellington, Junior Wells, Phil Wiggins, Kim Wilson, Mitch Woods, Marva Wright, Mighty Joe Young, and Zora Young.

Thanks also to Bruce Bastin, Michael Coats (Glodow & Coats Publicity), Larry Cohn (Columbia/Legacy Roots 'n' Blues series producer), Vera Daimwood (Mississippi Department of Economic & Community Development), Patrick Day (Day & Night Productions), Kathleen Finigan (Pegasus Productions), Jeff Hannausch, Michael Heatley, Steve Hecht, Tad Jones, Stephen LaVere, Gary Nesbit, Terri Reilly, Ben Sandmel, Mary Schmidt and Dawne Massey (Memphis Convention and Visitor's Bureau), Kat Stratton (Blue Cat Productions), Jeff Tamarkin (*Goldmine* magazine), and Dee Tango, typist extraordinarie.

A very extra special thanks must go to Bill Dahl (*Living Blues*), Ron Edwards (St. Louis Blues Society), Michael Frank (Earwig Records), Lee Hildebrand, Bruce Iglauer (Alligator Records), Daniel Jacoubovitch (Modern Blues Recordings), Peter Lee (Fat Possum Records), Chuck Nevitt (Dallas Blues Society), Jim O'Neal (Rooster Blues Records), Dick Shurman, and Richard Skelly (Jersey Shore Jazz & Blues Foundation) for reading portions of the manuscript and generously offering comments and corrections, as well as providing information and support via telephone calls and letters. Their help was invaluable.

Finally, I owe much to Eileen Rehbein and Eric Clarke of Almost Live CDs, the best CD store on the Jersey Shore, for getting me the blues discs I needed and for helping with record catalog information; to my agent, Sandy Choron, for setting up my relationship with Penguin, a great publishing house; to my editors at Penguin, Roger Devine and especially David Stanford, whose advice, guidance, patience, and friendship were much appreciated; and finally to my family—Cindy, my wife, and my three children, Jaron, Jenna, and Jake—all of whom understood just how important this book became to me over the three and a half years it took to write and research it and who provided the love and support necessary for me to finish it. Thanks and love to all of you.

Introduction

This is a book about the blues. More specifically, it's a book about the artists who have helped make the blues one of the richest and most enduring music forms in the American music treasury. It is intended to be a helpful and much-used reference book, a companion to your discovery of the blues; or, if you are already a veteran blues fan, a tool with which you might gain a broader view of the many artists who created this great body of music.

The Big Book of Blues is a biographical encyclopedia. There are more than six hundred entries in it; most of them sketch a blues artist's life and career and include a succinct examination of the contributions he or she has made to the form. A few entries profile significant blues and blues-based bands. An artist who began his career as a member of a band and later achieved fame as a soloist or became a prominent studio musician or sideman may have a separate biographical listing in addition to being included in the band entry. A name in SMALL CAPITALS indicates a separate entry for the artist elsewhere in the book. A list of recordings appears after each biographical entry. Not by any means meant to be a full discography, each "Essential Listening" list is comprised of those albums that are, well, essential to gaining an understanding and appreciation of each artist's work and blues slant.

At the very beginning of this project I was confronted with a fundamental problem: how to define *the blues*. The strictest interpretation of the form would have meant a leaner book: Some previous authors of blues books have limited themselves to African-American blues artists. I decided to include both black and white American bluesmen and -women, as well as important British artists in the book.

The blues was born out of the African-American experience in this country, principally in the South in the early part of this century. But some white blues musicians, especially those from the 1960s on, have made notable contributions to the music and ought not to be deleted from the book merely because of their skin color. I can't imagine *The Big Book of Blues* not including, for instance, Paul Butterfield, Charlie Musselwhite, Johnny Winter, and Stevie Ray Vaughan, or, for that matter, Eric Clapton and John Mayall.

Though British by birth, Clapton and Mayall have indeed had an impact on the blues and deserve recognition, as do other important English bluesmen. And as for white American artists like Winter or the late Stevie Ray Vaughan, it's safe to say that without their input, the blues revival that's currently going in pop music might not have happened at all.

Because there are no hard lines separating blues from rhythm & blues, soul-blues, gospel-blues, boogie-woogie, blues-based swing, the earliest rock & roll, and blues-rock, I've also included the major artists and bands who were or are prominent in these blues hybrids. This might offend some purists, but I decided to be thorough and provide as broad a picture of the blues as possible.

But the bulk of the book is about true blues. All blues idioms—first-generation country blues, jug-band music and the songster style, the classic blues of the 1920s, Mississippi Delta blues, Piedmont and East Coast blues, Texas blues, Memphis blues, St. Louis blues, pre- and postwar Chicago blues, Detroit blues, West Coast blues, the modern blues of the 1960s, the postmodern scene, and contemporary blues—are represented by their major artists, and many of their minor and lesser-known ones.

When I began *The Big Book of Blues* I felt I already knew much about the history of the music, and I estimated that this biographical encyclopedia would include some 350 entries. The number proved to be closer to 650. My research showed me that there are far more blues artists who have contributed in some way to the music since its birth nearly a century ago than I originally thought. Researching the lives and music of these men and women was, for me, like taking a graduate course in Advanced Blues History. I doubt this is anything like the final word, but I hope *The Big Book of Blues* will help fans and students of the blues better understand the music and the many artists who have made it such an emotionally rich and vibrant form.

In preparing these biographical sketches I wanted to go beyond the database feel of many music-reference books that merely record basic biographical information and notable achievements strung together in short phrases with semicolons and no sense of narrative. I wanted the entries to be concise, yet interesting and fun to read. Only you, the reader, will know whether I've succeeded or not.

The information I used to write this book came from a wide variety of sources. As is the case with most encyclopedias, much of the material used to compose the biographical sketches was taken from secondary sources (see the bibliography at the end of this book). Great works in blues literature such as Sheldon Harris's *Blues Who's Who*, Robert Palmer's *Deep Blues*, Mike Rowe's *Chicago Blues*, Bruce Bastin's *Red River Blues*, Paul Oliver's *The Meaning of the Blues*, David Evans's *Big Road Blues*, Peter Guralnick's *The Listener's Guide to the Blues*, and the *Blackwell Guide to Recorded Blues*, to name just some, were simply invaluable, as were the many excellent articles contained in such periodicals as *Living Blues, Juke Blues, Blues and Rhythm*, and *Goldmine*.

I greatly appreciate the pioneering work done by these dedicated blues historians. They were some of the first blues writers and researchers to experience the time-consuming, often tedious process of poring through birth records, old newspapers and magazines, and record-company files in a quest to document blues history. Without them and their much-admired work, *The Big Book of Blues* would not exist.

In addition to culling information from previously published sources, I also conducted interviews with well over a hundred artists, (some of whom, I'm sad to say, are now deceased), in order to gain additional information about their lives and music and of other artists with whom they were familiar. Tracking down some of these bluesmen and -women often proved to be difficult, as was the search to confirm and follow up on the stories they told.

I spent many hours going through the blues files at the Institute of Jazz Studies on the Rutgers University campus in Newark, New Jersey, which, fortunately, is but twenty minutes from my home. I made two trips to the Blues Archives at the University of Mississippi in Oxford, plus a pair of extended trips to both Chicago and Memphis, and one to San Francisco, not to mention numerous excursions into New York City—all in the name of blues research.

As any blues historian or journalist can attest, obtaining accurate information on blues artists and their careers can be a frustrating or seemingly impossible task. This is especially true when dealing with pre–World War II artists. In a few instances, even something as mundane as a birthdate is unverifiable because a birth certificate might not exist or has never been found. Whenever I ran into such a situation, I went with the birthdate and birthplace that was most frequently listed in the sources at hand. The same was done for an artist's death date and place of death and key aspects of his or her recording career and life.

Despite my attempt to make *The Big Book of Blues* as complete as possible, not every blues artist who ever played a blues progression, sang a blues tune, or made a blues record is included here. If an artist is not included and should be, it's probably because I couldn't find enough information to create a meaningful biographical sketch. The sketches are also not entirely objective. One of my goals was to assess each artist's contribution to the blues and his or her place in blues history, which required making judgments based on what I have been able to learn. Others may have more or new information, and I welcome correspondence, corrections, and criticism.

This book comes out at an awkward time because so many previously out-of-print blues albums, both foreign and domestic, are now becoming increasing available on compact disc. If there is a startling omission in the "Essential Listening" list following a biographical sketch, it's probably because the album in question is still out-of-print or in the process of going back into print. To list in the book all vinyl released by each artist would perhaps have been valuable to the blues record collector but not the general fan, to whom this book is addressed. I leave that task to another author, one with the perseverance and skill required to present a complete discography. My attention is on the works that are currently and readily available.

Most of the recordings cited here are distributed by U.S. record companies and can be purchased at mainstream music stores. In some cases, however, recordings listed have been issued by European labels or even Japanese companies. These recordings will generally be more difficult for fans to find, but the reality is that the Europeans especially have done a masterful job of rereleasing old blues gems by many blues masters. That's why a number of European imports must be viewed as crucial—they are recordings with which one must be familiar to comprehend and appreciate a particular artist's work.

Researching and writing this book took a great deal of time and energy. In truth, it was a labor of love. As a music journalist, I have written extensively in many publications, not only about the blues, but about rock, jazz, and reggae as well. As a fan, I have spent countless hours listening to music from those three genres. Yet, in the end, it's the blues to which I always return, each time with a greater appreciation and emotional attachment to the music than in the past. Maybe it's because without the blues we wouldn't have rock, jazz, or reggae— or funk or rap, either. The blues is the foundation of America's pop music legacy. It is the music form that has spawned so many other forms. For me it's impossible to think of American pop music without thinking of the blues first.

But my personal relationship with the blues goes even deeper than this. To me the blues, in its many shades and offshoots, says more about the human spirit, more about the soul, more about life itself, than any other music I know. I love its raw honesty, its simplicity (although not all blues forms are simple in structure), its passion, its culture, its folk-music–like qualities, and its ability to reinvent itself again and again.

Maybe Mississippi Fred McDowell said it best more than twenty years ago backstage at the Philadelphia Folk Festival. ''The blues,'' he explained to me, ''it jus' keeps goin' on, goin' on. Kill the blues and what have you got left? Nothin'. Know why? 'Cause the blues is the story of life and the spice of life. You get what I'm sayin'?''

I did. And I still do. I hope you do, too.

—Robert Santelli

THE BIG BOOK OF BLUES

A.

◄ ACES, THE

(aka the Four Aces, the Nightcats, the Jukes) Original members: Louis Myers (guitar, harmonica, vocals) (born September 18, 1929, Byhalia, Miss.); David Myers (guitar, bass, vocals) (born October 30, 1926, Byhalia, Miss.); Junior Wells (harmonica, vocals) (born December 9, 1934, Memphis, Tenn.); Fred Below (drums) (born September 16, 1926, Chicago, Ill.; died August 13, 1988, Chicago, Ill.)

The Aces was one of the earliest and most influential of the electric Chicago blues bands. In the early 1950s the group's only rival was the MUDDY WATERS Band. Fronted first by JUNIOR WELLS and then LITTLE WALTER Jacobs, two of Chicago's most expressive harmonica players, the group's nucleus was comprised of brothers LOUIS and DAVID MYERS on guitars and drummer FRED BELOW.

Rather than play the blues using slow, drawn-out tempos and riffs inspired by the rural sounds of the Mississippi Delta—the kind Waters and his band often preferred—the Aces employed urban-flavored shuffle rhythms and a sharper sense of swing, which gave their blues a clipped and more rhythmically driven sound. Under Little Walter's leadership, the Aces toured regularly and, in some instances, was the first band to introduce the biting, electrified sound of Chicago blues to an area. Also, many of Little Walter's most memorable Checker (Chess) recordings and post–Muddy Waters performances were made with the Aces (then known as the Jukes or Nightcats) or a version of the group.

The Aces began in 1950 as an extention of an earlier band, the Little Boys, which eventually became known as the Three Deuces (the Myers brothers and Junior Wells). The group played house-rent parties on Chicago's South Side and occasional club dates. Eventually the trio changed its name to the Three Aces. When Below joined the band in 1950, the Three Aces became simply the Aces.

Junior Wells left the Aces in 1952. He was replaced by Little Walter. (Walter had left the Muddy Waters band after his solo record, "Juke," made it to number one on the R&B charts that year.) Ironically, Wells was hired to take his place in the Muddy Waters band. Little Walter was a superb harp player, but he left a lot to be desired as a bandleader. Under his reign, ego and money squabbles took their toll on the band; by 1954 the Aces' framework had begun to disintegrate. That year Louis Myers left the band and was replaced by guitarist ROBERT JR. LOCKWOOD. Brother David quit in 1955, and was replaced by LUTHER TUCKER. Below also quit that year, leaving no original member left in the group.

Over the years members of the original Aces have reunited on numerous occasions. In the 1970s, the group recorded and toured in Europe, where it developed a loyal following. It also performed at the Chicago Blues Festival and in the city's leading blues clubs, thus ensuring that the band's legacy lived on.

Essential Listening:
The Best of Little Walter/MCA-Chess (CHD 9192)
The Best of Little Walter, Volume Two/MCA-Chess (CHD 9292)
Kings of Chicago Blues, Volume One/Vogue (LDM 3017)
Steady Rollin' Man (Robert Jr. Lockwood)/Delmark (DD 630)

◄ ACE, BUDDY

(aka The Silver Fox of the Blues) (born Jimmy Land, November 11, 1936, Jasper, Tex.)

A rhythm & blues balladeer whose vocal style is lined with gospel and blues strains, Buddy Ace grew up in Houston, Texas, where he performed in gospel groups with fellow singer Joe Tex. Influenced by rhythm & blues artists such as Lou Rawls, BOBBY "BLUE" BLAND, and IVORY JOE HUNTER, Ace moved out of gospel and into R&B in the early 1950s. He toured Texas and other parts of the Southwest with Bland and JUNIOR PARKER, and in 1955 signed a recording contract with Duke-Peacock Records. Ace remained with Duke some fifteen years despite marginal commercial success.

Ace moved to Los Angeles in 1959 and did some recording for Specialty Records, but returned to Houston two years later to work with Parker and Joe Hinton. Ace recorded his two best-known singles on the Duke label in the mid-'60s. "Nothing in the World Can Hurt Me (Except You)" was released in 1966 and made it to number 25 on the R&B charts. "Hold On (To This Old Fool)" followed in 1967.

In 1970 Ace moved back to Los Angeles; ten years later he moved up the California coast to Oakland where he became a regular on the Bay Area's soul-blues circuit. Ace moved to Sacramento in 1987, but often returned to Texas to perform. In 1991 he toured Germany and released his first album, *Don't Hurt No More*, on the EveJim label. He continues to record and perform.

Essential Listening:
Don't Hurt No More/EveJim Records (2018)

◄ ACE, JOHNNY

(born John Alexander, June 9, 1929, Memphis, Tenn.; died December 25, 1954, Houston, Tex.)

Johnny Ace was a gifted rhythm & blues singer whose tragic death has long overshadowed his music. Ace died Christmas night 1954 backstage at the Houston City Auditorium. During intermission at a show there that featured him and blues singer BIG MAMA THORNTON, Ace jokingly put a pistol to his head and fired. The only bullet in the revolver killed him instantly.

Born and raised in Memphis, Ace served in the U.S. Navy during World War II. After the war he became part of Memphis's Beale Street scene, performing as both a singer and piano player in clubs there with BOBBY "BLUE" BLAND, B.B. KING, and others. In the late 1940s Ace was a member of the Beale Streeters, a loosely formed group that included Bland, pianist ROSCO GORDON, and drummer Earl Forest.

Ace's smooth, plaintive croon led Duke Records to offer him a recording contract in 1952. Although his career was short, he recorded a batch of R&B hits for Duke, including two number-1 tunes "My Song" (1952) and "The Clock" (1953), along with "Cross My Heart," "Saving My Love for You," "Please Forgive Me," and "Never Let Go," all of which were top-10 hits in 1953 and 1954. "Pledging My Love," Ace's biggest hit, was released posthumously in 1955. It topped the R&B charts and even made it to number 17 on the pop charts. "Pledging My Love" was the most popular rhythm & blues record of the year; its success helped introduce black R&B to white audiences.

Essential Listening:
Johnny Ace Memorial Album/MCA (27014)

◄ ADAMS, FAYE

(born Faye Tuell, c. 1932, Newark, N.J.)

Faye Adams was a female blues and rhythm & blues singer who is best remembered for her three Herald hits, "Shake a Hand" and "I'll Be True," both of which made it to number 1 on the R&B charts in 1953, and "Hurts Me to My Heart," which made it to the top slot in 1954.

Adams's vocal style, like many other blues shouters of the period, was built from her experience singing gospel as a youth. Adams and two of her sisters sang as the Tuell Sisters in Newark, New Jersey, churches and on a local Newark radio station, where they had their own gospel program. Adams eventually shifted from gospel to blues and rhythm & blues. She sang in Newark and New York clubs as Faye Scruggs after marrying Tommy Scruggs in 1942. Her break came when she joined Joe Morris's Blues Cavalcade in 1952, replacing Little Laurie Tate. Her debut recording with Morris and the Blues Cavalcade, "I'm Going to Leave You," was released on the Atlantic label in 1953. When Morris's contract with Atlantic expired later that year, Scruggs and Morris signed a recording contract with the Herald label, and Scruggs changed her name to Adams. Although she scored with three number-1 singles in 1953 and 1954 and toured with the Top Ten Rhythm & Blues show in 1955, Adams began to fade from the R&B scene with the advent of rock and roll. In 1957 she left Herald and signed with Imperial Records, with whom she had a minor hit with "Keeper of My Heart." Adams also recorded for the Lido, Warwick, Savoy, and Prestige labels in the early 1960s before returning to gospel music and the church. Adams still lives in New Jersey.

Essential Listening:
Shake a Hand—Golden Classics/Collectables (Col 5122)

◄ ADAMS, JOHNNY

(born Lathan John Adams, January 5, 1932, New Orleans, La.)

Johnny Adams is a New Orleans rhythm & blues singer whose wide vocal range, falsetto rises, and soulful, velvety tones have earned him the nicknames "The Tan Canary" and "The Tan Nightingale." Adams toiled for years in relative obscurity until releasing a series of acclaimed albums on the Rounder label in the 1980s.

He began his career as a gospel singer, performing with such New Orleans groups as the Soul Revivers and Bessie Griffen and the Soul Consolators. In 1959 he turned to rhythm & blues and signed a recording contract with Ric/Ron Records. His first single was "I Won't Cry," which was popular in New Orleans but failed to make the national R&B charts. Adams placed only one single on the R&B charts; a song he recorded for Ric, "A Losing Battle" peaked at number 27 in 1962. It was written and produced by Mac Rebennack, aka DR. JOHN.

After brief stints with the Watch and Pace Maker labels in the mid-'60s, Adams signed with SSS International Records. In 1968 the label released the pop-flavored R&B tune "Release Me," which Adams had originally recorded for Watch. It made it to number 34 on the R&B charts and even dented the pop charts that year. Adams released two other singles of the same ilk in 1969: "Reconsider Me," which broke into the pop top 30 (number 8 on the R&B charts), and "I Can't Be All Bad," which went to number 45 on the R&B charts and number 89 on the pop version.

In the '70s Adams continued to record, mostly for local New Orleans labels. Then in 1985 he signed with Rounder Records. His debut album for the label, *From the Heart*, was well received and gave Adams his first taste of national exposure since the late 1960s.

Adams's bluesiest albums are *Walking on a Tightrope* and *Room with a View of the Blues*, both of which were released by Rounder in late 1980s. However, his most acclaimed work has been *Johnny Adams Sings Doc Pomus: The Real Me*, a Pomus tribute that included appearances by pianist DR. JOHN and guitarist DUKE ROBILLARD. Adams continues to record and perform.

Essential Listening:

From the Heart/Rounder (CD 2044)

After Dark/Rounder (CD 2049)

Room with a View of the Blues/Rounder (CD 2059)

I Won't Cry: The Original Ron Recordings/Rounder (CD 2083)

Walking on a Tightrope/Rounder (2095)

Johnny Adams Sings Doc Pomus: The Real Me/Rounder (CD 2109)

◄ AGEE, RAY

(born April 10, 1930, Dixons Mills, Ala.; died c. 1990, location unknown)

A West Coast rhythm & blues singer whose smooth and relaxed vocal style was not unlike CHARLES BROWN's, Ray Agee made a number of mostly overlooked records in the 1950s and 1960s. Agee suffered from polio as a child and was left permanently disabled by the disease. After moving with his family from Alabama to Los Angeles in the 1930s, Agee and his brothers formed a gospel group called the Agee Brothers. The group often performed in local churches.

Despite his gospel roots, Agee eventually turned toward blues and rhythm & blues and began recording in 1952. Throughout his career Agee recorded prolifically, though much of his recording catalogue, with the exception of his work with the Modern and Aladdin labels, is found on little-known labels such as Mar-Jan, Check, Solid Soul, and Krafton. Some of Agee's later records include guitar work by Bay Area artist JOHNNY HEARTSMAN.

By the mid-'70s Agee had disappeared from the rhythm & blues scene. He supposedly died sometime around 1990.

Essential Listening:
Tin Pan Alley/Diving Duck (4301)
Somebody Messed Up/Krafton (KRS 1011)
Black Night Is Gone/Mr. R&B (1005)
I'm Not Looking Back/Mr. R&B (1003)

◄ AKERS, GARFIELD

(born c. 1902, Brights, Miss.; died c. 1962, Memphis, Tenn.)

Garfield Akers was a first-generation Mississippi bluesman whose singular, repetitive guitar style influenced a number of later bluesmen, including ROBERT WILKINS and JOHN LEE HOOKER. Akers was also know for his high-pitched vocal wail. Akers was born in Mississippi around the turn of the century where he learned to play guitar and worked house parties and dances before settling in the Hernando area.

Akers often worked with guitarist JOE CALLICOTT who accompanied Akers during his first recording session for Vocalion in 1929. Akers also recorded for Brunswick in 1930. In all, four of Akers's recordings were released: his trademark "Cottonfield Blues, Parts 1 and 2," "Dough Roller Blues," and "Jumpin' and Shoutin' Blues." Akers continued to work around Memphis in the 1930s and again in the early 1950s. He gradually faded from the city's blues scene toward the end of the decade. He died around 1962, possibly earlier.

Essential Listening:
Delta Blues, Vol. 2 (1929–1939) (Various Artists)/Document (DLP 533)

◄ ALEXANDER, TEXAS

(born Alger Alexander, c. 1880 or 1900, Leona, Tex.; died c. 1955, Houston, Tex.)

A first-generation East Texas blues singer, Alger "Texas" Alexander developed a vocal style closely linked to the field hollers, work shouts, and prison songs he heard around him in the early 1900s. Little is known about his personal life other than that he was an older cousin of LIGHTNIN' HOPKINS, periodically worked in cotton fields and on railroad gangs, and sang at picnics and socials.

Alexander also lived for a while in the Deep Ellum section of Dallas and allegedly spent time in prison for murder.

Unlike most other bluesmen of his era, Alexander never learned how to play the guitar or any other instrument. Thus, he often performed with such noted guitarists as LONNIE JOHNSON, DENNIS "LITTLE HAT" JONES, J.T. "FUNNY PAPA" SMITH, LOWELL FULSON, and Hopkins. He first recorded in 1927 for the Okeh label; in all, he recorded more than sixty titles, most of which were released prior to 1930. Some of the sessions were done with the MISSISSIPPI SHEIKS, others with noted jazz trumpeter King Oliver, pianist CLARENCE WILLIAMS, and some of the previously mentioned guitarists.

Many of Alexander's best songs possessed prison or work themes and reflected East Texas culture. Some of his better songs—"Section Gang Blues," "Levee Camp Moan," "Penitentiary Moan Blues," and "Texas Troublesome Blues"— attest to this and, at the same time, explicitly depict the powerful vocal delivery he employed in these and most of the other songs he recorded.

Alexander continued to drift and sing the blues through the 1940s. In 1947 he recorded with Lightnin' Hopkins for Aladdin; three years later he cut a couple of sides for the tiny Freedom label. These final recordings attracted little attention. Alexander eventually faded from the Texas blues scene. He died sometime around 1955 in Houston.

Essential Listening:
Texas Alexander, Volume 1/Matchbox (MSE 206)
Texas Alexander, Volume 2/Matchbox (MSE 214)
Texas Alexander, Volume 3/Matchbox (MSE 220)
Texas Troublesome Blues/Agram Blues (AB 2009)

◄ ALIX, MAY (MAE)

(born Liza Mae Alix, August 31, 1904, Chicago, Ill.; death information unknown)

May Alix was a blues-based cabaret singer in the 1920s. She is best known for the two 1926 recordings she made with LOUIS ARMSTRONG and His Hot Fives. Both tunes—"Big Butter and Egg Man" and "Sunset Cafe Stomp"—feature Alix's strong and stagy vocals and Armstrong's perfectly executed cornet solos. Armstrong once remarked that Alix was one of his favorite vocalists.

Born and raised in Chicago, Alix worked in the city's cabarets and nightclubs. She later went to New York, where she had a stay at the famous Cotton Club in Harlem with the Duke Ellington Orchestra. In addition to recording with Armstrong, Alix also recorded with the Jimmy Noone Orchestra in 1929 and 1930 on the Vocalion label. For the remainder of her career, which ended circa 1940, Alix performed in Chicago nightclubs. During early stages in their careers, fellow cabaret singers ALBERTA HUNTER, Edna Hicks, and Edmonia Henderson occasionally used May (also Mae) Alix as their pseudonym, presumably to take advantage of Alix's popularity.

Essential Listening:
Louis Armstrong and His Hot Fives, Vol. II/Columbia (44253)

◄ ALLEN, LEE
(born July 2, 1926, Pittsburgh, Kans.)

In the 1950s tenor saxophonist Lee Allen played on dozens of hit records made by many of the great New Orleans rhythm & blues artists, including FATS DOMINO, LITTLE RICHARD, PAUL GAYTEN, HUEY "PIANO" SMITH, and LLOYD PRICE. Along with Alvin "Red" Tyler, Allen helped make the saxophone a key instrument in New Orleans R&B. Allen's sharp sense of order and line gave his sax style resiliency, grit, and true rocking energy as heard on classics like Little Richard's "Tutti Frutti."

Unlike many of his Crescent City contemporaries, Allen wasn't born in New Orleans. A musician and athlete while growing up in Denver, Colorado, Allen came to New Orleans in 1944 after accepting a scholarship to Xavier University. Allen never graduated, but he found plenty of work, first with Paul Gayten's band and then with bandleader and record producer DAVE BARTHOLOMEW.

Allen made his living doing session work and playing in New Orleans clubs until 1956 when he signed a solo recording contract with Aladdin and cut the song "Shimmy," which failed to muster much interest. A year later Allen recorded for a smaller label, Ember. "Walkin' with Mr. Lee," an instrumental, was successful enough for him to put together his own band and tour, working as a bandleader until 1961, when he joined Fats Domino's band. Allen stayed with Domino until 1965, when, with the collapse of New Orleans R&B, he moved to Los Angeles.

Unable to find much session or club work on the West Coast, Allen returned to the Domino band and stayed with it for most of the 1970s. In the '80s, Allen enjoyed a mild comeback, thanks to the California roots-rock group, the Blasters, who featured his sax work on their 1981 self-titled album for the Slash label. Allen continued to work with the Blasters until the group dissolved in the mid-1980s.

Essential Listening:
Walkin' with Mr. Lee—Golden Classics/Collectables (Col 583)
A History of New Orleans Rhythm & Blues, Vol. 1 (1950–1958) (Various Artists)/
    Rhino (RN 70076)
The Blasters Collection/Slash–Warner Bros. (9 26451-2)

◄ ALLISON, LUTHER
(born August 17, 1939, Mayflower, Ark.)

Luther Allison came of age as a Chicago blues guitarist in the late 1960s with a West Side style influenced by the likes of FREDDIE KING and MAGIC SAM. However, his marginal recording success in the U.S. and his interest in blues-rock often blurred his stature in the blues community. Allison's "wah-wah" guitar antics left some blues fans disappointed with his shift toward rock at the peak of his career.

Allison grew up on gospel. After his family moved to Chicago in 1951 he became a regular member of a gospel group, the Southern Travellers. Eventually he became fascinated with the blues and learned the rudiments of the music, mostly by listening to older brother Ollie Lee. Luther played in Ollie Lee's band from 1954 to 1957, then formed a group with another brother, Grant, called the Rolling Stones. They later changed the name of the band to the Four Jivers.

Allison also played Chicago clubs as a sideman and performed with mentors Freddie King and Magic Sam. But it wasn't until he began performing at such blues fests as the Ann Arbor Blues Festival in Michigan and at rock venues like the Fillmore East and Fillmore West (in New York and San Francisco, respectively) that Allison began to attract attention outside Chicago blues circles. Early recording efforts on the Delmark label contained West Side blues tracks juxtaposed with blues-rock doodlings such as "Bloomington Closer," which appeared on his *Love Me Mama* album, recorded in 1969.

A short-lived recording contract with Gordy Records in the 1970s failed to ignite Allison's career. He spent the remainder of the decade and most of the 1980s recording for labels such as Black and Blue, Encore, and Blind Pig, and doing festival and club dates in the U.S. and Europe. Allison eventually moved to France, where he continues to perform.

Essential Listening:
Love Me Mama/Delmark (DS 625)
Serious/Blind Pig (BP 2287)
Love Me Papa/Evidence (ECD 26015-2)

◄ ALLISON, MOSE

(born November 11, 1927, Tippo, Miss.)

Throughout his career, Mississippi Delta–born pianist Mose Allison has bridged the gap between jazz and blues with albums that have explored both forms. Although Allison is often labeled a jazz artist, his music is rich with blues undertones and shadings, and he has contributed to the blues song treasury such gems as "Parchman Farm" and "Young Man's Blues"; yet Allison's detached keyboard style and breezy vocals are far removed from the grit and earthiness of the Delta bluesmen he heard growing up in Mississippi.

Allison learned how to play piano as a child. After serving in the army and playing in the Army Band, he studied English and philosophy at Louisiana State University and earned a B.A. degree in 1950. He moved to New York in 1956 and worked his way into the city's vibrant jazz scene, playing with Zoot Sims, Al Cohn, Bob Brookmeyer, Stan Getz, and other noted jazz musicians. Allison's feathery keyboards and vocals were perfectly tailored for a trio setting (piano, bass, drums). In 1957 he began recording for the Prestige label, recording at least eight albums in a two year span (1957–1959). Allison left Prestige for Columbia in 1960 and then moved on to Atlantic Records in 1962; he remained with the label until 1978, releasing nearly a dozen more albums, though none were successful enough commercially to move Allison beyond his cult status. In 1982 he signed with Elektra and recorded two albums with the label before moving to Blue Note–Capitol. Allison continues to perform and record.

Essential Listening:
Greatest Hits (The Prestige Collection)/Prestige (OJCCC 6004-2)
The Best of Mose Allison/Atlantic (1542-2)
I Don't Worry About a Thing/Rhino-Atlantic (R2-71417)

◄ ALLMAN BROTHERS BAND, THE

Original members: Duane Allman (guitar) (born November 20, 1946, Nashville, Tenn.; died October 29, 1971, Macon, Ga.); Gregg Allman (organ, vocals) (born December 8, 1947, Nashville, Tenn.); Berry Oakley (bass) (born April 4, 1948, Chicago, Ill.; died November 11, 1972, Macon, Ga.); Dickey Betts (guitar, vocals) (born December 12, 1943, West Palm Beach, Fla.); Jai Johanny Johanson (aka Jaimoe) (drums) (born John Lee Johnson, July 8, 1944, Ocean Springs, Miss.); Butch Trucks (drums) (born May 11, 1947, Jacksonville, Fla.)

The Allman Brothers Band was never an authentic blues band, but both Duane Allman, its gifted lead guitarist, and brother Gregg, who plays organ and sings, were much influenced by the blues and always included the blues in their repertoire. The band's earliest albums are ripe with jazz- and rock-influenced interpretations of blues standards that in the late '60s and early '70s expanded the parameters of blues-rock. In addition, Duane Allman's stirring slide guitar work recalled the genius of blues guitarist ELMORE JAMES, while Gregg's raw, sandpaper vocals possessed enough in the way of blues feeling for him to be considered one of the greatest white blues-influenced singers rock has ever produced.

In 1965 the Florida-based Allman brothers formed the Allman Joys and released a little-noticed version of WILLIE DIXON's "Spoonful." Shortly afterwards, the brothers moved to Los Angeles, formed the group Hour Glass, and released two albums for Liberty Records, *Hour Glass* (1967) and *Power of Love* (1968). After these two efforts failed, they returned to Florida and ultimately formed the Allman Brothers Band with second guitarist Dickey Betts, bass player Berry Oakley, and drummers Butch Trucks and Jai Johanny Johanson.

The group's first four albums—*The Allman Brothers Band* (1969); *Idlewild South* (1970); the classic live album *At Fillmore East* (1971); and the combination live/studio effort *Eat a Peach* (1972)—all contain moments of blues-rock brilliance and together stand as a testament to the veracity of blues-rock as a viable hybrid music form. But the deaths of Duane Allman in 1971 and Berry Oakley in 1972 in separate motorcycle crashes altered the band's direction: after their passing, the Allman Brothers Band ventured away from the blues and farther into rock. Though the group has split up on at least two occasions, it re-formed in the late '80s and continues to record and perform.

Essential Listening:
The Allman Brothers Band/Polydor (823 653-2)
Idlewild South/Polydor (833 334-2)
At Fillmore East/Mobile Fidelity Sound Labs (UDCD 2-558)
Eat a Peach/Polydor (823 654-2)
The Fillmore Concerts/Polydor (314 517-294)

◄ ALTHEIMER, JOSH

(born 1910, Pine Bluff, Ark.; died November 18, 1940, Chicago, Ill.)

An early Chicago blues pianist best known for his richly percussive accompaniments, Josh Altheimer played on a number of LESTER MELROSE–sponsored recording sessions in the 1930s for the Bluebird label. Along with fellow blues pianists LEROY CARR, WALTER DAVIS, BLIND JOHN DAVIS, SPECKLED RED, and ROOSEVELT SYKES, Altheimer helped define the parameters of the pre–World War II Chicago blues piano style.

Very little is known about Altheimer's life, which was tragically ended at age thirty by a fatal case of pneumonia. Altheimer never recorded on his own. His best work can be found on recordings by BIG BILL BROONZY and JOHN LEE "SONNY BOY" WILLIAMSON.

Essential Listening:

Big Bill's Blues (Big Bill Broonzy)/Portrait (RJ 44089)

◄ AMERSON, RICH

(born c. 1887, Livingston, Ala.; death information unknown)

A relatively obscure Alabama blues harmonica player and singer who recorded some sides for the Folkways label in the early 1950s, Rich Amerson drew most of his vocal inspiration from old field hollers and shouts.

A farmer by trade, Amerson was born in Alabama and performed in local jukes and at Saturday night socials. In the late 1930s he recorded for the Library of Congress, which brought him some regional acclaim. However, Amerson was never able to use it to build a commercial recording career. His last known recordings can be heard on the compilation album, *Negro Folk Music of Alabama, Vol. 1: Secular.* Afterwards Amerson disappeared from Alabama's blues scene. It is presumed he continued to work house parties and such until his death.

Essential Listening:

Negro Folk Music of Alabama, Vol. 1: Secular (Various Artists)/Folkways (4475)
Blues Masters, Vol. 10—Blues Roots (Various Artists)/Rhino (R2-71135)

◄ AMMONS, ALBERT

(born September 23, 1907, Chicago, Ill.; died December 5, 1949, Chicago, Ill.)

Albert Ammons was a major boogie-woogie pianist, who, along with MEADE "LUX" LEWIS and PETE JOHNSON, helped make the romping boogie-woogie piano style popular in the late 1930s and 1940s. In 1938 Ammons and his colleagues performed at John Hammond's Spirituals to Swing concert at Carnegie Hall in New York. That legendary show led to a series of recordings with the Library of Congress, as well as with the Vocalion and Blue Note labels. These recordings documented Ammons's style, which was influenced by first-generation boogie-woogie stylists such as JIMMY YANCEY and PINE TOP SMITH. In fact, Ammons's trademark tune, "Boogie Woogie Stomp," is based on Smith's classic "Pine Top's Boogie Woogie."

Born in Chicago, Ammons grew up listening to the city's blues and barrelhouse piano players. While driving a taxi, he met fellow driver and pianist Meade "Lux" Lewis. The two musicians became good friends, even sharing living space in the apartment house where Pine Top Smith resided. The three pianists often jammed together and exchanged musical ideas.

Ammons played Chicago clubs in the early '30s and made his first recordings with his group, the Rhythm Kings, in 1936. After the Spirituals to Swing concert, Ammons played the Cafe Society, the popular New York club that featured major boogie-woogie artists like Lewis and Johnson, and performed with noted jazz artists such as Benny Goodman and Harry James. In 1949, he joined Lionel Hampton's band, but bad health made the stint a short one. Ammons died shortly thereafter at age 42. His son, Gene, became a noted jazz saxophone player.

Essential Listening:
King of Blues and Boogie Woogie/Oldie Blues (2807)
Albert Ammons, Volume 2/Oldie Blues (2822)
The King of the Boogie Woogie (1939–1949)/Blues Classic (BC 27)

◄ ANDERSON, LITTLE WILLIE

(born May 21, 1920, West Memphis, Ark.; died June 20, 1991, Chicago, Ill.)

A Chicago harmonica player, Little Willie Anderson built his harp style and stage presence almost exclusively from that of his idol, LITTLE WALTER Jacobs. Anderson was born in West Memphis, Arkansas, where he first began playing blues harmonica by watching and listening to his father play. By the time his family moved to Chicago in 1939, Anderson was a competent harp player, though it wasn't until he met Little Walter in the 1950s that his abilities matured.

Anderson eventually became a constant companion of Little Walter's, even acting as his personal assistant whenever he performed in Chicago clubs. On occasion, Anderson substituted for Little Walter onstage. Though Anderson recorded some in the 1970s—he released an album recorded in 1979 on the B.O.B. label and contributed several songs shortly thereafter to an anthology—his career never progressed much beyond his reputation as a Little Walter clone. He did, however, work with a number of noted Chicago bluesmen other than Little Walter, including JIMMY JOHNSON, SMOKEY SMOTHERS, JOHNNY YOUNG, and, for a brief time, MUDDY WATERS. Anderson died in 1991.

Essential Listening:
Swinging the Blues/B.O.B. (BOB 2701)
Low Blows (Various Artists)/Rooster Blues (7610)

◄ ANDERSON, PINK

(born Pinkney Anderson, February 12, 1900, Laurens, S.C.; died October 12, 1974, Spartanburg, S.C.)

Pink Anderson was a South Carolina songster and early bluesman who spent most of his life traveling with medicine shows and performing a rich repertoire of old minstrel tunes, folk numbers, rags, and early blues. His guitar playing echoed the hushed, sensitive blues style of the Carolinas, though it rarely contained the elaborate fingerpicking techniques of East Coast bluesmen such as BLIND BOY FULLER and BLIND BLAKE.

Anderson was born in Laurens, South Carolina, at the turn of the century. As a child he hustled pennies by singing and dancing in the streets of nearby Spartanburg. Sometime around 1915 Anderson teamed up with SIMMIE DOOLEY, a popular Piedmont-region songster. Together they worked Doctor W. R. Kerr's Indian Remedy Company Medicine Show and other cure-all outfits. The duo's only known recordings were four sides for Columbia Records in 1928.

Sometime thereafter, Anderson and Dooley parted company. Dooley faded from the medicine show/blues scene, while Anderson continued to travel the medicine show circuit right on up to the mid-'50s when illness finally slowed him down. In the early '60s, young folk fans discovered his music. He recorded for the Prestige-Bluesville label in the early '60s and appeared in the 1963 documentary, *The Blues*. The British art-rock band Pink Floyd was inspired enough by Anderson to make his first name their own ("Floyd" came from bluesman FLOYD COUNCIL). Anderson died in 1974.

Essential Listening:
Carolina Blues Man, Vol. 1/Prestige-Bluesville (OBCCD 504-2)

◄ ANIMALS, THE

Original members: Eric Burdon (vocals) (born May 11, 1941, Newcastle upon Tyne, England); Alan Price (organ) (born April 19, 1942, Durham, England); Bryan "Chas" Chandler (bass) (born December 18, 1948, Newcastle upon Tyne, England); John Steel (drums) (born February 4, 1941, Gateshead, England); Hilton Valentine (guitar) (born May 21, 1943, North Shields, England)

Like many other early-'60s British pop groups, the Animals based much of their initial sound on American blues and rhythm & blues. Lead singer Eric Burdon was a passionate blues record collector as well as a keen student of the music. He sought to instill an authentic blues feel into the Animals' renditions of such classics as JOHN LEE HOOKER's "Boom Boom" and Sam Cooke's "Bring It on Home to Me" with his scrappy, charcoal vocals. The band's initial success was due, in large part, to Burdon's blues commitment.

The Alan Price Combo became the Animals in 1962 after Burdon joined the band as its vocalist. The Animals's second single, "House of the Rising Sun," reached number 1 on both the British and American pop charts in 1964. While the band continued to have chart success with other singles, namely "It's My Life" and "We Gotta Get Out of This Place," it steadily moved away from its original blues base. The Animals broke up in 1966, but Burdon re-formed the band shortly thereafter, calling it Eric Burdon and the Animals. The new Animals embraced flower power and acid rock, as evidenced by the group's 1967 hit single "San Franciscan Nights," and two hits in 1968, "Monterey" and "Sky Pilot." The Animals broke up for the final time in late 1968. Burdon went on to form the group War.

Essential Listening:
The Best of the Animals/Abkco (CD 4324)

◄ ARCHIBALD

(aka Archie Boy) (born Leon Gross, September 14, 1912, New Orleans, La.;
died January 8, 1973, New Orleans, La.)

Archibald was an early New Orleans blues piano player who influenced the styles of more popular Crescent City rhythm & blues pianists like FATS DOMINO, JAMES BOOKER, ALAN TOUSSAINT, and DR. JOHN. Although Archibald is best remembered outside of New Orleans for his one hit, a spirited version of the familiar folksong "Stag-O-Lee" that he called "Stack-A-Lee (Parts I & II)," Archibald, along with TUTS WASHINGTON and PROFESSOR LONGHAIR, helped define the bluesy barrelhouse piano style for which New Orleans is especially known.

Born Leon Gross in New Orleans just before World War I, Archibald taught himself how to play piano. He began playing house parties and picnics before becoming a mainstay in the city's whorehouses and clubs in the 1930s and 1940s. His nickname, Archie Boy, later became simply Archibald.

Archibald served in the army during World War II. When he returned to New Orleans he resumed his clubwork. In 1950 he began recording for the Imperial label. "Stack-A-Lee (Parts I & II)," his first record, made it to number 10 on the R&B charts that year. Though Archibald's recording career ended in 1952, he continued performing in New Orleans until his death in 1973.

Essential Listening:
The New Orleans Sessions/Krazy Kat (7409)

◄ ARMSTRONG, LOUIS

(aka Satchmo, Pops, Dippermouth, Satchelmouth) (born Daniel Louis
Armstrong, August 4, 1901, New Orleans, La.; died July 6, 1971,
New York, N.Y.)

New Orleans–born trumpeter and jazz legend Louis Armstrong recorded with many of the great female classic blues singers of the 1920s, including BESSIE SMITH and MA RAINEY. His colorful solo work helped give classic blues the vitality and sophistication it needed to appeal to urban audiences, especially up North. Often Armstrong built his cornet (small trumpet) passages into musical dialogue with the blues singers he backed. Few jazz artists were as important as Armstrong in developing the classic blues sound of the 1920s.

Yet it was in early jazz that Armstrong made his greatest contributions. In the 1920s no musician did more to heighten the artistic merit of jazz than Armstrong. The exceedingly rich tones he cultivated from his cornet, his extraordinary range on the instrument, and his superb phrasing talents enabled him to expand the frontiers of improvisation with his solos.

Armstrong played on countless jazz sessions in the '20s, first with his mentor, King Oliver. In 1923 King Oliver and His Creole Jazz Band recorded some of the first jazz records by black musicians. Later Armstrong played with his own groups, the Hot Fives and the Hot Sevens, which included such noted musicians as trombone player Kid Ory, clarinetist Johnny Dodds, and pianist Lil Hardin Armstrong, his second wife. Armstrong eventually became a pop performer and personality and one of America's most beloved entertainers. He died in 1971.

Essential Listening:
Louis Armstrong—The Hot Fives, Vol I/Columbia (CK 44049)
Louis Armstrong—The Hot Fives and Hot Sevens, Vol. II/Columbia (CK 44253)
Louis Armstrong—The Hot Fives and Hot Sevens, Vol. III/Columbia (CK 44422)
Louis Armstrong of New Orleans/MCA (MCAD-42328)
Bessie Smith/The Complete Recordings, Vol. 2/Columbia/Legacy (C2K 47471)

◄ ARNOLD, BILLY BOY

(born William Arnold, September 16, 1935, Chicago, Ill.)

A disciple of JOHN LEE "SONNY BOY" WILLIAMSON, Billy Boy Arnold is a journeyman harp player and vocalist whose best recordings were made for Vee-Jay Records in the mid-1950s. As a youth, Arnold copiously imitated Williamson's harp style. Later, however, after also being influenced by LITTLE WALTER and JUNIOR WELLS, Arnold developed more of an original harp sound, though he never really strayed too far from his Sonny Boy roots.

Arnold played on Chicago street corners with BO DIDDLEY before making his recording debut at age seventeen on the Cool label. However, it was the songs he cut with Vee-Jay from 1955 to 1957, principally the tune "I Wish You Would," that gave Arnold credibility in the Chicago blues community and enabled him to perform alongside artists such as HOWLIN' WOLF, MUDDY WATERS, and EARL HOOKER in the late '50s.

Arnold did some occasional recording in the '60s and was a regular performer in Chicago blues clubs, but nothing he cut matched his '50s work. In 1975 he went to Europe with Bo Diddley, JOHNNY "GUITAR" WATSON, and other bluesmen as part of a blues package tour. Subsequent trips to Europe led to the recording of the album *Ten Million Dollars*, for the French Blue Phoenix label in 1984. Arnold continued to work Chicago blues clubs in the late '80s. In 1992 he performed at the San Francisco Blues Festival. He continues to reside in Chicago.

Essential Listening:
Crying and Pleading/Charly (CRB 1016)
Blow the Back Off It/Red Lightnin' (0014)

◄ ARNOLD, KOKOMO

(aka Gitfiddle Jim) (born James Arnold, February 15, 1901, Lovejoy, Ga.; died November 8, 1968, Chicago, Ill.)

A left-handed slide guitarist who influenced the likes of ROBERT JOHNSON, ELMORE JAMES, and other noted slide guitarists, Kokomo Arnold made a number of recordings in the 1930s memorable for the dramatic intensity of his slide technique. Arnold's trademarks were his wild and unpredictable sense of time, his penchant for sliding the bottleneck up and down the neck of his guitar as fast as possible, and his occasional use of the vocal falsetto to accent or embellish his guitar antics.

As a young man, Arnold regarded his career as a recording artist as secondary to his work as a bootlegger. Born and raised in Georgia where a cousin, John Wiggs, taught him the basics of the guitar, Arnold drifted up North, working as a farmhand in New York State and as a steelworker in Pittsburgh, before settling in Chicago in 1929 where he set up his bootlegging operation.

In 1930 Arnold went to Memphis and made his recording debut. He cut two sides for the Victor label, "Rainy Night Blues" and "Paddlin' Blues," under the name Gitfiddle Jim. Though they sold few copies, Arnold's first recordings detailed his engrossing guitar and vocal style. The latter song was played with such speed that Arnold's voice could hardly keep up with his fingers.

In 1934 Arnold recorded for Decca; two of the tracks he cut became classics. Not only did "Old Kokomo Blues" give Arnold his nickname and celebrity status in Chicago blues circles, but the song, based on SCRAPPER BLACKWELL's "Kokomo Blues," was later reworked by Robert Johnson and retitled "Sweet Home Chicago." The second track, "Milk Cow Blues," was interpreted by Elvis Presley in 1954 for Sun Records.

Arnold cut more tracks for Decca in the late '30s before fading from the blues scene. He was rediscovered by the young, mostly white folk audience in the early '60s, but didn't take advantage of the new interest in blues like other older blues men did. Arnold died of a heart attack in 1968.

Essential Listening:
*Kokomo Arnold, Vol. 1 (Complete Recorded Works in Chronological Order, May 17, 1930 to March 15, 1935)/*Document (DOCD 5037)
*Bottleneck Guitar: Trendsetters of the 1930s/*Yazoo (1049)

◄ AUGUST, LYNN

(born Joseph Leonard, August, August 7, 1948, Lafayette, La.)

A zydeco accordion player and singer, Lynn August maintains a strong commitment to blues, much the way one of his chief influences, CLIFTON CHENIER, did. Born in Louisiana, August went blind before he was a year old. By the time he was eight, he had developed a passion for the music of artists like RAY CHARLES, GUITAR SLIM, and the Soul Stirrers and began entertaining relatives and friends at get-togethers by playing the harmonica and singing. Eventually August switched to the washtub and then the drums.

August played drums in local bars around Lafayette in the early '60s, often teaming up with the flamboyant rhythm & blues artist Esquerita, and then with Jay Nelson, who later recorded for the Excello label. It was Esquerita who inspired August to learn how to play piano; August switched to the Hammond B-3 organ in 1964, and though he recorded a few locally released singles, he was relegated to playing lounges in Holiday Inns and other hotels until he joined zydeco accordionist Marcel Dugas's band in 1977. August was a full-time member of the Dugas band until 1979, at which time he went back to playing the hotel lounge circuit.

August finally picked up the accordion in 1987; a year later he recorded his first album, *Party Time*, which was released on the Maison de Soul label and included August's developing brand of blues-influenced zydeco. *Zydeco Groove*, his second album, came out in 1989. By this time August had become popular on the Louisiana zydeco circuit. After a performance at the legendary New Orleans club Tipitina's, August was offered a recording contract with Black Top Records. His Black Top debut, *Creole Cruiser*, which contained Chenier-styled zydeco liberally splashed with blues, came out in early 1992. A follow-up album, *Sauce Piquante*, was released by Black Top a year later. August continues to record and perform regularly.

Essential Listening:

Creole Cruiser/Black Top (BT 1074)

Sauce Piquante/Black Top (BT 1092)

◄ AUSTIN, LOVIE

(born Cora Calhoun, September 19, 1887, Chattanooga, Tenn.; died July 10, 1972, Chicago, Ill.)

Lovie Austin was a popular bandleader, session musician, composer, and arranger during the 1920s classic blues era. She and Lil Hardin Armstrong are often ranked as two of the best female jazz-blues piano players of the period. Schooled in music theory—she studied music at Roger Williams University and Knoxville College in her native Tennessee—Austin's well-defined percussive piano style can be heard on recordings by MA RAINEY, IDA COX, ETHEL WATERS, and ALBERTA HUNTER. When not leading her own band, the Blues Serenaders, which usually included Tommy Ladnier on cornet and Jimmy O'Bryant on clarinet, Austin also worked with many of the other top jazz musicians of the 1920s, namely Louis Armstrong, Kid Ory, and Johnny Dodds. Austin's skills as songwriter can be heard in the classic "Down Hearted Blues," a tune she co-wrote with Hunter. Singer BESSIE SMITH turned the song into a hit in 1923.

Austin spent the early years of her career playing vaudeville shows. In the mid-1920s she moved to Chicago and worked as a house musician for Paramount Records. However, her role in the recording studio was often more than simply playing the piano. Frequently she helped with song arrangements and was instrumental in laying the musical foundation from which many classic blues singers sprang to stardom. When the classic blues craze began to wither in the early 1930s, Austin settled into the position of musical director for the Monogram Theater in Chicago. After World War II she became a Chicago dance-school pianist and performed and recorded occasionally. She died in 1972.

Essential Listening:

Queen of the Blues/Biograph (Bio 12032)

B.

◄ BABY FACE LEROY

(born Leroy Foster, February 12, 1923, Algoma, Miss.; died May 26, 1958, Chicago, Ill.)

Baby Face Leroy was a drummer, guitarist, and singer whose work with MUDDY WATERS, LITTLE WALTER, SUNNYLAND SLIM, and FLOYD JONES in the late 1940s and early 1950s contributed to the birth of the modern Chicago blues sound. Named for his youthful looks, Baby Face was a spirited performer whose exuberant vocal shouts and clipped guitar style were admired by Waters and other Chicago bluesmen at the time. Baby Face was a member of Waters's earliest band, playing both guitar and drums.

Not much is known about Baby Face Leroy's personal life other than that he was born and raised in the South, came to Chicago in the early 1940s, and played with JOHN LEE "SONNY BOY" WILLIAMSON, SUNNYLAND SLIM, and other bluesmen on city street corners and in small clubs. In a short time he became one of the most popular bluesmen on the scene, appreciated by other musicians mostly because of his sprightly personality and his ability to consume large quantities of alcohol.

Baby Face Leroy recorded for a number of early Chicago blues labels, including Aristocrat (Chess), Parkway, J.O.B., and Savoy. In the mid-'50s he performed with Homesick James and Snooky Pryor, among others, before fading from the Chicago blues scene. He died in 1958 of a massive heart attack, due, most likely, to his excessive drinking and racy lifestyle.

Essential Listening:
Baby Face Leroy and Floyd Jones/Flyright (584)

◄ BAILEY, DEFORD

(born December 14, 1899, Nashville, Tenn.; died July 2, 1982, Nashville, Tenn.)

Harmonica player Deford Bailey was the first black artist to appear on the Nashville-based WSM country radio program "The Grand Ole Opry." He was a steady performer on the show from 1925 to 1941 and was one of its most popular performers prior to 1930. Although Bailey played black country music, which evolved out of old-time string band music (Bailey called it "black hillbilly"), he occasionally played blues or blues-flavored numbers on the show and his harp style was blues-based. Bailey's trademark tune was "Pan American

Blues," a novelty number based on the freight train–like sounds he drew from his harp. In 1928 he also recorded some blues tunes for Victor Records.

Bailey stayed with the Grand Ole Opry show until World War II. Few blues or country harmonica players of the period could match Bailey's creative antics with the harp. But because his sound was not true blues, Bailey is not always mentioned with other early blues harmonica players, such as NOAH LEWIS of Cannon's Jug Band Stompers or WILL SHADE of the MEMPHIS JUG BAND, as having played a part in the development of early blues harmonica styles. Yet there can be little doubt that many black blues harmonica players were well aware of Bailey's harp talents and regularly listened to him on the radio. Bailey died in 1982.

Essential Listening:
Harmonica Showcase, 1927–1931/Matchbox (218)

◄ BAKER, ETTA

(born March, 31, 1913, Caldwell, N.C.)

An instrumentalist who specializes in the Piedmont blues guitar style, Etta Baker's two- and three-finger picking technique is reminiscent of the traditional styles of Elizabeth (LIBBA) COTTEN and BLIND BOY FULLER. Born and raised in North Carolina, Baker learned how to play guitar, fiddle, banjo, and piano as a youth and often played with her father and sister at picnics and house parties.

In 1936 she married and put aside her musical ambitions to raise a family. Twenty years later Baker made her recording debut; five of her songs were included on the compilation album *Instrumental Music of the Southern Appalachians*, released on the Tradition label. Yet it wasn't until 1973, at age sixty, that Baker began performing regularly at folk and blues fests and in small clubs. Her first full-length album, *One-Dime Blues*, was released by Rounder in 1991. Baker continues to perform and record.

Essential Listening:
One-Dime Blues/Rounder (2112)

◄ BAKER, LAVERN

(born Dolores Williams, November 11, 1929, Chicago, Ill.)

Lavern Baker was a popular rhythm & blues singer in the 1950s whose vocal style did much to influence early rock & roll. Her 1954–55 record, "Tweedle Dee," was one of the first black rock & roll records to cross over onto the white pop charts.

After growing up in Chicago and listening to and singing gospel in the Baptist church, Baker began her career in R&B in 1946 when she billed herself as Little Miss Sharecropper and began playing Chicago clubs. She recorded for Columbia, RCA-Victor (with the Eddie Penigar Band), National, and King (with Todd Rhodes and his Orchestra) before signing with Atlantic Records as a solo artist in 1954. Now calling herself Lavern Baker, she recorded "Tweedle Dee" along with a number of other R&B songs such as "Jim Dandy" and "I Cried a Tear" that featured her well-shaped, sassy vocals. Georgia Gibbs and other white singers often covered Baker's songs. Gibbs's version of "Tweedle Dee" made it to number 2 on the pop charts in 1955. (Baker's peaked at number 14.)

Shortly after the success of "Tweedle Dee," Baker became a major attraction on the burgeoning rock & roll circuit. She often headlined disc jockey Alan Freed's Rock 'n' Roll Jubilee shows and appeared in two of his movies, *Mister Rock And Roll* and *Rock Rock Rock*. Baker was a mainstay on the charts in the 1950s; fifteen of her songs made it onto the R&B charts, while a third of them crossed over to the pop charts, making her one of the most popular artists of rock & roll's earliest period.

Baker continued to record with Atlantic into the early 1960s. "See See Rider," her last hit, was released in 1962. Baker left Atlantic in 1963 and signed with Brunswick Records. However, her career was in decline by then. In the late '60s, after entertaining troops in Vietnam, Baker relocated to the Philippines, where she worked as entertainment director at the Subic Bay military base. In 1990 she launched a comeback by replacing singer Ruth Brown in the hit Broadway musical *Black and Blue*. A year later Baker was voted into the Rock & Roll Hall of Fame. She still occasionally performs.

Essential Listening:
Soul on Fire: The Best of Lavern Baker/Atlantic (7 82311-2)
Lavern Baker Sings Bessie Smith/Atlantic Jazz (7 90980 2)

◄ BAKER, MICKEY

(born McHouston Baker, October 15, 1925, Louisville, Ky.)

In 1956 Mickey Baker teamed up with wife and former guitar student Sylvia Vanderpool (aka Robinson) as Mickey & Sylvia to record the pop classic "Love Is Strange," which contained Baker's memorable blues guitar break and Vanderpool's subtle yet sexy vocal delivery. The song, a million-seller, made it to number 1 on the R&B charts and number 11 on the pop charts.

Baker's place in blues history, however, extends beyond the commercial success of "Love Is Strange." During the 1950s he was a highly regarded session guitarist whose work was found on records by NAPPY BROWN, RAY CHARLES, RUTH BROWN, SONNY TERRY, CHAMPION JACK DUPREE, AMOS MILBURN, Little Willie John, and the Coasters, to name just a few. Along with pianist Henry Van Walls, bass player Lloyd Trotman, saxophonist KING CURTIS, and drummer Connie Kay, Baker helped create the noted 1950s Atlantic R&B sound, although he also worked for a variety of other labels during his career, including Savoy, King, and Aladdin.

Baker was born in Kentucky and came to New York around 1940. He worked in both blues and jazz formats. In 1953 he met Sylvia Vanderpool. In addition to giving her guitar lessons, the two got involved romantically. Deciding to work together, they recorded for the Cat and Rainbow labels, though the material they cut was largely ignored. That changed after the startling success of "Love Is Strange." Mickey & Sylvia toured with various rock & roll package shows and had a follow-up hit with "There Oughta Be a Law," which went to number 8 on the R&B charts in 1957.

The stardom that accompanied Baker's recording success did not, however, fit with his shy, quiet personality. Eventually, marital squabbles and musical differences led Baker and Vanderpool to split. In 1961 Baker moved to Paris where he continued his career as a sideman and session guitarist, working with MEMPHIS SLIM, Champion Jack Dupree, and other bluesmen who came to Europe to record and tour in the '60s and '70s. Sylvia went on to form Sugar Hill Records, an early and influential rap label.

Beginning in 1960 Baker also wrote a number of guitar instruction books, including *Mickey Baker's Analysis of the Blues for Guitar* and *Jazz Guitar*. Baker still records, though sporadically.

Essential Listening:
Ruth Brown: Miss Rhythm (Greatest Hits and More)/Atlantic (7 82061-2)
The Birth of Soul (Ray Charles)/Atlantic (82310)
The Legendary Mickey Baker/Shanachie (97019)

◄ BALDRY, LONG JOHN

(born John Baldry, January 12, 1941, East Maddon-Doveshire, England)

Long John Baldry was one of the early leaders of the British blues-rock scene. His deep, parched voice was ideally suited for the blues, and his penchant for playing with musicians that would one day find fame in the rock world was surpassed in British blues circles only by JOHN MAYALL and ALEXIS KORNER.

Baldry began his career as a folksinger; after befriending Ramblin' Jack Elliot, the American folk artist, Baldry frequently toured Europe with him in the late '50s. By the early '60s, however, Baldry had discovered the blues. Stints with Alexis Korner's Blues Incorporated (which also included singer Mick Jagger and drummer Charlie Watts, later of the ROLLING STONES) and the CYRIL DAVIES R&B All-Stars followed. After Davies's death in 1964, Baldry formed the Hoochie Coochie Men, made up mostly of Davies's All-Stars, followed by the group Steampacket, which featured vocalist Rod Stewart, and finally Bluesology, which included keyboards player Reg Dwight (Elton John).

In the late '60s Baldry turned to pop; one of his records, "Let the Heartaches Begin," reached the top of the British charts in 1968. But in the early '70s, Baldry was back singing blues-rock. His song "Don't Try to Lay No Boogie-Woogie on the King of Rock 'n' Roll" was a minor hit in the U.S. in 1971. Baldry faded from the scene in the mid-'70s after allegedly spending time in a mental institution. In 1980 he became a Canadian citizen. Since then Baldry has performed in Canadian clubs and recorded only sporadically.

Essential Listening:
It Still Ain't Easy/Stony Plain (STP 1163)

◄ BALL, MARCIA

(born March 20, 1949, Orange, Tex.)

Marcia Ball, a keyboard player and rhythm & blues singer whose influences include PROFESSOR LONGHAIR, ETTA JAMES, and Tina Turner, was one of the architects of the Austin Sound in the early '70s. Born in Texas and raised in Louisiana, Ball came from a family of musicians. She began taking piano lessons at five, which she continued until she was fourteen. In 1966 Ball attended Louisiana State University and played in the blues-based rock band Gum.

Ball moved to Austin in 1970 where she performed in the city's clubs with the progressive country group Freda and the Firedogs. After the band dissolved in 1974, Ball launched a solo career. A year later she released a single, "I Want to Be a Cowboy's Sweetheart." Since then Ball has released four solo albums, plus one she did with fellow Austin singers LOU ANN BARTON and ANGELA STREHLI, called *Dreams Come True*. All of her albums contain a mix of rhythm & blues, country swing, rock, and blues. Ball was voted into the Austin Music Hall of Fame in 1990. She continues to record and perform.

Essential Listening:
Soulful Dress/Rounder (3078)
Hot Tamale Baby/Rounder (3095)
Gatorhythms/Rounder (3101)
Dreams Come True/Antone's (ANT 0014)

◄ BALLARD, HANK

(born November 18, 1936, Detroit, Mich.)

In the early 1950s, gospel-tinged vocalist Hank Ballard and his group, the Midnighters, which included influential guitarist Alonzo Tucker, recorded some of the raciest songs in rhythm & blues. Hits such as "Work with Me, Annie" and "Sexy Ways," which Ballard had penned, and "Annie Had a Baby" (written by King label owner Syd Nathan under the pseudonym Lois Mann), had enough sexual intonations wedged behind their lyrics for many radio stations to refuse them airplay. The ban had little effect on sales or popularity, however. Both "Work with Me, Annie" and "Annie Had a Baby" made it to number 1 on the R&B charts in 1954, while "Sexy Ways" peaked at number 2. But Ballard is best known for his song "The Twist," which, after Chubby Checker recorded it in 1960, launched the dance rock craze in the early '60s.

Born in Detroit, Ballard worked on an auto assembly line before joining the Royals in 1953. The group's first hit, "Get It," for the Federal label (number 6 on the R&B charts) came out in 1953. A year later the Royals changed their name to the Midnighters to avoid confusion with the 5 Royals and enjoyed its most successful string of hits. The three records mentioned above, plus the third song of the "Annie" trilogy—"Annie's Aunt Fannie"—made the Midnighters one of 1954's biggest R&B groups.

The Midnighters continued to record for Federal until switching to King (Federal was a subsidiary of the King label) in 1959 and changing their name to Hank Ballard & the Midnighters. Although "Teardrops on Your Letter" made it to number 4 on the charts that year, its B-side, "The Twist," is the more historically important tune. While Checker's version of the song raced up the charts in 1960, Ballard & the Midnighters' original version was rereleased and made it to number 6 that same year. Four other noted Ballard numbers—"Finger Poppin' Time,"

"Let's Go, Let's Go, Let's Go," "The Hoochi Coochi Coo," and "The Float" backed with "The Switch-A-Roo"—went top 10 in 1960 and 1961.

However, by 1963 Ballard & the Midnighters' tenure as recording artists was up; two years later the group disbanded. Ballard then attempted a career as a solo artist. In 1968 he cut "How You Gonna Get Respect (When You Haven't Cut Your Process Yet)?" with the group the Dapps, and in 1974 recorded the novelty number "Let's Go Streaking." Neither record attracted much attention. Ballard next worked his way onto the oldies circuit in the late '70s. He continues to perform on occasion.

Essential Listening:
20 Hits: Hank Ballard & the Midnighters/King (5003X)

◄ BARBECUE BOB

(born Robert Hicks, September 11, 1902, Walnut Grove, Ga.; died October 21, 1931, Lithonia, Ga.)

Barbecue Bob was one of Atlanta's most noted blues artists in the 1920s. He played a twelve-string guitar, often with a bottleneck, and sang in strong, husky tones with occasional falsetto shadings. He supposedly got his nickname from a Columbia Records scout who discovered him when he was performing at a local barbecue pit called Tidwell's. An early publicity photo has Barbecue Bob dressed in a white chef's outfit strumming his guitar.

Barbecue Bob learned to play guitar from his older brother CHARLEY HICKS, who often went by the name Charley Lincoln. In the early 1920s, the two brothers moved to Atlanta and began playing parties and dances there. Barbecue Bob began recording in 1927, and though he only continued until 1930, he recorded nearly 70 sides, including "Going Up the Country," "Darktown Gamblin'," "Mississippi Heavy Water Blues," and "Yo Yo Blues." He died in 1931 at age twenty-nine of pneumonia and tuberculosis.

Essential Listening:
Barbecue Bob (Robert Hicks), 1927–30/Matchbox (MSE 1009)
Chocolate to the Bone/Yazoo (2005)
Complete Recorded Works, Vol. 2 (April 21, 1928–November 3, 1929)/Document (DOCD 5047)
Complete Recorded Works, Vol. 3 (November 6, 1929–December 8, 1930)/Document (DOCD 5048)

◄ BARNES, BOOBA

(born Roosevelt Barnes, September 25, 1936, Longwood, Miss.)

A Mississippi Delta blues guitarist and singer, Booba Barnes's brand of the blues is raw and jagged and stems from years of playing juke joints, including his own, the Playboy Club, in Greenville, Mississippi. Inspired by HOWLIN' WOLF, Barnes began his career as a harmonica player. By 1960 he was also playing guitar in a Delta band called the Swinging Gold Coasters. Barnes moved to Chicago in 1964 and performed on and off in the city's blues clubs. In 1971 he returned to Mississippi, formed a new band, and began playing jukes in and around Greenville.

Barnes opened his Playboy Club in 1985; it quickly became one of the Delta's best-known juke joints. He and his group, the Playboys, have been the house band at the club since its inception. Their popularity eventually spread beyond the Delta, leading to the release of their first album, *The Heartbroken Man*, in 1990 on the Delta-based Rooster Blues label. Since then, Barnes and his band have toured the U.S. and Europe. He continues to record and perform.

Essential Listening:
The Heartbroken Man/Rooster Blues (R 72623)

◄ BARTHOLOMEW, DAVE

(born December 24, 1920, Edgar, La.)

Dave Bartholomew, a producer, bandleader, composer, and arranger, was the major architect of the New Orleans rhythm & blues sound in the 1950s. His biggest artist was FATS DOMINO, for whom he wrote and arranged songs and produced records, but he also worked with other noted New Orleans R&B artists, including LLOYD PRICE, Shirley & Lee, EARL KING, and SMILEY LEWIS.

Bartholomew began his career as a trumpet player. He learned the rudiments of arranging while playing in an army band during World War II. After the war, he formed a jazz-flavored R&B band of his own that included sax players Red Tyler and LEE ALLEN and drummer Earl Palmer. The band quickly became New Orleans' most popular group in the late '40s.

Bartholomew began his career as a recording artist in 1947 with the release of "She's Got Great Big Eyes (And Great Big Thighs)" for the Deluxe label. But by 1950 he had turned most of his attention to record producing and arranging and began working for Lew Chudd's Imperial label. Bartholomew's success with Domino around this time led the two to form a partnership that resulted in the sale of millions of records. Beginning in 1950 with "The Fat Man," Domino's first hit for Imperial Records (it made it to number 2 on the R&B charts), Bartholomew produced and often cowrote many of Domino's hits in the 1950s. He also had success with Price and Shirley & Lee in 1952. Price's "Lawdy Miss Clawdy" (Specialty), which Bartholomew arranged, made it to number 1 on the R&B charts, while Shirley & Lee's "I'm Gone" (Aladdin) peaked at number 2. Bartholomew also cowrote "I Hear You Knocking" for Smiley Lewis, a tune that went to number 2 on the R&B charts in 1955. The success of these artists only solidified Bartholomew's reputation as one of New Orleans' top R&B producers.

Eventually Bartholomew signed an exclusive, long-term contract with Imperial Records that lasted until 1963 when the label was purchased by Liberty Records. At that time, rather than relocate to the West Coast where the company was based, Bartholomew retired from producing records and returned to his role as bandleader and jazz musician. In 1991 he was inducted into the Rock & Roll Hall of Fame.

Essential Listening:
The Classic New Orleans R&B Band Sound: The Best of Dave Bartholomew/
   Stateside (SSL 6036)
Antoine "Fats" Domino: They Call Me the Fat Man (The Legendary Imperial
   Recordings)/Capitol/EMI (96784)
Regal Records in New Orleans (with Paul Gayten)/Specialty (SPCD 2169-2)
Spirit of New Orleans: The Genius of Dave Bartholomew/EMI–Imperial (0777-
   7-80184-21)

◄ BARTON, LOU ANN

(born February 17, 1954, Fort Worth, Tex.)

A fixture on the Austin, Texas, blues scene since the early 1970s, Lou Ann
Barton is a sassy blues and rhythm & blues belter whose voice bears the unmis-
takable influences of IRMA THOMAS and Wanda Jackson. After moving from Fort
Worth to Austin in the early '70s, Barton began singing in the city's bars and
music clubs. Stints with an early version of the FABULOUS THUNDERBIRDS, ROOM-
FUL OF BLUES, and STEVIE RAY VAUGHAN's Double Trouble followed.

Barton's recording career began in 1982 on the Asylum label. Her debut album, *Old Enough*, was coproduced by Jerry Wexler and Glenn Frey. Though it
received some positive press, the album quickly faded into obscurity. In 1986
Barton released her second album, *Forbidden Tones*, on the independent Spin-
dletop label. In 1989 she signed with the Austin-based Antone's label and released
Read My Lips, an album that features Barton's hell-bent vocals at their best and
includes cameo appearances by friends such as guitarist JIMMIE VAUGHAN and
harmonica player Kim Wilson from the Fabulous Thunderbirds, and sax player
David "Fathead" Newman. The album received glowing reviews in *Rolling Stone*
and other major music publications, though it still failed to elevate Barton beyond
her regional star status. Barton also recorded *Dreams Come True* with fellow
Austin singers MARCIA BALL and ANGELA STREHLI in 1990. She continues to
record and perform.

Essential Listening:
Read My Lips/Antone's (Ant 0009CD)
Dreams Come True (with Marcia Ball and Angela Strehli)/Antone's (Ant 0014)
Old Enough/Antone's (Ant 0021)

◄ BASIE, COUNT

*(born William Basie, August 21, 1904, Red Bank, N.J.; died April 26, 1984,
Hollywood, Fla.)*

Of all the major big band jazz leaders of both the pre– and post–World War
II periods, it was Count Basie who cultivated one of the warmest relationships
with the blues. Not only did he employ great blues and blues-based singers in
his bands—JIMMY RUSHING, HELEN HUMES, Billie Holiday, and later, JOE WIL-
LIAMS all sang for Basie—but virtually all of his catalogue was woven with bluesy

rhythmic threads, and his piano playing almost always contained strong blues notions.

Though born in New Jersey, Basie learned the rudiments of the blues in New York, where, as a youth, he often backed blues singers in Harlem clubs. By his early '20s, Basie began playing piano in vaudeville troupes that toured the South. In 1928 he joined WALTER PAGE's Blue Devils, the hottest of the Kansas City blues-based swing bands, after being stranded in Kansas City and meeting Jimmy Rushing, the band's vocalist. However, Basie soon jumped to BENNIE MOTEN's band, another Kansas City group with strong blues ties. In 1935, after Moten's sudden death, Basie began his own band with musicians from Moten's outfit. From the start, Basie integrated generous elements of the blues into his band's repertoire. With top-notch soloists, such as the saxophone players Herschel Evans and Lester Young, trumpeter Buck Clayton, trombonist Dickie Wells; a rhythm section that included drummer Jo Jones, bass player Walter Page, and rhythm guitarist Freddie Green, and the blues singers out in front of the band, Basie broadly defined the jazz-blues link.

Basie's relationship with the blues became more apparent to his mainstream audience when Joe Williams joined the band. In 1955, with Williams singing, the Basie Band cut its one and only hit single, "Everyday I Have the Blues." The song made it to number 2 on the R&B charts.

Basie continued leading his band through the 1960s and early 1970s. In 1976 he suffered a heart attack, and though he recovered, Basie performed only when his health permitted. He died of cancer in 1984. His band has continued on under the leadership of Thad Jones and then Frank Foster, both longtime members of the Basie Orchestra.

Essential Listening:
Count Basie Swings—Joe Williams Sings/Verve (6 8488)
One O'Clock Jump/MCA–Decca (42324)
The Essential Count Basie, Vol. 1/Columbia (CK 40608)
The Essential Count Basie, Vol. 2/Columbia (CK 40835)
The Complete Decca Recordings/GRP–Decca (GRD-3-611)

◄ BELL, CAREY

(born Carey Bell Harrington, November 14, 1936, Macon, Miss.)

A Chicago-based harmonica player whose style incorporates the flair of LITTLE WALTER Jacobs and the subtle sensuality of BIG WALTER HORTON, Carey Bell has worked as both a sideman and bandleader and is noted for his work on the double-reed chromatic harp.

Born and raised in Mississippi where he taught himself the rudiments of his instrument, it wasn't until Bell moved to Chicago with his godfather, pianist Lovie Lee, and became a member of Lee's band that Bell began his career in earnest. Bell also performed with DAVID "HONEYBOY" EDWARDS and JOHNNY YOUNG, took harp lessons from Little Walter, appeared on albums by EARL HOOKER and MUDDY WATERS, and in 1969 made his debut as a featured recording artist. His album, *Carey Bell's Blues Harp*, was released on the Delmark label. Although it sparked little interest outside serious blues circles, the album enabled Bell to rise, if only temporarily, above sideman status. Three years later he was a featured guest on Big Walter Horton's Alligator album, *Big Walter Horton with Carey Bell*, which drew further attention to Bell and placed him on a par with Chicago's other harp masters.

In the 1970s and 1980s Bell toured extensively with WILLIE DIXON's Chicago Blues All-Stars, as well as with his own band, the Carey Bell Blues Band, which often included his son, guitarist LURRIE BELL. He also recorded with the Bob Riedy Blues Band and appeared in the blues documentary *Sincerely, the Blues*. In 1984 Bell and his son recorded *Son of a Gun* for the Rooster Blues label. In 1988 Bell began an association with the Maryland-based band Tough Luck, which resulted in an album for Blind Pig Records called *Mellow Down Easy*, released in 1991. A year earlier Bell was part of Alligator Records' critically acclaimed *Harp Attack!*, a super-session album that also featured Chicago harp standouts JAMES COTTON, JUNIOR WELLS, and BILLY BRANCH. Bell continues to record and perform.

Essential Listening:
Caley Bell's Blues Harp/Delmark (622)
Big Walter Horton with Carey Bell/Alligator/ (ALCD 4702)
Harp Attack! (Carey Bell, James Cotton, Junior Wells, Billy Branch)/Alligator (ALCD 4790)
Mellow Down Easy/Blind Pig (BP 74291)
Son of a Gun (with Lurrie Bell)/Rooster Blues (2617)

◄ BELL, ED

(born c. 1905, Alabama; died c. 1960, Alabama)

The guitar style of this early Alabama bluesman was fleshed with interesting riffs and chord structures, while his vocals contained the same vigor and coarseness heard in traditional field hollers. Little is known of Bell's life. Born in Alabama, he became part of the Greenville blues scene and played local parties and fish fries. He recorded for Paramount and Columbia Records in 1927 and 1930, respectively, but during the Depression he sold his guitar and gave up the blues for good. Bell died sometime around 1960 in Alabama.

Essential Listening:
Alabama Blues (Various Artists)/Yazoo (1006)
Ed Bell's Mamlish Moan/Mamlish (3811)

◄ BELL, LURRIE

(born December 13, 1958, Chicago, Ill.)

Lurrie Bell, the son of harmonica player CAREY BELL, is a Chicago-based blues guitarist and a founding member of the 1970s group the SONS OF BLUES. Bell grew up in a blues household. His father's band, the Carey Bell Blues Band, often rehearsed in the Bells' Chicago apartment. After he taught himself how to play guitar, Lurrie often sat in with his father's band during rehearsals and later in club performances. In 1977, Bell, along with bass player Freddie Dixon, son of WILLIE DIXON, and harp player BILLY BRANCH, formed the Sons of Blues. The group was represented on two Alligator Records anthologies, *Living Chicago Blues, Vol. 3* and *The New Bluebloods* though Bell did not play on the latter album.

Bell left the Sons of Blues in 1982. He spent the rest of the 1980s as a free-lance session musician and a member of KOKO TAYLOR's touring band. In 1984 he and his father recorded the album *Son of a Gun* for Rooster Blues. He also recorded *Everybody Wants to Win* for the JSP label. Bell continues to play Chicago clubs.

Essential Listening:
Living Chicago Blues, Vol. 3/Alligator (AL 7703)
Son of a Gun (with Carey Bell)/Rooster Blues (R 2617)
Everybody Wants to Win/JSP (227)

◄ BELOW, FRED

(born September 16, 1926, Chicago, Ill.; died August 13, 1988, Chicago, Ill.)

Fred Below was the most respected and in-demand Chicago blues drummer during the 1950s, and he created one of the music's most often-heard backbeats. Born in Chicago, Below attended DuSable High School, famous for the number of jazz musicians that had been students there, and later the Roy C. Knapp School of Percussion. Influenced by Gene Krupa, Chick Webb, and Buddy Rich, Below began his career as a jazz drummer. After a double stint in the army—he served during World War II and from 1948 to 1950 and was a member of the 427th Army Band—Below abandoned jazz because of lack of work in Chicago and turned to the blues. In 1950 he joined the group the ACES, which, at the time, included harmonica player–singer JUNIOR WELLS and brothers DAVID and LOUIS MYERS on guitars. Although his first attempts at keeping a blues backbeat were rough and unsteady, Below eventually developed into one of the deans of Chicago blues drummers. His swinging, jazz-flavored drumming—he often said he kept a "blues beat with a jazz feel"—could be heard on records by LITTLE WALTER, MUDDY WATERS, WILLIE DIXON, SONNY BOY WILLIAMSON (Rice Miller), OTIS RUSH, ELMORE JAMES, JIMMY REED, CHUCK BERRY, BO DIDDLEY, and dozens of other Chicago artists in the 1950s and 1960s.

Below left the Aces in 1955 and became the house drummer at Chess Records. His drumbeat was as much an influence on rock & roll as it was on early electric blues. It was Below's backbeat that propelled such Chuck Berry classics as "Roll Over Beethoven," "School Day," "Sweet Little Sixteen," "Johnny B. Goode," and "Memphis."

Below continued to perform and record with various artists, as well as work with the Aces in numerous reunions, right up until his death in 1988.

Essential Listening:
The Best of Little Walter/MCA-Chess (CHD 9192)
The Best of Little Walter, Volume TWO/MCA-Chess (CHD 9292)
Kings of Chicago Blues, Volume One/Vogue (LDM 3017)

Chuck Berry (box set)/MCA-Chess (CHD3-80,001)
The Chess Box (Various Artists)/MCA-Chess (CHD4-9340)

◄ BELVIN, JESSE

(born December 15, 1932, Texarkana, Ark.; died February 6, 1960, Little Rock, Ark.)

Jesse Belvin was a composer and blues balladeer who frequently crossed over into the pop and doo-wop genres in the 1950s. Born in Arkansas and raised in Los Angeles, Belvin began his career in 1951 as the singer in BIG JAY MCNEELY's band. While serving in the army in 1954, he wrote "Earth Angel" for the doo-wop group the Penguins. The song became one of the best-selling and most-popular doo-wop records ever made.

Belvin continued to write hits for himself and others; he recorded "Goodnight My Love," a top-10 R&B hit in 1956, and wrote "Girl of My Dreams" for the Cliques that same year. With a voice that was smooth and silky, not far from a NAT KING COLE croon, and a recording sound that often featured thick layers of orchestration, Belvin was part of the easy-flowing West Coast rhythm & blues style made popular in the 1950s by fellow artists such as PERCY MAYFIELD and CHARLES BROWN.

Belvin's career was cut tragically short when in 1960 he and his wife, Jo Anne, were killed in an automobile accident. He was twenty-six years old.

Essential Listening:
Jesse Belvin: The Blues Balladeer/Specialty (SPCD 7003)
Goodnight My Love/Flair-Virgin (V2-86301)

◄ BENNETT, WAYNE

(born December 13, 1933, Sulphur, Okla.; died November 18, 1992, New Orleans, La.)

Though not a solo artist, Wayne Bennett ranks as one of the great rhythm & blues guitarists. Most of Bennett's career was spent working with singer BOBBY "BLUE" BLAND, with whom he helped define blues-flavored R&B. Bennett's cupped, seamless guitar sound cushioned Bland's richly textured vocals and easily integrated itself into Bland's mesh of blues, soul, and gospel. Bennett played on numerous Bland classics, including "Turn On Your Love Light," "I Pity the Fool," and Bland's version of "Stormy Monday." He also appeared on records by JIMMY REED, WILLIE DIXON, OTIS RUSH, BUDDY GUY, JIMMY ROGERS, and PERCY MAYFIELD, among others.

Bennett's biggest influence was T-BONE WALKER. After growing up in Oklahoma, Bennett joined AMOS MILBURN's band in 1951. After a stint in the army Bennett flirted with jazz. But it wasn't until he moved to Chicago in 1958 and joined the Blues Consolidated Revue, which featured both Bland and JUNIOR PARKER, that Bennett began to make his mark as a blues guitarist. For three years Bennett toured with the package during which time he developed his distinctive guitar sound. In 1961 the revue broke up and Bennett went with Bland. For more than two decades the two toured and recorded together. Bennett began to slow down in the mid-1980s, due to health problems. He moved to New Orleans, where he performed with blues singer MARVA WRIGHT and did session work for the Black Top label, along with occasional roadwork with Bland. He suffered a fatal heart attack in 1992.

Essential Listening:
The Best of Bobby Bland/MCA (27013)
The Best of Bobby Bland, Vol. 2/MCA (4MC27045)

◄ BENTLEY, GLADYS

(born August 12, 1907, Pennsylvania; died January 18, 1960, Los Angeles, Calif.)

A New York–based cabaret singer and piano player in the 1920s, Gladys Bentley built her repertoire on risqué blues songs, some of which included unmasked references to lesbianism. Bentley began her career after moving to New York sometime in the mid-'20s, where she quickly established herself as a popular performer, especially in Harlem. A large woman with masculine traits, Bentley projected a mysterious edge regarding sexual preference. Some of her fans even believed she was a male transvestite.

Bentley recorded for the Okeh label in 1928 and continued to work New York nightclubs until the mid-1930s. Eventually she moved to the West Coast, where she occasionally recorded and performed in the 1950s. Bentley died in 1960.

Essential Listening:
Mean Mothers: Independent Women's Blues, Vol. 1 (Various Artists)/Rosetta (1300)

◄ BENTON, BUSTER

(born Ollie Benton, July 19, 1932, Texarkana, Ark.)

Journeyman singer-guitarist Buster Benton has been a blues performer since he moved to Chicago in 1959, though only since he began making records for the Ichiban label in the late 1980s has he attracted much attention outside the Windy City. Benton's guitar playing is steeped in the style of B.B. KING; his licks are airy and spare, yet rich in soul and sensitivity.

Benton grew up in Arkansas where he sang gospel as a youth. After resettling in Chicago, Benton did studio work for JOHN LEE HOOKER, JIMMY REED, and MIGHTY JOE YOUNG; he also recorded some obscure singles under his own name. In 1971 Benton began playing in WILLIE DIXON's band. Three years later Benton had a minor hit with the song "Spider in My Stew," which he rerecorded as the title track of his 1978 debut album, released by Ronn Records. Benton's follow-up album on Ronn, *Buster Benton Is the Feeling*, came out in 1980, but it failed to enlarge his reputation as a recording artist.

Benton spent the early 1980s playing clubs and doing occasional session work in Chicago and touring Europe. He recorded a couple of albums for the French Black and Blue label, *The First Time in Europe* and *Blues at the Top*, before he signed with Ichiban in 1987. Benton released three albums with the label, including *I Like to Hear My Guitar Sing* in 1991. He continues to record and perform.

Essential Listening:
I Like to Hear My Guitar Sing/Ichiban (ICH 1129)
Blues at the Top/Evidence (ECD 26030-2)

◄ BERRY, CHUCK

(born Charles Berry, October 18, 1926, St. Louis, Mo.)

Chuck Berry was as important to the early development of rock & roll as Elvis Presley, but for different reasons. Berry was one of rock & roll's first great lyricists; his witty, wonderfully expressive interpretations of American culture often went beyond worn-thin themes of teenage puppy love. Berry also gave rock & roll some of its earliest trademark guitar licks. One of them, the shuffling, boogie-woogie influenced riff that appears in the classic song "Johnny B. Goode," is a primary tool in any rock guitarist's repertoire. Berry also blended rhythm & blues, country, swing, and blues strains into his music, which made him one of rock & roll's first great stylistic innovators. Finally, Berry broke the color line and helped make rock & roll acknowledge its black roots.

Like LITTLE RICHARD, FATS DOMINO, and other pioneering black rock & rollers, Berry began his career as a rhythm & blues performer. Though he was influenced by jazz guitarist Charlie Christian and by Carl Hogan (the guitar player in rhythm & blues artist LOUIS JORDAN's Tympany Five), two of Berry's biggest influences were MUDDY WATERS and HOWLIN' WOLF. Berry also recorded for Chess, the major blues label in the 1950s, and used blues musicians on his records. Bass player WILLIE DIXON, drummers FRED BELOW and ODIE PAYNE, JR., and pianists JOHNNIE JOHNSON and LAFAYETTE LEAKE played on many of Berry's best recordings, all of which were made in Chicago. Though Berry drifted away from the blues when he became a rock & roll icon in the 1960s, blues subtleties remained solidly woven into his music.

Born and raised in St. Louis, Berry developed an early fascination for the guitar. With local jazz guitarist Ira Harris as an early teacher, Berry learned the rudiments of the instrument on a four-string tenor guitar. By 1950, however, he had changed over to a six-string electric. Two years later Berry began playing professional engagements in St. Louis clubs. On New Year's Eve in 1952 he played with the Sir John's Trio. The combo was led by pianist Johnnie Johnson and included drummer Eddie Hardy. Berry incorporated elements of country into the Sir John's Trio sound, but he also brought in some Muddy Waters songs. In effect, Berry's blend of blues and country eventually turned the Sir John's Trio into a prototype rock & roll band, though history has not accorded it that honor.

Berry's connection with Muddy Waters didn't end there. In 1955, Berry traveled to Chicago where he ran into Waters, and asked him where he should inquire about doing some recording. Waters told him to see LEONARD CHESS at Chess Records. Berry took Waters's advice, and a few weeks later, Berry, Johnson, Willie Dixon, and drummer Jasper Thomas recorded a country-flavored blues tune called "Ida Red" (later changed to "Maybellene"), along with another tune titled "Wee Wee Hours." The record went to number 1 on the R&B charts and number 5 on the pop charts in 1955.

The Chess label had enjoyed considerable commercial success with artists such as Waters and LITTLE WALTER, but their appeal to that point lay principally in the blues and rhythm & blues markets. With the addition of Berry on the Chess roster, the label was able to attract a wider record-buying audience. By the end of 1956, Berry was selling more records than anyone else on Chess because white teens had picked up on his infectious sound and his records were routinely crossing over onto the pop charts. Berry's chart success would continue throughout the 1950s.

Berry had a batch of hits from 1956 through 1958, many of which became rock & roll standards. "Roll Over Beethoven," "School Day," "Rock & Roll Music," "Sweet Little Sixteen," "Reelin' and Rockin'," "Little Queenie," and the quintessential rock & roll song, "Johnny B. Goode," are just some of his early masterpieces. These, along with appearances in early rock & roll films such as *Rock, Rock, Rock* and *Mister Rock & Roll* and numerous cross-country tours with rock & roll package shows made Berry a major star.

Despite changes in rock trends and styles, Berry continued to recycle the classic blues-flavored rock & roll sound he created in the 1950s. Occasional run ins with the law blighted Berry's career, though he always rebounded from these and has retained his status as one of rock & roll's most influential original artists. His trademark double-string guitar riff, his instantly recognizable duckwalk, and his long-standing defiance and arrogance are all part of his legacy. Inducted into the Blues Foundation's Hall of Fame in 1985 and the Rock & Roll Hall of Fame in 1986, Chuck Berry released his autobiography (*Chuck Berry: The Autobiography*) in 1987. That same year the Chuck Berry rockumentary, *Hail! Hail! Rock 'n' Roll*, was also released. Shot at the Fox Theatre in St. Louis, the film included guest appearances by ROLLING STONES guitarist Keith Richards and Bruce Springsteen. Berry continues to perform on occasion.

Essential Listening:
Chuck Berry (box set)/MCA-Chess (CHD3-80,001)
The Great Twenty-Eight/Chess (CH 8201)

◄ BIG BAD SMITTY

(born John Henry Smith, February 11, 1940, Vicksburg, Miss.)

A St. Louis–based guitarist and singer, Big Bad Smitty has a blues style that's derived, in part, from HOWLIN' WOLF and LIGHTNIN' HOPKINS. Smitty was born in Mississippi, where he played blues clubs in and around Jackson, occasionally with BOOBA BARNES, SAM MYERS, and other local blues artists. In 1966 Smitty relocated to St. Louis and played with the bar band Little Weaver and the Dynamites, performing in city clubs and jukes in other parts of Missouri and Illinois.

Smitty continued his career as a journeyman blues artist through the early 1990s. An occasional track on an anthology album (*Going to Mississippi*/White Label, *Genuine Mississippi Blues*/Ace) and regular club performances finally resulted in the recording of his debut album, *Mean Disposition*, on the Genes label and a couple of European tours. Smitty continues to perform regularly with the Big Bad Smitty Blues Band.

Essential Listening:

Mean Disposition/Genes-Adelphi (GCD 4128)

◄ BIG MACEO

(born Major Merriweather, March 31, 1905, Atlanta, Ga.; died February 23, 1953, Chicago, Ill.)

Big Maceo was one of the most influential blues piano players of the 1940s. His hammering, heavy-handed style had an impact on virtually every post–World War II blues pianist of note, especially OTIS SPANN, JOHNNY JONES and EDDIE BOYD. With a hazy, weathered voice and a piano style built on thick, pumping bass notes, Maceo, often with TAMPA RED on guitar, cut a number of classic Chicago piano numbers from 1941 to 1946. His biggest hit, "Worried Life Blues," has become a standard in the blues piano catalogue and remains Maceo's trademark tune.

By most accounts, Big Maceo was born in 1905 in Atlanta, where he taught himself how to play piano. When he was around twenty he moved with his family to Detroit. Shortly after his arrival he began playing house-rent parties and clubs. A growing desire to record led Maceo to move to Chicago in 1941. There he met the popular blues guitarist Tampa Red. They soon became best friends and performing partners. Red introduced Big Maceo to producer LESTER MELROSE of Bluebird Records who signed him to a recording contract. Big Maceo's first record was "Worried Life Blues," which, in 1941, promptly became a blues hit and made him a star in Chicago blues circles. Other classics such as "Chicago Breakdown," "Texas Stomp," and "Detroit Jump" followed.

Maceo's piano style evolved from the bluesy musings of earlier blues piano players like LEROY CARR, ROOSEVELT SYKES, and JOSH ALTHEIMER, as well as from the rolling, boogie-woogie sounds of MEADE "LUX" LEWIS and ALBERT AMMONS. In all, Big Maceo cut some thirty sides, most of them exceptional, before his career was cut short in 1946 by a debilitating stroke. Though Big Maceo continued to record sporadically up until his death in 1953, he was never able to recapture the power or passion of his prestroke recordings.

Essential Listening:

Big Maceo, Volume One: King of Chicago Blues Piano/Blues Classics (BC 28)

Big Maceo, Volume Two/Blues Classics (BC 29)

Grinder Man Blues: Masters of the Blues Piano/RCA Heritage (2098-2-R)

◄ BIG MAYBELLE

(born Mabel Smith, May 1, 1924, Jackson, Tenn.; died January 23, 1972, Cleveland, Ohio)

Big Maybelle was a classic 1950s rhythm & blues belter who could sing with the booming intensity of BESSIE SMITH and BIG MAMA THORNTON or caress a ballad with the sensitivity of Billie Holiday. Like Holiday, Big Maybelle allegedly suffered from heroin addiction throughout most of her career; her drug problem prevented her from ever reaching her full potential as a recording artist and performer.

Born Mabel Smith, Big Maybelle sang gospel as a child in Jackson, Tennessee, and by her teens had switched to rhythm & blues. She sang first with Dave Clark's Memphis Band and the all-female Sweethearts of Rhythm, then with Christine Chatman's Orchestra, with whom she made her debut as a recording artist in 1944, and with TINY BRADSHAW's Orchestra from 1947 to 1950. Big Maybelle signed a solo recording contract with Okeh Records in 1952 and made it into the top 10 of the R&B charts three times the following year. She also became one of the Apollo Theater's most popular performers during the early '50s.

When Big Maybelle's Okeh contract expired in 1956, she signed with the Newark-based Savoy Records, but her increasingly heavy heroin habit took its toll on her career. Her biggest hit, "Candy," was filled with lyrical irony. Big Maybelle continued to record and perform throughout the '60s. She died of diabetes in 1972.

Essential Listening:
Blues, Candy & Big Maybelle/Savoy Jazz (ZDS 1168)
The Okeh Sessions/Epic (EG 38453)

◄ THE BIG THREE TRIO

Original members: Willie Dixon (bass, vocals) (born July 1, 1915, Vicksburg, Miss.; died January 29, 1992, Burbank, Calif.); Leonard "Baby Doo" Caston (piano, vocals) (born June 2, 1917, Sumrall, Miss.; died August 22, 1987, Minneapolis, Minn.); Bernardo Dennis (guitar, vocals) (birth information unknown)

The Big Three Trio was a slick 1940s Chicago combo that featured seamless, three-part harmonies and a repertoire of soft blues, boogie-woogie, pop, and novelty numbers. Its sound was far removed from the more roughed-up, roots-oriented blues that was beginning to surface in the city around the same time from artists such as MUDDY WATERS and groups like the ACES.

In the early 1940s, bass player WILLIE DIXON and pianist Leonard "Baby Doo" Caston were both members of the Five Breezes, which recorded for the Bluebird label. When the Five Breezes broke up, Dixon went with the Four Jumps of Jive, while Caston and his group, the Rhythm Rascals, signed on with the USO during World War II and played for American servicemen all over the world. In 1946, Dixon and Caston, along with guitarist Bernardo Dennis, formed the Big Three Trio. The group cut a few sides with a couple of small labels before signing a recording contract with Columbia Records in 1947. That same year Ollie Crawford replaced Dennis on guitar.

The Big Three Trio frequently toured the South and made some interesting recordings for Columbia, most of which were built around the group's sweet vocals and Caston's versatile piano passages. The trio broke up in 1952. Willie Dixon went on to become Chess Records's main songwriter, producer, and arranger, working with MUDDY WATERS, CHUCK BERRY, and other major Chess artists.

Essential Listening:
Willie Dixon—The Big Three Trio/Columbia (CK 46216)

◄ BIG TIME SARAH

(born Sarah Streeter, January 31, 1953, Coldwater, Miss.)

A Chicago blues belter whose deep, gruff voice is an ideal vehicle for carrying traditional blues themes of betrayal and broken love, and for documenting in song the wars between men and women, Big Time Sarah is a singer in the tradition of BIG MAMA THORNTON, BIG MAYBELLE, and other big-voiced blues women.

Born in Mississippi, she came to Chicago with her family in 1960 and began singing in church. By her early teens she had fallen for the blues. Sarah's earliest experience singing in Chicago blues clubs came with the ACES. Other artists such as MAGIC SLIM and BUDDY GUY also encouraged her by giving her stage time. In the late '70s Sarah toured with SUNNYLAND SLIM and then ERWIN HELFER, though most of her performing was done in Chicago blues clubs such as B.L.U.E.S., Kingston Mines, and Biddy Mulligan's.

Sarah formed her own band, the BTS Express, in 1989 and soon became one of the principal female blues singers in Chicago. In 1993 she recorded her debut album, *Lay It on 'Em Girls*, for Delmark Records. Big Time Sarah continues to perform regularly.

Essential Listening:
Lay It on 'Em Girls/Delmark (DD 659)

◄ BIG TWIST

(born Larry Nolan, September 22, 1937, Terre Haute, Ind.; died March 14, 1990, Broadview, Ill.)

Larry "Big Twist" Nolan was the affable lead singer of the horn-dominated group, Big Twist and the MELLOW FELLOWS, which included guitarist Pete Special and saxophonist Terry Ogilini. Before he joined the band in 1970, Twist, a journeyman musician and singer who performed everything from blues to pop in Midwest bar bands was living in the college town of Carbondale, Illinois. When he agreed to become the Mellow Fellows' lead singer, Twist was playing drums in a country outfit.

For much of the 1970s, Big Twist and the Mellow Fellows built their repertoire on a blend of soul, R&B, blues, and rock, and performed at college fraternity parties, beer joints, and clubs throughout the Midwest. In 1978 the band relocated to Chicago; a year later Twist and the Mellow Fellows recorded their self-titled debut album for the Flying Fish label.

One other Flying Fish album, *One Track Mind*, followed in 1982 before the band switched to Alligator Records. Twist and the Mellow Fellows' subsequent album, *Playing for Keeps*, enabled the band to break out beyond its regional following and attract national attention. But on his way to becoming a recording artist, Twist suffered from bouts of ill health, brought on by kidney problems and his often excessive weight. In 1986 he recorded one more album with the Mellow Fellows and Alligator, *Live from Chicago!—Bigger than Life!!*, before increasing problems with diabetes made it impossible for him to perform with the same vigor he had in better days, or to record with the band. Big Twist died in 1990. The Mellow Fellows continued on until guitarist Pete Special left the band. At that point it changed its name to the Chicago Rhythm & Blues Kings. The band continues to perform.

Essential Listening:
Big Twist and the Mellow Fellows/Flying Fish (FF 70229)
One Track Mind/Flying Fish (FF 268)
Playing for Keeps/Alligator (AL 4732)
Live from Chicago!—Bigger than Life!!/Alligator (AL 4755)

◀ BIHARI BROTHERS, THE

The Bihari brothers—Jules, Joe, Saul, and Lester—owned Modern Records and its subsidiary labels: RPM, Kent, Crown, Flair, and Meteor. Together, the brothers released records by major blues and rhythm & blues artists in the late 1940s and 1950s, including B.B. KING, JOHN LEE HOOKER, ELMORE JAMES, JIMMY WITHERSPOON, ETTA JAMES, PEE WEE CRAYTON, and JOHNNY "GUITAR" WATSON. In the process, they helped bring credence to the post–World War II West Coast blues and rhythm & blues scenes.

Modern, the mother label, was formed in 1945 after Jules, a jukebox sales representative, couldn't get the R&B records his customers requested. With Jules overseeing the recording process, Joe handling sales, and Saul running the manufacturing end of the label, the Biharis went into the record business. Based in Los Angeles, the company recorded its own artists and either leased or bought masters from independent producers such as BOB GEDDINS in Oakland, Bill Quinn in Houston, and SAM PHILLIPS in Memphis.

Capitalizing on the postwar R&B boom, Modern was successful from the outset. In 1948, the Bihari brothers formed their first subsidiary, RPM; the label's first big hit was B.B. King's "Three O'Clock Blues" in 1951. In the meantime the fourth Bihari brother, Lester, had gone to Memphis, formed Meteor Records, and hired IKE TURNER as chief scout, taking the place of Phillips, who had gone on to form his own Sun Records. By the mid-'50s, the Crown subsidiary began releasing albums, while Kent concentrated on singles.

Modern's importance to blues and rhythm & blues began to wane in the 1960s as pop music tastes shifted to rock & roll. Eventually the brothers sold off their labels and faded from the blues scene.

Essential Listening:
The Fifties: R&B Vocal Groups (Various Artists)/Flair-Virgin (V2-86305)
The Fifties: Juke Joint Blues (Various Artists)/Flair-Virgin (V2-86304)
Juke Box R&B (Various Artists)/Flair-Virgin (V2-86302)
R&B Confidential No. 1: The Flair Label (Various Artists)/Flair-Virgin
  (V2-86303)

◄ BISHOP, ELVIN

(born October 21, 1942, Tulsa, Okla.)

As a blues guitarist, Elvin Bishop is best known for his work as an original member of the PAUL BUTTERFIELD Blues Band, the groundbreaking group that helped introduce electric Chicago-style blues to rock audiences in the mid-'60s. Bishop also had a successful blues-flavored career as a rock artist. In 1976 his song "Fooled Around and Fell in Love," sung by Mickey Thomas (later of the Jefferson Starship), reached number 3 on the pop charts.

Bishop was born and raised in Tulsa, Oklahoma, where he learned about the blues by listening to the radio and collecting blues records. A scholarship to the University of Chicago enabled him to move to the Windy City in 1959. He met harmonica player and singer Paul Butterfield at the university, and the two white musicians played black blues clubs, often sitting in with noted bluesmen such as guitarists OTIS RUSH and BUDDY GUY.

Butterfield formed the Paul Butterfield Blues Band in 1963, which included Bishop and later MIKE BLOOMFIELD on guitars. Their lively dual-guitar solos, heard most prominently on the thirteen-minute-plus song "East-West," the title track of the group's second album, set the stage for the soaring twin-guitar dialogue of Dickey Betts and Duane Allman of the ALLMAN BROTHERS BAND a couple of years later.

Bishop recorded three albums with the Paul Butterfield Blues Band before embarking on a solo career. He signed a contract with Epic Records in 1970 and released four albums that contained a poppish blend of blues, rock, country, gospel, and rhythm & blues. Although his albums sold moderately well, it wasn't until Bishop signed with Capricorn in 1974 that his solo career took off. "Travelin' Shoes," off his Capricorn debut, *Let It Flow*, almost made it into the top 40. *Struttin' My Stuff*, Bishop's follow-up album, included "Fooled Around and Fell in Love."

As rock moved away from its blues and R&B roots in the late '70s, Bishop began to fade from the scene, and his alledged problems with drugs and alcohol began to take their toll. Bishop resurfaced in 1988 after he signed a new recording contract with Alligator Records. Both *Big Fun* (1988) and *Don't Let the Bossman Get You Down!* (1991) contain Bishop's delectable, bluesy mix of American music. Bishop continues to record and perform, and lives in the San Francisco Bay area, where he moved after leaving the Butterfield Band in the late '60s.

Essential Listening:

The Paul Butterfield Blues Band (Paul Butterfield Blues Band)/Elektra (7294-2)

East-West (Paul Butterfield Blues Band)/Elektra (7315-2)

The Resurrection of Pigboy Crabshaw (Paul Butterfield Blues Band)/Elektra (74014-2)

Big Fun/Alligator (AL 4767)

Don't Let the Bossman Get You Down!/Alligator (AL 4791)

◄ BLACK ACE, THE

(aka B. K. Turner) (born Babe Karo Lemon Turner, December 21, 1905, Hughes Springs, Tex.; died November 7, 1972, Fort Worth, Tex.)

Babe Turner, better known as the Black Ace, was a Texas country bluesman who played a steel-bodied Hawaiian-style slide guitar. Born on a farm a few miles from the Louisiana-Texas border, Turner taught himself how to play the guitar and occasionally performed at house parties in the Hughes Springs area in the late 1920s. Later Turner teamed up with bluesman OSCAR "BUDDY" WOODS, who taught him how to play the Hawaiian steel guitar laid across his knees. Together they performed regularly around Shreveport, Louisiana, during the Depression.

Sometime in the mid-1930s Turner relocated to Fort Worth, Texas, where he frequently performed on KFJZ radio. In 1937 the Black Ace, as he was then called, recorded six sides for the Decca label. Turner continued to perform at parties and on radio programs until he was drafted into the armed forces during World War II. After being discharged, Turner picked cotton and held assorted menial jobs before being rediscovered by blues record producers Chris Strachwitz and Paul Oliver. Turner recorded for Strachwitz's Arhoolie label in 1960. In 1962 he appeared in the documentary, *The Blues*. Ten years later he died of cancer.

Essential Listening:

I'm the Boss Card in Your Hand/Arhoolie (CD 374)

◄ BLACKWELL, SCRAPPER

(born Francis Blackwell, February 21, 1903, Syracuse, S.C.; died October 7, 1962, Indianapolis, Ind.)

Scrapper Blackwell ranks with LONNIE JOHNSON as one of the earliest and most influential urban blues guitarists. His single-string style of playing helped bridge the gap between roughed-up rural blues and the slicker sounds of urban blues. Blackwell and his piano-playing partner, LEROY CARR, also popularized guitar-piano blues duets in the late 1920s and 1930s. Together they made a number of superlative recordings, including "How Long How Long Blues" and "My Own Lonesome Blues," and set the standards by which other guitar-piano duets would be judged.

Though Blackwell was born in the South, he grew up and spent most of his life in Indianapolis, where he taught himself to play guitar. Blackwell was a successful moonshiner before he was a recording artist. It wasn't until Carr persuaded Blackwell to record with him in 1928 for the Vocalion label that Blackwell considered a career in music. The overwhelmingly positive reaction to the duo's debut recording, "How Long How Long Blues," convinced Blackwell that the blues was worth taking seriously. Later in 1928 Blackwell also recorded as a solo artist for Vocalion. His song "Kokomo Blues" was later transformed into KO-KOMO ARNOLD's "Old Kokomo Blues" and Robert Johnson's "Sweet Home Chicago." Blackwell also recorded with BERTHA "CHIPPIE" HILL, GEORGIA TOM

DORSEY, Black Bottom McPhail, and others, though his most memorable recordings were done with Carr.

Blackwell's guitar style was less urbane than Lonnie Johnson's, with whom he's often compared, though Blackwell possessed much of Johnson's technical prowess. Blackwell was also the perfect accompanist. He and Carr seemed to have had an intimate understanding of each other's skills and preferences when it came to playing the blues, and rarely did they compete with each other, musically. In fact, few blues musicians of the time complemented each other with more memorable results.

When Carr died in 1935 at age thirty, Blackwell was heartbroken and not long thereafter quit music. He worked as a manual laborer in Indianapolis, a forgotten artist until 1959 when he resumed his recording career. Blackwell was on the verge of a comeback when he was shot to death in Indianapolis in 1962.

Essential Listening:
The Virtuoso Guitar of Scrapper Blackwell/Yazoo (L 1019)
Blues Before Sunrise (Leroy Carr)/Portrait (RK 44122)

◄ BLAKE, BLIND

*(aka Blind Arthur) (born Arthur Phelps or Arthur Blake, early 1890s,
Jacksonville, Fla.; died c. 1933, Fla.)*

Blind Blake was a first-generation blues guitarist whose intricate sense of phrasing and complex finger-picking technique made him one of the music's first great stylists. Blake incorporated broad strokes of ragtime and jazz into his blues, which led to a wide-open, swinging guitar style later mimicked by many East Coast blues guitarists.

Almost nothing is known about Blake's life. He was probably born in Jacksonville, Florida, in the early 1890s, though some blues historians believe he came from the Georgia Sea Islands. Being blind, Blake most likely earned a meager living playing for change on street corners or for Saturday night dances and fish fries. Sometime in the 1920s he went to Chicago and was probably living in the city when he signed a recording contract with Paramount Records in 1926. His first recorded side, "West Coast Blues," was a hit and led to a recording career that lasted until 1932. In all, Blake recorded nearly eighty titles and, along with BLIND LEMON JEFFERSON, was one of the blues' most popular male artists in the 1920s. Their success helped arouse interest in rural blues, which led to the discovery of numerous country blues guitarists in the 1930s. Blake died around 1933, probably in Florida. He was inducted into the Blues Foundation's Hall of Fame in 1990.

Essential Listening:
Ragtime Guitar's Foremost Fingerpicker/Yazoo (1068)
Blind Blake, Vol. 1 (1926–27)/Document (DOCD 5024)
Blind Blake, Vol. 2 (1927–28)/Document (DOCD 5025)
Blind Blake, Vol. 3 (1928–29)/Document (DOCD 5026)
Blind Blake, Vol. 4 (1929–32)/Document (DOCD 5027)

◄ BLAND, BOBBY "BLUE"

(born January 27, 1930, Rosemark, Tenn.)

In the 1950s and early 1960s Bobby "Blue" Bland was one of the main creators of the modern soul-blues sound. Along with artists such as Sam Cooke, RAY CHARLES, and JUNIOR PARKER, Bland developed a sound that mixed gospel with blues and R&B and colored it with a shimmering soul sensibility. Bland's particular style of soul-blues was punctuated with big-band brassiness and slick, B.B. KING–flavored guitar riffs. A compelling singer who could go from a falsetto to a gospel growl in one song, Bland easily ranks as one of the great soul-blues vocalists of all time.

Bland was born and raised in Rosemark, a small town just outside Memphis. In 1947 he moved to the city with his mother and began his career, first as a singer in the gospel group the Miniatures, then in the loosely knit blues group the Beale Streeters, which included such future blues stars as JOHNNY ACE, B.B. King, Junior Parker, and ROSCO GORDON.

Bland's earliest recording period was from 1950 to 1952, when he cut sides for the Modern and Chess labels. Getting drafted into the army in 1952 temporarily waylaid his career, but Bland was discharged in 1954, and shortly thereafter he began a long-term relationship with Duke Records that would result in dozens of records, many of them big sellers in the R&B market.

Bland's first Duke single, "It's My Life, Baby," was released in 1955. Two years later, he scored with the seminal Texas shuffle "Farther Up the Road," which went to number 1 on the R&B charts. Follow-up records included two 1961 hits, "I Pity the Fool," which also made it to number 1 on the R&B charts, and "Turn on Your Love Light," which went to number 2. "That's the Way Love Is," a 1963 release, gave Bland his third number 1 hit.

From 1957 to 1961 Bland played the chitlin' circuit with Junior Parker and his band, the Blue Flames. But in 1961 Bland broke with Parker, went out on his own, and rose to his greatest popularity. Because Bland neither composed nor played an instrument, he relied on others for songs and inspired instrumentation. Joe Scott, his bandleader and arranger, and for years one of Duke label owner DON ROBEY's chief talent scouts, helped create Bland's horn-heavy, big-band sound. Just as important to Bland's sound was guitarist WAYNE BENNETT, who complemented the horns and Bland's vocals with clipped, jazz-influenced solos, a la T-BONE WALKER and B.B. King.

Bland worked with Scott and Bennett until 1968 when the band broke up, partially the result of Bland's alledged alcohol problems. But Bland resuscitated his career in 1972, this time with producer Steve Garrie and bandleader Ernie Fields, Jr. Rather than dwell on R&B ballads, Garrie gave Bland a punchier, blues-based sound that resulted in two of his more commercially successful albums: *California Album* (1973) and *Dreamer* (1974). Both works were released on the ABC-Dunhill label, the company that purchased Duke in 1972.

Despite Bland's incredibly extensive recording catalogue, his long-term success on the R&B charts, and his near-constant touring (often with longtime friend B.B. King), he rarely crossed over into the pop realm. Dozens of blues and R&B-

influenced rock vocalists have, however, credited Bland as a main influence. Throughout the '70s, '80s, and early '90s, he continued to record, mostly for the Jackson, Mississippi, blues label, Malaco. Bland was inducted into the Blues Foundation's Hall of Fame in 1981 and the Rock & Roll Hall of Fame in 1992. He continues to perform regularly.

Essential Listening:
The Best of Bobby Bland/MCA (27013)
Two Steps from the Blues/MCA (27036)
The Best of Bobby Bland, Volume 2/MCA (4 MC 27045)
The "3B" Blues Boy—The Blues Years, 1952–1959/Ace (CDCHD 302)
Touch of the Blues and Spotlighting the Man/Mobile Fidelity (MFCD 770)
First Class Blues/Malaco (MAL 5000)
Midnight Run/Malaco (MAL 7450)
Portrait of the Blues/Malaco (MAL 7458)

◄ BLOCK, RORY

(born November 6, 1949, New York, N.Y.)

A country blues-style guitarist and singer whose influences include ROBERT JOHNSON, MISSISSIPPI FRED MCDOWELL, CHARLEY PATTON, and other pre–World War II bluesmen, Rory Block is one of just a handful of white women who have interpreted the rough-edged sounds of Mississippi Delta blues. Like BONNIE RAITT, Block has kept the traditional sounds of Delta blues alive and given the form a fresh, female point of view.

Block grew up around folk music; her father, a fiddle and banjo player, owned a sandal shop in New York's Greenwich Village in the early '60s. The shop was a hangout for many of the Village's folksingers, including John Sebastian and Tim Hardin. Block played the recorder as a child, and then switched to guitar. She took classical guitar lessons until she discovered the blues at age fourteen. Getting occasional lessons from the likes of MISSISSIPPI JOHN HURT, REV. BLIND GARY DAVIS, and SON HOUSE, Block became obsessed with detailing the finer points of the blues in her playing.

Block left New York in her midteens with fellow blues guitarist Stefan Grossman, with whom she would later record a blues guitar instructional album (*How to Play Blues Guitar*), and went to California. She played coffeehouses and clubs, but eventually quit performing to start a family. By the time she resumed her career in the mid-70s, interest in country blues had slowed to a trickle.

Block recorded albums for the RCA and Chrysalis labels, which featured a sloshy mix of rhythm & blues, pop, and even disco, before she signed with Rounder Records in 1981. Rounder encouraged Block to go back to playing acoustic country blues. Her debut album for the label, *High Heeled Blues*, was released the following year and received critical accolades from *Rolling Stone* and other music magazines. Block's other Rounder albums, especially *Mama's Blues* and *Ain't I a Woman*, have garnered similar praise. On these works, Block mixed traditional blues tunes by her mentors with original blues and occasional pop ballads. Block continues to perform and record.

Essential Listening:
High Heeled Blues/Rounder (3061)
Blue Horizon/Rounder (3073)
Rhinestones & Steel Strings/Rounder (3085)
I've Got a Rock in My Sock/Rounder (3097)
House of Hearts/Rounder (3104)
Mama's Blues/Rounder (3117)
Best Blues and Originals/Rounder (11525)
Ain't I a Woman/Rounder (3120)

◄ BLOOMFIELD, MIKE

(born July 28, 1944, Chicago, Ill.; died February 15, 1981, San Francisco, Calif.)

Mike Bloomfield was one of the first great blues-rock guitarists. His strikingly original work in the mid-'60s with the PAUL BUTTERFIELD Blues Band cut the path that dozens of other white, blues-influenced rock guitarists, including ERIC CLAPTON, Jimmy Page, and JOHNNY WINTER, would follow in the late 1960s.

Bloomfield was born and raised in Chicago. As a fledgling blues guitarist he was audacious enough to sit in with many of the black bluesmen performing in South Side clubs in the early '60s. Thus, unlike many of his white British blues-rock contemporaries, Bloomfield was given a rare, hands-on education by blues masters such as MUDDY WATERS, OTIS RUSH, and MAGIC SAM.

Bloomfield performed with singer Nick Gravenites and harmonica player CHARLIE MUSSELWHITE before joining Paul Butterfield's band in 1965. Bloomfield's stunning lead-guitar work on the band's self-titled debut and its follow-up, *East-West*, made him highly respected among both black and white blues musicians.

Bloomfield quit the Butterfield Blues Band in 1967; a year later he and Gravenites formed the innovative but short-lived ELECTRIC FLAG, a progressive San Francisco–based blues-rock band that featured a horn section and a driving rhythm section. After the demise of the Electric Flag in 1968, Bloomfield's career began a downward spiral from which it never recovered. The ill-advised *Super Session* album he recorded with Stephen Stills and Al Kooper in 1968 received mixed reviews. Bloomfield also developed a heroin habit that nearly destroyed his ability to play guitar.

In 1973, Bloomfield joined Triumvirate, a blues "supergroup" that also included DR. JOHN on keyboards and JOHN HAMMOND, JR., on guitar. The band was a flop. For the remainder of the '70s Bloomfield earned a living by scoring pornographic movies (in the late '60s he had written the music for such counter-culture film classics as *The Trip, Medium Cool*, and Andy Warhol's *Bad*) and recording poorly distributed solo albums. However, one album, *If You Love These Blues, Play 'Em as You Please*, was nominated for a Grammy in 1977. But Bloomfield's reluctance to tour, due mostly to nagging problems with drugs and insomnia, cursed any serious comeback. In 1981 he died of a drug overdose.

Essential Listening:
The Paul Butterfield Blues Band/Elektra (7294-2)
East-West (Paul Butterfield Blues Band)/Elektra (7315-2)
A Long Time Comin' (The Electric Flag)/Columbia (CS 9597)
If You Love These Blues, Play 'Em as You Please/Guitar Player (KT 5006)
The Best of Mike Bloomfield/Allegiance (7115)

◄ BLUE, LITTLE JOE

(born Joe Valery, September 23, 1934, Vicksburg, Miss.; died April 22, 1990, Reno, Nev.)

Guitarist and singer Little Joe Blue was an unheralded bluesman who briefly recorded for the Checker (Chess) label in the mid-1960s and later become part of the San Francisco Bay Area blues scene. His style, a blend of B.B. KING and LOWELL FULSON influences, endeared him to a small circle of blues fans, mostly on the West Coast, where he lived for the better part of his career.

Though born in Mississippi, Blue grew up in Louisiana. By 1951 he had settled in Detroit, where he worked on the auto assembly lines. Blue worked with BOBO JENKINS and other Motor City blues artists but was unable to expand his career beyond the local scene. After moving to California, Blue recorded three singles for Checker in 1966—"Dirty Work Goin' On," "My Tomorrow," and "Me and My Woman"—but none of the records attracted much attention. Blue continued to work small clubs, with an occasional tour of Europe with the American Blues Legends package. In 1977 he moved to Dallas and performed in local clubs there until relocating to Reno, Nevada. He died of cancer in 1990.

Essential Listening:
Dirty Work Going On/Evejim (1991)
I'm Doing All Right Again/Evejim (4009)

◄ BLUES BOY WILLIE

(born William McFalls, November 28, 1946, Memphis, Tex.)

Blues Boy Willie is a Texas-based singer whose influences include PERCY MAYFIELD and Little Willie Littlefield. He blends chitlin' circuit soul with rhythm & blues and Texas blues and is known both for his syrupy romantic ballads and his sense of humor. Blues Boy's most popular songs, "Be Who" and "Be Who 2," the title tracks from his second and third albums, respectively, contain amusing, bawdy dialogue against a funky bass backdrop.

Blues Boy began his professional singing career at age eight. After paying his dues by performing in countless Texas bars and roadhouses, he signed a recording contract with Ichiban Records in 1988 and teamed up with longtime friend and labelmate Gary B.B. Coleman to make his debut album, *Strange Things Happening*. Coleman also produced the follow-up album, *Be Who*, which remained on the R&B charts for 21 weeks, and its sequel, *Be Who 2*. Blues Boy Willie continues to record and perform.

Essential Listening:
Strange Things Happening/Ichiban (Ich 1038)
Be Who/Ichiban (Ich 1064)
Be Who 2/Ichiban (Ich 1119)
I've Got the Blues/Ichiban (Ich 1145)

◄ BLUES BROTHERS, THE

Original members: John Belushi (aka Jake Blues) (singer) (born January 24,
1949, Chicago, Ill.; died March 5, 1982, Los Angeles, Calif.); Dan Aykroyd
(aka Elwood Blues) (singer, harmonica) (born July 1, 1952, Ottawa, Canada)

It's debatable whether the Blues Brothers was a sincere tribute or a smart rip-
off of the Stax-Volt soul sound that originated out of Memphis in the late '60s.
The Blues Brothers were actors John Belushi (Jake Blues) and Dan Aykroyd
(Elwood Blues), two cast members of "Saturday Night Live," the popular late-
night TV program that regularly features live music and comedic skits. Belushi
and Aykroyd were both avid soul and blues fans; together in 1977 they created
the "Blues Brothers" concept by covering soul classics like Sam & Dave's "Soul
Man" and JOHNNIE TAYLOR's "Who's Making Love," dressing in sloppy suits,
sunglasses and fedoras, and peppering their dialogue with blues slang.

The Blues Brothers' popularity on "Saturday Night Live" prompted the duo
in 1978 to record a live album, *Briefcase Full of Blues*, that featured Belushi's
scraggly voice and Aykroyd's amateur harmonica riffs. What gave the Blues
Brothers credence was its back-up band, comprised of such Stax-Volt session
men as guitarist Steve Cropper and bass player Donald "Duck" Dunn and blues
guitarist MATT "GUITAR" MURPHY. Two more albums, the live *Made in America*
and the soundtrack to the movie, *The Blues Brothers*, were released in 1980. But
the accidental drug overdose of John Belushi in early 1982 ended the Blues
Brothers at the peak of their success. A greatest hits album, *The Best of the Blues*
Brothers, was released later that year.

Essential Listening:
The Best of the Blues Brothers/Atlantic (19331)

◄ BLUES INCORPORATED

Original members: Cyril Davies (harmonica, vocals) (born 1932, England; died
January 7, 1964, England); Alexis Korner (guitar, vocals) (born April 19,
1928, Paris, France; died January 2, 1984); Charlie Watts (drums) (born June
2, 1941, Islington, England); Dick Heckstall-Smith (saxophone) (born
September 26, 1943, Ludlow, England); Andy Hogenboom (bass) (birth
information unknown)

Blues Incorporated was the seminal English blues band that paved the way for
the rhythm & blues and later the blues-rock crazes that swept the country in the
1960s. The group was formed in London in 1961, and in all likelihood it was
one of England's first white electric blues bands.

Blues Incorporated was founded by harmonica player CYRIL DAVIES. Known for performing weekly at London's famed Marquee Club, Blues Incorporated inspired dozens of other young musicians to explore the blues and R&B, including Mick Jagger, who often sang with the group. Later, Blues Incorporated included such British blues-rock stalwarts as bass player Jack Bruce and drummer Ginger Baker (both of whom would play in CREAM with ERIC CLAPTON), keyboards player GRAHAM BOND (who would go on to form the Graham Bond Organisation), and singer LONG JOHN BALDRY.

Because of Blues Incorporated's drift toward jazz-flavored blues, Davies, a staunch admirer of Chicago-style blues, quit the group in late 1962 and formed Cyril Davies' R&B All-Stars. Watts took up with Mick Jagger and the ROLLING STONES, while Bruce replaced Andy Hogenboom on bass. This left guitarist-singer ALEXIS KORNER leading the group. The revolving musician policy, in effect, turned Blues Incorporated into a proving ground for young musicians who used the band to gain valuable stage experience and then leave for greener pastures. Blues Incorporated finally dissolved in 1967. Alexis Korner went on to form the group New Church and share the unofficial title of Britain's elder blues statesman with JOHN MAYALL until his death in 1984.

Essential Listening:
R&B from the Marquee/Deram

◄ BLUES PROJECT, THE

Original members: Danny Kalb (guitar, vocals) (born September 19, 1942, Brooklyn, N.Y.); Roy Blumenfeld (drums) (born May 11, 1944, Bronx, N.Y.); Andy Kulberg (bass, flute) (born April 30, 1944, Buffalo, N.Y.); Steve Katz (guitar, harmonica, vocals) (born May 9, 1945, Brooklyn, N.Y.); Tommy Flanders (vocals) (birth information unknown); Al Kooper (keyboards, vocals) (born February 5, 1944, Brooklyn, N.Y.)

In the mid-1960s the Blues Project was New York's first and most popular blues-rock band, and helped ignite interest in electric blues in the city. Formed by guitarist Danny Kalb, the group made its debut in 1965 at the Cafe Au Go Go in Greenwich Village. Less than a year later, the Blues Project recorded its first album there: *Live at Cafe Au Go Go.*

Despite its name, the Blues Project was not a strict blues band. Kalb had strong blues, rock, and folk roots, while the other members of the band had similar musical interests. However, near-constant dissension in the group over its musical direction weakened the Blues Project's output. Nonetheless, the band's debut recording, and its follow-up album and only studio effort, *Projections* (1966), were innovative studies in electric blues. (The Blues Project released a third album, *Live at Town Hall*, in 1967.)

The Blues Project disbanded in 1967 after keyboards player Al Kooper left the group. Kooper went on to form Blood, Sweat and Tears, and was later joined by Steve Katz. Kulberg and drummer Blumenfeld formed Sea Train, Kalb eventually became a session musician, and singer Tommy Flanders attempted a solo career. In 1971 Kalb put together a new version of the Blues Project, which included Blumenfeld. The resulting album, *Lazarus*, mustered little interest. In the summer of 1972 Kooper reunited all the original members of the band (minus Flanders) and performed in Central Park. *Reunion*, a live album that resulted from the concert, was released in 1973.

Essential Listening:
The Best of the Blues Project/Rhino (R2-70165)

◄ BLUESBREAKERS, THE

Original members: John Mayall (keyboards, harmonica, vocals) (born November 29, 1943, Manchester, England); John McVie (bass) (born November 26, 1945, London, England); Bernie Watson (guitar) (birth information unknown); Keith Robertson (drums) (birth information unknown)

The list of musicians who in the '60s and '70s were members of JOHN MAY-ALL's legendary group, the Bluesbreakers, reads like a Who's Who of British blues-rockers. In addition to its most famous member, guitarist ERIC CLAPTON, Bluesbreakers' alumni include guitarists Mick Taylor (ROLLING STONES), Peter Green (FLEETWOOD MAC), Harvey Mandel (CANNED HEAT), Jon Mark (Mark-Almond Band), and Jimmy McCulloch (Paul McCartney's Wings); bassists John McVie (Fleetwood Mac), Jack Bruce (CREAM), and Andy Fraser (Free); drummers Mick Fleetwood (Fleetwood Mac), Aynsley Dunbar (Frank Zappa and the Mothers of Invention), Keef Hartley (Keef Hartley Band), Jon Hiseman (Colosseum), and Hughie Flint (McGuiness-Flint); and reedsman John Almond (Mark-Almond Band).

Mayall, a fanatical blues record collector and blues musician, began the Bluesbreakers in 1963. From the outset, Mayall insisted that the band's rendition of American blues be as pure as possible. Despite an almost constantly changing lineup, Mayall's band became the most respected blues unit in England in the mid-'60s, while Mayall became a father figure to many of the musicians he hired. The Bluesbreakers achieved its greatest fame during the Clapton years of 1965 and 1966. The band's 1966 album, *Bluesbreakers—John Mayall with Eric Clapton*, might well be the best British blues album ever made.

Clapton left the Bluesbreakers in 1966 to form Cream, which also included Bluesbreaker bass player Jack Bruce. Mayall's Bluesbreakers also gave birth to Fleetwood Mac and other groups. Mayall often said in interviews that he didn't mind musicians using his band as a springboard in which to jump to bigger and more notable projects. Mayall, who lives in the U.S., continues to record and perform with the latest version of the Bluesbreakers, which includes guitarist Coco Montoya.

Essential Listening:
Bluesbreakers—John Mayall with Eric Clapton/London (800 086-2)
London Blues (1964–1969)/Polydor-Deram (844 302-2)

◄ BLUZBLASTERS, THE

Original members: Doug Newby (saxophone, vocals) (born October 22, 1949, Surry, Va.); Jimmy Williams (guitar, vocals) (born December 14, 1962, South Carolina); Glenn Foster (bass) (born April 8, 1961, Virginia Beach, Va.); Phil Riddle (drums) (born June 11, 1960, Danville, Va.)

The Bluzblasters, a Norfolk, Virginia, bar band, formed in 1987 under the leadership of saxophonist/singer Doug Newby and guitarist/singer Jimmy Williams. Prior to forming the band, Newby had worked with blues artists such as LITTLE JOHNNY TAYLOR and KENNY NEAL.

The Bluzblasters performed in clubs and bars in the Virginia and Washington, D.C., areas. The group gained a reputation for its driving brand of R&B and blues, which led to a recording contract with King Snake Records. The Bluzblasters' debut album, *Get Blasted*, was released in 1989. Frequent tours up and down the East Coast, dates in Switzerland and Italy, and an appearance at the tenth annual w.c. HANDY Awards show in Memphis followed. By late 1990, Hill had been replaced by Kelly Morris, while Phil Riddle had replaced George Smith on drums, and Williams had become a part-time member of the band. Also during this time, the Bluzblasters began backing soul-blues singer FRANKIE LEE; when Lee left New Jersey and relocated in Norfolk, the Lee/Bluzblasters connection solidified. The relationship resulted in a new recording contract with Flying Fish and the group's second album, *Sooner or Later*, which was released in 1992. However, in late 1992, Lee moved to Oakland, severing his relationship with the Bluzblasters, who continue to perform regularly.

Essential Listening:
Get Blasted/King Snake (KS 016)
Sooner or Later/Flying Fish (FF 0595)

◄ BO, EDDIE

(born Edwin Bocage, September 20, 1930, New Orleans, La.)

Eddie Bo was a singer, piano player, and record producer who contributed to the New Orleans rhythm & blues scene in the 1950s and early 1960s. Both his piano and vocal style contained blues and jazz elements, as did the bands he regularly led in the city's nightclubs.

Bo began his recording career for Ace Records in 1954; however, his earliest records attracted little attention outside the Crescent City. Bo also recorded for Apollo, Chess, and Ric Records in the 1950s; none of the singles he released for these labels charted either. Bo switched to Swan in 1962 and cut "Check Mr. Popeye," a bouncy R&B tune later covered by Southside Johnny and the Asbury Jukes, and spent the rest of the decade doing session work and cutting the occasional single.

In 1969 Bo recorded "Hook and Sling, Part I" for Scram Records; it was Bo's only semblance of a hit, peaking at number 13 on R&B charts. Bo spent most of the '70s working as a New Orleans producer. He remains semiactive in New Orleans R&B, mostly working with local labels.

Essential Listening:
Check Mr. Popeye/Rounder (2077)
Keys to the Crescent City (with Art Neville, Charles Brown, Willie Tee)/Rounder
  (2087)

◄ BOGAN, LUCILLE

*(aka Bessie Jackson) (born April 1, 1897, Amory, Miss.; died August 10, 1948,
Los Angeles, Calif.)*

Best known to blues record collectors and historians for writing and singing
"Shave 'Em Dry," one of the bawdiest blues songs ever recorded ("I got nipples
on my titties big as the end of my thumb/I got somethin' 'tween my legs'll make
a dead man come"), Lucille Bogan often explored explicit sexual themes and
tales of prostitution in her blues. She was a classic blues singer whose vocal
phrasings, tone, and understanding of blues subtleties were as authentic as many
of the other more noted blueswomen of the 1920s. But her reputation for risqué
lyrics and her blatant dealings with controversial topics such as lesbianism and
adultery often overshadowed any of her other contributions to early blues.

Bogan was born in Mississippi but raised in Birmingham, Alabama. Little is
known of her early life until 1923, when she made her first recordings for the
Okeh label in New York. She also recorded for the Paramount and Brunswick
labels in the late 1920s after she relocated to Chicago. In addition to lesbianism,
Bogan also sang about prostitution ("Stew Meat Blues," "Tricks Ain't Walkin'
No More"), alcoholism ("Sloppy Drunk Blues," "Cravin' Whiskey Blues"),
and abusive men ("Dirty Treatin' Blues," "Women Won't Need No Men").

From 1933 to 1935, Bogan, using the pseudonym Bessie Jackson, teamed up
with pianist WALTER ROLAND. The duo recorded for the American Record Company. It was during this two-year period that Bogan recorded "Shave 'Em Dry."
Two versions of the song were cut; an unreleased version of the song contained
far dirtier lyrics than the "cleaned-up" version that was released in 1935. (The
unexpurgated version has since been released; it is available on the *Hot Nuts and
Lollipops* CD compilation.)

ARC did not renew Bogan's recording contract in 1935 and she eventually
returned to Birmingham, where she was active in the city's blues scene, managing
the group Bogan's Birmingham Busters. Sometime in the late 1930s or early
1940s Bogan moved to the West Coast. She died in Los Angeles in 1948.

Essential Listening:
Hot Nuts and Lollipops (Various Artists)/Columbia (CK 46783)
Lucille Bogan & Walter Roland, 1927–1935/Yazoo (1017)

◄ BOLLIN, ZUZU

*(born A. D. Bollin, September 5, 1922, Frisco, Tex.; died October 26, 1990,
West Dallas, Tex.)*

A journeyman jump-blues singer and guitarist from the Dallas area, ZuZu
Bollin recorded four sides for the tiny Torch label in 1951 and 1952. Despite an

attractive baritone voice and a guitar style that was considerably influenced by T-BONE WALKER, Bollin's popularity never went much beyond Texas. When his solo career failed to take off, Bollin played in R&B singer PERCY MAYFIELD's band and backed such bluesmen as FRANKIE LEE SIMS before working with JIMMY REED in the late 1950s. By 1963, however, Bollin's aspirations to continue with a music career had evaporated, and he went into the dry cleaning business in Dallas.

In 1987, Bollin was rediscovered by Chuck Nevitt of the Dallas Blues Society, who coaxed him to record his first album, *Texas Bluesman*. Though the record attracted little national attention, it received enough acclaim in Texas blues circles for Bollin to launch a comeback. He began playing blues clubs, including regular appearances at the popular Austin blues club, Antone's, until his death in 1990. A year later, Antone's Records rereleased *Texas Bluesman*. The album was praised in *Rolling Stone* and other music publications.

Essential Listening:
Texas Bluesman/Antone's (ANT 0018)

◄ BOND, GRAHAM

(born October 28, 1937, Romford, England; died May 8, 1974, London, England)

Graham Bond was the leader of the Graham Bond Organisation, an innovative '60s British rhythm & blues band that, aside from Bond on organ, included drummer Ginger Baker, bass player Jack Bruce, and later, guitarist John McLaughlin. Although Bond began his career as a jazz saxophonist, he made his mark in the fledgling British blues scene, first as a member of BLUES INCORPORATED, which he joined in 1962, then with his own band the following year.

Bond was the first musician in London to work the organ into a blues and R&B framework. Though the Graham Bond Organisation did not have the clout or commercial success in the States that many of the other British Invasion bands did in the mid-'60s, it was a much-respected outfit in England. However, when Bruce and Baker left Bond to form CREAM with ERIC CLAPTON in 1966, the group began to fizzle. Bond broke up the band in 1968. After making a few unspectacular records, including one in 1972 called *Two Heads Are Better Than One* with Cream lyricist Pete Brown, and a brief reunion with Baker in Ginger Baker's Air Force, Bond formed the short-lived group Magus in 1973 with British folkie Carolanne Pegg. Money problems, excessive drug use, and a passion for the occult led Bond to a nervous breakdown in 1973. In 1974 he was found dead in a London subway station.

Essential Listening:
Mighty Graham Bond/Pulsar
Live at Klook's Kleek/Charly

◄ BONDS, SON

*(aka Brother Son Bonds, Brownville Son Bonds) (born March 16, 1909,
Brownsville, Tenn.; died August 31, 1947, Dyersburg, Tenn.)*

Son Bonds was a country blues guitarist and singer who came out of the same
Brownsville, Tennessee, scene that produced SLEEPY JOHN ESTES, HAMMIE NIXON,
and YANK RACHELL. Though Bonds was primarily a bluesman, he also sang and
recorded some gospel music under the name Brother Son Bonds.

In the late 1920s and early 1930s, Bonds often worked the streets of Brownsville and occasional house parties with harmonica player Hammie Nixon. His raw
country blues sound was not unlike other bluesmen from east Tennessee. When
Bonds began recording in 1934 for the Decca label, he cut solo sides as well as
sides with Nixon; the two musicians billed themselves as Hammie & Son. In
1941 Bonds also recorded for the Chicago-based Bluebird label with the Delta
Boys. The group included singer-guitarist Sleepy John Estes. Bonds died six years
later when he was accidentally shot.

Essential Listening:
Complete Recordings in Chronological Order/Wolf (129)

◄ BONNER, JUKE BOY

*(born Weldon Bonner, March 22, 1932, Bellville, Tex.; died June 28, 1978,
Houston, Tex.)*

Juke Boy Bonner was a multi-instrumentalist who often performed as a one-
man band. He played guitar, drums, harmonica, and various percussive instruments and mostly recorded for the Arhoolie label. Many of Bonner's original
songs were well-crafted works that went beyond the traditional blues themes of
heartache and tormented love; he wrote about racial conditions and personal experiences. But his popularity never rose above cult status.

Called Juke Boy because he sang along with jukebox records as a child, Bonner was mostly self-taught. He sang in a gospel group while in school but drifted
toward the blues by the time he was a teen. In 1948 he won a talent contest in
Houston and began appearing on KLEE radio and playing blues clubs and house
parties. Bonner moved to California in 1954; three years later he made his recording debut on BOB GEDDINS's Irma label and began performing as a one-man
band. He returned to Houston and remained there for the rest of his life, though
he toured regularly, working with the American Folk Blues Festival in England
and Europe in 1969 (the tour included a performance at the Royal Albert Hall),
playing the Ann Arbor Blues Festival in 1970, and the Montreux Blues Festival
in Switzerland in 1975. Although Bonner's best recording efforts were with Arhoolie, he continued to record with smaller labels, including Sonet and Home
Cookin', throughout the '70s. He died in 1978 of cirrhosis of the liver.

Essential Listening:
I'm Going Back to the Country/Arhoolie (1036)
The Struggle/Arhoolie (1045)

The One Man Trio/Flyright (548)
They Call Me "Juke Boy"/Ace (CHD 269)

◄ BOOGIE WOOGIE RED

(born Vernon Harrison, October 18, 1925, Rayville, La.; died July 2, 1992, Detroit, Mich.)

Blues pianist Boogie Woogie Red had been a mainstay of the Detroit blues scene since the 1940s. He performed with SONNY BOY WILLIAMSON (Rice Miller), JOHN LEE HOOKER, and BABY BOY WARREN, and also recorded as a solo artist. In the mid-1970s he was the first artist signed to the Blind Pig label.

Born in Louisiana, Boogie Woogie Red's family relocated to Detroit when he was two years old. He taught himself how to play piano and played local bars in the years just prior to World War II. After the war, Red teamed up with Williamson and remained with the noted harmonica player until Red moved briefly to Chicago in the late 1940s. When he returned to Detroit, Red began a longtime relationship with Baby Boy Warren that lasted until the mid-1970s. Red also played in John Lee Hooker's band in and around Detroit in the early 1950s.

However, with the rise of soul music in the Motor City in the 1960s, the Detroit blues scene all but disappeared and club work for Red dried up. He resumed his blues career in the early 1970s with Baby Boy Warren, playing the prestigious Ann Arbor Blues Festival and even touring Europe as part of the American Blues Legends package. After an extended stay at the Blind Pig club in Ann Arbor, Boogie Woogie Red recorded the album *Live at the Blind Pig* for the newly formed Blind Pig label in 1975. A Boogie Woogie Red follow-up album, *Red Hot*, was released by the label in 1977 and featured more of his rollicking barrelhouse piano passages. Red continued to play clubs in and around Detroit in the '80s and appeared on a 1991 Blind Pig compilation album called *Blue Ivory*, which also included tracks by ROOSEVELT SYKES and HENRY GRAY. Red died in 1992.

Essential Listening:
Red Hot/Blind Pig (003-77)
Blue Ivory (with Roosevelt Sykes, Henry Gray, and Mr. B)/Blind Pig (BP 74591)

◄ BOOK BINDER, ROY

(born Roy Bookbinder, October 5, 1943, New York, N.Y.)

Guitarist Roy Book Binder is a modern-day songster and storyteller whose synthesis of Piedmont blues, early country music, and bluegrass goes by the name hillbilly blues. Born in New York, Book Binder listened to rhythm & blues and early rock & roll before serving in the navy from 1962 to 1965. While in the navy Book Binder was introduced to the blues and began playing guitar. After his discharge he enrolled in Rhode Island Junior College and then the New School for Social Research in New York, but quit after meeting bluesman REV. BLIND GARY DAVIS in 1967. Book Binder became Davis's chauffeur and learned the finer points of Piedmont blues from him.

Book Binder began his recording career by cutting some sides for the Kicking Mule and Blue Goose labels in 1968. The next year he toured England with HOMESICK JAMES and ARTHUR "BIG BOY" CRUDUP. In 1970 Book Binder recorded his first album, *Travelin' Man*, for Adelphi and began to tour regularly. From 1973 to 1976 he usually worked with fiddle player Fats Kaplin. The duo recorded two albums for Blue Goose: *Git Fiddle Shuffle* in 1973 and *Ragtime Millionaire* in 1976. In 1976 Book Binder also moved into a motor home, which enabled him to remain, almost literally, on the road year-round, except for tours of Europe.

Book Binder recorded the album *Goin' Back to Tampa* as a solo artist for Flying Fish in 1979, then spent nearly ten years on the road, playing folk and blues festivals, college coffeehouses, and small clubs. He also developed a country and bluegrass audience for his hillbilly blues by frequently appearing on the TNN cable television program "Nashville Now."

Book Binder finally resumed his recording career when he signed with Rounder Records in 1988 and cut the album *Bookaroo!* In 1992 he released *The Hillbilly Blues Cats*, an album that featured harmonica player Rock Bottom. Book Binder continues to reside in a motor home and tours most of the year.

Essential Listening:
Goin' Back to Tampa/Flying Fish (098)
Bookaroo!/Rounder (3107)
The Hillbilly Blues Cats/Rounder (3121)

◄ BOOKER, JAMES

(born December 17, 1939, New Orleans, La.; died November 8, 1983, New Orleans, La.)

James Booker was a New Orleans keyboards player whose mental problems and drug addiction often prevented him from fulfilling his musical genius. Adept at both the piano and organ, Booker worked as a session musician, club performer, and touring sideman, as well as a solo recording artist. Influenced by the early New Orleans pianists TUTS WASHINGTON and ARCHIBALD, Booker was best known for his stunning piano phrasing and his smooth, liquidlike solos. Despite his talents, his recording output under his own name was sparse and his fame fleeting.

Booker was born in New Orleans but raised in Mississippi, where he learned how to play piano. At age fourteen he returned to New Orleans and promptly got a job playing blues and gospel piano on the radio station WMRY. Shortly thereafter, in 1953, Booker began his recording career, cutting tracks for the Imperial label and working with his own band, Booker Boy and the Rhythmaires. Though his early records attracted little attention, Booker had plenty of work as an accompanist, backing Shirley & Lee, EARL KING, SMILEY LEWIS, FATS DOMINO, Joe Tex, LLOYD PRICE, and HUEY "PIANO" SMITH, among others, either in the recording studio or on the road. In the mid-'50s Booker also briefly recorded for Chess and Ace before enrolling at Southern University in 1959 to study music.

A year later Booker cut his one and only hit single; "Gonzo," an organ instrumental recorded for the Peacock label, reached 3 number on the R&B charts in 1960. By this time, however, Booker had developed a serious drug problem. He worked on and off in the 1960s with B.B. KING, Joe Tex, LITTLE RICHARD, and others, but in 1970 was arrested for drug possession and sent to Angola State Prison in Louisiana. After his release, Booker moved to New York where he got session work with rock artists like Ringo Starr and the Doobie Brothers.

By 1975 Booker was back in New Orleans; he played the city's Jazz & Heritage Festival that year sporting a patch over his left eye (he supposedly lost half his sight in a drug mishap) and resurrected his reputation as a galvanizing piano player. His set's success at the fest led to a recording contract with Island Records, which released *Junco Partner* in 1976. Booker toured Europe in the late '70s and played the Montreux Jazz Festival in 1978 before returning to New Orleans. With his behavior growing more odd and his inability to control his drug problem growing more severe, Booker sank into the lower levels of the New Orleans club scene, performing erratically and getting sicker. In 1982 he recorded the album *Classified* for Rounder. In 1983 he died of a heart attack. He was forty-three years old.

Essential Listening:
New Orleans Piano Wizard: Live!/Rounder (2027)
Classified/Rounder (2036)
Junco Partner/Hannibal-Rykodisc (HNCD 1359)

◄ BOYD, EDDIE

(born November 25, 1914, Clarksdale, Miss.)

A popular post–World War II Chicago blues piano player and singer, Eddie Boyd is best known for his 1952 hit, "Five Long Years," which has since become a blues standard. Later in his career Boyd was one of a handful of blues artists who resettled in Europe and performed and recorded regularly there at a time when most bluesmen in the U.S. were barely scraping out a living.

Boyd was born and raised in the Mississippi Delta. As a youth he taught himself how to play piano and guitar, and he worked the jukes in and around the Delta before moving to Memphis in 1936. In the five years that he lived in Memphis, Boyd often performed in Beale Street blues clubs with his band, the Dixie Rhythm Boys. With recording on his mind, Boyd left Memphis for Chicago in 1941. There he worked in the city's blues joints with JOHNNY SHINES, JOHN LEE "SONNY BOY" WILLIAMSON, and an old Delta friend, MUDDY WATERS. The steadiest work came from Williamson, who also used Boyd in the recording studio.

In 1948 Boyd recorded with J.T. Brown's Boogie Band. These and other recording sessions led to his own contract with the J.O.B. label in 1951. A year later, Boyd recorded his song, "Five Long Years," which made it to the top of the R&B charts. In 1953 Boyd placed two more recordings in the R&B top 10: "24 Hours" and "Third Degree," both of which made it to number 3 on the charts. Boyd next recorded for Chess, though he was never able to match the triumph of "Five Long Years."

In the late '50s and early '60s Boyd recorded for a batch of small blues labels like Esquire, Mojo, and Palos. He made his first tour of Europe in 1965 as part of the American Folk Blues Festival package. Succeeding tours of England and the continent led to recording dates with JOHN MAYALL'S BLUESBREAKERS. The warm response to his brand of blues and the ease with which he obtained work convinced Boyd to move permanently to Europe in the late '60s. He first lived in Paris, then in 1971 moved to Helsinki, Finland, where he was acknowledged as a blues great.

Boyd continued to perform and record regularly in Europe into the '90s.

Essential Listening:

Eddie Boyd and His Blues Band/Crosscut (1002)

Ratting and Running Around/Crown Prince (400)

◄ BRACEY, ISHMAN

(aka Ishmon Bracey) (born January 9, 1901, Byram, Miss.; died February 12, 1970, Jackson, Miss.)

An early Mississippi Delta blues singer and guitarist, Ishman Bracey often worked with fellow bluesmen TOMMY JOHNSON and CHARLIE MCCOY in the Jackson area. His coarse vocals and penchant for bending his guitar strings to achieve a potent blues tone were his trademarks. During his youth Bracey supposedly served as a guide for BLIND LEMON JEFFERSON whenever the Texas bluesman worked the Delta. Later, like many other blues musicians of the time, Bracey played socials and picnics as well as on street corners for spare change.

Bracey made his first recordings in Memphis in 1928 for the Victor label. Two years later he traveled to Grafton, Wisconsin, to record for Paramount. Bracey continued to live the life of a bluesman until the late 1930s when he increasingly turned to religion. He all but abandoned his blues roots when he became an ordained minister sometime in the late 1940s or early 1950s. Bracey continued to play music, but it was mostly old religious standards. He died in 1970.

Essential Listening:

Ishman Bracey/Wolf (WSE 105)

◄ BRADFORD, PERRY

(born February 14, 1893, Montgomery, Ala.; died April 20, 1970, New York, N.Y.)

In 1920 Perry Bradford, a composer, arranger, producer, and pianist, made music history when he convinced Fred Hager of Okeh Records in New York to record MAMIE SMITH, a relatively unknown black singer. Smith sang two Bradford originals, "That Thing Called Love" and "You Can't Keep a Good Man Down." The record sold between fifty thousand and a hundred thousand copies, mostly to blacks. Its success surprised everyone but Bradford, who fervently believed blacks would buy records made by black artists.

Smith recorded a follow-up record a few months later, "Crazy Blues" backed with "It's Right Here for You," which were also Bradford originals. "Crazy Blues" was the first blues song ever recorded by a singer, white or black. Its amazing success—the record reputedly sold seventy-five thousand copies the first month of its release—not only helped create the "race record" market, but it also ushered in what became known as the Classic Blues Era.

Prior to 1920, Bradford had worked minstrel shows; however, after the Smith recordings, he went on to work with jazz artists like LOUIS ARMSTRONG and James P. Johnson, as well as other female blues singers of the period, namely ALBERTA HUNTER and EDITH WILSON. Bradford's songs and arrangements helped define the jazz-flavored blues style of the 1920s.

However, once the Depression hit and nearly destroyed the fledgling recording industry, Bradford's contributions to jazz and blues withered, though he continued in the business. Later on in his life he wrote his autobiography; called *Born with the Blues*, it was published in 1965. Bradford died in 1970.

Essential Listening:
Mamie Smith, Vol 1 (1920–1921)/Document (DLP 551)

◄ BRADSHAW, TINY

(born Myron Bradshaw, September 23, 1905, Youngstown, Ohio; died November 26, 1958, Cincinnati, Ohio)

Tiny Bradshaw began his career in big band jazz, but he had his biggest success as a rhythm & blues singer in the early 1950s. Born in Ohio, Bradshaw attended Wilberforce University and studied psychology before moving to New York to begin a career in music. One of his first stints was with Marion Hardy's Alabamians, the group that at one time had included Bradshaw's soon-to-be mentor, bandleader Cab Calloway. In 1934 Bradshaw started his own band, based in part on the style and sound of Calloway's big band. For a while Bradshaw's band featured vocalist Ella Fitzgerald, but he was better known for hiring superior saxophonists such as Sonny Stitt, Red Prysock, and Sil Austin.

Bradshaw's band recorded for the Decca label and worked regularly in the 1930s and 1940s. Shortly after the end of World War II they toured Japan, playing USO clubs. But with the big band era ending, Bradshaw, who could sing the blues convincingly, shifted from jazz to rhythm & blues and began recording for the King label as an R&B and jump blues shouter. In 1950 he registered two hits: "Well, Oh Well," which peaked at number 2 on the R&B charts, and "I'm Going to Have Myself a Ball," which made it to number 5. Bradshaw continued to record for King in the early '50s and perform with small R&B combos until his health began to fail. He died of a stroke in 1958.

Essential Listening:
Great Composer/King (KCD 653)
Breaking Up the House/Charly (CRB 1092)

◄ BRAGGS, AL "TNT"

(born 1934, Houston, Tex.)

Al Braggs began his singing career with the Blues Consolidated Revue, a late-1950s R&B package show based in Texas that featured BOBBY "BLUE" BLAND

and JUNIOR PARKER as the headliners. Braggs lacked an original style; he built up a following by imitating Bland's soul-blues vocal phrasing and incorporating gospel and rock & roll dynamics into his delivery. Braggs's forte was showmanship onstage. Known for his flips, jumps, and other histrionics, Braggs was an ideal show opener for the Revue, and beginning in 1959 he recorded for Don Robey's Peacock label, though his singles never dented the charts.

In 1961, when Bland and Parker parted and the Revue dissolved, Braggs continued on with Bland, even writing songs for him. Bland made Braggs's "Call on Me" a major hit in 1963. Braggs remained with Bland until around 1965 when he started a solo career. Although he continued to release occasional singles on the Peacock label, none of them attracted much attention. Braggs ended his association with Peacock in 1969. From that point on he performed in roadhouses and bars in and around Texas, gradually fading from the national blues and R&B scenes. He continues to perform on occasion.

◄ BRANCH, BILLY

(born October 3, 1953, Great Lakes, Ill.)

Since his arrival in Chicago in 1969, harmonica player Billy Branch has worked as a session musician and band member with a number of prominent blues musicians, including WILLIE DIXON, JOHNNY WINTER, and SON SEALS. He is also a founder of the group, the SONS OF BLUES. Branch's stock as a contemporary harp stylist appreciated after he recorded the critically acclaimed album *Harp Attack!* in 1990 with blues harp masters JUNIOR WELLS, JAMES COTTON, and CAREY BELL for Alligator Records.

Although he was born just outside Chicago, Branch was raised in southern California. He returned to Chicago in 1969 and enrolled at the University of Illinois as a political science major. First prize in a 1973 blues harp contest enabled him to secure work in Chicago blues clubs, often with the Sons of Blues, a group that then included guitarist LURRIE BELL, son of Carey Bell, and bass player Freddie Dixon, son of bass legend Willie Dixon. The band was represented on two Alligator Records anthologies—*Living Chicago Blues, Vol. 3* and *The New Bluebloods*—and recorded the album *Where's the Money* for the Red Beans label.

Branch's increasing exposure in the blues community led to recording dates with such Alligator artists as LONNIE BROOKS and KOKO TAYLOR. Branch also replaced Carey Bell in Willie Dixon's Chicago All-Stars band. Branch continues to work with the Sons of Blues and as a sideman.

Essential Listening:
Where's the Money/Red Beans (RB 004)
Living Chicago Blues, Vol. 3/Alligator (AL 7703)
The New Bluebloods/Alligator (AL 7707)
Harp Attack! (with James Cotton, Junior Wells, and Carey Bell)/Alligator (AL 4790)

◄ BRENSTON, JACKIE

(born August 15, 1930, Clarksdale, Miss.; died December 15, 1979, Memphis, Tenn.)

Jackie Brenston is best known for his song "Rocket 88," which SAM PHILLIPS once called the first rock & roll record ever made. Brenston, a saxophone player and singer from Clarksdale, Mississippi, wrote the song and recorded it with IKE TURNER's band in early 1951 at the Sun Recording Studio in Memphis. Phillips, the studio owner, sold the song to Chess Records. With its chugging R&B rhythm and a musical foundation that was strikingly similar to JIMMY LIGGINS's "Cadillac Boogie" (the Rocket 88 was an Oldsmobile), "Rocket 88" climbed to the top of the R&B charts and, overall, was the second most successful R&B record of 1951, yielding only to the Dominoes' "Sixty Minute Man."

Whether "Rocket 88" was indeed the first rock & roll record is subject to discussion. But the song did sound and feel like a rock & roll record, and it did provide an important link to the black R&B records that preceded it. The success of "Rocket 88" also prompted Phillips to start his own record company, Sun Records, in 1952 and to record a young Elvis Presley two years later.

Brenston was largely a one-hit wonder. He released a few more singles between 1951 and 1953, but none of them came close to matching the success he enjoyed with "Rocket 88." Brenston wound up playing sax in LOWELL FULSON's band until 1955 when he teamed up with Turner again. He remained a member of Turner's band until 1962. By the mid-'60s Brenston had faded from the music scene. He died in Memphis in 1979.

Essential Listening:

Rocket 88/Chess (GCh 8107)

Blue Flames: A Sun Blues Collection (Various Artists)/Rhino-Sun (R2-70962)

◄ BREWER, JIM

(aka Blind Jim Brewer) (born October 3, 1920, Brookhaven, Miss.; died June 3, 1988, Chicago, Ill.)

A longtime Chicago street singer, Jim Brewer's repertoire included both religious and secular blues. For many years he played his BIG BILL BROONZY–influenced blues in front of the open-air market on Maxwell Street, the legendary hangout for blues singers who relied on tips to survive.

Mississippi-born, Brewer lost his sight as a young child and turned to music to eke out a living. When his family moved to Chicago in 1940, Brewer began his career on the city's streets, where he played both blues and religious standards. As he matured as a singer and guitar player, his raw Delta style lost some of its rough edge. In the early '60s, Brewer began to play blues and folk festivals, along with colleges and clubs such as Chicago's No Exit Cafe, where he was a regular performer into the early '70s. He occasionally recorded for small labels like Heritage and Testament and appeared in the 1970 blues documentary *Blues Like Showers of Rain.* He continued to perform until his death in 1988.

Essential Listening:
Tough Luck/Earwig (LPS 4904)

◄ BRIM, JOHN

(born April 10, 1922, Hopkinsville, Ky.)

John Brim is a much-overlooked early Chess artist whose handful of songs recorded in the 1950s never received the promotional push from the label that other records got. Part of Brim's problem was his rather pedestrian vocals and guitar style. His real talent lay in songwriting. Tightly constructed Brim compositions such as "Tough Times," "Ice Cream Man," and "Rattlesnake" were as good as most of the best material being released by Chess in the early and mid-'50s.

Brim taught himself how to play guitar by listening to BIG BILL BROONZY and TAMPA RED records. He moved from Kentucky to Indianapolis in 1941 and then to Chicago in 1945 where he occasionally performed with MUDDY WATERS, JOHN LEE "SONNY BOY" WILLIAMSON, and EDDIE BOYD. Eventually he and his wife, Grace, who played drums, teamed up with BIG MACEO Merriweather. They stayed with Merriweather until his death in 1953. That same year the Brims moved to Gary, Indiana, and formed John Brim and His Gary Kings. During this time Brim signed with Chess and, backed by stellar musicians such as LITTLE WALTER and WILLIE DIXON, recorded the best of his Chess material. Brim's records failed to attract much attention, however, and for the remainder of his career, which stretched well into the 1980s, he was forced to play small clubs and sporadically record on small labels to earn his living. In 1979 the rock group Van Halen recorded Brim's signature tune, "Ice Cream Man." Brim stills performs on occasion in Chicago and Gary, Indiana, blues clubs.

Essential Listening:
Whose Muddy Shoes/(Elmore James and John Brim)/MCA-Chess (CHD 9114)

◄ BROOKS, LONNIE

(aka Guitar Junior) (born Lee Baker, Jr., December 18, 1933, Dubuisson, La.)

Louisiana-born guitarist Lonnie Brooks began his recording career shuffling between rock & roll and rhythm & blues. After backing up zydeco legend CLIFTON CHENIER in the mid-'50s, Brooks, then called Guitar Junior, signed a recording contract with the Louisiana-based Goldband label in 1957. His first single, an R&B ballad called "Family Rules," was a regional hit that year. A followup single, "The Crawl," was more rock-flavored. Though these records failed to make the national R&B charts, they led Brooks to a slot in Sam Cooke's touring troupe.

Eager to further his career, Brooks moved to Chicago in 1960. He dropped his Guitar Junior tag, since bluesman LUTHER "GUITAR JR." JOHNSON was already established in Chicago with the same moniker, and changed his name to Lonnie Brooks. Brooks also began to change his musical outlook; he became more immersed in Chicago-style blues, which led to a recording contract with Mercury

Records. Throughout the '60s, Brooks recorded some singles for Mercury and small Chicago-based labels such as Midas, USA, Chirrup, and Palos, before registering his first hit, "Let It All Hang Out," for the Chess label in 1967.

In 1969 Brooks recorded *Broke and Hungry*, his first album. Released by Capitol, the record featured a return to Brooks's Louisiana roots. For the album, Brooks dug up his Guitar Junior nickname and interpreted tunes by PROFESSOR LONGHAIR, GUITAR SLIM, and LIGHTNIN' SLIM, but *Broke and Hungry* bombed.

Brooks performed in Chicago clubs playing blues, rock, and R&B throughout much of the '70s. In 1975 he toured France as part of a blues package and released the European album *Sweet Home Chicago*. In 1978, four of his songs were included on Alligator Records' *Living Chicago Blues, Vol. 3* album, which led to a recording contract with the label. *Bayou Lightning* was released in 1979 and featured Brooks's unique blend of swamp rock, R&B, and straight Chicago blues. Other albums Brooks has recorded for Alligator include *Turn on the Light, Hot Shot, Satisfaction Guaranteed*, and the live recording *Live from Chicago—Bayou Lightning Strikes*. Brooks continues to record and perform.

Essential Listening:
Bayou Lightning/Alligator (AL 4714)
Turn on the Light/Alligator (AL 4721)
Hot Shot/Alligator (AL 4731)
Wound Up Tight/Alligator (AL 4751)
Live from Chicago—Bayou Lightning Strikes/Alligator (AL 5759)
Satisfaction Guaranteed/Alligator (AL 4799)
Let's Talk It Over/Delmark (DD660)

◄ BROONZY, BIG BILL

(born June 26, 1893, Scott, Miss.; died August 15, 1958, Chicago, Ill.)

Big Bill Broonzy was a seminal figure in Chicago's pre–World War II blues scene and one of the most acclaimed artists the blues has ever produced. A prolific songwriter and recording artist, Broonzy was one of the first artists to link the coarse, rough-edged qualities of rural blues with the more polished sounds of urban blues in the 1930s, a decade which saw him as one of the blues' best-selling recording artists. He recorded as a solo performer but also played on hundreds of other sessions during the course of his long recording career.

Broonzy's brand of blues stretched from ragtime-influenced and hokum blues, to solo acoustic country blues, to city blues backed with jazz musicians, to traditional folk blues and spirituals. Almost always his songs possessed a pithy narrative quality, while the melodies and manner of delivery were decidedly warm and supple. Broonzy was also a guiding light for many young bluesmen; often he took artists of lesser stature under his wing and helped them secure recording sessions and performance dates.

Broonzy was born into a Mississippi sharecropping family. By the time his family had moved to Arkansas, young Broonzy had already learned the rudiments of the fiddle. By age fourteen he was working for tips at country dances and picnics. Broonzy served in the army during World War I. Upon being discharged, he returned to Arkansas and farming, only to decide that he wanted to make his living as a singer and guitar player. Sometime in the early 1920s he moved to Chicago where, under the auspices of PAPA CHARLIE JACKSON, he learned how to play blues guitar.

Broonzy's enthusiasm for the blues and his ability to create a buzz wherever he played enabled him by 1930 to ascend to the top of the then-fledgling blues hierarchy. Although his earliest recordings smacked of entertaining hokum and ragtime blues, he eventually matured into a respected country-flavored blues guitarist and vocalist, often performing with the other top blues artists in Chicago at that time, namely, MEMPHIS MINNIE, TAMPA RED, JAZZ GILLUM, LONNIE JOHNSON, and JOHN LEE "SONNY BOY" WILLIAMSON.

Broonzy was a major artist on the Chicago blues scene during the 1930s. But despite his success, he never could live solely off his earnings as a musician. In his lifetime he held numerous menial jobs, including that of a janitor and a maintenance man. His stature as a blues artist grew far beyond the boundaries of the Chicago and Southern blues communities after his acclaimed performances at John Hammond's famous Spirituals to Swing concert series in 1938 and 1939 at Carnegie Hall in New York City. This newfound fame helped Broonzy maintain his role as a father of Chicago blues until World War II, when the arrival on the blues scene of the electric guitar and new artists like MUDDY WATERS pushed his brand of blues into the background. Rather than retire, Broonzy opted for a new role—that of a folk-bluesman. In 1951 he toured Europe, performing standard blues, but also traditional folk tunes and spirituals, to appreciative audiences. He returned to Europe the following year with pianist BLIND JOHN DAVIS. Not only did Broonzy help introduce blues to Europe, especially in France and the British Isles, but he also opened the door for other American blues artists to tour there as well.

In 1955 Broonzy, with help from writer Yannick Bruynoghe, told the story of his life in the book *Big Bill's Blues*. Originally published in London, the book was one of the earliest autobiographies penned by a bluesman. Two years later, Broonzy was diagnosed with throat cancer. Although he continued to perform, often with great pain, Broonzy died of the disease in 1958. He was inducted into the Blues Foundation's Hall of Fame in 1980.

Essential Listening:
The Young Bill Broonzy, 1928–1935/Yazoo (1011)
Do That Guitar Thing/Yazoo (1035)
Big Bill's Blues/Portrait (RK 44089)
Good Time Tonight/Columbia (CK 46219)
Big Bill Broonzy and Washboard Sam/MCA-Chess (CHD 9251)
Big Bill Broonzy Sings Folk Songs/Smithsonian Folkways (CD SF 40023)
Big Bill Broonzy, 1934–1947/Story of Blues (3504)

◄ BROWN, ADA

(born Ada Scott, May 1, 1890, Kansas City, Kans.; died March 31, 1950, Kansas City, Kans.)

Ada Brown was a blues and vaudeville singer who recorded during the 1920s at the height of the Classic Blues era. Her signature song, "Evil Mama Blues," was recorded with the BENNIE MOTEN Band for the Okeh label in 1923. Brown worked the dance halls in the Kansas City area, often with Moten's band, in the early '20s. After her second and last recording session in 1926 for the Vocalion label, Brown toured regularly with various musical revues through the 1930s and early 1940s. During this time she occasionally appeared with Bill "Bojangles" Robinson in such musical productions as *Brown Buddies, Jangleland, Going to Town*, and *Memphis Bound*. In 1943 she sang "That Ain't Right" with Fats Waller in the film *Stormy Weather*.

Brown retired from the stage sometime around 1945 and returned to Kansas City. She died of a kidney ailment in 1950.

Essential Listening:
Female Blues Singers, Vol. 3 (1924–1929)/Selmerphone (SHN 4014)

◄ BROWN, ANDREW

(born February 25, 1937, Jackson, Miss.; died December 11, 1985, Harvey, Ill.)

Andrew Brown was an underrated and underappreciated blues guitarist and singer whose small body of recorded work showed flashes of brilliance, as well as inspiration from the likes of FREDDIE KING, MAGIC SAM, and LITTLE MILTON. Brown was born in Jackson, Mississippi; he moved to Chicago in 1946 and worked his way into the city's vibrant blues scene. His stature among Chicago's biggest artists grew through the 1950s, but a stint in the army from 1960 to 1962 derailed his career.

After Brown was discharged, he relocated to Harvey, a suburb of Chicago. Although he cut a small batch of singles in the early '60s, most notably "You Better Stop" for the USA label and "Can't Let You Go" and "You Ought to Be Ashamed" for the 4 Brothers label, Brown could not make a living playing blues and worked in a steel mill until a heart attack and back injury forced him to retire from manual labor.

In 1980 Brown contributed three tracks to Alligator Records' *Living Chicago Blues* series (volume 4), which led to a recording contract with the Dutch Black Magic label. His 1982 debut album, *Big Brown's Chicago Blues*, won a W.C. HANDY Award. Brown's follow-up album, *On the Case*, came out in 1985 on the Double Trouble label, just prior to his death of lung cancer in 1986.

Essential Listening:
Living Chicago Blues, Vol. IV/Alligator (ALCD 7704)
Big Brown's Chicago Blues/Black Magic (9001)
On the Case/Double Trouble (DT 3010)

◄ BROWN, BUSTER

(born August 11, 1914, Criss, Ga.; died January 31, 1976, Brooklyn, N.Y.)

Buster Brown is known for his one and only hit, "Fannie Mae," a catchy rhythm & blues number he recorded for the New York–based Fire label in 1960. "Fannie Mae," with its swinging New Orleans–style beat, made it to number 1 on the rhythm & blues charts and number 38 on the pop charts that year.

Before signing with Fire, Brown was a little-known blues singer and harmonica player from Georgia who worked clubs and dances in his home state and Florida. Sometime in the mid-'50s Brown moved to New York, where he performed occasionally in Harlem clubs. He was discovered by Fire label owner Bobby Robinson in 1959. After "Fannie Mae," Fire released Brown's "Is You Is or Is You Ain't My Baby" and "Sugar Babe." Neither song, however, was able to match the popularity of "Fannie Mae."

Brown continued to release records for a number of other labels in the 1960s, including Gwenn, Checker, and Blue Horizon with little success. He died in 1976.

Essential Listening:

Good News/Charly (CRB 1209)

The New King of the Blues/Collectables (COL 5110)

◄ BROWN, CHARLES

(born September 13, 1922, Texas City, Tex.)

In the late 1940s and early 1950s Charles Brown, first as a member of Johnny Moore's Three Blazers and then as a solo artist, popularized a brand of blues often called "cocktail" or "nightclub" blues. West Coast in origin, this new blues shunned the rawness and rough edges of country blues or early Chicago blues. Instead it relied on cool and sentimental melodies, urbane arrangements, silky vocals, and piano and guitar riffs that flowed sweetly, usually from a small combo. Brown, a vocal crooner, not a shouter, was a piano player who tickled the keys rather than hammered them, and he epitomized this new blues idiom.

Unlike many blues artists, Brown was brought up in a black middle-class home. As a youth in Texas he studied classical piano and went to Prairie View A&M where he earned a B.S. degree in chemistry. Before embarking on his music career, Brown taught science and math at Carver High School in Baytown, Texas, and worked as a civil service chemist at the Pine Bluff Arsenal in Arkansas before being transferred to California. He settled in the Bay Area, where he briefly attended the University of California and began playing piano in small clubs. He moved to Los Angeles in 1944, working as an elevator operator by day and playing lounges and clubs like the Chicken Shack at night.

That year Brown joined with guitarist Johnny Moore (whose brother Oscar played guitar in the popular NAT KING COLE Trio) and bass player Eddie Williams, and together they formed Johnny Moore's Three Blazers. Inspired by Cole's combo, the trio began recording in 1945 for the Exclusive and Atlas labels. A year later the Three Blazers switched to the Philo/Aladdin label and cut "Drifting Blues," a song Brown had written as a youth back in Texas. It featured Brown's smooth vocals and his bluesy, appealingly mellow piano style. The song went to number 2 on *Billboard* magazine's R&B charts; *Cash Box*, another music industry trade magazine, voted it R&B Record of the Year in 1946.

"Drifting Blues" was the first of a string of late-'40s hits for Moore's Three Blazers, including the instant classic, "Merry Christmas, Baby," which went to number 3 on the charts in 1947. However, by 1948 Brown had grown tired of not getting the same wages or billing as Moore. Brown left the Three Blazers in early 1949 and was replaced by Billy Valentine. Brown then formed the Charles Brown Trio, signed his own recording contract with Aladdin, and recorded a number of hits from 1949 to 1952 that made him one of the most popular R&B artists of the period. He scored with such R&B chestnuts as "Get Yourself Another Fool," "Trouble Blues" (number 1 in 1949 for fifteen weeks), "In the Evening When the Sun Goes Down," "Black Night" (number 1 in 1951 for fourteen weeks), "I'll Always Be in Love with You," "Seven Long Days," and "Hard Times," before the lounge blues era began to wane and attention turned toward rock & roll. Although Brown continued to record throughout most of the '50s for a variety of small rhythm & blues labels, he never regained the popularity he enjoyed from 1945 to 1952.

Brown spent the 1960s and 1970s sporadically recording for labels like King, Jewel, and Imperial and working small clubs. In 1983 he performed regularly at the New York club, Tramps, which led to some renewed interest in his brand of soft blues. Three years later in 1986 he recorded a new album, *One More for the Road*, for Blueside Records. The label folded in 1988, and Alligator Records rereleased the album the following year.

Interest in Brown heightened after his appearance with singer RUTH BROWN (no relation) in the public television documentary "*That Rhythm . . . Those Blues*," and in 1990 blues-pop singer BONNIE RAITT invited Brown to open up for her during her acclaimed summer tour. That same year Brown signed a recording contract with the Bullseye Blues label. His 1990 album, *All My Life*, was the label's debut release. It featured liner notes by Raitt and guest appearances by Ruth Brown and DR. JOHN. *Someone to Love*, Brown's Bullseye follow-up, came out in 1992. Brown continues to record and perform.

Essential Listening:
Driftin' Blues: The Best of Charles Brown/EMI (CDP 7-97989-2)
One More for the Road/Alligator (AL 4771)
All My Life/Bullseye Blues (BB 9501)
Someone to Love/Bullseye Blues (BB 9514)

◄ BROWN, CLARENCE "GATEMOUTH"

(born April 18, 1924, Vinton, La.)

Clarence "Gatemouth" Brown's importance to the development of Texas blues is surpassed by only a handful of other artists, most prominently BLIND LEMON JEFFERSON, LIGHTNIN' HOPKINS, and T-BONE WALKER. By blending intriguing strains of jazz, country, and Cajun music into his blues, by incorporating the fiddle into blues instrumentation, and by drawing the same kind of passages out of his guitar that, say, a trumpet player might draw out of his horn, Brown expanded the parameters of traditional Texas blues. As a young guitarist, Brown was greatly influenced by Walker, whom he considered his mentor. But rather than ape Walker's style, Brown used it as a springboard to create a guitar sound that might caress the listener one moment and kick him in the shins the next.

Although Brown was born in Louisiana, his family moved to Orange, Texas, shortly after his birth. Brown grew up surrounded by music; his father played a variety of stringed instruments, including fiddle and guitar, and performed at weekend house parties and fish fries. By the time he was ten Brown knew how to play the fiddle. He would also learn to play the guitar, drums, harmonica, mandolin, and bass.

Brown played in a few bands, including the Brown Skin Models, before he went into the army during World War II. After being discharged he returned to Texas. One night in 1945 Brown filled in for Walker at the Bronze Peacock, a Houston nightclub owned by DON ROBEY. His performance was such a triumph that Robey offered Brown additional dates in his club as well as his services as manager. Brown accepted, and while he fronted big bands in Texas, Robey secured him a recording contract with the West Coast-based Aladdin label in 1947. Brown cut four sides for Aladdin, but the records received little promotion and sold poorly. Upset at the lack of attention Brown was getting as an Aladdin artist, Robey decided to form his own record company out of Houston. He called the new label Peacock (after his club). Brown became the company's first recording artist.

Although Brown was under contract with Peacock from 1947 to 1960 and recorded more than fifty singles for the label, he had only one real hit, "Mary Is Fine," which peaked at number 8 on the R&B charts in 1949. (The songs "Okie Dokie Stomp," "Dirty Work at the Crossroads," and "Just Got Lucky" were regional hits in the South.) Brown also made little money; for many of the songs he wrote, he reluctantly shared authorship with D. (Deadric) Malone, a Robey pseudonym. Despite Brown's lack of commercial success in the '40s and '50s, he influenced a whole generation of Texas blues guitarists, and songs of his such as "Pale Dry Boogie" and "Okie Dokie Stomp" became part of the Texas blues repertoire.

After parting company with Peacock, Brown found it difficult to sustain his recording career. Eventually he left Texas for Nashville, where he led the house band on the syndicated television show "The Beat," which featured appearances by nationally known rhythm & blues artists. Brown also worked with country singer Roy Clark and recorded some country singles while in Nashville, but his career remained stagnant.

It wasn't until Brown and his eclectic blues sound was discovered by European audiences in the early '70s that his career got back on track. During the '70s he toured Europe regularly and recorded for overseas labels like Black and Blue, a French company. Brown also toured the Soviet Union and Africa under the auspices of the U.S. State Department. In the late '70s he recorded albums for Real Records and MCA Records in the U.S., which led to a recording contract with Rounder Records. Rounder released *Alright Again!*, which won a Grammy for best blues recording of 1982. Brown recorded other albums for Rounder, including *One More Mile* and *Real Life*, before switching to Alligator Records in 1986.

That year Alligator released the Grammy-nominated *Pressure Cooker*, a collection of Brown's best songs recorded on European labels in the '70s. In 1989 Alligator released *Standing My Ground*, which featured a collection of brand new Brown songs done in a potpourri of styles: big band, hard blues, swing, and Texas funk, all highlighted by Brown's guitar and fiddle work. Despite advancing age, Brown continues to record and perform.

Essential Listening:
Alright Again/Rounder (2028)
The Original Peacock Recordings/Rounder (2039)
One More Mile/Rounder (2034)
Real Life/Rounder (2054)
Texas Swing/Rounder (11527)
Pressure Cooker/Alligator (AL 4745)
Stand My Ground/Alligator (AL 4779)

◄ BROWN, HENRY

(born July 25, 1906, Troy, Tenn.; died June 28, 1981, St. Louis, Mo.)

Henry Brown was a member of the St. Louis school of piano blues in the 1920s and 1930s. Although his recorded output was neither extensive nor particularly innovative, Brown nonetheless was a popular performer in the city, thanks to a clipped, economical keyboard style and an ability to play slow and easy blues as well as uptempo boogie-woogie. Along with ROOSEVELT SYKES, WALTER DAVIS, SPECKLED RED, and other St. Louis blues pianists, Brown helped make the city a blues piano hotspot during this period.

Little is known about Brown's early years. At age twelve he and his family moved to the Deep Morgan section of St. Louis where he developed his piano skills by listening to blues pianists playing clubs and house parties. By the late '20s, Brown worked his way into the city's blues circuit, often performing with friend and trombonist Ike Rodgers and guitarist HENRY TOWNSEND. Brown's first recordings were for Paramount in 1929. These were followed by sessions with Brunswick and Paramount again in 1930. Brown also accompanied singer Mary Johnson. Two of his best-known songs from this, his first recording period, are "Deep Morgan Blues" and "Henry Brown Blues."

During the Depression, Brown often worked in a small band setting in and around St. Louis. He remained a fixture on the city's blues scene up until World War II, when he was drafted into the army. Put into Special Services, Brown entertained troops in England. Brown returned to St. Louis after the war and continued to perform in small clubs. He was rediscovered by blues historian Paul Oliver in the late '50s. In addition to resuming his recording career in the '60s, cutting sides for the Euphonic and Adelphi labels, Brown also worked as the pianist aboard the Mississippi riverboat, *Becky Thatcher*. Brown continued to work, though irregularly, until his death in 1981.

Essential Listening:
Paramount, 1929–30. The Piano Blues, Volume One/Magpie (PY 4401)
Parmount, 1929–30. The Piano Blues, Volume Two/Magpie (PY 4417)
The Blues in St. Louis: Edith Johnson and Henry Brown/Folkways (FS 38150)

◄ BROWN, NAPPY

(born Napoleon Brown Culp, October 12, 1929, Charlotte, N.C.)

Nappy Brown's big, soulfully smooth voice is firmly rooted in the gospel music he sang in the late 1940s and early 1950s before he became a blues-based rhythm & blues singer of note for Savoy Records. Brown sang gospel with the Golden Bells, then the Selah Jubilee Singers, and finally with the Heavenly Lights, with whom he cut the single "Jesus Said It" in 1954. The following year Brown moved to Newark, New Jersey, and signed a solo contract with Art Lubinsky's Savoy label. From 1955 to 1961, Brown recorded a set of powerfully sung R&B records, including his hits "Don't Be Angry" (which made it to number 2 on the R&B charts in 1955), "Pitter Patter," and "It Don't Hurt No More."

Brown faded from the R&B recording scene in the 1960s and lost touch with the direction of black pop music. He returned to North Carolina and his gospel roots, performing and recording with the Bell Jubilee Singers for the Gibrailere label. In the late '70s, he briefly resumed his relationship with Savoy and recorded a gospel album under the name Brother Napoleon Brown and the Southern Sisters.

In the early '80s Brown left gospel again and returned to rhythm & blues. He recorded an album with blues guitarist TINSLEY ELLIS's back-up band, the Heartfixers, called *Tore Up*, which Alligator Records released in 1984. Brown then began to play clubs and blues festivals and in 1989 recorded *Something Gonna Jump Out the Bushes!* for Black Top Records and *Apples & Lemons* for Ichiban Records. A second Ichiban album, *Aw! Shucks*, came out in 1991. Brown continues to record and perform.

Essential Listening:
Tore Up/Alligator (AL 4792)
Something Gonna Jump Out the Bushes!/Black Top (BT 1039)
Apples & Lemons/Ichiban (1056)
Aw! Shucks/Ichiban (9006)

◄ BROWN, ROY

(born September 10, 1925, New Orleans, La.; died May 25, 1981, Los Angeles, Calif.)

Roy Brown was a rhythm & blues singer and piano player and a major influence on rock & roll. At home singing slow, soulful ballads or shouting the blues, Brown influenced everyone from Elvis Presley and JUNIOR PARKER to B.B. KING, Jackie Wilson, and James Brown. He is best known for his song "Good Rockin' Tonight." Fellow R&B singer WYNONIE HARRIS made the song into a big R&B hit in 1948, while Presley and Pat Boone recorded hit versions in the 1950s.

Brown was born in New Orleans. As a youth he sang gospel with the Rookie

Four. After the death of his mother he moved to Los Angeles in 1942 and began a career as a professional boxer. But Brown was most interested in becoming an entertainer. In 1945 he entered and won some amateur singing contests in L.A. before returning to Louisiana, where he began singing in nightclubs. In 1947 he recorded his "Good Rockin' Tonight" for the DeLuxe label. The record made it to number 13 on the R&B charts; a year later Harris, Brown's mentor, took his interpretation of the song to the top of the charts.

Brown's best years as a recording artist were from 1949 to 1951. In 1949 he had seven top-10 R&B hits; in 1950 he had four more, including "Hard Luck Blues," which made it to number 1, and "Love Don't Love Nobody," which made it to number 2. During this time, Brown practically defined the term "rocking blues" and paved the way for rock & roll.

But after 1951 Brown's career began to fade as he failed to make the transition to rock & roll, unlike some of his R&B contemporaries, even though his sound had many rock & roll elements. A contract with Imperial Records in 1956 resulted in two mild hits, a reworking of Buddy Knox's "Party Doll" and FATS DOMINO's "Let the Four Winds Blow," but they weren't strong enough to jumpstart his career.

Brown recorded for a number of small labels in the 1960s. In 1970 his appearance with JOHNNY OTIS at the Monterey Jazz Festival led to a short-lived contract with Mercury Records, but the singles he cut for the label were quickly forgotten. Brown died of a heart attack in 1981, the year he was inducted into the Blues Foundation's Hall of Fame.

Essential Listening:
Hard Luck Blues/King (5036X)
Laughing But Crying/Route 66 (KIX 2)
Good Rockin' Tonight/Route 66 (KIX 6)
I Feel That Young Man's Rhythm/Route 66 (KIX 26)

◄ BROWN, RUTH

(born Ruth Weston, January 30, 1928, Portsmouth, Va.)

One of Atlantic Records' most successful recording artists in the 1950s, rhythm & blues singer Ruth Brown shunned a hard, raw vocal style for one more polished and pop-oriented. From 1949 to 1955 Brown was a regular on the R&B charts. Songs such as "5-10-15 Hours" (1952), "Mama, He Treats Your Daughter Mean" (1953), and "Mambo Baby" (1954) all made it to number 1. Their success helped establish Atlantic Records as a major rhythm & blues label.

Brown grew up singing in her father's church choir in Portsmouth, Virginia. She began her professional singing career with the LUCKY MILLINDER Band in the mid-1940s. In 1948 she auditioned for (and won a contract with) Atlantic Records, but enroute to her first recording session for the label she was seriously injured in an automobile accident, which stalled her debut for a year. In 1949, still on crutches, Brown launched her recording career when she cut the tune "So Long." Her follow-up recording, "Teardrops from My Eyes," was released in 1950; it became her first number 1 single.

By 1955 Brown had begun to cross over into the white rock & roll and pop markets. She often toured with other R&B artists who had jumped over to rock & roll and was the star of several Alan Freed shows. In 1957 she had a top-40 pop hit with Leiber and Stoller's "Lucky Lips." Brown continued to record for Atlantic until 1960. A short stint with Phillips Records followed, but it produced no more hits.

Brown eventually retired from recording, though she staged a successful comeback in the 1970s. She performed in a number of musicals, including a touring version of *Guys and Dolls*. Then, in the 1980s, Brown appeared on Broadway in *Black and Blue* and won a Tony Award for her performance. She also appeared in the films *Under the Rainbow* and *Hairspray*. In the late 1980s Brown began recording for the Fantasy label; her performance on her 1989 album, *Blues on Broadway*, won her a Grammy for best female jazz vocalist. Brown was inducted into the Rock & Roll Hall of Fame in 1993. She continues to record and perform.

Essential Listening:
Miss Rhythm: Greatest Hits and More/Atlantic (7 82061-2)
Have a Good Time/Fantasy (9661)
Blues on Broadway/Fantasy (9662)
Fine and Mellow/Fantasy (9663)

◄ BROWN, WALTER

(born c. August 1917, Dallas, Tex.; died c. June 1956, Lawton, Okla.)

Blues shouter Walter Brown sang with JAY MCSHANN's orchestra in the early 1940s, giving the Kansas City big band a strong blues sound. Brown was also a composer; two of his songs, "Confessin' the Blues" and "Hootie Blues," became big sellers in the 1940s and remain his trademark tunes.

As a youth in Dallas, Brown sang in local clubs before being discovered by McShann in 1940. Brown worked with McShann's band from 1941 to 1945. On his own, Brown worked with the Earl Hines Orchestra and in small combos with TINY GRIMES and McShann. He also recorded for a number of companies, including Capitol, Mercury, and Peacock. But Brown never duplicated the success he enjoyed singing with McShann's big band. Much of his decline could be traced to drug addiction, which allegedly led to his death in 1956.

Essential Listening:
The Early Bird Charlie Parker/MCA (1338)
Blues from Kansas City: The Jay McShann Orchestra/Decca (GRD 614)

◄ BROWN, WILLIE

(born c. August 6, 1900, Clarksdale, Miss.; died c. December 30, 1952, Tunica, Miss.)

Willie Brown, a protégé of CHARLEY PATTON, played in Mississippi Delta juke joints and at plantation dances in the 1920s and 1930s. Along with Patton, TOMMY JOHNSON, and SON HOUSE, Brown helped create the biting Delta blues sound and was a major influence on ROBERT JOHNSON.

Brown was born into a sharecropping family and lived on Jim Yeager's plantation near Drew, Mississippi. By the time he was in his early twenties, he had begun performing with Patton in area jukes as well as on the Will Dockery plantation, just outside of Clarksdale. Sometime around 1929 Brown began playing with Son House and established a musical relationship with him that lasted throughout the 1930s and most of the 1940s.

Brown's only recordings were done in 1930 for Paramount Records in Grafton, Wisconsin, and for the Library of Congress in Mississippi in 1941 before he moved to Rochester, New York, with Son House. Brown eventually returned to the Delta, where he died of a heart attack in 1952.

Essential Listening:

Son House and the Great Delta Blues Singers (1928–1930)/Document (DOCD 5002)

◄ BUCHANAN, ROY

(born September 23, 1939, Ozark, Ark.; died August 18, 1988, Fairfax, Va.)

White blues-rock guitarist Roy Buchanan was one of the hybrid form's most innovative stylists in the 1970s and 1980s. Known for his scintillating harmonics and his wailing, note-filled solos, Buchanan broke new ground as a guitarist, even though he never enjoyed widespread popularity.

Buchanan grew up listening to gospel and early rhythm & blues and early on played the lap steel guitar. By the time he was fifteen, he was a blossoming guitarist, good enough to play with Dale Hawkins of "Suzy Q" fame. Buchanan's recording debut was on Hawkins's "My Babe" in 1957.

Buchanan next played with Ronnie Hawkins, whose band included guitarist Robbie Robertson and drummer Levon Helm, both of whom went on to be members of the late-'60s and '70s rock group the Band. In the 1960s Buchanan led his own bands and toured the East Coast, building his reputation as a guitar virtuoso in the process. Buchanan was well-known among the prominent rock artists of the day; supposedly the ROLLING STONES asked Buchanan to join the band after the departure of Brian Jones, and he declined. English blues-rock guitarists ERIC CLAPTON and Jeff Beck were both influenced by Buchanan's unique style.

Buchanan's reputation grew after a public television documentary on him and his guitar style aired in 1971. Called *The Best Unknown Guitarist in the World*, the program led to a recording contract with Polydor Records the following year. Buchanan cut five albums for Polydor from 1972 to 1975. In 1976 he signed with Atlantic Records and released three more albums. Most of his recordings were critically acclaimed, but they failed to push him beyond cult-star status.

Frustrated over lack of artistic control in the recording studio, Buchanan retired from recording in 1981, but was coaxed into a comeback by Alligator Records four years later. His debut album for the label, *When a Guitar Plays the Blues*, was Buchanan's first true blues album, though many of his earlier efforts were very much blues-influenced. Buchanan followed with two more recordings for Alligator, *Dancing on the Edge* in 1986 and the classic *Hot Wires* in 1987. In

1988 he committed suicide in a Virginia jail after being arrested for public intoxication.

Essential Listening:
When a Guitar Plays the Blues/Alligator (AL 4741)
Dancing on the Edge/Alligator (AL 4747)
Hot Wires/Alligator (AL 4756)
Guitar on Fire: The Atlantic Sessions/Rhino (71235)

◄ BUCKWHEAT ZYDECO

Bandleader: Stanley Dural, Jr. (born November 17, 1947, Lafayette, La.)

Led by accordion and keyboards player Stanley "Buckwheat" Dural, Jr., Buckwheat Zydeco took up where zydeco pioneer CLIFTON CHENIER and his Red Hot Louisiana Band left off. In the 1980s Dural and Buckwheat Zydeco moved zydeco into the mainstream by adding liberal doses of R&B, blues, rock, soul, and pop to the Louisiana dance music; by touring with the Irish rock group U2, blues-rock guitarist ERIC CLAPTON, and bluesman ROBERT CRAY; and by becoming the best known and most-recorded zydeco act of the decade. Though some zydeco purists have looked with disfavor on Dural's dilution of zydeco, thanks, in part, to him zydeco became a viable part of the American roots music renaissance of the mid and late 1980s.

Dural was born and raised in Louisiana. By the time he was twelve years old, he had learned how to play piano and organ and was jamming with local bands. Dural's first musical interests centered on R&B and blues, and later soul. He played the chitlin' circuit with R&B combos and worked as a sideman with CLARENCE "GATEMOUTH" BROWN and Joe Tex. His group, Buckwheat and the Hitchhikers, contained fifteen members and played a funk-soul-R&B hybrid.

Dural became interested in zydeco music after joining Chenier's Red Hot Louisiana Band in the 1970s. Dural's passion for zydeco grew, resulting in the formation of Buckwheat Zydeco in 1979. Dural mixed his R&B roots with zydeco and rock, which gave the band crossover appeal. Dural and Buckwheat Zydeco recorded for Black Top, Rounder, and other labels before signing with Island Records in 1987, making the group the first zydeco act to land a contract with a major record company.

Buckwheat Zydeco's debut album on Island, *On a Night Like This*, was nominated for a Grammy. Another Island album, *Where There's Smoke, There's Fire*, contained a cameo appearance by Eric Clapton, whose stirring guitar solo on Buckwheat's version of the Clapton classic "Why Does Love Have to Be So Sad" was one of the album's highpoints.

Buckwheat Zydeco next moved to the Point Blank–Charisma label. The group's 1992 album, *On Track*, included a wild zydeco version of the rock classic "Hey Joe," as the band continued to move in new zydeco-pop directions.

Essential Listening:
100 Percent Fortified/Black Top (BT 1024)
Turning Point/Rounder (2045)
Taking It Home/Rounder (90961)

Buckwheat Zydeco's Party/Rounder (11528)
On Track/Point Blank–Charisma (91822-2)
Menagerie: The Essential Zydeco Collected/Mango (162-539929-2)

◄ BUFORD, MOJO

(born George Buford, November 10, 1929, Hernando, Miss.)

George "Mojo" Buford played harmonica for MUDDY WATERS on and off from 1959 until the latter's death in 1983. Buford has also fronted his own band and played blues clubs and festivals in the States and abroad during this thirty-year-plus period.

Buford was born in Mississippi and raised in Memphis. He learned the basics of blues harp from his father and by listening to the records of LITTLE WALTER Jacobs, his main harp influence. Buford moved to Chicago in 1952 and formed the Savage Boys, which eventually became known as the Muddy Waters Jr. Band. His working relationship with Waters, his mentor, began in 1959 after he replaced harp player JAMES COTTON in the Muddy Waters Band. Buford left the Waters band in 1962 when he decided to relocate to Minneapolis to work and record with his own band, the Chi-fours. The group recorded one album, *Shades of Folk Blues*, for the Folk Art label.

Buford came back to the Waters band for a one-year stint in 1967 after harmonica player George Smith left the group. In 1968 he returned to Minneapolis and formed the Mojo Buford Blues Band. Buford resumed his relationship with Waters in 1971, often touring with him when not working with his own band. Buford remained with Waters until 1974. In the 1980s Buford recorded albums for labels such as Rooster Blues and JSP. Buford still performs regularly.

Essential Listening:
State of the Harp/JSP (CD 233)
Chicago Blues Summit/Rooster Blues (R 7603)

◄ BUMBLE BEE SLIM

(born Amos Easton, May 7, 1905, Brunswick, Ga.; died April 1968, Los Angeles, Calif.)

Bumble Bee Slim was one of Chicago's most productive and popular blues recording artists in the 1930s. Despite his success, Bumble Bee is not usually considered a principal architect of the Chicago blues style, mainly because he borrowed much of his easy and relaxed vocal mannerisms from his mentor, LEROY CARR, and much of his guitar style from Carr's accompanist, SCRAPPER BLACK-WELL. Nonetheless, Bumble Bee recorded extensively in the mid-1930s, working mostly for the Bluebird, Decca, and Vocalion labels; in 1935 alone he cut nearly thirty sides, more than many early blues artists recorded in their entire careers.

Born Amos Easton in Georgia, Bumble Bee left home as a youth, joined a circus, and traveled throughout much of the South and Midwest before settling in Indianapolis, where he worked halls and house rent parties. In the early '30s Bumble Bee moved to Chicago where he began his recording career. Although he lacked originality, he was a prolific songwriter and his records sold well during the Depression years. He recorded with such noted pianists as Black Bob and CRIPPLE CLARENCE LOFTON, as well as with guitarist BIG BILL BROONZY.

In the mid-'30s Bumble Bee moved back to Georgia and settled there, only to migrate to Los Angeles in the 1940s. Bumble Bee recorded for a few West Coast labels, including Specialty, in the 1950s, and for Pacific Jazz. He died in 1968.

Essential Listening:
Bumble Bee Slim, 1932–34/Blues Documents (2085)
Bumble Bee Slim, 1931–1937/Document (506)
Bumble Bee Slim, 1931–1937/Story of Blues (3501)

◄ BURNS, EDDIE
(born February 8, 1928, Belzoni, Miss.)

Guitarist and harmonica player Eddie Burns was a member of the post–World War II blues scene in Detroit. He helped JOHN LEE HOOKER shape his biting, Delta-influenced blues in the late 1940s and early 1950s with his expressive harp playing and toughened-up guitar accompaniments.

Burns was born in Mississippi, where his grandfather ran a juke joint. Inspired by SONNY BOY WILLIAMSON (Rice Miller), Burns taught himself how to play guitar and harmonica as a youth. Burns left Mississippi in 1946, worked for the railroad for a couple of years, and moved to Detroit in 1948. Burns worked with guitarist John T. Smith at Detroit house parties before he met John Lee Hooker and began playing with him. Burns also began his recording career in 1948, cutting "Notoriety Woman" and "Pupu's Boogie." Burns also cut some sides for the Checker (Chess) and Modern labels in 1954, but his records attracted little attention. Based principally out of Detroit, Burns eventually returned to his role as accompanist, which lasted through the 1950s and 1960s.

In 1975 Burns toured Europe with the American Blues Legends package. Since then, he has resumed his solo career, cutting albums for small blues labels like Moonshine and Blue Suite and doing occasional session work.

Essential Listening:
Treat Me Like I Treat You/Moonshine (ELP 106)
Detroit/Evidence (ECD 26024-2)

◄ BURNSIDE, R.L.
(born November 23, 1926, Oxford, Miss.)

R.L. Burnside is a northern Mississippi guitarist whose whiskered, bristly blues recalls an earlier style heard from the likes of MISSISSIPPI FRED MCDOWELL and BUKKA WHITE. Burnside learned how to play guitar by watching McDowell and MUDDY WATERS perform at Delta house parties. When he was old enough, he began playing area juke joints and developed a percussive guitar style that made him a Mississippi hill country favorite. Burnside didn't record until the late '60s when some of his music appeared on the anthology *Mississippi Delta Blues, Vol. 2*, released on the Arhoolie label.

Burnside toured Europe for the first time in 1971 and has since cultivated a small but loyal audience there for his brand of Mississippi blues. He recorded two albums, *Country Blues* and *R.L. Burnside*, for the Dutch label Swingmaster, and *Mississippi Blues* for Arion, a French company. Burnside has also performed at U.S. folk and blues festivals and tours occasionally. *Bad Luck City* was released in 1991 on the Mississippi-based Fat Possum label. Burnside continues to record and perform.

Essential Listening:
Mississippi Blues/Arion (ARN 33765)
Bad Luck City/Fat Possum (FP 1001)

◄ BURRIS, J.C.

(born John Burris, 1928, Kings Mountain, N.C.; died May 15, 1988, Kings Mountain, N.C.)

J.C. Burris was a part of the San Francisco Bay area blues scene from the early 1960s to his death in 1988. A harmonica player and vocalist, Burris maintained much of the country blues style he learned from his uncle, SONNY TERRY. In addition to playing harp, Burris also played the bones, the dancing doll (he called his doll Mister Jack), and other traditional percussive folk instruments.

Burris was born and raised in North Carolina. In 1949 he moved to New York City, where he learned the finer points of blues harmonica from Terry. Burris worked his way into the New York folk-blues scene in the 1950s by playing clubs and coffeehouses, occasionally performing with his uncle. Burris's first recording experience was with Terry; he cut sides as Terry's accompanist for the Folkways label in the late '50s.

Burris moved to the West Coast in 1959, settling in San Francisco a year later. He became a popular performer in the city's blues scene, playing his brand of North Carolina rural blues with its accent on Sonny Terry–styled harp. In 1975 Burris recorded his debut album, *One of These Mornings*, for the Arhoolie label. He continued to live and perform in the Bay Area right up until his death at age sixty.

Essential Listening:
One of These Mornings/Arhoolie (1075)

◄ BURSE, CHARLIE

(born August 25, 1901, Decatur, Ala.; died December 20, 1965, Memphis, Tenn.)

Charlie Burse was a member of the MEMPHIS JUG BAND in the late 1920s and early 1930s before he led his own band, the Memphis Mudcats. A skilled guitarist and a sprightly entertainer, Burse and his longtime partner, the harmonica player WILL SHADE, were fixtures on the Memphis blues scene until their deaths in the mid-'60s.

Burse was born and raised in Alabama where he learned to play banjo and guitar. In 1928 he relocated to Memphis, where he met Shade and joined his Memphis Jug Band. Burse toured and recorded with the band, which was one of the best and most popular of all jug bands of the late-'20s jug band craze. He and Shade also played together in the short-lived Picanniny Jug Band in 1932 before one last recording session with the Memphis Jug Band two years later.

In 1939 Burse put together his own band, the Memphis Mudcats, without Shade. Possessing a more modern sound than the traditional jug band—a bass replaced the jug and a saxophone replaced the harmonica—the Mudcats, whose steady members remain unknown, recorded for the Vocalion label. The group did not last long, however, and soon Burse was back performing with Shade. The two bluesmen continued to work Memphis house parties and street corners for nearly a quarter century. They also recorded for Folkways in the mid-1950s. Burse died in 1965.

Essential Listening:
Good Time Blues (Harmonicas, Kazoos, Washboards & Cow-Bells)/Columbia (CK 46780)
Charlie Burse and James De Berry/Old Tramp (OT 1214)

◄ BUTLER, GEORGE "WILD CHILD"

(born October 1, 1936, Autaugaville, Ala.)

A journeyman harmonica player and singer, George "Wild Child" Butler began his blues career in his native Alabama in the late 1950s. As a child he had not only taught himself how to play the harmonica, but had also built his own instrument from a discarded Prince Albert tobacco can. Butler cut his first record, "Achin' All Over," for the tiny Sharp label in 1963. However, it wasn't until his move to Chicago in 1966 and his signing of a recording contract that year with Jewel Records that he began to attract some attention in the blues community. While with Jewel, Butler recorded a number of sides, some of which contained backing from bass player WILLIE DIXON and guitarist JIMMY DAWKINS. During this time Butler also worked with LIGHTNIN' HOPKINS in Houston, appearing on some of Hopkins's late '60s recordings.

Butler left Jewel in 1968 and a year later signed with Mercury Records, for which he cut *Keep on Doing What You're Doing*, an album that received little notice. A subsequent album for Roots Records, *Funky Butt Lover*, recorded in 1976, was later reworked and rereleased as *Lickin' Gravy* for Rooster Blues in 1990. Butler often toured with guitarist JIMMY ROGERS in the 1980s, shelving his solo career. But after Butler moved to Windsor, Canada, in 1985, he began performing with his own band. In 1991 he resumed his recording career with the release of *Mean Old Blues* on the Bullseye Blues label. Butler continues to record and perform.

Essential Listening:
Open Up Baby/Charly (CRB 1104)
Lickin' Gravy/Rooster Blues (7611)
These Mean Old Blues/Bullseye Blues (BB 9518)

◄ BUTTERBEANS & SUSIE

(Butterbeans, born Jody Edwards, July 19, 1895; died October 28, 1967.
Susie, born Susie Hawthorn, 1896, Pensacola, Fla.; died December 5, 1963,
Chicago, Ill.)

Butterbeans & Susie was a popular vaudeville duo in the 1920s, spicing home-spun satirical skits on marriage and other male-female relationships with blues songs. The duo made a number of recordings for Okeh Records in the mid and late 1920s and frequently traveled the same TOBA (Theater Owners Booking Agency) circuit worked by blues singers.

Susie Hawthorn began her stage career when she joined a circus in her mid-teens. She married Jody "Butterbeans" Edwards sometime around 1915. The two developed an act, the Butterbeans & Susie Revue, that appealed to rural and urban audiences alike. Despite the near collapse of the recording industry in the early Depression years and the decrease in popularity of classic blues singers, Butterbeans & Susie continued to work what was left of the vaudeville circuit in the 1930s and early 1940s.

Essential Listening:
Daddy's Got the Mojo/Bluetime (2009)
Elevator Papa, Switchboard Mama/JSP (JSP CD 329)

◄ BUTTERFIELD, PAUL

(born December 17, 1942, Chicago, Ill.; died May 3, 1987, Los Angeles, Calif.)

A vocalist and harmonica player whose style evolved from his listening to LITTLE WALTER Jacobs and other Chicago blues harp greats, Paul Butterfield was one of the first white blues stars. As the leader of the Paul Butterfield Blues Band, he helped electric Chicago blues gain a foothold in mid-'60s rock circles, which, in turn, inspired the creation of the American blues-rock movement of the late '60s.

Butterfield was born and raised in Chicago and discovered the blues at an early age. By the time he was sixteen, he had already taught himself how to play harmonica and began sitting in with such noted bluesmen as MAGIC SAM, OTIS RUSH, and HOWLIN' WOLF in Chicago clubs. Butterfield met guitarist ELVIN BISHOP when the two aspiring musicians were students at the University of Chicago in the early '60s. In 1963 Butterfield formed the Paul Butterfield Blues Band. Two years later, the racially mixed group, which included Bishop and MIKE BLOOMFIELD on guitars, MARK NAFTALIN on keyboards, and black bluesmen Jerome Arnold on bass and SAM LAY on drums, recorded its self-titled debut album for Elektra. That summer the band appeared at the prestigious Newport Folk Festival. The group played its own set and then backed up Bob Dylan for his now-legendary electric set that shocked folk purists who believed folksingers should never perform with anything but acoustic instruments.

The Paul Butterfield Blues Band built upon the success of its debut, which contained a surprisingly authentic interpretation of Chicago blues, with its second album, *East-West*, in 1966. A more ambitious album that was fed with jazz and rock themes, *East-West* featured a thirteen-minute title track of orgiastic guitar passages by Bishop and Bloomfield and drumming by Billy Davenport, who had replaced Sam Lay in the group.

The Butterfield Blues Band strayed even farther from its original blues base on its third album, *The Resurrection of Pigboy Crabshaw*, released in 1967. The album was recorded without Bloomfield (who had left the band to form his own group, the ELECTRIC FLAG) but with a brass section that included future jazz artist David Sanborn on saxophone. Although the album contained moments of brilliance, Butterfield's turn toward rhythm & blues and jazz confounded many of the group's original blues fans.

The Paul Butterfield Blues Band released two more albums in the 1960s—*In My Own Dream* (1968) and *Keep on Moving* (1969)—and performed at the Woodstock rock festival in 1969, but it was increasingly obvious that the band's best days were over. In 1972 Butterfield finally dissolved the group and formed Better Days, made up of bass player Billy Rich, drummer Chris Parker, pianist Ronnie Barron, guitarist Amos Garrett, and second vocalist Geoff Muldar. Better Days recorded two imaginative though uneven albums, *Paul Butterfield's Better Days* and *It All Comes Back*, before the project fizzled.

Butterfield remained a member of the blues-influenced rock scene in the 1970s. He performed in the farewell concert for the Band in 1976 and appeared in the resulting documentary, *The Last Waltz*. He also toured with ex–Band members Levon Helm and Rick Danko. Two more Butterfield albums followed: *Put It in Your Ear* (1976) and *North/South* (1981). Both flopped.

Butterfield spent his remaining years battling drug and alcohol addiction and trying to refocus his musical goals. He died of a drug-related heart attack in 1987.

Essential Listening:
The Paul Butterfield Blues Band/Elektra (7294-2)
East-West/Elektra (7315-2)
The Resurrection of Pigboy Crabshaw/Elektra (74015-2)
Paul Butterfield's Better Days/Rhino (R21Y 70877)

C.

◄ CAGE, BUTCH

(born James Cage, March 16, 1894, Hamburg, Miss.; died c. 1975, Zachary, La.)

Butch Cage was a Louisiana fiddle player whose style harked back to the pre-blues days of the nineteenth century when black string bands played country dances and socials. Though Cage recorded only sparingly and late in his life, he nonetheless provided music historians with an invaluable link to the past.

Cage learned to play the fife before the fiddle and often worked parties and picnics in the Hamburg, Mississippi, area before he settled in Zachary, Louisiana, around 1927. Once in Louisiana, Cage began a musical partnership with guitarist Willie Thomas that lasted more than forty years. Their popular renditions of string tune standards and primal country blues gave them work at country dances and backwoods socials until being discovered by Dr. Harry Oster of the Louisiana Folklore Society. Oster recorded Cage and Thomas for the Folk-Lyric label in 1960. The recordings enabled Cage and Thomas to work occasionally outside Louisiana, mostly at folk festivals, in the 1960s and early 1970s. The duo also appeared in the British documentary *Blues Like Showers of Rain* in 1970. Cage died in Louisiana in 1975.

Essential Listening:
Country Negro Jam Session/Arhoolie (2018)

◄ CAIN, CHRIS

(born November 19, 1955, San Jose, Calif.)

California guitarist-singer Chris Cain began the Chris Cain Band in 1982. As a guitarist Cain has been influenced by B.B. KING and ALBERT KING, as well as jazz-rock artists Larry Carlton and Robben Ford. Cain's band reflects his roots; the group's music is a typical West Coast blend of jazz and blues.

Cain's debut record, *Late Night City Blues*, was released in 1987 on the Blue Rock'it label. The increased exposure that came from frequent club tours of the U.S. and Europe led to W.C. HANDY Award nominations in 1988 for guitarist of the year and blues band of the year. In 1990 Cain signed with Blind Pig Records and recorded the album *Cuttin' Loose*. His follow-up record for the label, *Can't Buy a Break*, was released in 1992. Cain and his band continue to record and perform.

Essential Listening:
Cuttin' Loose/Blind Pig (BP 4090)
Can't Buy a Break/Blind Pig (BP 5000)

◄ CALLICOTT, JOE

(aka Joe Calicott, Joe Calicutt, Mississippi Joe Callicott) (born October 11, 1901, Nesbit, Miss.; died c. 1969, Nesbit, Miss.)

Joe Callicott was an early Mississippi blues guitarist and singer, who, along with fellow bluesman GARFIELD AKERS, played dances and house parties in the 1920s and later toured with traveling medicine shows. Callicott also occasionally worked with blues guitarist FRANK STOKES, one of his main influences, in Memphis. Unlike other noted country bluesmen of the time, Callicott recorded only one tune, "Traveling Mama Blues" in 1930 for the Brunswick label, though he did accompany Akers during his recording dates. However, in 1967, folklorist George Mitchell discovered Callicott during a recording trip down South. Mitchell convinced Callicott to record some of his songs, the results of which can be heard on the Arhoolie label's *Mississippi Delta Blues, Vol. 2* and other anthology albums. Shortly after the album was released, Callicott passed away.

Essential Listening:
Mississippi Delta Blues, Vol. 2/Arhoolie (1042)
Son House and the Great Delta Blues Singers (1928–1930)/Document (DOCD
  5002)

◄ CAMPBELL, EDDIE C.

(born May 6, 1939, Duncan, Miss.)

An underrated journeyman Chicago guitarist and singer who now lives and works in Europe, Eddie C. Campbell counts among his influences MAGIC SAM and HOWLIN' WOLF and possesses a style that strongly recalls the classic sounds of West Side blues. Born in Mississippi, Campbell and his family moved to Chicago when he was six. Encouraged by MUDDY WATERS, Campbell learned how to play guitar and broke into Chicago's blues scene in the 1960s, backing up numerous artists including Waters, LITTLE WALTER, OTIS RUSH, Wolf, and Magic Sam. In the 1970s he worked with JIMMY REED, PERCY MAYFIELD, KOKO TAYLOR, and WILLIE DIXON, among others, before recording his album *King of the Jungle* on the Mr. Blues label in 1977.

Campbell performed in Europe for the first time in 1979 when he toured with the American Blues Legends package. He moved to Europe in 1983 and established himself as one of the most popular blues artists in Germany. In 1985 Rooster Blues Records rereleased *King of the Jungle*. Campbell continues to perform, mostly in Europe.

Essential Listening:
King of the Jungle/Rooster Blues (R 7602)

◄ CAMPBELL, JOHN

(born January 20, 1952, Shreveport, La.; died June 13, 1993, New York, N.Y.)

Blues guitarist and singer John Campbell was born in Louisiana and, as a youth, was involved in a drag racing accident that claimed his right eye and scarred his face. During long months of recuperation, Campbell discovered the blues and taught himself how to play guitar. He performed in juke joints and roadhouses in Louisiana and Texas before moving to New York in 1985.

Campbell played various Big Apple clubs, opening for JIMMIE ROGERS, PINE-TOP PERKINS, and other visiting bluesmen. When club gigs weren't available, he played street corners and subways for spare change. Campbell eventually settled into steady work at Crossroads, a club in the Soho section of Manhattan, which eventually led to his recording contract. His 1991 debut album, *One Believer*, won critical praise for its stark, detached imagery and the guitarmanship that graces most of the cuts. Campbell's 1993 follow-up album, *Howlin Mercy*, received similar acclaim. However, a few months after its release, Campbell suffered a fatal heart attack. He was forty-one years old.

Essential Listening:
One Believer/Elektra (9 61086-2)
Howlin Mercy/Elektra (961440-2)

◄ CANNED HEAT

Original members: Bob Hite (vocals, harmonica) (born February 26, 1945, Torrance, Calif.; died April 5, 1981, Venice, Calif.); Alan Wilson (guitar, harmonica, vocals) (born July 4, 1943, Boston, Mass.; died September 3, 1970, Torrance, Calif.); Henry Vestine (guitar) (born December 24, 1944, Washington, D.C.); Larry Taylor (bass) (born June 26, 1942, Brooklyn, N.Y.); Frank Cook (drums) (birth information unknown)

Canned Heat, a California-based boogie-blues group with rock undertones, was formed in 1966 out of a short-lived jug band begun by blues buffs Bob Hite and Alan Wilson. Inspired by the driving sounds of blues guitarist JOHN LEE HOOKER, with whom the group would record the album *Hooker 'n' Heat* in 1970, Canned Heat was the most popular of the American white blues groups of the late 1960s.

Hite, nicknamed "The Bear" because of his physical size—he stood over six feet tall and weighed over three hundred pounds—was a fanatical blues record collector whose knowledge of prewar blues was extensive. Wilson, called "Blind Owl" because of his poor vision, was a music major in college and understood the musical subtleties of the blues. Together, Hite and Wilson sought to recreate the traditional jug band sounds of the 1930s with their first band in 1965. When the experiment failed, the group, now called Canned Heat, reformed in 1966 with guitarist Henry Vestine, bass player Larry Taylor, and drummer Frank Cook. Canned Heat's aim was to give boogie-blues an electric rock jolt. The group quickly became the house band at the hip L.A. club the Kaleidoscope, and increasing popularity in L.A. blues circles led to a recording contract with Liberty Records in 1967.

Canned Heat's best years were from 1967 to 1970. The band played the Monterey Pop Festival in 1967 and Woodstock in 1969. The group also toured Europe, had three pop top-40 hits—"On the Road Again" (number 16 in 1968), "Going Up to the Country" (number 11 in 1968), and a reworking of Wilbert Harrison's "Let's Work Together" (number 26 in 1970)—and recorded *Hooker 'n' Heat* with John Lee Hooker, just months before Wilson died of a drug overdose in 1970.

Though Canned Heat carried on after Wilson's death, the band never regained its momentum, and with blues-rock becoming passe in the mid-'70s, the band faded into obscurity. Hite died of a heart attack in 1981.

Essential Listening:
The Best of Canned Heat/EMI Manhattan (CDP 748377 2)
Hooker 'n' Heat/EMI (CDP 7-97896-2)

◄ CANNON, GUS

(aka Banjo Joe) (born September 12, 1883, Red Banks, Miss.; died October 15, 1979, Memphis, Tenn.)

Gus Cannon's group, the Jug Stompers, was one of the best Memphis-based jug bands to record in the late '20s. The group was formed in 1928 by Cannon, a banjo player, supposedly after he heard WILL "Son" SHADE's MEMPHIS JUG BAND and was asked by Victor Records to form a similar ensemble. A year earlier Cannon had recorded six sides for Paramount Records with BLIND BLAKE in Chicago. For those records Cannon used the nickname Banjo Joe.

Before settling in Memphis in 1916, Cannon had lived in Clarksdale, Mississippi, at a time when the raw, earthy sound of Delta blues was beginning to take shape. Influenced by early blues as well as the pop, folk, and old minstrel songs he heard and learned while working with medicine shows, Cannon's banjo style was diverse and inventive. On occasion he'd set the instrument on his lap and slide a knife up and down its neck, much like a bottleneck blues guitarist would. To capitalize on the jug craze that swept Memphis in the late '20s, Cannon rigged a jug around his neck so that he could blow into it and play banjo at the same time.

In addition to featuring Cannon's banjo and jug playing, the songs the Jug Stompers recorded for the Victor label also featured the innovative harmonica work of NOAH LEWIS, whose style cut through the band's good-timey sound and injected it with a genuine dose of blues. Other members of the Jug Stompers included guitarists Ashley Thompson, Hosea Woods, and Elijah Avery.

Though the popularity of jug band music remained strong in Memphis, Louisville, and other mid-South cities, the Depression cut the Jug Stompers' chances of recording after the early 1930s. Cannon continued to work on and off with members of the Jug Stompers in the mid-1930s and later performed as a solo artist in Memphis's W.C. HANDY Park, working for tips.

Cannon's recording career was reactivated in 1956 when he recorded for the

Folkways label. In the '60s he played folk and blues festivals and clubs, occasionally with fellow Memphis bluesman FURRY LEWIS. He also appeared in two documentary films, *The Blues* and *The Devil's Music: A History of the Blues*, and recorded with Lewis and BUKKA WHITE for the Adelphi label in 1969. A Cannon song, "Walk Right In," was redone by the Rooftop Singers, a '60s folk-pop group, and made it to the top of the pop charts in early 1963.

Cannon died in 1979 at the age of ninety-six.

Essential Listening:
Cannon's Jug Stompers/Yazoo (1082/3)
Memphis Blues: Gus Cannon and Robert Wilkins/Wolf (WSE 108)

◄ CAROLINA SLIM

(aka Country Paul, Lazy Slim Jim, Jammin' Jim) (born Edward Harris, August 22, 1923, Leasburg, N.C.; died October 22, 1953, Newark, N.J.)

Carolina Slim was a country blues guitarist and singer from North Carolina who was as adept at creating LIGHTNIN' HOPKINS–like blues as he was BLIND BOY FULLER–style down-home blues. Born in North Carolina, Slim learned the basics of blues guitar from his father. Apparently he wandered the South playing for tips and spare change before being approached by the Savoy label to record in 1950. Since the label was based in Newark, New Jersey, Slim reportedly moved there later that year and recorded sides for the label and its subsidiaries, Acorn and Sharp, under his own name as well as the pseudonyms Lazy Slim Jim and Jammin' Jim. (Slim also recorded some sides for the King label in the early '50s and used the pseudonym Country Paul.)

Slim's future as a recording artist seemed bright; his records were not commercial failures, though Savoy's main blues concern at the time was more urban jump blues and R&B than country blues. Slim reportedly entered a Newark hospital for back surgery in 1953 and unfortunately suffered a fatal heart attack during the operation. He was just thirty years old.

Essential Listening:
Carolina Blues & Boogie/Travelin' Man (TM 805)
Blues Go Away from Me/Savoy (SJL 1153)

◄ CARR, LEROY

(born March 27, 1905, Nashville, Tenn.; died April 1935, Indianapolis, Ind.)

Pianist Leroy Carr was one of the first great urban bluesmen. He and his partner, guitarist SCRAPPER BLACKWELL, helped give the blues a more polished, urbane edge in the late 1920s and early 1930s and set the stage for a number of blues piano-guitar duos to follow in their paths. The success Carr and Blackwell enjoyed as recording artists also led many record companies to search for blues talent in urban centers, rather than just scouring rural areas like the Mississippi Delta and East Texas for new artists.

Carr isn't known as an innovative piano stylist, but his relaxed, understated playing proved just right for his plaintive vocals. And with Blackwell's sophisticated single-string guitar passages answering Carr's vocals and complementing his piano riffs, the duo was able to introduce a brand new sound to the blues. No blues duo was more popular from 1928 to 1935, the year Carr died at the age of thirty.

Carr was born in Nashville but grew up in Indianapolis. After teaching himself how to play the piano, he quit school and began a life of travel that included a stint with a circus, a stay in the army, marriage, a short-lived career as a bootlegger, and countless nights playing the piano for house parties and dances throughout the upper South and Midwest.

Carr's recording career didn't begin until he met Blackwell in 1928. They cut Carr's classic "How Long Long Blues" for the Vocalion label that same year. The song became an instant best-seller and led to a stunning seven-year stretch for Carr, during which time he would write and record with Blackwell such blues chestnuts as "Blues Before Sunrise," "Mean Mistreater Mama," "Shady Lane Blues," and "Prison Bound."

Carr, however, was drinking heavily throughout the period. The all-night parties and endless carousing took their toll, and at the height of his career, Carr died of acute alcoholism. He left behind a catalogue of great blues and would come to influence to some degree virtually every pianist who followed him in the pre–World War II period. Carr was inducted into the Blues Foundation's Hall of Fame in 1982.

Essential Listening:
Blues Before Sunrise/Portrait (RK 44122)
Singing the Blues/Biograph (BLP C-9)
Leroy Carr, 1930–1935/Magpie (CD 07)
Naptown Blues/Yazoo (1036)

◄ CARR, SAM

(born April 17, 1926, Friars Point, Miss.)

Delta blues drummer Sam Carr is the son of ROBERT NIGHTHAWK. He began his career playing bass in his father's band in the 1940s and acting as the group's doorman and chauffeur. In the early 1950s Carr moved to St. Louis where he formed a band that included FRANK FROST on guitar and lead vocals and Little Willie Foster on harmonica (Carr played bass and guitar). The band backed up SONNY BOY WILLIAMSON (Rice Miller) until 1959, at which point Carr and Frost moved back to Mississippi. Carr, who by now was playing drums, and Frost, who was playing guitar and harmonica and singing, performed in Delta jukes and at local dances.

In 1962 guitarist BIG JACK JOHNSON joined the group, which was now called Frank Frost and the Nighthawks. The band cut two albums. Interest in the group petered out in the early '70s. However in 1978 they signed a recording contract with the Chicago-based Earwig label. Now calling themselves the JELLY ROLL KINGS, the trio released *Rockin' the Juke Joint Down* in 1979. Carr continues to perform with the band.

Essential Listening:
Rockin' the Juke Joint Down/Earwig (CD 4901)

◄ CARTER, BO

(born Armenter Chatmon, March 21, 1893, Bolton, Miss.; died September 21, 1964, Memphis, Tenn.)

A member of the Mississippi Delta's famous Chatmon family, Bo Carter was a ribald bluesman whose songs were soaked with sexual motifs and double entendres. Songs such as "My Pencil Won't Write No More," "Pussy Cat Blues," "Ram Rod Daddy," and "Banana in Your Fruit Basket," all recorded in the 1930s, contained clever vocal phrasings and often hilarious lyrics that were backed by intricate and rhythmic guitar riffs.

Before Carter went blind in the late 1920s and settled into a life as a street singer, he frequently played in the Chatmon family string band. Performing not just blues, but also ragtime and syncopated dance tunes, mostly for white audiences, the Chatmon family band included Carter's brothers, Lonnie and SAM CHATMON, who later played together as the MISSISSIPPI SHEIKS. Carter, too, performed with the Sheiks on occasion during the 1930s, but he remains best known as a solo artist.

While he built his repertoire on bawdy blues, Carter was not known as a womanizer; according to his brother Sam, writing racy blues songs was simply a way for Carter to earn a living. During the 1930s, Carter recorded more than a hundred titles for a variety of labels. His popularity began to wane in the early 1940s and he retired from performing and recording. He died in Memphis in 1964.

Essential Listening:
Greatest Hits/Yazoo (1014)
Twist It Babe/Yazoo (1034)
Please Warm My Weiner/Yazoo (1043)
Banana in Your Fruit Basket/Yazoo (1064)

◄ CEPHAS, JOHN

(aka Bowling Green John Cephas) (born September 4, 1930, Washington, D.C.)

Virginia-based John Cephas is a blues guitarist and singer and one half of the duo Cephas & Wiggins (PHIL WIGGINS plays harmonica). Often compared to the old blues duo of SONNY TERRY and BROWNIE MCGHEE, Cephas & Wiggins mostly perform in the Piedmont blues style, the bouncy, ragtime-influenced blues from the eastern seaboard that's built around a complex finger-picking style.

Traditionalist in their approach and repertoire, Cephas & Wiggins have toured the world, often under the auspices of the U.S. State Department. They also have played many of the major folk and blues festivals, and have been honored for preserving Piedmont blues by the Blues Foundation and the federal government.

Cephas was born into a deeply religious family in Washington, D.C., but was raised in Bowling Green, Virginia. His father was a Baptist preacher, and Cephas's first introduction to music was gospel. Upon learning how to play guitar and listening to the records of BLIND BOY FULLER, BLIND BLAKE, and the REV. BLIND GARY DAVIS—all early pioneers in Piedmont blues—Cephas switched from spiritual to secular music. In the early '70s Cephas met Wilbert "Big Chief" Ellis, an old barrelhouse piano player from New York, and the two played house parties together around Washington, D.C. In 1976 Cephas was introduced to harmonica player Phil Wiggins at the Smithsonian Institution's Festival of American Folklife. Intrigued by the younger Wiggins's interest in traditional Piedmont blues, Cephas invited the harmonica player to perform with him and Ellis. Shortly thereafter the three bluesmen formed the Barrelhouse Rockers, which also included bass player James Bellamy. But the group was short-lived; it disbanded when Ellis died in 1977.

The end of the group meant the beginning of the Cephas & Wiggins duo. Traveling extensively, the two musicians developed a following among traditional blues fans in the U.S. as well as in Europe. Their success abroad led to two recordings in the early '80s for the German L&R label: *Living Country Blues, Vol. I, Bowling Green John Cephas & Harmonica Phil Wiggins from Virginia, U.S.A.* and *Sweet Bitter Blues*. Cephas & Wiggins spent much of the '80s abroad, playing not only in Europe but also Africa, Central and South America, and the Soviet Union.

In 1987, the duo's first American release, *Dog Days of August*, won a W.C. HANDY Award for the best traditional blues album of the year, while the duo was named blues entertainers of the year. Two years later Cephas won a National Heritage Fellowship award for preserving the Piedmont blues tradition. Cephas & Wiggins continue to record and perform.

Essential Listening:
Dog Days of August/Flying Fish (394)
Guitar Man/Flying Fish (90470)
Flip, Flop, and Fly/Flying Fish (FF 70580)

◄ CHARLES, BOBBY

(born Robert Charles Guidry, February 21, 1938, Abbeville, La.)

More remembered for the songs he wrote than the records he made, Bobby Charles was part of the New Orleans rhythm & blues scene in the 1950s and early 1960s. A Cajun from south Louisiana, Charles wrote slow bluesy ballads as well as up-tempo swamp-rockers. The first white artist to sign with the Chess label, Charles recorded "(See You) Later Alligator" in 1956; the song made it to number 14 on the R&B charts. Bill Haley & the Comets cut a version of the song, shortly after Charles released his record, and had the bigger hit. Charles's follow-up single, "Time Will Tell," fared slightly better than "(See You) Later Alligator"; it made it to number 11 on the charts that same year.

Charles also penned "Walking to New Orleans," which FATS DOMINO turned into a number 2 R&B hit in 1960, and "But I Do" for CLARENCE "FROGMAN" HENRY, which made it to number 9 on the charts in 1961. Charles started his own label, Hub City Records, in 1963, but it attracted little attention and was short-lived. Some country records he recorded for the Jewel label also came and went. By the late '60s Charles had all but disappeared from the New Orleans scene; he eventually relocated to Woodstock, New York, where in 1972 he recorded a comeback album, *Bobby Charles*, for the Bearsville label. Even though it included cameos by the Band and DR. JOHN, the album fizzled. In 1976 Charles appeared in the Band's farewell concert and movie, *The Last Waltz*. Charles returned to Louisiana in the late '70s and has continued to write songs.

Essential Listening:
Clean Water/Zensor (2242)
Louisiana Days/Pony Canyon (PCCY 00082)

◄ CHARLES, RAY

(born Ray Charles Robinson, September 23, 1930, Albany, Ga.)

In his long career, Ray Charles has worked in a variety of genres, including blues, R&B, soul, country, and pop. He is often referred to as the father of soul; by mixing blues, gospel, and rhythm & blues in the mid-1950s, Charles blazed a trail in black music that just about every soul singer of note in the 1960s would follow.

Charles was born in Georgia but raised in Greenville, Florida. He began to lose his sight at age five due to glaucoma that went untreated. By the time he was seven, he was blind. As a child he attended the St. Augustine School for the Deaf and Blind where he learned to play a variety of instruments, ultimately settling on the piano. After leaving school Charles played in north Florida bands before he moved to Seattle in 1948 and formed the McSon Trio, later called the Maxine Trio. At the time Charles was greatly influenced by crooners NAT KING COLE, CHARLES BROWN, and the rest of the West Coast school of soft blues. He sought to imitate his idols with lightly textured vocals and feathery piano riffs.

Charles began his recording career in 1949 when he and his trio cut "Confession Blues" for the Downbeat label. The record went to number 2 that year on the R&B charts. A stint with Swingtime Records in the early 1950s resulted in two more hit singles, "Baby Let Me Hold Your Hand" in 1951 and "Kiss Me Baby" in 1952. Both records made it into the R&B top 10. In late 1952, Atlantic purchased Charles's contract from Swingtime, and he began his most memorable blues and R&B period. From 1954 to 1960, Charles placed nearly two dozen records on the R&B charts, including the number 1 hits "I've Got a Woman" and "A Fool for You" (1955), "Drown in My Own Tears" (1956), and "What'd I Say (Part I)" (1959). Another cherry, Charles's version of "Georgia on My Mind," made it to number 3 on the charts in 1960 and won him two Grammys: one for best male recording and the other for best rhythm & blues recording.

During this period Charles shed his Nat King Cole coating and developed a recording and performing style that was steeped in blues and gospel. The crooning qualities in his voice gave way to more gritty and bluesy tones. His piano work took on a sharper R&B edge, and he often performed with a horn section. Early in the 1950s Charles worked with blues guitarists LOWELL FULSON and GUITAR

SLIM. It was Charles who arranged and played on Slim's trademark tune, "The Things that I Used to Do." By the time he scored with "What'd I Say," which has become one of his signature songs and an important link between blues, R&B, soul, and rock, Charles had become one of the biggest black artists in the music business.

Charles's contract with Atlantic expired in 1960, and he signed with ABC-Paramount. Although "Georgia on My Mind" and his three number 1s in 1961— "One Mint Julep," "Hit the Road Jack" (written by PERCY MAYFIELD), and "Unchain My Heart"—were done in a rhythm & blues style, Charles began his move into country and pop music the following year after registering yet another number 1, "I Can't Stop Loving You." His 1962 album, *Modern Sounds in Country Music*, also went to the top of the album charts.

Charles's career was nearly destroyed when he was arrested for heroin use in 1965, but his remarkable tenacity kept his career going through the '60s and '70s. In 1980 he appeared in the movie *The Blues Brothers*; two years later he was inducted into the Blues Foundation's Hall of Fame. In 1986 he was inducted into the Rock & Roll Hall of Fame.

Charles got a big boost in 1991 when he began making Pepsi Cola television commercials. The wide exposure and acclaim the commercials received revived his sagging career. He continues to record and perform regularly.

Essential Listening:

The Birth of Soul (*The Complete Atlantic Rhythm & Blues Recordings*)/Atlantic (82310)

◄ CHATMON, SAM

(aka Sam Chatman) (born January 10, 1897, Bolton, Miss.; died February 2, 1983, Hollandale, Miss.)

Sam Chatmon was a songster, itinerant bluesman, and multi-instrumentalist whose family was well-known in Mississippi for its broad musical talents. The Chatmon family string band, of which Sam was a sometimes member in his youth, regularly performed for white audiences in the early 1900s. In addition to playing first generation blues, the Chatmon band also played rags, ballads, and popular dance tunes of the day. Two of Sam Chatmon's brothers, fiddle player Lonnie Chatmon and guitarist BO CARTER (Armenter Chatmon), were also noted bluesmen. Lonnie and Bo Carter, and on occasion Sam, often performed with guitarist WALTER VINSON as the MISSISSIPPI SHEIKS. Carter also had his own solo career in the 1930s as a bawdy blues singer.

In addition to playing guitar, Sam Chatmon also played banjo, bass, mandolin, and harmonica. Like other bluesmen of the day, Chatmon performed at parties and on street corners throughout much of Mississippi for small pay and tips. In the 1930s he recorded with the Sheiks as well as with brother Lonnie as the Chatman Brothers, and continued his wanderings with medicine and minstrel shows throughout the South. In the early 1940s, Chatmon settled down in Hollandale, Mississippi, and worked on area plantations. He was rediscovered in 1960 and began a new chapter of his career, this time as a folk-blues artist.

Chatmon recorded for the Arhoolie label in 1960, which led to recordings with a number of other labels in the '60s and '70s. He also toured extensively during these two decades, capitalizing on the blues revival that had swept through folk circles. He played many of the largest and best-known folk festivals, including the Smithsonian Festival of American Folklife in Washington, D.C., in 1972, the Mariposa fest in Toronto in 1974, and the New Orleans Jazz & Heritage Festival in 1976. Chatmon continued to record and perform until his death in 1984.

Essential Listening:

Stop and Listen (Mississippi Sheiks)/Yazoo (2006)

Mississippi Sheiks, Vol. 1 (1930)/Document (DOCD 5083)

Mississippi Sheiks, Vol. 2 (1930–1931)/Document (DOCD 5084)

Mississippi Sheiks, Vol. 3 (1931–1934)/Document (DOCD 5085)

Mississippi Sheiks & Chatman Brothers (Lonnie & Sam), Vol. 4 (1934–1936)/
   Document (DOCD 5086)

Sam Chatmon and His Barbecue Boys/Flying Fish (FF 202)

Sam Chatmon's Advice/Rounder (2018)

◄ CHAVIS, BOOZOO

(born Wilson Chavis)

In 1954 Boozoo Chavis, a Lake Charles, Louisiana, accordion player, recorded "Paper in My Shoe," the first zydeco hit song. Although Chavis, who had learned to play accordion by watching and listening to his father perform on Saturday nights, might well have turned such initial success into a full-fledged career, he chose horse training over music and eventually left the zydeco scene.

Some twenty years later Chavis launched a comeback. Though his one-chord accordion vamps and sandpapery voice sounded raw and gritty when compared to the slicker zydeco sounds emanating out of Louisiana bayous by the mid-'80s, Chavis worked hard to overcome his mistrust of record companies and his fear of flying and reestablished himself as a zydeco master. A recording contract with the Maison de Soul label resulted in three albums—*Louisiana Zydeco Music, Boozoo Zydeco!*, and *Zydeco Homebrew*—as well as a reputation for playing dance music that was driven by bluesy vocal wails and accordion riffs that paid little mind to convention or form.

In 1991 Chavis recorded a self-titled album for Elektra Records that was part of the label's critically acclaimed American Explorer series. The record enabled Chavis to tour outside Louisiana and widen his claim as one of the true pioneers of zydeco. Chavis continues to tour and record with his band, the Magic Sounds, which includes sons Charles and Rellis on rub-board and drums, respectively.

Essential Listening:

Boozoo Chavis/Elektra (961146-2)

The Lake Charles Atomic Bomb/Rounder (2097)

◄ CHEATHAM, JIMMY AND JEANNIE

(Jimmy Cheatham born Birmingham, Ala.; Jeannie Cheatham born Akron, Ohio)

Jimmy Cheatham, bass trombonist and bandleader, and Jeannie Cheatham, singer and pianist, are a husband-and-wife team that falls into a Kansas City–style jazz-blues category. Although Jimmy Cheatham is formally trained, having studied at the New York Conservatory of Modern Music and other institutes, and possesses a jazz sophistication, a good portion of his and his wife's catalogue is blues-based.

The two musicians met in 1956 and married in 1959. In the '50s Jeannie Cheatham worked with Dakota Staton, JIMMY RUSHING, JIMMY WITHERSPOON, and other jazz and jazz-based blues artists. While living in New York in the 1960s Jimmy Cheatham worked as Chico Hamilton's music director, and in 1972 worked briefly with the Duke Ellington Orchestra. To complement their performance careers, Jimmy Cheatham taught in the jazz program, first at Benington College in Vermont, then at the University of Wisconsin in Madison in the mid-'70s. Currently Cheatham heads the jazz studies program at the University of California at San Diego.

In 1983 Jeannie Cheatham was featured in the documentary *Three Generations of Blues*, with singers SIPPIE WALLACE and BIG MAMA THORNTON. Increased exposure led to a recording contract with Concord Records a year later. The Cheathams also ran weekly jam sessions in two San Diego hotels, the Sheraton and Bahia, from 1978 to 1984. When Jimmy Cheatham isn't teaching, the duo tours with its band, Sweet Baby Blues. The Cheathams' most recent album, *Blues and the Boogie Masters*, was released on Concord in 1993.

Essential Listening:
Sweet Baby Blues/Concord (CJ 258)
Midnight Mama/Concord (CJ 297)
Homeward Bound/Concord (CJ 321)
Back to the Neighborhood/Concord (CJ 373)
Luv in the Afternoon/Concord (CCD 4429)
Basket Full of Blues/Concord (CCD 4501)

◄ CHENIER, CLIFTON

(born June 25, 1925, Opelousas, La.; died December 12, 1987, Lafayette, La.)

Clifton Chenier was the king of zydeco music. By mixing the Cajun-laced French Louisiana music with generous helpings of blues, R&B, and rock & roll, Chenier introduced zydeco into the pop music realm and kept it there by recording and touring extensively throughout the 1960s and 1970s and playing some of the most exuberant dance music American pop has ever known. Chenier played the accordion, the lead instrument in zydeco, and often sang in a roughed-up French patois that helped make the music attractive to blues fans. Chenier also knew how to make a splash onstage; he often wore a cape and crown during his performances. His natty gold tooth only enhanced his regal presence.

Born in Louisiana to sharecropper parents, Chenier was taught to play the accordion by his father. In 1947, he followed his older brother, Cleveland, to Lake Charles and worked in the oil fields. On weekends Clifton and Cleveland, who played washboard, performed together. Influenced by the R&B sounds of FATS DOMINO, PROFESSOR LONGHAIR, and JOE and JIMMY LIGGINS, the Cheniers played accordion-based rhythm & blues rather than straight zydeco. In 1954, Chenier signed with Elko Records and began his recording career with the single "Cliston [sic] Blues"/"Louisiana Stomp." The record was a regional success. Shortly thereafter, Elko sold Chenier's contract to Post Records, an offshoot of Imperial, but Chenier failed to broaden his audience while with Post.

In 1955 he signed with Specialty and had a hit with the zydeco-flavored "Ay-Tete-Fee." Chenier began touring Louisiana and Texas with his Zodico Ramblers, which at that time included blues guitarist PHILLIP WALKER. By 1956 Chenier was established enough as an R&B artist to quit his oil refinery job and devote full-time to music. He left Specialty for Chess in 1957, but a drop in interest in R&B by Chess and record buyers caused his career to flounder.

In 1964 Chris Strachwitz of Arhoolie Records signed Chenier to a recording contract and convinced him to go farther in the direction of zydeco, a move which gave his career new life. Later that year his first album, *Louisiana Blues and Zydeco*, was released on Arhoolie, and the song "Louisiana Blues" was a hit in Louisiana and Texas. Chenier released *Bon Ton Roulet* in 1965, an album that produced the popular song "Black Gal." A widely hailed set at the 1966 Berkeley Blues Festival in Berkeley, California, helped broaden interest in Chenier and zydeco.

From that point on, Chenier began a nearly nonstop touring schedule that included festival appearances and dates in the U.S., Canada, and Europe. A number of Arhoolie albums followed, including the classic *Bogulosa Boogie* in 1976. Playing in front of his Red Hot Louisiana Band, which featured brother Cleveland, tenor sax player Blind John Hart, and guitarist Paul Senegal, Chenier, more than any other artist before or after him, popularized zydeco in America and Europe and demonstrated its strong ties to blues, rock, and R&B.

By the late 1970s, Chenier began suffering from diabetes and slowed his touring pace considerably. In 1982 Alligator Records released the album *I'm Here*. But as his illness grew more serious, his potent live performances became a mere memory. Chenier died in 1987.

Essential Listening:
Bogulusa Boogie/Arhoolie (347)
Red Hot Louisiana Band/Arhoolie (1078)
60 Minutes with the King of Zydeco/Arhoolie (301)
Live at St. Mark's/Arhoolie (313)
The King of Zydeco/Arhoolie (335)
I'm Here/Alligator (4729)
Louisiana Blues and Zydeco/Arhoolie (329)
King of the Bayous/Arhoolie (339)
Bon Ton Roulet! & More/Arhoolie (345)
Sings the Blues/Arhoolie (1097)

Live at the San Francisco Blues Festival/Arhoolie (1093)
Zydeco Dynamite: The Clifton Chenier Anthology/Rhino (71194)

◄ CHESS, LEONARD AND PHIL

(birth information unknown)

Phil and Leonard Chess, owners of Chess Records, did more to document and foster Chicago blues in the 1950s than any other record executives. At the height of the company's success in the mid-1950s, the Chess artist roster read like a blues who's who: MUDDY WATERS, WILLIE DIXON, HOWLIN' WOLF, LITTLE WALTER, SONNY BOY WILLIAMSON (Rice Miller), and ELMORE JAMES all recorded for Chess, not to mention dozens of other blues artists. Chess was also instrumental in early rock & roll. Both CHUCK BERRY and BO DIDDLEY recorded for Chess, as did the Dells, the Monotones, and CLARENCE "FROGMAN" HENRY.

Chess recordings, whether they were blues, rock & roll, or R&B, almost always possessed a sound that emphasized a tight rhythm section (drummer FRED BELOW and bass player Willie Dixon played on many a session), roughed-up guitar licks, and enough space so that the vocals were not buried in the instrumentation. Under the production guidance of Leonard Chess, the label turned out hit after hit in the 1950s, effectively altering the course of American pop music.

The Chez family came to America from Poland and settled in Chicago in 1928. Shortly thereafter the family changed its name to Chess. After Prohibition the family got into the liquor business, eventually purchasing taverns such as the famed Macomba Lounge on the city's South Side. Noticing that the black blues artists playing their bars lacked a place to record, the Chess brothers bought into the Aristocrat label in 1947. The label's first artists were jazz bands like Jump Jackson's Orchestra or R&B groups like the Five Blazes. One of their first blues artists was Muddy Waters. In 1948 he recorded "I Can't Be Satisfied" backed with "Feel Like Going Home." The commercial success of the record—it sold out in less than twenty-four hours—confirmed what the Chess brothers believed: blues was indeed a marketable music.

After buying out their Aristocrat partner in 1950, Phil and Leonard renamed their label Chess. Two years later they began the Checker label, a Chess subsidiary. Chess not only recorded its own artists, but leased masters made by independent producers such as SAM PHILLIPS in Memphis. From Phillips, Chess got recordings by JACKIE BRENSTON and Howlin' Wolf, among other blues artists. Brenston's "Rocket 88" was released in 1950 and is considered by some music historians to be the very first rock & roll record. But it was Muddy Waters who was the label's biggest and most influential artist in the early 1950s, followed by harmonica player and former Waters band member Little Walter. Together these two artists played a major role in the development of early Chicago blues, as did Chess record producers such as Willie Dixon and Ralph Bass.

Chess continued to record blues acts until the early 1960s. It had also broadened its subsidiary base to include the Argo and Cadet labels. In 1969 Leonard Chess, the creative force behind the company, died. The Chess catalog was sold to MCA Records, which in the 1980s began a comprehensive reissue program, making the great Chess albums available on CD.

Essential Listening:
Chess Blues (Various Artists)/MCA–Chess (CHD 4-9340)

◄ CHICAGO BOB

(born Robert Nelson, July 4, 1944, Bogalusa, La.)

A harmonica player and singer, Chicago Bob worked for years in relative obscurity as a sideman before gaining some recognition for his 1992 album *Hit and Run Lover*, on the Ichiban label. Bob taught himself the basics of the blues harmonica and used tips from Louisiana bluesmen such as LAZY LESTER and SLIM HARPO to refine his blues style. His earliest professional performances were with Harpo, who liked Bob's easy-flowing harp solos.

In the early '60s Bob moved from Louisiana to Chicago, where he met MUDDY WATERS and many of the city's other noted bluesmen. It was Waters who gave Bob his nickname and with whom Bob occasionally performed in local clubs. Around 1965 Bob began a ten-year stint with LUTHER ''GEORGIA BOY'' JOHNSON that ended shortly before Johnson's death in 1976. Bob moved to Atlanta the following year and settled into the city's blues scene, working with his own band, Dry Ice, and then with the Heartfixers, with whom he recorded. In 1987 Bob recorded *Just Your Fool* with guitarist J.T. Speed for High Water Records. The album's popularity in Atlanta blues circles prompted Ichiban to sign Bob and release *Hit and Run Lover*. He continues to perform.

Essential Listening:
Hit and Run Lover/Ichiban (ICH 9019)

◄ CLAPTON, ERIC

(born April 30, 1945, Ripley, Surrey, England)

In the 1960s, guitarist Eric Clapton was England's most respected and best-loved blues artist, and its first great guitar hero. The phrase ''Clapton Is God'' was a familiar one in British blues circles. As a member of the YARDBIRDS, then JOHN MAYALL'S BLUESBREAKERS, and finally CREAM (rock's first supergroup), Clapton forged a bond between blues and rock that remains strong today. In helping to create the blues-rock hybrid, Clapton elevated the blues-induced rock guitar solo to new heights. Since then, Clapton has relied less and less on the blues, but he still remains an ambassador of the music and one of its biggest concert attractions.

Clapton didn't begin playing guitar in earnest until he was seventeen. In 1963 he joined his first band, the R&B-based Roosters. But in a period of a few months, Clapton moved to the popish Casey Jones and the Engineers, and then to the Yardbirds, with whom he stayed until 1965. By this time, Clapton had become a devoted student of the three KINGS—B.B., FREDDIE, and ALBERT—as well other major bluesmen like MUDDY WATERS, LITTLE WALTER, and ROBERT JOHNSON.

Clapton played on the Yardbirds' big 1965 hit ''For Your Love,'' but when the group sought a more rock and pop direction, Clapton quit. Invited to join one of Britain's best blues bands, John Mayall's Bluesbreakers, Clapton settled into a position where his deep interest in the blues could flourish. The classic Bluesbreakers album released in 1966, *Bluesbreakers—John Mayall with Eric Clapton*, contained Clapton's now-classic renditions of Freddie King's "Hideaway," OTIS RUSH's "All of Your Love," and Robert Johnson's "Ramblin' on My Mind." But Clapton soon outgrew the Bluesbreakers, and in 1966 he formed Cream with drummer Ginger Baker and bass player Jack Bruce.

Cream was the first major psychedelic blues band. The trio's repertoire contained a good portion of blues standards: Hambone Willie Newbern's "Rollin' and Tumblin'," Albert King's "Born Under a Bad Sign," WILLIE DIXON's "Spoonful," and Robert Johnson's "Crossroads," a song that has become Clapton's signature piece. However, the use of mind-expanding drugs by its members and a desire to broaden the traditional blues structure to include orgies of feedback, wahwah guitar sounds, bloated solos, and splashy rock excess made Cream far more than a typical blues band.

Despite Cream's critical and commercial success, the band broke up amid ego squabbles in late 1968. Clapton formed the supergroup Blind Faith with Baker, keyboards player Steve Winwood from Traffic, and bass player Rick Grech the following year. One album and one tour later the short-lived Blind Faith went the way of Cream.

Clapton entered the 1970s with a growing heroin habit and a self-confidence problem that stemmed in part from the pressure put on him by adoring fans who insisted that he was a guitar deity. Clapton played with John Lennon in his post-Beatles group the Plastic Ono Band and with Delaney and Bonnie, the American R&B group that opened Blind Faith's U.S. shows. Then, in 1970, he recorded his first solo album, *Eric Clapton*. On this album, Clapton, for the first time, not only played lead guitar but sang all the lead vocals. The album produced the top-20 single "After Midnight."

Some of Clapton's best blues guitar work was featured on the 1970 album *Layla and Other Love Songs*, recorded by his new group, Derek and the Dominoes, which included slide guitarist Duane Allman of the ALLMAN BROTHERS BAND. Spurred by Clapton's angst-filled love for Patti Harrison, former wife of Beatle George Harrison, his passion for the blues, drugs, and the inspiration of playing with Allman, these sessions produced some of the most moving rock and blues-rock guitar work of all time. Songs such as "Tell the Truth," "Have You Ever Loved a Woman," "Key to the Highway," and "Layla" (a song many critics believe to be the greatest guitar song in rock history) opened up a new dimension in blues-rock and proved that Clapton was indeed a guitar genius.

Derek and the Dominoes, like Clapton's earlier bands, was short-lived: *Layla* was its only studio album. After a couple of live performances, Clapton retreated back to England, where for two years he battled his addiction to heroin. He surfaced in 1973 and resumed his solo career, free of drugs and moving in the direction of pop and rock. Although nearly all of his '70s and '80s solo albums contain a token blues number or two, Clapton had all but abandoned the blues as a recording artist. Live, however, he continued to spice his shows with blues favorites like "Crossroads" and "Motherless Children," the hit off his 1974 solo effort *461 Ocean Boulevard*.

Clapton's commitment to the blues was rekindled with the rise in popularity of STEVIE RAY VAUGHAN and ROBERT CRAY and the late 1980s blues revival that they helped spur. Clapton performed with Vaughan the night the latter was killed in a helicopter crash in 1990.

The year 1993 was a particularly special one for Clapton. He and his old group Cream were inducted into the Rock & Roll Hall of Fame and his live album, *Unplugged*, won six Grammy Awards. Clapton continues to record and perform, occasionally hinting of a full-fledged return to the blues.

Essential Listening:
Eric Clapton: Crossroads (box set)/Polydor (835)
24 Nights/Reprise (9 26420-2)
Five Live Yardbirds/Rhino (R2 70189)
Bluesbreakers—John Mayall with Eric Clapton/London (800 086-2)
Fresh Cream/Polygram (827 576-2)
Disraeli Gears (Cream)/Polygram (2970)
Goodbye (Cream)/Polydor (823 660-2 Y-1)
Unplugged/Reprise (9 45024-2)

◄ CLARKE, WILLIAM

(born March 21, 1951, Inglewood, Calif.)

A Los Angeles–based vocalist and harmonica player strongly influenced by GEORGE "HARMONICA" SMITH (who for years was a member of MUDDY WATERS's band), William Clarke worked with Smith from 1977 until Smith's death in 1983. However, it wasn't until the release of *Blowin' Like Hell*, Clarke's album on Alligator Records in 1990, that he attracted serious attention outside California blues circles. The album introduced his jazz-flavored, West Coast brand of jump blues along with his lyrical, flowing harp style. "Must Be Jelly," a song off the album, won Clarke a W.C. HANDY Award for blues song of the year in 1991.

Clarke discovered the blues in the '60s by listening to the ROLLING STONES and other British blues-rock bands. In addition to playing with Smith, Clarke logged time with local L.A. blues luminaries such as Ironing Board Sam, R. S. Rankin, Smokey Wilson, and Shakey Jake Harris. Clarke recorded five albums —*Hittin' Heavy* (Good Time, 1978), *Blues From Los Angeles* (Hittin' Heavy, 1980), *Can't You Hear Me Calling* (Watch Dog, 1983), *Tip of the Top* (Satch, 1987), and *Rockin' the Boat* (Riviera, 1988)—and received six W.C. Handy Award nominations before signing with Alligator and releasing *Blowin' Like Hell*.

A full-time blues musician since 1987, Clarke performs regularly in the U.S. and Europe. *Serious Intentions*, his follow-up album to *Blowin' Like Hell*, was released by Alligator in 1992.

Essential Listening:
Rockin' the Boat/Riviera (LP-RR 503)
Blowin' Like Hell/Alligator (ALCD 4788)
Serious Intentions/Alligator (ALCD 4806)

◄ CLAY, FRANCIS

(born November 16, 1923, Rock Island, Ill.)

Francis Clay played drums with MUDDY WATERS from 1957 until 1962. In addition to performing on such noted Waters recordings as "Got My Mojo Working" and "She's Nineteen Years Old," Clay also played with Waters at the now-legendary Newport Jazz Festival in 1960 when Waters introduced electric blues to jazz fans. Like most early blues drummers, Clay began his career in jazz. After he moved to Chicago in 1947, he played with a variety of jazz artists, including Gene Ammons and (Papa) John Creach. Clay didn't begin to play the blues until he was asked to fill in with Waters in 1957. Impressed with Clay's beat, Waters offered him a full-time position in the band.

Clay spent the next five years with Waters before going with harmonica player JAMES COTTON in 1962. By 1965, however, Clay was back with Waters, playing on and off until 1966, when he rejoined Cotton. Clay also recorded with a number of prominent blues artists, including LIGHTNIN' HOPKINS, BIG MAMA THORNTON, JOHN LEE HOOKER, and VICTORIA SPIVEY. Bad knees eventually forced Clay to retire from both performing and recording. He currently resides in the Bay Area.

Essential Listening:

The Chess Box (Muddy Waters)/MCA-Chess (CHD3-80002)

◄ CLAY, OTIS

(born February 11, 1942, Warshaw, Miss.)

Otis Clay is a soul-blues singer whose style is steeped with gospel shouts and wails, and recalls the vocal brilliance of Otis Redding and O. V. WRIGHT. Clay was born in Mississippi in 1942 and moved to Chicago as a youth. In the early 1960s he sang with gospel groups, including the Pilgrim Harmonizers, the Gospel Songbirds, and the Sensational Nightingales, which led in 1965 to a career as a rhythm & blues artist. Clay recorded for the One-derful label until the company folded in 1968, then he switched to the Atlantic subsidiary label, Cotillion.

Through the '70s and '80s, Clay became well-established in traditional R&B circles, especially down South and in Japan, but he failed to make much of an impact with more contemporary R&B listeners. Clay attracted some attention in 1991 when the Bullseye Blues label rereleased his classic *Soul Man—Live in Japan* album. Recorded in Tokyo in 1983, the album demonstrates Clay's soulful fervor and his strong gospel underpinnings. In 1992, Bullseye Blues released *I'll Treat You Right*, Clay's first real studio effort since the '60s. A 1993 album, *The Gospel Truth*, came out on the Blind Pig label. He continues to record and perform.

Essential Listening:

Soul Man—Live in Japan/Bullseye Blues (BB 9513)
I'll Treat You Right/Bullseye Blues (BB 9520)
The Gospel Truth/Blind Pig (BPCD 5005)

◄ CLEARWATER, EDDY

*(aka Guitar Eddy, the Chief) (born Edward Harrington, January 10, 1935,
Macon, Miss.)*

Guitarist/singer Eddy Clearwater is best-known as an interpreter of rock &
roll–flavored blues, often paying tribute in his music to his biggest influence,
CHUCK BERRY. A self-taught left-handed guitar player, Clearwater was born in
Macon, Mississippi. He moved to Birmingham, Alabama, when he was thirteen
years old. Clearwater sang and played guitar in the church, but it was his exposure
to both country & western music and the blues that had the biggest impact on
his eventual style.

Clearwater moved to Chicago in the early 1950s, called himself Guitar Eddy,
and worked into the blues club scene there. By the time he began recording for
the Atomic-H label in the late '50s, he had changed his name to "Clear Waters"
(as opposed to MUDDY WATERS), later modified to Clearwater, and developed a
guitar style that included both Chuck Berry and West Side (OTIS RUSH, MAGIC
SAM) blues licks. Clearwater later began wearing an Indian headdress when he
performed, thus acquiring a new nickname: "the Chief."

In addition to recording for Atomic-H, Clearwater cut singles for a variety of
other labels in the early 1960s, including Federal and LaSalle. Throughout the
'60s and '70s, he played as much rock & roll and rhythm & blues as he did
blues, and more often than not his audience was white.

In 1980 Clearwater signed a recording contract with Rooster Blues and released his first U.S. album, *The Chief*. He recorded another studio album, *Flimdoozie* (1986), and a like effort, *Real Good Time—Live!* (1990), for Rooster Blues
as well as one album, *Red Lightnin'*, for the British label before signing with
Blind Pig Records and releasing *Help Yourself* in 1992. Clearwater continues to
perform regularly in blues clubs and at blues festivals, both in the U.S. and
abroad.

Essential Listening:
2 x 9/Charly (1025)
The Chief/Rooster Blues (2615)
Flimdoozie/Rooster Blues (2622)
Help Yourself/Blind Pig (BP 74792)
Blues Hang Out/Evidence (ECD 26008-2)

◄ COBBS, WILLIE

(born July 15, 1932, Smale, Ark.)

For most of Willie Cobbs's career, he's been a little-known harmonica player
and singer who penned the classic "You Don't Love Me," a tune made popular
by the ALLMAN BROTHERS BAND in the early '70s and recorded by a number of
other blues artists. More recently, though, Cobbs has begun an acting career. He
appeared in the movie *Mississippi Masala*, in which he played a bluesman and
performed two of his songs, "Angel from Heaven" and "Sad Feeling." He also
had a part in *The Firm* and the made-for-TV movie *Memphis*.

Born in Arkansas, Cobbs sang gospel before he began singing and playing the blues. After moving to Chicago in 1951, Cobbs played for tips on Maxwell Street and occasionally sat in with LITTLE WALTER and MUDDY WATERS in local clubs. He served in the armed forces in the mid-'50s. Upon his discharge, Cobbs returned to Chicago and resumed his blues career. In 1961 he cut "You Don't Love Me" for the Mojo label and followed it with more than two dozen other singles for a variety of labels, including Vee-Jay, JOB, and Philwood. It wasn't, however, until Cobbs released the albums *Down to Earth* for Rooster Blues and *Hey Little Girl*, a compilation of singles from his own Wilco label, that his popularity began to grow beyond the Mississippi Delta. Cobbs has performed at the King Biscuit Blues Festival in Helena, Arkansas, and the Chicago Blues Festival. He continues to record and perform.

Essential Listening:
Hey Little Girl/Wilco (824)
Down to Earth/Rooster Blues (72628)

◄ COLE, NAT KING

(born Nathaniel Coles, March 17, 1919, Montgomery, Ala.; died February 15, 1965, Santa Monica, Calif.)

Crooner Nat King Cole was one of the first great black superstars. For nearly two decades, from the early 1940s to the early 1960s, Cole dominated the rhythm & blues charts and was a regular on the pop charts, amassing dozens of hit singles and albums, including classics like "All for You," "Straighten Up and Fly Right," "Get Your Kicks on Route 66," "(I Love You) For Sentimental Reasons," "Mona Lisa," and "Unforgettable."

Although Cole was a pop balladeer, not a true blues singer, he nonetheless influenced an entire genre of blues. Many post–World War II blues artists who had settled on the West Coast and played piano, most notably CHARLES BROWN and RAY CHARLES, were moved by Cole's silky smooth vocals and his soft, feathery piano style.

Cole was born in Alabama but raised in Chicago in a strict religious household: his father was a Baptist minister. Cole's earliest musical experiences were in gospel, but by the time he was in his teens he had discovered jazz. Influenced by jazz pianist Earl "Fatha" Hines, Cole started the King Cole Trio in 1939, with guitarist Oscar Moore and bassist Wesley Prince. A year later, Cole and the trio began recording for Decca. One of the songs they cut for the label was "That Ain't Right," one of Cole's few true blues numbers.

In 1943, Cole began his relationship with Capitol Records, which would last for the rest of his career. Many of the tunes Cole cut in the 1940s for the label featured the gorgeous interplay of Cole's delicately presented but soulful piano riffs and Moore's, and later Joe Comfort's, wonderfully tailored guitar passages. On top of the instrumentation, of course, were Cole's intimate and warm vocals.

With this winning combination Cole was able to cross musical boundaries as well as those of race (he was quite popular with white audiences, although racists repeatedly tried to sabotage his career). In 1956 bigots from the White Citizen

Council beat him up in Birmingham, Alabama, during a concert stopover in the city.

Cole appeared in numerous films and hosted both radio and television shows. He recorded Christmas and pop albums and was often called "the sepia Sinatra." A heavy smoker, Cole eventually developed lung cancer, which forced him to end his career in 1964. He died the following year. His daughter, Natalie Cole, is a singer.

Essential Listening:
Jumpin' at Capitol: The Best of the Nat King Cole Trio/Rhino (R2-71009)
Nat King Cole: The Capitol Collector's Series/Capitol (CDP7-93590-2)
Hit That Jive, Jack: The Earliest Recordings, 1940–41/Decca-MCA
    (MCAD-42350)

◄ COLEMAN, GARY "B.B."

(born January 1, 1947, Paris, Tex.)

A producer, arranger, songwriter, talent scout, booking agent, and recording artist, Gary "B.B." Coleman (the initials are a tribute to B.B. KING, one of his mentors) has been one of the main shapers of the Ichiban Records catalog. Thanks to Coleman's many talents, Ichiban became a major blues label in the late 1980s. In addition to recording his own albums, Coleman produced albums by other Ichiban artists and often wrote many of the songs on them. He also brought to the label such bluesmen as BLUES BOY WILLIE, BUSTER BENTON, CHICK WILLIS, and the LEGENDARY BLUES BAND and engineered the comebacks of LITTLE JOHNNY TAYLOR and Clarence Carter.

Coleman grew up listening to the blues; when he was fifteen years old he began working with FREDDIE KING. He backed up LIGHTNIN' HOPKINS and played Texas blues clubs with his own band, and also booked blues artists into clubs in Texas, Oklahoma, and Colorado. In 1985 he formed his own record label, Mr. B's Records, to record his music, and released the single "One-Eyed Woman" and the album *Nothin' But the Blues*. Coleman caught the attention of Ichiban, which signed him a year later and rereleased *Nothin' But the Blues*. Coleman then turned himself into a veritable blues machine, recording more than a half dozen albums, producing another thirty or so, scouring the South for new artists, and writing songs such as Blues Boy Willie's trio of hits, "Be Who?," "Be Who 2," and "Be Who 3." Coleman continues to produce records and explore new ways of delivering chitlin' circuit funk-blues and pop-blues.

Essential Listening:
Nothin' but the Blues/Ichiban (Ich 1005)
If You Can Beat Me Rockin'/Ichiban (Ich 1015)
Dancin' My Blues Away/Ichiban (Ich 1049)
Best of Gary B.B. Coleman/Ichiban (Ich 1065)
Too Much Weekend/Ichiban (Ich 1140)

◄ COLEMAN, JAYBIRD

(born Burl Coleman, May 20, 1896, Gainesville, Ala.; died June 28, 1950, Tuskegee, Ala.)

A first-generation blues harmonica player, Jaybird Coleman developed a harp style in which he used his instrument as if it was an extension of his voice. Coleman's unique way of playing the harp derived from the traditional call and response vocal patterns of field laborers. Although Coleman's recording output is sparse—he recorded just eleven songs between 1927 and 1930—his reputation as a harp stylist is solid.

Coleman was born into an Alabama sharecropping family in 1896. He taught himself how to play harmonica and performed at picnics and parties. He served in the army during World War I and after his discharge settled in the Birmingham area, where he occasionally teamed up with the Birmingham Jug Band in the 1920s. He also performed as a solo artist, often working street corners for tips.

In 1927 Coleman recorded for the Gennett, Silvertone, and Black Patti labels; three years later he recorded with the Birmingham Jug Band for the Okeh label. Coleman continued as a street musician throughout much of the 1930s and early 1940s before fading from the Alabama blues scene. He died of cancer in 1950.

Essential Listening:
Alabama Harmonica Kings (1927–30)/Wolf (WSE 127)

◄ COLLINS, ALBERT

(born October 1, 1932, Leona, Tex.)

A leading exponent of the Texas blues guitar tradition, Albert Collins was one of the first artists to achieve stardom during the 1980s blues revival, along with STEVIE RAY VAUGHAN and ROBERT CRAY. Collins recorded seven acclaimed albums for Alligator Records from 1977 to 1987, including the Grammy Award winner *Showdown!* (with fellow guitarists Cray and JOHNNY COPELAND). The success of these albums helped spur an increasing interest in contemporary blues and confirmed Alligator as the leading label in the new blues scene.

As a stylist, Collins has influenced a number of guitarists, including Cray. His use of minor tunings and a capo placed high on the neck of his guitar, plus his percussive picking technique and insistence on lean, sparsely laid solos enabled Collins to develop the "icy" guitar sound that has become his trademark.

A cousin of the legendary LIGHTNIN' HOPKINS, Collins was born and raised in Texas. While growing up in Houston, he studied piano and guitar and was deeply influenced by the guitar styles of Hopkins, T-BONE WALKER, GUITAR SLIM, and CLARENCE "GATEMOUTH" BROWN. Collins formed his first band, the Rhythm Rockers, in 1952 and played Houston clubs, often sharing the stage with other young Houston guitarists such as Johnny Copeland and JOHNNY "GUITAR" WATSON. Collins next joined the Piney Brown Orchestra and toured the South before securing his first recording contract with Kangaroo Records in 1958. That year he recorded "The Freeze," a regional instrumental hit that led to other "cool" releases such as "Frosty," "Frost-Bite," "Thaw Out," "Icy Blues," and "Sno-Cone" for Kangaroo and other small labels.

Though Collins moved to Kansas City in 1966, he still performed regularly in Houston. Meeting Bob "Bear" Hite of the California blues-rock group CANNED HEAT during one of his Houston performances in 1967, led to a record contract with Imperial Records and a move to Los Angeles in 1969. Collins recorded three funk-blues albums for Imperial: *Love Can Be Found Anywhere (Even in a Guitar), Trash Talkin'*, and *The Compleat Albert Collins*, which were aimed as much at black soul audiences as they were traditional blues fans. Collins left Imperial in 1972 and became the first act signed to Bill Szymczyk's Tumbleweed Records. His only album for the short-lived label, *There's Gotta Be a Change*, attracted little attention.

Collins didn't record again until he signed with Alligator in 1977. His debut album for the label, *Ice Pickin'*, was a resounding critical triumph and was nominated for a Grammy. It included some of Collins's most fierce and chilling guitar work and demonstrated that he was also a capable vocalist. Two follow-up albums, *Frostbite* (1980) and *Frozen Alive!* (1981), also received Grammy nominations and solidified Collins's position as Alligator's leading act. *Don't Loose Your Cool* won the W.C. HANDY Award for best contemporary blues album of 1983, while *Live in Japan* (1984) remains a vivid testament to Collins's power as a concert performer. In 1985 he jammed with GEORGE THOROGOOD at Live Aid in front of a television audience of 1.8 billion people.

Collins recorded two more albums for Alligator, *Showdown!* (1985) and *Cold Snap* (1986), before signing with Point Blank–Charisma in 1991. *Showdown!* elevated the art of contemporary blues guitar to new heights and nudged Collins close to blues superstar status. On *Cold Snap* Collins turned in his best full-length studio effort since *Ice Pickin'*.

In 1991 Collins released his self-titled debut for Point Blank–Charisma. He continues to tour throughout the year and remains one of the blues' most respected guitarists.

Essential Listening:
The Complete Imperial Recordings/EMI (CDP 7-96740-2)
Ice Pickin'/Alligator (AL 4713)
Frostbite/Alligator (AL 4719)
Frozen Alive!/Alligator (AL 4725)
Don't Lose Your Cool/Alligator (AL 4730)
Live in Japan/Alligator (AL 4733)
Showdown! (with Robert Cray and Johnny Copeland)/Alligator (AL 4743)
Cold Snap/Alligator (AL 4752)
Albert Collins/Point Blank–Charisma (2-91583)

◄ COLLINS, SAM

(aka Crying Sam Collins, Jim Foster) (born August 11, 1887, La.; died October 20, 1949, Chicago, Ill.)

Sam Collins was an early country bluesman whose lightly textured slide-guitar work and near-falsetto voice were apt vehicles for his gospel-flavored blues. Almost nothing is known about Collins's early life. He was born in Louisiana but probably was raised in Mississippi around the McComb area. Unlike other bluesmen of the period who used the slide technique as a slashing complement to a harsh vocal delivery, Collins kept his guitar style in line with his clear, almost schooled vocals.

Collins often worked with KING SOLOMON HILL at Mississippi house parties and other socials. In 1927 he began his recording career, which lasted until 1932. He recorded for a number of labels, including Gennett and the American Record Company, often under the pseudonym Jim Foster. In the 1930s Collins followed the path of other Mississippi Delta bluesmen and made his way to Chicago where he performed occasionally. He died in 1949.

Essential Listening:
Jailhouse Blues/Yazoo (1079)
Sam Collins, 1927–1931/Document (DOCD 6001)

◄ CONNOR, JOANNA

(born August 31, 1962, Brooklyn, N.Y.)

Joanna Connor is a singer and guitarist known for her searing slide work. Like RORY BLOCK, SUE FOLEY, and BONNIE RAITT, Connor has given contemporary blues guitar a refreshing female slant.

Connor was born in Brooklyn, New York, but raised in Worcester, Massachusetts. She began playing guitar as a child; by the time she was ten years old, she had turned professional. Connor played clubs throughout New England until 1984, when she relocated to Chicago. A year later she joined Dion Payton's 43rd Street Blues Band, one of the city's most popular blues bar groups. Using her role in the band as a means to showcase her guitar talent, Connor's reputation in Chicago blues circles enabled her to form her own band in 1987. The Joanna Connor Band played the Windy City bar circuit and Midwest college campuses. In 1989 she signed a recording contract with Blind Pig Records. The success of her debut, *Believe It!*, enabled Connor to perform at festivals, both in the U.S. and abroad, and to move beyond bar-band status.

On Connor's second Blind Pig album—*Fight*, released in 1992—she moved away from hard blues and explored rock and rhythm & blues paths. She continues to record and perform.

Essential Listening:
Believe It!/Blind Pig (BP 3289)
Fight/Blind Pig (BPCD 5002)

◄ COPELAND, JOHNNY

(aka Johnny Clyde Copeland) (born March 27, 1937, Haynesville, La.)

Guitarist and singer Johnny Copeland came out of the same early 1950s Houston blues scene that spawned fellow guitarists ALBERT COLLINS and JOHNNY "GUITAR" WATSON. Though he began recording in 1958, it wasn't until 1980, when he signed a recording contract with the Rounder label, that Copeland began to attract national and international attention. Known for his blazing live performances and his adventurous spirit, Copeland was the first American bluesman to record in Africa and one of the first to play behind the Iron Curtain. Copeland's career peaked in 1986 when he won a Grammy and a W.C. HANDY Award for his performance on *Showdown!*, the Alligator-released blues album of the year that also included the guitar mastery of Albert Collins and ROBERT CRAY.

Copeland was born in Louisiana and raised in Arkansas, but it was in Houston that he cut his teeth as a bluesman. In the early 1950s he began playing in the city's blues clubs and later worked with Joe Hughes and with the Dukes of Rhythm. The group occasionally toured Texas and other parts of the Southwest, playing behind BIG MAMA THORNTON, SONNY BOY WILLIAMSON (Rice Miller), and FREDDIE KING. As a guitarist, Copeland was deeply influenced by T-BONE WALKER; he also was easily able to cross over from hard Texas blues to rhythm & blues and even to blues-rock. His first recording, "Rock 'n' Roll Lily," was a mild regional success in 1958; it led to some thirty singles, recorded on a variety of mostly small independent labels in the early '60s, with limited results.

In 1975, rather than follow the Texas blues migration to the West Coast, Copeland looked east and moved to New York. Within a couple of years he was a regular in New York blues clubs, and became known for his slashing, firebrand Texas style. Copeland's East Coast success led to his recording contract in 1980 with Rounder. The albums *Copeland Special* (1981) and *Make My Home Where I Hang My Hat* (1982) were critically acclaimed; their success enabled Copeland to tour the U.S. and Europe and expand his following. In 1982 he embarked on a ten-nation tour of Africa; his experiences there inspired him to record his third Rounder album, *Bringing It All Back Home* (1984), in Nigeria using some African musicians.

Although *Bringing It All Back Home* sparked interest in Copeland outside blues circles, it was the album *Showdown!* that made him a major blues figure in the latter half of the 1980s. The classic work contained some of Copeland's most inspired guitar work. Two other Rounder releases followed: the live *Ain't Nothin' But a Party* (1988) and *Boom Boom* (1989). Since then Copeland has continued to record and perform regularly.

Essential Listening:

Copeland Special/Rounder (2025)
Make My Home Where I Hang My Hat/Rounder (2030)
Bringing It All Back Home/Rounder (2050)
Showdown! (with Albert Collins and Robert Cray)/Alligator (4743)
Ain't Nothin but a Party/Rounder (205)
Boom Boom/Rounder (2060)

◄ COPLEY, AL

(born Providence, R.I.)

One of the original members of the Westerly, Rhode Island, group ROOMFUL OF BLUES in the early '70s, keyboards player Al Copley moved to Brussels, Belgium, in 1989, where he later signed a recording contract with Black Top Records and launched a solo career. His two Black Top albums, *Automatic Overdrive* (1989) and *Royal Blue* (1990), feature Copley's polished blues and boogie-woogie piano style.

Copley has also done considerable session work, most notably on *Tuff Enuff*, the mid-'80s breakthrough album for the FABULOUS THUNDERBIRDS. Copley played on all but one track. He has also worked with BIG JOE TURNER, ROY BROWN, and EDDIE "CLEANHEAD" VINSON. Copley continues to record and perform.

Essential Listening:
Automatic Overdrive/Black Top (BT 1047)
Royal Blue/Black Top (BT 1054)

◄ COTTEN, LIBBA

(born Elizabeth Cotten, January 1895, Chapel Hill, N.C.; died June 29, 1987, Syracuse, N.Y.)

A folksinger who performed into her nineties, Libba Cotten's soft, homespun music possessed a special warmth and intimacy and contained strains of country blues, ragtime, and old-time Appalachian mountain music. Despite playing music all her life, Cotten didn't begin recording and performing outside family circles until she was well past sixty. "Freight Train," her most noted tune, was written when she was just twelve years old and has long been considered an American folk song classic.

Born and raised in North Carolina, Cotten taught herself how to play guitar; she played it upside down and left-handed, and developed an interesting two-finger picking style. Cotten worked most of her life as a domestic, first in North Carolina, and then in the Washington, D.C., area for the famous folk-singing Seeger family (ethnomusicologist Charles Seeger, his wife, Ruth, and their children, Pete, Mike, and Peggy). In 1958 Mike Seeger recorded Cotten for Folkways Records. The album was called *Folksongs and Instrumentals with Guitar*. Its acclaim enabled Cotten to perform at various folk and blues festivals, including the prestigious Newport Folk Festival in 1964 and the Smithsonian Festival of American Folklife from 1968 to 1971. In 1972 Cotten won the National Folk Association's Burl Ives Award for her contribution to American folk music.

Cotten continued to record and perform throughout the '70s and early '80s. Her last album, *Elizabeth Cotten Live!*, recorded in 1985, won a Grammy for best traditional folk music recording. Cotten's songs have been recorded by the Grateful Dead, Taj Mahal, and Peter, Paul and Mary, among others. She died in 1987.

Essential Listening:
Elizabeth Cotten Live!/Arhoolie (1089)

Negro Folk Songs and Tunes/Folkways (FG 3526)
Freight Train and Other North Carolina Folk Songs and Tunes/Smithsonian Folkways (40009)

◄ COTTON, JAMES

(born July 1, 1935, Tunica, Miss.)

James Cotton ranks with the best of the modern Chicago blues harmonica players. Though his style was an outgrowth of his tuteluge with SONNY BOY WILLIAMSON (Rice Miller), Cotton came into his own as a harp player in the mid-1950s when he was a member of the famed MUDDY WATERS Band. Since then, Cotton has fronted his own bands and recorded extensively. He remains one of the deans of the blues harp.

Cotton became interested in the harmonica in the early 1940s after hearing Williamson's "King Biscuit Time" show on KFFA, the Helena, Arkansas, radio station. Not yet a teen, Cotton nonetheless went to Helena, found Williamson, and asked the harp master to teach him the basics of the instrument. On and off for some six years, Cotton lived, worked, and traveled with Williamson. Cotton also worked with HOWLIN' WOLF and WILLIE NIX in West Memphis blues clubs in the late 1940s. He and JUNIOR PARKER shared harp responsibilities in Wolf's band. Cotton played on Wolf's early Sun Records sessions, and in 1953 and 1954, using the Wolf band, he recorded four of his own songs, including the classic "Cotton Crop Blues," which features Cotton's roughly chiseled vocals, but not his harp playing.

Cotton's increasing popularity in Memphis led Muddy Waters to offer him the harmonica slot in his band, replacing GEORGE "HARMONICA" SMITH. Cotton accepted Waters's invitation and in 1955 moved to Chicago. He remained with Waters until 1966, touring with the band and appearing on much of the material Waters cut for Chess during this period. Cotton also recorded with other prominent Chicago blues musicians, including OTIS SPANN and JOHNNY YOUNG.

Cotton formed his own band in 1966 and secured a recording contract with Verve Records the following year. He recorded four albums for Verve. His reputation as the former harmonica player for Muddy Waters enabled him to cross over into the fast-growing blues-rock market where Waters was an elder statesman. Cotton often performed at the Fillmore East (New York) and West (San Francisco) in the late '60s, opening for many blues-rock acts. He also performed at the 1968 and 1969 Sky River Rock Festivals in Washington and at the Miami Pop Festival in 1968.

In the '70s and '80s Cotton continued to lead his own band, as well as work with JOHNNY WINTER and Muddy Waters again. A 1974 album for Buddah Records, *100% Cotton*, was critically praised but failed to enlarge Cotton's audience. In 1984 Cotton signed with Alligator Records and released *High Compression*, an album that featured a traditional blues band and included pianist PINETOP PERKINS and guitarist MAGIC SLIM. *High Compression* was followed by *Live from Chicago—Mr. Superharp Himself* in 1986, which was nominated for a Grammy.

Cotton jumped to Antone's Records in 1988 and released a second live recording. Called *James Cotton Live*, the album was recorded at Antone's, the popular Austin, Texas, blues club. It too was nominated for a Grammy and gave new energy to Cotton's career. The following year, Cotton, along with Chicago harp players CAREY BELL, JUNIOR WELLS, and BILLY BRANCH, recorded *Harp Attack!* for Alligator Records, which gave further momentum to the Cotton comeback. Since then, Antone's has released *Mighty Long Time*, perhaps Cotton's finest studio album as a solo artist. He remains a regular on the blues circuit.

Essential Listening:
Mystery Train (with Junior Parker and Pat Hare)/Rounder (SS 38)
High Compression/Alligator (AL 4737)
Live from Chicago—Mr. Superharp Himself/Alligator (AL 4746)
James Cotton Live/Antone's (ANT 0007)
Mighty Long Time/Antone's (ANT 0015)
Harp Attack! (with Carey Bell, Junior Wells, and Billy Branch)/Alligator (AL 4790)

◄ COUNCIL, FLOYD

(born September 2, 1911, Chapel Hill, N.C.; died June 1976, Sanford, N.C.)

Guitarist Floyd Council was a member of the pre–World War II North Carolina blues scene and a frequent accompanist of BLIND BOY FULLER, one of its most noted performers. After teaching himself how to play guitar, Council spent time playing for spare change on Chapel Hill street corners. He met Fuller in the late 1920s, and the two bluesmen often worked house parties and picnics together.

In 1937, Council went to New York with Fuller and harmonica player SONNY TERRY and recorded for the American Record Company and Vocalion label as a backing artist and solo performer using the nickname "Dipper Boy" and "The Devil's Daddy-in-Law." By the start of World War II, Fuller had died and Terry had relocated to New York City. Council remained in North Carolina and continued to work clubs and socials in the Chapel Hill area. He quit performing in the 1960s. Around 1970 he suffered a debilitating stroke and died in 1976. The British rock band Pink Floyd took the first part of its name from Pink Anderson and the last from Council, two of the band's favorite American bluesmen.

Essential Listening:
Carolina Blues (1936–50)/HK (4006)

◄ COUSIN JOE

(born Pleasant Joseph, December 20, 1907, Wallace, La.; died October 2, 1989, New Orleans, La.)

A fixture in New Orleans blues circles for some forty years, Cousin Joe was a pianist, singer, and witty songwriter whose popularity unfortunately never matched his talent.

Born Pleasant Joseph in Wallace, Louisiana, Joe moved to New Orleans at age two or three, where, as a youth, he spent part of each year working in the country cutting sugar cane. Joe learned how to sing in church; he also wrote hymns. By age twenty he had learned to play the ukulele and the guitar. Eventually he taught himself to play piano and began playing parties and clubs in New Orleans. In the late '30s he traveled to Dallas and Cincinnati, playing the blues, and briefly returned to New Orleans before moving to New York in 1942, where he began his recording career and got his nickname. In New York Joe worked mostly with jazz artists, backing up jazz legend Sidney Bechet and singing with Earl Bostic and TINY GRIMES's band. He cut his first records using the monikers Pleasant Joe ("Saw Mill Man Blues") and Brother Joshua ("Lightning Struck the Poorhouse"). Joe recorded other tracks for Gotham, Savoy, and Decca, though none of his records attracted much interest.

By 1948 Joe was back in New Orleans, where he recorded locally and played piano blues in the French Quarter for the next decade and a half. Joe's career was recharged in 1964 after he toured England with MUDDY WATERS and REV. BLIND GARY DAVIS as part of the performance package Blues and Gospel Train. Throughout the rest of the '60s and right on through the mid-'80s, Joe continued to perform and occasionally tour Europe. He also recorded for the English Big Bear label and the French Black & Blue label, as well as for Bluesway in the U.S. In 1985 he cut his final album, *Relaxin' in New Orleans*, for Great Southern. Two years later the University of Chicago Press published his autobiography, *Cousin Joe: Blues from New Orleans*. He died in 1989.

Essential Listening:
Cousin Joe from New Orleans in His Prime/Oldie Blues (8008)
Bad Luck Blues/Black & Blue (33.549)
Relaxin' in New Orleans/Great Southern (GS 11011)

◄ COX, IDA

(aka Julia Powers, Jane Smith, Velma Bradley, Kate Lewis) (born Ida Prather, February 25, 1896, Toccoa, Ga.; died November 10, 1967, Knoxsville, Tenn.)

In many ways, Ida Cox may have been the complete classic blues artist of the 1920s. Although she didn't possess the rugged blues voice of a BESSIE SMITH or MA RAINEY, Cox had a convincing blues delivery that made her one of the more popular female singers of the era. More important, though, Cox symbolized the new, liberated spirit of some black American blueswomen in the '20s with her stylish urban outlook, lavish wardrobe, and business acumen. Cox wrote many of her own songs, often produced her own stage shows, and managed her own touring company, appropriately called Raisin' Cain.

Cox was born Ida Prather in Toccoa, Georgia, in 1896. Like nearly all her contemporaries, she left home at an early age and worked the Southern tent show and vaudeville circuit as a comedienne and singer. She spent some time with pianist Jelly Roll Morton before signing a recording contract with Paramount in 1923.

Paramount billed her as the Uncrowned Queen of the Blues, though her singing style was as much influenced by vaudeville as by the blues. Many of the seventy-eight songs Cox recorded for the label through 1929, and with other labels like Broadway and Silvertone (using pseudonyms such as Kate Lewis, Velma Bradley,

Julia Powers, and Jane Smith) dealt with themes specifically suited for female audiences. Cox seemed to sing directly to black women who saw themselves trapped by demeaning racial and social conditions, yet longed for dignity and respect, especially from the men in their lives.

One of Cox's most enduring songs, "Wild Women Don't Have the Blues," hinted at sexual freedom. Another tune, "Mean Papa Turn Your Key," took a light-hearted look at love. Two other Cox classics, "Pink Slip Blues," which dealt with the woes of unemployment, and "Last Mile Blues," a song about capital punishment, revealed a decidely female view of social issues.

With many blues fans Cox is best remembered for her gloomy graveyard songs—"Graveyard Dream Blues," "New Graveyard Dream Blues," "Coffin Blues," "Bone Orchard Blues," and "Cemetery Blues"—in which the bluesy tones of Cox's vocals were richly evident. Cox continued to perform and occasionally record throughout the 1930s. She appeared in John Hammond's celebrated Spirituals to Swing concert at Carnegie Hall in 1939. Cox also recorded with jazz artists Charlie Christian, J.C. Higgenbottom, Lionel Hampton, HOT LIPS PAGE, and Fletcher Henderson for the Vocalion and Okeh labels that same year. Later, in the early '60s, she recorded with Coleman Hawkins before retiring to Knoxville, Tennessee. She died of cancer in 1967.

Essential Listening:
Ida Cox/Collector's Classics (CC 56)
Ida Cox & Bertha Chippie Hill/Queen-disc (Q 048)
Wild Women Don't Have the Blues/Rosetta (1304)

◄ CRAY, ROBERT

(born August 1, 1953, Columbus, Ga.)

Robert Cray has been one of the most important black blues artists to emerge on the blues and pop scenes since the 1960s. Along with fellow guitarists ALBERT COLLINS and STEVIE RAY VAUGHAN, Robert Cray helped jumpstart interest in the blues in the 1980s with his innovative guitar work and soul-soaked vocals. He played a major role in the blues renaissance of that decade.

Cray has become one of contemporary blues' most venerated and successful recording artists; since he began his recording career in 1979, he has won three Grammy Awards. Cray's most celebrated album, *Strong Persuader*, has sold over a million units. Not only has Cray done much to resurrect the blues, but in the process he has broken down the traditional parameters that limited the music's growth and prevented it from becoming an integral part of contemporary music. Cray has embedded his blues with large chunks of soul, rhythm & blues, gospel, and pop. Because of this liberal approach and other factors, the blues has become as popular in the pop framework as it was during the 1960s, the music's last golden period.

Cray was born in Columbus, Georgia, but since his father was in the military he spent his childhood moving from one home to the next, with stops in Virginia, California, and Germany before his family finally settled in Tacoma, Washington, in 1968. Cray began studying piano while living in Germany. His earliest influences were RAY CHARLES, Sam Cooke, and other early soul artists. Around the time of the Beatles-led British invasion of America, Cray switched from keyboards to guitar. Playing in a variety of local garage bands, Cray became a proficient rock guitarist. However, it wasn't until he met guitarist Albert Collins in 1969 that he became interested in the blues.

With bass player Richard Cousins, Cray formed the Robert Cray Band in 1974. The band backed visiting blues artists and developed a strong local following in the Tacoma area. A chance meeting with John Belushi led Cray to a part in the movie *Animal House* as the bass player in the group Otis Day and the Knights. In 1978, Cray and his band signed a recording contract with Tomato Records and the following year cut their debut album, *Who's Been Talkin'*. The record wasn't released until 1980 and garnered only minimal interest. For his next album, Cray switched to Hightone Records; the classic *Bad Influence* was released in 1983 and contained enough striking examples of Cray's soul-blues sound to make a slight dent in the pop scene, which, at the time, was dominated by British new wave bands.

False Accusations, Cray's third album, was a sharper-edged, more defined soul-blues record than its predecessor, yet it still failed to reach many ears. Cray's breakthrough came on *Showdown!*, the 1985 album he made with fellow guitarists Albert Collins and JOHNNY COPELAND. Not only did *Showdown!* win a Grammy award and ultimately sell over a quarter of a million units, but it introduced Cray's inventive guitar style to a wide blues audience and paved the way for Cray's *Strong Persuader* album on Mercury in 1986, which contained the hit song "Smoking Gun" and won Cray a second straight Grammy.

Cray toured the U.S., Canada, Europe, and the Far East, appeared with CHUCK BERRY, Keith Richards, and other rock guitarists in the movie *Hail! Hail! Rock 'n' Roll*, performed with ERIC CLAPTON, and became one of the guiding forces behind contemporary blues. His next album, *Don't Be Afraid of the Dark*, released in 1989, won him his third Grammy, and, like *Strong Persuader*, registered sales of over one million. Though *Midnight Stroll*, his sixth album, saw Cray moving away from the blues and deeper into soul and rhythm & blues, the record didn't hurt Cray's standing with blues fans.

In 1991 Cray performed with guitarists Eric Clapton, JIMMIE VAUGHAN, Albert Collins, BUDDY GUY, and pianist JOHNNIE JOHNSON at the Royal Albert Hall in London. Later that year Clapton released his double-disc live album, *24 Nights*, which was made up of material from the Royal Albert Hall shows and included Cray's playing. Cray continues to record and perform.

Essential Listening:
Who's Been Talkin'/Tomato (269653)
Bad Influence/Hightone (8001)
False Accusations/Hightone (8005)
Showdown!/Alligator (4743)
Strong Persuader/Mercury (830 568-1)
Don't Be Afraid of the Dark/Mercury (834 923-1)
Midnight Stroll/Mercury (846 652)
I Was Warned/Mercury (314 512 721-2)

◄ CRAYTON, PEE WEE

(born Connie Crayton, December 18, 1914, Rockdale, Tex.; died June 25, 1985, Los Angeles, Calif.)

Guitarist Pee Wee Crayton was a disciple of T-BONE WALKER and a shaper of the West Coast blues sound. His guitar style was jazz-influenced and included the kind of single-note solos and chordal patterns that recalled Walker's sound, often in great detail, as well as that of two other mentors, jazzmen Charlie Christian and Kenny Burrell.

Crayton was born and raised in Texas but moved to Los Angeles in 1935. He performed with IVORY JOE HUNTER in West Coast clubs and recorded with him in 1946. Crayton eventually resettled in the Bay Area, though he continued to perform in L.A., where, in 1948, he signed a recording contract with Modern Records and cut the bulk of the material he's best known for, including "Blues After Hours," a number 1 R&B hit that year, "Texas Hop," "I Love You So," and "I'm Still in Love with You."

Crayton recorded for Vee-Jay, Imperial, and a variety of labels in the 1950s, but he was never able to match the success he enjoyed while with Modern. His career continued largely on the strength of touring and session work with artists such as CLARENCE "GATEMOUTH" BROWN, ROY MILTON, BIG MAYBELLE, and BIG JOE TURNER. Work with bandleader JOHNNY OTIS in 1970 led to a recording deal with Vanguard, which released Crayton's first album, *Things I Used to Do*, in 1971. He continued to record for small labels and tour regularly into the early 1980s. He died in 1985.

Essential Listening:
Things I Used to Do/Vanguard (VMD 6566)
Make Room for Pee Wee/Murray Brothers (1005)

◄ CREAM

Members: Eric Clapton (guitar, vocals) (born March 30, 1945, Ripley, England); Ginger Baker (drums) (born August 19, 1939, Lewisham, England); Jack Bruce (bass, vocals) (born May 14, 1943, Lanarkshire, Scotland)

Cream was a British psychedelic blues-rock band that featured the guitar work of ERIC CLAPTON and the distortion of American blues into a nearly unrecognizable though intriguing form in the late '60s. Although the trio is best known for nonblues classics such as "Sunshine of Your Love" and "White Room," its live shows were often long improvised blues jams. A riveting version of Robert Johnson's "Crossroad Blues" (shortened to "Crossroads") became one of the band's showstopping tunes in concert and catapulted Clapton into blues-rock superstardom. The group even released a live version of the song as a single in 1969; it made it to number 28 on the pop charts. Other blues songs Cream recorded and performed in concert included ALBERT KING's "Born Under a Bad Sign," WILLIE DIXON's "Spoonful," and SKIP JAMES's "I'm So Glad."

Cream was formed in 1966. All three musicians had blues backgrounds of some sort. Baker and Bruce had both played with the GRAHAM BOND Organisation, an early British blues outfit, while Clapton had logged time with the YARDBIRDS and JOHN MAYALL'S BLUESBREAKERS. Though Cream was critically hailed and on the cutting edge of the burgeoning blues-rock scene, ego squabbles stifled its output and caused it to dissolve in late 1968. Cream released only two full studio albums: *Fresh Cream* in 1966 and *Disraeli Gears* in 1967. A third album, *Wheels of Fire*, released in 1968, had both studio and live tracks on it. Cream's last concert, which was filmed and recorded, occurred at the Royal Albert Hall in London in November 1968. The ensuing documentary and album were each called, appropriately, *Goodbye*.

Shortly thereafter, Clapton and Baker formed the rock supergroup Blind Faith, with keyboards player Stevie Winwood, while Bruce embarked on a solo career. Clapton later began a solo career of his own that continues today. Cream was inducted into the Rock & Roll Hall of Fame in 1993.

Essential Listening:
Fresh Cream/RSO (827 576-2)
Disraeli Gears/RSO (823 636-2)
Wheels of Fire/RSO (827 578-2)
Goodbye/Polygram (823 660-2-Y-1)

◄ CRUDUP, ARTHUR "BIG BOY"

(aka Elmore Jones, Percy Crudup) (born August 24, 1905, Forest, Miss.; died March 28, 1974, Nassawadox, Va.)

Arthur "Big Boy" Crudup will forever be known as the author of "That's All Right (Mama)," the first song Elvis Presley recorded. Released on the Sun label in 1954, the record launched Presley's phenomenal career and explicitly linked blues with early rock & roll. Crudup wrote other blues classics, including "Rock Me Mama," "Mean Ol' Frisco," and "My Baby Left Me," which have been covered by artists such as B.B. KING, BIG MAMA THORNTON, and BOBBY "BLUE" BLAND and remain part of most basic blues repertoires.

Born and raised in Mississippi, Crudup began his career singing in gospel groups and church choirs. He began playing the blues after going to Chicago in 1939. Working the city's street corners for spare change, Crudup was discovered by blues producer LESTER MELROSE, who signed him to a recording contract with the Bluebird label. Not much of a guitar player, Crudup had, however, a powerful vocal style that intermeshed gospel wails and field holler shouts.

His relationship with Melrose ended in 1947 after Crudup found out he was not being paid royalties for his hit songs. He returned to Mississippi where he operated a successful bootlegging business and continued to record with RCA in the late 1940s and early 1950s.

Crudup frequently toured with SONNY BOY WILLIAMSON (RICE MILLER) and ELMORE JAMES. But by the mid-1950s he had all but quit his career as a songwriter and bluesman. Angered at repeatedly being cheated out of money due him, Crudup faded from the blues scene until blues aficionado Dick Waterman rediscovered him in Mississippi in the mid-'60s. Waterman worked to secure money owed Crudup and convinced him to end his self-imposed retirement. Crudup began recording again; he released albums on the Delmark and Liberty labels. A film documentary based on his life—*Arthur Crudup: Born in the Blues*—came out in 1973. He also toured the U.S. and Europe before his death in 1974.

Essential Listening:

Mean Ol' Frisco/Collectables (5130)

Give Me a 32-20/Crown Prince (IG 403)

Crudup's Mood/Delmark (621)

◄ CURTIS, PECK

(born James Curtis, March 7, 1912, Benoit, Miss.; died November 1, 1970, Helena, Ark.)

James "Peck" Curtis was as much an old-fashioned entertainer as he was a bluesman. Not only did he play washboard, drums, and, early on, the jug, but Curtis was also a hot-stepping tap dancer. In short, Curtis used whatever was available to drum or scrape or tap out percussive parts in a blues framework.

Curtis was born in Mississippi but raised in Arkansas. Some of his earliest performing was with jug bands in and around Memphis. After traveling the South playing with vaudeville shows, Curtis teamed up with ROBERT JR. LOCKWOOD and SONNY BOY WILLIAMSON (Rice Miller) as the King Biscuit Entertainers in 1942. Together they played the King Biscuit radio show that was broadcast live on KFFA out of Helena, Arkansas, each afternoon. Throughout the decade Curtis continued to play on and off with Williamson and then with guitarist-singer HOUSTON STACKHOUSE in the 1950s and 1960s. He died in 1970.

Essential Listening:

King Biscuit Time (Sonny Boy Williamson)/Arhoolie (CD 310)

Mississippi Delta Blues, Vol. 1 (Various Artists)/Arhoolie (1041)

D.

◄ DAVENPORT, COW COW

(born Charles Davenport, April 23, 1894, Anniston, Ala.; died December 2, 1956, Cleveland, Ohio)

Cow Cow Davenport was one of the earliest boogie-woogie pianists. His walking bass figures and rag-flavored rhythms along with his trademark tune, "Cow Cow Blues," helped give life to the fledgling boogie-woogie piano style in the 1920s. Davenport had some piano training as a youth but was mostly self-taught. Basing his early style on what he heard from ragtime piano players, Davenport worked with carnivals and vaudeville troupes, eventually creating an act called Davenport and Co. with singer Dora Carr. Together they played the TOBA (Theater Owners' Booking Association) circuit in the early 1920s and recorded together in 1924.

Although the duo was fairly successful, Carr left Davenport in the mid-'20s, after which Davenport wrote "Cow Cow Blues," one of the most popular boogie-woogie piano tunes ever recorded. The original version of the song came out on the Okeh label, but Davenport later recorded the song with other labels. He also worked with other singers, including Iva(y) Smith, with whom he established an act called the Chicago Steppers and recorded "Jim Crow Blues," his noted song about racism.

Davenport's career dried up during the Depression. He allegedly spent some time in prison for debts and tried his hand in business with little success. Although he continued to perform sporadically in the late 1930s and 1940s, he gradually disappeared from the blues scene. He died in 1956.

Essential Listening:
"Cow Cow" Davenport, 1927–29/Document (557)
Cow Cow Davenport/Oldie Blues (2811)

◄ DAVENPORT, JED

(birth and death information unknown)

Along with WILL SHADE and NOAH LEWIS, Jed Davenport was one of the best Memphis harmonica players in the late 1920s and 1930s. Like Shade, who formed the MEMPHIS JUG BAND, and Lewis, who played with GUS CANNON's Jug Stompers, Davenport used a jug band format to showcase his harp talents. Not as well-known as the Memphis Jug Band or Cannon's Jug Stompers, his band, the Beale

St. Jug Band, played traditional romp and stomp Memphis-style jug band music, often highlighted with Davenport's dynamic solos.

Little is known of Davenport's life: he probably was born in Mississippi. In his late teens he moved to Memphis, where he played his harmonica on street corners for spare change. He traveled with tent shows but by the late 1920s was back playing around Memphis. He formed the Beale St. Jug Band in 1930 during the heyday of the city's jug band era. The group recorded for Vocalion that same year. Loosely knit, the Beale St. Jug Band often included MEMPHIS MINNIE and Kansas JOE MCCOY on guitars, in addition to Charlie Pierce on fiddle. Davenport played on some Memphis Minnie records and frequently accompanied other Memphis musicians in the studio. As the Memphis jug band craze began to wane in the mid-1930s, Davenport played with numerous Memphis-based artists in the city's clubs and parks, occasionally with saxophone player Dub Jenkins and bass player Al Jackson. In addition to playing harmonica, he also played trumpet, jug, and other instruments.

By the 1940s, Davenport had faded from the Memphis blues scene, though he is said to have remained in Memphis playing Beale Street for tips. He is believed to have died sometime in the 1960s.

Essential Listening:
The Great Jug Bands, 1926–1934 (Various Artists)/Historical (HLP 36)

◄ DAVENPORT, LESTER

(born January 16, 1932, Tchula, Miss.)

In 1955 Chicago blues harmonica player Lester Davenport replaced BILLY BOY ARNOLD in BO DIDDLEY's band and gained respect in blues circles for his smooth, fluid harp phrasing. Davenport, who was born in Mississippi and came to Chicago in 1946, taught himself how to play the blues harp. He had performed with SMOKEY SMOTHERS and BIG BOY SPIRES before joining Diddley's band. Davenport recorded some sides with Diddley for Chess and toured with him until 1961 when he formed his own group and began playing Chicago clubs.

Davenport kicked around the Windy City blues scene, splitting his time playing harmonica and drums. He backed up SUNNYLAND SLIM, JUNIOR WELLS, KANSAS CITY RED, and other Chicago bluesmen, but never made enough money to quit his day job as a commercial paint sprayer. In 1979 Davenport toured Europe as part of the American Blues Legends tour. The resulting album, *American Blues Legends 1979* on the Big Bear label featured Davenport on drums and bass guitar. Other package tours of Europe and the U.S. followed until the mid-1980s when Davenport signed on as the harmonica player for the blues-rock group the KINSEY REPORT. In 1992 he recorded his debut solo album, *When the Blues Hit You*, for Earwig Records. Davenport continues to perform.

Essential Listening:
American Blues Legends 1979/Big Bear (23)
When the Blues Hit You/Earwig (4923)

◄ DAVIES, CYRIL

(born 1932, Denham, England; died January 7, 1964, England)

Harmonica player and singer Cyril Davies was a co-founder of BLUES INCOR-PORATED, an early British blues band that set the stage for the British blues-rock scene of the '60s and influenced such bands as the ROLLING STONES, the YARDBIRDS, and CREAM. Davies began his career in the early 1950s as a jazz and skiffle musician before turning all of his attention to blues in 1955. After performing as a solo artist at the London Blues and Barrelhouse Club, he formed Blues Incorporated with ALEXIS KORNER in 1961. The group's drummer was Charlie Watts, who later joined the Rolling Stones. Unhappy with the band's increasing interest in jazz-flavored blues, Davies left Blues Incorporated in 1962 and formed Cyril Davies' R&B All-Stars, a more traditional blues and R&B band that included among its members guitarist Jeff Beck, piano player Nicky Hopkins, and singer LONG JOHN BALDRY. The All-Stars were a popular club attraction in London in 1963, but their run came to a sudden end when Davies died of leukemia in early 1964.

Essential Listening:
R&B from the Marquee/Deram
The Legendary Cyril Davies/Folklore

◄ DAVIS, REV. BLIND GARY

(born April 30, 1896, Larens, S.C.; died May 5, 1972, Hammonton, N.J.)

Rev. Blind Gary Davis was a gospel-blues singer whose gruffy, salt-of-the-earth vocals and intricate finger-picking techniques on the six- and twelve-string guitar gave his music great vitality. He had considerable impact on both blues and blues-flavored folk musicians. In addition to influencing the guitar styles of BLIND BOY FULLER, JOHN CEPHAS, and TAJ MAHAL, Davis, a major force in the East Coast/Piedmont blues school, also touched the folk and rock styles of Bob Dylan, DAVE VAN RONK, Ry Cooder, and Jorma Kaukonen. Davis brought together sacred and secular music the way BLIND WILLIE JOHNSON and only a handful of others were able to do before him.

Using a performance and recording style that emphasized emotional honesty and a unique, homespun folk quality, Davis made gospel and the blues seem like perfect partners. He had a long and prolific recording career, and many of his best songs, such as "Samson and Delilah," "Candy Man," and "Cocaine Blues," have become standards and been reinterpreted by dozens of artists.

Information on Davis's early life is sketchy. Despite doing numerous interviews in his life, Davis was, for some reason, reluctant to confirm details about his blindness. Some accounts trace his blindness to birth; others say he lost his eyesight when he was a young man. By the time he was a teen, he had taught himself how to play harmonica, banjo, and guitar and had already begun performing at house parties and picnics in the Laurens, South Carolina, area. Davis eventually left South Carolina and by the late 1920s had settled in Durham, North Carolina, playing blues on street corners for spare change.

Sometime during the early 1930s, Davis became interested in salvation and religious music. Eventually he was ordained a Baptist minister and began mixing gospel music with the blues. He often played revival meetings and lumber camps, using his loud, emotionally charged vocals to send a religious message, and his stirring guitar picking to give it a rich, bluesy sound.

While in Durham, Davis met up with Blind Boy Fuller, another innovative finger-picking blues guitar stylist from the Piedmont school. Together the two artists traveled to New York in 1935 to record for the American Record Company. Believing that there would be more opportunity for him to perform and record in New York, Davis moved there around 1940 and lived in the city for the rest of his life. Along with BROWNIE MCGHEE, another Piedmont blues guitarist who had come to New York to live, Davis began to record regularly for a variety of labels, including Riverside and Folk-Lyric. He also worked the streets of Harlem, gaining fame as a blues-playing preacher.

By the late 1950s, Davis was known enough through his recordings and performances in New York to assume a major role in the folk-music revival underway at the time. White folk-blues artists like Dave Van Ronk studied Davis's finger-picking style and adopted his mix of gospel and blues. Davis played the era's major folk festivals, including Newport and also Mariposa in Toronto. He also became a regular performer in coffeehouses and folk clubs like Gerdes Folk City in New York, and continued to record, cutting albums for larger labels such as Folkways, Vanguard, Prestige, and Bluesville.

Davis was one of the most in-demand blues performers on the folk-festival circuit prior to the "rediscovery" of Mississippi Delta blues artists in the early '60s. He remained a popular attraction throughout the decade. He toured England in 1964 and was the subject of a short film, *Blind Gary Davis*, in New York that same year. Davis made repeat performances at the Newport Folk Festival, Mariposa, the Philadelphia Folk Festival, and numerous other fests and went back to England at least two other times. In 1972, while enroute to a concert in southern New Jersey, Davis suffered a fatal heart attack. He was seventy-six years old.

Essential Listening:
Say No to the Devil/Original Blues Classics (519)
Reverend Gary Davis/Yazoo (1023)
When I Die I'll Live Again/Fantasy (24704)
From Blues to Gospel/Biograph (BCD 123)
Blues & Ragtime/Shanachie (97024)

◄ DAVIS, JAMES "THUNDERBIRD"

(born November 10, 1938, Mobile, Ala.; died January 24, 1991, St. Paul, Minn.)

James "Thunderbird" Davis, a gospel-influenced rhythm & blues singer, recorded for Duke Records in the early 1960s. Despite a voice rich in tone and emotional fervor, most of the material he cut for Duke, including his best-known songs, "Blue Monday" and "Your Turn to Cry," attracted little attention outside dedicated R&B circles. It wasn't until Davis began a serious comeback in the late 1980s that his career started to blossom. Unfortunately, while performing onstage in St. Paul, Minnesota, in 1991, Davis suffered a fatal heart attack.

Davis was born in Mobile, Alabama, and learned how to sing gospel before switching to rhythm & blues in 1957. Discovered by GUITAR SLIM, Davis spent the late 1950s opening shows for Slim. The exposure led to a recording contract with the Duke label in 1961. Davis stayed with Duke until 1965. During the '60s and early '70s he often toured with Joe Tex and O.V. WRIGHT, opening shows for these R&B artists the way he did for Guitar Slim. By the mid-1970s, however, Davis had faded from the touring and recording scene. He was rediscovered during the late 1980s blues boom and signed to a recording contract with Black Top Records. His debut album, *Check Out Time*, was released in 1989 and was well received. Davis was getting ready to record a follow-up album when he died.

Essential Listening:
Check Out Time/Black Top (1043)
Angels in Houston (Various Artists)/Rounder (2011)

◄ DAVIS, BLIND JOHN

(born John Henry Davis, December 7, 1913, Hattiesburg, Miss.; died October 12, 1985, Chicago, Ill.)

Blind John Davis, a noted session piano player for LESTER MELROSE's Bluebird label in the 1930s and 1940s, recorded with many of Chicago's best prewar blues artists, including TAMPA RED, BIG BILL BROONZY, and JOHN LEE "SONNY BOY" WILLIAMSON. Blind since he was nine years old, Davis began playing the piano as a teen after his father, a speakeasy owner during Prohibition, promised to hire him to perform in his club. Davis incorporated blues, ragtime, jazz, and boogie-woogie into his playing and became known for his versatility and smooth, easily accessible keyboard style.

In addition to doing sessions for Bluebird, Davis led his own band, playing house parties and cocktail lounges in and around Chicago. He recorded as a solo artist in 1938 for the Vocalion label, but his reputation was greatest as an accompanist, and much of his best work can be heard on Broonzy and Williamson records. In 1952, he and Broonzy toured Europe, opening the door for other Chicago blues artists to follow.

Davis returned to Europe often during the next twenty years, where he developed a particularly loyal following. When not on the road, he performed with drummer Judge Riley in Chicago clubs. In 1977 Alligator Records released *Stomping on a Saturday Night*, an album recorded at Club Popular in Bonn, Germany, and previously released in Europe. Another solo album, *You Better Cut That Out*, was released by Red Beans Records in 1985. Davis died of a heart attack that year.

Essential Listening:
Stomping on a Saturday Night/Alligator (AL 4709)
You Better Cut That Out/Red Beans (RB 008)
Blind John Davis, 1938–1939/Story of Blues (3520)

◄ DAVIS, LARRY

(born December 4, 1936, Kansas City, Mo.)

Larry Davis is a soul-blues singer and guitarist who, despite winning four W.C. HANDY Awards in 1982, including artist of the year, has never achieved the commercial success of many of his blues colleagues. Born in Kansas City but raised in Arkansas, Davis came onto the blues scene in the 1950s as the bass player in a bar band that included guitarist FENTON ROBINSON. The band impressed BOBBY "BLUE" BLAND enough for him to recommend the group to DON ROBEY, who signed Davis to his Duke label. Though he cut two memorable tunes for Duke in the 1960s, "Texas Flood," a song covered by STEVIE RAY VAUGHAN twenty years later, and "Angels in Houston," Davis attracted little attention.

Davis played bass in ALBERT KING's band before switching to guitar in the late 1960s. In 1972 he was in a motorcycle accident and severely damaged his hand. A few years later, he suffered a stroke. These setbacks prompted Davis to retire from performing and recording. But in 1981 he was encouraged to launch a comeback by Rooster Blues label owner Jim O'Neal, who admired Davis's gospel-drenched, soul-blues vocal delivery and his complementing guitar work. Davis recorded his debut album, *Funny Stuff*, for Rooster Blues. In addition to winning the coveted artist of the year award, presented at the W.C. Handy Awards in 1982, Davis also walked away with contemporary blues album of the year and two other W. C. Handy Awards. Yet because Davis's sound lacked the riveting dynamics of blues-rock or the harsher Chicago blues sound that '80s rock and pop audiences preferred, he fell back into the blues shadows. A second album, *I Ain't Beggin' Nobody*, on the Pulsar label came and went. Davis next signed with Bullseye Blues and recorded *Sooner or Later* in 1991. Though the album garnered much critical praise, it did not elevate Davis to the blues stardom. He continues to record and perform.

Essential Listening:
Angels in Houston (Various Artists)/Rounder (2031)
Funny Stuff/Rooster Blues (R 2616)
I Ain't Beggin' Nobody/Pulsar (1001)
Sooner or Later/Bullseye Blues (9511)

◄ DAVIS, MAXWELL

(born Thomas Maxwell Davis, 1916, Independence, Kans.; died September 18, 1970, Los Angeles, Calif.)

Maxwell Davis was one of the principal builders of the West Coast rhythm & blues sound in the late 1940s and 1950s. His skill as a bandleader and tenor sax sideman and his vision as an arranger, producer, songwriter, and talent scout had great impact on post–World War II black music. His influence was evident in the music of everyone from PERCY MAYFIELD and JIMMY WITHERSPOON to FLOYD DIXON and T-BONE WALKER. Davis also worked with B.B. KING, CLARENCE

"GATEMOUTH" BROWN, JESSE BELVIN, ETTA JAMES, JOHNNY "GUITAR" WATSON, BIG JOE TURNER, and many other prominent blues and R&B artists.

In addition to his studio work with other artists, Davis released numerous records under his own name and led many bands and orchestras in his long career. Yet despite his critical importance to West Coast R&B, Davis never achieved the fame he helped other artists enjoy, mostly because his best work was done behind the scenes and away from the limelight.

Davis was born in Kansas during World War I; by the time he was in his late teens he was a convincing saxophonist whose biggest influence was jazz sax player Coleman Hawkins. In 1937 Davis moved to Los Angeles where he secured work with the Fletcher Henderson Orchestra. Eventually he began writing and arranging songs, producing recording sessions, working as an A&R man for West Coast R&B labels like Aladdin and Modern, and creating a rhythm & blues sound that was blues-based but had strong, swinging links to jazz. By the mid-1950s Davis had become the patriarch of West Coast R&B.

With the advent of rock & roll, Davis's brand of rhythm & blues began a slow fade from the pop scene, though he continued to record and perform. He never registered any major hits—his 1956 record "Slow Walk" for the Mecury label was his only semblance of a hit—but Davis released dozens of titles, even in the 1960s when R&B had all but disappeared from the charts. Davis continued to direct West Coast orchestras and play piano, he worked right up until his fatal heart attack in 1970.

Essential Listening:
Father of West Coast R&B/Ace (CHAD 239)
Maxwell Davis/Official (6064)

◄ DAVIS, TYRONE

(born May 4, 1938, Greenville, Miss.)

A soul singer with strong blues undertones, Tyrone Davis has been a star on the chitlin' circuit since the late 1960s when his chart-topping record "Can I Change My Mind" sold more than a million copies. Since then Davis has placed dozens of songs on the charts, including "Turn Back the Hands of Time," which in 1970 made it to number 1 on the R&B charts and number 3 on the pop charts, and "Turning Point," which hit number 1 on the R&B charts in 1975.

Born in Mississippi, Davis moved to Saginaw, Michigan, as a teen to live with his father, a minister, before settling in Chicago in 1959. He worked as a valet for bluesman FREDDIE KING and became friends with soul-blues singer OTIS CLAY, then began his own career in 1962. In the '60s Davis often performed under the name Tyrone the Wonder Boy. He signed with Dakar Records in 1968. His first record was "Can I Change My Mind," and its huge success led to a slew of singles recorded in the 1970s for Dakar and later Columbia, with whom he signed in 1977.

Davis moved effortlessly into the disco era, making records with hearty dance grooves. "Give It Up (Turn It Loose)" peaked at number 2 on the R&B charts in 1976. In the 1980s Davis continued playing one-nighters on the chitlin' circuit, appealing mostly to women who enjoyed his sexy stage antics. Davis continued to record for small labels such as Highrise, Ocean Front, and Future. In 1991 he signed with Ichiban Records and released the albums *I'll Always Love You* and *Something's Mighty Wrong*. Davis continues to record and perform.

Essential Listening:
Greatest Hits: Tyrone Davis/Rhino (R2-70533)

◄ DAVIS, WALTER

(born March 1, 1912, Grenada, Miss.; died October 22, 1963, St. Louis, Mo.)

Pianist Walter Davis was part of the pre–World War II St. Louis blues scene that spawned other popular singer-pianists such as PEETIE WHEATSTRAW, ROOSEVELT SYKES, ST. LOUIS JIMMY ODEN, and HENRY BROWN. Influenced by LEROY CARR, Davis was noted more for his dark, almost gloomy vocals than for his pedestrian piano style. He recorded regularly in the 1930s and was often accompanied by guitarist HENRY TOWNSEND on many of his best sides.

Davis grew up in the Mississippi Delta and learned to play piano. In the mid-1920s he left the Delta for St. Louis and settled into the city's growing blues scene, playing clubs and house parties, usually with Townsend. Davis was also a popular performer in East St. Louis, Illinois, which at the time also had a thriving blues scenes.

Davis began his recording career in 1930 with the Victor label. He later recorded for Bluebird and Bullet. In all, Davis cut some 150 sides between 1930 and 1952. After suffering a stroke, Davis got deeply involved in religion and ultimately became a preacher. He died in 1963.

Essential Listening:
Walter Davis/Cripple Clarence Lofton/Yazoo (1025)
Walter Davis, 1930–33/Old Tramp (1213)
Walter Davis, Vol. 1/Blues Documents (2084)

◄ DAWKINS, JIMMY

(born October 24, 1936, Tchula, Miss.)

Blues guitarist Jimmy Dawkins has spent much of his career in the shadows of more celebrated Chicago blues artists, but his guitar style—full of tension and prickly solos—makes him an important, though largely unsung, artist in the post-'60s blues hierarchy. Growing up in Mississippi, Dawkins taught himself how to play guitar in the early 1950s. When he moved north to Chicago in 1955, he played for tips on the city's street corners. Eventually he obtained sideman work with WILLIE DIXON, MAGIC SAM, and BIG WALTER HORTON. Dawkins also did studio work for Sonny Thompson, JOHNNY YOUNG, and other Chicago bluesmen, and formed his own band.

In 1969, after nearly a decade of apprentice work on blues stages and in recording studios, Dawkins signed a recording contract with Delmark Records, which released his debut album, *Fast Fingers*. Though the record attracted little attention in the U.S., it won France's Grand Prix du Disque de Jazz in 1971 for best jazz/blues album of the year. Dawkins recorded two other albums for Delmark, *All for Business* in 1975 and *Blisterstring* in 1976, both of which were favorably reviewed. He also recorded for the French Black and Blue and Vogue labels and the Excello label in the early '70s. Dawkins spent most of his time in the '70s and '80s playing festivals and clubs. In 1992 he signed with the Earwig label and released *Kant Sheck Dees Bluze*. Dawkins continues to record and perform.

Essential Listening:
Fast Fingers/Delmark (DS 623)
All For Business/Delmark (DS 634)
Blisterstring/Delmark (DS 641)
Kant Sheck Dees Bluze/Earwig (4920)
Tribute to Orange/Evidence (ECD 26031-2)

◄ DETROIT JUNIOR

(born Emery Williams, Jr., October 26, 1931, Haynes, Ark.)

A piano player and occasional guitarist, Detroit Junior was a member of the Motor City's blues scene in the early 1950s. By 1956, though, he had settled in Chicago where he played with Morris Pejoe, J. T. Brown, and EDDIE TAYLOR before forging a full-time working relationship with harmonica player Little Mack Simmons, with whom he recorded for the Bea & Baby label. Detroit Junior's signature song, "Money Tree," was recorded in 1960 and featured his humorous blues twist. The song's success in Chicago was enough for him to make records with a variety of labels through the '60s and to work with HOWLIN' WOLF's band until the legendary bluesman's death in 1976.

In 1971 Detroit Junior recorded *Chicago Urban Blues* for Antilles, a subsidiary of Island Records. But the album received little attention and Junior went back to playing piano in Chicago blues clubs. Alligator Records included four of his songs on volume 4 of its *Living Chicago Blues* series, released in 1980. Detroit Junior continues to play Chicago clubs as a sideman.

Essential Listening:
Living Chicago Blues, Vol. 4 (Various Artists)/Alligator (AL 7704)

◄ DIDDLEY, BO

(born Otha Ellas Bates McDaniels, December 30, 1928, McComb, Miss.)

Bo Diddley's music more often rides under the banners of rock & roll and R&B than that of blues, but his signature guitar sound—proto-funk and thickly textured, and featuring the famous "Bo Diddley beat" (aka "Shave 'n' a haircut, two bits")—is blues-derived. Diddley recorded with blues musicians during his tenure with Chess Records in the 1950s and 1960s, and plenty of his songs are built on blues themes. Like CHUCK BERRY, he falls somewhere between blues and R&B-based rock & roll, appealing to fans of both genres.

Diddley was born in Mississippi but brought up in Chicago. As a youth his main interests were boxing (which is where he picked up his nickname) and music. Though he was well-versed in spirituals and sanctified church music, Diddley also took violin lessons and studied classical music. By age thirteen, however, he had discovered the guitar and the blues by way of JOHN LEE HOOKER's "Boogie Chillen." Diddley abandoned the violin but incorporated his church music roots into his sound, which accounts, in part, for the distinctive rhythmic muscle of so many of his songs.

Diddley began playing Chicago street corners in the late 1940s. After forming his first group, the Hipsters, which included Diddley's longtime percussionist, Jerome Green, Diddley moved from the streets into Chicago clubs. Blues harmonica player BILLY BOY ARNOLD was added to the group, and Diddley changed its name to the Langley Avenue Jive Cats (Diddley lived on Langley Avenue, as did bass player Roosevelt Jackson). In 1955 Diddley signed a recording contract with Checker (Chess) Records and released his first single, "Bo Diddley" backed with "I'm a Man." While the former song contained the kind of lyrics that kids might sing when playing street games ("Hey Bo Diddley, have you heard?/My pretty baby says she's a bird"), the latter song was mostly autobiographical and had a lively blues slant. Other Diddley classics followed: "Who Do You Love" (1956), "Hey Bo Diddley" (1957), "Mona (I Need You Baby)" (1957), "Say Man" (1958), "Road Runner" (1959), and a version of WILLIE DIXON's "You Can't Judge a Book by Its Cover" (1962).

Diddley moved to Washington, D.C., in 1958; it was there that he designed his trademark square guitar. In the late '50s and early '60s he toured with rock & roll package shows and made albums with titles like *Bo Diddley Is a Gunslinger* (1960), *Bo Diddley Is a Lover* (1961), and *Bo Diddley Is a Twister* (1962), appealing primarily to a rock & roll crowd. When the guitar-heavy surfing craze swept rock & roll in 1963, Diddley recorded albums like *Surfin' with Bo Diddley* and *Bo Diddley's Beach Party*.

Although Diddley's influence on early-'60s British invasion rock bands like the Beatles, the ROLLING STONES, the YARDBIRDS, and the Who was substantial, his popularity waned in America until he was forced to make his living on the oldies circuit. In 1969 he recorded *Black Gladiator*, one of his most inspired albums, but it failed to sell many copies.

Diddley continued to tour in the '70s and '80s; he opened some shows for the British punk-rock band the Clash in 1979, and in 1987 was inducted into the Rock & Roll Hall of Fame. Diddley's most successful comeback came from an odd source: a Nike sneakers commercial in the late 1980s that featured Diddley and football/baseball superstar Bo Jackson. Diddley continues to perform.

Essential Listening:
Go Bo Diddley/MCA-Chess
Bo Diddley: The Chess Box/MCA-Chess (CHC 2-19502)

◄ DIXIELAND JUG BLOWERS

Members: Clifford Hayes (violin); Earl McDonald (jug); Henry Clifford (jug); Johnny Dodds (clarinet) (born April 12, 1892, New Orleans, La.; died August 8, 1940, Chicago, Ill.)

The Louisville-based Dixieland Jug Blowers helped ignite the Memphis jug band craze in the late 1920s. WILL "Son" SHADE, a Memphis musician, was inspired to start his own band, the MEMPHIS JUG BAND, after hearing records made by the Dixieland Jug Blowers. The Memphis Jug Band ultimately became one of the most popular and most recorded of all jug bands. Its success prompted the creation of another popular and influential jug band, Cannon's Jug Stompers.

Unlike the jug bands from Memphis, which based their brand of jug band music on the blues, the Dixieland Jug Blowers were more jazz oriented. The group included noted New Orleans clarinet player Johnny Dodds, along with violinist Clifford Hayes and jug players Earl McDonald and Henry Clifford. Though the Dixieland Jug Blowers was led by Hayes and featured Dodds, it was McDonald who exerted the most influence. His ability to use the jug to create a trombonelike sound inspired other jug players to create similar sounds in the late '20s and early '30s.

McDonald later formed his own jug band, the Original Louisville Jug Band, and recorded for Columbia Records. He also did side work as a session musician for classic blues singer SARA MARTIN and white country-folk-blues singer JIMMIE RODGERS.

Essential Listening:
The Jug, Jook, and Washboard Bands/Blues Classics (BC 2)

◄ DIXON, FLOYD

(born February 8, 1929, Marshall, Tex.)

Floyd Dixon was one of a number of Texas blues and R&B artists who came to the West Coast in the 1940s. A piano player and singer, Dixon was particularly versatile; not only did he embrace a variety of blues and R&B styles, but he could also croon like CHARLES BROWN one moment and rock like LITTLE RICHARD the next. Traditional and cocktail lounge blues, slick R&B, pop, and rock & roll were all included in Dixon's repertoire at one time or another in his career.

Dixon taught himself how to play piano. After he and his family moved to Los Angeles in the mid-'40s, he decided to become a professional singer. He won a few amateur talent contests in L.A., and bandleader JOHNNY OTIS encouraged Dixon to seek a recording contract. Shortly thereafter, he signed with Modern Records. His first record, "Dallas Blues," was released by the label in 1949. From that point on, he recorded for a variety of labels—Modern, Supreme, Aladdin, and Specialty—as he sought to find his niche in the West Coast rhythm & blues scene. Dixon's biggest hits were with Aladdin: "Telephone Blues" and "Call Operator 210" both hit near the top of the R&B charts in 1951 and 1952, respectively. "Hey Bartender," a song he wrote and recorded in 1954 for the Cat label, was made popular again in the late '70s by the BLUES BROTHERS, a band featuring actors John Belushi and Dan Aykroyd.

Dixon spent the rest of his career doing R&B package tours and performing one-nighters around the U.S. Although he continued to record into the 1970s with a number of small independent labels, he was never able to match the success he had enjoyed in the early 1950s.

Essential Listening:
Marshall, Texas Is My Home/Specialty (SPCD 7011-2)

◄ DIXON, WILLIE

(born July 1, 1915, Vicksburg, Miss.; died January 29, 1992, Burbank, Calif.)

Willie Dixon was the quintessential behind-the-scenes bluesman. As a composer, producer, arranger, bass player, recording artist, session musician, talent scout, and bandleader for Chess Records in the 1950s and early 1960s, Dixon did more to shape postwar Chicago blues than perhaps any other artist save MUDDY WATERS. Dixon, in fact, was a key catalyst in Waters's success; such Waters staples as "Hoochie Coochie Man" and "I Just Want to Make Love to You" were penned by Dixon. He also wrote the HOWLIN' WOLF classics "Evil," "Spoonful," "I Ain't Superstitious," "Little Red Rooster," and "Back Door Man," as well as the LITTLE WALTER gem "My Babe" and SONNY BOY WILLIAMSON's (Rice Miller) hit, "Bring It on Home."

Dixon also helped forge a bond between blues and rock & roll. He played on numerous CHUCK BERRY sides in the 1950s, and in the 1960s a number of his best songs were reinterpreted by English and American blues-rock bands. CREAM ("Spoonful"), LED ZEPPELIN ("I Can't Quit You Baby" and "You Shook Me"), and the Doors ("Back Door Man") are just some of the rock groups that recorded Willie Dixon compositions.

Over the years Dixon has been one of the blues' most effective and respected ambassadors. In an attempt to give something back to the music, he created the Blues Heaven Foundation in 1982 with royalty money from his song catalog. The aim of the nonprofit organization, which is still active, is to keep the blues alive through such programs as blues-in-the-schools and scholarship funds. Blues Heaven also gives financial aid to destitute blues artists.

Dixon was born in Vicksburg, Mississippi. His mother wrote and recited religious poetry, which, at an early age, made Dixon aware of rhyming schemes and meter. Musically his first influences were also religious. Early on he sang with the Union Jubilee Singers, a gospel quartet that had its own radio program on the Vicksburg station WQBC. Dixon pursued a career as a professional boxer before turning to music full-time. In 1936 he left Mississippi for Chicago; a year later he was the Illinois State Golden Gloves heavyweight champion in the novice category. Once Dixon even sparred with Joe Louis. But despite such early success, his pro career lasted only four fights. A brawl with his manager over money in the boxing commissioner's office ended whatever professional fight dreams Dixon might have harbored.

Shortly afterwards, Dixon began his career as a musician. In 1939 he began playing the bass and, along with guitarist Leonard "Baby Doo" Caston, formed the Five Breezes. The group played Chicago clubs and did a little recording until 1941 when Dixon, who had declared himself a conscientious objector, was arrested for refusing to serve in the U.S. armed forces. While Dixon was in prison, Caston formed the Rhythm Rascals, a trio that played USO clubs in the Pacific, North Africa, and Europe.

After serving his sentence Dixon formed a new group, the Four Jumps of Jive, which regularly performed in Chicago clubs and recorded for Mercury in 1945. That same year Caston returned to Chicago and resumed his musical partnership with Dixon. The two formed the BIG THREE TRIO with guitarist Bernardo Dennis, who was later replaced by Ollie Crawford. With a repertoire of soft blues, boogie-woogie, pop, and novelty numbers, the Big Three landed a recording contract, first with Bullet Records and then in 1947 with Columbia Records. The Big Three remained active until 1952.

While playing with the Big Three Trio, Dixon was also jamming with Muddy Waters and other bluesmen in the clubs of Chicago's South Side. During one late-night jam at the Macomba Lounge Dixon met PHIL and LEONARD CHESS, the club's owners. The Chess brothers had recently started Chess Records, and they offered Dixon a part-time job with the label in 1948. He accepted, and after the breakup of the Big Three Trio, Dixon went to work for Chess full-time.

Dixon wrote some songs for Eddie Boyd and even released a few tracks under his own name for Chess in 1953. But it wasn't until 1954, when Waters recorded Dixon's "Hoochie Coochie Man," Howlin' Wolf recorded "Evil," and Little Walter & His Jukes cut "Mellow Down Easy," that Dixon's reputation in the Chicago blues community blossomed. Dixon also began to work as a session musician; he played bass in the Chess house band, recording with Waters, Berry, BO DIDDLEY, Little Walter, and JIMMY WITHERSPOON, among others. Dixon also began arranging and producing sessions for Chess, but it was his composing talent that was most in demand. In addition to the above-mentioned originals, Dixon also wrote such blues standards as "The Seventh Son," "Wang Dang Doodle," and "You Can't Judge a Book by Its Cover," all of which were covered by a number of blues artists. Dixon kept a solo recording career going, but it never matched the success he enjoyed as a songwriter and recording session ace.

Dixon's tenure with Chess was interrupted in 1957 when he went to work for Cobra Records. During the two years that the label was in existence, Dixon worked with MAGIC SAM, OTIS RUSH, and BUDDY GUY—the three guitarists who would create the West Side Sound of the Chicago blues in the late '50s and '60s. When Cobra folded, Dixon returned to Chess and stayed with the company through most of the 1960s. During this time he performed with the American Folk Blues Festival package in Europe and formed the Chicago Blues All-Stars as his flexible touring and recording band.

During the 1970s Dixon released albums on the Ovation, Columbia and Yambo labels and toured regularly. In the 1980s he released albums on the Pausa label, though none of them attracted much attention outside hardcore blues circles.

Dixon also got involved with movie soundtrack work, scoring music for *The Color of Money* and producing Bo Diddley's version of "Who Do You Love" in *La Bamba*.

In 1980 Dixon was inducted into the Blues Foundation's Hall of Fame. He continued playing club dates and festivals, both in the U.S. and abroad. In 1988 he signed a recording contract with Bug/Capitol and released the critically acclaimed album *Hidden Charms*. A year later he published his autobiography, *I Am the Blues* (written with Don Snowden). By 1990, Dixon's ill health forced him to perform only part-time with the Chicago Blues All-Stars, though he remained active with his Blues Heaven Foundation. He died of a heart ailment in 1992.

Essential Listening:
Willie Dixon: The Big Three Trio/Columbia (CK 46216)
Willie Dixon: The Chess Box/MCA-Chess (CHD2-16500)
Hidden Charms/Capitol (C1 90595)
I Am the Blues/Mobile Fidelity (MFCD 872)
Willie Dixon and His Chicago Blues Band/Spivey (1016)

◄ DOMINO, FATS

(born Antoine Domino, February 26, 1928, New Orleans, La.)

Pianist and singer Fats Domino was the most popular of all the rhythm & blues artists to come out of New Orleans in the 1950s. Much of his allure grew from his warm, insouciant vocals and the easy-riding rhythms that flowed from his piano. But some of Domino's charm lay in his embraceable personality and his incessant smile. He was the perfect counterpart, both musically and visually, to another R&B recording artist, LITTLE RICHARD, who, in the 1950s, took the music to its most radical edge.

Domino was a regular visitor to the upper echelon of the R&B charts from 1950 to 1963. Working with New Orleans producer/arranger/bandleader/songwriter DAVE BARTHOLOMEW, Domino cut a long string of hits for the Imperial label. Many of his records also crossed over onto the pop charts where they enjoyed even greater success and helped break the color line that once prevented R&B records from attracting pop audiences. Songs such as "Blueberry Hill," "Ain't It a Shame," "I'm Walkin'," "Whole Lotta Loving," and "Walkin' to New Orleans" have become rock & roll classics.

Domino was born and raised in New Orleans. He learned to play piano as a child, and by the time he was in his early teens he was already playing New Orleans bars and clubs. Bartholomew discovered Domino in 1948 and helped him get a recording contract with Imperial the following year. The debut Bartholomew-Domino release for the label, "The Fat Man," was a big hit in 1949 and 1950. It set in motion the trademark Domino sound: smooth and bluesy piano rhythms set against the backdrop of Bartholomew's band—which included Red Tyler on sax and Earl Palmer on drums—and, of course, Domino's lightly salted R&B vocals. Domino was Imperial's biggest artist in the 1950s; his success ignited interest in other New Orleans artists and played a major role in shaping the city's golden age of R&B and early rock, which lasted into the early 1960s.

Domino's first crossover hit was "Ain't It a Shame" in 1955, which Pat Boone also turned into a smash with his milky version of the song that same year. Two 1956 hits, "Blueberry Hill" and "I'm in Love Again," made Domino a major pop star. Domino also appeared in the rock & roll film *The Girl Can't Help It* that year and was a headlining act on rock & roll package tours. In 1957 came more Domino hits: "I'm Walkin'," "Blue Monday," "It's You I Love," "Valley of Tears," and "The Big Beat."

Domino continued recording with Imperial until 1962. By that time the New Orleans Sound had begun to wane on the pop charts, and Domino looked for a new start with the ABC label. But neither the records he made with ABC in 1963 and 1964, nor those he made with Mercury or Reprise later on in the decade, matched those from his Imperial years. By the early '70s Domino had settled into the oldies circuit, often playing Las Vegas nightclubs and other glitzy venues. Domino lives in New Orleans and continues to tour.

Essential Listening:
My Blue Heaven: The Best of Fats Domino, Vol. 1/EMI (CDP 7-92808-2)
"They Call Me the Fat Man . . .": The Legendary Imperial Recordings/EMI-Capitol (96784)

◄ DOOLEY, SIMMIE

(aka Blind Simmie) (born Simeon Dooley, July 5, 1881, Hartwell, Ga.; died January 27, 1961, Spartanburg, S.C.)

Blues singer and guitarist Blind Simmie Dooley was a frequent companion of Piedmont bluesman PINK ANDERSON. The two traveled together and played street corners for tips in the 1920s, mostly in South Carolina. Little is known of Dooley's personal life. Like Anderson, Dooley worked the medicine show circuit through the South in the early 1900s and probably was self-taught on guitar. He also played kazoo.

After Anderson befriended him, the two musicians worked in and around Spartanburg, South Carolina. Dooley's only known recording session was done with Anderson in 1928 for the Columbia label. Dooley eventually dropped out of the South Carolina blues scene in the 1930s. He reportedly lived in Spartanburg until his death in 1961.

Essential Listening:
Songsters and Saints: Vocal Traditions on Race Records/Matchbox
   Bluesmasters (MSEx 2001/2002)
Georgia String Bands (1928–1930)/Blues Documents (BD 2002)

◄ DORSEY, GEORGIA TOM

(aka Barrelhouse Tom) (born July 1, 1899, Villa Rica, Ga.; died January 23, 1993, Chicago, Ill.)

Pianist Georgia Tom Dorsey is best known for his work as a gospel singer, songwriter, and publisher. But before he found religion in the early 1930s, Dorsey was a bluesman whose contributions to early Chicago blues were significant.

Dorsey was born and raised in Georgia. His father was a Baptist minister and his mother a church organist. Dorsey learned to sing in church choirs and studied the piano, learning how to read music, before he left for Chicago in 1916. He continued to study music in Chicago at the College of Composition and Arranging while working in local clubs as a pianist. He also worked briefly with classic blues singer MA RAINEY during the early 1920s.

In 1928 Dorsey teamed up with guitarist TAMPA RED and formed a piano-guitar duo that rivaled that of pianist LEROY CARR and guitarist SCRAPPER BLACKWELL. Dorsey and Tampa Red began recording for the Vocalion label in 1928. Their most noted tune, "It's Tight Like That," became an instant blues classic with its clever double entendre lyrics and rag-flavored rhythm. Dorsey and Tampa Red also performed and recorded as the Hokum Boys, which, at times, included singer Bob Robinson. Although Dorsey was in demand as a recording artist (he also recorded with the Hokum Jug Band and as a solo performer), as well as an accompanist (he resumed working with Ma Rainey during this time), and as an arranger and recording session organizer (he worked for Brunswick Records), Dorsey drifted away from the blues around 1930 after discovering gospel music.

Dorsey employed the same songwriting, performing, and organizational talents that he used in his blues career to build a new career in gospel. In the early 1930s, he formed his own gospel music publishing company and began to write gospel tunes. He also became the choral director of Chicago's Pilgrim Baptist Church. Dorsey worked with singer Sallie Martin, recorded and toured extensively on his own, later worked with Mahalia Jackson, and penned such gospel standards as "Precious Lord" and "Peace in the Valley." Few artists have had a more profound impact on gospel. Dorsey died in 1993.

Essential Listening:
Come on Mama, Do That Dance/Yazoo (1041)

◄ DORSEY, LEE

(born Irving Lee Dorsey, December 4, 1926, New Orleans, La.; died December 1, 1986, New Orleans, La.)

Singer Lee Dorsey was one of New Orleans's most popular R&B artists in the 1960s. Working with producer-songwriter ALLEN TOUSSAINT, Dorsey had a batch of top-10 hits that featured a funky Crescent City beat. Of all the other New Orleans R&B artists, only FATS DOMINO enjoyed similar success in the '60s.

Dorsey was born in New Orleans, but his family moved to Portland, Oregon, when he was about ten. After serving in the navy during World War II, Dorsey returned to Portland where, despite standing just over five feet tall, he became a boxer.

Dorsey moved back to New Orleans in 1955 and began working in an autobody shop, where he was discovered by record producer Reynauld Richard, who signed him to Rex, a local label. The resulting single, "Rock Pretty Baby"/ "Lonely Evening," was a local hit in 1958 (both songs were penned by Dorsey). Dorsey's follow-up, "Lottie-Mo," attracted enough attention outside Louisiana for him to appear on Dick Clark's TV program, "American Bandstand."

In 1961 Dorsey signed with Bobby Robinson's Fire/Fury label. The two wrote the novelty nursery-rhyme number "Ya Ya," which was arranged by Allen Toussaint. The song shot to number 1 on the R&B charts and number 7 on the pop charts, making Dorsey New Orleans's newest R&B star. Dorsey's follow-up, "Do Re Mi," written by Earl King, made it to number 22 on the R&B charts in 1962. Fire/Fury folded in 1963 and Dorsey went back to the body-shop business. In 1965, when Toussaint returned from a two-year stint in the army, he resumed his relationship with Dorsey. Toussaint wrote and produced the songs and Dorsey sang them, and the two managed to maintain a New Orleans presence on the R&B charts, despite decreasing interest in the city's sound in the mid- and late '60s.

Together Toussaint and Dorsey cut "Ride Your Pony" in 1965 for Amy Records, which peaked at number 7 on the R&B charts. In 1966, Dorsey's greatest year, he landed three songs in the top 10—"Get Out of My Life, Woman," "Working in the Coal Mine," and "Holy Cow"—all on the Amy label. Though Dorsey continued to make records, including "Sneakin' Sally Through the Alley" (later coverd by rocker Robert Palmer) and "Yes We Can" (later covered by the Pointer Sisters and retitled "Yes We Can Can"), none of them matched his earlier success. A cameo appearance on Southside Johnny and the Asbury Jukes' debut album, *I Don't Want to Go Home*, in 1976 helped Dorsey ink a new recording contract with ABC in 1977, but little came of it. Dorsey eventually returned to the body-shop business. He died of emphysema in 1986.

Essential Listening:
Golden Classics/Collectables (COL 5082)

◄ DOUGLAS, K.C.

(born November 21, 1913, Sharon, Miss.; died October 18, 1975, Berkeley, Calif.)

K.C. Douglas, a transplanted Mississippi Delta bluesman, moved to the Bay Area in the 1940s and remained there the rest of his life. Douglas was one of the few West Coast bluesmen who retained his rural Delta style; despite the rise of electric blues in the 1950s and 1960s, Douglas continued to play accoustic blues that recalled the style of his biggest influence, TOMMY JOHNSON.

Douglas was born in the Delta in 1913. Although he grew up listening to the blues, it wasn't until he was in his early twenties that he learned how to play the guitar. Once he became proficient enough on the instrument to perform, Douglas began working Delta house parties and jukes, often with Johnson. In the 1940s, after moving to the West Coast, he played small bars and parties, both as a solo artist and with a small combo. Douglas also began his recording career at this time. He released a few singles, most notably "Mercury Boogie," a tune later covered by the Steve Miller Band and David Lindley, and an album on the tiny Cook label. But it wasn't until the folk-blues revival of the early '60s and his album *K.C.'s Blues*, on the Bluesville label, that Douglas began to attract white listeners and play folk and blues festivals. Douglas was a frequent performer at the Berkeley and San Francisco Blues fests and was a regular on the Bay Area coffeehouse and blues circuit until his death in 1975.

Essential Listening:
K.C.'s Blues/Bluesville (OBCCD 533-2)

◄ DR. JOHN

(aka Mac Rebennack) (born Malcolm Rebennack, November 21, 1940, New Orleans, La.)

Dr. John is the spiritual and musical embodiment of New Orleans. Since the 1950s he has used Crescent City blues, R&B, funk, jazz, rock, and pop as ingredients in his musical gumbo, and he remains one of the city's most personable ambassadors. Over the years, Dr. John has played on hundreds of recordings made by dozens of artists and has worked as an arranger, producer, sideman, and talent scout. He also has penned hundreds of compositions and has performed at just about every major jazz and blues festival, both in the U.S. and abroad. In short, Dr. John is a New Orleans original and one of the shapers of that city's post–World War II musical legacy.

Born and raised in New Orleans, Mac Rebennack (he didn't begin calling himself Dr. John until 1968) was surrounded by music as a child. His father owned a record store that specialized in black music, and he also repaired club sound systems, often taking his son with him on jobs. By hanging out at his father's store, young Mac was exposed to jazz, blues, and early R&B. By age fourteen he could play the piano and guitar and began working recording sessions at Cosimo Matassa's recording studio where he befriended such New Orleans luminaries as JAMES BOOKER, PROFESSOR LONGHAIR, and ALLEN TOUSSAINT.

By the mid-1950s Rebennack was a main cog in the New Orleans music-making machine. Ace Records employed him as a songwriter, and he worked as a producer and A&R man for Ric and Ron Records, in addition to Specialty, Minit, and other labels. Rebennack also did studio work for Chess and Mercury and, despite being white, was a founding member of the AFO (All for One) black music co-operative and label.

In a 1961 barroom fight, Rebbenack lost the tip of his ring finger on his right hand when a gun he sought to take away from his adversary went off. The tip of the finger was repaired, but Rebennack lost feeling in it. The injury forced him to change the way he played guitar and prompted him to learn the bass. Fortunately it didn't affect his piano playing, as the piano was becoming his main instrument.

With work opportunities for musicians fading in New Orleans in the mid-'60s,

Rebennack joined other Cresent City players who moved to the West Coast to seek work. Rebennack became a studio musician and often worked with rock & roll producer Phil Spector. In 1968, he began his solo career; using studio time given to him by Sonny & Cher, Rebennack recorded his debut album, *Gris Gris*, which was picked up by Atco Records that year. Changing his name to Dr. John Creaux the Night Tripper (later shortened to Dr. John) and creating a psychedelicized voodoo persona, complete with wild Mardi Gras costumes and headdresses, Rebennack reinvented traditional New Orleans sounds in a pop setting.

After *Gris Gris*, Dr. John recorded the albums *Babylon and Remedies* and *The Sun, Moon & Herbs* before scoring with *Gumbo*, an album that was filled with New Orleans roots music. The 1972 work contained flavorful versions of New Orleans standards like "Iko Iko" and "Tipitina." The follow-up Atco record, *In the Right Place*, featured Dr. John's biggest pop hit, "Right Place, Wrong Time," which made it to number 9 on the charts in 1973. Dr. John next joined Triumvirate, a short-lived supergroup that also included blues guitarists MIKE BLOOMFIELD and JOHN HAMMOND, JR. Their self-titled album sank without a trace in 1974.

For the rest of the 1970s and well into the 1980s, Dr. John continued to make records. Along the way he explored a variety of rock and pop paths with mixed results. He also continued his busy career as a studio musician and club performer. His recording career was revitalized in 1990 with the release of the album *In a Sentimental Mood*, which included an infectious rendition of "Makin' Whoopee," cut as a duet with singer Rickie Lee Jones.

In 1992 Dr. John once again returned to his New Orleans roots with the album *Goin' Back to New Orleans*. He continues to record and perform.

Essential Listening:
Gris Gris/Alligator (AL 3904)
Gumbo/Alligator (AL 3901)
The Ultimate Dr. John/Warner Brothers
Goin' Back to New Orleans/Warner Brothers (9 26940-2)

◄ DR. ROSS

(born Isaiah Ross, October 21, 1925, Tunica, Miss.; died May 28, 1993, Flint, Mich.)

Dr. Ross was a one-man blues band; he sang and played drums, guitar, and harmonica. The roots of his raw Mississippi Delta blues style can be traced to the influences of JOHN LEE HOOKER and JOHN LEE "SONNY BOY" WILLIAMSON, but Ross was no mere imitator. He created a distinctive romping sound that featured boogie rhythms and supple harp riffs.

Ross was born in the Delta and learned how to play harmonica at an early age. While serving in the army during World War II, he bought a guitar and performed at USO shows. After the war, Ross returned to Mississippi where he performed regularly on Clarksdale's WROX radio station and later on WDIA in Memphis. His band, the Jump and Jive Boys (later renamed Dr. Ross and the Interns), played Delta parties and dances. Ross also served in the army during the Korean War. After his discharge in 1951, SAM PHILLIPS recorded him for Chess Records. When Phillips left Chess to form Sun, Ross followed. Ross's specialty was the boogie, as heard in "Dr. Ross's Boogie," "Jukebox Boogie," and "Boogie Disease"—his signature songs. However, with the arrival of Elvis Presley, Phillips's attention shifted from the blues to rock & roll, which prompted Ross to leave Memphis (and Sun) in 1954 and move to Flint, Michigan, where he worked in the auto industry and occasionally performed as a one-man band.

In the 1970s and 1980s Ross recorded for a few tiny blues labels and performed at blues fests in the U.S. and Europe. He died in 1993.

Essential Listening:
Boogie Disease/Arhoolie (CD 371)

◄ DUPREE, CHAMPION JACK

(born William Thomas Dupree, July 23, 1909, New Orleans, La.; died January 21, 1992, Hanover, Germany)

Champion Jack Dupree was one of the last remaining barrelhouse piano players whose career dated back to the mid-1920s. More a quick-witted entertainer and raconteur than a piano stylist, Dupree was best known for his blend of bluesy keyboard rhythms and bawdy stories that artfully depicted the spirit of blues culture.

Born in New Orleans, Dupree was orphaned as a baby when his parents died in a fire reputedly set by the Ku Klux Klan. Like New Orleans jazz great LOUIS ARMSTRONG, Dupree grew up in the city's Colored Waifs' Home for Boys where he learned how to play piano. By the time he was in his teens, he was hustling money on New Orleans street corners. Picking up the finer points of barrelhouse piano from Crescent City musicians Willie Hall ("Drive 'Em Down") and Don Bowers, Dupree later worked the bordellos and bars in the city's French Quarter.

Dupree left New Orleans around 1930 and eventually wound up in Chicago, where he played house parties and small clubs. Dupree, however, did not become a mainstay in the city's blues scene, leaving for Detroit after a year spent selling bootleg whiskey and playing piano at the Continental Cafe. He let music become a part-time job while he pursued a career as a professional boxer, based out of Indianapolis. In all, Dupree fought more than a hundred bouts and, for a time, was the lightweight champion of Indiana. Dupree's music career broadened in 1940, when he recorded for the first time in Chicago for producer Lester Melrose.

Dupree was drafted into the navy in 1942. While serving as a cook in the Pacific, he was captured by the Japanese and spent two years as a prisoner of war. He returned to the States after the war and moved to New York, where he recorded for a number of labels, including Savoy and King, and occasionally worked as a cook. Dupree recorded twenty-six titles from 1953 to 1955, including "Walking the Blues," a duet with Mr. Bear (Teddy McRae). The song made it to number 6 on the R&B charts in 1955. In the late '50s, Dupree recorded for Groove and Vik Records.

Tired of the prejudice and racism that still existed in America, Dupree moved first to Paris, then to Zurich, Switzerland, in 1959. He also lived in Denmark and England before moving to Germany in the mid-'70s. Along the way Dupree recorded for nearly a dozen European jazz and blues labels. He built a loyal following on the Continent that enabled him to live in relative comfort.

Dupree returned to the U.S. in 1990 to play the New Orleans Jazz & Heritage Festival and record *Back Home in New Orleans* for Bullseye Blues Records, an album that demonstrated he had lost little of his entertaining charm, despite his advanced age. In 1991 Dupree recorded a second album for Bullseye, *Forever and Ever*, and did a repeat performance at the New Orleans Jazz & Heritage Fest. He also played the Chicago Blues Festival that year. Dupree died in 1992.

Essential Listening:

Shake Baby Shake/Detour (33-007)

Blues for Everbody/King (5037X)

Junker Blues/Travelin' Man (807)

Back Home in New Orleans/Bullseye Blues (BB 9502)

Forever and Ever/Bullseye Blues (BB 9512)

New Orleans Barrelhouse Boogie/Columbia-Legacy (CK 528 34)

E.

◄ EAGLIN, SNOOKS

(born Fird Eaglin, January 21, 1936, New Orleans, La.)

Although Snooks Eaglin is a local legend in New Orleans blues and R&B circles, his reputation as a multifaceted guitarist and singer never much reached beyond Louisiana with any consistency until the late 1980s. Eaglin, blind since he was a baby, is as much a throwback to the old-style street entertainer as he is a serious bluesman. His repertoire is made up of everything from true blues and classic Crescent City R&B to eccentric renditions of pop tunes.

Eaglin taught himself to play guitar and spent his early youth performing on New Orleans street corners and singing in church. By his midteens he had joined ALLEN TOUSSAINT's band, the Flamingos, and penned the R&B classic "Lucille" for LITTLE RICHARD. The first phase of Eaglin's recording career was short but sweet; in 1960 he recorded for the Folk-Lyric, Folkways, and Prestige/Bluesville labels before he switched to Imperial. He then recorded some ten R&B singles before leaving the label in 1961. Except for the album *Possum Up a Simmon Tree*, recorded for the Arhoolie label in 1971, and some recordings he made with PROFESSOR LONGHAIR that same year, Eaglin rarely recorded until he signed with Black Top Records in 1987. Since then he's cut *Baby, You Can Get Your Gun!* and *Out of Nowhere*. Eaglin continues to perform regularly in New Orleans, and during the summer months he performs at folk and blues festivals around the country.

Essential Listening:
Country Boy in New Orleans/Arhoolie (CD 348)
Baby, You Can Get Your Gun!/Black Top (BT 1037)
Out of Nowhere/Black Top (BT 1046)

◄ EARL, RONNIE

(born March 10, 1953, New York, N.Y.)

Ronnie Earl is one of the principal guitar stylists of contemporary blues. Along with JOHNNY WINTER, the late STEVIE RAY VAUGHAN and his brother JIMMIE, ANSON FUNDERBURGH, and DUKE ROBILLARD, Earl has helped keep a white presence in guitar blues.

Born and raised in New York, Earl later moved to Boston. He didn't begin playing guitar until he went to a MUDDY WATERS concert in 1975. The show so moved him that he dedicated himself to learning and then mastering the blues guitar. Earl became proficient enough on his instrument to replace Robillard in ROOMFUL OF BLUES in 1980. During Earl's eight-year tenure with the band, the group went from being a popular regional act to being one of the most respected white blues bands in America. The group recorded an album with EDDIE "CLEAN-HEAD" VINSON (*Eddie "Cleanhead" Vinson & Roomful of Blues*) in 1982 and one with BIG JOE TURNER (*Blues Train*) in 1983. Both albums were released on the Muse label. Roomful of Blues also released albums without guest artists. Most of them featured Earl's T-BONE WALKER–influenced guitar licks.

During the 1980s, Earl released three critically acclaimed solo albums backed by his own band, the Broadcasters. *Smokin'* and *They Call Me Mr. Earl* were released on the Black Top label, while *I Like It When It Rains* came out on the Antone's label. The albums increased Earl's exposure as a recording artist in his own right and led to his exit from Roomful of Blues in 1988. Since then, Earl has continued to record for Black Top and perform regularly in the U.S. and Europe.

Essential Listening:
Deep Blues/Black Top (BT 1033)
Soul Searching/Black Top (BT 1042)
I Like It When It Rains/Antone's (002)
Smokin'/Black Top (BT 1023)
Test of Time/Black Top (BT 1082)

◄ EDWARDS, ARCHIE

(born September 4, 1918, Union Hall, Va.)

A Piedmont blues singer and guitarist, Archie Edwards played the blues for nearly half a century before it became his full-time vocation. Influenced by MISSISSIPPI JOHN HURT, BLIND BOY FULLER, and BLIND LEMON JEFFERSON, Edwards taught himself how to play guitar as a youth; he also mastered the harmonica and five-string banjo. Edwards performed at family parties and occasional dances in Virginia in the late 1930s. In 1941 he enlisted in the army and served until the end of the war. In 1946 he relocated to Washington, D.C., and worked for the government until he retired in 1981.

That same year Edwards recorded his first album, *The Road Is Rough and Rocky*, for the German L+R label. In 1982 he was part of a blues package that toured Europe. After his return home, Edwards began performing at U.S. blues festivals and on college campuses. His second album, *Blues and Bones*, was released on the Maple Shade label in 1991. Edwards continues to perform.

Essential Listening:
The Road Is Rough and Rocky/L+R (42.036)

◄ EDWARDS, BERNICE

(aka Moanin' Bernice Edwards) (birth and death information unknown)

Bernice Edwards was a little-known but interesting Houston piano player and singer in the late 1920s. She was a close friend of SIPPIE WALLACE, the classic blues singer, and of the famous Thomas family, which included two noted piano players, GEORGE and HERSAL (Hersal reportedly taught her the rudiments of the keyboard). After leaving Houston for Chicago in the mid-1920s, Edwards signed a recording contract with the Vocalion label. In 1928 she recorded some twelve songs for the label, but they attracted little attention. Her final recording session took place in Fort Worth in 1935. Edwards then found religion, and she left the blues behind.

Essential Listening:

Good Time Blues (Harmonicas, Kazoos, Washboards & Cow-Bells)/Columbia (CK 46780)

◄ EDWARDS, DAVID "HONEYBOY"

(born June 28, 1915, Shaw, Miss.)

David "Honeyboy" Edwards is one of the few remaining original practitioners of the acoustic Delta blues style. Though Edwards took up electric blues in the 1960s and has since worked on occasion with a band, he still performs authentic solo acoustic country blues and is living testament of the music's vitality.

Edwards was born in Mississippi and taught himself how to play the guitar by listening to area bluesmen like TOMMY MCCLENNAN and ROBERT PETWAY. By the age of 14 he was playing Delta juke joints and picnics with BIG JOE WILLIAMS. Later he played with McClennan, ROBERT JOHNSON, BIG JOE WILLIAMS, BIG WALTER HORTON, and YANK RACHELL and traveled frequently through the South with them.

Edwards started his recording career in 1942 when he cut some fifteen sides for ALAN LOMAX and the Library of Congress. His first commercial session didn't occur until 1951 in Houston when he recorded for the American Record Company under the name Mr. Honey. Edwards then went to Chicago in 1953 to record four songs for Chess. The song "Drop Down Mama" was the only one issued, and that was in 1970. Edwards settled in Chicago in 1956. He relied on street-corner and small club performances to remain part of the Chicago blues scene during the late 1950s.

Edwards continued to perform throughout the 1960s and 1970s in Chicago with Big Walter Horton, JOHNNY TEMPLE, FLOYD JONES, KANSAS CITY RED, and others, with occasional trips South to play juke joints there. In the mid-'60s he resumed his recording career with the Adelphi/Blue Horizon label and began to play some festivals.

Edwards toured Europe and Japan in the 1970s and 1980s and has performed at the Smithsonian's Festival of American Folklife, the Chicago Blues Festival, and the San Francisco Blues Festival, among others. He currently records for the

Chicago-based Earwig label, which released his *Delta Bluesman* album in 1992. The work includes Edwards's original Library of Congress recordings and newer material. Despite advanced age, "Honeyboy" Edwards continues to perform regularly worldwide.

Essential Listening:
Mississippi Delta Blues Man/Folkways (3539)
Walking Blues/Flyright (541)
Old Friends/Earwig (4902)
Delta Bluesman/Earwig (4922)

◄ ELECTRIC FLAG

Original members: Michael Bloomfield (guitar) (born July 28, 1944, Chicago, Ill.; died February 15, 1981, San Francisco, Calif.); Buddy Miles (drums); Nick Gravenites (vocals); Barry Goldberg (keyboards); Harvey Brooks (bass); Marcus Doubleday (trumpet); Peter Strazza (tenor saxophone); Herbie Rich (baritone saxophone)

The Electric Flag was a noble late-'60s experiment that failed, not because of its music but because of strained egos and poor leadership. The brainchild of blues guitarist MIKE BLOOMFIELD, the Electric Flag sought to blend blues with jazz and rock. Yet what made the Electric Flag's sound so interesting was its hot, soulful horn section, its funk-driven rhythms, and the way Bloomfield incorporated the brass into a jazz-flavored blues-rock format.

Based in San Francisco, the band came together in 1967 after Bloomfield left the PAUL BUTTERFIELD Band. Bloomfield put together a solid rhythm section, with Buddy Miles on drums and Harvey Brooks on bass, and spiced it with Barry Goldberg's piano and Nick Gravenites's vocals. The horn section was filled out with Herbie Rich and Peter Strazza on saxophones and Marcus Doubleday on trumpet.

The band's first appearance was at the legendary Monterey Pop Festival in 1967. The group received promising reviews as did its debut album, *A Long Time Comin'*, released the following year on CBS. Unfortunately, personality differences and a lack of sharp musical focus cut the band's future short. The self-titled follow-up album, released in 1969, didn't build on the ground gained by *A Long Time Comin'* and the band folded. Its short life wasn't in vain, however. The Electric Flag opened doors for the Chicago Transit Authority (later called simply Chicago), Ten Wheel Drive, and other rock horn bands. An attempt to resurrect the Electric Flag in 1974 led to production of the group's third and final album, *The Band Kept Playing*.

Essential Listening:
A Long Time Comin'/CBS (9597)

◄ ELLIS, BIG CHIEF

(born Walter Ellis, Birmingham, Ala.; died December 21, 1977, Birmingham, Ala.)

A member of the New York City blues scene in the 1940s and early '50s, Walter "Big Chief" Ellis was a pianist who often backed other transplanted Southern bluesmen in the Big Apple, including BROWNIE MCGHEE, STICKS MCGHEE, and SONNY TERRY.

Born in Birmingham, Alabama, Ellis taught himself how to play piano and worked house parties and such until he left Alabama in 1936 and began traveling the South, eventually winding up in New York. Ellis's earliest recordings were with the Continental and Sittin' In With labels, for which he used the name Big Boy Ellis. Ellis also worked in New York studios with Tarheel Slim, MICKEY BAKER, and Leroy Dallas before he retired from performing and recording around 1952.

In 1972 Ellis moved to Washington, D.C., and opened up a liquor store. Shortly thereafter he resumed his music career and began performing in local clubs and at area folk and blues fests with his group, the Barrelhouse Rockers, which included guitarist JOHN CEPHAS and harmonica player PHIL WIGGINS. Ellis recorded a single for the Rounder label, "Dices Blues," and an album, *Big Chief Ellis*, for Trix Records, before he died in 1977.

Essential Listening:
Big Chief Ellis/Trix (3316)
Folk Blues/Continental (CLP 16003)

◄ ELLIS, TINSLEY

(born June 4, 1957, Atlanta, Ga.)

Tinsley Ellis is a white blues guitarist who, like JOHNNY WINTER and STEVIE RAY VAUGHAN, soaked up the influences of great black blues players such as FREDDIE and ALBERT KING and BUDDY GUY. Born and raised in Atlanta, Ellis spent his formative years first as the guitarist in an Atlanta bar band, the Alley Cats, and later as the co-leader of another Atlanta blues band, the Heartfixers, with vocalist Chicago Bob (Bob Nelson). The latter group was named for an Albert King song, "Heartfixin' Business," and recorded three albums—*Live at the Moonshadow, Tore Up* (with rhythm & blues singer NAPPY BROWN), and *Cool on It*—for Landslide Records.

In 1988 Ellis disbanded the Heartfixers, formed the Tinsley Ellis Band, and recorded *Georgia Blue*, his debut album on Alligator Records. The album also marked Ellis's first attempt at singing lead. Both *Georgia Blue* and Ellis's follow-up album, *Fanning the Flames* (1989), contain a collage of blues styles and offshoots, including rhythm & blues, New Orleans funk, and Texas blues-rock. In 1991 Alligator rereleased *Cool on It*, and in 1992 came *Trouble Time*, an album that featured more of Ellis's burning blues-rock guitar. Ellis continues to record and perform.

Essential Listening:
Georgia Blue/Alligator (ALCD 4765)
Fanning the Flames/Alligator (ALCD 4778)
Cool on It/Alligator (ALCD 3905)
Trouble Time/Alligator (ALCD 4805)

◄ EMERSON, BILLY "THE KID"

(born December 21, 1925, Tarpon Springs, Fla.)

Billy "The Kid" Emerson recorded for Memphis-based Sun Records in the early 1950s. A more successful songwriter than he was a recording artist, Emerson's most popular tune, "Red Hot," was turned into a rockabilly hit by Billy Riley and His Little Green Men in 1957. The song was later covered by Sam the Sham and Robert Gordon.

Emerson came to the attention of Sun owner SAM PHILLIPS in 1954 by way of IKE TURNER. A pianist, Emerson logged time in Turner's band, the Kings of Rhythm, before forming his own band. Emerson recorded five singles for Sun before leaving the label in 1956. Frustrated with his lack of success in Memphis, Emerson moved to Chicago and signed with Vee-Jay Records. Although songs like "You Never Miss the Water" and "If You Won't Stay Home" were full-blown rockers, they suffered the same fate as Emerson's Sun singles and never cracked the top-40 pop or R&B charts. Emerson eventually faded from the recording scene.

Essential Listening:
Little Fine Healthy Thing/Charly (CR 30187)
Crazy 'Bout Automobiles/Charly (CFM 602)

◄ ESTES, SLEEPY JOHN

(born January 25, 1904, Ripley, Tenn.; died June, 5, 1977, Brownsville, Tenn.)

Sleepy John Estes was a Tennessee-based singer and guitarist whose crying vocals and handcrafted songs were well-entrenched in the country blues tradition. Estes wrote down-home blues songs that revealed much about his personal experiences, as well as songs that commented on social conditions, especially those of the 1930s. His vocal style recalled elements of the traditional field holler, while his guitar work, though limited, possessed a simplistic purity that became popular with folk-blues fans in the 1960s.

Estes was born into a sharecropping family just outside Ripley, Tennessee, but was raised in Brownsville. He lost sight in his right eye after an accident that occurred during his youth. Estes learned to play guitar and began performing at area parties and picnics, often with mandolin player YANK RACHELL. In the 1920s, Estes, Rachell, and harmonica/jug player HAMMIE NIXON went to Memphis and performed in a jug band on street corners and in parks.

Estes began his recording career in 1929 with Victor. Two years later, he and Nixon relocated to Chicago, where, during the 1930s, Estes recorded for Decca. Estes also recorded for Bluebird from 1940 to 1941. "Someday, Baby" (also known as "Worried Life Blues"), his most noted Bluebird release, eventually became one of Estes's trademark numbers and a blues standard.

Estes, who got his nickname because of his propensity to take naps, returned to Tennessee and ended the first phase of his recording career. He lived and worked out of Brownsville and occasionally ventured into Memphis to perform. Estes and Nixon recorded for SAM PHILLIPS at the Sun Studios in Memphis in the early 1950s. By this time, however, he had lost the sight in his left eye, leaving him totally blind. Estes faded from the blues scene in the 1950s; many blues fans believed he had died in obscurity.

In 1962 Estes was rediscovered, living in poverty in Brownsville. Thanks to the folk-blues craze his career was revived. He appeared in two documentaries: *Citizen South, Citizen North* in 1962 and *The Blues* in 1963. He also signed a recording contract with Delmark Records and recorded *The Legend of Sleepy John Estes* and other albums in the 1960s. He began touring and performing regularly, playing concerts, clubs, and folk and blues festivals. In 1964 he played the Newport Folk Festival and went to Europe with the American Folk Blues Festival package. He returned to the Newport Folk Festival in 1969 and also played the Ann Arbor Blues Festival that year. Estes was featured at the Smithsonian's Festival of American Folklife in 1970 and 1973 and later toured both Europe and Japan. He enlarged his recording catalog with more releases from Delmark and small labels like Fontana. Estes died in 1977.

Essential Listening:
First Recordings with Yank Rachell and Noah Lewis/JSP (601)
The Legend of Sleepy John Estes/Delmark (DD 603)
Electric Sleep/Delmark (DD 619)
I Ain't Gonna Be Worried No More, 1929–1941/Yazoo (2004)
Brownsville Blues/Delmark (613)

◄ EVANS, ELGIN

(born Elga Edmonds; birth and death information unknown)
Elgin Evans was MUDDY WATERS's first full-time drummer. Prior to Evans joining Waters's band, multi-instrumentalist Baby Face Leroy Foster had played drums when a song called for a backbeat. But by 1950, Evans, a raw, simple thumper who seldom exhibited a sense of swing in his playing, was the drummer.

Almost nothing is known about Elgin Evans's life, except for the period during the early 1950s when he played with Waters and other early Chess artists such as LITTLE WALTER and MEMPHIS MINNIE. Evans first recorded with Waters in late 1950. During the session, the group, which included Big Crawford on bass, Little Walter on harmonica, and Waters on guitar, recorded "Louisiana Blues" and "The Evans Shuffle" (dedicated to Chicago disc jockey Sam Evans, one of the city's first disc jockeys to play Waters on the radio, not to Elgin). On the former song, Evans played washboard instead of drums. On the latter, he did not play at all.

By 1951, Evans was playing drums on most of Waters's material and can be heard on such Waters classics as "Hoochie Coochie Man" and "I Just Want to

Make Love to You.'' In 1954 he was replaced by jazz-turned-blues drummer FRED BELOW. In the early '50s Evans recorded with Little Walter, and played on Walter's classic instrumental, "Juke," in 1952. Evans eventually disappeared from the Chicago blues scene.

Essential Listening:

Muddy Waters: The Chess Box/MCA-Chess (CH6 80002)

F.

◄ FABULOUS THUNDERBIRDS, THE

Original members: Jimmie Vaughan (guitar) (born March 20, 1951, Dallas, Tex.); Kim Wilson (vocals, harmonica) (born January 6, 1951); Keith Ferguson (bass) (birth information unknown); Mike Buck (drums) (birth information unknown)

In the late 1970s the Fabulous Thunderbirds helped bring attention to the Austin, Texas, blues scene, and they played a significant role in the 1980s blues renaissance. The group's vigorous, bar-band sound was built on a foundation of Texas blues, R&B, soul, and rock & roll and featured the guitar work of JIMMIE VAUGHAN (brother of STEVIE RAY VAUGHAN) and the harmonica prowess of singer Kim Wilson.

The Fabulous Thunderbirds was formed in 1974 by Vaughan and Wilson and included bass player Keith Ferguson, drummer Mike Buck, and for a brief spell, LOU ANN BARTON. Early on, the T-Birds had few fans. Eventually, through sheer persistence, the Thunderbirds became the house band at the popular Austin blues club Antone's, where they backed up visiting blues artists and created their own repertoire of blues and R&B.

In 1979 the T-Birds recorded their self-titled debut album for the Takoma label. The band then moved to Chrysalis Records and recorded three more albums, *What's the Word* (1980), *Butt Rockin'* (1981), and *T-Bird Rhythm* (1982). By this time Fran Christina, the former dummer for ROOMFUL OF BLUES, had replaced Mike Buck. In the early 1980s the T-Birds also opened shows for the ROLLING STONES and ERIC CLAPTON. Though their records received enthusiastic reviews from the music press, the T-Birds seemed caught in a cult-following dead end that resulted in disappointing album sales.

Chrysalis dropped the Thunderbirds after *T-Bird Rhythm*, and the group went without a recording contract until 1986, when it signed with the CBS subsidiary label Epic/Associated. By this time bass player Keith Ferguson had left the group and been replaced by Preston Hubbard, also formerly of Roomful of Blues. The T-Birds' Epic debut, *Tuff Enuff*, was recorded in London in 1986. Produced by Dave Edmunds, it turned out to be the breakthrough album the band had long hoped for. The title song, released as a single, made it into the top 10 on the pop charts, while the album peaked at number 13. That same year the T-Birds won a W.C. HANDY Award for best blues band.

Two follow-up albums, *Hot Number* (1987) and *Powerful Stuff* (1989), were solid enough but failed to surpass *Tuff Enuff* either in terms of commercial success or critical acclaim. Soon after, the T-Birds lost the services of Vaughan, who left the band to work with brother Stevie Ray and also launch a solo career. Vaughan was replaced by guitarist DUKE ROBILLARD, yet another refugee from Roomful of Blues. Kid Bangham was added as a rhythm guitarist to fill out the band's sound.

In 1991 the T-Birds released *Walk That Walk, Talk That Talk* on Epic/Associated, while Chrysalis issued a compilation of early T-Birds material called *The Essential Fabulous Thunderbirds Collection*. The band continues to record and perform.

Essential Listening:
Tuff Enuff/Epic/Associated (40304)
The Essential Fabulous Thunderbirds Collection/Chrysalis (F2-21851)
Hot Stuff: The Greatest Hits/Epic/Associated (2K 53007)

◄ FLEETWOOD MAC

Original members: Mick Fleetwood (drums) (born June 24, 1942, London, England); John McVie (bass) (born November 26, 1945, London, England); Peter Green (guitar, vocals) (born October 29, 1946, London, England); Jeremy Spencer (guitar) (born July 4, 1948, West Hartlepool, England)

In rock and pop circles, Fleetwood Mac will always be remembered as one of the most commercially successful bands of the 1970s. The albums *Fleetwood Mac* and *Rumours* each sold millions of copies and rocketed members of the band to superstar status. But during its formative years in the late 1960s, Fleetwood Mac was a blues-rock band and an integral part of England's thriving blues-rock scene.

Three of the band's founding members—drummer Mick Fleetwood, bass player John McVie, and guitarist Peter Green—logged time in JOHN MAYALL'S BLUESBREAKERS, one of England's seminal blues bands. Fleetwood Mac formed in 1967; its original lineup included second singer-guitarist Jeremy Spencer. (Bob Brunning was actually Fleetwood Mac's original bass player, but he was replaced by McVie shortly after the band's inception.)

With Green's fascination with the guitar style of B.B. KING and Spencer's near obsession with slide guitarist ELMORE JAMES, Fleetwood Mac's earliest albums— the self-titled debut (not to be confused with the 1975 album of the same name) and *English Rose*, both released in 1968—were rich with American blues strains. By the end of the year Fleetwood Mac added a third guitarist, Danny Kirwan.

Fleetwood Mac's third album, *The Pious Bird of Good Omen* (1969), was a curious mix of B-sides and tracks from the group's previous two albums. But *Fleetwood Mac in Chicago*, also recorded in 1969, featured appearances by WILLIE DIXON, OTIS SPANN, and other Chicago bluesmen. When Fleetwood Mac released *Then Play On* (1969), its first U.S. album, it became clear that the group had begun to abandon its original blues path. The following year Peter Green found religion and left the group. Jeremy Spencer did the same in 1971; he joined a religious cult called Children of God.

Fleetwood Mac moved to the U.S. in 1974 and became a pop-rock band that found its niche when American rockers Lindsey Buckingham and Stevie Nicks joined the fold. After the gargantuan success of the albums *Fleetwood Mac* and *Rumours*, the band found it difficult to maintain such a high level of sales and acclaim and gradually began a slide in the mid-1980s that led to the exit of both Buckingham and Nicks and the end of the band. Their hit "Don't Stop" was adopted as a themesong by Bill Clinton during his 1992 presidential campaign, and the group reunited to play it at an inaugural gala concert.

Essential Listening:
Live in Concert: The Original Fleetwood Mac/Pair (PCD 2-1208)
Fleetwood Mac in Chicago/Sire

◄ FOGHAT

Original members: "Lonesome" Dave Peverett (guitar, vocals); Roger Earl (drums); Rod Price (guitar); Tone Stevens (bass)

The British band Foghat formed in 1971 at the tail end of the late '60s blues-rock period after guitarist "Lonesome" Dave Peverett, drummer Roger Earl, and bass player Tone Stevens left the group SAVOY BROWN, an earlier British blues-rock outfit, and joined up with second guitarist Rod Price. Foghat toured the U.S. regularly in the early '70s, developing a reputation as a hard-playing, boogie-driven band. Thanks to near-constant touring, Foghat managed to keep fans interested in blues rock at a time when the hybrid form had all but run its course. Albums such as its self-titled debut, *Rock and Roll Outlaws*, and *Energized* were all built on blues foundations, though most of the songs were rockers.

In 1974 bass player Nick Jameson replaced Stevens; a year later the band released its most acclaimed album, *Fool for the City*, and the hit single, "Slow Ride," followed by "Drivin' Wheel" and a live version of the WILLIE DIXON blues chestnut "I Just Want to Make Love to You." Jameson left Foghat in 1976 and was replaced by Craig MacGregor. By this time Foghat had transformed itself into a hard rock band with blues underpinnings, as evidenced by the hits "Stone Blue" in 1978 and "Third Time Lucky (First Time I Was a Fool)" in 1979.

Flushed with its American success, Foghat relocated to New York in the late '70s. Various versions of the band continued to perform into the '80s with diminishing results.

Essential Listening:
The Best of Foghat, Vol. I/Rhino (70088)
The Best of Foghat, Vol. II/Rhino (70516)

◄ FOLEY, SUE

(born March 29, 1968, Ottawa, Canada)

A Canadian-born guitarist and singer, Sue Foley is part of the female-laced Austin, Texas, blues scene that has produced such artists as LOU ANN BARTON, MARCIA BALL, and ANGELA STREHLI. Unlike her colleagues, Foley is an electric guitarist, which makes her a rarity in blues circles. Her style is drawn from a variety of influences, including SLIM HARPO, T-BONE WALKER, and EARL HOOKER.

Foley was born in Ottawa. As a youth she listened to the ROLLING STONES and other blues-based rock groups, but she didn't become enamored with the blues until seeing Chicago harmonica player JAMES COTTON in concert when she was fifteen. Determined to learn blues guitar, Foley jammed regularly in Ottawa blues clubs before moving to Vancouver and forming a band. In 1990 she sent a demo tape to Clifford Antone of Antone's Records, who invited her to Austin, Texas, for an audition. Foley wound up relocating to Austin and signing a recording contract with Antone's. Her debut album, *Young Girl Blues*, was released in 1992.

Essential Listening:
Young Girl Blues/Antone's (ANT 0019)

◄ THE CHARLES FORD BAND

Original members: Robben Ford (guitar, vocals) (born December 16, 1951, Woodlake, Calif.); Mark Ford (harmonica) (born October 21, 1953, Ukiah, Calif.); Patrick Ford (drums) (born February 19, 1949, Woodlake, Calif.); Stanley Poplin (bass) (birth information unknown)

In 1971 the Charles Ford Band, which included three brothers—guitarist Robben, harmonica player Mark, and drummer Pat—played clubs in the San Francisco Bay area. The band developed a reputation as an unconventional blues group that paid scant attention to tradition, mixing elements of blues, jazz, country, and rock into its sound. Although the band remained intact less than a year, it left its mark on the Bay Area music scene.

Prior to forming the Charles Ford Band, Pat, Robben, and Mark Ford played in a northern California group, the Ford Blues Band. The Charles Ford Band, named after the brothers' father, Charles, a country musician, first came together in 1970 after Pat and Robben Ford moved from Ukiah, California, down to San Jose. The group also included harmonica player Gary Smith and bass player Stan Poplin.

Shortly after the Charles Ford Band's inception, Robben and Pat Ford dissolved it to join blues harmonica player CHARLIE MUSSELWHITE's backup group. But their stay with Musselwhite was short; after a few months they quit and reformed the Charles Ford Band. Mark Ford replaced Gary Smith on harp, while Stan Poplin resumed his old slot as bass player. The group's first recording was actually made after it had broken up a second time: coming together in the recording studio in an attempt to document its sound, the band cut its critically landed debut album in 1972 for the Arhoolie label. A second album, *A Reunion*, was recorded live ten years later for Pat Ford's fledgling label, Blue Rock'it.

In the 1980s Mark Ford formed the Mark Ford Band, while Robben Ford became a blues and jazz session guitarist. In 1992 Robben released the critically lauded album *Robben Ford & the Blue Line* for Stretch Records. Pat Ford has continued to head the Blue Rock'it label and lead the Ford Blues Band.

Essential Listening:
The Charles Ford Band/Arhoolie (CD 353)
A Reunion/Blue Rock'it (101)

◄ FRAN, CAROL

(born October 23, 1933, Lafayette, La.)

A Louisiana-born rhythm & blues singer, Carol Fran began singing professionally at age fifteen with Joe Lutcher's band, then moved into the New Orleans cabaret circuit. Fran began her recording career in 1958 when she cut her song "Emitt Lee" for the Excello label. It was a hit in the Gulf Coast region, and its success landed Fran a spot opening up for GUITAR SLIM and the chance to record three more singles for Excello. Her relationship with the Louisiana label ended in 1962.

Fran next recorded with Lyric and Port Records, but the few singles she cut for these labels in the '60s did little to make her a more nationally known singer. Fran settled into a long time engagement at the New Orleans R&B club Dew Drop Inn and worked with the Joe Tex Revue in the late '60s. In the mid-'70s she moved to Houston where she met and married CLARENCE HOLLIMON, the guitarist for BOBBY "BLUE" BLAND, Little JUNIOR PARKER, CHARLES BROWN, and other noted R&B artists. Fran and Holliman began working Houston clubs and cocktail lounges as a duo. In 1990 they appeared on the Black Top Records' compilation, *Gulf Coast Blues*, which led to their first album, *Soul Sensation*, released by Black Top in 1992. Fran and Hollimon continue to perform together.

Essential Listening:
Gulf Coast Blues, Vol. 1/Black Top (CD BT 1055)
Soul Sensation/Black Top (BT 1071)

◄ FREEMAN, DENNY

(born August 7, 1944, Orlando, Fla.)

A longtime member of the Texas blues scene, blues guitarist Denny Freeman has spent most of his career working in the shadow of JIMMIE and STEVIE RAY VAUGHAN and other more noted guitarists from the Lone Star state. Freeman grew up in Dallas, where he played rock and rhythm & blues guitar in a number of garage groups. In the 1970s, he and Stevie Ray Vaughan were the two guitarists in Paul Ray & the Cobras, a popular Texas bar band. After leaving the Cobras in 1982, Freeman, who settled in Austin and became a familiar figure on the city's growing blues scene, played in LOU ANN BARTON's band before joining ANGELA STREHLI's band that same year.

Despite kudos from local musicians like the Vaughan brothers, Freeman was unable to cash in on the attention Austin musicians received from major labels after the success of Stevie Ray's Double Trouble and Jimmie's group, the FABULOUS THUNDERBIRDS, partly because of his reluctance to sing. Freeman nonetheless released two albums, *Blues Cruise* in 1986 and *Out of the Blue* in 1988, on Amazing Records. Freeman moved to Los Angeles in 1992, but he frequently returns to Austin to perform.

Essential Listening:
Blues Cruise/Amazing Records (AMCD)

◄ FROST, FRANK

(born April 15, 1936, Augusta, Ark.)

Multi-instrumentalist and singer Frank Frost is best known as a harmonica player whose style is plainly inspired by that of SONNY BOY WILLIAMSON (Rice Miller). Frost learned the finer points of blues harp from Williamson when he played guitar in Williamson's band in the late 1950s. In addition to harmonica, Frost plays keyboards, particularly organ, and, at times, second guitar, in the Mississippi Delta–based trio the JELLY ROLL KINGS. The group also includes drummer SAM CARR and guitarist BIG JACK JOHNSON.

Frost learned how to play piano as a youth and often accompanied church choirs in Arkansas. In 1951 he moved to St. Louis where he played behind harmonica player Little Willie Foster. While in St. Louis Frost met drummer Sam Carr who invited him to play guitar, harmonica, and sing in his band. Soon the group was backing Sonny Boy Williamson and doing occasional club dates of its own. The association with Williamson lasted until 1959. That year Frost and Carr returned to the Delta where, in 1962, the duo added guitarist Big Jack Johnson; Frost switched to organ, and the group became known as Frank Frost and the NIGHTHAWKS. The band recorded *Big Boss Man!* for the Phillips International label the following year, as well as another album for the Jewel label in 1966. In addition to playing Delta juke joints in the '60s, Frost and the Nighthawks also backed Carr's father, ROBERT NIGHTHAWK, whenever he performed in Mississippi.

Frank Frost and the Nighthawks remained loosely knit for some years—and were sometimes practically nonexistent—until 1978 when they signed a recording contract with the Chicago-based Earwig label and became the Jelly Roll Kings. *Rockin' the Juke Joint Down*, the band's third album (its first as the Jelly Roll Kings), was released the following year. Afterwards, the band worked on a semiregular basis, mostly in Delta juke joints, though the group did tour Holland twice in the early '80s, enjoying considerable fan support.

In 1990 Frost released his first solo album, *Midnight Prowler*, also on the Earwig label. He continues to perform with the Jelly Roll Kings and on his own with local bands in Helena, Arkansas.

Essential Listening:
Rockin' the Juke Joint Down (with the Jelly Roll Kings)/Earwig (LPS 4901)
Midnight Prowler/Earwig (CD 4914)

◄ FULLER, BLIND BOY

(born Fulton Allen, July 10, 1907, Wadesboro, N.C.; died February 13, 1941, Durham, N.C.)

Not only was Blind Boy Fuller one of the most recorded bluesmen in the 1930s, but he was also one of the most popular. From 1935 to 1940 Fuller recorded 135 songs for the American Record Company. He sang and played in a variety of blues styles: some of Fuller's songs are full-blown rags; others are good examples of the Piedmont blues guitar style that featured intricate finger-picking passages; still others contain rough-cut bottleneck guitar playing. In short, few bluesmen from this period were more stylistically versatile than Blind Boy Fuller.

Fuller learned how to play guitar at an early age. Although not blind at birth, he lost his sight in the late 1920s, which is when he turned to music as his main means of income. He mostly played on North Carolina street corners and in front of tobacco houses in the early '30s. Sometime during this period he and his wife, Cora Mae Allen, settled in Durham. In 1935, James Baxter Long (aka J.B. Long), a Durham record retailer, heard Fuller perform and was impressed enough to contact the American Record Company to inquire about the possibility of recording Fuller. Long gave the guitarist his "Blind Boy Fuller" tag and secured a contract for him from ARC. Thanks to Long, who, in effect, became Fuller's manager and producer, Fuller's career blossomed. Long took him up to ARC's New York studios to record and made certain that both he and Fuller received the financial renumeration due them.

Some of Fuller's recordings were solo efforts. But on many of his best recorded pieces he was accompanied by REV. BLIND GARY DAVIS on guitar and/or Bull City Red (George Washington) on the washboard. Later, harmonica player SONNY TERRY also recorded with Fuller. Unlike one of his main influences, BLIND BLAKE, Blind Boy Fuller possessed a hardy, full-bodied voice that was as supple as his guitar style. Fuller wrote many of the songs he recorded. Some of them, especially "Step It Up and Go" and "Truckin' My Blues Away," have become standards in the East Coast blues repertoire.

Fuller died in 1941 at the age of thirty-two, of blood poisoning resulting from a kidney ailment.

Essential Listening:

Truckin' My Blues Away/Yazoo (1060)
East Coast Piedmont Style/Columbia (CK 46777)
Blind Boy Fuller, Vol. 1, (1935–36)/Document (5091)
Blind Boy Fuller, Vol. 2, (1937)/Document (5092)
Blind Boy Fuller, Vol. 3, (1937)/Document (5093)
Blind Boy Fuller, Vol. 4, (1937–38)/Document (5094)
Blind Boy Fuller, Vol. 5, (1938–40)/Document (5095)
Blind Boy Fuller, Vol. 6, (1940)/Document (5096)

◄ FULLER, JESSE

(born March 12, 1896, Jonesboro, Ga.; died January 29, 1976, Oakland, Calif.)

A country blues singer and one-man band, Jesse Fuller wrote the classic "San Francisco Bay Blues" and influenced numerous early-'60s white folk-blues artists. Fuller played twelve-string guitar with a Piedmont-inspired finger-picking style, as did many bluesmen from Georgia. He was equally known for playing the "fotdella," a homemade bass that was made with piano strings and played with a foot pedal. When he added the swish of a cymbal, the wail of a harmonica and kazoo, and the rhythmic chatter of a washboard, Fuller's sound was nearly that of a traditional jug band.

Though Fuller learned how to play guitar as a youth, he didn't begin his blues career in earnest until the early 1950s. Prior to then, Fuller hoboed through the South and West, winding up in the early 1920s in Los Angeles, where he worked as an extra in films, including *The Thief of Baghdad, East of Suez,* and *End of the World.* Fuller eventually moved to the Bay Area and worked odd jobs, performing at parties and on street corners. In 1951, at age fifty-five, he decided to pursue music full-time. In 1954 he wrote "San Francisco Bay Blues," which became his trademark tune. Fuller drew attention with his one-man band routine, and in 1955 he began his recording career with the release of the album *Folk Blues: Working on the Railroad with Jesse Fuller.* The LP included "San Francisco Bay Blues." Recording sessions for the Good Time Jazz, Bluesville, and Prestige labels followed.

Fuller performed extensively in the '60s and early '70s. He toured Europe, played at the famous 1964 Newport Folk Festival as well as dozens of other blues and folk festivals in the '60s, and was a regular on the college coffeehouse circuit. By spicing his repertoire with folk and religious numbers, rags, and country blues, Fuller embodied the style and soul of a traditional songster. He died in 1976.

Essential Listening:
San Francisco Bay Blues/Good Time Jazz (OBCCD 537-2)
Jesse Fuller's Favorites/Prestige (OBCCD 528-2)
Frisco Bound/Arhoolie (CD 360)
The Lone Cat/Good Time Jazz (OBCCD 526-2)

◄ FULLER, JOHNNY

(born April 20, 1929, Edwards, Miss.)

A Bay Area singer, Johnny Fuller has included in his repertoire downhome blues, R&B, rock & roll, and gospel-influenced soul. Fuller was born in Mississippi but raised in California. As a teen he sang gospel music, but by the early 1950s he had switched to secular music, particularly rhythm & blues. Fuller was influenced by R&B ballad singer JOHNNY ACE. One of Fuller's best-known songs, "Johnny Ace's Last Letter," was a tribute to Ace, who died in 1954.

In the mid and late 1950s, Fuller, who in addition to singing played guitar and piano, toured with various rock & roll and rhythm & blues package shows. He also recorded for Aladdin and other labels, though his recording career never moved above the journeyman level. Fuller spent most of the 1960s and 1970s working blues clubs in the Bay Area and recording sporadically on local labels.

Essential Listening:
Fool's Paradise/Diving Duck (4303)
Fuller's Blues/Diving Duck (4311)

◄ FULSON, LOWELL

(aka Lowell Fulsom) (born March 31, 1921, Tulsa, Okla.)

Guitarist-singer Lowell Fulson was one of the West Coast's leading blues artists in the late 1940s and 1950s, having written and recorded such classics as

"Three O'Clock Blues," "Blue Shadows," and "Reconsider Baby." His jazzy blues style, often created with pianist LLOYD GLENN and supplemented with a full-bodied horn section, epitomized the softer, smoother California blues sound.

Born in Oklahoma to black and Choctaw Indian parents, Fulson's first experience with music came in the form of gospel and country music. By the time he was a teen, he had developed a taste for blues. Fulson played for awhile with an Oklahoma string band before beginning an association with country bluesman TEXAS ALEXANDER and moving to Gainesville, Texas.

Fulson backed up Alexander from 1940 until he was drafted into the navy in 1943. While in the service Fulson was stationed in Oakland where he met blues record producer BOB GEDDINS. After his discharge from the service, Fulson began his recording career with Geddins. Beginning in 1946 he recorded for Geddins's Down Town, Gilt Edge, and Down Beat labels before switching to Swingtime in 1950. His version of the Memphis Slim tune, "Nobody Loves Me," which he called "Everyday I Have the Blues," made it to number 3 on the R&B charts that year. Fulson followed up the hit with "Blue Shadows," which made it to number 1 a few months later.

In 1954, Fulson signed with the Chess subsidiary label, Checker, and immediately scored with "Reconsider Baby," which peaked at number 3 on the R&B charts. Fulson stayed with Checker until 1962. During this time he recorded and toured regularly, often with package shows working the West Coast and Southwest. In 1964, Fulson signed with Kent Records, which changed the spelling of his last name to Fulsom. One of Fulson's Kent releases, "Tramp," made it to number 5 on the charts in 1967, but as black music shifted more and more away from the blues, Fulson's career began to fade.

Fulson later recorded for the Jewel label and spent most of the '70s and '80s working the blues club circuit and performing at blues festivals, both in the U.S. and Europe. In 1984 he recorded the album *One More Blues* for the French Blue Phoenix label, and then *It's a Good Day* for Rounder Records, before signing a contract with Bullseye Blues Records in 1991. *Hold On*, his Bullseye debut, was released the following year. Fulson continues to record and perform.

Essential Listening:
Lowell Fulson/Arhoolic (2003)
Lowell Fulson/Blues Boy (302)
The Blues Got Me Down/Diving Duck (DD 4306)
Baby Won't You Jump with Me/Crown Prince (IG 407/408)
Lowell Fulson/Chess (2-92504)
Hung Down Road/MCA-Chess (CHD 9325)
It's a Good Day/Rounder (2088)
Hold On/Bullseye Blues (BB 9525)

◄ FUNDERBURGH, ANSON

(born November 14, 1954, Plano, Tex.)

Anson Funderburgh was part of the white blues-guitarist generation that came of age in the 1980s and included JIMMIE and STEVIE RAY VAUGHAN, RONNIE EARL, and DUKE ROBILLARD, among others. Funderburgh's guitar style, an interesting mix of Chicago and Texas blues, was well documented on record during the decade. With his band, the Rockets, Funderburgh released six albums on the Black Top label. *Sins*, released in 1988, won a W.C. HANDY Award for best contemporary blues album of the year. Funderburgh and the Rockets also won "Best Blues Band" that year.

Funderburgh grew up in Plano, Texas. After he taught himself the basics of blues guitar by listening to the records of FREDDIE KING, MAGIC SAM, and B.B. KING, Funderburgh played in a series of bands in the 1970s, including one called Delta Road, before forming the Rockets in 1978 with singer and harmonica player DARRELL NULISCH. Funderburgh and the Rockets built a solid regional following in Texas and attracted the attention of Hammond and Nauman Scott, two blues fans who were set to launch a blues record label, Black Top. Funderburgh and the Rockets signed a contract with the label, and in 1981 *Talk to You By Hand*, their debut album, was Black Top's maiden record.

Due in part to a grueling tour schedule—Funderburgh often played three hundred dates a year in the '80s—the Rockets' roster changed often. Since the departure of Nulisch in 1986, the group has featured harmonica player and vocalist SAM MYERS, a veteran bluesman who in the 1950s recorded as a solo artist and worked with ELMORE JAMES. Myers gave the Rockets a solid front man who also had vital links with black blues.

Since then, Funderburgh and the Rockets have broadened their following beyond the Southeast and have continued to issue well-received albums. The group's most recent releases include *Rack 'em Up, Tell Me What I Want to Hear*, and *Thru the Years: A Retrospective*, all of which are on Black Top.

Essential Listening:
Talk to You by Hand/Black Top (1001)
She Knocks Me Out/Black Top (1022)
Sins/Black Top (1038)
Thru the Years: A Retrospective/Black Top (BT 1077)

G.

◄ GAINES, GRADY

(born May 14, 1934, Waskom, Tex.)

Rhythm & blues saxophone player and bandleader Grady Gaines began his career in Houston in the early 1950s as a session musician for Duke/Peacock Records. Gaines backed such noted artists as JOHNNY ACE, CLARENCE "GATE-MOUTH" BROWN, and BOBBY "BLUE" BLAND, before accepting the lead position with the R&B group the Upsetters and working with LITTLE RICHARD in 1955. Though Gaines and the Upsetters recorded only sparingly with Little Richard, they did play on "Keep A Knockin'," a number-two hit in 1957 and made up his regular touring band from 1955 until 1958, when he abandoned rock & roll to become a minister. In addition to recording and touring with Little Richard, Gaines and the Upsetters appeared in three teen rock films with him: *Don't Knock the Rock* and *The Girl Can't Help It* (both 1956) and *Mister Rock and Roll* (1957).

For a brief spell in the late '50s Gaines and the Upsetters backed James Brown, who was hired to take Little Richard's place in the rock & roll package shows. In 1962, the group worked with Little Willie John and Sam Cooke. It also recorded with Cooke, appearing on such Cooke classics as "Bring It on Home to Me" and "Twisting the Night Away." The group remained with Cooke until his death in 1964. The Upsetters then worked R&B package shows, appearing behind such artists as Jackie Wilson, Gladys Knight and the Pips, BO DIDDLEY, Diana Ross and the Supremes, and Joe Tex. In 1968 Gaines gave up leadership of the Upsetters to join Joe Tex, then LITTLE JOHNNY TAYLOR, and finally Joe Tex again until 1972. That same year Gaines formed Grady Gaines and the Crown Jewels to work the Continental Showcase, the Houston club owned by Duke/Peacock label owner DON ROBEY.

After Robey's death in 1975, Gaines returned to the road, backing R&B singers Curtis Mayfield and Millie Jackson. Gaines retired in 1980 but launched a comeback in 1985 that resulted in a recording contract with Black Top Records. His debut album, *Full Gain*, was released in 1987. Gaines continues to record and perform with his group, Grady Gaines and the Texas Upsetters.

Essential Listening:
Gulf Coast Blues, Vol. 1/Black Top (BT 1055)
Blues-A-Rama, Vol. 4/Black Top (BT 1057)
Full Gain/Black Top (BT 1041)
Horn of Plenty/Black Top (BT 1084)

◄ GAITHER, BILL

(aka Leroy's Buddy) (born 1908, Tennessee; death information unknown)

Bill Gaither was a blues guitarist and singer who recorded regularly in the late 1930s and early 1940s. Deeply influenced by pianist LEROY CARR, Gaither came to be called "Leroy's Buddy," as he imitated Carr's slow, bluesy vocal and recording style, leaving little room for his own originality to mature. When Carr died in 1935, Gaither penned "The Life of Leroy Carr" as a tribute to his friend and mentor.

Taking a cue from Carr and his guitarist, SCRAPPER BLACKWELL, Gaither often recorded as part of a duo. During the most prolific period of his career—1935 to 1941—he used a number of pianists to accompany him in the recording studio, but Honey Hill was his favorite. During the war years Gaither faded from the recording scene.

Essential Listening:
Leroy's Buddy/Document (CD 3503-2)
Bill Gaither, 1935–1941/Story of Blues (3503)

◄ GALLAGHER, RORY

(born March 2, 1949, Ballyshannon, Ireland)

In the early 1970s, blues guitarist Rory Gallagher was Ireland's answer to Johnny Winter. Gallagher's passion for loud, power-packed bottleneck riffs and stinging solos—and his commitment to American blues at a time when the blues-rock flood of the mid-'60s was starting to recede—endeared him to diehard fans in Europe and the U.S.

Gallagher began his career in the early '60s by playing guitar in an Irish cover band called the Fontana Showband, later called the Impact. When the band broke up in 1965, Gallagher formed Taste, a blues-based rock trio that included bass player Charlie McCracken and drummer John Wilson. The group released a few pedestrian albums in Great Britain before breaking up in 1971. Gallagher then became a solo artist and released his self-titled debut on the Polydor label that same year. The album was warmly received both in England and the U.S. Contributing to MUDDY WATERS's *London Sessions* album in 1972 increased his reputation among American blues fans. Gallagher spent the rest of the '70s trying to broaden his support with a batch of albums on the Chrysalis and Polydor labels, nearly all of which contained recycled blues guitar lines and figures. Gallagher all but faded from the American blues scene in the '80s, but in 1990 he staged a comeback with his album *Fresh Evidence*. Gallagher continues to perform and record.

Essential Listening:
Irish Tour '74/Polygram (PD 9501)
The London Muddy Waters Sessions/MCA-Chess (9298)
Fresh Evidence/Polygram (1370)

◄ GANT, CECIL

(aka Pvt. Cecil Gant) (born April 4, 1913, Nashville, Tenn.; died February 4, 1951, Nashville, Tenn.)

Cecil Gant's rise to stardom in the mid-1940s reads like a Hollywood movie script. A private in the army during World War II, Gant attended a war-bond rally in Los Angeles in 1944. During a break in the entertainment, Gant (a pianist, he'd played roadhouses and clubs in the South before joining the army) asked for and got permission to go onstage and perform a couple of songs. His short performance at the rally was so well-received that Gant was asked to perform at other bond rallies in the L.A. area. His rising popularity led to a recording contract with Gilt Edge Records. In late 1944 he recorded the ballad "I Wonder," which shot to the top of the Billboard charts and made Gant one of rhythm & blues' hottest recording artists.

Gant's smooth, vocal croon was only one aspect of his talent. His thumping, boogie blues piano style helped chart the course rock & roll piano players like Jerry Lee Lewis would follow in the 1950s. Gant even recorded songs, such as "We're Gonna Rock" and "Rock Little Baby," that contained rock & roll lyrics as well as rhythms. But despite his numerous recordings with the Bullet, Down Beat, Swing Time, and Imperial labels, Gant was never able to match the success he enjoyed with "I Wonder." A serious drinking problem exacerbated his frustration and ultimately led to pneumonia, which killed him in 1951.

Essential Listening:
Cecil Gant/Krazy Kat (CD 03)
I'm Still Singing the Blues Today/Oldie Blues (8004)

◄ GARLAND, TERRY

(born June 3, 1953, Johnson City, Tenn.)

More an interpreter of traditional country blues styles than a contemporary blues innovator, Terry Garland is a National Steel slide guitarist and singer who includes in his repertoire both downhome Mississippi Delta and Piedmont blues.

Garland was born and raised in Tennessee, where his first musical influences were rock & rollers like Elvis Presley, Carl Perkins, and Jerry Lee Lewis. Eventually Garland discovered the blues and worked in a succession of blues and blues-based rock bands throughout the South before finally leaving the bar-band circuit and becoming a solo blues artist. Garland began playing small blues clubs and festivals in the late '80s, capitalizing on the commercial reemergence of the blues. In 1991 he recorded his first album, *Trouble in Mind*, for First Warning Records. The work features Garland's interpretation of BLIND WILLIE MCTELL's "Ain't Long Before Day," BUKKA WHITE's "Aberdeen," and JIMMY REED's "Upside Your Head," as well as the harmonica work of Mark Wenner of the NIGHTHAWKS. Garland's second album, *Edge of the Valley*, was released in 1992. He performs regularly in East Coast blues clubs and at blues and folk festivals.

Essential Listening:
Trouble in Mind/First Warning (72705-75701-2)
Edge of the Valley/First Warning (72705-75713-2)

◄ GARLOW, CLARENCE

(born February 27, 1911, Welsh, La.; died July 24, 1986, Beaumont, Tex.)

Clarence Garlow is best known for his 1950 hit "Bon Ton Roula," a rhythm & blues–laced zydeco song that helped introduce the Louisiana music form to a national audience. Garlow was born in Louisiana but raised in nearby Beaumont, Texas. His first instrument was the fiddle; he later learned how to play the accordion and guitar. Garlow worked outside music, mostly with the post office, until 1949 when he put together a band, began playing jukes and dances in the Houston area, and signed a recording contract with Marcy's Records. Though the label was short-lived, Marcy's did release "Bon Ton Roula" (French for "Let the Good Times Roll"), which made it onto the R&B charts and became an instant zydeco classic in Louisiana and East Texas.

After Marcy's demise, Garlow moved from one label to the next but never could repeat the success he enjoyed with "Bon Ton Roula." In 1953 he cut "New Bon Ton Roulay" for the Aladdin label, but it attracted little attention. Garlow even flirted with rock & roll. In 1957 he recorded yet another version of "Bon Ton Roula" for the Goldband label, but it, too, failed to resuscitate Garlow's recording career.

Garlow was more influential as a behind-the-scenes player than as a recording artist. In 1952 he opened his Bon Ton Drive-In, a Beaumont club that provided a place for blues and zydeco artists such as CLIFTON CHENIER to perform. Garlow also worked as a radio disc jockey on Beaumont's KJET, spinning blues, zyedco, and R&B records. In 1984 Garlow launched a comeback as a performer and began playing East Texas clubs again. Shortly before his death in 1986, Garlow performed at the New Orleans Jazz & Heritage Festival with longtime friend Clifton Chenier.

Essential Listening:
Clarence Garlow, 1951–1958/Flyright (586)

◄ GAYTEN, PAUL

(born January 29, 1920, Kentwood, La.; died March 26, 1991, Los Angeles, Calif.)

Rhythm & blues bandleader and pianist Paul Gayten recorded for the DeLuxe and Regal labels in the late 1940s and had two hits, "True" and "Since I Fell For You," with his orchestra and vocalist Annie Laurie. However, his biggest contribution to the blues was as a producer, arranger, and talent scout. After touring extensively in the years immediately after World War II, Gayten dissolved his band in 1950 and began working out of New Orleans as a producer and occasional session pianist. His knowledge of the Crescent City's blues and R&B scenes prompted Chess to hire him (he filled nearly the same role in New Orleans that WILLIE DIXON filled for Chess in Chicago). Gayten discovered many new artists for Chess, including CLARENCE "FROGMAN" HENRY, EDDIE BO, and BOBBY CHARLES. He also produced and arranged their records.

Gayten moved to Los Angeles in the early '60s and started his own record company, Pzazz, which focused less on blues and R&B and more on jazz. Gayten remained an elder statesman of the L.A. jazz and blues scenes until his death in 1991.

Essential Listening:
Paul Gayten: The Chess King/MCA-Chess (9294)
Paul Gayten and Dave Bartholomew/(Regal Records in New Orleans)
    Specialty (SPCD 2169-2)

◄ GEDDINS, BOB

(born 1913, Marlin, Tex.; died February 16, 1991, Oakland, Calif.)

Bob Geddins was a founder of the Oakland blues scene. As a songwriter, producer, and record company owner, he gave focus to the city's fledgling blues community in the years immediately after World War II and recorded many of the artists that later would become established West Coast blues performers. Geddins was born in Texas, where he became a fan of country blues. When he moved to Los Angeles in 1933, he opened a record shop, selling mostly blues and gospel recordings to fellow blacks, who, like him, had come from the Southwest to California for better economic opportunities.

Geddins moved up the coast to Oakland in 1939 and in 1945 began Big Town Recordings. Although his first success was with gospel—"If Jesus Had to Pray, What About Me?" by the Rising Star Gospel Singers—Geddins was most interested in recording Southwest-style blues. In the late 1940s and 1950s Geddins recorded such artists as LOWELL FULSON, JIMMY MCCRACKLIN, JUKE BOY BONNER, ETTA JAMES, BIG MAMA THORNTON, JIMMY WILSON, JOHNNY FULLER, and RAY AGEE. He released their records on Big Town and his other labels—Down Town, Cavatone, Irma, Plaid, Art-Tone, Rhythm. Geddins also produced and leased sides for such major West Coast labels as Specialty, Modern, Aladdin, and Imperial.

With the decline of blues and R&B in the early '60s, Geddins eventually dropped out of the recording scene. He opened a radio and television repair shop in Oakland. Only occasionally did he return to the recording studio to produce a blues session. Geddins died of cancer in 1991.

Essential Listening:
Oakland Blues/Arhoolie (2008)

◄ GEREMIA, PAUL

(born April 21, 1944, Providence, R.I.)

A folk-blues interpreter, singer-guitarist Paul Geremia began his career in the mid-'60s, playing coffeehouses and college campuses from Boston to New York. His guitar style is mostly drawn from the Piedmont blues school. Much of his elaborate finger-picking technique has been influenced by the work of BLIND WILLIE MCTELL and MISSISSIPPI JOHN HURT.

Born in Providence, Rhode Island, Geremia discovered folk music by listening to records made by Pete Seeger and Ramblin' Jack Elliott. Geremia played harmonica before picking up the guitar. In 1964 he attended the Newport Folk Festival, where he heard bluesmen such as SKIP JAMES and ROBERT PETE WILLIAMS and took up the blues as a full-time career a short time later. Geremia's debut album, *Just Enough*, came out on the Folkways label in 1968.

Like ROY BOOK BINDER, JOHN HAMMOND, JR., and other white folk-blues artists, Geremia has spent much of his career playing small clubs and performing at folk and blues fests, both in the U.S. and abroad. He recorded two albums in the '70s, a self-titled work for Sire in 1971 and *Hard Life Rockin' Chair* for Adelphi in 1973. Two other albums were recorded in the '80s for Flying Fish: *I Really Don't Mind Livin'* (1983) and *My Kinda Place* (1987). In 1993 he signed a new record contract with Red House Records and released *Gamblin' Woman Blues*. All of Geremia's albums contain complex blues guitar arrangements and renditions of blues classics as well as original numbers. Geremia continues to record and perform.

Essential Listening:
I Really Don't Mind Livin'/Flying Fish (FF 270)
My Kinda Place/Flying Fish (FF 395)
Gamblin' Woman Blues/Red House (RHR 54)

◄ GIBSON, CLIFFORD

(born April 17, 1901, Louisville, Ky.; died December 21, 1963, St. Louis, Mo.)

Blues guitarist Clifford Gibson was a contemporary of noted guitarist LONNIE JOHNSON. Both Gibson and Johnson were based out of St. Louis in the late 1920s and early 1930s, the period when Gibson recorded for the Victor and QRS labels. Like Johnson, Gibson's guitar playing centered on the single-string style, but Johnson was the more popular musician, having recorded literally dozens of sides during his long recording career compared to Gibson's twenty-four known sides.

Little is known of Gibson's early years. He probably moved from Louisville to St. Louis sometime in the early 1920s and began playing clubs and street corners to survive. In 1929 he recorded for the QRS label in New York and two years later for the Victor label. His recording career cut short by the Depression, Gibson continued to perform in and around St. Louis for tips and spare change right on up to his death in 1963.

Essential Listening:
Beat You Doing It/Yazoo (1027)

◄ GILLUM, JAZZ

(born William Gillum, September 11, 1904, Indianola, Miss.; died March 29, 1966, Chicago, Ill.)

Jazz Gillum was one of Chicago's most popular harmonica players in the 1930s and early 1940s. Though JOHN LEE "SONNY BOY" WILLIAMSON was more influential and enjoyed greater commercial success, Gillum worked regularly with such artists as BIG BILL BROONZY and WASHBOARD SAM and helped make the harmonica a vital instrument in prewar Chicago blues.

Gillum was born and raised in Mississippi, where he learned to play harmonica. He played house parties and street corners for spare change before moving to Chicago in 1923. Gillum teamed up with Broonzy in the mid-1920s and began accompanying other blues artists in the recording studio. In 1934, Gillum began a long-term association with LESTER MELROSE and the Bluebird label, which didn't end until the late 1940s. During that time, Gillum recorded many sides with Broonzy and with Washboard Sam, as well as recording under his own name. Gillum was primarily an interpretative artist rather than a composer, and he often covered tunes by Broonzy and Washboard Sam. In 1942, Gillum was drafted into the army. After the war he recorded a bit with Bluebird and Victor, but the metamorphosis of Chicago blues in the postwar years into a more hard-edged electric sound left Gillum behind. He eventually faded from the city's blues scene. In 1966 he was shot and killed.

Essential Listening:
Jazz Gillum, 1938–47/Travelin' Man (808)
Roll Dem Bones, 1938–47/Wolf (WBJ 002)

◄ GLENN, LLOYD

(born November 21, 1909, San Antonio, Tex.; died May 23, 1985, Los Angeles, Calif.)

Pianist Lloyd Glenn helped established the West Coast blues sound in the 1940s and 1950s. Though he recorded as a solo artist for labels like Aladdin, Swing Time, and Imperial, Glenn's best work was as a sideman and arranger. His lilting, jazz-flavored piano style contained elements of Texas blues as well as the rhythmic punch of boogie-woogie pianists, first heard from artists such as JIMMY YANCEY and MEADE "LUX" LEWIS.

Glenn was born and raised in San Antonio, Texas. In the late 1920s he began working with bands such as the Royal Aces and Boots & His Buddies in and around Texas, gaining experience as a pianist and arranger. By the time he had moved to Los Angeles in 1942, Glenn had perfected his engaging piano style, which enabled him to work into the West Coast blues scene, working with stride piano player Walter Johnson and doing arrangements for labels like Crown and Black & White. Glenn played piano and arranged music for T-BONE WALKER, LOWELL FULSON, B.B. KING, and BIG JOE TURNER, among many others. From 1949 to 1953 Glenn recorded for the Swing Time label; however, his recording session work for other artists overshadowed his own career as a recording artist. Glenn continued to perform, mostly in West Coast clubs, through the early '80s. He died in 1985.

Essential Listening:
Texas Man/Jukebox Lil (608)
After Hours/Oldie Blues (8002)

◄ GORDON, ROSCO

(aka Roscoe Gordon) (born 1934, Memphis, Tenn.)

A fixture on the Memphis blues scene in the late 1940s and 1950s, pianist Rosco Gordon personified the talented but eccentric blues artist. He sang in a style that emphasized wails, moans, and weird diction slurs and played a boogie-influenced brand of blues piano. In the early 1950s Gordon, JOHNNY ACE, BOBBY "BLUE" BLAND, Earl Forest, and others were frequently called the Beale Streeters, an informal group of Memphis's best blues and R&B musicians that recorded and broadcast together.

Gordon began his recording career with producer SAM PHILLIPS in 1951. His song "Booted" came out on both the Chess and RPM (Modern) labels and went to the top of the R&B charts in 1952. Phillips also leased other Gordon material to Duke Records. After contract squabbles between RPM and Chess over who owned Gordon's recording rights were straightened out, he spent the early 1950s recording for RPM. Except for "No More Doggin'," which went to number 3 on the R&B charts in 1952, Gordon was unable to match the success of "Booted" in the 1950s. In 1955, Gordon left RPM and signed with Phillips's Sun Records. He recorded a number of tunes, including R&B rockers "She's My Baby," "I'm Gonna Shake It," and "Let's Get High," and odd numbers like "Do the Chicken" and "Cheese and Crackers." Gordon ended his relationship with Phillips and Sun in 1958. The next year he signed with Vee-Jay Records; his song "Just a Little Bit" was a hit on the R&B and pop charts in 1960 and seemed to revive his career. But Gordon's success was short-lived. With the demise of rhythm & blues in the early '60s, the promise of his career began to ebb. In 1962 he moved to New York and briefly recorded for Columbia Records, but none of the sides were ever released. Gordon next signed with ABC-Paramount, which was also a short-lived affair, and then with the Old Town label. In 1969 Gordon formed his own record company, called Bab-Roc; the label was the only musical outlet left to him. Gordon continued to release occasional singles through the '70s. He eventually faded from the blues and R&B scenes.

Essential Listening:
Let's Get High/Charly (CD 213)

◄ GRAVES, BLIND ROOSEVELT

(birth and death information unknown)

Blues guitarist Blind Roosevelt Graves and his tambourine-playing brother, Uaroy, made up two-thirds of the MISSISSIPPI JOOK BAND, a mid-1930s good-time blues trio that played upbeat dance numbers and wailing rags. The third member of the Jook Band was pianist Cooney Vaughn.

Little is known of Graves's early life, other than that he and his brother were based out of Hattiesburg, Mississippi, and often performed together in Delta juke joints. Before forming the Jook Band, the Graves brothers recorded for the Paramount and the American Record Company, beginning in 1929. Easily moving from blues to gospel and back again, Blind Roosevelt Graves, like BLIND WILLIE

JOHNSON and other sightless bluesmen, felt it necessary to perform both secular and religious numbers. Graves eventually disappeared from the blues scene.

Essential Listening:
Blind Roosevelt Graves/Wolf (110)

◄ GRAY, HENRY

(born January 19, 1925, Kenner, La.)

A blues pianist, Henry Gray was a much-in-demand session player in Chicago in the 1950s and 1960s, recording behind such stalwarts as JIMMY REED, LITTLE WALTER, BILLY BOY ARNOLD, and BO DIDDLEY. But Gray is best known as HOWLIN' WOLF's pianist. He performed and recorded with Wolf from 1956 to 1968 and, more recently, as a solo artist.

Gray was born and raised in Louisiana, where he taught himself how to play piano. He played house parties and church services before being drafted into the army during World War II. Influenced by the piano mastery of BIG MACEO, Gray moved to Chicago in 1946 and filled the piano slot in Little Hudson's Red Devil Trio. By 1952 he was working with bluesman Morris Pejoe. The additional exposure in the Chicago club scene enabled Gray to get work as a session pianist for the Chess and Vee-Jay labels and to fill the piano position in Howlin' Wolf's band.

When Gray ended his twelve-year tenure with Wolf in 1968, he left Chicago and returned to Louisiana, where he performed regularly in and around Baton Rouge. Eventually he formed his own band, the Henry Gray Cats. In 1977 Gray toured Europe and did some recording in Germany. For the rest of the '70s and most of the '80s he remained a relatively obscure blues artist in the States. A recording contract with the Blind Pig label led to the release of his first American album, *Lucky Man*, in 1988. Since then, Gray has played festivals and worked the club circuit, both in the U.S. and abroad.

Essential Listening:
Lucky Man/Blind Pig (2788)

◄ GREEN, LIL

(born December 22, 1919, Miss.; died April 14, 1954, Chicago, Ill.)

Lil Green was a popular Chicago-based, blues-flavored rhythm & blues vocalist who often worked with BIG BILL BROONZY in the 1940s. Green's expressive voice and understanding of vocal shadings as well as her composing skills—she wrote her best-known song, ''Romance in the Dark''—made her popular, but she still ranked below such leading female R&B figures of the day as DINAH WASHINGTON, Helen Humes, and (Little) ESTHER PHILLIPS.

Born in Mississippi, Green and her family moved to Chicago in 1929. She worked small Chicago clubs in the late 1930s before being discovered by blues producer LESTER MELROSE and signing a recording contract with Bluebird Records in 1939. Green toured with Broonzy in a small combo and with larger ensembles, such as the TINY BRADSHAW Orchestra, throughout the early and mid-1940s. Later in the decade she toured with the Howard Callender Orchestra and recorded for the Aladdin and Atlantic labels, before fading from the scene. In 1954, when she was thirty-five years old, Green died of pneumonia.

Essential Listening:
*Lil Green, 1940–47/*Rosetta (1310)

◄ GRIMES, TINY

(born Lloyd Grimes, July 7, 1916, Newport News, Va.; died March 4, 1989, New York, N.Y.)

Guitarist Tiny Grimes, who played both tenor (or four-string) and six-string models, was also a rhythm & blues bandleader in the late 1940s and early 1950s and an accompanist to jazz pianist Art Tatum. Grimes played drums and some piano before he switched to the guitar in the mid-'30s. Influenced by the silky electric guitar figures of Charlie Christian, Grimes played with the group The Cats and the Fiddle in the early 1940s. He then joined a jazz trio that featured Tatum and drummer Slam Stewart before forming the Tiny Grimes Quartet in 1944, which featured saxophonist Charlie Parker.

However it was the rhythm & blues band the Rockin' Highlanders that best showcased Grimes's blues guitar talents. He and his band, which often wore Scottish kilts onstage, were one of the first acts signed to Atlantic Records in 1947. In 1952, Grimes employed SCREAMIN' JAY HAWKINS as his pianist and main singer, but Hawkins remained with him for barely a year before starting his solo career.

Grimes continued to tour throughout the 1950s, though his best rhythm & blues years were behind him. In the early 1970s he resumed his career, working in a jazz format with trumpeter Roy Eldridge and pianist LLOYD GLENN, releasing albums on the Muse, Sonet, and Classic Jazz labels and playing New York City clubs. Grimes died in 1989.

Essential Listening:
*Tiny Grimes and His Rockin' Highlanders/*Krazy Kat (KKCD 01)
*Tiny Grimes, featuring Screaming Jay Hawkins, Vol. 1/*Collectables (5034)
*Tiny Grimes and His Rockin' Highlanders, Vol. 2/*Collectables (5317)
*Tiny Grimes and Friends/*Collectables (5321)

◄ GUITAR GABRIEL

(aka Nyles Jones) (born Robert Jones, October 12, 1925, Atlanta, Ga.)

Known for his wild hats and an eclectic brand of blues that includes elements from all the major schools of blues as well as from gospel, Guitar Gabriel is a journeyman blues guitarist and singer whose career began in the late 1940s. Born in Atlanta, he and his family moved to Winston-Salem, North Carolina, when he was a child. Influenced by his father, Sonny Jones, a local blues artist, Gabriel got work as a sideman after serving in the army during World War II. He logged time with LIGHTNIN' HOPKINS, KING CURTIS, and a crop of other blues artists in the postwar years.

After relocating to Pittsburgh in the mid-'60s, Gabriel recorded his debut solo album, *My South, My Blues*, for the Gemini label in 1970. A single off the record, ''Welfare Blues,'' received considerable notice in the blues community, though it failed to advance Gabriel's career. (*My South, My Blues* was rereleased in 1988 on the Jambalaya label as *Nyles Jones, the Welfare Blues.*)

Eventually Gabriel returned to the Winston-Salem area, remaining inactive as a bluesman until 1991. That year he joined the group Brothers in the Kitchen and performed in clubs and at festivals. The band self-released the album *Do You Know What It Means to Have a Friend?* (Karibu) and continues to perform.

Essential Listening:
Nyles Jones, the Welfare Blues/Jambalaya

◄ GUITAR KELLEY

(born Arthur Kelley, November 14, 1924, Clinton, La.)

Guitar Kelley is a Louisiana bluesman whose downhome guitar and vocal styles are good examples of unfiltered swamp blues. Kelley grew up in rural Louisiana and taught himself how to play guitar. In the late 1940s he began playing house-rent parties and country picnics, often with fellow bluesman LIGHT-NIN' SLIM. Kelley continued to play his blues in Louisiana jukes in the 1950s and 1960s, with Slim and with SILAS HOGAN.

Kelley finally got his chance to record in 1970 when the Arhoolie label became interested in Baton Rouge–area blues and released a compilation album, *Louisiana Blues*, that featured a few of Kelley's songs. Though Kelley attracted only marginal attention outside Louisiana and was never able to muster enough interest in his music to tour much outside his home state, he played the New Orleans Jazz & Heritage Festival in 1972 and became a popular performer in Baton Rouge blues clubs thereafter.

Essential Listening:
Louisiana Blues (various artists)/Arhoolie (1054)

◄ GUITAR SHORTY

(born David Kearney, September 8, 1939, Houston, Tex.)

A protégé of GUITAR SLIM, Guitar Shorty is known more for his flashy, acrobatic live performances than for his recordings, which, despite a career that extends back to the mid-1950s, have been few. Shorty first recorded in 1957 for the Cobra label. He also toured with fellow guitarists OTIS RUSH and Guitar Slim in the late 1950s. In 1959 he recorded three singles for the tiny Pull label, none of which attracted much attention. He then entered a phase that saw him working clubs in the U.S. and Canada, making the most out of his wild, no-holds-barred stage show, which featured flips, kicks, and headstands delivered with the same kind of reckless energy exhibited by Guitar Slim.

Shorty resumed his domestic recording career in 1984 when he cut a four-song EP, *Down Home Blues*, for Big J Records. A year later he signed with Olive Branch Records, which released a couple of singles, including his theme song,

"They Call Me Guitar Shorty." In 1991 the English label JSP released his album *My Way on the Highway*, which won a W.C. Handy Award the following year for best contemporary foreign blues album. Shorty then signed with Black Top Records in 1993 and released the album *Topsy Turvy*. He continues to tour extensively on the blues club circuit in the U.S. and Canada.

Essential Listening:
Jericho Alley Blues, Volume Two/Diving Duck (4313)
On the Rampage/Olive Branch (ER 5456)
My Way on the Highway/JSP
Topsy Turvy/Black Top (BT-1094)

◄ GUITAR SLIM

(born Eddie Jones, December 10, 1926, Greenwood, Miss.; died February 7, 1959, New York, N.Y.)

Although he died at age thirty-two, Guitar Slim's place in blues history is well-assured. Aside from recording "The Things I Used to Do," a million-selling hit in 1954 and one of the most influential songs to come out of New Orleans's early R&B period, Slim was an invigorating performer and a guitarist whose slashing, volume-heavy sound contained nearly all the essentials that rock guitarists would later employ.

To also call Slim a pioneering rock & roll performer would not be stretching the truth. His sound might have been firmly rooted in gospel and blues-influenced R&B, but his delivery was certainly rock & roll–oriented. Slim dressed as loudly as he played; cherry-red suits and white shoes were favorites. He also walked and danced his way through club audiences, thanks to a guitar cord that some say was two hundred feet long. In short, Slim packed his most audacious and ego-inflated personality traits into his live shows and left his fans screaming for more.

Born and raised in the Mississippi Delta, little is known of Slim's early life except that he was a flashy dancer and a ladies' man in local juke joints. In 1944 he went into the army. When he returned home in 1946, he stayed little more than a year before leaving the Delta for good. He wound up in New Orleans in 1950, where he teamed up with HUEY "PIANO" SMITH in a blues trio. Slim signed his first recording contract with Imperial Records in 1951 and recorded a few sides with the Nashville-based J-B label before switching to Specialty in 1953. Late that year, with RAY CHARLES on piano, Slim cut "The Things I Used to Do," which shot to the top of *Billboard*'s R&B chart and became the best-selling R&B record of 1954. The song contained Slim's gospel-soaked vocals and enough unique guitar riffs to make it a seminal New Orleans R&B tune.

Slim continued to record for Specialty until 1956 but never repeated the success he experienced with "The Things I Used to Do." When Specialty dropped him, Slim signed with Atco and recorded for the Atlantic subsidiary through 1958, with little chart success. A heavy drinker and womanizer, Slim's fast-paced lifestyle caught up with him in New York in 1959. He contracted pneumonia and died on February 7, just a few days after the plane crash that killed rock & rollers Buddy Holly, Ritchie Valens, and the Big Bopper.

Essential Listening:
Guitar Slim: Sufferin' Mind/Specialty (SPCD 7007-2)
The Things That I Used to Do/Ace (CHD 110)

◄ GUY, BUDDY

(born George Guy, July 30, 1936, Lettsworth, La.)

During his heyday in the 1960s, Buddy Guy, along with OTIS RUSH and MAGIC SAM, moved the blues guitar into its postmodern era. With a style built on the stinging single-string poetics of B.B. KING and the colorful freneticism of GUITAR SLIM, Guy was both a popular session player and a successful solo artist. His gospel-flecked voice and his wailing, edgy guitar intensity endeared him to white blues-rock fans, who often compared him to JIMI HENDRIX. Even Guy's guitar-playing peers marveled at the manner in which he was able to transpose a solo into a boundless orgiastic experience. Hendrix is said to have admitted to being profoundly influenced by Guy, while ERIC CLAPTON has called him the greatest blues guitarist ever. In fact, few blues musicians today can match Guy's white-knuckled ability to make a guitar solo the ultimate blues statement.

Guy was born and raised in Louisiana and began playing professionally in and around Baton Rouge in the early 1950s. It wasn't until he relocated to Chicago in 1957 that his career took shape. Befriended by MUDDY WATERS, Guy worked himself into the city's thriving blues scene. In 1958 he beat both Magic Sam and Otis Rush in a club-sponsored "Battle of the Blues" contest, which led Sam to recommend him to Eli Toscano, owner of the Artistic and Cobra labels. Guy recorded two singles for Artistic, "Sit and Cry" and "This Is the End," before the company went bankrupt.

Guy signed with Chess Records in 1960 and became an in-demand session guitarist there, backing such noted artists as Waters, WILLIE DIXON, LITTLE WAL-TER, SONNY BOY WILLIAMSON (Rice Miller), and KOKO TAYLOR. In 1962 his own record, "Stone Crazy," went to number 12 on the R&B charts. Guy left Chess in 1967 and moved to the Vanguard label, where he cut such respected albums as *A Man and the Blues, This Is Buddy Guy*, and *Hold That Plane!* He had also formed a professional relationship with harp player JUNIOR WELLS. The duo proved especially popular with white blues fans of the late '60s and early '70s, though they never reaped many financial rewards.

Guy's records were good, but his live shows were better. Part of it was due to his unpredictable nature; he could mimic HOWLIN' WOLF and Guitar Slim in one boisterous set, and in the next settle into a study of soul-blues that was far removed from the onstage frenzy for which he was known. For much of the '70s and '80s Guy had to rely on his live performances to earn a living. Though he continued to record, his albums were erratic affairs that all too often conspicuously lacked the power and passion of the Chess and Vanguard efforts. Guy continued to play blues clubs in the U.S. and at blues fests in Europe, with little attention from the rock crowd that had adopted him in the late '60s. That changed in 1989 when Guy opened his now-famous blues club, Legends, in Chicago. The club has become a stop-off point for visiting bluesmen and blues-influenced rockers.

In 1991 Eric Clapton invited Guy to perform with him at the Royal Albert Hall in London. His stunning performances with Clapton led to a recording contract with the Silvertone label and the release of *Damn Right, I've Got the Blues*, an acclaimed comeback album that included cameo appearances by Clapton, Jeff Beck, and Mark Knopfler. A follow-up album, *Feels Like Rain*, came out in 1993. Guy continues to perform and record. He is the brother of blues guitarist PHIL GUY.

Essential Listening:
The Complete Chess Studio Recordings/MCA-Chess (CHD2-9337)
Damn Right, I've Got the Blues/Silvertone (1462-2-J)
Alone and Acoustic/Alligator (AL 4802)
I Was Walking Through the Woods/MCA-Chess (9315)
A Man and the Blues/Vanguard (VMD 79272)
Stone Crazy!/Alligator (4723)
Hold That Plane!/Vanguard (VMD 79323)
This Is Buddy Guy/Vanguard (VMD 79290)
My Time After Awhile/Vanguard (VMD 141/42)
The Very Best of Buddy Guy/Rhino (R2-70280)
Feels Like Rain/Silvertone (01241-41-2)

◄ GUY, PHIL

(born April 28, 1940, Lettsworth, La.)

Blues guitarist Phil Guy has long been in the shadow of his older, more-famous brother, Buddy. Yet Phil Guy has fronted his own band, the Chicago Machine, and has recorded a number of albums since he followed his brother to Chicago in 1969.

Phil learned how to play on a guitar left in the Guy home by Buddy after he had relocated to Baton Rouge to play with Louisiana bluesman RAFUL NEAL. When Buddy returned home during breaks in touring, he taught his younger brother the essential elements of the blues guitar until Phil was good enough to take Buddy's place in the Neal band in 1959.

Phil Guy stayed with Raful Neal for a decade before settling in Chicago. He joined Buddy's touring band on the eve of a tour of Africa in 1970 and remained with it until 1975, when Buddy, frustrated over his inability to secure a recording contract, temporarily retired from touring. That same year Phil recorded his first album, *The High Energy Blues* on the JSP label, and formed Phil Guy and the Chicago Machine. Since then, Guy has recorded other albums for JSP and Red Lightnin' and has become a familiar figure on the Chicago-blues club scene, occasionally opening shows for Buddy at his club, Legends, with the Chicago Machine.

Essential Listening:
All Star Chicago Blues Session/JSP (CD 214)
Tina Nu/JSP (CD 226)

H.

◄ HAMMOND, JR., JOHN

(born November 13, 1942, New York, N.Y.)

Few white blues artists have stayed true to traditional country blues the way John Hammond has. Since discovering the form in the late 1950s, Hammond has become one of country blues' most consistent interpreters, and is particularly known for his slashing slide style derived from the Mississippi Delta. His richly authentic delivery and his acute concern for the preservation of country blues have enabled him to sustain a career that spans four decades and includes the release of more than twenty albums.

The son of legendary talent scout/producer John Hammond, who was responsible for signing such acts as Billie Holiday, Bob Dylan, Bruce Springsteen, and STEVIE RAY VAUGHAN to Columbia Records, Hammond taught himself how to play guitar and harmonica by listening to blues records, especially those of his main influence, ROBERT JOHNSON. After a successful stand at New York's Gerdes Folk City in 1962, Hammond signed a recording contract with Vanguard Records. The label released his self-titled debut shortly after his triumphant appearance at the 1963 Newport Folk Festival. On that and subsequent albums, Hammond delivered a raw, invigorating blues sound that appealed to the growing folk-blues crowd. After a successful tour of England, Hammond returned home to make albums that featured musicians who would later form the Band. Other artists Hammond worked with included ROLLING STONES bass player Bill Wyman and guitarists Duane Allman and JIMI HENDRIX.

Although Hammond was steeped in country blues, he was not limited by it. An early-'70s album for Columbia, *I'm Satisfied*, featured a big band on some cuts. Triumvirate, a short-lived blues-rock trio that, in addition to Hammond, featured DR. JOHN on keyboards, and MIKE BLOOMFIELD on guitar, recorded an album of the same name, also for Columbia, during that time.

By the mid-'70s Hammond had largely given up on experimentation with bands and blues offshoots and settled in as a solo artist, though he did record his 1979 album, *Hot Tracks*, with the Washington, D.C.–based blues band the NIGHT-HAWKS. Hammond won his only Grammy in 1985 for his appearance on *Blues Explosion*, a collection of tunes taken from the Montreux Jazz Festival that included performances by STEVIE RAY VAUGHAN and KOKO TAYLOR. For the remainder of the '80s, Hammond toured extensively in the U.S. and abroad, playing clubs, concerts, and outdoor blues and folk festivals. He also recorded for the Flying Fish label. In 1992 he jumped to Point Blank–Charisma Records and released *Got Love If You Want It*, a work that featured Hammond in both solo and band settings. Hammond continues to record and perform.

Essential Listening:
The Best of John Hammond/Vanguard (VCD 11/12)
John Hammond/Rounder (11532)
Live/Rounder (3074)
Got Love If You Want It/Point Blank–Charisma (92146-2)

◄ **HANDY, W.C.**
(born William Christopher Handy, November 16, 1873, Florence, Ala.; died March 28, 1958, New York, N.Y.)

W.C. Handy called himself "the Father of the Blues." While Handy did not invent the blues form, he was one of the first to use the term "blues" in a song title ("Memphis Blues" in 1912) and include "blue notes" (flatted thirds and sevenths) in a published composition. Handy did as much as any early pioneer of the blues to promote the music form and push for its inclusion in the early 1900s American music vernacular. As a songwriter, bandleader, and publisher, Handy became synonymous with the blues, though his relationship with the music was always distanced due to his cultivated musical standards. He called the blues a "primitive music" and alluded to its "disturbing monotony," yet Handy remained a blues champion until his last days. To honor Handy's contribution to the blues, the Memphis city fathers named a park after him, and each year the Blues Foundation honors selected blues artists and their work with W.C. Handy Awards, the blues equivalent of a Grammy.

Handy was born in Alabama and studied music as a youth. He played cornet in bands traveling the South with minstrel and tent shows. According to Handy it was in 1892, during the course of his travels, that he first heard Delta blues. After playing with Mahara's Minstrels, he assumed the troupe's music directorship in 1896 and performed light classical pieces, popular dance numbers of the day, and rags throughout the Mississippi Delta in the late 1800s and early 1900s. In 1908 he was requested to write a campaign song to help elect E. H. "Boss" Crump mayor of Memphis. Handy obliged; the original title of the song he composed was "Mr. Crump." Handy later changed it to "Memphis Blues" and published it in 1912. The song became a big hit. Purists have debated whether or not "Memphis Blues" is indeed a true blues. Regardless of the musical technicalities, the song inspired other composers to pen "blues" songs, including PERRY BRADFORD, who wrote "Crazy Blues" for singer MAMIE SMITH. Smith recorded the song in 1920, marking the first time a blues song was recorded. The tune ushered in the classic blues period of the 1920s.

Handy published "St. Louis Blues" and "Yellow Dog Blues" in 1914 and "Beale Street Blues" in 1916, among others, and in 1917 moved to New York City, where he recorded with his own band until 1923. In 1922, he founded the Handy Record Company, but the label folded before it issued any recordings. In the 1920s and 1930s Handy worked with a number of orchestras. In 1938 he penned his autobiography, *Father of the Blues*. Due to failing eyesight, Handy faded from the performing scene in the 1940s. He died in 1958.

Essential Listening:
W.C. Handy: Father of the Blues/DRG Records (SL 5192)

◄ HARE, PAT

(born Auburn "Pat" Hare, December 20, 1930, Cherry Valley, Ark.; died September 26, 1980, St. Paul, Minn.)

Pat Hare was a blues guitarist whose distorted, ornery tone and ripping style gave many of the records on which he performed an urgency and tension few other players could produce. He broke onto the Memphis blues scene as a member of HOWLIN' WOLF's first band in 1948. In 1952 he came to the attention of SAM PHILLIPS, who recruited Hare to work as a Sun Records session guitarist. In the two years that he was with Sun, Hare recorded with JUNIOR PARKER, JAMES COTTON, and other Memphis bluesmen, as well as recording a few solo sides. One song, "I'm Gonna Murder My Baby," expressed the violent side of Hare's personality and predicted the act that would end his career a decade later.

Hare left Memphis and Sun with Junior Parker in 1954 and resettled in Houston. After touring with Parker and the R&B-heavy Blues Consolidated package, which also included BOBBY "BLUE" BLAND and BIG MAMA THORNTON, Hare moved to Chicago and joined the MUDDY WATERS Band. Hare's raw guitar sound helped give the Waters band a particularly rough edge. But during his time in Chicago, Hare's drinking problems grew worse; after Waters's now-legendary appearance with his band at the Newport Jazz Festival in 1960, Hare was fired. In 1963 he moved to Minneapolis to work with MOJO BUFORD, but shortly thereafter was arrested for murdering his girlfriend and a policeman. He was convicted in 1964 and sent to prison for life. He died in 1980.

Essential Listening:
Mystery Train (with Junior Parker and James Cotton)/Rounder (SS 38)
Muddy Waters: The Chess Box/MCA-Chess (31268)

◄ HARMAN, JAMES

(born June 8, 1946, Anniston, Ala.)

Singer and harmonica player James Harman has been a fixture on the southern California blues scene since the early '70s when he moved to the West Coast after stays in Chicago, New York, New Orleans, and Miami. As the leader first of the Icehouse Blues Band and then the R&B/blues–based James Harman Band, Harman cultivated a small but loyal following in California blues clubs, often backing established bluesmen such as EDDIE "CLEANHEAD" VINSON, T-BONE WALKER, FREDDIE KING, and BIG JOE TURNER onstage.

Harman began his recording career in 1981 with *This Band Won't Behave*, an EP that he released on his own Icepick label. Two years later Harman signed with Enigma Records and released *Thank You Baby*, followed by *Those Dangerous Gentlemens* on Rhino Records in 1987. All three albums contained a bar-band brand of blues that relied on Harman's soulful vocals and sense of humor. In 1988 Harman and his band jumped to the Rivera label and released the album *Extra Napkins*. Also that year Harman's song "Kiss of Fire" was included in the soundtrack for the film *The Accused*, which starred Jodie Foster. Harman used the exposure to broaden his audience; he and his band toured Europe in 1989 and played a number of European blues festivals.

In order to take advantage of the James Harman Band's increasing reputation as a energetic live act, Rivera released *Strictly Live . . . in '85* in 1990. The following year Harman jumped to the Black Top label and recorded *Do Not Disturb*, a concept album that humorously examines the perils of motel living and life on the road. A follow-up album, *Two Sides to Every Story*, was released in 1993. Harman continues to record and perform.

Essential Listening:
Strictly Live . . . in '85!/Rivera (LP-RR 506)
Do Not Disturb/Black Top (BT 1065)
Those Dangerous Gentlemens/Rhino (70837-2)
Extra Napkins/Rivera (LP-RR 505)
Two Sides to Every Story/Black Top (BT 1091)

◄ HARPO, SLIM

(aka Harmonica Slim) (born James Moore, January 11, 1924, Baton Rouge, La.; died January 31, 1970, Baton Rouge, La.)

Slim Harpo was one of the principal purveyors of Louisiana swamp blues. Along with LIGHTNIN' SLIM, with whom he regularly recorded and performed, Harpo practically defined the Excello Records' blues sound in the 1950s and 1960s with raw yet easy-flowing rhythms and roots-flavored but rather glum tones. Harpo played harmonica and guitar and sang with a nasal texture that gave his recordings their distinctive quality. He was one of Excello's most consistent and best-selling recording artists.

Harpo began his career in the 1940s, playing juke joints, parties, and picnics under the name Harmonica Slim. After years of building a following in and around Baton Rouge, Harpo got the opportunity to record as an accompanist to Lightnin' Slim for the Excello label in 1955. In 1957 he cut one of his most noted songs, "I'm a King Bee," which was later covered by the ROLLING STONES. Harpo continued to record with Excello and work with Lightnin' Slim throughout the South. In 1961 he recorded a second hit, "Rainin' in My Heart." A third, "Baby Scratch My Back," came out in 1966 and led to a chance at a big break-through that year when he opened for R&B/soul singer James Brown at Madison Square Garden in New York. The performance led Harpo to venture into rock territory in the late '60s. He performed at such noted rock venues as the Electric Circus, the Fillmore East, and the Scene in New York as well as the Whiskey A-Go-Go in Los Angeles before suffering a fatal heart attack in 1970. He was forty-six years old when he died. Harpo was inducted into the Blues Foundation's Hall of Fame in 1985.

Essential Listening:
The Best of Slim Harpo/Rhino (R1-70169)
I'm a King Bee/Flyright (FLYCD 05)

◄ HARRIS, PEPPERMINT

(born Harrison Nelson, July 17, 1925, Texarkana, Tex.)

A Houston-based rhythm & blues singer and guitarist, Peppermint Harris made his mark in the early '50s with two hits, "Rainin' in My Heart" (1950) and "I Got Loaded" (1951). The latter song made it to number 1 on the R&B charts.

Influenced by Texas bluesmen LIGHTNIN' HOPKINS and CLARENCE "GATE-MOUTH" BROWN, Harris bought his first guitar while serving in the navy during World War II. After the war he came back to Houston and began performing in area nightclubs. He cut his first records for Gold Star in 1947, but it wasn't until he signed with the New York–based Sittin' In With label and recorded "Rainin' in My Heart" that he attracted attention outside Texas. On the strength of the chart success of "Rainin' in My Heart," Harris signed a contract with the L.A.–based Aladdin label in 1951.

Harris's tenure with Aladdin lasted only until 1953. He bounced from one label to the next for the rest of his career. He continued to write for a variety of artists, including ALBERT KING, B.B. KING, ETTA JAMES, and BOBBY "BLUE" BLAND, and recorded into the mid-'80s, but little became of his singles. Harris has continued to perform and record on occasion.

Essential Listening:
I Got Loaded/Route 66 (KIX 23)
Houston Can't Be Heaven/Ace (CHD 267)

◄ HARRIS, WYNONIE

(born August 24, 1915, Omaha, Nebr.; died June 14, 1969, Los Angeles, Calif.)

Wynonie Harris was a blues shouter whose hell-raising vocals, razor-sharp stage moves, and lady-killing looks made him the most serious rival of BIG JOE TURNER, the dean of R&B belters, in the late 1940s and early 1950s. Harris turned nearly every song he recorded into a powerful example of R&B's rousing sexual suggestiveness. Many of Harris's risqué stage moves were reputedly copied by Elvis Presley. Confident to the point of arrogance, which irritated many of his associates, Harris made a number of great R&B records during the music's heyday and undoubtedly paved the way for the flood of rock & roll artists who followed him.

Harris was born in Omaha, where he began his singing career in 1934. Making frequent trips to Kansas City where he heard Big Joe Turner, Harris developed an effective vocal shout style that was perfectly suited for jump blues. After a stint in Los Angeles in the early 1940s, during which time he appeared as a dancer in the film *Hit Parade 1943*, Harris returned to the Midwest and signed on in 1944 with LUCKY MILLINDER's band, replacing vocalist Trevor Bacon. Shortly thereafter, Harris and the Lucky Millinder Band booked time in a New

York studio and cut "Hurry Hurry" and "Who Threw the Whiskey in the Well?" for the Decca label.

Harris wasted little time starting his solo career. In 1945 he returned to Los Angeles and signed a recording contract with Philo and then Apollo. In 1947 Harris signed with King Records, with whom he cut many of his biggest and best records. It was his version of "Good Rockin' Tonight," a song singer ROY BROWN first cut in 1947, that shot to the top of the R&B charts in 1948 and established Harris as one of King's best-selling artists. Harris had a number of other hit songs on the King label, including "Good Morning Judge," "Lovin' Machine," and "Bloodshot Eyes." Like these, many of the songs Harris cut dealt with alcohol ("Drinkin' Wine, Spo-Dee-O-Dee") or sex ("I Like My Baby's Pudding").

Harris toured with Big Joe Turner in 1949 and remained a major R&B artist through 1954 when he ended his tenure with King. Harris was unable to make the jump into the more lucrative rock & roll field—and stay there—in the mid and late '50s, and he gradually slipped from the scene. He attempted a few comebacks and recorded with Atco and other labels in the 1960s, but none of his records came close to matching his earlier success. He died of cancer in 1969.

Essential Listening:
Good Rockin' Tonight/Charly (CD 244)
Good Rockin' Blues/Gusto (5040X)

◄ HARRISON, WILBERT

(born January 5, 1929, Charlotte, N.C.)

Wilbert Harrison is best known for his version of the Leiber and Stoller song "Kansas City," which topped the R&B and pop charts in 1959. A capable singer, Harrison bounced around the R&B scene in the 1950s, recording for the Rockin', DeLuxe, Chart, and Savoy labels, and playing clubs up and down the East Coast. The success of "Kansas City" made him a star. Harrison performed in R&B and rock & roll road package shows and continued to record for a number of labels in the 1960s.

After a string of singles, most of which failed to dent the charts, and time spent performing as a one-man band, Harrison scored a semblance of a hit one last time in 1969 with the song "Let's Work Together." Although the record only made it to number 32 on the pop charts, its infectious shuffle rhythm and Harrison's easy-flowing delivery inspired the blues-rock group Canned Heat to cut its version of the song.

Harrison continued to work through the 1970s and into the 1980s but was never able to come close to matching the success of either "Kansas City" or "Let's Work Together." He eventually retired from performing and recording.

Essential Listening:
Lovin' Operator/Charly (CRB 1102)

◄ HAWKINS, SCREAMIN' JAY

(born July 18, 1929, Cleveland, Ohio)

No other R&B artist has possessed the strange charm, black humor, or onstage histrionics of singer and pianist Screamin' Jay Hawkins. Wearing capes and weird clothes, using a flaming coffin as a prop, working with all sorts of smoke boxes and voodoo accoutrements, and projecting an image of a man besieged by lunacy, Hawkins made his stage show far more important than his music. He was a pioneer in the kinds of theatrics later used by rock artists such as Arthur Brown, David Bowie, and Alice Cooper.

Although Hawkins was interested in music at an early age, he became a boxer before he turned to rhythm & blues, and was a Golden Gloves champion in 1943. While serving in the army in the late '40s, he worked with Special Services, performing as a singer and pianist in GI clubs and USOs in Europe and the Far East. When Hawkins was discharged in 1952, he joined TINY GRIMES's Rocking Highlanders. After his stint with Grimes, Hawkins worked one-nighters on his own and with R&B artists like FATS DOMINO.

Hawkins signed a recording contract with Okeh Records in 1956 and released his most famous song, "I Put a Spell on You." The record's success in both R&B and rock & roll circles enabled Hawkins to secure a spot on Alan Freed's package shows and in the 1957 movie *Mister Rock & Roll*. Hawkins continued to tour and record for a variety of labels through the mid-'60s and into the '70s, though he'd been relegated to the oldies circuit, and few, if any, of his records were taken seriously. Hawkins appeared in the movie *American Hot Wax* in 1978 and has toured and recorded on and off since then.

Essential Listening:
Voodoo Jive: The Best of Screamin' Jay Hawkins/Rhino (R2-70947)
Real Life/EPM (FDC 5509)

◄ HEARTSMAN, JOHNNY

(born February 9, 1937, San Fernando, Calif.)

From the mid-1950s to the late 1960s, Johnny Heartsman was a popular Oakland-based studio musician who recorded and worked with many of the Bay Area's best bluesmen, including JIMMY MCCRACKLIN and JIMMY WILSON. He frequently worked for producer BOB GEDDINS, and on occasion made his own records. One of them, "Johnny's House Party," made it into the top 20 of the R&B charts in 1957. For a time, Heartsman also played bass in McCracklin's group, the Blues Blasters.

In addition to bass, Heartsman plays flute, organ, piano, and trombone, but he is best known as a guitarist. His delicate, highly dynamic style is juiced with light jazzy tones and textures. Heartsman's tenure as one of the Bay Area's busiest session musicians ended when he left to tour with a top-40 cover band in the early '70s. Heartsman eventually returned to California in 1975 and settled in Sacramento. He began playing blues again, often performing at the San Francisco Blues Festival and popular West Coast blues clubs. In 1991 he recorded his first widely released album, *The Touch*, for Alligator Records. Two previous albums, *Music of My Heart*, on the Cat 'N Hat label (1983), and *Sacramento*, on the German Crosscut label (1988), were poorly distributed and received little attention. Heartsman continues to record and perform.

Essential Listening:
Sacramento/Crosscut (1018)
The Touch/Alligator (AL 4800)

◄ HEGAMIN, LUCILLE

(aka Fanny Baker) (born Lucille Nelson, November 29, 1894 or 1897, Macon, Ga.; died March 1, 1970, New York, N.Y.)

Lucille Hegamin was the second black vaudeville-blues singer to record in 1920. She cut "The Jazz Me Blues" and "Everybody's Blues" for Arto Records in November of that year, just a few months after MAMIE SMITH had recorded "Crazy Blues," the first blues song to appear on disc.

Although not a pure blues singer in the tradition of, say, BESSIE SMITH, Hegamin seemed as comfortable singing the blues as she was singing the pop and vaudeville hits of the day. Light-skinned and attractive and born with a cool, well-rounded voice, Hegamin became one of the biggest names in blues circles in the early 1920s. Her signature song, "He May Be Your Man, But He Comes to See Me Sometimes," is considered one of the era's most memorable numbers.

Hegamin was born in Macon, Georgia, hence her first stage nickname, the Georgia Peach. Although she had little or no vocal training, she began working the tent-show circuit in the South in her midteens. In 1914 she married piano player Bill Hegamin. The duo eventually wound up in Chicago, where Hegamin sang with jazz pianists Jelly Roll Morton and Tony Jackson. She and her husband moved to Los Angeles before ultimately settling in New York in 1919. In New York she sang in cabarets and nightclubs and was signed by Arto in 1920. Her follow-up to "The Jazz Me Blues" was "Arkansas Blues," a song that solidified her reputation as one of the more popular black singers of the era.

After Hegamin's contract with Arto expired, she signed with Cameo and eventually became known as the Cameo Girl. In all, Hegamin recorded some forty songs with Cameo before she slid from the scene in the 1930s. In the early 1960s, Hegamin returned to recording, thanks to the support and urging of fellow classic blues singer VICTORIA SPIVEY. Hegamin cut songs for Spivey's self-named label as well as for the Prestige-Bluesville label. She died in 1970.

Essential Listening:
Songs We Taught Your Mother (Alberta Hunter, Lucille Hegamin,
    Victoria Spivey)/Prestige-Bluesville (OBCCD 520-2)

◄ HELFER, ERWIN

(born January 20, 1936, Chicago, Ill.)

Erwin Helfer, a Chicago pianist, is a throwback to the days when boogie-woogie players such as PINE TOP SMITH, ALBERT AMMONS, and PETE JOHNSON jacked up bass lines and rhythms and made some of the most romping piano blues ever heard. Helfer has kept alive this form, whether playing solo, in duets with other Chicago blues pianists like JIMMY WALKER, or as an accompanist for blues singers like ESTELLE "MAMA" YANCEY.

Helfer was born and raised in Chicago, and as a child was more interested in classical music than blues. Once Helfer discovered the blues he enrolled at Tulane University in New Orleans, where he spent time outside of class soaking up the piano style of such Crescent City pianists as ARCHIBALD and PROFESSOR LONG-HAIR. Helfer began his professional career when Mama Yancey, wife of pianist and boogie-woogie pioneer JIMMY YANCEY, coaxed him to fill in for her accompanist, LITTLE BROTHER MONTGOMERY. His initial performance with Yancey led to a long-term professional partnership with the singer that lasted to her death in 1986 at age ninety.

Helfer began his recording career in the late '70s with the Chicago-based Flying Fish label. *On the Sunny Side of the Street*, released in 1979, featured Helfer playing in both blues and jazz styles. In 1982 Helfer began his own record company, Red Beans, and released albums by Mama Yancey, BLIND JOHN DAVIS, JOHNNY "BIG MOOSE" WALKER, and other Chicago blues artists. Helfer continues to live and work out of Chicago.

Essential Listening:
Erwin Helfer and Friends/Flying Fish (210)
Erwin Helfer Plays Chicago Piano/Red Beans (010)

◄ HEMPHILL, JESSE MAE

(born October 6, 1934, Senatobia, Miss.)

Jesse Mae Hemphill is a blues artist from the Mississippi Delta region whose repertoire is a combination of traditional blues and originals written from a distinctively female viewpoint.

Hemphill comes from a long line of blues musicians; her grandfather was reputedly recorded by folklorist ALAN LOMAX during one of his southern field trips in the 1940s. Hemphill learned how to play guitar and drums by watching her relatives perform at picnics and parties in the Mississippi Delta. She sang with pickup blues bands until the early 1980s when she opted for a solo career and began accompanying herself on guitar and percussion. Hemphill released her debut album, *She-Wolf*, for the Vogue label in 1981; her first American album, *Feelin' Good*, was released by High Water Records in the late 1980s. Hemphill won back-to-back W.C. HANDY Awards for best traditional female blues artist in 1987 and 1988. She continues to perform.

Essential Listening:
She-Wolf/Vogue (513-501)
Feelin' Good/High Water (1012)

◄ HENDERSON, ROSA

(born Rosa Deschamps, November 24, 1896, Henderson, Ky.; died April 6, 1968, New York, N.Y.)

Rosa Henderson is considered by some jazz and blues historians to be one of the most overlooked of the classic blues vocalists. She was a popular blues-vaudeville singer in her day: She recorded nearly a hundred songs between 1923 and 1931. Henderson's delivery was significantly sweeter and more conservative than those of blues queens MA RAINEY and BESSIE SMITH, both of whom had passionate, soulful, and rough-edged vocal styles. Henderson often sounded more like a cabaret singer than a blueswoman. Still, songs such as "Penitentiary Blues," "Back Wood Blues," "Strut Yo' Puddy," and "Can't Be Bothered with No Sheik" reveal her to have been a singer with more emotional depth than she's been given credit for.

Another reason why Henderson has been forgotten by all but the staunchest students of the classic blues period stems from the fact that she used nearly a dozen pseudonyms during her recording career. In order to sidestep contract limitations Henderson made recordings under the names Flora Dale, Bessie Williams, Sally Ritz, Rosa Green, Mae Harris, Mamie Harrie, Josephine Thomas, Sara Johnson, and Gladys White. This strategy allowed her to record more songs and make more money but practically destroyed her identity as a historically important classic blues artist.

Born Rosa Deschamps, Henderson performed in tent and vaudeville shows throughout the South. After their marriage, she and Douglas "Slim" Henderson worked as a duo. They made their way north, ending up in New York where she was offered her first recording contract. Throughout the '20s she recorded on a variety of labels, including Paramount, Columbia, Vocalion, and Victor. In the 1930s Henderson, like other vaudeville-blues singers, saw her career wane. She died in 1968.

Essential Listening:
Mean Mothers: Independent Women's Blues, Vol. 1/Rosetta (1300)
Rare and Hot, 1923–1926/Historical Records (14)
The Blues, 1923 to 1933 (Various Artists)/ABC (836 046-2)
Rosa Henderson, 1923–1924/Blues Documents (BD 2105)

◄ HENDRIX, JIMI

(aka Jimmy James) (born James Hendrix, November 27, 1942, Seattle, Wash.; died September 18, 1970, London, England)

Although Jimi Hendrix will be remembered as rock's most innovative and revolutionary guitarist, he had the natural instincts of a bluesman and in fact built much of his early repertoire from the blues. Live, Hendrix played plenty of blues; his sets were almost always filled with long, extended jams based on blues chord progressions heard in such gems as "Red House" and "California Night."

Some of what Hendrix did with feedback, fuzz tones, distortion, and volume elaborated on the styles of blues guitarists PAT HARE and GUITAR SLIM. With his screeching solos, Hendrix shattered rock and blues traditions regarding how long and in what capacity solos should be delivered. He broke down barriers between blues and rock so that his guitar ideas flowed freely from one idiom to the other. His influence can be heard in the guitar styles of bluesmen MAGIC SAM, BUDDY GUY, and, later on, STEVIE RAY VAUGHAN.

Hendrix's earliest influences came from MUDDY WATERS, B.B. KING, Guitar Slim, and CHUCK BERRY. After a stint in the army from 1959 to 1961, Hendrix, working under the name Jimmy James, became a respected sideman, playing behind such soul and R&B artists as LITTLE RICHARD, KING CURTIS, and the Isley Brothers. In 1964 Hendrix moved to New York City and formed his own band, Jimmy James and Blue Flames, which mostly played JIMMY REED, MEMPHIS SLIM, Muddy Waters, and ROBERT JOHNSON covers. Barely surviving in the Greenwich Village folk and blues scene, Hendrix nonetheless became a regular at the Cafe Wha? For a brief spell, he played with blues guitarist and singer JOHN HAMMOND, JR., before he was approached by Chas Chandler, the former bass player of the English blues-rock group the ANIMALS. Chandler invited Hendrix to go to London and start a new group, which Chandler would manage. Hendrix took the offer, moved to London in 1966, and formed the Jimi Hendrix Experience with drummer Mitch Mitchell and bass player Noel Redding.

The Experience's debut album, *Are You Experienced?*, contained a number of Hendrix classics, including "Purple Haze," "Manic Depression," and "Foxy Lady." On this album, Hendrix introduced to the rock world his awesome guitar prowess and proceeded to redefine the standards by which all other rock guitarists would subsequently be judged. Hendrix's legendary performance at the Monterey Pop Festival in 1967, at which he burned his guitar in an orgiastic climax, only increased the hoopla surrounding him and his band.

Are You Experienced? was a startling work that still ranks as one of the greatest debut albums in rock history. On his two 1968 releases, *Axis: Bold as Love* and *Electric Ladyland*, Hendrix continued his probe into psychedelia and the sonic stratosphere, yet still managed to keep his relationship with the blues solid.

In 1969 Hendrix dissolved the Experience. After playing the Woodstock festival, Hendrix formed the Band of Gypsys with old army chum and bass player Billy Cox and former ELECTRIC FLAG drummer Buddy Miles. Hendrix had built his own recording studio, Electric Ladyland, in Greenwich Village and recorded regularly in 1970. Going off in a jazz direction, Hendrix played with guitarists John McLaughlin and Larry Coryell and planned to record with trumpet player Miles Davis.

After a performance at the Isle of Wight rock festival in late summer of 1970, Hendrix went to London. There on September 18 he died in his sleep, choking on vomit after ingesting a heavy dose of barbiturates. He was twenty-seven years old. Hendrix was inducted into the Rock & Roll Hall of Fame in 1992.

Essential Listening:
Are You Experienced?/Reprise (RS-6261-2)
Axis: Bold as Love/Reprise (RS 6281)
Electric Ladyland/Reprise (zRS 6307)
Smash Hits/Reprise (MSK 2276)

Band of Gypsys/Capitol (STAO 472)
The Cry of Love/Reprise (MS 2034)
The Essential Jimi Hendrix, Vol. 1/Reprise (2Rs 2245)
The Essential Jimi Hendrix, Vol. 2/Reprise (HS 2293)
Live at Winterland/Rykodisc (RCD 20038)
Lifelines: The Jimi Hendrix Story/Reprise (9 26435-2)
Stages, 1967–1970/Reprise (9 26732-2)

◄ HENRY, CLARENCE "FROGMAN"

(born March 19, 1937, Algiers, La.)

A New Orleans R&B singer and piano player who counted FATS DOMINO and PROFESSOR LONGHAIR as his main influences, Clarence "Frogman" Henry broke onto the national R&B scene in 1956 with his hit "Ain't Got No Home." In the song Henry displayed his wide vocal range, from a falsetto to a "froggy" groan, thereby earning his nickname.

Henry grew up on blues and early R&B. In his late teens he moved to New Orleans to work as a musician and singer. He began with the Bobby Mitchell Band but soon struck out on his own, leading his own group. In 1956 he signed a recording contract with Argo Records, the Chess subsidiary label, and cut "Ain't Got No Home," which made it into the top 10 on the R&B charts and the top 20 on the pop charts.

Henry spent the next four years touring with R&B and rock & roll package shows and playing New Orleans clubs on the fame he generated with "Ain't Got No Home." In 1961 he returned to the charts with a flurry of hits, including "But I Do" and "You Always Hurt the One You Love." Argo released his first album that year, and Henry again toured the U.S. and appeared on network television. He opened shows for the Beatles in 1964 and the ROLLING STONES in 1965. But by the late '60s Henry and his brand of New Orleans R&B began to wither from the pop scene. Henry stayed active in the music business by working oldies shows with other '50s R&B artists with close links to rock & roll. He continues to perform today.

Essential Listening:
You Always Hurt the One You Love/Argo (4009)
Down on Bourbon Street/CFH (101)

◄ HICKS, CHARLEY

(aka Laughing Charley, Charlie Lincoln) (born March 11, 1900, Lithonia, Ga.; died September 28, 1963, Cairo, Ga.)

Charley Hicks, a guitarist and singer and brother of BARBECUE BOB (Robert Hicks), was part of the Atlanta blues scene that flourished in the 1920s. As well as recording with his brother as a duo, Hicks recorded as a solo artist, though he never achieved the commercial success or popularity alone that his brother did. Still, his twelve-string guitar work and plaintive vocal style were representative of the Atlanta blues school of the 1920s.

Born and raised in the Georgia countryside, the Hicks brothers played picnics and parties before they moved to Atlanta sometime around 1920. Working Decatur Street, the city's famous strip where Georgia bluesmen played for spare change, the Hicks brothers came into contact with other Atlanta bluesmen such as PEG LEG HOWELL, BUDDY MOSS, BLIND WILLIE MCTELL, and CURLEY WEAVER.

The Hicks brothers began their recording careers as solo artists in 1927 with Columbia Records, also cutting some tracks as a duo. One of the songs they recorded together, "It Won't Be Long Now," became a modest hit for Columbia. The record's success prompted the label to release more individual sides by the brothers, in addition to another duet, "Darktown Gamblin." But the record failed to match the success of "It Won't Be Long Now."

With Robert Hicks's records selling better than his brother's, Charley Hicks's recording career had ended by 1930. In 1931 Robert died suddenly of pneumonia. Heartbroken by his brother's death, Charley Hicks quit performing and drifted into a life of alcoholism. In 1956 he was arrested for murder and sent to prison, where he died in 1963.

◄ HILL, BERTHA "CHIPPIE"

(born March 15, 1905, Charleston, S.C.; died May 7, 1950, New York, N.Y.)

Bertha "Chippie" Hill isn't always mentioned in the same breath with MA RAINEY, BESSIE SMITH, CLARA SMITH, and IDA COX as the best of the classic blues singers from the 1920s; yet her authentic, southern-rooted blues voice, developed during years working the TOBA (Theatre Owners' Booking Association) circuit and touring with the Rabbit Foot Minstrels, made her nearly as popular—especially with black audiences—as her more celebrated counterparts.

Hill came from a family of sixteen children. In her early teens she left home to become a singer and dancer and wound up in New York City, where she danced with ETHEL WATERS, a popular cabaret performer and sometimes blues singer. During a stint at Leroy's, a noted New York nightclub, Hill was nicknamed "Chippie" because of her young age (she was fourteen at the time) and diminutive size.

She first recorded for the Okeh label in Chicago in 1925. Backed by cornet player LOUIS ARMSTRONG and pianist Richard Jones on songs such as "Low Land Blues" and "Kid Man Blues" that year and on "Georgia Man" and "Trouble in Mind" with the same musicians in 1926, Hill demonstrated her ability to belt out a hardened and earthy blues style, not unlike that which was heard from male country blues singers at the time.

In the mid-'20s Hill performed with jazz bandleader and trumpet player King Oliver. Later in her career she sang with the Jimmie Noone Orchestra and with the Kid Ory Band. She died in 1950, a victim of a hit-and-run auto accident in New York.

Chippie Hill's recording catalog is small when compared to other noted blues singers of the era. Her most memorable recordings were done for Okeh from 1925 to 1927. Absent from the recording studio in the 1930s, Hill staged a comeback in 1946 with LOVIE AUSTIN's Blues Serenaders and recorded for Rudi

Blesh's Circle label. However, nothing of what she recorded for Blesh matched the raw beauty of her Okeh material.

Essential Listening:
Ida Cox & Bertha Chippie Hill/Queen-disc (Q 048)

◄ HILL, KING SOLOMON

(born Joe Holmes, c. 1897, McComb, Miss.; died c. 1949, Sibley, La.)

King Solomon Hill was an obscure but interesting slide guitarist and singer whose few existing recordings reveal a downhome blues sensibility and a primitive guitar style with ragged notes and irregular rhythms. Little is known about Hill's life. He was probably born in McComb, Mississippi, around the turn of the century. Undoubtedly self-taught on the guitar, Hill played parties and juke joints and often traveled to Louisiana, where he eventually settled.

There are reports of Hill working with SAM COLLINS, RAMBLIN' THOMAS, and even BLIND LEMON JEFFERSON. Hill was well-known enough to be offered a recording contract with Paramount. His only known recordings were made in Paramount's Grafton, Wisconsin, studios in 1932 and released later that year. All of the tracks feature Hill's wailing, upper-range vocals and his crude, though occasionally compelling, guitar work. For most of the 1930s, Hill worked Louisiana and Texas jukes before disappearing from the scene. He lived in Sibley, Louisiana, and is thought to have died around 1949.

Essential Listening:
Blues from the Western States (1929–1949) (Various Artists)/Yazoo (L 1032)
Giants of Country Blues, Volume 1 (1927–1932) (Various Artists)/Wolf
   (WSE 116)

◄ HILL, Z.Z.

(born Arzell Hill, September 30, 1935, Naples, Tex.; died April 27, 1984, Dallas, Tex.)

More than any other artist in the 1980s, singer Z.Z. Hill was most responsible for resurrecting interest in the blues with Southern black audiences and record buyers. Remarkably, his album *Down Home* spent nearly two years on the black charts in the early 1980s. At the time, Hill's popularity was greater than that of even B.B. KING and other veteran bluesmen, though he was little known to white listeners. Tragically, Hill died in 1984, at the peak of his fame, as the result of injuries suffered in an auto accident.

It wasn't that Hill had created a startling new blues sound; nor, with the exception of "Down Home Blues," which had become one of the most familiar blues songs of the 1980s, was much of what he recorded traditional down-home blues. Hill's music was a soul-blues hybrid, with strong links to BOBBY "BLUE" BLAND. *Down Home* was the right record at the right time, and was as important an album to the 1980s blues revival as ROBERT CRAY's *Strong Persuader* and STEVIE RAY VAUGHAN's *Texas Flood*.

Hill's earliest musical experiences were in gospel; as a youth he sang in church choirs. After moving to Dallas in 1953 he began playing in bands on the local club circuit. With the arrival of soul music in the early '60s, Hill was greatly influenced by Sam Cooke. He fused soul with blues and recorded for a variety of labels, including United Artists and CBS, with only marginal commercial success. In the late '70s Hill even flirted with disco. It wasn't until he signed on with the Malaco label in 1980 that his career took off like a shot.

Hill's first self-titled album was well received by black record buyers who knew Hill from his many one-nighters on the chitlin' circuit. But *Down Home*, his second Malaco release, made him a star. It also solidified the financial standing of Malaco and helped make Malaco *the* contemporary blues label for black blues fans, as Alligator was and remains for whites. In all, Hill made five albums for Malaco from 1980 to 1984. He was forty-nine years old when he died.

Essential Listening:
Z.Z. Hill/Malaco (7402)
Down Home/Malaco (7406)
In Memoriam, 1935–84/Malaco (7426)

◄ HOGAN, SILAS

(born September 15, 1911, Westover, La.)

A longtime presence on the Baton Rouge blues scene, Silas Hogan recorded for Excello Records in the early 1960s. His relaxed, easygoing blues failed to catch on beyond Baton Rouge with any consistency, but Hogan has been a familiar figure in the city's local blues community for more than three decades.

Although Hogan taught himself how to play the guitar and played house parties and picnics in the late 1920s and 1930s, his career didn't take a firm shape until he formed his band, the Rhythm Ramblers, in 1956. The group played around Baton Rouge and developed enough of a following for Excello Records to offer Hogan a contract. From 1962 to 1966, Hogan recorded some eight singles. Thereafter he continued to perform in Baton Rouge blues clubs, but bad health and a lack of recognition outside Louisiana and the Gulf Coast region prevented Hogan from performing in other parts of the U.S.

Hogan garnered some wider exposure in the early '70s when tracks of his appeared on Baton Rouge blues compilations issued by Arhoolie and Excello. He continued to perform in and around Baton Rouge throughout the rest of the 1970s before fading from the scene.

Essential Listening:
Trouble/Excello (Ex8019)
I'm a Free Hearted Man/Flyright (595)
Louisiana Blues (Various Artists)/Arhoolie (1054)

◄ HOGG, SMOKEY

(born Andrew Hogg, January 27, 1914, Cushing, Tex.; died May 1, 1960, McKinney, Tex.)

Smokey Hogg, a journeyman Texas blues guitarist and singer and the cousin of LIGHTNIN' HOPKINS, was a prolific recording artist. Influenced by the likes of BLIND LEMON JEFFERSON, BIG BILL BROONZY, and PEETIE WHEATSTRAW, Hogg had a couple of hits with the songs "Long Tall Mama" (1948) and "Little School Girl" (1950). His delivery was centered around coarse, country blues tones and figures.

Hogg learned how to play guitar from his father. As a youth he worked with BLACK ACE at local picnics and taverns. He first recorded in 1937 when he cut some sides for the Decca label in Dallas. The session initiated what would become a twenty-year recording career in which Hogg cut for a variety of labels, including Exclusive, Blue Bonnet, Modern, Specialty, Imperial, Federal, and Show Time. Hogg served in the army during World War II. After his discharge, he built a following on the West Coast as did other Texas blues artists who had gone to California during the war years. Hogg worked both Texas and the West Coast, playing jukes, rent parties, and picnics until his death in 1960.

Essential Listening:
Angels in Harlem/Specialty (SPCD 7020-2)
Goin' Back Home/Krazy Kat (7421)
Too Late Old Man—Jivin' Little Woman/Crown Prince (409)

◄ HOLE, DAVE

(born March 30, 1948, Heswall Cheshire, England)

A blues-rock slide guitarist and singer from Australia, Dave Hole attracted attention in the U.S. when Alligator Records rereleased his self-produced debut album, *Short Fuse Blues*, in 1992. Hole's unconventional guitar technique—he plays with his hand over the top of the guitar and the slide tubing on his index finger instead of his pinky—and his wailing solos made him one of the most important blues guitar discoveries of the early '90s.

Hole was born in England, but by the time he was four years old his family had relocated to Perth, in western Australia. Hole was introduced to the blues when a friend played him a MUDDY WATERS record. Shortly thereafter he began learning the basics of blues guitar by listening to records by BLIND LEMON JEFFERSON, ELMORE JAMES, MISSISSIPPI FRED MCDOWELL, and ROBERT JOHNSON. A soccer injury to his little finger led to his unorthodox slide guitar style.

Hole played Perth clubs until 1972 when he moved to London and worked in a pub band for two years. By 1974 he was back in Australia where he resumed his career as a blues-rock performer. In 1990 Hole recorded *Short Fuse Blues* and sold it at club gigs. On a lark he sent a copy of the album to *Guitar Player* magazine. Editor Jas Obrecht lavishly praised *Short Fuse Blues* in a review and followed it with a feature story on Hole. The articles caught the interest of Al-

ligator Records owner Bruce Iglauer, who made Hole his company's first foreign
signing. Hole's second album, *Working Overtime*, came out in 1993.
    Essential Listening:
Short Fuse Blues/Alligator (ALCD 4807)
Working Overtime/Alligator (ALCD 4814)

◄ HOLLIMON, CLARENCE

(born 1937, Houston, Tex.)
    In the 1950s and 1960s, Clarence Hollimon, a rhythm & blues guitarist with
a lilting, blues-flavored style, toured and recorded with BOBBY "BLUE" BLAND,
JUNIOR PARKER, CHARLES BROWN, BIG MAMA THORNTON, and a number of other
Duke/Peacock artists. His best known guitar work can be heard on such R&B
classics as Bland's "Farther on Up the Road" and Parker's "Next Time You
See Me, Things Won't Be the Same."
    Born and raised in Houston, Hollimon began his career with the Bill Harvey
Orchestra while still in high school, followed by a road stint with Thornton in
the early 1950s. Hollimon spent the last half of the decade working with Charles
Brown and as a session guitarist for Duke-Peacock. Hollimon left Brown in 1960,
but continued to work with Duke-Peacock, recording with such Houston-based
blues and R&B artists as O.V. WRIGHT and BUDDY ACE.
    In the mid-'70s, Hollimon met and married singer CAROL FRAN, and the two began
performing as a duo in Houston clubs. In 1987 saxophone player GRADY GAINES used
Hollimon on his album *Full Gain*, for Black Top Records, which led to a recording
contract with the label for Hollimon and Fran. Their debut album, *Soul Sensation*,
was released in 1992. Hollimon continues to perform with Fran and do session work.
    Essential Listening:
Soul Sensation/Black Top (BT 1071)
Gulf Coast Blues, Vol. 1/Black Top (BT 1055)

◄ HOLMES BROTHERS, THE

Members: Wendell Holmes (guitar) (born December 19, 1943, Plainfield, N.J.);
Sherman Holmes (bass) (born September 29, 1939, Plainfield, N.J.); Popsy
Dixon (drums) (born July 26, 1942, Virginia Beach, Va.); Gib Wharton (pedal
steel guitar) (born September 15, 1955, Mineral Wells, Tex.)
    The Holmes Brothers began in 1980 as a New York bar band whose repertoire
was built on an eclectic mix of blues, soul, gospel, and R&B. Three of the four
band members—bass player Sherman Holmes, guitarist Wendell Holmes, and
drummer Popsy Dixon—learned about the various forms of music they played
by listening to the radio in the 1950s. The fourth member of the band, pedal steel
guitarist Gib Wharton, joined in 1989 and brought a country music influence to
the Holmes Brothers' sound.
    Sherman Holmes moved to New York in 1959 after studying music theory
and composition at Virginia State. After Wendell completed high school, he
joined his older brother in New York. The two musicians played in a few bands

before forming the Sevilles, in 1963. The group lasted for some three years, after which the brothers played in a succession of cover and top-40 bar bands until forming the Holmes Brothers.

The group signed a recording contract with Rounder Records in 1989, and *In the Spirit* was released that year. The record garnered mostly glowing reviews and led to a series of performances outside New York and five European tours in just two years. The follow-up album, *Where It's At*, came out in 1991. Still based in New York, the Holmes Brothers continue to record and perform.

Essential Listening:
In the Spirit/Rounder (2056)
Where It's At/Rounder (2111)

◄ HOMESICK JAMES

(born James Williamson, May 3, 1905, Somerville, Tenn.)

Homesick James is a slide guitarist whose rather imaginative approach to tunings and time has often made his style sound crude and wild. As a singer, Homesick's wailing moans hark back to Mississippi Delta field hollers. He was born in Tennessee and is self-taught on guitar, though both parents played instruments—his father the drums and his mother the guitar. By the time he was in his early teens he had left home and began hoboing through the South, playing guitar for tips on street corners and in parks. On the road Homesick met and played with a number of prominent bluesmen, including mandolin player YANK RACHELL and guitarists SLEEPY JOHN ESTES and BIG JOE WILLIAMS.

Homesick formed his own group, the Dusters, and began his recording career in the late 1930s; he cut some sides in 1937 for RCA in Memphis and recorded with Buddy Doyle on the Vocalion label two years later. In the early 1950s, after years of juke joint work and traveling through the South, Homesick settled in Chicago and began sitting in with his cousin, slide guitarist ELMORE JAMES. Homesick usually played bass with James, both in clubs and in the recording studio, and by 1958 he was a permanent member of the Elmore James Band. It was in Homesick's Chicago apartment that James died in 1963.

For the rest of his career Homesick was a familiar figure on the Chicago blues scene, playing clubs and recording for blues labels like Delmark, Prestige Bluesville, and Black and Blue. In 1970 he toured Europe for the first time with the American Blues Festival package. He has also played numerous blues fests over the years, including the Ann Arbor and Chicago Blues festivals. Now in his late eighties, Homesick continues to perform and record. He resides in Nashville, Tennessee, where in 1992 he recorded the album *Sweet Home Tennessee* for the Appaloosa label.

Essential Listening:
Shake Your Moneymaker/Krazy Kat (790)
Blues on the Southside/Prestige-Bluesville (7388)
Goin' Back Home/Trix (3315)
Goin' Back in the Times/Earwig (4929)
Sweet Home Tennessee/Appaloosa (APP 6109)

◄ HOOKER, EARL

(born January 15, 1930, Clarksdale, Miss.; died April 21, 1970, Chicago, Ill.)

A cousin of JOHN LEE HOOKER, Earl Hooker was a Chicago slide guitarist in the same league as ELMORE JAMES, HOUND DOG TAYLOR, and his mentor, ROBERT NIGHTHAWK. Some Chicago blues guitarists even consider Hooker to have been the greatest slide player ever. Hooker never achieved the success that James did mainly because Hooker rarely sang. Realizing that his voice lacked texture and range, Hooker concentrated on being a blues instrumentalist. Many of his best works contain superbly crafted guitar work, but without vocals they lacked broad commercial appeal.

Hooker was born in the Mississippi Delta where he taught himself the basics of blues guitar. When his family moved to Chicago in the early 1940s, he attended Lyon & Healy Music School. From the knowledge he gained there, Hooker eventually became proficient on the drums and piano as well as on such stringed instruments as the banjo and mandolin. While a teen, Hooker performed on Chicago street corners, occasionally with BO DIDDLEY. He also developed a friendship with slide guitarist Robert Nighthawk, which led to Hooker's interest in slide guitar and some performances with Nighthawk's group outside Chicago. In 1949 Hooker moved to Memphis, joined IKE TURNER's band, and toured the South. Being in Memphis led to some performances with harmonica ace SONNY BOY WILLIAMSON (Rice Miller) on his KFFA radio program, "King Biscuit Time," and to Hooker's first recording dates. Hooker cut some sides for the Rockin' label in 1952, followed by dates with King Records in 1953.

By the mid-'50s Hooker was back in Chicago and fronting his own band. He became a steady figure on the Chicago blues scene, and regularly traveled to cities such as Gary and Indianapolis, Indiana, playing blues clubs. Hooker also kept recording, although most of his material was cut for small labels like Bea & Baby and Chief, and rarely attracted much attention outside Chicago-area blues circles.

With the exception of a 1965 European tour with Joe Hinton (which included an appearance on the English pop music television show "Ready Steady Go!") and a return trip overseas with the American Folk Blues Festival package, Hooker spent most of the '60s playing Chicago clubs with his own band and often with harp player JUNIOR WELLS. Hooker also recorded during the '60s for such labels as Arhoolie, Bluesway, and Blue Thumb, frequently playing a double-necked guitar. In 1969 he recorded an album, *Hooker and Steve*, with organist Steve Miller (not the San Francisco rock guitarist Steve Miller) for Arhoolie. With increased attention on blues guitarists and, thanks to Duane Allman, the rising popularity of the slide guitar in rock, Hooker seemed destined to break beyond his cult status. Unfortunately he died of tuberculosis in 1970. He was forty years old.

Essential Listening:
Two Bugs and a Roach/Arhoolie (CD 324)
Blue Guitar/P-Vine (PCD 2124)
Play Your Guitar Mr. Hooker!/Black Top (BT-1093)

◄ HOOKER, JOHN LEE

(born August 17, 1920, Clarksdale, Miss.)

John Lee Hooker is one of the giants of post–World War II blues, on a par with MUDDY WATERS, B.B. KING, WILLIE DIXON, HOWLIN' WOLF, and LIGHTNIN' HOPKINS. Known as the father of the boogie, an incessant one-chord exercise in blues intensity and undying rhythm, Hooker's sound is also a study in deep blues. From his guitar come shadowy tones, open tunings, feverish note clusters, and that familiar chugging rhythm that has been his blues signature—all of which hark back to the music's formative years.

Hooker also owns one of the most distinctive voices in blues. It reaches down deep and comes together slowly and with careful consideration. It's soaked with sexuality, spiced with arrogance, and contains layers of weathered, bassy textures. Hear John Lee Hooker once and both his voice and his guitar are thereafter unmistakable and unforgettable.

Unlike the other major blues figures of the late 1940s and 1950s who hailed from Chicago, Texas, or Memphis, Hooker made his mark in Detroit and became the Motor City's biggest blues star. He cut nearly as many recordings as Lightnin' Hopkins—the artist many blues historians believe to be the most recorded in the music's history. Because Hooker recorded under a number of pseudonyms to escape contractual obligations, his recording catalog is a confusing maze of albums and singles.

Hooker not only was popular with black blues audiences, but in the early '60s he influenced an entire generation of British blues-rockers. Groups such as the ANIMALS (the band had a major hit in 1964 with Hooker's "Boom Boom"), the ROLLING STONES, JOHN MAYALL and the BLUESBREAKERS, and early FLEETWOOD MAC all borrowed extensively from Hooker. In the U.S., CANNED HEAT built much of its late-'60s repertoire from Hooker's boogie rhythms. More recently, blues-rockers such as JOHNNY WINTER and GEORGE THOROGOOD have reinterpreted the Hooker boogie, while Bruce Springsteen made "Boom Boom" one of his concert highpoints in the late '80s.

Hooker was born in Clarksdale, Mississippi, and was taught the basics of blues guitar by his stepfather, Will Moore. As a child, Hooker learned to sing in church, and he professed an interest in religious music, particularly gospel, during adolescence. Sometime around age fifteen, Hooker left the Delta and went to Memphis, where he worked as an usher in a Beale Street theater and played his guitar on street corners for spare change. He returned to Mississippi for a short while but left again, this time for Cincinnati, where he sang in such gospel groups as the Fairfield Four and the Big Six.

Hooker moved to Detroit in 1943, hoping to cash in on assembly-line work there during the height of World War II. He wound up a janitor in an automotive plant and played clubs and house parties in Detroit's black neighborhoods. His recording career began in 1948 when he recorded his seminal blues number, "Boogie Chillen." Released on the Modern label, the song introduced Hooker's penchant for hypnotic, one-chord guitar ramblings and his deep, chilling vocals. "Boogie Chillen" was a throwback to prewar country blues and the antithesis of the slick rhythm & blues that filled out the charts in the years immediately following World War II. Incredibly, "Boogie Chillen" made it all the way to number 1 on the R&B charts in early 1949 and today is considered one of the all-time classic songs in the blues treasury.

Hooker recorded extensively between 1949 and 1952. His blues appeared on a variety of labels under a variety of pseudonyms, including Birmingham Sam, Delta John, Texas Slim, Johnny Lee, John Williams, Boogie Man, and John Lee Booker. Modern released Hooker's classic "Crawlin' Kingsnake" in 1949 and his biggest hit, "I'm in the Mood," in 1951, but other Hooker material surfaced on the Regal, Gone, Staff, and Sensation labels. Despite the name deception, he never changed his sound. Always his guitar work was dark and Delta-laced and deceptively simple in structure. Hooker's guitar riffs were also supported by the rhythmic stomping of his feet, which gave many of his songs an increased intensity.

Hooker recorded for Chess from 1952 to about 1954; during this time he also toured with Muddy Waters and performed on his own. As in the past, he continued to record for other labels, despite his Chess connection. Hooker songs appeared on the Gotham, Savoy, and Specialty labels, among others. But the label Hooker was most associated with in the late '50s and early '60s was Vee-Jay Records. Hooker stayed with the label until 1964. Two of Hooker's best-known hits from this period, "Dimples" (1956) and "Boom Boom" (1962) had a profound effect on the British blues scene. Oddly, his influence abroad in the early '60s was stronger than it was in the U.S. where he had returned to a solo acoustic blues style in order to take advantage of the growing folk-blues revival going on in cities like New York and San Francisco and on many college campuses.

Hooker continued to record and perform extensively throughout the 1960s; he was at home in either an acoustic or electric format. He toured England and continental Europe in 1962, and performed at the Newport Folk Festival in 1960 and 1963 and at the Newport Jazz Festival in 1964. He returned to England and the Continent every year from 1964 to 1969, while back home in the States he played hip rock clubs like The Scene and Electric Circus in New York as more and more rock fans picked up on his blues.

Hooker left Detroit and moved to Oakland in 1970; that same year he cut the album *Hooker 'n' Heat* with blues-rock group Canned Heat and further solidified his standing with rock audiences. Hooker also continued to make his own records. From the early '70s came *Endless Boogie, Never Get Out of These Blues Alive*, and *Free Beer and Chicken*, to name just some of them. Much of the material on these albums was recycled songs or ideas and boogie rhythms that did little else except keep stores stocked with new John Lee Hooker vinyl.

By the late 1970s, Hooker seemed destined to fade into the blues woodwork. His sound had gone stale and interest in the blues was not yet what it would be later in the 1980s. But Hooker hung on, thanks to the continuous reissue of previously recorded material by labels such as Charly, GNP Crescendo, Chameleon, and Chess. In 1980 Hooker was inducted into the Blues Foundation's Hall of Fame.

Hooker's career continued to sag until 1989 when the Chameleon label released *The Healer*, an album of newly recorded material produced by Hooker's former guitarist Roy Rogers. *The Healer* included a guest appearance by longtime Hooker fan BONNIE RAITT, plus other cameos from Carlos Santana, ROBERT CRAY, George Thorogood, and others. To the surprise of Hooker and everyone else, *The Healer* not only sold better than any other Hooker album had and earned many enthusiastic reviews, but it also won a Grammy Award for best blues recording. Suddenly Hooker was hot. In early 1990 he was inducted into the Rock & Roll Hall of Fame. Later that year he was honored at a special tribute concert in New York's Madison Square Garden that featured Raitt, Joe Cocker, Huey Lewis, Ry Cooder, BO DIDDLEY, Mick Fleetwood, Gregg Allman, Al Kooper, Johnny Winter, Willie Dixon, ALBERT COLLINS, and others.

Before year's end, Hooker signed with Point Blank/Charisma Records, and for an encore he and Rogers cut *Mr. Lucky*, which, like its predecessor, was stocked with big-name guests (Collins, Cooder, Cray, Winter, Santana, Van Morrison, JOHN HAMMOND, JR., Keith Richards, and others). It, too, registered impressive sales and reviews, although on most tracks Hooker took a backseat to his admirers or else wasn't able to work up enough steam to get his husky vocals out in front of all the layers of instrumentation.

Hooker currently lives outside of Los Angeles. He continues to record and tour, and, with B.B. King, shares the honor of being elder statesman of the blues.

Essential Listening:
The Ultimate Collection: 1948–1990/Rhino (R2-70572)
The Hook/Chameleon (D2-74794)
John Lee Hooker Plays & Sings the Blues/Chess (MCA) (CHD 9199)
The Healer/Chameleon (74808-2)
The Real Folk Blues/MCA-Chess (CHD 9271)
That's My Story/Riverside (OBCCD 538-2)
Hooker 'N Heat/EMI (Liberty) (CDP 7-97896-2)
More Real Folk Blues and The Missing Album/MCA-Chess (CHD 9329)
Mr. Lucky/Point Blank–Charisma (91724-2)
The Best of John Lee Hooker/MCA-Chess (MCAD 10539)
Boom Boom/Point Blank–Charisma (86553)

◄ HOPKINS, LIGHTNIN'

(born Sam Hopkins, March 15, 1912, Centerville, Tex.; died January 30, 1982, Houston, Tex.)

Lightnin' Hopkins was a Texas blues great whose career spanned six decades and who, in all probability, made more recordings than any other blues artist. He was a prolific songwriter, a master raconteur, and a convincing performer. His guitar style, with its ragged rhythms and carefree collection of meter and structure, could never be considered conventional. But it did possess a remarkable durability and authenticity, and it almost always seemed the ideal vehicle to carry his songs and complement his dry, sagebrush-scratched vocals.

When it came to recording or performing, Hopkins often improvised with wit and humor. He made up verses as he went along, or else altered lyrics as he saw fit. Hopkins was, in the end, a tremendously important blues figure—one of the most influential country blues artists of the post–World War II period. In Texas only BLIND LEMON JEFFERSON and T-BONE WALKER have had as much impact on the state's blues legacy.

Hopkins was born in Centerville, Texas, and learned guitar from his older brother Joel, himself a blues musician. In 1920, when he was eight years old, Hopkins met and performed with Blind Lemon Jefferson at a country picnic. The opportunity to play alongside Jefferson left a profound mark on the young Hopkins. The incident so strengthened his desire to become a blues musician that by the time he was in his early teens he was accompanying his popular blues vocalist cousin, TEXAS ALEXANDER, at house parties and picnics and traveling all over East Texas. Hopkins continued to perform on and off with Alexander until the mid-'30s when Hopkins was sent to a prison work farm for an unknown offense.

Upon his release, Hopkins resumed his partnership with Alexander. They performed on Houston street corners and in small clubs, and periodically traveled to Mississippi and other southern states to play parties and juke joints. In 1946 a talent scout for Aladdin Records discovered the duo in Houston and offered them a recording contract. Hopkins followed up on the offer; Alexander didn't. When Hopkins cut his first songs later that year in Los Angeles, it was with Wilson "Thunder" Smith, a Houston pianist, not his cousin. During Hopkins's debut recording session, he was given the nickname "Lightnin' " and Aladdin billed the duo as Thunder and Lightnin' on its first releases.

Hopkins tasted success with the song "Katie May," which became a hit in the Southwest. Aladdin called Hopkins and Smith back to Los Angeles the following year to make more recordings. A second session later in 1947 was scheduled just with Hopkins. Given his erratic approach to singing and playing the blues, Hopkins was at his best when he performed with no accompaniment.

In all, Hopkins recorded forty-three sides for Aladdin. At the same time he was also making records for Gold Star in Houston, occasionally recording the exact same songs he cut in L.A. with Aladdin. During his career, Hopkins recorded for more than twenty labels, making his discography one of the longest and most complicated in blues history.

Hopkins recorded regularly from 1946 to 1954, cutting dozens of songs, not only with Aladdin and Gold Star but also with Mainstream, Mercury, Herald, and other labels. But because none of Hopkins's releases ever sold remarkably well, his first recording phase ended as interest in electric blues, particularly Chicago-made, picked up. Hopkins went back to playing Houston clubs and parties until he was rediscovered by blues historian and record producer Sam Charters in 1959. Under Charters's guidance, Hopkins resumed his recording career, this time cutting material for Folkways, Prestige/Bluesville, Arhoolie, and other labels in the 1960s.

Though Hopkins continued to work out of Houston and played there often, he broadened his popularity considerably during the folk-blues revival of the early '60s. In the year after meeting Charters, Hopkins went from playing small blues joints in Houston to sharing a bill at Carnegie Hall in New York with Pete Seeger and Joan Baez. His raw blues sound and narrative talents made him a popular performer on the concert and coffeehouse circuit and a regular at folk and blues festivals. In 1964 he toured with the American Folk Blues Festival package in England and continental Europe and afterwards returned to Carnegie Hall. The following year he was a featured performer at the Newport Folk Festival.

His simple, traditional interpretation of the blues influenced a number of white folk-blues artists. By the late 1960s, Hopkins's appeal had even begun to pour over into rock territory. For one Bay Area concert, Hopkins headlined over the popular acid-rock group Jefferson Airplane. At another he performed with the Grateful Dead. All along, Hopkins kept on recording for practically any label that would pay him cash up front.

Hopkins remained busy as both a recording and performing artist in the 1970s. He contributed to the soundtrack of the movie *Sounder* in 1972, appeared in a number of blues documentaries, played the New Orleans Jazz & Heritage Festival and Carnegie Hall again, toured Europe, recorded for the Sonet label, and continued to maintain his traditionalist blues style, even though interest in his brand of country blues had, by the late '70s, all but dried up. Hopkins was inducted into the Blues Foundation's Hall of Fame in 1980. He died of cancer in 1982.

Essential Listening:

The Complete Prestige/Bluesville Recordings/Prestige/Bluesville (7PCD 4406-2)
The Complete Aladdin Recordings/EMI (CDP 7-96843-2)
Lightnin' Hopkins/Smithsonian/Folkways (CD SF 40019)
Texas Blues/Arhoolie (CD 302)
The Herald Recordings—1954/Collectables (Col.-CD 5121)
The Lost Texas Tapes, Vol. 1–5/Collectables (Col. 5201, 5202, 5203, 5204, 5205)
Drinkin' in the Blues/Collectables (Col.-CD 5143)
Prison Blues/Collectables (Col.-CD 5144)
Mama and Papa Hopkins/Collectables (Col.-CD 5145)
Nothin' but the Blues/Collectables (Col.-CD 5146)
Mojo Hand/Collectables (Col.-CD 5111)
Houston's King of the Blues/Blues Classics (30)
The Gold Star Sessions, Vol. 1/Arhoolie (CD 330)
The Gold Star Sessions, Vol. 2/Arhoolie (CD 337)
Lightin' New York/Story of Blues (79010)
The Complete Candid Otis Spann/Lightnin' Hopkins Sessions/
  Mosaic Records (MD3-139)

◄ HORTON, BIG WALTER

(aka "Shakey" Horton) (born April 6, 1917, Horn Lake, Miss.; died December 8, 1981, Chicago, Ill.)

Big Walter "Shakey" Horton ranks with LITTLE WALTER Jacobs, SONNY BOY WILLIAMSON (Rice Miller), JUNIOR WELLS, and JAMES COTTON among the most influential harmonica stylists of Chicago's postwar blues scene. Of the five, Horton is the least celebrated, mostly because he made few recordings on his own during his most productive years, preferring the role of the consummate harp sideman. Horton's harmonica style was also more sweet-toned and less dependent on dynamics than the others. Often his solos seemed to soothe the soul rather than agitate it. Horton's creative harp riffs and warm, supple phrasing have graced records made by JOHNNY SHINES, WILLIE DIXON, and OTIS RUSH, among other noted post–World War II bluesmen.

Horton was born in Mississippi at the end of World War I but early on moved to Memphis with his mother. In the late 1920s he briefly performed and recorded with the MEMPHIS JUG BAND and worked the Southern dance and picnic circuit when he wasn't playing on Memphis street corners. Horton made his way to Chicago in the late 1940s but came back to Memphis to play on records released by Modern/RPM and Sun. Horton returned to Chicago in 1953 after accepting an invitation from longtime friend EDDIE TAYLOR to play in his band. Horton next found work in MUDDY WATERS's band, replacing harp player JUNIOR WELLS, who had been drafted. Horton played with Waters for about a year, then teamed up with Johnny Shines, JIMMY ROGERS, Otis Rush, and others in the recording studio and onstage in Chicago blues clubs. Horton can be heard on numerous Chess, Cobra, and States sides recorded in the 1950s. In the '60s Horton moved freely from Rogers and Shines to JOHNNY YOUNG and HOWLIN' WOLF.

Throughout the '70s Horton supplemented his blues club and recording work with regular appearances at folk and blues festivals, often with Willie Dixon's Chicago Blues All-Stars. In 1972 he recorded with fellow harp player CAREY BELL for Alligator Records. The resulting album, *Big Walter Horton with Carey Bell*, featured a number of harp duets between the student and his teacher. Horton continued to record occasionally until his death in 1981. He was inducted into the Blues Foundation's Hall of Fame a year later.

Essential Listening:
Big Walter Horton with Carey Bell/Alligator (4702)
Can't Keep Lovin' You/Blind Pig (1484)
Fine Cuts/Blind Pig (006-78)
Mouth Harp Maestro/Ace (CHD 252)
The Soul of the Blues Harmonica/Chess (9268)
Live at the El Mocambo/Red Lightnin' (RLCD 0088)

◄ HOUSE, SON

(born Eddie James, Jr., March 21, 1902, Riverton, Miss.; died October 19, 1988, Detroit, Mich.)

A major blues figure, Son House was one of the originators of the Mississippi Delta blues style. Along with CHARLEY PATTON and WILLIE BROWN, House defined early Delta blues in the late 1920s and 1930s with his irregular, often furious guitar work and his intensely emotional vocals. So profound was House's blues style that he was the main influence of the legendary bluesman ROBERT JOHNSON, as well as MUDDY WATERS.

House sang and played his guitar with compelling urgency and conviction. His brand of the blues was streaked with both preacher passion and raw, manly desires, which seemed to turn many of his songs into battles between good and evil, sin and redemption.

House was born on a Delta plantation. Early on he took up with the church and actually became a Baptist pastor by the time he turned twenty. But he straddled the sacred and secular worlds, which led to troubles with women and alcohol. He had also discovered the power of the blues. After spending time in Louisiana in the early 1920s, House returned to the Delta in 1926 and learned how to play guitar. He worked local juke joints and house parties until 1928, when he shot and killed a man, allegedly in self-defense. House was sent to Parchman Farm, an infamous Mississippi penitentiary, that year. A year later, a judge reexamined his case and ordered him released from prison.

House left Clarksdale for Lula, Mississippi, where he met Charley Patton and Willie Brown. He performed and traveled with them to Grafton, Wisconsin, in 1930, where all three blues guitarists recorded sides for the Paramount label. One of the songs House recorded, ''Preachin' the Blues,'' was a powerful, personalized account of how the blues stole his soul away from the Baptist church.

House continued to perform on occasion with Patton and Brown until Patton's death in 1934. For the remainder of his time in Mississippi, House worked jukes and dances with Brown and as a solo artist. In 1941, ALAN LOMAX recorded Son House for the Library of Congress. Lomax returned to Mississippi in 1942 and recorded House a second time. The following year House moved to Rochester, New York, and simply disappeared from the blues scene until 1964. Hailed as the greatest surviving original Delta bluesman, House became a hero to the young, white, folk-blues crowd of the early '60s. He performed at the 1964 Newport Folk Festival; a year later House played Carnegie Hall and signed a recording contract with CBS Records. His album *Father of the Folk Blues* (later renamed *Death Letter*) was a critical success and led to appearances at many of the major folk and blues festivals in the U.S. and Europe. In 1969 he was the subject of a blues documentary, called simply *Son House.*

By 1971 House fell into ill health. Although he did perform at the occasional festival in the early 1970s, his blues career had come to end. In 1976 he moved to Detroit. He was inducted into the Blues Foundation's Hall of Fame in 1980. Son House died in 1988.

Essential Listening:

*Delta Blues: The Original Library of Congress Sessions from Field
    Recordings 1941–1942*/Biograph (BCD 118 ADD)
Father of the Delta Blues: The Complete 1965 Sessions/Columbia (48867)
Death Letter/Edsel (EDCD 167)
Masters of the Delta Blues: The Friends of Charlie Patton/Yazoo (2002)

◄ HOWELL, PEG LEG

(born Josua Howell, March 5, 1888, Eatonton, Ga.; died August 11, 1966, Atlanta, Ga.)

An early and influential member of the Atlanta blues community in the 1920s, guitarist and singer Peg Leg Howell was also one of the first to record. His debut session occurred in 1926; it marked Columbia Records' entry into the country blues market. Howell's brand of blues was based on country dance and folk idioms and occasional rags, but he also recorded straight blues, incorporating finger-picking and slide guitar techniques into his guitar style.

Howell was raised in rural Georgia and taught himself how to play guitar. An argument with a brother-in-law in 1916 resulted in a gunshot wound to his leg, which led to amputation and his nickname, "Peg Leg." Unable to work as a farm laborer, Howell turned to music to earn a living. He drifted to Atlanta in the early 1920s, where he played street corners for spare change. Howell also got involved in bootlegging at this time. In 1925 he was arrested for selling liquor and spent a year in prison. When he was released, Howell returned to busking in Atlanta. A Columbia Records scout heard Howell in 1926 and offered him a recording contract. For his first recording session Howell cut "New Prison Blues," a tune he had learned while incarcerated. The song sold enough copies for Columbia to send Howell back into the recording studio the following year.

Howell continued to record until 1929. In addition to solo sides, he cut songs with his street group, Peg Leg Howell and His Gang, which included second guitarist Henry Williams and fiddle player Eddie Anthony. "Beaver Slide Rag," an uptempo dance number recorded in 1927, was the group's only semblance of a hit. After Howell's recording career ended, he resorted to playing with Williams and Anthony on Decatur Street, Atlanta's famed blues street, for tips. After Williams's incarceration (he eventually died in prison) and Anthony's death in 1934, Howell gradually withered from the city's blues scene. In 1952, as a result of diabetes, he lost his second leg. Howell lived in obscurity until 1963 when he was rediscovered and recorded for the Testament label. He died in 1966.

Essential Listening:
Peg Leg Howell, Vol. 1/Matchbox (221)
Peg Leg Howell, Vol. 2/Matchbox (205)

◄ HOWLIN' WOLF

(born Chester Arthur Burnett, June 10, 1910, West Point, Miss.; died January 10, 1976, Hines, Ill.)

Howlin' Wolf was possibly the most electrifying performer in modern blues history and a recording artist whose only rivals among his contemporaries were SONNY BOY WILLIAMSON (Rice Miller), LITTLE WALTER, and MUDDY WATERS. Like these artists, Wolf was a dean of electric Chicago blues during the genre's heyday in the 1950s and early 1960s. A large, intimidating man who stood well over six feet tall and weighed close to three hundred pounds, Wolf's gripping histrionics and sheer physical intensity gave new meaning to the blues nearly every time he performed. He would jump about the stage like an angry man trying to work off dangerous steam, or wriggle on the floor as if he was in unbearable pain, or whoop and howl and hoot like someone who had succumbed to the worst of demons. Wolf acted out his most potent blues; he became the living embodiment of its most powerful forces.

Musically, Wolf was an amalgam of blues styles. His originality lay in the way he crafted all his influences into one invigorating form. He learned how to play guitar by watching and listening to CHARLEY PATTON, from whom he also picked up valuable performing pointers (Patton was known to accent his perform-ances with all kinds of pre–rock & roll showmanship). Wolf was taught how to play harmonica by none other than Sonny Boy Williamson (Rice Miller) after the harp player had married Wolf's half-sister. Finally, Wolf learned the art of ex-panding the range of his cracked, gruff voice with yodels and moans from the likes of TOMMY JOHNSON and the blues-influenced country singer JIMMIE RODG-ERS. When Wolf merged all of these elements and projected them from his mas-sive frame, the results could stir even the most passive or skeptical listener.

That Wolf didn't begin to record until the onset of middle age gave him plenty of time to absorb the meaning of the blues. He spent his first forty or so years balancing the life of a bluesman with that of a farmer. He knew better than many of the celebrated blues artists who came after him, of the unbreakable bond the blues had with the land and the labor that went into working it, especially in the Delta.

Though Wolf played both guitar and harp, he was a master of neither. He also was a traditionalist who refused to let his blues change with the times and grow into something it hadn't been when he began playing back in the late 1920s. But in the end, Wolf demonstrated again and again that his blues was a timeless form that could transcend styles and eras without growing moss or sounding stale.

Wolf was born Chester Arthur Burnett, named after the late–nineteenth century American president. He was nicknamed "Howlin' Wolf" as a child, supposedly a reflection of his mischievous behavior. Wolf learned of the blues early in his life; Charley Patton and WILLIE BROWN, in particular, often played plantation picnics and area juke joints that Wolf frequented. After Wolf picked up the guitar, he began playing those same places. Throughout the late 1920s and 1930s, Wolf tilled the land on his father's farm during the week and on weekends sang the blues. He often played guitar and harmonica simultaneously, using a harmonica rack to keep the instrument close to his mouth, and, on occasion, he shared performance time with ROBERT JOHNSON, ROBERT JR. LOCKWOOD, and Tommy Johnson, as well as Patton and Brown.

Wolf served in the army during World War II. When he returned to Mississippi in 1945, he resumed farming and performing blues locally. But Wolf itched for an opportunity to record and take his blues beyond the Delta. In 1948 he moved to West Memphis, Arkansas, just across the river from Memphis, Tennessee, and put together a band that, at different times, included harmonica players JAMES COTTON and JUNIOR PARKER and guitarists PAT HARE, MATT "GUITAR" MURPHY, and Willie Johnson, and secured a slot on local radio station KWEM playing blues and endorsing agriculture equipment.

IKE TURNER, at the time a record scout for Memphis producer SAM PHILLIPS, heard Howlin' Wolf and recommended that Phillips record Wolf. Wolf went into the studio with Phillips in 1951 and recorded two songs, "Moanin' at Midnight" and "How Many More Years." The tunes were leased to Chess Records, who released them in 1952.

Wolf cut other material for Phillips, which Phillips farmed out to Chess and

RPM (a subsidiary of Modern Records). A grapple for the rights to Wolf's best sides was eventually won by Chess. In 1953 Howlin' Wolf moved to Chicago and called the city home for the rest of his life. Almost at once he began to compete with Chess's mainstay, Muddy Waters, for the songs of WILLIE DIXON, whose prolific output kept Waters and other bluesmen on the Chess roster well stocked with material. From Dixon, Wolf got and recorded classics like "Spoonful," "Little Red Rooster," "Evil," "Back Door Man," and "I Ain't Superstitious." Although Wolf wasn't considered a great blues composer, he wrote "Moanin' at Midnight," "Smokestack Lightning," and "Killing Floor," as well as a number of other tunes.

The competition between Wolf and Waters extended beyond Dixon's songs and remained with them into the '60s and '70s. Wolf was a suspicious man who seemed to measure people by how threatening they were to him. Like Waters, Wolf was also a proud man who found it hard to shake hands with his chief rival. Some blues historians have suggested that the competition that existed between them actually forced both Waters and Wolf to rise to great blues heights.

In the early '60s, Wolf played overseas with the American Blues Festival package and regularly performed in noted Chicago clubs. In 1965 he appeared on the American rock television show "Shindig" with the ROLLING STONES. Throughout the rest of the decade, Wolf strengthened his ties with rock, culminating with a rock-sounding album released in 1969 called *The Howlin' Wolf Album*, followed by another, *The London Howlin' Wolf Sessions*, recorded in England in 1970 with guitarist ERIC CLAPTON, bass player Bill Wyman and drummer Charlie Watts of the Rolling Stones, Beatles drummer Ringo Starr, and other British rock stalwarts.

By the early 1970s Howlin' Wolf was beginning to slow down. He had already suffered a heart attack, and an auto accident in 1970 caused irreparable damage to his kidney and necessitated frequent dialysis treatments. Despite ill health, Howlin' Wolf continued to record and perform. In 1972 he recorded a live album, *Live and Cookin' At Alice's Revisited*, at the Chicago club. He also cut a second "London" album, *London Revisited*, with Muddy Waters, and another studio album, *Back Door Wolf*, which included the songs "Watergate Blues" and the autobiographical "Moving." Wolf's last performance was in Chicago with B.B. KING in November of 1975. Two months later he died of kidney failure. Howlin' Wolf was inducted into Blues Foundation's Hall of Fame in 1980 and the Rock & Roll Hall of Fame in 1991.

Essential Listening:
Howlin' Wolf (box set)/MCA-Chess (CHC3-9332)
Memphis Days: The Definition Edition, Vol. 1/Bear Family (BCD 15460)
Memphis Days, Vol. II/Bear Family (BCD 15500)
Moanin' in the Moonlight/MCA-Chess (CHD 5908)
The Real Folk Blues/MCA-Chess (9273)
More Real Folk Blues/MCA-Chess (9279)
The London Howlin' Wolf Sessions/MCA-Chess (9297)
Change My Way/MCA-Chess (93001)

◄ HUGHES, JOE "GUITAR"

(born September 29, 1937, Houston, Tex.)

A Houston-based guitarist strongly influenced by T-BONE WALKER, Joe Hughes spent most of his career backing up more noted Texas bluesmen like BOBBY "BLUE" BLAND and AL "TNT" BRAGGS before launching his solo career in 1989. Hughes's debut album, *If You Want to See the Blues*, was released that year on the Black Top label.

Hughes spent his formative years listening to records by Walker and CLARENCE "GATEMOUTH" BROWN and watching his Houston neighbor JOHNNY "GUITAR" WATSON perform. Hughes formed his first band, the Dukes of Rhythm, in 1953. The group included second guitarist JOHNNY COPELAND and worked Houston blues clubs and dances. In the '60s Hughes played with GRADY GAINES and the Upsetters, then with Bland, with whom he also recorded, and finally with Al Braggs. During the '70s and most of the '80s, Hughes worked locally in Houston. Since his record deal and the release of *If You Want to See the Blues*, Hughes has toured extensively, often performing with Gaines and the Upsetters as part of blues festival packages.

Essential Listening:
If You Want to See the Blues/Black Top (BT 1050)

◄ HUMES, HELEN

(born June 23, 1913, Louisville, Ky.; died September 13, 1981, Santa Monica, Calif.)

Helen Humes was a blues and pop singer best known for her work with the COUNT BASIE Band in the late 1930s and early '40s. Humes usually shared the microphone with blues shouter JIMMY RUSHING and handled the band's mellower tunes and ballads. Together, they helped make the Basie band one of the best of the swing era.

Humes was born into a middle-class black family in Louisville, Kentucky. After formal piano and vocal lessons, Humes was discovered at age fourteen by blues guitarist Sylvester Weaver, who took her to St. Louis to record in 1927. Her recording debut featured LONNIE JOHNSON on guitar. Other recording sessions followed in New York, but little came of them. Humes continued to sing in New York cabarets until 1938, when legendary talent scout John Hammond heard her and was so impressed with her vocal clarity that he coaxed her into joining the Count Basie Band, taking the place of Billie Holiday, who had recently left for a solo career. (A year earlier Basie himself had offered Humes the job, but she'd turned him down.)

From 1938 to 1942, Humes toured and recorded with the Basie Band, playing in the now legendary 1938 Hammond-produced "From Spirituals to Swing" concert at Carnegie Hall in New York City and crisscrossing the U.S. in a flurry of one-night stands. Humes left the Basie band in 1942 to work as a solo act. She often headlined the Cafe Society club in New York before going to California in 1944 and singing with Norman Granz's Jazz at the Philharmonic orchestra into the early '50s. Humes also recorded soundtracks for such films as *Panic in the Streets* and *My Blue Heaven*. In the mid-'50s she sang with vibraphonist Red Norvo's band and continued to record, while in the early '60s she was a featured artist with the American Folk Blues Festival package that toured Europe and included T-BONE WALKER and JOHN LEE HOOKER, among other blues greats. But by the mid-'60s Humes's career had practically dried up, and she moved back to Louisville to be with her family.

In 1973 Humes was invited to perform at the Newport Jazz Festival, and her well-received set revived her career. Later that year she toured Europe and recorded the album *Helen Comes Back* for the French Black and Blue label. She continued to tour and perform and released her final album, *Helen*, in 1981, the same year she died of cancer.

Essential Listening:
Be-Baba-Leba: The Rhythm and Blues Years/Savoy (SJL 1159)
Count Basie: The Complete Decca Recordings/GRP-Decca (GRD 3-611)

◄ HUNTER, ALBERTA

(born April 1, 1895, Memphis, Tenn.; died October 17, 1984, New York, N.Y.)

In the 1920s singer Alberta Hunter helped bridge the gap between classic blues and cabaret flavored pop music. In the process, she and other singers like LUCILLE HEGAMIN, ETHEL WATERS, and EDITH WILSON introduced white audiences to the emotional vigor of the blues. Thanks to her vocal versatility and her urbane delivery, which accented her warm, engaging vibrato, Hunter's career extended far beyond the classic blues era of the 1920s. She continued to record and perform as a blues-based cabaret singer until her self-imposed retirement in the 1950s. But then in 1977, at the ripe age of eighty-two, she began a comeback of sorts, mostly performing in New York clubs like the Cookery in Greenwich Village until her death in 1984 at the age of eighty-eight.

Hunter was born in Memphis, Tennessee. At age twelve she ran away to Chicago where she began her singing career. At first most of her work was in flop joints and seedy saloons. Gradually, however, she made her way up the performing ladder, ultimately singing in Chicago's leading cabarets, before moving to New York in 1921 and launching her recording career.

Hunter recorded for the Black Swan label upon arriving in New York. But in 1922 she switched to Paramount, for which she recorded much of her best material. Hunter wrote many of the songs she recorded; one of them, ''Down Hearted Blues,'' was a big hit for blues great BESSIE SMITH in 1923. Smith had heard Hunter's version of the tune and decided to make it her first recording. Hunter's connection to Bessie Smith didn't stop there. In 1923 Hunter replaced Smith in the *How Come?* revue, then playing at Harlem's Apollo Theater. Hunter's stint in the revue brought her much-needed recognition in New York and enabled her to go on to a flourishing career as a cabaret singer.

Throughout the remainder of the 1920s Hunter recorded on the Biltmore label under the pseudonym Alberta Prime; on the Gennett label as Josephine Beatty; and on the Okeh, Victor, and Columbia labels under her own name. Her live performances were as important to the definition of good classic blues as were her best late-'20s records, namely, "Your Jelly Roll Is Good," "Sugar," "Beale Street Blues," and "Take That Thing Away." In 1927 she performed in England and continental Europe, working into her repertoire jazz and show standards to go with her blues and pop songs. In the '30s she went overseas on a number of occasions, playing clubs and performing in concert in Western Europe as well as the Middle East and Russia. At home she performed at the Cotton Club in Harlem and appeared with LOUIS ARMSTRONG and the Teddy Hill Band.

During World War II, Hunter spent much time abroad entertaining troops in China, Burma, India, Korea, and Europe under the auspices of the USO. After the war she continued to work in U.S. and Canadian clubs before retiring from the stage in 1956. In the early '60s she recorded for the Prestige/Bluesville, Riverside, and Folkways labels.

In 1977, Hunter's reappearance on the New York cabaret scene led to a new recording contract with Columbia Records. Hunter continued to perform up until the time of her death.

Essential Listening:
Young Alberta Hunter/Jass (CD 6)
Amtrak Blues/Columbia (PC 36430)
With Lovie Austin and Her Blues Serenaders/Original Blues Classic (510)
The Blues, 1923 to 1933 (Various Artists)/ABC (836 046-2)

◄ HUNTER, IVORY JOE

(born October 10, 1914, Weirgate, Tex.; died November 8, 1974, Memphis, Tenn.)

Pianist and singer Ivory Joe Hunter was a prolific songwriter and recording artist, specializing in pop-tinted rhythm & blues ballads in the 1940s and 1950s. When interest in rhythm & blues waned in the 1960s, he switched to country music.

Hunter learned how to play piano as a youth and was performing professionally in the Beaumont, Texas, area by his midteens. In 1933 he recorded under the name Ivory Joe White for the Library of Congress. But it wasn't until he migrated to California in 1942 that his career began to take shape. He started his own record label, Ivory Records, in Oakland in 1945. It folded shortly after its inception, and Hunter went on to help create Pacific Records, for which he also recorded.

Hunter performed with his own R&B combo up and down the coast and recorded for the Excelsior, 4-Star, and King labels in the late 1940s before signing with MGM Records in 1949. He had big hits in 1950 with "I Almost Lost My Mind" and "I Need You So," which went to number 1 and 2, respectively, on the R&B charts. Hunter charted with additional MGM records until 1954 when he switched to Atlantic. He continued to score on the charts with such hits as "Since I Met You Baby" (1956), "Empty Arms" (1957), and "Yes I Want You" (1958).

The decline of rhythm & blues and Hunter's interest in country music led him to Nashville in the early '60s. There he worked as a country songwriter and performed with the Grand Ole Opry. In 1970 he attempted a recording comeback with the album *The Return of Ivory Joe Hunter* on the Epic label. The album attracted some attention, but Hunter's health stopped his comeback plans. He was diagnosed with cancer and died from the disease in 1974.

Essential Listening:
Sixteen of His Greatest Hits/King (KCD 605)
Seventh Street Boogie/Route 66 (KIX 4)
Jumping at the Dew Drop Inn/Route 66 (KIX 15)

◄ HURT, MISSISSIPPI JOHN

(born July 3, 1893, Teoc, Miss.; died November 2, 1966, Grenada, Miss.)

Mississippi John Hurt was a songster whose repertoire included a caressing, gentle version of the blues, handed-down folk songs, light rags, and ballads. Apart from a brief recording career in the late 1920s, Hurt lived nearly all of his life in obscurity until being rediscovered by folk fan Tom Hoskins in 1963. During the three years before his death in 1966, Hurt performed his soft-spoken, finger picked blues and folk tunes at college coffeehouses and numerous festivals, including the Newport Folk Festival (1963 to 1965). A favorite with the early-'60s folk crowd, who were touched by his untroubled voice and equally tranquil guitar picking, Hurt also appeared on national television, performed in the blues documentary *This Hour Has Seven Days*, and recorded three albums for Vanguard Records.

Hurt was raised in Mississippi, where he taught himself how to play guitar. He worked as a farmhand and often performed at local dances and socials. Hurt was discovered by an Okeh Records talent scout in 1928 and sent to Memphis and New York where he recorded thirteen sides, only seven of which were ever released. Hurt returned to Mississippi where he continued to do farm work and occasional performances in the Avalon area until age seventy-one, when Hoskins found him.

Hurt was a major influence on the many folk artists who came of age in the early 1960s. Everyone from Bob Dylan down has paid tribute to Hurt's inventive finger-picking technique and his humble brand of blues.

Essential Listening:
1928 Sessions/Yazoo (1065)
The Best of Mississippi John Hurt/Vanguard (VCD 19/20)
Today!/Vanguard (VMD 79220)
Last Sessions/Vanguard (VMD 79327)

◄ HUTTO, J.B.

(born Joseph Benjamin Hutto, April 29, 1926, Blackville, S.C.; died June 12, 1983, Harvey, Ill.)

J.B. Hutto was a rough-hewn Chicago slide guitarist and singer whose riveting style can be traced to his main influence, ELMORE JAMES. Like fellow slide guitarist and contemporary HOUND DOG TAYLOR, Hutto cared more about the emotional impact of his music than refining his screeching slide solos or his husky, down-home vocals. During the late '60s and early '70s, Hutto's gripping guitar work reminded blues fans that just because the blues had become urbanized didn't mean the music had to sacrifice its grit or primal drive.

Born in South Carolina and raised in Georgia, Hutto's first musical encounter was with gospel. He played the drums and piano before he picked up the guitar, so that when he and his family relocated to Chicago in 1949 with the hope of finding better employment opportunities, Hutto found work as a drummer with a local bar band, Johnny Ferguson and His Twisters. Eventually Hutto quit the band to form his own group, the Hawks, which played basement parties and occasional clubs. Lack of success prompted Hutto to dissolve the band and leave the music business in the mid-'50s.

Inspired by the searing slide sounds of Elmore James, Hutto returned to the blues in the mid-'60s and signed a recording contract with the Vanguard label. Hutto also recorded for Delmark Records. Two of his Delmark releases, *Hawk Squat* (1968) and *Slidewinder* (1973), contain his most inspired guitar work.

Throughout the '70s, Hutto performed in blues clubs and at blues and folk festivals in the U.S. and recorded for a variety of small independent labels. Before Hutto died, he passed along some of his slide guitar secrets to his nephew, Ed Williams, aka LIL' ED WILLIAMS, the leader of Lil' Ed and the Blues Imperials. Hutto was inducted into the Blues Foundation's Hall of Fame in 1985, two years after his death.

Essential Listening:
Hawk Squat/Delmark (DD 617)
Slidewinder/Delmark (DD 636)
Slideslinger/Varrick (003)
J.B. Hutto and the Hawks/Testament (2213)

I

▶

◄ IGLAUER, BRUCE

(born July 10, 1947, Ann Arbor, Mich.)

The owner of Alligator Records, Bruce Iglauer had as much to do with the 1980s blues revival as any one artist. Iglauer, a self-professed blues fanatic, built his record company with not only business acumen but a zeal for the artists he signed and the blues he helped them create in the recording studio. In the label's first twenty years, Alligator artists have won more than two dozen Grammy nominations, close to fifty W.C. HANDY Awards, and other distinctions from the music industry. Its 1985 Grammy Award–winning album *Showdown!*, with ROBERT CRAY, ALBERT COLLINS, and JOHNNY COPELAND, has sold over a quarter million units. No other contemporary blues label has come close to matching Alligator's commercial and critical success.

A native of Cincinnati, Iglauer moved to Chicago in 1970 to work as a shipping clerk for Delmark Records and be closer to the city's blues scene. Discovering HOUND DOG TAYLOR playing in a small Chicago bar called Florence's and falling for Taylor's raw blues sound, Iglauer approached Delmark owner Bob Koester about recording Taylor and his band, the HouseRockers. When Koester refused, Iglauer set out to record Taylor himself and, in the process, set up his own record company. Calling his living-room label Alligator, Iglauer recorded Hound Dog Taylor and the HouseRockers and became the band's manager.

Iglauer built his label slowly, releasing just nine albums in seven years. But in 1978 Alligator released seven, including critically acclaimed works by blues guitar great Albert Collins (*Ice Pickin'*) and singer KOKO TAYLOR (*The Earthshaker*). By the end of the year, Alligator had earned six Grammy nominations—one each for nearly half of its records.

In the early '80s Iglauer brought increased respect to Alligator when he released an album (*I'm Here*) by zydeco king CLIFTON CHENIER and signed blues guitarists JOHNNY WINTER and SON SEALS and harmonica player JAMES COTTON. Alligator's big breakthrough came in 1985 with the release of *Showdown!*, judged by many blues critics to be one of the top blues albums of the decade. The latter half of the '80s saw Alligator enlarge its roster considerably. Iglauer released albums by such highly regarded contemporary blues acts as LIL' ED [WILLIAMS] and the Blues Imperials, LUCKY PETERSON, the KINSEY REPORT, WILLIAM CLARKE, and SAFFIRE—THE UPPITY BLUES WOMEN.

In 1991 Alligator was honored at the Chicago Blues Festival, and Iglauer released a double-disc anthology that documented the label's history, called *The Alligator Records 20th Anniversary Collection*. Alligator continues to operate at the vanguard of contemporary blues.

Essential Listening:

The Alligator Records 20th Anniversary Collection/Alligator (ALCD 105/6)

J ▶

◀ JACKSON, BULLMOOSE

(born Benjamin Jackson, 1919, Cleveland, Ohio; died July 31, 1989, Cleveland, Ohio)

A singer and saxophonist, Bullmoose Jackson was a member of the LUCKY MILLINDER Orchestra in the early 1940s before beginning a solo career in 1947. He helped make rhythm & blues popular during the decade with his wailing vocals and honking sax solos.

Jackson was born in Cleveland. While in high school in the 1930s, he formed the Harlem Hotshots. By 1943 he was singing with Millinder's Orchestra, replacing WYNONIE HARRIS. Jackson continued to work with Millinder through the war years. But with the rise of R&B, Jackson left Millinder, buttressed by his 1946 hit, "I Know Who Threw the Whiskey in the Well . . ." Released on the Queen label, the song reached number 4 on the R&B charts that year.

The following year Jackson had his first number 1 hit with "I Love You, Yes I Do" on the King label. The record's success led to a number of other late '40s R&B hits for Jackson, including "I Can't Go on Without You," which hit number 1 in 1948 and made Jackson, along with LOUIS JORDAN, ROY MILTON, BIG JOE TURNER, and Harris, one of the biggest stars in rhythm & blues.

Although the hits dried up for Jackson after 1949, he continued to perform, often with R&B package shows, before retiring from music in the mid-1950s. Jackson worked at Howard University in Washington, D.C., until he was coaxed back into performing by the Pittsburgh bar band the Flashcats. Jackson worked with the band from 1983 to 1986 and recorded *Moosemania!* with the Flashcats on the Bogus label. Jackson died in 1989.

Essential Listening:
Big Fat Mamas Are Back in Style Again/Route 66 (KIX 14)
Moose on the Loose/Saxophonograph (BP 506)

◀ JACKSON, JIM

(born 1890, Hernando, Miss.; died 1937, Hernando, Miss.)

Although singer-guitarist Jim Jackson was best known for his song "Kansas City Blues," which was one of the biggest-selling blues records of the 1920s (it reputedly sold close to a million copies), much of his repertoire was made up of minstrel and pop songs, rags, and novelty numbers.

Jackson was born in Mississippi, where he taught himself how to play guitar.

He spent most of his youth working with minstrel and medicine shows in the South, ultimately winding up in Memphis in the early 1920s, where he fell in with the city's bluesmen. Jackson often worked the city's street corners for spare change with GUS CANNON and WILL SHADE. He began his recording career in 1927 with the Vocalion label. The success of Jackson's debut release, "Jim Jackson's Kansas City Blues" (later shortened to "Kansas City Blues"), made him a star and enabled him to continue recording through 1930, occasionally with pianist SPECKLED RED.

When Jackson performed, he blended tall tales and roguish humor with his blues and minstrel songs. He continued to travel with minstrel or medicine shows until his death in 1937.

Essential Listening:
Jim Jackson, 1928–1930/Blues Documents (BD-613)

◄ JACKSON, JOHN

(born February 25, 1924, Woodville, Va.)

An elder on the Washington, D.C., blues scene, John Jackson is one of the last remaining songsters whose guitar style and song repertoire are a potpourri of blues, rag, folk, country, and old ballads. Although his popularity is based primarily in the Southeast, Jackson has toured in Europe, played numerous folk and blues festivals, and has recorded a batch of albums that depict his traditional folk-blues slant.

Born in Virginia, Jackson learned to play guitar and banjo as a child by listening to old 78s by artists like BLIND BLAKE, picking up tidbits from his father, a country blues guitarist, and learning from itinerant musicians. Eventually Jackson began to play house parties and picnics in Rappahannock County. However, despite his development as a songster and his warm, affable delivery, Jackson was not able to devote all his time to music. His desire to remain in Virginia and not take to the road inhibited whatever big-time musical ambitions he had. In 1950 Jackson moved to Fairfax, Virginia, where he worked as a gravedigger during the week and on weekends played in local clubs and at social functions.

During the folk-blues revival in the '60s, Jackson was recorded by Arhoolie Records. One album he cut for the label, *John Jackson in Europe*, was recorded in Germany in 1969. Jackson continued to perform and occasionally record in the '70s and '80s. Two of his albums, *Step It Up & Go* and *Deep in the Bottom*, came out on the Rounder label. Jackson still performs, playing mostly blues and folk festivals on the Eastern Seaboard.

Essential Listening:
Blues and Country Dance Songs from Virginia/Arhoolie (1025)
More Blues and Country Dance Songs/Arhoolie (1035)
John Jackson in Europe/Arhoolie (1047)
Step It Up & Go/Rounder (2019)
Deep in the Bottom/Rounder (2032)

◄ JACKSON, LIL' SON

(born Melvin Jackson, August 17, 1916, Tyler, Tex.; died May 30, 1976, Dallas, Tex.)

Part of the post–World War II Texas blues scene, country bluesman Lil' Son Jackson recorded for the Gold Star and Imperial labels and was a regional blues favorite until he retired from performing and recording in 1955. Jackson learned how to play blues guitar by listening to the records of BLIND LEMON JEFFERSON, LONNIE JOHNSON, and TEXAS ALEXANDER. He sang occasionally at house parties and family get-togethers, and formed a group, the Blue Eagle Four, in the late 1930s. But it wasn't until after he had served in the army during World War II that he considered a career in music.

In 1946 Jackson cut a cheap demo and sent it to Bill Quinn, owner of the Houston-based Gold Star label, who gave Jackson a contract. One of the songs Jackson recorded for Gold Star, "Freedom Train Blues," made it into the R&B top 10 in 1948. Quinn wanted Jackson to remain a country blues solo performer, but Jackson, hoping to capitalize on the growing popularity of rhythm & blues, sought to build a band around his sound. Their differences caused Jackson to leave Gold Star and sign with Imperial in 1950, with whom he recorded until 1954. That year Jackson suffered serious injuries in an auto crash. Following his recuperation, he retired from performing and recording and went back to work as an auto mechanic, the job he'd had before the war years.

In 1960 producer Chris Strachwitz coaxed Jackson out of retirement and convinced him to record a self-titled album for Strachwitz's Arhoolie label. Jackson also recorded for Houston producer Roy Ames in 1963, but little came of the session and Jackson eventually went back into retirement. Jackson died of cancer in 1976.

Essential Listening:
Lil' Son Jackson/Arhoolie (F 1004)
Texas Blues: Bill Quinn's Gold Star Recordings (Various Artists)/Arhoolie (352)

◄ JACKSON, PAPA CHARLIE

(born c. 1890, New Orleans, La.; died c. 1938, Chicago, Ill.)

Papa Charlie Jackson was one of the first country blues artists to make a record and the first to achieve significant commercial success. In 1924 he cut "Papa's Lawdy Lawdy Blues" and "Airy Man Blues" for the Paramount label and, in the process, ended the domination of recorded blues by female artists, which had begun in 1920 with MAMIE SMITH. Unlike other bluesmen, who accompanied themselves on guitar or piano, Jackson played a banjo—more precisely, a six-stringed version, which he strummed and picked like a guitar. His bawdy and humorous tunes were early versions of what soon became known as hokum blues.

Almost nothing is known of Jackson's life other than that he came from New Orleans and most likely worked with minstrel and vaudeville shows throughout the South in the early 1900s. Sometime around 1919 or 1920, he settled in Chicago and began playing on Maxwell Street for tips. He is reputed to have taught BIG BILL BROONZY how to play guitar. In 1924 he was discovered by a Paramount Record scout who set up a recording session with Jackson in Grafton, Wisconsin. His first record sold well enough, especially with rural record buyers, that Paramount requested others. In all, Jackson is said to have recorded more than sixty sides. He also worked with MA RAINEY, IDA COX, and BLIND BLAKE. Jackson remained in Chicago in the 1930s, playing street corners, clubs, and house parties. He is believed to have died around 1938.

Essential Listening:
Fat Mouth/Yazoo (1029)

◀ JACKSON, WILLIS "GATOR"

(aka Gator Tail Jackson) (born April 25, 1932, Miami, Fla.; died October 25, 1987)

Saxophonist Willis "Gator" Jackson helped bridge the gaps separating rhythm & blues, soul, and jazz in the 1950s and '60s. After attending Florida A&M, Jackson came to New York in 1948 and joined the Cootie Williams band, with whom he recorded a year later. During the session Jackson, the featured soloist, cut "Gator Tail, Parts One and Two," which launched his career and gave him his nickname.

Jackson's tenor sax style featured the kind of hot, honking solos that made rhythm & blues popular in the post–World War II years. His link to R&B was solidified after he married singer Ruth Brown in the early '50s and played on a number of her hit records. Jackson also signed his own recording contract with Atlantic, Brown's label, though he never matched his wife's recording success.

With the decline of rhythm & blues in the '60s, Jackson moved into soul-jazz and began a recording relationship with the Prestige label that lasted until 1971. In all, Jackson recorded some twenty-five albums for Prestige. During the '70s and early '80s Jackson continued to record and perform, often touring in Europe and working with Richard "Groove" Holmes in New York and New Jersey clubs. Jackson died in 1987.

Essential Listening:
Call of the Gator/Delmark (DD-460)

◀ JAMES, ELMORE

(born Elmore Brooks, January 27, 1918, Richland, Miss.; died May 24, 1963, Chicago, Ill.)

A disciple of ROBERT JOHNSON, Elmore James was the single most important slide guitar stylist of the post–World War II period. Not only did James significantly affect the course of slide guitar blues, but he also had a profound influence on a generation of blues-rock guitarists who sought to imitate his frenzied, emotional sound. Everyone from ERIC CLAPTON and Peter Green in England, to Duane Allman and JOHNNY WINTER in the States was moved by James's slide technique and the way he incorporated it into a hard-driving, hard-rocking blues format.

In addition to his slide guitar skills, James was also a stirring singer and songwriter. He often shouted when he sang so as to match the soaring qualities of his guitar work. Although James was never very comfortable in the studio, his recordings of original songs such as "Shake Your Money Maker" and "Done Somebody Wrong" were some of the best rocking blues ever heard. He also was a slow blues master; in two certified classics, TAMPA RED's "It Hurts Me Too" and his own "The Sky Is Crying," James filled both his guitar work and vocals with layers of scorched, sorrowful passion.

But it was with the Robert Johnson tune "I Believe I'll Dust My Broom" (which James re-invented and shortened to "Dust My Broom") that James made his biggest mark in the blues. Throughout his eleven-year recording career, which stretched from 1952 to his death in 1963, James recorded a number of similar-sounding songs, all built on the distinctive slide salvos learned from Johnson and used in "Dust My Broom." Songs such as "I Believe," "Dust My Blues," and "Wild About You Baby" were little more than takes on "Dust My Broom."

James was born into a Mississippi Delta sharecropping family. He taught himself the rudiments of the blues on a one-string homemade guitar and was playing juke joints around the Belzoni area when he met Robert Johnson sometime around 1937. Johnson died a year later, but he left an indelible mark on James, who made Johnson's slide guitar technique the most important element in his own style. At this time James also became friends with SONNY BOY WILLIAMSON (Rice Miller). The two bluesmen began performing together; James often played guitar behind Sonny Boy during his radio broadcasts and on his earliest recordings, as well as in Delta jukes.

In 1943 James served in the Pacific theater with the U.S. Navy. Upon his discharge in 1945, he returned to the Delta and formed one of the very first electric blues bands there, while MUDDY WATERS was doing the same up in Chicago. In 1952 James recorded "Dust My Broom" for the Mississippi-based Trumpet Records. James's bristling slide guitar work and knotty vocals enabled the song to become the fledgling label's first hit and one of the biggest records on the R&B charts that year.

The song's success led other record companies to offer James recording contracts. After considerable pressing by Joe Bihari, James agreed to go to Chicago and record for the BIHARI BROTHERS' Meteor Records, a subsidiary of the popular Modern label. James formed a Chicago band, the Broomdusters, at this time, which included pianist JOHNNY JONES, drummer ODIE PAYNE, JR., sax player J.T. Brown, and, on occasion, second guitarist-bassist HOMESICK JAMES (a cousin) or guitarist EDDIE TAYLOR.

While living in Chicago, James periodically returned to the Delta, which enabled him to keep in touch with the region's more rough-edged blues and at the same time, unintentionally, made James a bridge between urban Chicago and rural Delta blues. Despite his popularity in both blues centers and his riveting sound, James never matched the success enjoyed by Muddy Waters during the postwar period. One reason was his inability to secure a long-standing contract with a recording company such as Chess (for whom Waters and most other noted '50s Chicago bluesmen recorded) that could get his music heard beyond the Windy

City and the Delta. Another reason might have been the repetitive quality of his sound. Despite the muscular intensity of his material, many of his songs possessed a sameness that could, on occasion, dull the senses.

Despite these disadvantages, James was able to record some of his best songs in the last couple of years before his death. "The Sky Is Crying" was recorded in 1959 and "Done Somebody Wrong" in 1961, both for New York–based Fire Records. James, in fact, was still at the peak of his career when he died in Chicago of a massive heart attack in 1963, just at the time young whites were beginning to discover the electric blues coming out of Chicago. James was inducted into the Blues Foundation's Hall of Fame in 1980.

Essential Listening:
Elmore James: King of the Slide Guitar (box set)/Capricorn (42006-2)
Whose Muddy Shoes (with John Brim)/MCA-Chess (CHD 9114)
Dust My Broom/Tomato (R2-70389)
Let's Cut It: The Very Best of Elmore James/Flair(Virgin) (2-91800)
The Sky Is Crying: The History of Elmore James/Rhino (71190)

◄ JAMES, ETTA

(born Jamesetta Hawkins, January 25, 1938, Los Angeles, Calif.)

In the 1950s and early 1960s Etta James was a sultry rhythm & blues singer who worked with bandleader JOHNNY OTIS and arranger MAXWELL DAVIS and who recorded a number of hits for the Modern and Argo labels. Her vocal style fell somewhere between that of DINAH WASHINGTON and BILLIE HOLIDAY. Although many of her early hits were R&B rave-ups, she later matured into a convincing ballad singer, as evidenced by hits such as "All I Could Do Was Cry" and "At Last."

James was born in Los Angeles but moved to San Francisco while still a youth. She learned to sing in church, but by her midteens was drawn to rhythm & blues. Johnny Otis discovered James in 1954 and took her back to Los Angeles where the two composed the song "Roll with Me, Henry" in response to Hank Ballard's 1954 R&B hits "Work with Me, Annie" and "Annie Had a Baby." Thinking the title too suggestive, James and Otis changed the song's title to "The Wallflower." It became a number 2 smash on the R&B charts for Modern. Singer Georgia Gibbs took the song, changed the title once again—this time to "Dance with Me Henry"—and in 1955 scored a number 1 pop hit with it. James had another R&B hit with "Good Rockin' Daddy" in 1955 and worked the R&B circuit with Otis and his band.

James jumped to the Chess subsidiary label, Argo, in 1960 and racked up a number of R&B and pop hits, including "All I Could Do Was Cry" in 1960, "Something's Got a Hold of Me" in 1961, "Stop the Wedding" in 1962, and "Pushover" in 1963. That year she left Argo and fell off the charts, thanks, in part, to alleged drug problems. In 1967 James began a third phase of her recording career when she began recording for Cadet, another Chess subsidiary. "Tell Mama," backed with "I'd Rather Go Blind," became her highest-charted hit, going to number 23 in 1968. But by 1971 James was without a recording contract

again as she continued to fight her alleged drug dependency. In 1973 she returned
to Chess. Finally drug-free, she worked her way back onto the R&B circuit,
playing one-nighters and reestablishing her reputation as a powerful, emotionally
expressive vocalist. In 1978 she opened for the ROLLING STONES and continued
to tour and record through the 1980s. James sang at the opening ceremonies of
the 1984 Olympic Games in Los Angeles. In 1990 she released an album, *Stickin'
to My Guns*, on Island Records that featured a contemporary funk sound. Two
years later James switched to Elektra Records and cut *The Right Time*, an album
Rolling Stone called "a masterpiece." James was inducted into the Rock & Roll
Hall of Fame in 1993. She continues to record and perform.

Essential Listening:
At Last/MCA-Chess (CHC 9266)
Second Time Around/MCA-Chess (CHD 9287)
Etta James Rocks the House/MCA-Chess (CH 9184)
Tell Mama/MCA-Chess (CHD 9269)
Her Greatest Sides, Vol. 1/MCA-Chess (CH 9110)
The Sweetest Peaches: The Chess Years, Vol. 1 (1960–1966)/MCA-Chess (CHD
    9280)
The Sweetest Peaches: The Chess Years, Vol. 2 (1967–1975)/MCA-Chess (CHD
    9281)
R&B Dynamite/Flair (Virgin) (2-91693)

◄ JAMES, SKIP

*(born Nehemiah James, June 9, 1902, Bentonia, Miss.; died October 3, 1969,
Philadelphia, Pa.)*

Skip James was the foremost practitioner of the so-called Bentonia school
of Mississippi blues. His vocal style featured high, haunting, falsetto phrases,
while his guitar scheme was based on a complicated picking technique and
eerie-sounding, mostly minor chords and tunings. Though his recording career
consisted of only the collection of sides he cut for Paramount Records in 1931
and a couple of albums in the 1960s, James influenced a number of Mississippi
bluesmen, including ROBERT JOHNSON, and is highly regarded among blues historians and collectors as one of the most intriguing stylists the music has ever
spawned.

James was born into a religious family; his father was a minister. He learned
how to play piano by taking some music lessons in high school and learned guitar
from his friend Henry Stuckey. James and Stuckey often performed together in
the 1920s and early 1930s at picnics and dances. In 1930 James was discovered
by H.P. Speir, a Jackson, Mississippi, record store owner. Speir sent James to
Grafton, Wisconsin, where he recorded twenty-six sides for Paramount Records
in two days. Thanks mostly to the Depression, which practically destroyed the
recording business in the 1930s, James's records failed to sell. Disappointed, he
quit playing the blues, moved to Dallas, and formed a gospel group called the
Dallas Texas Jubilee Singers to back his father's preaching. James also became
a preacher himself, and was ordained as a Baptist minister in 1932 and as a

Methodist minister in 1946. After frequent travels and tours throughout the South, he returned to Mississippi in the mid-1940s.

James worked outside of music through most of the 1940s and 1950s. In 1964, he was discovered by folk guitarist John Fahey and friends Bill Barth and Henry Vestine (Vestine would later play with the blues-rock group CANNED HEAT) and coaxed to perform at the 1964 Newport Folk Festival in Rhode Island. James's triumphant performance at the festival enabled him to tour folk and blues clubs and play other fests, often with MISSISSIPPI JOHN HURT. James also recorded for the Vanguard label in the '60s. His two albums, *Skip James Today!* and *Devil Got My Woman*, depict James's lonely falsetto and his melancholy guitar style.

James moved to Philadelphia in the mid-'60s, where he died of cancer in 1969. He was inducted into the Blues Foundation's Hall of Fame in 1992.

Essential Listening:
The Complete 1931 Sessions/Yazoo (1072)
Skip James Today!/Vanguard (VMD 79219)
Devil Got My Woman/Vanguard (VMD 79273)

◄ JEFFERSON, BLIND LEMON

(aka Deacon L. J. Bates) (born July 1897, Couchman, Tex.; died December 1929, Chicago, Ill.)

Blind Lemon Jefferson was one of the most influential country bluesmen the genre has known, as well as one of its first commercially successful recording artists. Jefferson's recording career was short; his nearly one hundred titles were all recorded between 1926 and 1929. But in that time he became one of the most popular male blues singers in black America. His success enabled other male blues artists to secure recording contracts in an era that was dominated by female classic blues singers such as BESSIE SMITH, MA RAINEY, and IDA COX.

Little of substance is known about Jefferson's personal life. One of seven children, he was born blind in the late 1800s in East Texas and, most likely, learned to play guitar as a means of scraping out a meager living. Jefferson's handicap didn't hamper his artistry or his resourcefulness as an itinerant blues-man. In 1917, after performing at house parties, picnics, and dances around Worthman in central Texas, Jefferson moved to the Deep Ellum section of Dallas, where he played on street corners for spare change. Jefferson's reputation as singer-guitarist grew to the point where he attracted regular patrons when he played, and he earned enough money through tin-cup offerings to support a wife and child.

Although Jefferson is known as a bluesman, he also sang and played religious hymns, spirituals, work songs, and folk tunes in the tradition of a Southern song-ster. His vocal style included many of the mannerisms that would later define blues singing, including an elastic, thinly veneered vocal whine. But it was Jefferson's guitar style that had the biggest impact on his contemporaries and future generations of bluesmen. Jefferson constructed intricate melodic structures punc-tuated with irregular phrasing that often expanded standard tempo patterns. He also used, to great effect, single-string arpeggios, repeating bass runs on the lower guitar strings, and interesting jazzlike improvisations, which gave his style wonderful color and charisma.

Jefferson was also a first-rate songwriter and permanently altered the relationship that blues singers of the time had with professional songwriters. Before Jefferson, nearly all of the female classic blues singers relied on songs written by outsiders. Jefferson recorded many of his own songs. Some were admittedly takeoffs on traditional folk-blues songs, but at his composing best, Jefferson artfully penned vivid lyrical accounts of early 1900s black culture in the South, especially Texas.

Part of Jefferson's early fame stemmed from his regular travels beyond Dallas. There are accounts of him performing in Oklahoma, the Mississippi Delta, Atlanta, and the Carolinas. But it wasn't until 1925, when Jefferson was recommended to Paramount Records by SAMMY PRICE, a Dallas piano player/record store employee, and was invited to Chicago to record, that he had his biggest impact. Jefferson recorded blues and spirituals, the latter under the pseudonym Deacon L. J. Bates. His recording success led Paramount to search for other male blues singer-guitarists. In late 1926 they discovered BLIND BLAKE, who along with Jefferson provided Paramount with the two biggest-selling country bluesmen of the decade. Jefferson also recorded some sides for the Okeh label in 1927, including "Match Box Blues" and "That Black Snake Moan."

Jefferson recorded a number of other self-penned classics. "See That My Grave Is Kept Clean" was an early blues spiritual tune that has been interpreted by countless blues musicians and has since become a permanent fixture in the country blues songbook. Jefferson also cut a number of East Texas folk-blues standards, including "Jack O'Diamonds" about the perils of gambling, "Boll Weevil Blues" about the dreaded insect that ravaged the East Texas cotton crop in the early twentieth century, and a revamped "See See Rider," which Jefferson called "Corrina Blues."

Blind Lemon Jefferson died just as the first great blues era was coming to a close. The fact that no official death certificate has ever been found has given rise to numerous accounts of his passing in December 1929. The most colorful had Jefferson freezing to death in a Chicago snowstorm. Another account blamed a heart attack for his demise. It's quite possible that Jefferson suffered a heart attack during a Chicago snowstorm.

Because Paramount's records were widely distributed both in the North and South, Jefferson's blues style was well-known among blues musicians. Many artists were influenced by his striking style, including a young T-BONE WALKER, who would walk with Jefferson to his favorite Dallas street corner in his Deep Ellum days, and who carried elements of the Jefferson style of blues guitar into electric blues in the late '30s and '40s. Other Jefferson disciples include LIGHTNIN' HOPKINS, B.B. KING, and a number of guitarists from the Virginia Piedmont region, including REV. BLIND GARY DAVIS and BLIND WILLIE MCTELL. Blind Lemon Jefferson was inducted into the Blues Foundation's Hall of Fame in 1980.

Essential Listening:
King of the Country Blues/Blind Lemon Jefferson/Yazoo (1069)
Blind Lemon Jefferson/Milestone (47022)

◄ JELLY ROLL KINGS

Original members: Jack Johnson (guitar, vocals) (born July 30, 1940, Lambert, Miss.); Sam Carr (drums) (born April 17, 1926, Friar's Point, Miss.); Frank Frost (harmonica, keyboards, vocals) (born April 15, 1936, Augusta, Ark.)

Originally called FRANK FROST and the Nighthawks, this Mississippi Delta–based trio became known as the Jelly Roll Kings in the mid-'70s. The Nighthawks, which played a jagged, roughed-up brand of juke-joint blues, released a couple of albums in the 1960s and also went by a variety of other names—Jelly Roll Frank Frost and the Jelly Roll Kings, the Blues Kings, Little SAM CARR and the Nighthawks, Big Jack and the Clippers—until the group settled on the Jelly Roll Kings. In 1978 the Kings signed a recording contract with the Chicago-based Earwig label; the following year the band released its third album, *Rockin' the Juke Joint Down*. The material on the album was, essentially, the set the Kings had been playing in area jukes when Earwig Records owner Michael Frank first heard the group in 1975.

Since then, both Johnson and Frost have begun separate solo careers. Frost released his *Midnight Prowler* album on Earwig in 1989. BIG JACK JOHNSON began his solo career two years earlier with the release of the album *The Oil Man*. In 1989 his follow-up effort, *Daddy, When Is Mama Comin Home?*, was also released on Earwig. Today, the Jelly Roll Kings continue to play Delta juke joints and blues festivals in the U.S. and Europe.

Essential Listening:
Rockin' the Juke Joint Down/Earwig (LPS 4901)

◄ JENKINS, BOBO

(born John Jenkins, January 6, 1915, Forkland, Ala.; died August 14, 1984, Detroit, Mich.)

Guitarist and singer Bobo Jenkins was a member of Detroit's post–World War II blues scene. Sharing clubwork with the likes of BABY BOY WARREN, EDDIE KIRKLAND, and JOHN LEE HOOKER, Jenkins played a roughed-up brand of blues that often included clever social commentary in the lyrics. Although Jenkins never made the charts with any of his records, two of his best-known tunes, "Democrat Blues" and "Watergate Blues," featured scathing looks at American politics and provided good examples of his composing skills.

Jenkins was born in Alabama, where he grew up on gospel. His earliest musical performances occurred in church. By the time he was in his midteens, Jenkins had left Alabama to wander through the South. In 1942 he was drafted into the armed forces. When he was discharged in 1944, he settled in Detroit and began working on an automobile assembly line. By this time he had also begun to teach himself how to play guitar. Eventually, he was performing in Motor City blues clubs.

Jenkins signed a recording contract with Chess in 1954. Though little came of the relationship with the blues label, Jenkins was able to use the experience to get recording time with other smaller labels throughout the '50s. In the 1960s and 1970s, he continued to perform in and around Detroit and to work in the auto industry. He started his own production company, Big Star, in the early '70s. Despite his persistence, Jenkins was never able to attract much attention outside Motor City blues circles. He died in 1984.

Essential Listening:
Detroit Blues: The Early 1950s (Various Artists)/Blues Classics (12)

◄ JENKINS, GUS

(born March 24, 1931, Birmingham, Ala.; died December 1985, Los Angeles, Calif.)

Gus Jenkins was a blues pianist and singer who recorded for Chess in the early 1950s but then moved to the West Coast, where he became a popular musician in the Los Angeles area blues scene.

Jenkins was born and raised in Birmingham, Alabama, where he learned to play the piano. After performing in Birmingham clubs and parties, he left Alabama and worked with various blues and rhythm & blues package shows, before winding up in Chicago in the late 1940s. Jenkins found studio work with Chess Records, though his recording output under his own name is meager.

Jenkins left Chicago in late 1953 and settled in Los Angeles. In the 1950s and '60s, he recorded with a number of small West Coast based independent record companies, including Flash, Combo, Catalina, General Artist, and his own Pioneer label. Jenkins also toured with bandleader JOHNNY OTIS and traveled with West Coast R&B revues. Sometime in the late 1960s, Jenkins, a Christian, converted to Islam and changed his name to Jaarone Pharaoh. He continued to perform, mostly in southern California, until his death in 1985.

Essential Listening:
Cold Love/Diving Duck (4309)

◄ JOHNSON, BLIND WILLIE

(born c. 1902, Marlin, Tex.; died c. 1947, Beaumont, Tex.)

A coarse-throated, gruff gospel singer who occasionally used the blues idiom to carry his religious messages, Blind Willie Johnson was also a superb slide guitarist. However, unlike more noted Delta slide players whose guitar styles frequently tore at a song's melody or charged it with uncontrolled passion, Johnson forged a style in which the notes he played were perfect accompaniments to the notes he sang.

Little is known of Johnson's life that can be substantiated. He was born around the turn of the century. Sometime between the ages of three and seven he was blinded, reputedly by a stepmother who threw lye into his eyes during a fight with his father. Johnson, like other blind bluesmen in the prewar period, earned his living by singing on Texas street corners. He also became a Baptist preacher. In 1927 he married and shortly thereafter relocated to Dallas, where he recorded for the Columbia label. A batch of the songs he cut ultimately became classics and served as his substantial contribution to gospel-blues. Among the songs for which Johnson is most known are "Motherless Children Have a Hard Time," "If I Had My Way," "Let Your Light Shine on Me," "You're Gonna Need Somebody on Your Bond," and "Jesus Make Up My Dying Bed."

Despite his brief career as a recording artist—he didn't record after 1930—Johnson continued to perform throughout the 1930s and 1940s. He died in 1947; reportedly his house burned to the ground and, after sleeping in its remains, he caught pneumonia.

Essential Listening:
Praise God I'm Satisfied/Yazoo (1058)
Sweeter as the Years Go By/Yazoo (1078)
The Complete Blind Willie Johnson/Columbia (C2K 52835)

◄ JOHNSON, BIG JACK

(born July 30, 1940, Lambert, Miss.)

A blues guitarist and vocalist from Clarksdale, Mississippi, Big Jack Johnson owns a sound that's rooted in traditional Delta blues yet contains elements of funk and soul. Unlike many other Delta bluesmen who left Mississippi for Chicago and other points north in the 1950s and '60s, Johnson stayed in the Delta, playing juke joints and house parties. He remained relatively unknown to blues fans outside of Mississippi until the release of his solo albums in the 1980s.

Inspired by his father to learn an instrument, Johnson taught himself to play guitar well enough to sit in with his father's group as early as age thirteen. In 1962 Johnson teamed up with fellow Delta musicians drummer SAM CARR and harmonica player FRANK FROST. Going by the name Frank Frost and the Nighthawks, the trio recorded *Hey Boss Man!* for SAM PHILLIPS's International label the following year. A second Nighthawks album came out on the Jewel label in 1966, as the group continued to work Delta jukes and dances. Eventually the group broke up; but in 1978, Earwig label president Michael Frank coaxed the three musicians to re-form and record the album *Rockin' the Juke Joint Down*. Released in 1979, the work won critical acclaim from the international blues community and enabled the JELLY ROLL KINGS (as they now billed themselves) to tour Holland twice. Still, the Kings remained a part-time unit while Johnson worked as a Clarksdale truckdriver to support his family.

In 1987 Johnson recorded his first solo album for Earwig, *The Oil Man*, followed by *Daddy, When Is Mama Comin Home?* in 1989. Fueled by Johnson's stinging guitar style, his big, husky vocals, and a penchant to write about topical themes (AIDS, wife abuse, the airline industry) the albums scored enough success to enable Johnson and the Jelly Roll Kings to perform at the Chicago Blues Festival in 1987 and 1991 and extend their fan base beyond the Delta. Johnson continues to record and perform.

Essential Listening:
The Oil Man/Earwig (4910)
Daddy, When Is Mama Comin Home?/Earwig (CD 4916)
Rockin' the Juke Joint Down (with the Jelly Roll Kings)/Earwig (4901)

◄ JOHNSON, JIMMY

(born Jimmy Thompson, November 25, 1928, Holly Springs, Miss.)

A fixture in Chicago blues clubs since the mid-1970s and the brother of soul-blues singer SYL JOHNSON, guitarist Jimmy Johnson is known for expanding the traditional parameters of the blues by writing songs with unconventional chord structures and sparse, though probing guitar passages.

Born in Mississippi, where he grew up listening to and singing gospel, Johnson moved first to Memphis and then to Chicago in 1950. Shortly after arriving in the Windy City, Johnson was drafted into the army, but he refused to serve and was dishonorably discharged. Johnson worked full-time as a welder until the early 1960s when he formed a rhythm & blues band to play Chicago clubs. On occasion, he also worked as a session guitarist with brother Syl and as a sideman with bluesmen such as ALBERT KING, SUNNYLAND SLIM, OTIS CLAY, and TYRONE DAVIS.

Johnson switched from R&B to straight Chicago blues when he joined the JIMMY DAWKINS Band in 1974. Two years later he formed his own blues band. Four tracks on Alligator Records' Living Chicago Blues series, a set of albums released in the late '70s that was dedicated to showcasing unsigned blues talent in the city, led Johnson to a recording contract with Delmark Records. His critically praised album *Johnson's Whacks* was recorded in 1978 when Johnson was fifty years old. "Ashes in My Ashtray," a plaintive, soul blues ballad from the album, won a 1980 W.C. HANDY Award for blues single of the year.

Johnson released one more album for Delmark, *North/South*, before jumping to Alligator Records. In 1985 the label released Johnson's *Bar Room Preacher*. Since then Johnson has struggled to find his niche in contemporary blues, though he remains a member of the Chicago blues scene.

Essential Listening:
Johnson's Whacks/Delmark (644)
North/South/Delmark (647)
Bar Room Preacher/Alligator (AL 4744)

◄ JOHNSON, JOHNNIE

(born July 8, 1924, Clarksdale, W.Va.)

As CHUCK BERRY's piano player from 1955 to 1973, Johnnie Johnson's blues-flavored rock & roll keyboards helped give dozens of Berry classics, including "Maybellene," "Roll Over Beethoven," and "Johnny B. Goode," their rhythmic drive. Johnson built his piano style from a mix of boogie-woogie blues, rhythm & blues, and big band swing that, when integrated with Berry's rollicking guitar licks, practically defined the sound of rock & roll in the mid-1950s.

Johnson grew up in West Virginia, where he taught himself to play the piano. At the outbreak of World War II, he moved to Detroit to work in the defense industry. Johnson joined the Marines in 1943 and played in a big band that toured the Pacific theater. After the war Johnson moved to Chicago, where he learned about the blues by listening to and occasionally sitting in with MUDDY WATERS, LITTLE MILTON, and other bluesmen, and then to St. Louis, where he worked with

ALBERT KING. Eventually he started his own group, the Johnnie Johnson Trio (aka Sir John's Trio), which played mostly jazz and R&B. In 1952, Johnson, who knew Chuck Berry primarily as a local black country & western artist, hired him to play a New Year's Eve date in St. Louis. The two eventually formed a musical partnership that lasted some thirty years.

Tired of touring, Johnson left Berry in the early 1970s and worked with a St. Louis group called the Sounds of the City, later renamed the Magnificent Five when Johnson assumed control. He also performed on occasion with Berry and appeared in the Berry rockumentary *Hail! Hail! Rock 'n' Roll* in 1987. The success of the film inspired Johnson to reclaim his place as one of the masters of blues-influenced rock & roll piano.

Also in 1987 Johnson released a solo album, *Blue Hand Johnnie*, on the Pulsar label. In 1991, his critically praised *Johnnie B. Bad* album was part of the debut release of Elektra Records' American Explorer Series. The album featured guest appearances by guitarists Keith Richards of the ROLLING STONES and ERIC CLAPTON and brought Johnson long-overdue recognition after years of living in Chuck Berry's shadow. Johnson continues to perform and record.

Essential Listening:
Chuck Berry: The Chess Box/MCA-Chess (CHD3-80,001)
Blue Hand Johnnie/Pulsar (1002)
Johnnie B. Bad/Elektra (9 61149-2)

◄ JOHNSON, LONNIE

(born Alonzo Johnson, February 8, 1894, New Orleans, La.; died June 16, 1970, Toronto, Canada)

Lonnie Johnson was the first great modern blues guitarist. His harmonically advanced and fluid style influenced everyone from ROBERT JOHNSON and Charlie Christian to T-BONE WALKER and B.B. KING. A prolific recording artist, Johnson's career extended from the mid-1920s to the late 1960s. He recorded hundreds of songs along the way as both a featured artist and an accompanist. Many of his recordings transcended the blues idiom and incorporated everything from jazz to pop; such was Johnson's amazing versatility. In terms of the blues, his most productive period was from 1925, the year he began his recording career, to approximately 1932. It was during this time that Johnson's influence as a guitar master was most felt and that the bulk of his best blues and blues-flavored recordings were released.

To call Johnson a pure blues guitarist would not be entirely accurate. More than any other early guitarist, Johnson brought the blues to jazz, and jazz to blues. Johnson had neither the raw country blues background that such contemporaries as BLIND LEMON JEFFERSON and BIG BILL BROONZY had, nor the roughed-up, often renegade guitar style practiced by Delta bluesmen like SON HOUSE and CHARLEY PATTON. Johnson's guitar style was clean and manicured. He selected his notes with careful consideration, thanks to an understanding of his instrument that ran deeper than that of nearly every other blues guitarist of the day. In a way, his approach to the guitar was polished to the point of being polite. Nevertheless,

Johnson's guitar style possessed feeling and a delightful sense of swing and sophistication. Johnson lived all his life in the city, and his guitar articulation reflected this. He was one of the first guitarists to experiment with single-string solos, an innovation that would be adopted by countless jazz and blues musicians later on, and he developed professional relationships with some of the top recording artists of the '20s.

Johnson was born into a large, musically inclined New Orleans family in the late 1800s. As a child growing up in this most musical of cities, Johnson was undoubtedly influenced by the early New Orleans jazz scene, and he developed a fondness for music in general that was a far cry from the relationships cultivated by Delta and East Texas country bluesmen of the same period.

Johnson's first instrument was the violin; as a child he often performed in his father's string band. Later he learned the banjo, mandolin, piano, and, of course, the guitar. In 1917 he traveled to London with a musical revue whose name is lost to history. When he returned two years later, he found that the infamous flu epidemic of 1919 had killed his mother and father and all of his siblings (accounts put their number at ten or twelve) save one brother, James. In a state of shock, Johnson left New Orleans to escape his personal pain and grief, and moved to St. Louis, where he and his brother got work on Mississippi steamboats playing in the jazz bands of Charlie Creath and Fate Marable. In 1925 Johnson entered a weekly blues contest held at the Booker T. Washington Theater in St. Louis. After he took first place in the contest, Okeh Records offered him a recording contract.

Although Johnson recorded a number of excellent self-penned songs in the mid- and late '20s in which he was the featured artist, his most memorable work occurred when he performed with musicians of equal genius. Johnson recorded with both LOUIS ARMSTRONG and Duke Ellington, as well as with fellow guitarist Eddie Lang. His exquisite back-and-forth solos with trumpeter Armstrong on "I'm Not Rough," "Hotter Than That," and "Savoy Blues," recorded with Armstrong's band in late 1927, remain special moments in early jazz history, as do the pieces he recorded with Duke Ellington's orchestra the same year. Johnson's guitar work on the Ellington classic "The Mooche" set the stage for the memorable contributions to jazz by guitarist Charlie Christian more than a decade later. And with Lang, Johnson recorded a number of much-admired duets that served as an inspiration and a guide for an entire generation of guitarists, blues and jazz alike.

Johnson also recorded with the classic blueswoman VICTORIA SPIVEY and the country blues singer TEXAS ALEXANDER, which revealed his versatility and proved that underneath the jazz musings he was indeed a blues guitarist. In seven years Johnson produced some 130 recordings, making him the most recorded male blues artist of the 1920s. Like other noted blues artists, Johnson's recording pace slowed to a trickle during the Depression, forcing him to find work outside of music in order to earn a living. But in the mid-'40s Johnson launched a comeback; he signed new recording contracts, first with Aladdin and then King Records, in 1947. His recording of the ballad "Tomorrow Night," released in early 1948, was a big hit with postwar pop and rhythm & blues audiences. The follow-up single, "I Know It's Love," in which Johnson played an electric (as opposed to his usual acoustic) guitar, as well as "Pleasing You," "So Tired," and "Confused," were all hits.

Johnson, however, had strayed from his blues and jazz roots. Many of his late-'40s and early-'50s recordings were aimed at mainstream tastes. When rock & roll supplanted rhythm & blues in the mid-'50s, Johnson was, once again, forced out of music. He was rediscovered one last time in the '60s and was able to capitalize on the decade's blues resurgence. Johnson toured as a folk-blues guitarist with varying degrees of success. In 1969 he was hit by a car in Toronto. He died a year later of complications from the accident. Johnson was inducted into the Blues Foundation's Hall of Fame in 1990.

Essential Listening:
Steppin on the Blues/Columbia (CK 46221)
The Hot Fives & Hot Sevens, Vol. II (with Louis Armstrong)/Columbia (CK 44422)
Blues by Lonnie Johnson/Original Blues Classics (502)
Lonnie Johnson, 1926–40/Blues Documents (2064)
Losing Game/Prestige-Bluesville (OBCCD 543-2)
The Complete Folkways Recordings/Smithsonian-Folkways (SF 40067)

◄ JOHNSON, LUTHER "GEORGIA BOY"

(aka "Snake Boy") (born Lucius Johnson, August 30, 1934, Davisboro, Ga.; died March 18, 1976, Boston, Mass.)

Luther "Georgia Boy" Johnson played guitar and bass in the MUDDY WATERS Band from 1967 to 1970. No relation to LUTHER "GUITAR JR" JOHNSON or LUTHER "HOUSEROCKER" JOHNSON, Luther "Georgia Boy" Johnson has, nonetheless, links to both bluesmen. It was "Guitar Jr." Johnson who eventually took Johnson's place in the Muddy Waters Band. Both Johnsons also resettled in Boston: "Georgia Boy" in the 1970s, "Guitar Jr." in the 1980s. Also, like Luther "Houserocker" Johnson, "Georgia Boy" was born in Georgia.

"Georgia Boy" Johnson learned how to play guitar as a child. He served in the army during the Korean War and often worked at USO clubs. After his discharge, Johnson worked blues clubs in Milwaukee. Sometime in the early '60s, he resettled in Chicago, where he fell in with some of the city's best blues artists, including pianist OTIS SPANN. In 1967 he joined the Waters band and recorded and toured with the group. By 1970 Johnson had formed his own group and began playing clubs, mostly around Boston, and touring Europe with packaged blues shows. He recorded for the French Black and Blue label before his death in 1976 of cancer.

Essential Listening:
Get Down to the Nitty Gritty/Roir (NRCD 5088)
They Call Me the Snake/Roir (NRCD 5114)

◄ JOHNSON, LUTHER "GUITAR JR."

(aka Luther Johnson, Jr.) (born April 11, 1939, Itta Bena, Miss.)

Luther "Guitar Jr." Johnson, not to be confused with Luther "Georgia Boy" Johnson or Luther "Houserocker" Johnson (no relation), is a journeyman guitarist whose style recalls the West Side sound of such Chicago guitar stalwarts as MAGIC SAM and OTIS RUSH. Before forming his own band, the Magic Rockers, Johnson played in MUDDY WATERS's band from 1972 to 1980.

Born in Mississippi, Johnson and his family moved to Chicago in 1955. Johnson's entry into the city's competitive blues scene was with Tall Milton Sheldon, for whom he played bass and sang. In the early '60s, Johnson, now nicknamed "Guitar Jr.," worked the West Side's blues clubs and fell under the influence of Magic Sam; he also worked with Sam, his mentor, for a couple of years in the mid-'60s. A growing reputation as a blues guitarist led to the position in Waters's band.

Johnson's first solo album, *Luther's Blues*, was recorded in 1976 with members of the Muddy Waters Band and released on the French Black and Blue label. Johnson's solo career got a boost when four of his songs were included on volume 4 (CD version) of Alligator Records' *Living Chicago Blues Series* in 1980. He next recorded with the NIGHTHAWKS, on the Adelphi label, and won a Grammy for his contribution to the 1984 Atlantic Records' compilation *Blues Explosion*. In 1982 Johnson moved to Boston and became one of the city's most popular blues acts. He recorded one album, *Doin' the Sugar Too*, for Rooster Blues in 1983 before signing with the Bullseye Blues label and recording *I Want to Groove with You* in 1990. Johnson continues to tour and record with the Magic Rockers.

Johnson should also not be confused with LONNIE BROOKS, who, early in his career, called himself Guitar Jr.

Essential Listening:

Luther's Blues/Evidence (ECD 26010)

Living Chicago Blues, Vol. 4 (Various Artists)/Alligator (AL 7704)

Doin' the Sugar Too/Rooster Blues (R 7607)

I Want to Groove with You/Bullseye Blues (BB 9506)

◄ JOHNSON, LUTHER "HOUSEROCKER"

(born July 15, 1939, Atlanta, Ga.)

No relation to Luther "Guitar Jr." Johnson or to Luther "Georgia Boy" Johnson, guitarists in the MUDDY WATERS's band in the 1960s and 1970s, Luther "Houserocker" Johnson is a guitarist and singer who records for the Ichiban label. Born and raised in Atlanta, Johnson taught himself how to play guitar mostly by listening to JIMMY REED and LIGHTNIN' SLIM records. As a teen he began backing up visiting blues artists such as JOHNNY WINTER and Omar and the Howlers in Atlanta clubs. Eventually he formed his own band, the Houserockers, and played clubs and bars throughout Georgia.

In 1989 Johnson signed a recording contract with Ichiban Records and released his debut, *Takin' a Bite Outta the Blues*. His follow-up album, *Houserockin'*

Daddy, was released in 1991 by Ichiban. Johnson continues to record and perform.

Essential Listening:

Takin' a Bite Outta the Blues/Ichiban (ICH 1060)

Houserockin' Daddy/Ichiban (ICH 9010)

◄ JOHNSON, PETE

(born March 25, 1904, Kansas City, Mo.; died March 23, 1967, Buffalo, N.Y.)

Pete Johnson was one of the great boogie-woogie pianists, ranking together with ALBERT AMMONS and MEADE ''LUX'' LEWIS as the most popular and artistically important boogie-woogie players of the late 1930s and early 1940s. Johnson teamed up regularly with blues shouter BIG JOE TURNER; their performance at John Hammond's legendary 1938 Spirituals to Swing concert at Carnegie Hall in New York City helped ignite renewed interest in boogie-woogie. Johnson's signature song was the romping ''Roll 'em Pete,'' now a staple in most boogie-woogie piano repertoires.

Johnson was born in Kansas City and learned to play drums before piano. He eventually got pointers on the keyboards from a variety of sources and listened intently to Fats Waller records in order to become proficient enough to begin playing Kansas City clubs and house parties in the early 1920s. Johnson's link with Turner began shortly thereafter. The two played the Sunset Cafe and other popular Kansas City nightspots into the mid-1930s when they were discovered by talent scout and producer John Hammond, who, at the time, was seeking artists to perform on his Spirituals to Swing bill. In 1938, Johnson and Turner traveled to New York and appeared on the ''Benny Goodman Camel Caravan Radio Show,'' followed by a slot in the Spirituals to Swing concert in December of that year.

The two musicians stayed on in New York, where, along with Albert Ammons and Meade ''Lux'' Lewis, they worked the Cafe Society club, one of New York's hippest jazz and blues venues. Billed as the Boogie Woogie Trio, Ammons, Lewis, and Johnson began performing regularly at the Cafe Society in 1939 and stayed there into the early '40s. During the rest of the decade Johnson frequently performed and recorded with Ammons as a duo.

Johnson moved to Buffalo, New York, in 1950. His career all but ended two years later when one of his fingers was partially severed in an accident. Johnson, however, continued to perform on and off during the 1950s. But due to his accident and the lack of interest in boogie-woogie, except as a nostalgic form, Johnson faded from the scene in the 1960s. He suffered a series of strokes before he died in 1967.

Essential Listening:

Pete Johnson, 1938–47/Document (535)

Big Joe Turner's Greatest Hits/Atlantic (81752)

Central Avenue Boogie/Delmark (DD 656)

Tell Me Pretty Baby (with Joe Turner)/Arhoolie (CD 333)

◄ JOHNSON, ROBERT

(born May 8, 1911, Hazelhurst, Miss.; died August 16, 1938, Greenwood, Miss.)

Robert Johnson is one of the most celebrated figures in blues history. Although he died when he was just twenty-seven years old, his impact on blues culture and blues mythology, as well as his influence on the development of blues guitar styles, has been substantial to say the least. A half-century after his death, Johnson still possessed the power and magnetism to play a major role in the latest blues revival. In 1990, Columbia Records kicked off its prestigious Roots 'n' Blues Series with *The Complete Recordings of Robert Johnson*, a two-disc boxed set with extensive liner notes, rare photos, and a fresh view of his music. According to series producer Larry Cohn, the set was expected to sell some 20,000 copies. Incredibly, it sold nearly a half-million units. It also won a Grammy Award, inspired a number of Robert Johnson cover stories in the music press, launched a brand new fascination with Johnson's music and his contribution to blues guitar, and hastened the reissuing of classic blues albums on compact disc by dozens of other companies.

If Robert Johnson had never been born, the blues might have seen fit to invent him, as his story has become the archetype of blues life. It reads so much like a film that it inevitably became one. Based loosely on the always sketchy details of his life, the mid-1980s movie *Crossroads* is something no true blues fan would ever consider anything more than mere entertainment. But that the Johnson legacy was compelling enough to warrant a full-length feature film tells us much about the impact he has had on our view of the blues.

Johnson's recording catalog adds up to a grand total of only twenty-nine tracks; it is criminally lean when compared to those of such blues giants as MUDDY WATERS, JOHN LEE HOOKER, LIGHTNIN' HOPKINS, and others. Yet most blues scholars and critics agree that there is more than enough musical evidence available to proclaim Johnson a musical genius, while his lyrics have been analyzed more closely perhaps than those of any other blues composer.

According to the myth, Johnson obtained his amazing guitar skills by selling his soul to the Devil. (That Johnson wrote songs about the Devil and explored in his music the fight of good against evil strengthened the myth, which endured after his death and grew larger as the years passed.) Aside from this Faustian explanation, we know little about how Johnson came to acquire his compelling skills, as both a songwriter and guitarist, in such a remarkably brief time.

He certainly had the physical tools to forge an unusual blues guitar style. A careful look at the photo that appears on the box of *The Complete Recordings of Robert Johnson* reveals the guitarist to have had extraordinarily large hands. Some of the chordal movements and note selections that grace his songs are practically impossible to achieve with normal-size fingers. Yet this physical trait doesn't explain where Johnson's inspiration came from.

Some of it can be indirectly traced and some perhaps inferred. Johnson's use of walking bass notes probably came from hearing first-generation boogie-woogie piano players. He certainly must have learned about guitar tone and texture from listening to LONNIE JOHNSON. And Delta greats such as CHARLEY PATTON, WILLIE BROWN, and SON HOUSE undoubtedly influenced his approach to the slide guitar. With all the traveling Johnson did in his short life, surely he picked up melodic and rhythmic ideas from other bluesmen he met. Yet what made all these influences jell was his blues passion and deeply rooted intensity. In the end, these are the things that made Johnson's guitar work truly special.

A few historians believe the influence of Johnson's guitar playing has been overstated. While his style has worked its way into modern blues and rock and has touched Muddy Waters, ELMORE JAMES, ROBERT JR. LOCKWOOD, JOHNNY SHINES, JOHN HAMMOND, JR., ERIC CLAPTON, and Keith Richards, to name a few prominent blues and rock guitarists, bluesmen other than Johnson have exerted far more sweeping influences. T-BONE WALKER and B.B. KING, for instance, have had a greater impact on the course of blues guitar history. Nonetheless, Johnson remains a vital source of inspiration, not to mention frustration, for those who seek to take blues guitar to a new, more spectacular level. Few other blues guitarists are held in higher esteem. It is also safe to say that no one who has surfaced since his passing has been able to match his unconventional guitar accomplishments, save, perhaps, JIMI HENDRIX.

Johnson was born illegitimate in 1911 to Julia Dodds and Noah Johnson. When he was three or four, Johnson's mother sent him to live with her husband, Charles Dodds, who was residing in Memphis and had taken a new name, Charles Spencer. As a youth, Johnson was known as Robert Spencer and Robert Dodds, but when he learned the identity of his real father, he assumed the name Johnson.

Before he absorbed the rudiments of the guitar, mostly by watching his older brother Charles play, Johnson had taught himself how to play harmonica. He learned, too, from watching Son House, Charley Patton, and Willie Brown play guitar at Delta picnics and parties. Not much is known about Johnson's personal life other than that by 1930 he had married and lost his wife, who died during childbirth, and that he had decided to become a bluesman. Johnson remarried in 1931, but spent most of his time wandering the Delta. Around 1933 or so, Johnson met up again with Son House and Willie Brown. What they heard Johnson play on guitar startled them.

In an amazingly short time, Johnson had turned into a blues guitar master, hence the myth that he made a deal with the Devil. Johnson's reputation as a guitarist spread as he worked as an itinerant bluesman, roaming the Delta. He also traveled to Memphis, St. Louis, Chicago, Detroit, and even to New York. Occasionally he traveled with fellow bluesman Johnny Shines and often met DAVID "HONEYBOY" EDWARDS and Robert Jr. Lockwood on the road. Most of the time, however, he traveled alone.

Johnson's only two recording sessions occurred just a couple of years before his death. The first session took place in November 1936 in a San Antonio, Texas, hotel room. During the three-day session Johnson cut sixteen sides for the American Record Company, including "I Believe I'll Dust My Broom," "Sweet Home Chicago," "Terraplane Blues," "Cross Road Blues," "Come on in My Kitchen," and "Walkin' Blues"—all acknowledged classics.

The second session occurred in June 1937 in a Dallas warehouse, producing still more Johnson classics, such as "Traveling Riverside Blues," "Love in Vain Blues," "Hell Hound on My Trail," and "Me and the Devil Blues." After this last session, Johnson resumed his wandering ways, ultimately winding up in Greenwood, Mississippi, where he was poisoned with strychnine-laced whiskey after a brief fling with the wife of a local juke-joint owner. Three days later he died.

Johnson was inducted into the Blues Foundation's Hall of Fame in 1980 and the Rock & Roll Hall of Fame in 1986.

Essential Listening:
The Complete Recordings of Robert Johnson/Columbia (C2K 46222)

◄ JOHNSON, SYL

(born Syl Thompson, July 1, 1939, Holly Springs, Miss.)

Syl Johnson began his career as a bluesman but made his biggest mark as a soul singer in the 1960s and 1970s. With the decline of soul in the '80s, Johnson, brother of blues guitarist JIMMY JOHNSON, returned to the blues, though with only limited results.

Born in Mississippi, Johnson learned how to play guitar at an early age. He moved with his family to Chicago in 1952 and worked his way into the Chicago blues scene, occasionally playing with MUDDY WATERS, JUNIOR WELLS, and other noted blues artists of the period. As a guitarist, Johnson was strongly influenced by the West Side sound of MAGIC SAM, and he played with his mentor in the late '50s. He also recorded with Wells, JIMMY REED, and BILLY BOY ARNOLD. In the early '60s, Johnson began to turn more to soul music instead of straight-ahead Chicago blues. After breaking in as a solo artist with the Federal label, Johnson later switched to Twilight Records. In 1967 he placed his first single on the R&B charts; "Come on Sock It to Me" made it to number 12.

Johnson continued to record for Twilight/Twinight until 1972 when he jumped to the Hi label. His greatest success with the label occurred with his version of the Al Green tune "Take Me to the River," which peaked at number 7 on the R&B charts in 1975. As interest in soul dwindled, so did interest in Syl Johnson as a soul singer. Other releases on the Hi label barely cracked the pop top 100, though many of them made it onto the R&B charts. Eventually, Johnson returned to the blues. In 1980 he recorded the album *Brings Out the Blues in Me* for his own Shama label. Johnson eventually dropped out of the Chicago blues scene and went into the restaurant business.

Essential Listening:
Brings Out the Blues in Me/Shama
Dresses Too Short/Twinight
Back for a Taste of Your Love/Hi
Diamond in the Rough/Hi
Total Explosion/Hi

◄ JOHNSON, TOMMY

(born c. 1896, Terry, Miss.; died November 1, 1956, Crystal Springs, Miss.)

Tommy Johnson was one of the most influential blues artists working in the Mississippi Delta in the 1920s and 1930s. Only famed bluesmen CHARLEY PATTON and SON HOUSE commanded greater respect and had more of an impact than he did. With a full-bodied voice that could be jacked up to an eerie falsetto and a compelling guitar style that, though rather limited, evoked shivering blues figures, Johnson helped define the early Delta blues sound. Had he recorded more—he made about a dozen recordings during his entire career—his status as a pioneering bluesman undoubtedly would be greater today with blues fans.

As it stands, much of the Johnson legacy concerns his live performances, his rowdy womanizing, his powerful drinking (when whiskey wasn't available, Johnson reportedly drank Sterno, denatured alcohol, or even shoe polish), and his spooky flirtations with the Devil. Johnson repeatedly told friends and admirers that he acquired his blues talent by selling his soul to the Devil. At times, Johnson did indeed seem like a man possessed. Taking a cue from Patton, Johnson often played his guitar behind his neck and back and made histrionics as much a part of his performance as his music. Johnson had a profound impact on HOWLIN' WOLF, who took Johnson's attention to showmanship to the next degree in the post–World War II years.

Johnson was born circa 1896 in southern Mississippi. By the time he was a teen, he had learned the rudiments of the guitar and had headed north to the Delta region, where he met Patton and Patton's longtime friend and musical companion WILLIE BROWN, both of whom influenced the way in which Johnson played and sang the blues. Johnson began working with Patton and Brown in Delta jukes and at plantation dances. Later in the 1920s, Johnson worked with CHARLIE MCCOY, ISHMAN BRACEY, and RUBIN LACY in the Jackson, Mississippi, area.

Johnson's recording career lasted but two years, from 1928 to 1930, during which time he cut sides for the Victor and Paramount labels. Among the songs that have since become blues standards are "Big Road Blues" and "Canned Heat Blues," the latter tune a haunting, autobiographical account of his alcohol addiction. In the 1960s, the California blues-rock group CANNED HEAT named itself after this song. Johnson continued to work Jackson jukes and parties into the 1950s, early on influencing ROBERT JOHNSON (not believed to be a relation) and countless other young bluesmen in the process, though his acute alcohol problems prevented any serious attempt at expanding his career outside Mississippi. Johnson died in 1956. He was inducted into the Blues Foundation's Hall of Fame in 1987.

Essential Listening:

Complete Recorded Works in Chronological Order/Document (DOCD 5001)
Tommy Johnson/Wolf (WSE 104)

◄ JONES, CASEY

(born July 26, 1939, Nitta Yuma, Miss.)

Casey Jones is a drummer and singer who has been a part of the Chicago blues scene since the mid-1950s. Jones moved from Mississippi to Chicago in 1956. Some of his earliest work was with MORRIS PEJOE, FREDDIE KING, and JIMMY JOHNSON. He formed his own bar band, Casey Jones and the Cannonball Express, in the early 1960s and became the featured vocalist.

In 1975 Jones joined HOWLIN' WOLF's band and remained with the group until Wolf died the following year. The exposure led to work with LONNIE BROOKS, ALBERT COLLINS and the Icebreakers, and JOHNNY WINTER. In 1983 Jones started his own label, Airwax, and released the solo album *Still Kickin'*. Anxious to front his own band again, Jones began playing Chicago clubs and recorded *Solid Blue*, which was leased to Rooster Blues Records in 1987. Jones next recorded *The Chi-Town Boogie Man*, and released it on Airwax. Jones remains active on the Chicago blues scene.

Essential Listening:
Solid Blues/Rooster Blues (R 7612)
Still Kickin'/Airwax (AW 3839)
The Chi-Town Boogie Man/Airwax (AW 590)

◄ JONES, CURTIS

(born August 18, 1906, Naples, Tex.; died September 11, 1971, Munich, Germany)

Curtis Jones was a Chicago blues pianist and singer best known for his pre–World War II classic "Lonesome Bedroom Blues." Jones's piano style was Texas-rooted, lightly layered, and often unassuming, but it contained plenty of blues feeling. He first learned how to play guitar as a youth, but later switched to piano and began playing clubs after moving to Dallas in his teens. Jones spent most of the 1920s developing his economical piano style. Sometime in the early '30s he left Dallas for Kansas City, where he played in clubs and at house parties. Eventually he made his way to Chicago in 1937. He signed a recording contract that same year with the Vocalion label and recorded "Lonesome Bedroom Blues," which would become his signature song. Jones also cut sides for Okeh and Bluebird before experiencing a ten-year lapse in his recording career, beginning in 1942.

By 1952, Jones was back recording again, this time with the Parrot label. He worked Chicago clubs and occasional out-of-town dates in Midwest cities throughout the 1950s. He continued his recording career with Prestige-Bluesville and Delmark in the early 1960s before moving to France in 1962. Jones spent the rest of his life performing in Europe and northern Africa and living the life of an expatriate bluesman. He died of heart failure in Munich, Germany, in 1971.

Essential Listening:
Lonesome Bedroom Blues/Delmark (DL 605)

Trouble Blues/Original Blues Classics (515)
Blues and Trouble/Oldie Blues (2824)

◄ JONES, DENNIS "LITTLE HAT"

(birth and death information unknown)

Dennis "Little Hat" Jones was a first-generation Texas blues guitarist who traveled and worked with the likes of TEXAS ALEXANDER and J.T. "FUNNY PAPA" SMITH. Despite recording only occasionally, Jones left his mark with a unique finger-picking guitar style and an insistence on big, rolling bass notes, the kind used by fellow guitarists Smith and BLIND LEMON JEFFERSON. Unfortunately, almost nothing is known of his life.

In addition to his guitar talent, Jones was a formidable singer. On songs such as "Cherry Street Blues" and "Little Hat Blues," Jones belted out his blues with the kind of passion heard in field hollers. Unfortunately, Jones's recording career spanned a meager two years; his last records were made in 1930.

Essential Listening:

Blues from the Western States, 1927–1949 (Various Artists)/Yazoo (1032)
Texas Blues Guitar, 1929–35/Blues Documents (2010)

◄ JONES, FLOYD

(born July 21, 1917, Marianna, Ark.; died December 19, 1989, Chicago, Ill.)

A pioneer of the post–World War II Chicago blues sound, guitarist Floyd Jones never received the recognition that his more-recorded contemporaries did. Though some of Jones's earliest recorded efforts contain the same roughed-up Delta-influenced musical elements found in the blues of MUDDY WATERS and other noted Chicago blues artists in the late 1940s, he recorded relatively little, compared to Waters and others, and thus was unable to attract the attention he deserved. Another reason for Jones's relative obscurity was the fact that he rarely ventured outside of Chicago. He held a day job throughout almost his entire career.

Jones reputedly acquired his first guitar from HOWLIN' WOLF in 1933, the year he began performing. Throughout the 1930s and early 1940s Jones wandered the South, playing juke joints and house parties. He met up with cousin Moody Jones in the mid-1940s, and the two bluesmen worked Chicago's Maxwell Street for tips. The Jones cousins often shared street corners with bluesmen SNOOKY PRYOR and HOMESICK JAMES. Jones recorded with Pryor and later SUNNYLAND SLIM before forming his own band and recording for Chess, J.O.B., and Vee-Jay Records. Known for his melancholy sound, some of Jones's best songs—"Stockyard Blues," "Dark Road," and "Hard Times"—contain poignant views of poverty and dillusionment.

Jones continued to record occasionally and perform in Chicago clubs throughout the 1960s and 1970s. Ill health forced him into retirement by the 1980s, although he did perform with longtime friend SMOKEY SMOTHERS at the 1986 Chicago Blues Festival. Jones died of heart failure in 1989.

Essential Listening:
Drop Down Mama (Various Artists)/MCA Chess (CH-93002)
Masters of Modern Blues, Vol. 3: Floyd Jones and Eddie Taylor/Testament (2214)

◄ JONES, JOHNNY

(aka Johnnie Jones, Little Johnnie Jones) (born November 1, 1924, Jackson, Miss.; died November 19, 1964, Chicago, Ill.)

A cousin of blues pianist OTIS SPANN, Johnny Jones was an influential and highly regarded Chicago blues pianist who recorded with ELMORE JAMES as well as many other blues stalwarts, including MUDDY WATERS, JIMMY REED, HOWLIN' WOLF, BILLY BOY ARNOLD, and MAGIC SAM. During the 1950s, Jones and James regularly performed at Sylvio's, the legendary Chicago blues club.

Jones was born in Mississippi and learned to play both piano and harmonica as a youth. Sometime in the mid-1940s, he and his family moved to Chicago. By 1947 he was playing dates with TAMPA RED. Jones also recorded with Tampa Red from 1949 to 1951. In 1950 Jones recorded for the Aristocrat (Chess) label, backing Muddy Waters on two sides and doing a pair of his own songs with Waters in support. Jones's "Big Town Playboy" is generally regarded by blues historians as an early postwar Chicago blues classic. Jones's most celebrated musical relationship was with slide guitarist James, with whom Jones first began performing around 1951. Later in the decade Jones teamed up with West Side guitarist Magic Sam. In the early '60s, Jones often worked as a session pianist; he appeared on Howlin' Wolf's seminal track, "Little Red Rooster," and also cut tracks with Jimmy Reed.

As a solo artist, Jones made no studio albums of his own and only recorded three singles. In the early '60s Jones developed lung problems, though he still continued to work. Cancer was diagnosed in 1963; Jones died in 1964.

Essential Listening:
Johnny Jones & Billy Boy Arnold/Alligator (AL 4717)

◄ JONES, MAGGIE

(born Fay Barnes, c. 1900, Hillsboro, Tex.; died, date and place unknown)

A little-remembered classic blues singer from Texas, Maggie Jones recorded for Columbia Records in the 1920s. Not much is known about Jones's formative years. In the early 1920s she reportedly moved to New York from Tennessee and supported herself by singing in local clubs. Eventually, she began working the TOBA (Theater Owners' Booking Association) circuit and might have even appeared on Broadway. In 1923 she recorded for the Black Swan, Victor, and Pathe labels as Fae (Faye) Barnes, but jumped to Paramount a year later and recorded as Maggie Jones. According to most classic blues historians, her best songs were recorded for Columbia from 1924 to 1926 when she was often accompanied in the recording studio by LOUIS ARMSTRONG, Fletcher Henderson, and CLARENCE WILLIAMS. In all, Jones cut some thirty-four sides for Columbia.

Not a particularly supple or invigorating vocalist, Jones's best material—

"Good Flat Time Blues," "North Bound Blues"—did, however, reflect her Texas roots and reveal her to have been an artist interested in singing about social issues. The former tune tells the story of a police raid on a whorehouse, while the latter deals with the Jim Crow oppression blacks faced in the South and the promise of less hardship and inequality up North.

Like so many other classic blues singers, Jones faded from the recording and performing scenes in the late '20s. Her last reported performance was in 1934 in Fort Worth, Texas.

Essential Listening:
Mean Mothers: Independent Women's Blues, Vol. 1 (Various Artists)/Rosetta (1300)

◄ JOPLIN, JANIS

(born January 19, 1943, Port Arthur, Tex.; died October 4, 1970, Hollywood, Calif.)

Janis Joplin was one of the greatest white female blues singers of all time. Although she came from the same mid-'60s San Francisco rock scene that spawned bands like the Grateful Dead and Jefferson Airplane, Joplin's screaming, gut-wrenching vocals were firmly based in the blues. Joplin frequently cited BESSIE SMITH as her chief inspiration and influence.

Joplin lived the life of a pained blueswoman bent on self-destruction. Alcohol and drug excess sapped her talent and eventually killed her. Her sexual promiscuity led to feelings of inadequacy and bouts with depression. She experienced difficulty in handling her growing fame. In the end, Joplin funneled all her problems into her music, which made it some of the rawest, most emotionally intense of the late-'60s rock period.

Joplin was born in Port Arthur, Texas, a town noted for its blues heritage. As a child, Joplin was fond of art and poetry and discovered both folk music and the blues. She sang in coffeehouses and folk clubs in Houston and Austin before going to California in 1965. Her initial stay on the West Coast was a short one; the following year she returned to Texas and began singing in an Austin country band. By luck, Joplin heard of a San Francisco blues-rock band, Big Brother and the Holding Company, that was looking for a lead singer. Joplin left Texas for a second time and moved to San Francisco, where, with Big Brother, her career took off.

Joplin and Big Brother released their self-titled debut album on the Mainstream label in early 1967 and performed at the Monterey Pop Festival that June along with other soon-to-be-famous San Francisco rock bands. The success of Joplin and Big Brother's performance landed the group a recording contract with CBS Records. Big Brother's major label debut, *Cheap Thrills*, became a best-seller in 1968, buoyed by the success of the single "Piece of My Heart," which showcased Joplin's tortured blues vocals.

Joplin left Big Brother after *Cheap Thrills* to form her own Kozmic Blues Band. In 1969 Joplin and the group released the album *I Got Dem Ol' Kozmic Blues Again, Mama*, which included one of Joplin's trademark numbers, "Try

(Just a Little Bit Harder).'' The Kozmic Blues Band was, however, a short-lived group. Joplin dissolved it and formed the Full Tilt Boogie Band, with whom she recorded her most-remembered album, *Pearl*. It included the number 1 hit ''Me and Bobby McGee.'' Joplin didn't live to share in the album's success. She died of a heroin overdose in 1970. *Pearl* was released posthumously.

Essential Listening:
Cheap Thrills/CBS (CB 9700)
I Got Dem Ol' Kozmic Blues Again, Mama/CBS (CB 9913)
Pearl/CBS (CB 30322)
Greatest Hits/CBS (CB 32168)

◄ JORDAN, CHARLEY

(born c. 1890, Mabelville, Ark.; died November 15, 1954, St. Louis, Mo.)

Charley Jordan was a popular St. Louis–based guitarist who often worked with piano player PEETIE WHEATSTRAW in the 1930s. Jordan led a colorful life before he settled into the St. Louis blues scene. He grew up in Arkansas, where he taught himself how to play guitar. After serving in the army at the close of World War I, Jordan worked as an itinerant bluesman, playing house parties and small clubs throughout the Delta.

Jordan moved to the St. Louis area in the mid-1920s and got involved in the bootlegging business, which nearly cost him his life. In 1928 he was shot and left partially disabled. Jordan recovered enough to work his way into the St. Louis blues scene, landing a recording contract with Vocalion Records in 1930 and beginning a partnership with Peetie Wheatstraw that would last through the '30s.

The Jordan/Wheatstraw duo became the most popular of the St. Louis guitar/piano teams. It was based on the Scrapper Blackwell/Leroy Carr duo that heralded the guitar/piano blues era of the '30s in cities such as Chicago, Indianapolis, and St. Louis. In addition to working with Wheatstraw, Jordan also acted as a talent scout for the Vocalion and Decca labels. After Jordan's relationship with Wheatstraw began to wither, he frequently performed with fellow guitarist BIG JOE WILLIAMS. Jordan faded from the blues scene in the 1940s. He died in 1954.

Essential Listening:
It Ain't Clean/Agram (2002)
Charley Jordan, 1932–1937/Document (518)
St. Louis Blues, 1929–37/Wolf (WSE 110)

◄ JORDAN, LOUIS

(born July 8, 1908, Brinkley, Ark.; died February 4, 1975, Los Angeles, Calif.)

Louis Jordan was the dean of jump blues in the late 1940s and one of the most popular rhythm & blues artists of the post–World War II period. Taking a cue from jazz bandleader Cab Calloway, Jordan was as much a showman as he was a saxophone player, bandleader, and songwriter. He was blessed with a warm sense of humor and the ability to reach beyond traditionally imposed racial barriers in pop music. Throughout his career, Jordan routinely crossed over into the white record-buying market. He sold millions of records, wrote numerous classic R&B tunes, and appeared in movies.

Jordan was born in Arkansas and learned the rudiments of the saxophone from his father, who was the bandleader for the Rabbit Foot Minstrels. Jordan attended Baptist College in Arkansas and majored in music. After a brief fling with the Rabbit Foot Minstrels, Jordan went north to Philadelphia and played in a variety of bands until he joined drummer Chick Webb's band in 1936. Jordan stayed with Webb until the bandleader's death in 1938. He then formed his own band, the Tympany Five (though the group almost always had more than five members), and signed a recording contract with Decca Records that lasted into the 1950s.

Jordan recorded a number of successful tunes, including "I'm Gonna Move to the Outskirts of Town" and "Five Guys Named Moe," before hitting big with "Caldonia," which was covered by Woody Herman in 1945. Other smashes followed: "Choo Choo Ch' Boogie," "Saturday Night Fish Fry," "Let the Good Times Roll," and "Is You Is, or Is You Ain't (Ma Baby)?" Jordan also criss-crossed the country playing countless one-nighters. Appearances in the films *Meet Miss Bobby Socks* and *Swing Parade of 1946* exposed Jordan's entertaining talents to even wider audiences. By the late 1940s Jordan's brand of jump blues had convincingly made its mark in pop music and Jordan was a major star.

In 1951 Jordan formed a big band, but dissolved it a year later. He ended his association with Decca in 1953 and signed on with Aladdin, hoping to revive his now-sagging career. But clearly Jordan's best days as a recording artist were behind him. Rock & roll was about to become the rage, and rhythm & blues was beginning its slow but steady slide. Still, Jordan continued to perform and record. Stints with Mercury in the late '50s and Ray Charles's Tangerine label in the early '60s kept him and his band working, but produced marginal recordings. Jordan kept performing in the late '60s, mostly as an oldies act. Still other records were cut for the French company Black and Blue, and for JSP in the early '70s. By 1973, Jordan had cut back on his performances and semiretired. He died of a heart attack in 1975. Jordan was inducted into the Blues Foundation's Hall of Fame in 1983 and the Rock & Roll Hall of Fame in 1987.

Essential Listening:

The Best of Louis Jordan/MCA (MCAD 4079)

Jivin' with Jordan/Charly (CDX7)

Five Guys Named Moe (Original Decca Recordings, Vol. 2)/MCA-Decca (MCAD 10503)

One Guy Named Louis: The Complete Aladdin Sessions/Capital Jazz (CDP 7 96804 2)

Mo' of the Best of Louis Jordan: Just Say Moe!/Rhino (R2-71144)

K.

◄ KANSAS CITY RED

(born Arthur Lee Stevenson, May 7, 1926, Drew, Miss.; died May 7, 1991, Chicago, Ill.)

Kansas City Red was a blues drummer who recorded little but toured and performed in Chicago clubs with dozens of noted blues artists, among them ROB-ERT NIGHTHAWK, EARL HOOKER, ELMORE JAMES, BIG WALTER HORTON, BLIND JOHN DAVIS, and JIMMY REED. Red became a musician when still living in Drew, Mississippi, his hometown, after he filled in for Nighthawk's errant drummer in 1944. Red continued playing drums for Nighthawk until 1946, when he began performing in Delta jukes, often with blues guitarist/singer DAVID "HONEYBOY" EDWARDS. Red eventually teamed up with guitarist Earl Hooker; however, the association landed the two musicians and bass player Ernest Lane in prison in 1950 after they were arrested for allegedly stealing audio equipment from a club they had played in Cairo, Illinois.

Upon his release from prison Red relocated to Chicago, where he remained for the rest of his life. He was a regular performer in Chicago blues clubs, backing a variety of artists. Red made his recording debut in 1975 when tracks of his appeared on two Barrelhouse recordings, *Bring Me Another Half Pint* and *Easy Baby and the House Rockers*. In 1979 he recorded the album *Old Friends* with Big Walter Horton, FLOYD JONES, and Honeyboy Edwards for the Earwig label. Kansas City Red died in 1991.

Essential Listening:
Old Friends (with Big Walter Horton, Floyd Jones, and Honeyboy Edwards)/
   Earwig (4902)

◄ K-DOE, ERNIE

(born Ernest Kador, Jr., February 22, 1936, New Orleans, La.)

Ernie K-Doe, a rollicking rhythm & blues singer whose rambunctious stage shows have kept him on the New Orleans R&B club circuit since the 1950s, had a hit song, "Mother-in-Law," in 1961. Written and produced by ALLEN TOUS-SAINT, "Mother-in-Law" topped both the R&B and pop charts that year and brought K-Doe his only true national exposure.

K-Doe was born and raised in New Orleans and sang in gospel groups before he moved to Chicago in 1953. While in the Windy City, K-Doe supposedly sang with the Moonglows and Flamingos, and on his own recorded a batch of blues

229

songs, which were never released, for United Records. A year later, K-Doe returned to New Orleans and formed his own group, the Blue Diamonds. Although the Blue Diamonds recorded a couple of sides for the Savoy label, neither the group nor its music attracted much attention. K-Doe then launched a solo career when he signed a recording contract with Specialty Records in 1955. K-Doe's reputation as an energetic performer made him a top club draw in New Orleans, though he was unable to dent the charts with any of the records he made. That changed when he signed with Minit in 1960 and began working with Toussaint. The third record he released with the label was "Mother-in-Law," which became his signature song.

K-Doe continued to record in the 1960s for Minit and then Duke, but was never able to match the success he had achieved with "Mother-in-Law." In the 1970s and 1980s he performed regularly in New Orleans clubs and fests and worked as a disc jockey. He continues to perform, mostly in small clubs.

Essential Listening:
Ernie K-Doe/Bandy (70004)
Ernie K-Doe: Vol. 2/Bandy (70004)
Mother-In-Law/Stateside (SSL6012)

◄ KENNER, CHRIS

*(born December 25, 1929, Kenner, La.; died January 25, 1976,
New Orleans, La.)*

Although Chris Kenner was a rhythm & blues recording artist, his real talent was in songwriting. Kenner's songs were recorded by a number of artists, including FATS DOMINO and Wilson Pickett. His two best-known songs are "I Like It Like That" and the classic dance-rocker "Land of a Thousand Dances," which Pickett recorded and turned into a best-seller in 1966.

Kenner began his career in gospel in the early 1950s but switched to R&B after recording one song, "Don't Let Her Pin That Charge on Me," in 1955 for the Baton label. In 1957 he signed with the Imperial label and wrote and recorded "Sick and Tired," which made it to number 13 on the R&B charts. A year later Fats Domino cut his version of the song; Domino's record made it to number 22 on the pop charts. In the '50s Kenner also recorded for the Ron and Ponchartrain labels.

Kenner's biggest hit as a singer came with "I Like It Like That," which he recorded for Instant Records. The song peaked at number 2 on both the R&B and pop charts and gave Kenner his biggest taste of success; the English rock group the Dave Clark Five had a top-10 hit with the song in 1965. Despite this exposure, Kenner's lack of vocal dexterity and stage charm, coupled with a serious drinking problem, stifled any chances of following up "I Like It Like That" with another hit. Kenner continued to record until he got in trouble with the law and was sent to prison in the late '60s. Upon his release in 1973, Kenner launched a half-hearted comeback that ended with his death in 1976.

Essential Listening:
The Name of the Place/Bandy (70015)
Land of a Thousand Dances/Peavine (6172)

◄ KENT, WILLIE

(born September 24, 1936, Shelby, Miss.)

A longtime bass player and vocalist on the Chicago blues club scene, Willie Kent and his band, the Gents, recorded their first album, *I'm What You Need*, on the Big Boy label in 1989. Kent's forte—sinewy vocals coupled with robust bass riffs—enabled him to develop a small but loyal following in the '70s and '80s.

Kent was born in Mississippi, where he was first introduced to the blues, specifically to the sounds of MUDDY WATERS and JOHN LEE HOOKER. He and his family moved to Chicago in the 1950s. Eventually, Kent worked his way into the club scene there, occasionally performing with EDDIE TAYLOR and other local bluesmen. As a band-leading bass player, Kent lacked the spotlight and attention normally afforded lead guitarists in blues club settings. However, he has endured as a blues artist whose tenacity has often equalled his talent. He continues to perform regularly in Chicago blues clubs.

Essential Listening:
Ain't It Nice/Delmark (DD 653)
Chicago Blues Session, Vol. 21/Wolf (120.867)

◄ KIMBROUGH, JUNIOR

(born David Kimbrough, July 28, 1930, Hudsonville, Miss.)

Little known outside the Mississippi hill country, Junior Kimbrough is a popular juke-joint owner and performer there whose unique, trance-inducing blues guitar style is dominated by eerily constructed riffs and raw, rocking rhythms.

Kimbrough grew up in Hudsonville, Mississippi, and learned how to play guitar by listening to bluesmen like MISSISSIPPI FRED MCDOWELL. In 1968 he made his first record: "Tramp" backed with "You Can't Leave Me" for the tiny Philwood label. Kimbrough's only other early recorded efforts occurred when he made "Keep Your Hands Off Her" backed with "I Feel Good Little Girl" for High Water and "All Night Long," a song that appeared on volume 2 of the Southland label's National Downhome Festival series. In 1992 Kimbrough was featured in the blues documentary *Deep Blues*, which preceded the recording of his debut album, *All Night Long*, for the Fat Possum label. Produced by blues historian Robert Palmer and recorded at Kimbrough's Mississippi juke joint, *All Night Long* received glowing reviews in *Rolling Stone* and other music magazines and brought some long overdue recognition to Kimbrough.

A contemporary of Mississippi bluesmen R.L. BURNSIDE and BOOBA BARNES, Kimbrough still leads juke joint get-togethers in the Delta and occasionally plays outside the region. He has performed in England and Holland as well as regional blues festivals. Kimbrough continues to record and perform.

Essential Listening:
All Night Long/Fat Possum (FP 1002)
Deep Blues (Various Artists)/Atlantic (82450)

◄ KIMBROUGH, LOTTIE

(aka Lottie Beamon) (born c. 1900, Kansas City, Mo.; death information unknown)

One of Kansas City's best-known classic blues singers in the 1920s, Lottie Kimbrough recorded extensively during the period under a variety of pseudonyms for a variety of labels. Kimbrough was born in Kansas City sometime around the turn of the century. She began her career in the early 1920s singing in the city's red-light clubs and bordellos. In 1925, using the name Lottie Beamon, Kimbrough cut her first records for Paramount, followed by sessions for the Kansas City–based Merrit Records, a label owned by black singer and entertainer Winston Holmes, who often sang with Kimbrough. Kimbrough's "City of the Dead" and "Cabbage Head Blues" were Merrit's best-selling records. Despite the success Holmes had with Kimbrough, the label folded in 1929.

In the mid- and late '20s Kimbrough also recorded for Gennett, using her own name, but for sides recorded for Champion she used the pseudonym Lottie Everson, for Supertone she used Lottie Brown, and for Superior, Martha Johnson. She also reputedly went by the names Clara Carey and Mae Moran. By 1930, Kimbrough had disappeared from the Kansas City blues scene.

Essential Listening:
Lottie Kimbrough and Winston Holmes (1928–29)/Wolf (WSE 114)
The Country Girls! (1927–1935) (Various Artists)/Original Jazz Library (OJL 6)

◄ KING, AL

(born Alvin Smith, August 8, 1926, Monroe, La.)

Blues singer-songwriter Al King first recorded in 1948 for John Dolphin's Hollywood Records and later released some singles in the 1950s and '60s. Although only one of them, "Think Twice Before You Speak," on the Sahara label, made it onto the charts (number 36 in 1966), King was known in Bay Area blues circles as a singer and composer whose talent surpassed his commercial success.

Born in Louisiana, King grew up listening to and singing gospel. He moved to Los Angeles in the mid-'40s and eventually landed a slot in the Johnny Otis Revue. Smith later moved up to the Bay Area, where he began working with bluesman JOHNNY HEARTSMAN, who played guitar on most of the records King cut in the '60s. In 1965 King started his own Flag label and linked up with Sahara, which leased some of King's Flag records, including the minor hit "Think Twice Before you Speak." In the late '60s and '70s King recorded for Kent and Modern and worked with noted producer/arranger Maxwell Davis.

King continued to perform, mostly in Bay Area blues clubs, through the 1980s.

Essential Listening:
On My Way/Diving Duck (4302)

◄ KING, ALBERT

(born Albert Nelson, April 25, 1923, Indianola, Miss.; died December 21, 1992, Memphis, Tenn.)

Bluesman Albert King was one of the premier electric guitar stylists of the post–World War II period. By playing left-handed and holding his guitar upside down (with the strings set for a right-handed player), and by concentrating on tone and intensity more than flash, King fashioned, over his long career, a sound that was both distinctive and highly influential. He was a master of the single-string solo and could bend strings to produce a particularly tormented blues sound that set his style apart from his contemporaries. A number of prominent artists, from ERIC CLAPTON and JIMI HENDRIX to MIKE BLOOMFIELD and STEVIE RAY VAUGHAN, borrowed heavily from King's guitar style.

King was also the first major blues guitarist to cross over into modern soul; his mid- and late 1960s recordings for the Stax label, cut with the same great session musicians who played on the recordings of Otis Redding, Sam & Dave, Eddie Floyd, and others, appealed to his established black audience while broadening his appeal with rock fans. Along with B.B. KING (no relation, though at times Albert suggested otherwise) and MUDDY WATERS, King helped nurture a white interest in blues when the music needed it most to survive.

King was born in Mississippi and taught himself how to play on a homemade guitar. Inspired by BLIND LEMON JEFFERSON, King quit singing in a family gospel group and took up the blues. He worked around Osceola, Arkansas, with a group called the In the Groove Boys before migrating north and ending up in Gary, Indiana, in the early 1950s. For a while, King played drums behind bluesman JIMMY REED. In 1953, King convinced Parrot label owner Al Benson to record him as a blues singer and guitarist. That year King cut "Bad Luck Blues" and "Be on Your Merry Way" for Parrot. Because King received little in the way of financial remuneration for the record, he left Parrot and eventually moved to St. Louis, where he recorded for the Bobbin and the King labels. In 1959 he had a minor hit on Bobbin with "I'm a Lonely Man." King's biggest release, "Don't Throw Your Love on Me So Strong," made it to number 14 on the R&B charts in 1961.

King didn't become a major blues figure until after he signed with Stax Records in 1966. Working with producer-drummer Al Jackson, Jr., guitarist Steve Cropper, keyboards ace Booker T. Jones, and bass player Donald "Duck" Dunn—aka Booker T. and the MGs—King created a blues sound that was laced with Memphis soul strains. Although the blues were dominant on songs such as "Laundromat Blues" and the classic "Born Under a Bad Sign," the tunes had Memphis soul underpinnings that gave King his crossover appeal. Not only was he the first blues artist to play the legendary San Francisco rock venue the Fillmore West, but he was also on the debut bill, sharing the stage opening night in 1968 with Jimi Hendrix and JOHN MAYALL. King went on to become a regular at the Fillmore; his album *Live Wire/Blues Power* was recorded there in 1968. King was also one of the first bluesman to record with a symphony orchestra: in

1969 he performed with the St. Louis Symphony, triumphantly bringing together the blues and classical music, if only for a fleeting moment.

During the 1970s King toured extensively, often playing to rock and soul crowds. He left Stax in 1974 to record for independent labels like Tomato and Fantasy. King was inducted into the Blues Foundation's Hall of Fame in 1983. He continued touring throughout the 1980s and early 1990s, playing festivals and concerts, often with B.B. King. He died of a heart attack in 1992, just prior to starting a major European tour.

Essential Listening:
Masterworks/Atlantic (AD 2-4002)
Live Wire/Blues Power/Stax (4128)
King of the Blues Guitar/Atlantic (8213-2)
Born Under a Bad Sign/Atlantic-Stax (7723)
Let's Have a Natural Ball/Modern Blues Recordings (723)
Laundromat Blues/Edsel (130)
I'm in a Phone Booth, Baby/Fantasy (9633)
Wednesday Night in San Francisco/Stax (MPS 8556)
Thursday Night in San Francisco/Stax (MPS 8557)
The Ultimate Collection/Rhino (71268)

◄ KING, B.B.

(born Riley B. King, September 16, 1925, Indianola, Miss.)

Since the late 1960s, when rock and pop audiences discovered him and his refined, majestic brand of the blues, guitarist and singer B.B. King has been the music's most successful concert artist and its most consistently recognized ambassador. He has been bestowed with more awards and honorary degrees than any other bluesman and has made the cause of preserving the blues his lifetime work. Almost singlehandedly he brought the blues out from the fringe of the American music spectrum and into its mainstream. Thanks to King, blues is now performed in the most prestigious venues and in front of audiences whose introduction to the blues often stems back to the first time they heard a B.B. King record.

King has also had a profound effect on the inner workings of rock & roll. Few, if any, bluesmen have exerted more influence on rock guitarists than King. Greats such as ERIC CLAPTON, Jeff Beck, and Jimmy Page, along with JOHNNY WINTER, Billy Gibbons, and STEVIE RAY VAUGHAN were all touched by King to some degree. As for blues guitarists, virtually every major stylist from the postwar period has, in some capacity, been influenced by the King style. A member of the Blues Hall of Fame and the Rock & Roll Hall of Fame, B.B. King has continued to be a vital performer and prolific recording artist despite advancing age and health problems. His graciousness and articulation, especially when discussing the meaning and significance of the blues, have done much to build respect for the music and its culture.

King's guitar style is essentially a consolidation of deep Mississippi blues and jazz, coupled with strains of gospel, rock, and pop. A trained ear can detect traces of BLIND LEMON JEFFERSON, T-BONE WALKER, and LONNIE JOHNSON in King's guitar solos, as well as those of jazz guitar legends Charlie Christian, Eddie Lang, and Django Reinhardt. King is the acknowledged master of the single-string guitar style and the technique called string bending, which is employed to embellish the emotional intensity of a guitar passage.

King is not a flashy or busy guitarist, yet his solos sting rather than soothe the senses. He often uses vibrato to accent notes and phrases, and he gives his guitar passages plenty of room to breathe within the context of a song's arrangement. At his best, King pushes his guitar solos to become an extension of his voice, so that the result is a practically seamless blues presentation. If there's been any criticism of King and his guitar style, it usually centers on his work being too slick and too neat. However, there is no denying the dynamics and tension that run through his best work. What King has done more than anything else is elevate the blues guitar solo to a high art. He has taken the blues guitar out of smokey clubs and funky roadhouses and relocated it to a more sophisticated setting, namely the concert stage.

Born in Mississippi, King's earliest interest in music came from the church, which is where he learned to sing gospel music. After being taught a few chords on the guitar by the minister of his church, King's interest started to extend beyond just singing. He began listening to guitar-playing bluesmen more intently and was moved by the jazz guitar work of Charlie Christian. As a young man King was a Mississippi Delta farmhand and tractor driver, working the fields during the week and playing music on weekends.

After World War II, King went to Memphis and stayed with his cousin, bluesman BUKKA WHITE, before returning to the Delta in late 1946. He did farm work for one more year before leaving it for good. In 1947, King moved to Memphis. He had heard harmonica player SONNY BOY WILLIAMSON (Rice Miller) perform on West Memphis radio station KWEM; King went to see Williamson and requested work. Williamson had him perform on his program, which led to other work for King on Memphis station WDIA, hawking an alcohol-based tonic called Pepticon and playing and singing blues songs for ten minutes every day.

In 1949, King became a full-time disc jockey on WDIA. Calling himself the Beale Street Blues Boy, later shortened to B.B., King got a blues and jazz education by listening to the records he spun on the air. He also gained some local fame as an on-the-air personality, which he translated into performing dates in Beale Street blues clubs. King worked with numerous musicians, including ROBERT JR. LOCKWOOD, who helped him broaden his blues view by showing him uncommon chords and jazz licks, and the Beale Streeters, an informal group of Memphis musicians (ROSCO GORDON, BOBBY "BLUE" BLAND, Earl Forest, JOHNNY ACE, etc.) that were lumped together for broadcasting and advertising purposes.

King's recording career began in 1949 when he cut four sides for the Nashville-based Bullet label. None of the songs made much of an impression on black record buyers. But in 1951 he recorded at SAM PHILLIPS's Sun studio for Modern/RPM and then, later in the year, at the Memphis YMCA. One of the songs from the latter session, "Three O'Clock Blues," launched King to blues stardom. The record lodged itself in the number 1 slot on the R&B charts and stayed there for seventeen weeks. King's startling success enabled him to go on tour and play as far north as the Apollo Theater in New York City. There were three more number 1 hits: "You Know I Love You" in 1952, "Please Love Me" in 1953, and "You Upset Me Baby" in 1954, all on the RPM label.

During the early and mid-1950s, King recorded prolifically, as he was to do throughout most of his career. Many of his best recordings were not original songs but interpretations of songs penned by other blues composers such as LOW-ELL FULSON, who wrote "Three O'Clock Blues," as well as Memphis Slim, who wrote "Everyday I Have the Blues," which King turned into a hit in 1955. From TAMPA RED, King got "Sweet Little Angel," one of his signature pieces. King was able to breathe new life into these songs and others with his increasingly sculptured guitar work and his powerful vocals.

Another factor in King's success was the sound of his band and the arrangements they used. King had been greatly influenced by the big band blues sound of Count Basie and Duke Ellington and wanted it for his own band, which usually consisted of between eleven and fourteen members. Under the astute direction of West Coast arranger MAXWELL DAVIS, who possessed a keen understanding of how to meld horns into a blues framework and give the resulting sound a sharp sense of swing, King's band had at its disposal some of the best big band blues arrangements ever created. So well crafted were they that King continued to use many of them right into the 1980s.

Throughout the 1950s King seemed to finish one tour only to begin another. In 1956, he reputedly did 342 shows. When not performing, he was recording. However, as the '60s dawned, King's popularity began to wane. Black interest in the blues began to shrink, thanks to the advent of soul and the more urban sounds of R&B, and whites were more fascinated with country bluesmen than a full-fledged blues band of the kind that King led. In 1962 King switched to the ABC/Paramount label with the hope of cultivating a new sound and attracting a new audience. It didn't work; though King's guitar work had never sounded stronger, his blues framework seemed, to some blues fans, stale. Nonetheless, in 1962, King recorded *Live at the Regal*, an album many blues critics contend is the greatest blues recording ever made. King's performance was classic; his guitar gushed with emotional fervor and his vocal delivery was impeccable. Yet the album's critical success did little to push King's career forward.

In the late '60s, B.B. King finally found a new and appreciative audience: rock fans. He began playing rock venues like the Fillmore (East and West) and rock festivals and opened concerts for the ROLLING STONES. Although not a gritty blues guitarist, the kind that most rock fans favored, King was regarded as a blues guitar master by the rock crowd. King solidified his standing within the realm of rock and pop with the success of his version of the Roy Hawkins tune "The Thrill Is Gone" in 1970. The record made it all the way to number 15 on the pop charts (and number 3 on the R&B charts) and reignited interest in King in black music circles.

After "The Thrill Is Gone," King became an elder statesman of the blues. He carried the music through the 1970s—on the whole, bad times for the blues—

with routinely inspiring live performances. He continued to make albums, but King's reluctance or inability to expand his sound or even probe new ideas made them only mildly interesting, except to serious blues guitar listeners and longtime King fans. During the decade King toured Europe regularly and played Las Vegas. He appeared on network television and survived the disco craze at the end of the 1970s. King continued to record and perform through the 1980s, adding Atlantic City to his list of performance locales. With the passing of MUDDY WATERS in 1983, King was looked upon more and more as dean of the blues.

King struck a responsive note with a new generation of rock fans when he forged a friendship with Irish supergroup U2 and appeared on its acclaimed album *Rattle and Hum* in 1988. His guitar and vocal performance on the song ''When Love Comes to Town'' proved that King could still belt out the blues in grand fashion. Although King now suffers from diabetes, his concert schedule remains packed solid and he still manages to make new records. His 1991 album, *There Is Always One More Time*, on MCA Records, was recorded with L.A. session musicians and contained a conscious, though uneven, attempt by King to work his blues into contemporary pop.

King was inducted into the Blues Foundation's Hall of Fame in 1980 and the Rock & Roll Hall of Fame in 1987. A CD box set compilation of some of King's best work, called *King of the Blues*, was released in 1992.

Essential Listening:
King of the Blues (box set)/MCA (D4-10677)
The Best of B.B. King, Vol. 1/Flair (Virgin) (86230)
Live at the Regal/Mobile Fidelity Sound Labs (UDCD 01-00548)
Live in Cook County Jail/MCA (27005)
Blues Is King/MCA (MCAD 31368)
The Rarest King/Blues Boy (301)
Lucille/BGO (BGOLP 36)
Completely Well/MCAD (31039)
Now Appearing at Ole Miss/MCA (MCAD 2-8016)
Live at the Apollo/GRP Records (GRD 9637)
Spotlight on Lucille/Flair (2-91693)

◄ KING, EARL

(born Solomon Johnson, February 7, 1934, New Orleans, La.)

Earl King was one of the architects of New Orleans rhythm & blues in the 1950s and early 1960s. Along with ALLEN TOUSSAINT, DAVE BARTHOLOMEW, FATS DOMINO, and DR. JOHN, King cooked up a soulful mix of blues, gospel, early rock & roll, and primal funk that helped make the Crescent City a major R&B center during the period. King's contributions came in many forms, though he is best known as a composer. His most interesting songs contain clever wordplay and unusual chord progressions that complement his quirky time structures, obviously influenced by New Orleans's traditional second-line rhythms. King's best songs have been covered by PROFESSOR LONGHAIR, Dr. John, JIMI HENDRIX, STEVIE RAY VAUGHAN, the Neville Brothers, and dozens of other name artists.

Guitarist King also worked as a sideman, playing on countless New Orleans recording sessions, and as a record producer. In the 1950s King was one of New Orleans's top recording artists, though his popularity never came close to reaching the level attained by Fats Domino, his contemporary. Still, King's 1955 classic, "Those Lonely Lonely Nights," released on the Ace label, sold nearly a quarter-million copies and influenced the sound of the New Orleans ballad well into the 1960s.

Heavily influenced by GUITAR SLIM, King began his career with Slim followed by a stint with New Orleans pianist HUEY "PIANO" SMITH. King's first recordings were made in 1953 for the Savoy label under the name Earl Johnson. A year later he signed with Specialty Records and recorded "A Mother's Love," an R&B nugget that gave him his first taste of regional success. Next came "Those Lonely Lonely Nights," King's biggest hit. In the late '50s, King occasionally recorded under the name Handsome Earl and continued to work as a studio musician. He signed with Imperial Records in 1960 and recorded a number of his best-known songs, including "Trick Bag" and "Come On, Let the Good Times Roll." Other noted King songs from the period are "Big Chief," which Professor Longhair turned into a regional hit, and the Mardi Gras standard "Street Parade."

King continued to record for a number of minor labels in the '60s and even did some session work for Motown, but in the '70s and '80s, most of his time was spent in the studio working as a producer or session player. King did, however, launch a comeback as a recording artist in the mid-'80s. He signed with Black Top Records and released two albums, *Glazed*, which he recorded with ROOMFUL OF BLUES, and *Sexual Telepathy*. A third solo album, *Hard River to Cross*, came out in 1993. King continues to record and perform.

Essential Listening:
Glazed/Black Top (1035)
Sexual Telepathy/Black Top (BT 1052)
Hard River to Cross/Black Top (BT 1090)

◄ KING, FREDDIE (FREDDY)

(born Freddie Christian, September 3, 1934, Gilmer, Tex.; died December 28, 1976, Dallas, Tex.)

Freddie King (no relation to any of the other blues guitarists named King) was one of the lynchpins of modern blues guitar. Along with OTIS RUSH, BUDDY GUY, and MAGIC SAM, King spearheaded Chicago's modern blues movement in the early '60s and helped set the stage for the blues-rock boom of the late '60s. His influence on such blues-rock titans as ERIC CLAPTON helped preserve a legacy characterized by searing, aggressive guitar solos and the welding of blues and rock into one cohesive sound.

Although Freddie King was born and raised in Texas, he matured as a musician in Chicago. His guitar style combined country and urban influences. As a child, King grew up on the music of such legendary country blues guitarists as BLIND LEMON JEFFERSON, LIGHTNIN' HOPKINS, and ARTHUR "BIG BOY" CRUDUP. After he and his family moved to Chicago in 1950, King began hanging out in clubs where the stinging, city-hot guitar work of such Mississippi Delta–rooted blues-men as MUDDY WATERS, JIMMY ROGERS, and EDDIE TAYLOR filled the air.

Though he first recorded in the 1950s—cutting sides for the obscure El-Bee label and doing a few session dates for Chess—King didn't begin to attract attention until after he signed with Federal Records in 1960. (Federal was a subsidiary of the Cincinnati-based King Record label.) Under the guidance of pianist and King Records A&R man Sonny Thompson, King's early-'60s sessions resulted in such stellar tunes as "Lonesome Whistle Blues" and "I'm Tore Down," as well as a potent rendition of the Bill Myles classic "Have You Ever Loved a Woman." (Eric Clapton did a version of the song during his Derek and the Dominos days.)

King also recorded numerous instrumentals in the early '60s. One song, "Hide Away," reached number 29 on the *Billboard* pop charts in 1961 and ranks among the most popular blues instrumentals ever recorded. Named for Mel's Hideaway Lounge, a noted Chicago blues club, the song showcased King's guitar prowess and inventiveness in combining catchy themes drawn from blues, rock, and rhythm & blues. Thanks to the popularity of twangy guitar instrumentals in the early '60s, King was able to move freely from blues to R&B to rock-flavored blues and novelty songs like "Bossa Nova Watusi Twist," "Monkey Donkey," and "Surf Monkey."

King's relationship with Federal/King ended in 1968. Although King's most productive period was over, he enjoyed a renaissance of sorts in the late '60s when English blues-rock guitarists such as Clapton, Mick Taylor, and Peter Green began covering King tunes and incorporating elements of his guitar style into their own. This brought King renewed recognition and a growing audience among blues-rock fans, plus new recording contract in 1968 with Cotillion, a subsidiary of Atlantic Records. Two years later King jumped to Shelter Records. His last recording contract was with RSO Records in 1974. Though the bulk of King's blues from this era leaned heavily toward funk and rock, his guitar work remained stylish and supple.

King was only forty-two years old when he died in 1976 of bleeding ulcers and heart failure.

Essential Listening:
Freddy King Sings/Modern Blues Recordings (722)
Just Pickin'/Modern Blues Recordings (721)
Getting Ready . . . /Shelter (8003)
Larger than Life/Polydor (831 816-1)
Let's Hide Away and Dance Away with Freddy King/King (773)
17 Original Greatest Hits/Federal (1036)

◀ KING, LITTLE JIMMY

(born Manuel Gales, December 4, 1968, Memphis, Tenn.)

Though guitarist Little Jimmy King got the latter half of his stage name after blues guitar great ALBERT KING "adopted" him as a son, King's guitar style is as much rock-oriented as it is influenced by his musical stepfather. The "Little

Jimmy'' tag is a tribute to King's affection for the blues-rock of JIMI HENDRIX.

King, a left-handed player, broke into the Memphis rock scene in the early 1980s but by 1986 had switched to blues. After a stint with a local group, Omni, King apprenticed with blues harp player MOJO BUFORD. In 1988 King formed his own blues group, Jimmy & the Soul Survivors. A year later King left the local Memphis blues scene to become Albert King's second guitarist. The two musicians forged a father-son relationship. When Little Jimmy left the band to pursue a solo career, he took the King moniker with him. He formed Little Jimmy King & the Memphis Soul Survivors and signed a recording contract with Bullseye Blues Records. His self-titled debut album was released in 1991. King's two older brothers, Eugene and Eric, are two-thirds of the Eric Gales Band, a blues-flavored hard rock trio not unlike the Jimi Hendrix Experience. King continues to record and perform. He lives in Memphis.

Essential Listening:

Little Jimmy King & the Memphis Soul Survivors/Bullseye Blues (BB 9509)

◄ KING CURTIS

(born Curtis Ousley, February 7, 1934, Fort Worth, Tex.; died August 31, 1971, New York, N.Y.)

King Curtis was one of the great rhythm & blues saxophonists. In the 1950s and 1960s his crisp, honking style punctuated dozens of hits, by everyone from the Coasters and the Shirelles to Wilson Pickett, FREDDIE KING, Donny Hathaway, and Aretha Franklin. That Curtis was able to transcend musical genres—he easily crossed over into pop, jazz, and rock territories—enhanced his popularity as both a session artist and bandleader. His signature piece, "Soul Twist," was a number 1 R&B hit in 1962, and has since become a sax standard.

Curtis was born in Texas, where he played sax in his high school marching band. Influenced by jazz legend Lester Young and R&B sax star LOUIS JORDAN, Curtis joined Lionel Hampton's band in 1950 then moved to New York in 1952. Curtis quickly found work as a session musician there; he also began making his own records, though they attracted little attention. His best work was being heard on other artists' records. In 1957 he played the famous sax solo on the Coasters' smash "Yakety Yak"; the song made him one of R&B's best-known sax session players.

Curtis's solo career kicked into gear with "Soul Twist," which temporarily restored the saxophone as a primary instrument in R&B and rock & roll. Other King Curtis R&B hits followed in the 1960s. "Memphis Soul Stew" and "Ode to Billy Joe" both landed in the R&B top 10 in 1967. But it was Curtis's work with Wilson Pickett, Sam & Dave, and especially Aretha Franklin that brought him the most recognition. Unfortunately in 1971, at the peak of his career, Curtis was murdered outside his apartment in New York City. He was thirty-seven years old.

Essential Listening:

King Curtis: Golden Classic/Collectables (Col 5119)

Enjoy . . . The Best of King Curtis/Collectables (Col 5156)

◄ KINSEY, BIG DADDY

(born Lester Kinsey, March 18, 1927, Pleasant Grove, Miss.)

A blues singer and guitarist, Big Daddy Kinsey is the father of Donald, Ralph, and Kenneth Kinsey of the blues-rock band the KINSEY REPORT. Prior to the late '80s, when his sons moved more in a rock and funk direction with their blues, Big Daddy fronted the Kinsey Report. Since then he has toured with the band as an opening act, using his sons as back-up musicians.

Kinsey was born in the Mississippi Delta, where he learned how to sing and play the guitar in church. Influenced as much by the blues as by gospel, Kinsey played parties in the Delta before moving to Gary, Indiana, in 1944. After a stint in the service, he returned to Gary to work in a steel mill. He eventually resumed his blues career by playing weekend dates with local groups such as the Soul Brothers and, in the late '60s, performing with oldest son Donald as Big Daddy and B.B. King, Jr. Kinsey senior eventually enlarged the group, bringing in son Ralph and billing the band Big Daddy Kinsey & His Fabulous Sons.

With his sons exploring rock and reggae during the 1970s and early 1980s, Big Daddy worked clubs and lounges with nonfamily musicians. However, by 1984, the Kinsey clan reunited and formed the Kinsey Report. That year the group, with Big Daddy Kinsey handling the lead vocals, signed with Rooster Blues and released the album *Bad Situation* in 1985. A year later, the Kinsey Report switched labels and signed with Alligator Records, releasing a couple of well-received blues-rock albums. Big Daddy Kinsey moved to Blind Pig Records and recorded a solo effort, *Can't Let Go*, in 1990. He continues to record and perform.

Essential Listening:
Bad Situation/Rooster Blues (R 2620)
Can't Let Go/Blind Pig (BP 3489)

◄ KINSEY REPORT, THE

Members: Donald Kinsey (lead guitar, vocals) (born May 12, 1953, Gary, Ind.); Ralph Kinsey (drums) (born April 26, 1952, Gary, Ind.); Kenneth Kinsey (bass) (born January 21, 1963); Ron Prince (rhythm guitar) (born July 21, 1956, Chicago, Ill.)

From its inception in the mid-'80s, the Kinsey Report has been most interested in creating a swirling mix of blues, rock, and funk-trimmed rhythm & blues, the results of which were punctuated with Donald Kinsey's stinging guitar solos. The Kinsey brothers—Donald, Ralph, and Kenneth—grew up in a traditional blues household in Gary, Indiana. Their father, Lester "BIG DADDY" KINSEY, was a Mississippi Delta–style blues singer who made certain his sons were well versed in down-home blues styles before they ventured off into other blues-related music forms. For a short time in the late '60s, Big Daddy and eldest son Donald performed together as Big Daddy and B.B. King, Jr. (One of Donald's earliest influences and heroes was B.B. KING.) Later, Big Daddy brought second son, Ralph, into the fold and called the new act Big Daddy Kinsey & His Fabulous Sons.

The band dissolved after Donald signed on with ALBERT KING as rhythm guitarist; he played on King's 1972 Stax album, *I Wanna Get Funky*.

In 1975 Donald Kinsey formed a blues-rock trio called White Lightning that included brother Ralph on drums and former King bass player Busta "Cherry" Jones. The band released an unheralded self-titled album on Island that same year. Through his link with Island, Donald Kinsey met Peter Tosh and Bob Marley, the label's biggest artists and reggae's biggest stars. Tosh hired Kinsey to play on his *Legalize It* album and tour as a member of his back-up band. Marley used Kinsey on *Rastaman Vibration* and asked him to become a member of the Wailers, Marley's back-up band. Kinsey accepted the offer and moved to Jamaica in 1976. However, after the bungled assassination attempt on Marley in Kingston, at which Kinsey was present, the guitarist left the band. He returned home and toured with the Staples Singers. Later, he toured and recorded with Tosh, playing guitar on the album *Bush Doctor*.

Wanting to lead his own band, Donald formed the Chosen Ones, a reggae-rock band, with brother Ralph and friend Ron Prince, and self-released a self-titled EP. Though the group was a forerunner of the Kinsey Report, the Chosen Ones was dissolved when Donald rejoined the Wailers for what turned out to be Marley's final U.S. tour in 1981. Kinsey also toured again with Tosh and played on his *Mama Africa* album.

When Donald Kinsey formed the Kinsey Report in 1984, the group also included younger brother Kenneth on bass. Originally called Big Daddy Kinsey and the Kinsey Report, since the lineup included Big Daddy as lead vocalist, the band released the album *Bad Situation* on the Rooster Blues label. However, when the band jumped to Alligator Records in 1984, Big Daddy Kinsey began a solo career, though he also toured with his sons. The Kinsey Report released the albums *Edge of the City* in 1987 and *Midnight Drive* in 1989 before switching to Point Blank–Charisma in 1991 and releasing the album *Powerhouse*. The Kinsey Report continues to record and perform.

Essential Listening:
Bad Situation/Rooster Blues (R 2620)
Edge of the City/Alligator (AL 4758)
Midnight Drive/Alligator (AL 4775)
Powerhouse/Point Blank–Charisma (2-91421)
Crossing Bridges/Point Blank–Charisma (V2-87004)

◄ KIRKLAND, EDDIE

(born August 16, 1928, Kingston, Jamaica)

Along with JOHN LEE HOOKER, BABY BOY WARREN, and BOBO JENKINS, Eddie Kirkland was a prominent member of the Detroit blues scene in the 1950s. An invigorating performer who, like HOWLIN' WOLF, worked wild-man histrionics into his live show, Kirkland has had more of an impact over the years as a performer than as a recording artist.

Born in Jamaica but raised in Alabama, Kirkland sang in his church choir and learned guitar from a local bluesman, Blind Murphy. During his teens, Kirkland boxed and played his guitar for tips in New Orleans before working his way north to Detroit in 1943. Kirkland teamed up with John Lee Hooker, with whom he performed and recorded in the early 1950s. However, his relationship with Hooker ended when the latter began touring regularly outside Detroit. Kirkland remained in Detroit, fronting his own band and becoming a mainstay on the city's blues scene. In 1961 Kirkland recorded with KING CURTIS and his band for the Prestige–Tru Sound label and then relocated to Georgia, where he worked in blues clubs around Macon. Kirkland's most active recording period was from the mid-'60s to the mid-'70s when he cut sides with Hooker for Bluesway and as a solo artist for the King, Volt, and Trix labels.

In the mid-'70s, Kirkland befriended the British blues-rock band Foghat, which, for a short while, exposed him to rock fans still interested in the blues. Since then, Kirkland has survived as a journeyman blues performer working small blues clubs and playing occasional festivals. His most recent album, *All Around the World*, was released on the Deluge label in 1993.

Essential Listening:
Detroit Blues: The Early 1950s (Various Artists)/Blues Classics (12)
It's the Blues Man!/Original Blues Classics (513)
All Around the World/Deluge (Del 3001)

◄ KORNER, ALEXIS
(born April 19, 1928, Paris, France; died January 2, 1984)

Guitarist Alexis Korner was a founder of BLUES INCORPORATED, an early British blues band that exerted great influence on the burgeoning blues and blues-rock scene in London in the early 1960s. To many young British blues-rockers, Korner, like JOHN MAYALL, was an important guiding figure. Future stars, including the ROLLING STONES' Mick Jagger and CREAM'S ERIC CLAPTON, were inspired by Korner's knowledge of American blues and jazz and by his performances with Blues Incorporated at London clubs like the Marquee.

Korner was born in Paris and spent his childhood in various parts of Europe before moving to England in 1939. A jazz fan, Korner played guitar and some piano. In the early 1950s he teamed up with Chris Barber, one of Britain's earliest jazz and blues authorities, in a series of jazz and skiffle groups before forming Blues Incorporated in 1961 with another British blues authority, CYRIL DAVIES. Though Davies quit the following year, Blues Incorporated lasted until 1967. After its demise, Korner spent the next couple of years working with up-and-coming blues rockers like LED ZEPPELIN's Robert Plant and Steve Marriott of Humble Pie. He then formed the group New Church in 1969, and followed it with CCS (the Collective Consciousness Society), which, in 1970, had a hit in England with its version of Led Zeppelin's "Whole Lotta Love." The following year, Korner recorded with B.B. KING in London. Additional Korner projects included the group Snape with Danish guitarist Peter Thorup, and Rocket 88, with pianist Ian Stewart, bass player Jack Bruce, and Rolling Stone drummer Charlie Watts. The makeshift group's self-titled album was released in 1981. Korner died in 1984.

Essential Listening:
Alexis Korner and Cyril Davies/Krazy Kat (789)
The Alexis Korner Collection, 1961–72/Collector Series (CCSLP 150)
R&B from the Marquee/Deram

◄ KUBEK, SMOKIN' JOE

(born November 30, 1956, Grove City, Pa.)

Smokin' Joe Kubek is a Dallas-based guitarist and bandleader whose synthesis of Texas blues and rock is not unlike the sound created by fellow Texan STEVIE RAY VAUGHAN in the 1980s.

When he was still in his teens, Kubek began his career backing bluesmen such as AL "TNT" BRAGGS and FREDDIE KING in Texas blues clubs. He eventually began leading his own Dallas bar bands; after meeting Bnois King, a guitarist and singer from Monroe, Louisiana, the two formed the Smokin' Joe Kubek Band and enlarged its performing territory to include all of Texas and the rest of the Southwest. In 1991 the band signed a recording contract with the Bullseye Blues label and released *Steppin' Out Texas Style*. The group also toured the U.S., playing clubs, college campuses, and blues festivals. The band's follow-up album, *Chain Smokin' Texas Style*, continued Kubek's penchant for raucous, roadhouse-rocking blues. Kubek and the band continue to record and perform.

Essential Listening:
Steppin' Out Texas Style/Bullseye Blues (BB 9510)
Chain Smokin' Texas Style/Bullseye Blues (BB 9524)

L▸

◄ LACY, RUBIN

(born January 2, 1901, Pelahatchie, Miss.; died c. 1972, Bakersfield, Calif.)

An important influence on blues great SON HOUSE, Rubin Lacy was part of the Jackson, Mississippi, blues scene in the 1920s—a scene that also included ISHMAN BRACEY, TOMMY JOHNSON, and CHARLIE MCCOY. Lacy recorded only two sides during his career as a bluesman, but his chiseled vocals and rummaging guitar style played a role in the early development of Delta blues.

Lacy was raised by his grandfather, a preacher. After learning how to play guitar, he left home and worked Mississippi juke joints. He drifted as far north as Illinois in the mid-1920s before returning to the Jackson area, where he frequently performed with the above-mentioned blues musicians and the popular Chatmon family. His two recordings—"Mississippi Jail House Groan" and "Ham Hound Crave"—were cut for Paramount in 1928, although he reputedly played on a number of other recordings made by Mississippi bluesmen. Sometime around 1932 Lacy quit the blues and became a Baptist minister. For the next two decades he preached in Mississippi churches. In the late 1950s Lacy moved to Los Angeles, and later settled in Bakersfield, where he died in or around 1972.

Essential Listening:
Mississippi Moaners, 1927–1942 (Various Artists)/Yazoo (1009)

◄ LASALLE, DENISE

(born Denise Craig, July 16, 1939, Leflore County, Miss.)

A soul-blues singer whose sassiness, feminist sensibility, and sexually charged lyrics have endeared her mostly to black female fans, Denise LaSalle comes from the same school of blues and R&B as Millie Jackson. LaSalle is also a successful songwriter; her song "Married but Not to Each Other" was a big country hit for Barbara Mandrell. She has also formed her own blues society—the National Association for Preservation of the Blues—which endorses and honors artists mostly in the soul-blues and rhythm & blues genres.

LaSalle was born in Mississippi, where her earliest musical influences were country and gospel. After moving to Chicago at age thirteen, she sang with all-female gospel group the Sacred Five. Eventually LaSalle began singing secular music. In 1962 she signed a recording contract with Chess Records, but released no records. Her first album, *A Love Reputation*, came out on the tiny Tarpon label in 1967 and later was distributed by Chess in Europe. LaSalle began recording with Westbound Records in 1970, then moved on to ABC and MCA in the mid-'70s. Much of the material she recorded was funk-based rhythm & blues.

LaSalle didn't turn to the blues until she signed with Malaco in the early 1980s. Since then she's released a number of soul-blues albums, including *Right Place, Right Time* and *Holding Down with the Blues*, and tours regularly.

Essential Listening:
Right Place, Right Time/Malaco (7417)
Love Talkin'/Malaco (7422)

◄ LAWHORN, SAMMY

(born July 12, 1935, Little Rock, Ark.; died April 29, 1990, Chicago, Ill.)

Sammy Lawhorn played guitar in the MUDDY WATERS Band from the mid-'60s to the mid-'70s. Noted for his well-crafted phrasing and dynamics, Lawhorn's guitar signature was the quivering sound he got when he used his tremelo bar. Lawhorn was born and raised in Arkansas; he learned how to play guitar in the late 1940s and occasionally performed with the King Biscuit Boys, a group led by SONNY BOY WILLIAMSON (Rice Miller) in Helena. Lawhorn went into the navy during the Korean War and stayed in the service until 1958. After being discharged, Lawhorn returned to Arkansas and began playing with bluesman WILLIE COBBS. By 1960, Lawhorn had settled in Chicago.

Lawhorn played Chicago's blues clubs; he eventually met Muddy Waters, who invited him to join his band. Lawhorn worked with Waters for a decade, both on the road and in the recording studio, before Lawhorn's alleged growing dependence on alcohol ended the relationship. Lawhorn returned to the Chicago club scene, performing regularly at Theresa's, one of the city's most famous blues clubs, until his death in 1990.

Essential Listening:
Muddy Waters: The Chess Box/MCA-Chess (CHC6-80002)

◄ LAY, SAM

(born March 20, 1935, Birmingham, Ala.)

Sam Lay is a veteran Chicago drummer who has played with many of the city's most celebrated post–World War II blues artists, including HOWLIN' WOLF, MUDDY WATERS, JIMMY REED, OTIS SPANN, and PAUL BUTTERFIELD. Lay is best known as a master of the shuffle beat, one of the blues' most essential rhythms. His "double shuffle," a beat he created after listening to the way sanctified churchgoers clap their hands, has become his drumming trademark.

Lay spent the early '60s playing in Howlin' Wolf's band before he and bass player Jerome Arnold left to join white bluesman Paul Butterfield's band, making it one of the first integrated blues groups in Chicago. Although Lay made only one album with the Butterfield band, the 1966 self-titled classic, it was a breakthrough record that helped spur the late-'60s blues revival. Lay also played drums on Waters's 1969 album, *Fathers and Sons*.

After his stint with Butterfield, Lay went on to work with WILLIE DIXON, BO

DIDDLEY, JOHN LEE HOOKER, HOUND DOG TAYLOR, JIMMY ROGERS, A.C. REED, and the SIEGEL-SCHWALL BAND, another black-white Chicago blues group. Lay currently works Chicago blues clubs with his own outfit, the Sam Lay Blues Band, and free-lances with other blues groups.

Essential Listening:
The Paul Butterfield Blues Band/Elektra (7294-2)
Fathers and Sons (Muddy Waters)/Chess (127)
The Siegel-Schwall Reunion Concert/Alligator (AL 4760)
The Sam Lay Band/Ichiban-Appaloosa

◄ LAZY LESTER

(born Leslie Johnson, June 20, 1933, Torras, La.)

Lazy Lester first surfaced as a blues artist in the mid-1950s, playing harmonica for fellow Louisiana bluesman LIGHTNIN' SLIM and doing session work for producer JAY MILLER and the Excello label. Lester's carefree and not very ambitious personality prompted Miller to call him "Lazy Lester."

As a harp player and vocalist, Lester borrowed heavily from JIMMY REED and LITTLE WALTER. Although his harmonica riffs were crisp and articulate, his vocals were too often one-dimensional and garbled. Despite this, Miller recorded Lester as a solo artist during the late '50s and early '60s, resulting in such singles as "I'm a Lover Not a Fighter" (covered by English rock band the Kinks), its B-side, "Sugar Coated Love," and "I Hear You Knockin'" (both tunes covered by Texas blues-rock group the FABULOUS THUNDERBIRDS), "Whoa Now," and "Lester's Stomp." While on Excello Lester also released one album, *True Blues*, and frequently appeared on Miller-produced songs by Lightnin' Slim, SLIM HARPO, KATIE WEBSTER, and other Excello artists. In addition to harmonica, Lester occasionally played guitar and percussion as a sideman.

From the mid-'60s to the mid-'80s Lester wallowed in obscurity, living in Louisiana and later relocating to Pontiac, Michigan, where his longtime friend Lightnin' Slim lived. In the wake of the late-'80s blues revival, Lester began touring again and recorded an album in 1987, *Lazy Lester Rides Again*, with the British blues band Blues'n Trouble. The album was released in the U.S. on the King Snake label. Flyright Records then released *Poor Boy Blues*, a compilation album of Lester's Excello material, and in 1988, Lester recorded *Harp and Soul* for Alligator Records. The album featured Lester's harp-fueled swamp blues—a curious blend of Louisiana blues and cajun and country music—and his Jimmy Reed–like vocal drone. Lazy Lester continues to perform.

Essential Listening:
Poor Boy Blues/Flyright (544)
Harp and Soul/Alligator (ALCD 4768)

◀ LEADBELLY

(born Huddie Ledbetter, January 21, 1888, Shiloh, La.; died December 6, 1949, New York, N.Y.)

More than any other black folk-blues artist of his time, Leadbelly helped expose his race's vast musical riches to white America, and, in the process, helped preserve a folk legacy that has become a significant part of this nation's musical treasury. Leadbelly was not a blues singer in the traditional sense; he was, rather, more of a songster, that is, one who played blues, spirituals, pop, and prison songs, as well as dance tunes and folk ballads. That many of his songs carried a blues spirit could be traced back to the days when Leadbelly learned about the blues from seminal Texas bluesman BLIND LEMON JEFFERSON. But Leadbelly's greatest contribution to American music was in the folk field. Leadbelly classics such as "Goodnight Irene," "The Midnight Special," "Rock Island Line," "Cotton Fields," and "Bring Me a Little Water, Sylvie" all contain black folk elements that many prewar bluesmen shunned, at least in the recording studio.

Leadbelly certainly led the life of a bluesman. Born and raised in rural Louisiana to hardworking sharecropper parents, he left home as a youth and wandered through Louisiana and East Texas. Though little is known about Leadbelly's early life—he rarely spoke of those days—it is assumed that sometime around 1915 he met Blind Lemon Jefferson and worked and traveled with the legendary bluesman. By this time, Leadbelly (who played guitar, mandolin, piano, and accordion) had settled on the twelve-string guitar as his instrument of choice. He had probably heard the guitar's rich, ringing sound from Mexican musicians who often played in Texas saloons and bordellos. Leadbelly also developed a wonderfully rhythmic guitar style in which he imitated the walking bass figures commonly employed by barrelhouse piano players on Fannin Street, the most celebrated street in Shreveport's red-light district, where Leadbelly was known to have worked in his early years.

A large, muscular man who had an explosive temper, Leadbelly had frequent run-ins with the law. The worst occurred in 1917 when he killed a man in Texas, was convicted of murder, and sentenced to a thirty-year prison term at the Huntsville Prison Farm. Six years were added to the sentence when he tried to escape. Yet Leadbelly was a shrewd prisoner. He used his musical talent to avoid harsh work details and, incredibly, was able to wrangle a pardon from Texas governor Pat Neff in 1925 after he composed and sang a tune for him pleading for freedom.

Leadbelly returned to the Lake Caddo district of Louisiana where he had been raised. But in 1930 he was arrested again, this time for assault with intent to murder. Leadbelly was sent to the Angola Prison Farm in Louisiana where, in 1933, JOHN and ALAN LOMAX discovered him. At Angola to record folk songs sung by prisoners, the Lomaxes were struck by Leadbelly's powerful voice and rhythmic guitar style as well as his wide knowledge of black folk songs. Thanks to the Lomaxes, who petitioned Louisiana governor O.K. Allen to pardon Leadbelly because of his folksinging resources, Leadbelly secured his freedom in 1934 and went to work for the Lomaxes as a chauffeur and occasional performer.

A year later, Leadbelly had taken a second wife and settled in New York City, where he became a favorite among left-leaning white folksingers of the 1930s. Leadbelly became friends and musical partners with Woody Guthrie and Pete Seeger as well as black bluesmen SONNY TERRY and BROWNIE MCGHEE. With them he performed at hootenannies and union halls, often in support of left-wing causes. That Leadbelly got involved with politics and remained for the rest of his days in New York, separated him from his rural Southern roots, and he thus forsook the chance to build a loyal black audience for his many recordings. From 1934 to his death in 1949, Leadbelly recorded for the Library of Congress and Folkways Records as well as other labels. Though his recordings were powerful examples of black folk music, what few were sold most likely went to white listeners.

Leadbelly did not, however, concern himself with just black folk music. Influenced by Guthrie and the other New York–based folksingers, Leadbelly wrote songs such as "Bourgeois Blues" and "Scottsboro Boys" that carried strong political messages. Despite his stature among white folksingers of the 1930s and 1940s, Leadbelly made little money. He and his wife lived constantly on the brink of poverty.

In 1949, after an unsuccessful trip to Paris where he had hoped to build a European following, Leadbelly was diagnosed as suffering from Lou Gehrig's disease, a sickness that destroys the muscular system. He died from the disease later that year. Ironically, in 1950, the Weavers, a folk group led by Pete Seeger, recorded Leadbelly's "Good Night Irene." The song went to number 1 on *Billboard*'s pop charts. Since then a number of artists and rock groups have recorded Leadbelly songs. In 1988, Columbia Records released *Folkways: A Vision Shared*, which contained renditions of Leadbelly and Woody Guthrie songs by such artists as TAJ MAHAL, Brian Wilson, Bruce Springsteen, Sweet Honey in the Rock, Bob Dylan, and John Mellencamp. The net profits went to purchase the Folkways Record catalog for the Smithsonian Institution. Leadbelly was inducted into the Blues Foundation's Hall of Fame in 1986 and the Rock & Roll Hall of Fame in 1988 as one of the music form's chief pioneers.

Essential Listening:
Midnight Special/Rounder (1044)
Gwine Dig a Hole to Put the Devil In/Rounder (1045)
Let It Shine on Me/Rounder (1046)
King of the 12-String Guitar/Columbia (CK 46776)
Alabama Bound/RCA (9600-2)
Leadbelly Sings Folk Songs/Smithsonian/Folkways (SF 40010)

◄ LEAKE, LAFAYETTE

(born c. 1920, Winona, Miss.; died August 14, 1990, Chicago, Ill.)

An inventive and versatile blues pianist, Lafayette Leake made his mark in the 1950s and '60s as a session player for Chess Records and as a recording and performing partner of WILLIE DIXON. Leake was an intensely private man, thus very little is known of his early life. Leonard "Baby Doo" Caston introduced Leake to Dixon around 1952 after the break-up of Caston's and Dixon's group,

the Big Three Trio. During the 1950s, Leake and Dixon recorded with MUDDY
WATERS and other Chess blues artists, including HOWLIN' WOLF, SONNY BOY
WILLIAMSON (Rice Miller), and LITTLE WALTER, as well as with rock & roll artist
CHUCK BERRY. Leake, along with fellow pianist JOHNNIE JOHNSON, helped define
the role the piano would play in the transition from blues to early rock & roll.

When Dixon began working with Cobra Records in 1958, he took Leake with
him as the company's session pianist. Leake played on blues guitarist OTIS RUSH's
Cobra recordings in the late '50s. He continued working with Dixon in the 1960s,
touring and recording with him as a side musician and as a member of Dixon's
Blues All-Stars. In the 1970s Leake quit the band and faded from the blues scene.
His last major public performance occurred in 1986 when he performed in Chuck
Berry's back-up band at the Chicago Blues Festival. He died of diabetes in 1990.

Essential Listening:
Otis Rush: 1956–1958, The Cobra Recordings/Paula (PCD 01)
Willie Dixon—The Chess Box/MCA-Chess (CHD2-16500)
Chess Blues (Various Artists)/MCA-Chess (CHD4-9340)

◄ LEAVY, CALVIN

(born 1941, Stuttgart, Ark.)

Little known outside of Arkansas, bluesman Calvin Leavy is best known for
"Cummins Prison Farm," which he recorded in 1969. This powerful song about
the notorious Arkansas prison revealed Leavy's deep blues intensity, and though
it only dented the R&B charts in 1970 (number 40), it has often been mentioned
as one of the best blues records released in the 1970s.

Leavy was born in Arkansas and learned how to sing and play guitar in church
gospel groups. Drawn more to soul-blues than traditional down-home blues,
Leavy inserted generous dollops of gospel and Southern soul into his delivery,
though his guitar work was often frenzied and jagged. Leavy played blues clubs
in Arkansas and served time at Cummins Prison Farm before signing a record
contract with the tiny Soul Beat label in the late '60s. Although "Cummins Prison
Farm" was a regional hit, Leavy was unable to use it as a springboard to become
nationally known. Leavy continued to perform in Arkansas until he was convicted
of a drug offense and returned to prison in Arkansas.

Essential Listening:
Cummins Prison Farm/P-Vine (2118)

◄ LED ZEPPELIN

Members: Robert Plant (vocals) (born August 20, 1948, Bromwich, England);
Jimmy Page (guitar) (born January 9, 1944, Heston, England); John Paul
Jones (bass) (born June 3, 1946, Sidcup, England); John Bonham (drums)
(born May 31, 1948, Redditch, England; died September 25, 1980, Windsor,
England)

Blues-based British supergroup Led Zeppelin grew from the ashes of an earlier
band, the YARDBIRDS, in 1968. With the release of its classic self-titled debut

album a year later, Led Zeppelin expanded the parameters of the new blues-rock hybrid with scorching, stentorian guitar work and booming bass and drums. In the process, the band introduced rock fans to the music of WILLIE DIXON with orgiastic renditions of "I Can't Quit You Baby" and "You Shook Me," both of which featured Robert Plant's screeching vocals and Jimmy Page's mind-blowing guitar solos.

Zeppelin was formed by Page after the Yardbirds, a group he had joined reluctantly in 1966, dissolved amid ego and artistic squabbles. Live, Led Zeppelin often covered songs by HOWLIN' WOLF and ALBERT KING, as well as Dixon, and used the blues to build the foundation for what would become heavy metal. By the time *Led Zeppelin II* was released in late 1969, the band had already begun to move beyond its blues-rock influences, venturing into previously unexplored hard-rock territories. Led Zeppelin went on to become one of the biggest bands in all of rock in the 1970s, as each succeeding album shot to the top of the charts and concerts were routine sellouts. The band broke up in 1980 after the death of drummer Bonham and the bad publicity that surrounded Page's frequent flirtations with the occult. In the 1980s Plant and Page began solo careers, amid regular calls for a Led Zeppelin reunion. Page's solo work, including his stint with the Firm, has been uneven and unspectacular, while Plant has managed to keep much of his credibility with interesting forays into jazz-rock, rhythm & blues, and progressive heavy metal.

Essential Listening:
Led Zeppelin/Atlantic (SD 19126-2).
Led Zeppelin (box set)/Atlantic (7 82144-2)

◄ LEE, FRANKIE

(born Frankie Lee Jones, April 29, 1941, Mart, Tex.)

A Texas-born rhythm & blues singer whose style recalls the gospel wail of Otis Redding and the soul-blues of BOBBY "BLUE" BLAND and Sam Cooke, Frankie Lee learned how to sing in church choirs and gospel groups. In the early '60s Lee left gospel and turned to rhythm & blues. He began his recording career in 1963 with DON ROBEY's Peacock Records as Little Frankie Lee. In the '60s the label released three Lee recordings—"Full-Time Lover" (a sequel to Little Johnny Taylor's "Part-Time Love"), "Taxi Blues," and "Hello, Mr. Blues"—but none of them attracted much attention outside Texas.

Lee spent the latter half of the '60s touring with ALBERT COLLINS and playing small clubs. In 1973, he moved out of Texas and settled in Oakland, where he played West Coast blues clubs, occasionally venturing back home for extended stays and occasional performances. Lee resumed his recording career in 1984 when Hightone Records released his album *The Ladies and the Babies*. The album contained a cameo appearance by Lee's cousin, JOHNNY "GUITAR" WATSON.

Lee moved east to New Jersey in the mid-'80s, hoping to restoke his career by playing blues clubs in the New York City area. He headlined the Jersey Shore Jazz & Blues Festival in 1988 and 1989, but then left New Jersey for Virginia where he began fronting the BLUZBLASTERS. Their album *Sooner or Later* was released in 1992 on the Flying Fish label. Later that year Lee ended his association with the Bluzblasters and moved back to the San Francisco Bay area, where he continues to perform.

Essential Listening:
The Ladies and the Babies/Hightone (HT 8004)
Sooner or Later (with the Bluzblasters)/Flying Fish (FF 70595)

◄ LEGENDARY BLUES BAND, THE

Original members: Willie Smith (drummer) (born 1935, Helena, Ark.); Calvin Jones (bass) (born 1926, Greenwood, Miss.); Pinetop Perkins (piano) (born July 7, 1913, Belzoni, Miss.); Jerry Portnoy (harmonica) (born November 25, 1943, Evanston, Ill.)

The Legendary Blues Band was formed in 1980 after drummer Willie Smith, bass player Calvin Jones, harmonica player Jerry Portnoy, and pianist Pinetop Perkins left the MUDDY WATERS Band. Smith, Jones, and Perkins had all been with Waters for about a dozen years. Portnoy had come aboard in 1974.

The Legendary Blues Band signed a contract with Rounder Records, employed Louis Myers to play guitar, and recorded the album *Life of Ease* in 1981. The band recorded its follow-up album, *Red Hot & Blue* in 1983. Perkins left in 1985, followed by Portnoy a year later. The band managed to stay together, however, with Jones and Smith sharing the leadership position and a variety of musicians filling out the group's lineup. Although the Legendary Blues Band had become a popular club act, the group was unable to sustain much momentum, due mostly to its ever-changing personnel. The band signed a new recording contract with Ichiban Records in 1989. That year Smith and Jones added guitarists SMOKEY SMOTHERS and Billy Flynn and harmonica player Mark Koenig to the band and recorded the album *Woke Up with the Blues*, which was nominated for a W.C. HANDY Award. Since then the group has continued to record and perform regularly on the blues club and blues festival circuit.

Essential Listening:
Life of Ease/Rounder (2029)
Red Hot & Blue/Rounder (2035)
Prime Time Blues/Ichiban (9015)

◄ LENOIR, J.B.

(born March 5, 1929, Monticello, Miss.; died April 29, 1967, Urbana, Ill.)

Unlike many blues composers who wrote mostly about the ups and downs of love, J.B. (the initials were his given name) Lenoir often penned songs of social commentary. Tunes such as "Everybody Wants to Know," which issued a stern warning about hunger in America, "Deep in Debt Blues," which dealt with poverty, and "Eisenhower Blues" and "Korea Blues," which explored issues of politics and war respectively, predated the protest-rock trend of the 1960s. Yet, inexplicably, despite the added virtues of a good voice and competent guitar skills, Lenoir was never able to achieve real commercial success in his career.

Born in Mississippi to guitar-playing parents, Lenoir learned how to play the instrument from his father. After apprenticing at house parties and picnics, Lenoir made his way to New Orleans, where he worked for a while with ELMORE JAMES and SONNY BOY WILLIAMSON (Rice Miller). From New Orleans, Lenoir headed north, winding up in Chicago in 1949. BIG BILL BROONZY befriended him and helped him work his way into the city's blues club scene. By 1951, Lenoir had signed a recording contract with Chess, then moved on to the J.O.B. label, followed by a stint with the Parrot label, and finally returning to Checker (Chess) in 1955, with whom he remained until 1958.

Lenoir was a popular player on the Chicago blues scene well into the '60s and continued to record with various small blues labels. A 1965 tour of Europe with the American Folk Blues Festival package led to a second tour in 1966 and a chance to expand his popularity beyond Chicago. But tragically, Lenoir was involved in a serious car wreck that year, which resulted in a fatal heart attack. He was thirty-eight years old when he died.

Essential Listening:
J.B. Lenoir, 1951–1954: His J.O.B. Recordings/Paula (PCD 4)
Natural Man/MCA-Chess (9323)

◄ LEWIS, FURRY

(born Walter Lewis, March 6, 1893, Greenwood, Miss., died September 14, 1981, Memphis, Tenn.)

From his rediscovery in the late 1950s until his death in 1981 at age eighty-eight, Furry Lewis played the role of a Memphis blues ambassador. Not only did he record and tour regularly, but Lewis appeared in movies (*W.W. and the Dixie Dance Kings* with actor Burt Reynolds), on television ("The Tonight Show" with Johnny Carson), and in the print media (*Playboy* did a feature on Lewis). Singer Joni Mitchell wrote a song about him, "Furry Sings the Blues," and Richard Fariña named his acclaimed '60s novel *Been Down So Long, Looks Like Up to Me* after a line in Lewis's song "I Will Turn Your Money Green."

Lewis possessed a unique sense of humor and showmanship that endeared him to blues fans. But he was also an accomplished if unconventional guitarist and an intriguing songwriter in his early days. His song lyrics were witty and well crafted, and although he recorded only twenty-three sides for the Vocalion and Victor labels between 1927 and 1929, his music has stood the test of time.

Lewis was born in the Mississippi Delta but moved to Memphis when he was a young boy. After teaching himself how to play the guitar, Lewis left home and traveled throughout the South, often working with medicine and minstrel shows. In 1916, a train mishap resulted in the loss of a leg; from that point on, Lewis walked on a peg leg. Lewis eventually returned to Memphis, where he worked street corners and parks with Memphis bluesmen such as WILL SHADE and GUS CANNON. Later, he performed with the MEMPHIS JUG BAND at house parties and picnics in and around the city. To supplement the tips he received from his music, Lewis began working with the Memphis Sanitation Department as a street cleaner in 1922. It was a job he held for some forty years.

Lewis was rediscovered in 1959 by blues historian and record producer Sam Charters. Lewis recorded for the Folkways label that year and went on to appear at numerous folk and blues festivals in the '60s and '70s. Lewis was featured in several blues documentaries, including *The Blues* in 1963 and *Roots of American Music: Country & Urban Music* in 1971. Lewis was a colorful raconteur, which made him a popular club and concert attraction on the blues circuit. Although he had lost some of his dexterity in his later years, he remained a versatile guitarist, capable of surprisingly intricate finger-picking techniques and slippery slide guitar riffs. Lewis remained active in the blues right on up to his death.

Essential Listening:
In His Prime, 1927–28/Yazoo (1050)
The Remaining Titles/Wolf (101)
Furry Lewis, 1927–1929/Wolf (WSE 101)

◄ LEWIS, MEADE LUX

(born Meade Lewis, September 4, 1905, Chicago, Ill.; died June 7, 1964, Minneapolis, Minn.)

Pianist Meade Lux Lewis helped establish boogie-woogie as a major blues piano style in the 1930s and 1940s. Along with fellow boogie-woogie pianists ALBERT AMMONS and PETE JOHNSON, Lewis took the rollicking piano form out of the clubs and cathouses and onto the concert stage in 1938 where its fast-flowing rhythms and charging solos delighted audiences and eventually laid the groundwork for rhythm & blues and later rock & roll.

Lewis was a master boogie-woogie craftsman. He was heavily influenced by such boogie-woogie pioneers as JIMMY YANCEY and PINE TOP SMITH. Lewis recorded "Honky Tonk Train Blues," his signature piece and a standard in the boogie-woogie repertoire, in 1927, though it wasn't released by Paramount Records until two years later. The piece ranks with "Yancey Special" and "Pine Top's Boogie Woogie" as the greatest recorded early examples of boogie-woogie piano.

Lewis was born in Chicago in 1905. In the mid-1920s he met Albert Ammons, a fellow pianist, who, like Lewis, drove a taxi for a living. Eventually they shared an apartment together in the same building where Pine Top Smith resided. All three pianists became good friends, often sharing ideas and jamming together. It is not surprising then that Lewis's "Honky Tonk Train Blues" bears a striking resemblance to Smith's "Pine Top's Boogie Woogie."

After the death of Smith in 1929 at age twenty-five and the onset of the Depression, interest in boogie-woogie faded, forcing Lewis to seek other forms of employment to supplement his meager income from playing the piano. Despite boogie-woogie's decline, Lewis continued to record in the 1930s, occasionally cutting sides as a session man playing behind singers George Hannah and Bob Robinson.

Lewis and Ammons were key figures in the boogie-woogie renaissance of the late 1930s and early 1940s. Contacted by talent scout John Hammond to play his 1938 Spirituals to Swing concert at Carnegie Hall in New York City, Lewis, along with Ammons and fellow pianist Pete Johnson, so excited concertgoers with their bristling boogie-woogie piano passages that the music's second craze began then and there. Lewis and his colleagues were booked to play the Cafe Society, a chic Manhattan club where the best boogie-woogie would be heard through 1941.

Lewis remained in New York until that year, at which time interest in boogie-woogie had begun to wither a second time. He relocated in Los Angeles, where he resumed his club work and recording career. Lewis recorded for the Asch label in 1944, though he and boogie-woogie were no longer vital parts of the blues scene. He also continued to perform, usually in small clubs and lounges. Lewis died in an automobile crash in 1964.

Essential Listening:
Meade Lux Lewis, 1927–1939/Document (DD 534)
Meade Lux Lewis, 1939–1954/Blues Documents (2031)
Meade Lux Lewis and Cripple Clarence Lofton/Euphonic (1209)
Tell Your Story/Oldie Blues (2805)
Meade Lux Lewis, Vol. 1/Oldie Blues (2820)
Chicago Piano Blues and Boogie Woogie, 1936–1951/Oldie Blues (2827)

◄ LEWIS, NOAH

(born September 3, 1895, Henning, Tenn.; died February 7, 1961, Ripley, Tenn.)

Noah Lewis was one of the most important blues harmonica players of the pre–World War II period. His acute sense of tone and his expressive, intricately woven solos set within the framework of early blues and jug band music went a long way toward setting the standards by which future harp players would be judged. Lewis also possessed incredible breath control; using his nose, he was able to play two harps at once as well as duplicate the sound of a train, birds, and a human whine.

Lewis was born in Henning, Tennessee, and taught himself how to play the harmonica. He played picnics and house parties and fell in with banjo player GUS CANNON and guitarist SLEEPY JOHN ESTES. By the 1920s Lewis was playing Memphis street corners and parks for tips. When Cannon formed the Jug Stompers in 1928, Lewis joined as the group's harmonica player. He recorded with the Jug Stompers and as a solo artist in the late 1920s for the Victor and Bluebird labels and continued to work the Memphis area as a pickup musician, street player, and occasional companion of Cannon in the early '30s. When the jug band fad began to fade, Lewis left Memphis and settled in Ripley, where he spent the remainder of his life. He died in 1961.

Essential Listening:
Gus Cannon's Jug Stompers/Yazoo (1082/83)

◄ LEWIS, SMILEY

(born Overton Amos Lemons, July 5, 1920, Union, La.; died October 7, 1966, New Orleans, La.)

A New Orleans rhythm & blues singer in the 1950s, Smiley Lewis is best known for his hit "I Hear You Knocking," which featured HUEY "PIANO" SMITH on piano. Lewis began his career by singing in clubs in and around New Orleans. Thanks to a gritty voice that was perfectly suited for down-home rhythm & blues, Lewis secured a contract with DeLuxe Records in 1947 and recorded under the name Smiling Lewis. By 1950 he had signed with the Imperial label and began a decade-long relationship with noted producer DAVE BARTHOLOMEW. Though Lewis experienced success on the R&B charts with "The Bells Are Ringing" (number 10) in 1952 and "I Hear You Knocking" (number 2) in 1955 and wrote other songs that artists such as Elvis Presley ("One Night") and FATS DOMINO ("Blue Monday") turned into pop hits, he was never able to cross over into the pop domain the way Domino and other New Orleans artists had.

Lewis stayed with Imperial until 1960. The following year he signed with Okeh but was unable to revive his career. Stints with the Dot and Loma labels followed but the results were the same. By the mid-'60s, Lewis was suffering from stomach cancer. He died of the ailment in 1966.

Essential Listening:
Smiley Lewis, Volume 1/K.C. (CD 01)
Smiley Lewis, Volume 2/K.C. (CD 02)

◄ LIGGINS, JIMMY

(born October 14, 1922, Newby, Okla.; died July 18, 1983, Durham, N.C.)

Jimmy Liggins, the younger brother of rhythm & blues bandleader, singer, and pianist JOE LIGGINS, was also an R&B singer and bandleader in the 1940s and 1950s. Unlike Joe, however, Jimmy played guitar, and his band's sound, though it featured a similar mix of swing, blues, and pop, possessed more rocking rhythms than Joe's band, the Honeydrippers. Jimmy Liggins tried a career in radio as a disc jockey and in sports as a boxer before he became his brother's chauffeur and then a bandleader in his own right in 1946.

Liggins signed with the Specialty label in 1947. From 1948 to 1953 he had three top-10 hits on the R&B charts: "Teardrop Blues" (1948), "Don't Put Me Down" (1949), and "Drunk" (1953). Other Jimmy Liggins trademark songs included "Cadillac Boogie" (the song that inspired Jackie Bronston's "Rocket 88," according to some music historians the very first rock 'n' roll record) and "I Ain't Drunk." Liggins toured the West Coast and Southwest with his band, the Drops of Joy, and catered to a jump blues audience. In 1949, Liggins was shot in the face in Jackson, Mississippi. Though the bullet broke his jaw and severed his tongue, he recovered and resumed his career. By 1954, Liggins had left Specialty for Aladdin. Though he continued to record, he was never able to recapture the success he achieved in the late '40s. In 1958 he started his own label, Duplex, which he kept until 1978. In the mid-'70s Liggins moved from

Los Angeles to Durham, N.C., where he opened a music school. He died in 1983.
   Essential Listening:
Jimmy Liggins and His Drops of Joy/Specialty (SPCD 7005)
Rough Weather Blues/Specialty (SPCD 7026)

◄ LIGGINS, JOE

(born 1915, Guthrie, Okla.; died July 26, 1987, Los Angeles, Calif.)
   Joe Liggins and the Honeydrippers were a popular rhythm & blues band in
the 1940s and 1950s. The outfit, which included saxophonist Willie Jackson,
based its sound on a mixture of pop, big band swing, and blues and featured
Liggins's rhythmic piano passages and smooth vocals. Liggins's biggest record,
"The Honeydripper" (number one in 1945), was rhythm & blues' first million-
selling instrumental.
   Liggins and his younger brother Jimmy, who was also a popular R&B bandleader, were born in Oklahoma. In 1932, when Joe was a teen, the family moved
to San Diego. Liggins had become proficient on piano and had studied some
music theory before he went to Los Angeles in 1939 and apprenticed in blues-
based combos, one of which included Illinois Jacquet on saxophone. By the mid-
1940s, Liggins had formed his own band; he signed a recording contract in 1945
with Exclusive Records. In the three years he was with the label, Liggins registered nearly a dozen hits, including "The Honeydripper" and "I Got a Right to
Cry," both considered R&B classics. When Exclusive folded in 1949, Liggins
joined his brother on the Specialty label. His song "Pink Champagne" made it
to number 1 on the R&B charts in 1950 and was voted R&B record of the year
by *Billboard Magazine*. Like the music of LOUIS JORDAN, AMOS MILBURN, and
other R&B bandleaders, Liggins's jump blues sound filled the gap between swing
and early rock & roll. But by the mid-1950s, Liggins's brand of R&B began to
wane in popularity and gave way to bands with harder-edged sounds. After Liggins left Specialty in late 1954, he moved to the Mercury label, then to Aladdin,
then back to Mercury in 1962, never matching the success he enjoyed with Specialty or Exclusive. However, Liggins and his band continued to play dates on
the West Coast through the mid-1980s, never really abandoning the jump blues
sound of the golden years of rhythm & blues. Liggins died in 1987.
   Essential Listening:
Joe Liggins & the Honeydrippers/Specialty (SPCD 7006)
Dripper's Boogie/Specialty (SPCD 7025-2)

◄ LIGHTNIN' SLIM

*(born Otis Hicks, March 13, 1913, St. Louis, Mo.; died July 27, 1974, Detroit,
Mich.)*
   Lightnin' Slim was one of the first post–World War II Baton Rouge blues
artist to record, thus paving the way for Louisiana swamp blues to become a
viable part of the blues market in the 1950s and early 1960s. Slim epitomized
down-home swamp blues with his slow drawl, primitive guitar sound, and rough-

cut recordings. He influenced virtually every major Baton Rouge bluesman to follow him into the recording studio, including SLIM HARPO, SILAS HOGAN, GUITAR KELLEY, and LAZY LESTER.

Slim was born in St. Louis but moved to Louisiana as a youth to work as a farmhand. His father taught him how to play guitar, but it wasn't until 1946, when he went to Baton Rouge, that he began to take performing seriously. Slim played small clubs and juke joints outside of Baton Rouge from 1946 until his discovery by record producer JAY MILLER in 1954. That year Miller recorded Slim's "Bad Luck Blues" for the Feature label. The record was important, for it captured the raw swamp blues sound that had been popular in Louisiana for years, but which no one had thought enough of to record. Slim also briefly recorded for Ace Records that year and continued to work Baton Rouge clubs. In 1955 he began recording for the Excello label. That same year he formed a loosely structured trio made up of harmonica player Lazy Lester and whatever drummer happened to be available at the time. Later, when Lester left to begin his own career, Slim played with harp man WHISPERING SMITH.

Slim's best-selling song, "Rooster Blues," made it to number 23 on the R&B charts in 1959. Although he continued to record for Excello until 1966, Slim was unable to match his previous success. He moved to Detroit in the mid-'60s and later joined Slim Harpo's band. In 1970 Slim launched a minor comeback when he re-signed with Excello and began touring England and continental Europe. He performed at the Montreux Jazz Festival in Switzerland in 1972 and played dates with the American Blues Legends package in Europe the following year. After returning home in 1973, Slim's health began to fail. He died of cancer in 1974.

Essential Listening:
Rooster Blues/Excello (8000)
Bell Ringer/Excello (8004)
Rollin' Stone/Flyright (CD 08)
Blue Lightning/Indigo (IGO 2002)

◄ LIL' ED WILLIAMS

(born April 8, 1955, Chicago, Ill.)

Blues guitarist and singer Lil' Ed Williams is the nephew of slide guitar legend J.B. HUTTO. In 1986 Williams was washing cars by day and playing guitar by night with his band, the Blues Imperials, in Chicago clubs when BRUCE IGLAUER of Alligator Records asked the group to record a song for *The New Bluebloods*, an album sampler of Chicago blues talent. Williams and the Blues Imperials cut the song "Young Thing" along with twenty-nine other songs—all in one session. Many of those songs were included on the band's debut album, *Roughhousin'*, released later that year on Alligator.

Born in Chicago, Williams grew up surrounded by the blues, but it wasn't until he was fifteen that he began to play guitar. Picking up tips from Hutto, Williams and his half-brother, bass player James "Pookie" Young, became proficient enough on their instruments to form the Blues Imperials in 1975 and begin playing Chicago blues clubs. In addition to Williams and Young, the original

Blues Imperials also consisted of drummer Louis Henderson and rhythm guitarist Dave Weld. Henderson and Weld left the band after the release of *Roughhousin'* and were replaced by drummer Kelly Littleton and second guitarist Mike Garrett.

The band's second album, *Chicken, Gravy & Biscuits*, was released in 1989; on it, Williams continued his mastery of high-flying barroom blues, complete with wailing guitar solos. Lil' Ed and the Blues Imperials continue to perform and record.

Essential Listening:
Roughhousin'/Alligator (AL 4749)
Chicken, Gravy & Biscuits/Alligator (AL 4772)
What You See Is What You Get/Alligator (AL 4808)

◄ LIPSCOMB, MANCE

(born April 9, 1895, Navasota, Tex.; died January 30, 1976, Navasota, Tex.)

Mance Lipscomb, a Texas sharecropper and self-described songster whose vast repertoire included everything from straight blues and spirituals to simple folk tunes and children's songs, didn't begin recording until he was sixty-five years old. In 1960 California folklorists Chris Strachwitz and Mack McCormick discovered Lipscomb in Navasota, Texas, and recorded him virtually on the spot. Most of the songs Lipscomb sang that day wound up on *Mance Lipscomb, Texas Songster*, his very first recording, and the debut release on Strachwitz's Arhoolie label later that year.

Lipscomb spent almost all of his working life in Brazos County, Texas, farming a twenty-acre plot of bottomland and on weekends performing at country dances, picnics, and house parties. Lipscomb's father, an emancipated slave and fiddler, taught him the rudiments of fiddling; later Lipscomb taught himself how to play guitar and eventually developed a supple, richly textured finger-picking style that complemented his hushed, easy-flowing vocals. Rather than just play the blues, Lipscomb, like fellow songsters LEADBELLY and JESSE FULLER, performed most types of roots music, since a songster's survival often depended on his performing versatility.

Lipscomb recorded five volumes of country blues and folk music for Arhoolie in the '60s and frequently performed at folk and blues festivals throughout the U.S. He also recorded one album, *Trouble in Mind*, for Reprise Records in 1970. His vast storehouse of songs and stories and his intricate finger-picking technique influenced many of the fledgling white folk artists caught up in the folk-blues boom of the early '60s.

Lipscomb's life and music have been well documented on film. He appeared in several '60s and early-'70s blues documentaries, including *The Blues* (1962), *The Blues According to Lightnin' Hopkins* (1968), *Blues Like Showers of Rain* (1970), *A Well Spent Life* (1971), and *Out of the Black into the Blues* (1972). Lipscomb retired from performing in 1974; he died two years later at age eighty-one.

Essential Listening:
Texas Songster/Arhoolie (306)

Texas Songster and Sharecropper/Arhoolie (1001)
Texas Songster, Vol. 2/Arhoolie (1023)
Texas Songster, Vol. 3/Arhoolie (1026)
Mance Lipscomb, Vol. 4/Arhoolie (1033)

◄ LITTLE CHARLIE AND THE NIGHTCATS

Members: Charlie Baty (guitar) (born July 10, 1953, Birmingham, Ala.); Rick Estrin (vocals, harmonica) (born October 5, 1950, San Francisco, Calif.); Dobie Strange (drums) (born November 15, 1948, Red Bluff, Calif.); Brad Lee Sexton (bass) (born November 11, 1948, South Carolina)

Little Charlie and the Nightcats, a northern California quartet, employ various shades of humor and barroom wit to brighten their blend of straight Chicago blues, jazz-flavored West Coast blues, Texas swing, rockabilly, and rhythm & blues.

Long a Bay Area bar band, the Nightcats took permanent shape in 1976 when Charlie Baty, then a harmonica player and vocalist who also happened to play guitar, teamed up with Rick Estrin, a self-taught, accomplished harp player and singer inspired by the styles of LITTLE WALTER, SONNY BOY WILLIAMSON (Rice Miller), and JAMES COTTON. With Baty on guitar and Estrin assuming the harp and vocal chores, plus Dobie Strange on drums and Jay Peterson on bass, Little Charlie and the Nightcats developed a loyal following among blues and roots-music fans in northern California.

In 1986 the group signed a recording contract with Alligator Records and released its debut album, *All the Way Crazy*, the following year. This recording and the others Little Charlie and the Nightcats have since made for Alligator contain lyrics steeped in playful repartee and a sense of swing that recalls the jump blues of LOUIS JORDAN.

In 1990 Brad Lee Sexton replaced Peterson on bass. Little Charlie and the Nightcats tour the U.S. and Europe extensively, performing at both small blues clubs and large outdoor festivals.

Essential Listening:
All the Way Crazy/Alligator (AL 4753)
Disturbing the Peace/Alligator (4761)
The Big Break!/Alligator (AL 4776)
Night Vision/Alligator (AL 4812)
Captured Live/Alligator (AL 4794)

◄ LITTLE MILTON

(born Milton Campbell, September 7, 1934, Inverness, Miss.)

Stylistically set somewhere between the soul-blues of BOBBY "BLUE" BLAND and the refined urban blues of B.B. KING, Little Milton has spent virtually all of his career in a blues limbo. His guitar craft has always gone unchallenged; his careful attention to texture and tone and his penchant for notes that sing instead of sting has made him a staple on the chitlin' circuit for some four decades. But his inability to create a clearly identifiable sound has prevented him from crossing over into pop markets and enjoying some of the acclaim that, for years, has gone to Bland and King.

Little Milton was born and raised in Mississippi. He taught himself how to play the guitar by listening to the radio and to local bluesmen performing at Delta picnics and house parties. Influenced as much by country music as he was by the blues, Little Milton soaked in guitar styles like a sponge. His first experience as a recording artist occurred when he was a member of WILLIE LOVE's band the Three Aces in 1951. The group recorded for the Trumpet label. Milton next worked with IKE TURNER, who recommended him to SAM PHILLIPS of Sun. Phillips recorded Little Milton in 1953 and 1954, but both his records and his brand of blues went unnoticed.

Little Milton recorded one single for the Meteor label in 1957 before moving to East St. Louis, Illinois, and signing with the fledgling Bobbin label in the mid-'50s. Milton's tenure with Bobbin resulted in his first semblance of a hit with "I'm a Lonely Man." He stayed with Bobbin until 1960, all the while developing a fan base on the chitlin' circuit.

Milton switched to Checker (Chess) in 1961; four years later he registered his first number 1 hit on the R&B charts with "We're Gonna Make It." Other hits for Chess followed until he left the label in 1969. Milton continued to make records and perform, recording for Stax and lesser-known labels like Glades and Golden Ear in the '70s and appearing at the Wattstax music festival in 1972. In the 1980s he jumped to the Jackson, Mississippi–based Malaco label, where he remains. Little Milton's albums sell at a steady clip and epitomize the modern soul-blues sound. In 1988 Milton was inducted into the Blues Foundation's Hall of Fame. He continues to perform regularly, mostly in the South.

Essential Listening:
We're Gonna Make It/Little Milton Sings Big Blues/Chess (CHD 5906)
The Sun Masters/Rounder (SS 35)
Movin' to the Country/Malaco (7445)
Age Ain't Nothin' but a Number/Modern Fidelity Sound Labs (MFCD 766)
The Blues Is Alright!/Evidence (ECD 260 26-2)

◄ LITTLE MIKE

(born Michael Markowitz, November 23, 1955, Queens, N.Y.)

Little Mike is a harmonica player, vocalist, and piano player whose band, the Tornadoes, plays a blue-collar brand of rocking blues. Born in New York, Little Mike grew up listening to records by JOHN LEE HOOKER, MUDDY WATERS, and LITTLE WALTER. In 1978 he formed the Tornadoes and began playing blues and rock bars in New York City. The band, which experienced numerous personnel changes over the years, also backed such bluesmen as PINETOP PERKINS, HUBERT SUMLIN, and JIMMY ROGERS on tour.

In 1988, Little Mike produced Perkins's album *After Hours* for Blind Pig Records. The following year he produced Sumlin's *Heart & Soul* album. In 1990 Blind Pig gave Little Mike & the Tornadoes their own recording contract. The band's debut, *Heart Attack*, features cameo appearances by Perkins, Sumlin, PAUL BUTTERFIELD, and others. The band's follow-up album, *Payday*, came out in 1992.

Little Mike & the Tornadoes have performed in blues clubs and at festivals, both in the U.S. and Europe. They continue to tour regularly.

Essential Listening:
Heart Attack/Blind Pig (BP 73990)
Payday/Blind Pig (BP 74992)

◄ LITTLE RICHARD

(born Richard Penniman, December 5, 1932, Macon, Ga.)

Little Richard was what happened when rhythm & blues turned into rock & roll. For three years—1955 through 1957—Little Richard practically ruled both the pop and R&B charts with some of the most frenetic piano-pounding music ever made. Smashes such as ''Tutti Frutti,'' ''Long Tall Sally,'' ''Lucille,'' and ''Good Golly Miss Molly'' gushed with unbridled sexual urgency and rhythms that romped and stomped and knocked over everything in their path. Little Richard's gospel-crazed shouting vocal style and wild piano antics only strengthened the music's vast energy and excitement. No other rhythm & blues artist endowed rock & roll with such glorious gifts.

Richard grew up in a religious household in Macon, Georgia. As a child he learned how to sing and play the piano in church. Because of problems stemming from his homosexuality and his growing desire to embark on a career as an entertainer, Richard left home when he was just fourteen years old and worked the chitlin' circuit with B. Brown and His Orchestra, and minstrel troupes like Sugarfoot Sam, the Tidy Jolly Steppers, and the Broadway Follies. While performing with the latter group in the late 1940s, Little Richard came into contact with BILLY WRIGHT, an R&B artist who employed the same gospel shout, wore the same kinds of outrageous clothes and makeup, and had the same kind of frenzied delivery that Little Richard would later call his own.

Richard began his recording career in 1951 when Wright contacted a disc jockey friend who set up a recording session at his Atlanta radio station (WGST). Backed by Wright's band, Richard cut four sides for RCA-Victor, including ''Every Hour,'' which was a minor hit in Georgia. Richard returned to the WGST studios in early 1952 and cut another four sides for RCA, though none proved to be hits. Richard continued to perform in and around Macon with his gospel-flavored group the Tempo-Toppers and then went to New Orleans and played rhythm & blues clubs. From New Orleans the band went to Houston, where the group attracted the attention of Duke-Peacock label owner DON ROBEY. Richard cut four songs for Robey in 1953 at one session and four more at another session that year, this time with R&B bandleader JOHNNY OTIS. The results were so disappointing that Robey refused to release any of the material. The double failure with Duke-Peacock prompted the breakup of the Tempo-Toppers.

In 1955, Richard signed a recording contract with Specialty Records. Brandishing a harder, more aggressive sound than what he had with the

Tempo-Toppers, Richard recorded "Tutti Frutti," a full-on rocker with sexual intonations built into the nonsense lyrics. The song went to number 2 on the R&B charts, and Little Richard's career took off like a shot. In 1956 "Long Tall Sally" made it to number 1, "Slippin' and Slidin' " to number 2, "Rip It Up" to number 1, and "Ready Teddy" to number 8. The following year, 1957, saw more chart success for Richard. "Lucille" took the top slot and "Jenny Jenny" wound up number 2, as did "Keep a Knockin'." Little Richard appeared on national television and in three mid-'50s rock & roll films: *Don't Knock the Rock* and *The Girl Can't Help It* in 1956 and *Mister Rock & Roll* in 1957.

Despite his success, Richard was having second thoughts about rock & roll and the excessive lifestyle he led. In a shocking about-face in 1957, Little Richard renounced the music and ended his career to attend Oakwood College in Huntsville, Alabama, and become a preacher. He remained out of rock & roll until 1964. By then the music had taken a new and different course. With Beatlemania sweeping the U.S., black R&B-flavored rock & roll had faded from the pop picture. For the most part, Little Richard was relegated to the oldies circuit.

The rest of Little Richard's career has had much less to do with blues and R&B than with Richard's self-serving flamboyance on- and offstage, back and forth steps with religion, and occasional comebacks that never quite materialized. Little Richard did make three creditable albums for the Reprise label in the early '70s—*The Rill Thing, King of Rock & Roll*, and *Second Coming*—but they failed to garner much attention beyond the Little Richard faithful. He played Las Vegas and kept recording on smaller labels. In his 1984 biography, *The Life and Times of Little Richard*, he talked openly about his homosexuality. Since then he has appeared at the Grammy Awards, has worked with young rock bands such as Fishbone, and was inducted into the Rock & Roll Hall of Fame in 1986.

Essential Listening:
The Specialty Sessions (box set)/Specialty (SPCD 8508)
The Georgia Peach/Specialty (SPCD 7012-2)

◄ LITTLE WALTER

(born Marion Walter Jacobs, May 1, 1930, Marksville, La.; died February 15, 1968, Chicago, Ill.)

Little Walter is considered by most blues historians to be the greatest and most influential of all the post–World War II harmonica players. As a stylist he redefined the instrument's blues presence by broadening its textural boundaries and creating brand-new tones. He made the harp an integral part of the new urban blues sound by demonstrating its effectiveness when amplified in a band setting. Little Walter was also a superb soloist. He rarely overplayed; his solos were sonic sculptures of carefully placed notes and gorgeous phrasing that gave urban blues a vitality it never before knew.

In addition to being a blues harp genius and an engaging singer, Little Walter was a talented songwriter and interpreter, plus an arranger, bandleader, and blues character. Little Walter staples such as "Blues with a Feeling," "My Babe," "Sad Hours," and "Juke" were major hits and have become part of the standard blues repertoire. In all, he placed fourteen songs into the top-10 *Billboard* R&B charts between 1952 and 1958. Backed by some of the best sidemen in Chicago, Little Walter routinely delivered energetic live sets in clubs and on the concert stage. He was one of the first Chicago bluesmen to play the Apollo Theater in Harlem, and his popularity was as great in England as in the U.S.

Little Walter was born in rural Louisiana and began playing the harp as a child. By the time he was twelve, he was playing New Orleans street corners for spare change. He worked his way up to Chicago with stops in Helena and St. Louis; along the way he picked up harp tips from BIG WALTER HORTON and SONNY BOY WILLIAMSON (Rice Miller). He even appeared on Williamson's "King Biscuit Time" show on KFFA in Helena.

Upon arriving in Chicago around 1946, Little Walter played his harmonica on Maxwell Street and quickly caught the attention of BIG BILL BROONZY. Work with Broonzy and TAMPA RED followed as did recording sessions with the Ora-Nelle and Parkway labels. But Walter's big break came when MUDDY WATERS sought out his harp riffs for his earliest Chess recordings in 1948. Little Walter gave Waters's hardened blues a heightened intensity with harp solos that beautifully underscored Waters's vocal grittiness and growl.

Little Walter also performed with Waters's original band. One of the songs they often opened with was a romping instrumental called "Your Cat Will Play" that prominently featured Little Walter's harp skills. The band also recorded the song; however, when it was released in 1952 on Checker Records, label owner LEONARD CHESS renamed it "Juke" and issued it under Little Walter's name. While touring in Louisiana, Little Walter heard of the song's startling success, quit Waters's band, and returned to Chicago. Little Walter lost no time in taking over a group called the ACES, led by another harp player, JUNIOR WELLS. (Wells then took Little Walter's spot in the Waters band.) Little Walter used the name Little Walter and His Night Cats for material that had been cut with Waters in 1952 as well as for early songs recorded with the Aces. By 1953, Little Walter was calling his band Little Walter and His Jukes. The group consisted of Louis and David Myers on guitars and FRED BELOW on drums, though later that year ROBERT JR. LOCKWOOD replaced Louis Myers. It was with the Jukes that Little Walter began his rapid rise to the top of the Chicago blues hierarchy.

Though no longer playing live with Waters and his band, Little Walter continued to record, on occasion, with the group, at the insistence of Leonard Chess. Together and apart they dominated the Chicago blues scene in the mid-'50s, sharing their power and prestige with only HOWLIN' WOLF. In 1954 Little Walter and His Jukes performed across the U.S.; in 1955, his song "My Babe" went to number 1 on the R&B charts. Although his touring pace slackened in the late '50s, Little Walter was part of a blues package show that toured continental Europe and Great Britain in 1962. The success he experienced in England led to a return tour in 1964, this time with the ROLLING STONES.

Back in the U.S., however, Little Walter's popularity began to fade. He recorded only sparingly, and his excessive drinking and eagerness to fight at the slightest provocation seemed to sap much of his creative energy. In 1968, after a particularly vicious street brawl, Little Walter died of coronary thrombosis. He was thirty-seven years old. Little Walter was inducted into the Blues Foundation's Hall of Fame in 1980.

Essential Listening:
The Best of Little Walter/Chess (MCA) (CHD 9192)
The Best of Little Walter, Vol. 2/Chess (MCA) (CHD 9292)
Hate to See You Go/Chess (9321)

◄ LITTLEJOHN, JOHNNY

(born John Funchess, April 16, 1931, Lake, Miss.)

An unheralded but compelling blues guitarist and singer, Johnny Littlejohn comes from the ELMORE JAMES school of slide guitar. Littlejohn has been a fixture on the Chicago blues club scene since his arrival in the city in 1953. With his wailing guitar technique and rough-cut vocals, Littlejohn has helped carry on the Chicago slide guitar legacy, despite marginal recording success and little media exposure.

Littlejohn was born in Mississippi and taught himself how to play the guitar. As a youth he apprenticed in Delta juke joints and at fish fries and picnics when not working a day job. In the early '50s Littlejohn moved to Michigan and, for a short while, played Detroit and Ann Arbor blues clubs. But it was only after he had relocated to Chicago and settled into the city's blues scene that his career began to take shape. Throughout the '50s and '60s Littlejohn fronted his own band and backed other bluesmen, often appearing with fellow guitarist JIMMY ROGERS. Although he has recorded two powerful albums—*John Littlejohn and the Chicago Blues Stars* for Arhoolie in 1968 and *So-Called Friends* for Rooster Blues in 1985—Littlejohn has been unable to break out beyond Chicago blues circles. He continues to perform in Chicago clubs, despite occasional ill-health.

Essential Listening:
John Littlejohn and the Chicago Blues Stars/Arhoolie (1043)
So-Called Friends/Rooster Blues (R 2621)
Chicago Blues Sessions, Vol. 13: John Littlejohn's Blues/Wolf (120.859)

◄ LOCKWOOD, ROBERT JR.

(born March 27, 1915, Marvel, Ark.)

More than any other blues musician save JOHNNY SHINES, Robert Jr. Lockwood has been the torchbearer of the ROBERT JOHNSON guitar legacy. Not only is Lockwood the stepson of Johnson, but it was Johnson who taught Lockwood how to play guitar in the 1930s. But Lockwood has been no mere imitator of the Johnson guitar style. An absorbing stylist in his own right, he remains one of the few country bluesmen to have incorporated jazz elements into traditional blues. He is known for his placement of unusual chord structures into the blues format, as well as for his superb accompaniments in band and duo settings.

Had Lockwood possessed a more vibrant blues voice and a more outgoing personality, his stature among mainstream blues fans would be much greater than it has been in recent years. But serious blues guitar students appreciate his style as something far more inventive and expressive than the typical country blues style.

Lockwood's first instrument was the organ. After Robert Johnson came into his life (Johnson took up with Lockwood's mother, Esther) Lockwood abandoned the organ for the guitar. Lockwood's career as a bluesman began when he was fifteen years old; he traveled the Mississippi Delta, playing juke joints and house parties with harmonica player SONNY BOY WILLIAMSON (Rice Miller). Lockwood eventually worked his way to Memphis, then St. Louis, and on to Chicago, where, in 1941, he began his career as a recording artist. Lockwood cut four sides for the Bluebird label. But instead of remaining in Chicago, Lockwood went back down South that same year to Helena, Arkansas, where he resumed his partnership with Williamson and became a regular performer on Williamson's "King Biscuit Time" radio program on station KFFA. Lockwood spent the 1940s working with the King Biscuit Boys in and around Helena. He also worked jukes and parties as a solo artist, playing the jazz-inflected blues that would eventually become his trademark.

Lockwood returned to Chicago in 1950, where he found work as an accompanist. By 1953 he was working as a sideman for Chess, though he never recorded for the label as a solo artist. He did, however, record for the Bea & Baby, J.O.B., and Decca labels. Lockwood remained in Chicago during the city's blues heyday in the 1950s, working with OTIS SPANN, SUNNYLAND SLIM, WILLIE MABON, and other bluesmen. When work began to dry up in Chicago, he relocated to Cleveland in 1961 and has remained there ever since. In Cleveland, Lockwood led his own band and played area clubs, but he maintained his relationship with Chicago, recording in the '70s for the Delmark label as well as for Trix and Advent.

In the early '80s Lockwood recorded *Hangin' On* and *Mister Blues Is Here to Stay* with Johnny Shines for Rounder Records. It marked the first time the two disciples of Robert Johnson had ever recorded together. Lockwood also continued to tour, playing festivals both in the U.S. and abroad.

In the late '80s, when interest in Robert Johnson reached an all-time high with blues fans, thanks to the reissue of Johnson's music in the box set *The Complete Recordings of Robert Johnson*, interest in Lockwood's connection to Johnson also increased and resulted in interviews and more concert dates. Anxious to retain control of his music, Lockwood started his own record company. His album *What's the Score* was the label's maiden release. In 1989 Lockwood was inducted into the Blues Foundation's Hall of Fame. He continues to tour.

Essential Listening:

Mister Blues Is Here to Stay/Rounder (2026)

Hangin' On (with Johnny Shines)/Rounder (2023)

Dust My Broom/Flyright (CD 10)

The Baddest New Guitar/P-Vine (PCD 2134)

Steady Rollin' Man/Delmark (DD 630)

◄ LOFTON, CRIPPLE CLARENCE

(born March 28, 1896, Kingsport, Tenn.; died January 9, 1957, Chicago, Ill.)

A pioneer of the boogie-woogie piano style, Cripple Clarence Lofton embellished his stage act with dance steps, whistles, hoots, odd sounds, and percussion, all executed with vaudeville showmanship. Along with COW COW DAVENPORT, PINE TOP SMITH, and JIMMY YANCEY, Lofton helped popularize boogie-woogie piano in Chicago in the 1920s. He was a regular on the rent-party circuit and in clubs, where he turned what might have been a routine piano performance into something of a tent-show act.

Lofton was nicknamed ''Cripple'' due to a birth defect that made him hobble, though not enough to prevent him from learning how to tap dance as a youth. That he was self-taught on piano was most likely the reason his piano style was mercurial and untrained. Lofton moved to Chicago in 1917 and began playing rent parties and small clubs. Word of his energetic stage act spread, and soon Lofton was among the most popular of the boogie-woogie piano players in Chicago. His popularity was such that he was eventually able to open his own Chicago club, the Big Apple, in the mid-1930s. Lofton also began his recording career at this time, cutting sides for a variety of labels, including Vocalion.

Lofton remained a familiar figure on the Chicago boogie-woogie scene throughout the 1930s and early 1940s, but once the boogie-woogie craze began to wane, Lofton, too, faded from the scene. Although he played an occasional show, he was essentially forced into retirement after World War II. He died in 1957.

Essential Listening:

Cripple Clarence Lofton and Walter Davis/Yazoo (1025)
Cripple Clarence Lofton and Meade Lux Lewis/Euphonic (1208)

◄ LOMAX, ALAN

(born January 31, 1915, Austin, Tex.)

The son of noted folklorist JOHN LOMAX, Alan continued his father's work, recording and collecting blues and folk songs for the Library of Congress and helping to preserve America's rich musical heritage. When he was in his teens, Alan accompanied his father on field trips in the South. He eventually became an assistant archivist at the Library of Congress, but Alan's best work was done in the field. In 1938 he produced a series of recordings with jazz pioneer Jelly Roll Morton that remains one of the genre's most valuable recorded documents. A book, *Mister Jelly Roll*, resulted from the project. Three years later, while searching for blues singer ROBERT JOHNSON (unbeknownst to Lomax, Johnson had died in 1938), Lomax and fellow folklorist John Work discovered and recorded bluesman MUDDY WATERS for the Library of Congress. Lomax went back and recorded Waters in 1942. These were Waters's very first recordings; they documented his roots as a country bluesman.

Lomax's interest in recording and documenting folk music spread beyond the United States. He did fieldwork in the Caribbean, the British Isles, and Europe and produced volumes of foreign folk music for such labels as Decca, Columbia, and Caedmon in the 1950s and 1960s. With the advent of the folk and blues revivals in the U.S. in the early '60s, Lomax got involved in producing concerts and working with folk festival organizers, along with penning *The Penguin Book of American Folksongs* in 1961 and *Folk Song Style and Culture* in 1968.

Lomax also worked in radio and wrote extensively on fieldwork and folk music for journals and folk magazines, staying actively involved in the preservation of American folk music through the 1980s. In the late 1980s, Lomax produced a critically hailed documentary series called *American Patchwork*, which dealt with various forms of American music. One film in the series, *The Land Where the Blues Began*, dealt with how field hollers and work songs led to the origins of the blues in the Mississippi Delta. In 1993 Lomax published a blues memoir by the same name.

◄ LOMAX, JOHN

(born September 23, 1867, Goodman, Miss.; died January 26, 1948, Greenville, Miss.)

Folklorist John Lomax was a pioneer in recording and collecting black field and folk songs, prison work chants, blues, and spirituals. Because of his efforts, folk-blues artists such as LEADBELLY and songs such as "Rock Island Line" and "John Henry" have become part of the American music treasury. In all, Lomax amassed some ten thousand recordings for the Library of Congress, including hundreds of blues songs that serve as the foundation of what we know about the origins and early development of the music.

Lomax was born in Mississippi but raised in Texas. He earned degrees in English from the University of Texas and Harvard in preparation for a teaching career but turned a boyhood fascination with cowboy songs into a career as a folklorist. Spurred on by friends at Harvard, Lomax returned to Texas to collect cowboy songs, and in 1910 he published *Cowboy Songs and Other Frontier Ballads*, followed by *Songs of the Cattle Trail and Cow Camp* in 1917. Lomax spent the next decade and a half in a variety of teaching positions and banking posts, until he returned once again to song collecting in the early 1930s. This time Lomax sought to collect and categorize black folk songs. With help from his son, ALAN LOMAX, he spent the early Depression years, particularly 1933, traveling the South with primitive recording equipment, recording itinerant bluesmen, prison inmates, and laborers. The results of his work were published in the book *American Ballads and Folksongs* in 1934. Earlier that year, Lomax had discovered and recorded Leadbelly at the Angola Prison Farm in Louisiana. Lomax helped Leadbelly secure a pardon from Governor O.K. Allen. Freed, Leadbelly began a career as a folk-blues recording artist and performer with Lomax as his manager, and, for a time, worked as a chauffeur for Lomax.

Lomax spent his remaining years in charge of the Archive of Folk Music at the Library of Congress and writing books about black music. In 1936 he published *Negro Folk Songs as Sung by Lead Belly*. Five years later he published *Our Singing Country*. These books helped spark interest in American folk music and blues and paved the way for continued research and field recordings down South by future folklorists and musicologists. Lomax died in 1948 at age eighty.

◄ LONESOME SUNDOWN

(born Cornelius Green, December 12, 1928, Donaldsonville, La.)

Lonesome Sundown's shimmering vibrato guitar style and strapping voice helped define the sound of Louisiana-based Excello Records in the mid-1950s and early 1960s. Lonesome remains a much-overlooked blues artist; he never had a major hit, and, except for a brief comeback attempt in the '70s, he retired from recording and performing relatively early.

Sundown began his career in the mid-'50s, sharing guitar responsibilities with PHILLIP WALKER in CLIFTON CHENIER's zydcco band. Sundown signed a solo recording contract with Excello Records in 1956, and JAY MILLER, the label's producer, nicknamed him Louisiana Sundown because, in Miller's view, his real name—Cornelius Green—lacked commercial appeal. Sundown recorded some sixteen singles and one album for Excello from 1956 to 1964, the year he gave up music for religion. Nearly every Excello song Sundown recorded, including the classic "My Home Is a Prison," contained stirring elements of blues, swamp soul, and rhythm & blues, which, when recorded, served to accent his deep, warm voice and distinctive guitar passages.

After Sundown left the blues, he joined the Church of the Lord Jesus Christ. He worked outside of music until 1977, when he was coaxed into a comeback by producers Bruce Bromberg and Dennis Walker of Joliet Records. The result was *Been Gone Too Long*, rereleased by Alligator Records in 1979 and by Hightone in 1991. The album featured Sundown's longtime friend Phillip Walker on guitar. Although *Been Gone Too Long* was an artistic triumph for Sundown, it failed to sell. Frustrated, Sundown returned to retirement in Louisiana, earning his living as a construction worker.

Essential Listening:
Lonesome Sundown/Excello (8012)
Lonesome Sundown/Flyright (16)
Been Gone Too Long/Hightone (8031)

◄ LOUIS, JOE HILL

(born Leslie Hill, September 23, 1921, Raines, Tenn.; died August 5, 1957, Memphis, Tenn.)

Joe Hill Louis was a Memphis-based one-man band in the 1940s and 1950s. He had his own radio show on WDIA and worked frequently with producer and record company owner SAM PHILLIPS.

Louis left home as a youth to hobo around Tennessee and Mississippi; he played harmonica and Jew's harp for spare change at picnics and on street corners. After learning how to play the drums and the guitar, Louis concocted a one-man band act and called it Joe Hill Louis, the Be-Bop Boy and His One-Man Band. Louis often played all his instruments at once, which left little room to grow proficient on one particular instrument. His sound was crude and raw, yet he became popular enough in and around Memphis that he recorded a couple sides for Columbia in the late 1940s and got his own radio show on WDIA as the Pepticon Boy.

Louis began his association with Phillips in 1950 when the producer and fledgling record company owner recorded him on his pre-Sun Phillips label. After the label folded, Phillips sold Louis's contract to RPM-Modern. Louis stayed with the label until 1953, recording a handful of primitive blues and boogies. He spent a brief time with Checker (Chess) and finally came back to Phillips and his Sun label, where he recorded as a solo artist and a session musician until his death in 1957.

Essential Listening:
Union Ave. Breakdown, Sun: The Roots of Rock, Vol. 12 (Various Artists)/Charly (CR 30127)

◄ LOUISIANA RED

(born Iverson Minter, March 23, 1936, Vicksburg, Miss.)

A journeyman Mississippi Delta blues guitarist and singer, Louisiana Red built his performing and recording style from a variety of sources, including JIMMY REED, MUDDY WATERS, and LIGHTNIN' HOPKINS. Born in Mississippi, Red's early life was not an easy one; his mother died shortly after giving birth and his father was reputedly lynched by the Ku Klux Klan. Red taught himself how to play harmonica and guitar. After migrating to Pittsburgh around 1945, where he played on street corners for spare change, Red moved to Chicago in 1949 and recorded briefly for the Checker (Chess) label.

Despite his inroads into the Chicago blues scene, Red spent most of the 1950s in the air force. Upon his discharge in 1958, Red bounced from gig to gig. He recorded his debut album, *Lowdown Back Porch Blues*, in the early '60s for the Roulette/Vogue label. Throughout the '60s, uncertainty over his career led Red to work as much outside of music as he did as a blues performer. In 1971 he recorded the album *Louisiana Red Sings the Blues* for Atlantic Records subsidiary Atco, but the album failed to sell and Red was dropped from the label's roster. In the years since, Red has performed in small blues bars and at occasional festivals and has recorded for labels such as L+R. He lives in Europe, where he continues to record and perform.

Essential Listening:
Lowdown Back Porch Blues/Vogue (522 004)
Midnight Rambler/Tomato (26934-2)

◄ LOVE, CLAYTON

(born November 15, 1927, Mattson, Miss.)

A St. Louis–based pianist and singer, Clayton Love bridged rhythm & blues and rock & roll in the 1950s as the singer and keyboard player in IKE TURNER'S

Kings of Rhythm. He also led his own group, Clayton Love & the Shufflers, and recorded for a variety of labels, including Trumpet, Aladdin, and Modern.

Love was born in the Mississippi Delta town of Mattson, but when he was twelve moved with his family to Clarksdale. There he met and became friends with Turner. Love sang and got started playing piano in local churches before serving in the navy. After being discharged, he attended Alcorn A&M College, planning on becoming a teacher.

In the early 1950s Love worked Delta clubs with the Shufflers. He landed a recording contract with the Jackson, Mississippi–based Trumpet label, which yielded the song "Shuffling with Love." Love also did session work with Aladdin and Modern before joining Turner's Kings of Rhythm, which brought him from the Delta to St. Louis. Love's tenure with the Kings of Rhythm lasted into the mid-'60s, at which point he became a teacher in the St. Louis school district. Love continued to play piano in hotel lounges and bars on weekends until the late 1980s, when he retired from teaching and resumed his music career. An album he made with fellow St. Louis pianists JOHNNIE JOHNSON and JIMMY VAUGHN, called *Rockin' Eighty-Eights*, was released by Modern Blues Recordings in 1991.

Essential Listening:
Rockin' Eighty-Eights/Modern Blues Recordings (MBCD 1201)
Strange Kind of Foolin' (with Jerry McCain and Tiny Kennedy)/Alligator Trumpet (AL 2701)

◄ LOVE, WILLIE

(born November 4, 1906, Duncan, Miss.; died August 19, 1953, Jackson, Miss.)

Piano player and singer Willie Love was a familiar figure on the Memphis, West Memphis, and Mississippi Delta blues scenes in the late 1940s and early 1950s, often working with guitarist JOE WILLIE WILKINS and drummer WILLIE NIX. Love, however, is also known for his work with SONNY BOY WILLIAMSON (Rice Miller). He played on some of Williamson's earliest recordings for the Trumpet label in 1951.

Love learned how to play piano as a youth in the Delta. Like so many other musicians from the region, Love played out-of-the-way juke joints and house parties and lived the life of an itinerant bluesman. He eventually made his way to Helena, Arkansas, in 1942 and began performing on radio station KFFA's "King Biscuit Time" blues program with Williamson, whom Love had met earlier that year in a Greenville, Mississippi, juke. Love, Williamson, Nix, and Wilkins often performed together in Delta jukes in the late 1940s as the Four Aces. Love also continued his radio work; for a while in 1949 he even had his own show on KWEM out of West Memphis.

In addition to recording with Williamson, Love recorded for Trumpet as a solo artist and as a member of the group that, without Williamson and the other Aces, was called nonetheless the Three Aces and often included saxophone player Otis Green, drummer Alex Wallace, and guitarist ELMORE JAMES. After a swing through the South working in Williamson's back-up band, Love contracted pneu-

monia, brought on by excessive drinking. The disease killed him in 1953. He was
forty-six years old.

Essential Listening:

Delta Blues—1951 (Big Joe Williams, Willie Love, Luther Huff)/Alligator-
Trumpet (ALCD 2702)

Clownin' with the World (Sonny Boy Williamson and Willie Love)/Alligator-
Trumpet (ALCD 2700)

◄ LUTCHER, NELLIE

(born October 15, 1915, Lake Charles, La.)

A rhythm & blues singer and pianist who in the late 1940s recorded a batch
of top-10 hits for Capitol Records, Nellie Lutcher combined jazz, blues, and pop
into an appealing style that enabled her to work into the early 1980s. Such songs
as "Hurry on Down" and "He's a Real Gone Guy" (both hit number 2 on the
R&B charts in 1947), along with "Fine Brown Frame" (number 2 in 1948) and
"Come and Get It Honey" (number 6 in 1948), are good examples of Lutcher's
smooth, bluesy vocals.

Born in Louisiana, Lutcher began her musical career in church. By the time
she was twenty, she had switched to secular music, moved to Los Angeles, and
began playing in local lounges. Lutcher was discovered by Capitol Records talent
scout and producer Dave Dexter, Jr., in 1947 after he heard her on a March of
Dimes fund-raising radio show. Lutcher scored hits for Capitol through 1950 and
toured the U.S. and the British Isles before her career waned. Despite the arrival
of rock & roll and decreasing interest in her breezy style of rhythm & blues,
Lutcher continued to perform, mostly in small clubs on the West Coast. She has
since retired from performing. Lutcher's brother is R&B saxophonist Joe Lutcher.

Essential Listening:

My Papa's Got to Have Everything/Jukebox Lil (1100)

Ditto from Me to You/Jukebox Lil (1103)

M.

◄ MABON, WILLIE

(born October 24, 1925, Hollywood, Tenn.; died April 19, 1985, Paris, France)

Willie Mabon was a Chicago blues pianist and singer popular in the early 1950s when he recorded for Chess. His roots lay in boogie-woogie and jazz, but he was equally influenced by the sophisticated blues piano riffs of BIG MACEO Merriweather and ROOSEVELT SYKES and the soft, sensuous vocals of CHARLES BROWN. Mabon taught himself the rudiments of piano playing, but when his family moved to Chicago in 1942, he was able to take formal piano lessons. After a stint in the marines during the last part of World War II, Mabon returned to Chicago and worked his way into the blues club scene there.

Mabon began his recording career by cutting sides as Big Willie for the Apollo label in 1949 and then switched to Aristocrat (Chess) the following year. He remained with Chess until 1956. During that time he scored two number 1 hits on the R&B charts: "I Don't Know" in 1952 and "I'm Mad" in 1953. Another record, "Poison Ivy," made it to number 7 on the charts in 1954 before Mabon's recording success began to wane.

Mabon continued his recording career with Federal and a number of small labels in the late '50s and '60s and performed in Chicago bars and lounges. In 1972 he toured Europe, where he built a loyal following, especially in France. Regular visits to Europe followed in the 1970s, either as a solo artist or with package shows. Mabon also recorded for European companies such as the French Black and Blue label. He died in Paris in 1985.

Essential Listening:
Willie Mabon/Chess (9189)
The Seventh Son/Crown Prince (IG 402)

◄ MAGIC SAM

(born Sam Maghett, February 14, 1937, Grenada, Miss.; died December 1, 1969, Chicago, Ill.)

Had Chicago guitarist and vocalist Magic Sam not suffered the heart attack that robbed him of his life and his blossoming career—he was just thirty-two years old when he died—his stature as a blues guitar stylist and singer would surely be greater than it is. One of the originators of the West Side guitar style, Magic Sam, along with such contemporaries as FREDDIE KING, OTIS RUSH, and

BUDDY GUY, helped forge the transition in Chicago from first-generation postwar electric blues to modern blues.

Magic Sam was born in the Mississippi Delta. His first guitar was homemade; he learned how to play it by listening to local country blues players at picnics and house parties. In his early teens Sam moved to Chicago, bent on building a career as a blues guitarist. Early influences included B.B. KING and MUDDY WATERS. Sam eventually landed a spot in Homesick James's band but soon formed his own band, playing Chicago blues clubs and recording for Cobra Records.

Sam was drafted into the army in 1959. After he deserted, he was caught and spent time in jail before being dishonorably discharged in 1961. He returned to Chicago that year and resumed his career. He recorded for the Chief label in the early '60s, but sustained himself primarily as a performer. Throughout the '60s he regularly played the popular Chicago blues club Sylvio's and other blues bars. Eventually, Sam began performing outside of Chicago. His most successful dates were in San Francisco at the Fillmore West and the Avalon Ballroom, attracting the growing segment of the Bay Area rock audience that was also tuned into the blues.

The most important performance of his career occurred at the 1969 Ann Arbor Blues Festival in Ann Arbor, Michigan. Critics and many fans who attended the fest considered his set the most memorable of the festival. It resulted in a number of prized bookings, both in the U.S. and Europe. Sam, however, died a few months after the Ann Arbor festival, never having the chance to capitalize on his growing reputation as a blues great.

As a guitarist, Magic Sam fell somewhere between Otis Rush and B.B. King. His guitar style was as innovative as Rush's and as fluid as King's, yet he packed it with snappy, skittering notes and well-constructed phrasing that shot his solos high above the basic blues arrangements from which they originated. What Magic Sam's vocals lacked in depth and texture, they more than made up for in ebullience and emotional intensity, making him one of Chicago's most exciting blues performers in the late '60s.

Considering the influence he exerted on future blues guitarists, Sam's studio recording catalog is small. His best material is found on the late-'60s Delmark recordings *West Side Soul* (his only studio album), *Black Magic*, and *Magic Sam Live*. The latter, two-disc release includes his now-legendary Ann Arbor Blues Festival set. Magic Sam was inducted into the Blues Foundation's Hall of Fame in 1982.

Essential Listening:
West Side Soul/Delmark (615)
Black Magic/Delmark (620)
Magic Sam Live/Delmark (DE 645)
West Side Guitar/Paula (PCD 02)
Give Me Time/Delmark (DD 654)
Magic Touch/Black Top (BT 1085)

◄ MAGIC SLIM

(born Morris Holt, August 7, 1937, Grenada, Miss.)

A Chicago guitarist and singer whose main contribution to the city's blues scene has been as an interpretative artist, Magic Slim's style is derived from MUDDY WATERS and nearly every major Chicago guitarist of the '60s, including MAGIC SAM (who gave his boyhood friend his nickname), OTIS RUSH, FREDDIE KING, and BUDDY GUY.

Born in Mississippi, Slim began in music as a piano player, but after he lost one of his fingers in a farming accident, he switched to guitar. In 1955 he moved to Chicago and for a while played bass in Magic Sam's band. But Slim failed to find a niche in the city's competitive blues scene and eventually returned to Mississippi.

His second attempt to crack the Chicago scene was more successful. Back living in the city in the early '60s, he made his first recording in 1966, and with his group the Teardrops, which included his brother Nick Holt on bass, he played Chicago's blues clubs, eventually taking over for HOUND DOG TAYLOR at Florence's, the popular blues bar on the city's South Side.

In 1978, after recording a batch of singles with a harmonica player called Little Hite, Slim and the Teardrops appeared on the Alligator album *Living Blues, Vol. 3*, a collection of songs by unsigned but locally popular blues acts. Slim's appearance on the acclaimed album led to other recordings, mostly on European labels. In 1982 Alligator released a compilation of Slim's material called *Raw Magic*. That same year he recorded the album *Grand Slam* for Rooster Blues, which included a remake of his first single, ''Scuffling,'' and won a W.C. HANDY Award. Slim and a new version of the Teardrops signed a recording contract with Blind Pig Records in 1990 and recorded *Gravel Road*, an album of soul-blues, straight blues, and R&B songs that illustrates Slim's bar-band versatility. Slim continues to record and perform.

Essential Listening:
Raw Magic/Alligator (AL 4728)
Grand Slam/Rooster Blues (R 2618)
Gravel Road/Blind Pig (BP 73690)
Highway Is My Home/Evidence (ECD 26012)

◄ MAHAL, TAJ

(born Henry St. Claire Fredericks, May 17, 1942, New York, N.Y.)

A longtime student of African-American music, Taj Mahal is a modern-day songster who incorporates into his repertoire country blues, ragtime, reggae, rhythm & blues, jazz, and folk music. Born in New York but raised in Springfield, Massachusetts, Mahal grew up in a musical family; his father was a jazz musician and his mother a gospel singer. By 1956 Mahal had begun performing as a folksinger. He continued to play while attending the University of Massachusetts in Amherst. In 1964 he worked his way into the Boston folk scene, playing coffeehouses and local colleges. A year later he moved to Los Angeles and met guitarist

Ry Cooder. Together they formed a band called the Rising Sons. Although the group quickly secured a recording contract with CBS Records, the Rising Sons dissolved before its album was released. (CBS finally released the album in 1992 as part of its Legacy series.)

Convinced that Mahal was a unique talent, CBS offered him a solo deal; in 1967, his self-titled debut album was released. The record introduced Mahal's eclectic approach to the blues and caught on with the folk-rock crowd. He then released a series of other acclaimed albums, the best being the two-record set *Giant Step/De Ole Folks at Home*, which includes his renditions of blues classics such as "Good Morning Little School Girl" and "Candy Man," and *Recycling the Blues & Other Related Stuff*, which features Mahal's interpretation of the standard "Sweet Home Chicago."

Mahal wrote music for and appeared in the early-'70s film *Sounder*. With the increasing popularity of reggae in the '70s, he also began to experiment with it and other Caribbean music forms. His album *Music Fuh Ya' (Musica Para Tu)*, released in 1976 on Warner Brothers, contained an intriguing mix of blues and reggae that, though it didn't sell as expected, was critically praised. Mahal also did the soundtrack for the 1977 film *Brothers* and the 1991 Broadway play *Mulebone*.

Mahal has continued his study of black music through the '80s and into the '90s. He has appeared at most of the major blues festivals in this country and abroad and has continued to record, though his most recent albums feature more rhythm & blues and pop than pure blues. Mahal lives on the Hawaiian island of Kuai.

Essential Listening:
Rising Sons (with Ry Cooder)/CBS (CK 52828)
The Best of Taj Mahal, Vol. 1/CBS (CK 36528)
Giant Step/De Ole Folks at Home/CBS (CGK 18)
Happy Just to Be Like I Am/Mobile Fidelity Sound Lab (MFCD 765)
Recycling the Blues & Other Related Stuff/Mobile Fidelity Sound Lab (MFCD 764)
Taj's Blues/Columbia (CK 52465)
Mulebone (soundtrack)/Gramavision (R2-79432)

◄ MARGOLIN, BOB

(born May 9, 1949, Boston, Mass.)

A Chicago blues interpreter, Bob Margolin played guitar in the MUDDY WATERS Band from 1973 to 1980. Influenced by the likes of CHUCK BERRY, JIMMY ROGERS, and Waters, Margolin carries on the tradition of a guitar style that's rooted in rural blues, yet has a distinct urban sensibility.

Before joining Waters's band, Margolin played with LUTHER "GEORGIA BOY" JOHNSON, who had played guitar for Waters in the 1960s. Margolin's association with Johnson led him to Waters's band, where, in addition to playing guitar behind Waters, he also carried out many of the band's day-to-day road managing responsibilities until 1978.

Margolin began a part-time solo career in 1980, fronting his own band, mostly in Southeast blues clubs. After the death of Muddy Waters in 1983, Margolin devoted himself full-time to his solo career. In 1989 he released his debut album, *The Old School*, followed two years later by *Chicago Blues*. Margolin currently lives in Greensboro, North Carolina, and continues to record and perform.

Essential Listening:
The Old School/Powerhouse (Ichiban) (P-105)
Chicago Blues/Powerhouse (Ichiban) (POW 4105)

◄ MARS, JOHNNY

(born December 7, 1942, Lawrence, S.C.)

A blues harmonica player whose biggest influence has been JIMI HENDRIX, Johnny Mars has spent much of his career drawing wild, psychedelicized blues notes out of his harp, attempting to do with his instrument what Hendrix did with his guitar.

Mars was born to sharecropping parents in South Carolina. When he was fourteen his family moved to New York State, where he played in local bands and listened to blues records by LITTLE WALTER and JIMMY REED. In the mid-'60s Mars saw Hendrix perform in New York City's Greenwich Village and was immediately taken by Hendrix's guitar pyrotechnics. Drawn by the rock revolution going on in San Francisco at the time, Mars moved to the Bay Area, where he performed with local bands and released one single, ''Deep in the Wilderness,'' for Mercury in 1967. The record, however, attracted little attention.

Frustrated by his inability to make further progress with U.S. blues and rock audiences, Mars moved to England in 1972, where he recorded a pair of albums for Big Bear—*Blues from Mars* and *Johnny Mars and the Oakland Boogie*—and performed regularly. In the mid-'80s he released a third album, *King of the Blues Harp*, on JSP, but it mustered little notice outside of England.

After a twenty-year hiatus, Mars returned to the Bay Area to play the 1992 San Francisco Blues Festival. He continues to perform, mostly in Europe.

Essential Listening:
Blues from Mars/Big Bear (2460 162)

◄ MARTIN, SARA

(born June 18, 1884, Louisville, Ky.; died May 24, 1955, Louisville, Ky.)

A 1920s classic blues singer, Sara Martin began her career in vaudeville. In 1922 she signed a recording contract with Okeh Records. Her best songs, ''Mean Tight Mama,'' ''Death Sting Me Blues,'' and ''Uncle Sam Blues,'' proved that Martin could be as sassy and as ribald as any of her classic blues counterparts. Because of her stage success, Martin frequently toured, performing on the TOBA (Theater Owners' Booking Association) circuit in the early '20s and, later on, playing theaters and clubs on the East Coast and throughout the South. Like other 1920s female blues singers, Martin wore extravagant costumes onstage and, in general, sought to live up to her celebrity status by adorning herself with layers of jewelry and gaudy clothes.

Martin retired from the stage in the early '30s. She returned to Louisville, where she dabbled in gospel singing and ran a nursing home. She died of a stroke in 1955.

Essential Listening:
Best of Blues, 1922–28/BOB (19)

◄ MAYALL, JOHN

(born November 29, 1933, Manchester, England)

John Mayall was the paternal guardian of British blues in the 1960s. His band the BLUESBREAKERS was something of a blues college for young musicians, who, under Mayall's guidance, got a first-class education in American blues. Everyone from guitarists ERIC CLAPTON and Mick Taylor to bass players Jack Bruce and John McVie to drummers Mick Fleetwood and Aynsley Dunbar spent time in the Bluesbreakers. Mayall, a competent singer, keyboards player, and harmonica player, gave the band and its long line of musicians a blues vision that was vital to the growth and popularity of the English blues scene in the '60s.

Mayall became interested in the blues as a child. From his father, a jazz musician, he inherited a record collection that included many American blues artists, including LITTLE WALTER, MUDDY WATERS, and SONNY BOY WILLIAMSON (Rice Miller). Mayall learned how to play guitar and ukelele during his school years, and his interest in jazz and blues increased. However, it wasn't until after Mayall had completed four years worth of service in the British army during the Korean War and had enrolled at the College of Art in Manchester that he began to forge a career in music.

In the mid-'50s he formed his own group, the Powerhouse Four, which in 1963 became the Bluesbreakers. A year later Mayall moved from Manchester to London and restructured the band. With Mayall on keyboards and vocals, the rest of the group consisted of Bernie Watson on guitar, John McVie on bass, and Keith Robertson on drums. The band played London blues and jazz clubs and backed up visiting American bluesmen. From the beginning, the group rarely had a steady lineup; musicians came into the band and left it with such regularity that it's surprising the group managed to endure. Mayall, however, was the one who kept it going with his dedication to the music and the musicians who played it. He even encouraged the revolving door atmosphere in which the band operated.

Mayall and the Bluesbreakers released a number of interesting British blues albums in the 1960s. The group's classic, however, was *Bluesbreakers—John Mayall with Eric Clapton*, released in 1966. The Bluesbreakers reached an artistic peak during Clapton's mid-'60s tenure (Clapton left in 1966 and formed Cream with Bluesbreaker bass player Jack Bruce and drummer Ginger Baker, formerly of the Graham Bond Organisation). Mayall continued the band with new personnel and released other noted albums, such as *The Turning Point* (1970), recorded live at New York's Fillmore East without a drummer and featuring some of Mayall's most compelling harmonica playing.

In 1971 Mayall released the two-record set *Back to the Roots*, which featured a reunion with former Bluesbreaker guitarists Clapton and Taylor and drummer Keef Hartley.

Despite the decline in interest of British-style blues, Mayall remained active as a recording artist and performer throughout the 1970s and 1980s. In the mid-'70s he resettled in the U.S. and recorded a few albums for Blue Thumb-ABC, including *A Banquet in the Blues* (1975) and *Last of the British Blues* (1978). In 1982 he staged a Bluesbreaker reunion tour with bass player McVie and guitarist Taylor. Two years later, Mayall began yet another version of the Bluesbreakers that featured guitarist Coco Montoya. Few of Mayall's recent albums have fared well commercially, yet he continues to record, sustained by an audience who still recognizes him as a major blues figure. His 1993 album, *Wake Up Call*, on Silvertone featured guest appearances by BUDDY GUY, ALBERT COLLINS, Mick Taylor, and Mavis Staples.

Essential Listening:
Bluesbreakers—John Mayall with Eric Clapton/London (800 086-2)
London Blues: John Mayall, 1964–1969/Deram (844 302-2)
Room to Move: John Mayall, 1969–1974/Deram (314 517 291-2)

◄ MAYFIELD, PERCY

(born August 12, 1920, Minden, La.; died August 11, 1984, Los Angeles, Calif.)

A gifted composer and tender vocalist, Percy Mayfield was known as the Poet of the Blues. Few songwriters in either blues or R&B possessed his talent to turn lyrics into passionate descriptions of heartache and love. Mayfield was also a major contributor to the rhythm & blues scene that surfaced in the early 1950s in Los Angeles. Often teaming up with noted arranger-musician Maxwell Davis, Mayfield's records were examples of emotional vigor and blues warmth.

Mayfield was born in Louisiana but raised in Houston. Early on his interest lay in songwriting. During World War II he moved to Los Angeles where he hoped he'd begin a career as an R&B songwriter. In 1948 Mayfield took one of his songs, "Two Years of Torture," to Supreme Records hoping that JIMMY WITHERSPOON would record it. Instead, Mayfield was coaxed into singing it himself. With a voice that in its softest moments resembled crooners like NAT KING COLE and CHARLES BROWN, Mayfield was impressive enough as a singer to secure a recording contract with Specialty Records in 1950. His first record for the label, "Please Send Me Someone to Love" backed with "Strange Things Happening" made it to number 1 on the R&B charts, establishing both Mayfield and the fledgling Specialty label as major players in West Coast rhythm & blues. Mayfield followed up his initial success with "Lost Love," which was also a hit in 1951. Mayfield's future as a songwriter/singer seemed infinitely bright until a 1952 car wreck permanently disfigured him. Though Mayfield continued to record for Specialty into 1955 and wrote and recorded a series of outstanding rhythm & blues numbers for the label, he never regained the momentum he enjoyed before his auto accident. Mayfield would continue to record with a number of labels, including Chess, Atlantic, and RCA, but his main contributions were in composing. In the late '50s he became RAY CHARLES's personal songwriter, penning, among other gems, "Hit the Road Jack," which went to number 1 in 1961. Mayfield also recorded for Charles's Tangerine label.

Mayfield's three RCA albums in the late '60s and '70s contain some of his best post-Specialty recordings, but they attracted little attention. Although his stature with record-buying R&B fans had diminished, his respect among recording artists continued to grow. "Please Send Me Someone to Love" is considered a blues standard, while artists from B.B. KING to JOHNNY WINTER have interpreted Mayfield's songs.

In the early '80s Mayfield performed at West Coast blues festivals and in Bay Area clubs, often with pianist MARK NAFTALIN. Mayfield died in 1984. His son is Curtis Mayfield, a popular R&B singer-composer who performed with the Impressions in the 1960s and then as a solo artist.

Essential Listening:
Percy Mayfield: Poet of the Blues/Specialty (CD 7001)
Percy Mayfield, Vol. 2: Memory Pain/Specialty (SPCD 7027-2)
Percy Mayfield Live/Winner (445)

◄ MCCAIN, JERRY

(born June 19, 1930, Gadsden, Ala.)

Singer and harmonica player Jerry McCain's best-known song, "She's Tuff," was made into a breakthrough hit by the FABULOUS THUNDERBIRDS in the mid-'80s. McCain's own recording career started in 1952 with the Trumpet label. He also recorded for Excello and Okeh and a handful of smaller companies with little success in the late '50s.

Determined not to quit playing the blues, however, McCain stuck with his music, playing small clubs in Alabama, occasionally touring with better-known artists like FREDDIE KING and RUFUS THOMAS, and recording for Ric, Continental, Jewel, and other small labels, when not working as a private investigator. In the early '60s, McCain signed with CBS Records; his version of Gene Ammons's "Red Top" was a regional hit, but he failed to record a suitable follow-up number and was dropped from the label.

Thanks to the success enjoyed by the Fabulous Thunderbirds with "She's Tuff," interest in McCain's music finally picked up again in the late 1980s. In 1989 he signed a recording contract with Ichiban Records. His debut album for the label, *Blues 'n Stuff*, gave his career new life and shone new light on his harp talents. McCain continues to record and perform.

Essential Listening:
Choo Choo Rock/White Label (9966)
Blues 'n Stuff/Ichiban (ICH 1047)
Love Desperado/Ichiban (ICH 9008)
Strange Kind of Feelin' (with Tiny Kennedy and Clayton Love)/Alligator-Trumpet (AL 2701)

◄ MCCALL, CASH

(born Morris Dollison, Jr., January 28, 1941, New Madrid, Mo.)

Cash McCall is best known as a songwriter, side musician, and producer, having worked in the studio or on the stage with such artists as WILLIE DIXON, KOKO TAYLOR, and ETTA JAMES, among others. McCall was born in Missouri and raised in Chicago, but it was in Mississippi, where he spent his teens, that he was first introduced to his main inspiration: gospel music. After serving in the army airborne, McCall received a medical discharge and returned to Chicago. He then began singing with a variety of gospel groups, including the Five Tones of Harmony, the Gospel Songbirds, and the Pilgrim Jubilees.

McCall eventually moved into blues and R&B and got a job writing songs for Onc-dcrful Rccords. IIe later switched to St. Lawrence Records, and when the tiny label was bought by Chess, McCall came with the package. Some of the songs McCall wrote while working at Chess include "Jealous Kind of Fellow" for Garland Green, "More and More" for LITTLE MILTON, "Bird Nest on the Ground" for MUDDY WATERS, and "I Prefer You" for Etta James. McCall also penned the song "That's How It Is" for OTIS CLAY (with whom he sang in the Gospel Songbirds) and had a minor hit of his own with "When You Wake Up" in 1966.

McCall recorded his first solo album, *Omega Man*, for Paula Records in 1973. A follow-up album, *No More Doggin'*, came out on the L+R label. McCall continued working as a studio musician and composer for James and other blues artists. In 1988 he co-produced Willie Dixon's *Hidden Charms* album, which won a Grammy Award. He also filled in for an ailing Dixon in 1991, fronting Dixon's Chicago Blues All-Stars at the Chicago Blues Festival and other fests around the U.S. McCall continues to remain active in the contemporary blues scene, performing with his group, the Cash McCall Express, and working as a songwriter and producer.

Essential Listening:
No More Doggin'/L+R (42.058)
Cash Up Front/Stone (1945)

◄ MCCLENNAN, TOMMY

(born April 8, 1908, Yazoo City, Miss.; died 1962, Chicago, Ill.)

Tommy McClennan was a rough-and-tumble Delta guitarist and singer whose blues style was equally coarse and harsh. McClennan paid little attention to form or structure; he was more apt to improvise vocally and slash out chords on his steel-bodied guitar. Yet McClennan's crudely constructed blues often packed considerable rage and emotional fervor. It was feeling more than finesse that made McClennan attractive enough for Bluebird record producer LESTER MELROSE to personally travel to the Delta in search of the bluesman and offer him the opportunity to record, which McClennan accepted in the late 1930s.

McClennan was born in the Mississippi Delta town of Yazoo City. His early years were spent picking cotton and playing his guitar for tips on street corners and in juke joints. Often accompanied by fellow guitarist ROBERT PETWAY, McClennan worked as a bluesman through the Depression years, rarely leaving the Delta. After Melrose made contact with him, McClennan went to Chicago and recorded for the Bluebird label, beginning in 1939. His trademark song, "Bottle Up and Go," was offensive to many northern black listeners because of the word "nigger," which McClennan insisted on keeping in its lyrics. McClennan split his time between the Delta and Chicago until 1942, when his relationship with Melrose ended. McClennan reportedly remained in Chicago and played small clubs and beer joints before fading from the scene in the 1950s. He died in 1962 of alcoholism.

Essential Listening:
Cotton Patch Blues/Travelin' Man (804)
Travelin' Highway Man/Travelin' Man (TMCD 06)

◄ MCCOY, CHARLIE

(born May 26, 1909, Jackson, Miss.; died July 26, 1959, Chicago, Ill.)

More known as an accompanist than a featured performer, Charlie McCoy recorded with numerous blues artists from the late 1920s well into the 1940s. Like his brother JOE MCCOY, he was a versatile guitarist whose repertoire included not only Mississippi blues but also hokum, string band music, and good-time dance songs.

Born in Jackson, Mississippi, McCoy taught himself how to play guitar. By the time he was in his teens, he was a key member of the city's blues scene, working with his brother Joe, plus WALTER VINSON, the Chatmon brothers, ISHMAN BRACEY, and TOMMY JOHNSON in area juke joints. He began his recording career when he accompanied Tommy Johnson on the sides Johnson cut for Victor Records in 1928. From that point on, McCoy recorded with Vinson, BIG BILL BROONZY, MEMPHIS MINNIE, JOHN LEE "SONNY BOY" WILLIAMSON, and Joe McCoy, as well as with his own groups, Papa Charlie's Boys and the Harlem Hamfats, with whom he recorded regularly from 1936 to 1939. McCoy's session work was cut back dramatically during the war years, due, in part, to the ban on recording imposed by the striking musicians' union and to the emergence of modern blues. He died in 1959.

Essential Listening:
Charlie McCoy/Earl (BD 602)
Charlie McCoy & Walter Vincson, 1928–1936/Earl Archives Blues Documents (BD 612)
Harlem Hamfats, 1936–1939/Document (DLP 547)

◄ MCCOY, JOE

(born May 11, 1905, Raymond, Miss.; died January 28, 1950, Chicago, Ill.)

Joe McCoy is better known by his slew of pseudonyms—Kansas Joe, Big Joe, Georgia Pine Boy, Hallelujah Joe, Hamfoot Ham, et al.—than he is by his real name. Although McCoy died at age forty-four of heart failure, he was actively involved in the Memphis and early Chicago blues scenes.

McCoy was born and raised in the Mississippi Delta, where he taught himself how to play guitar and worked picnics and parties around Jackson with his brother CHARLIE MCCOY and local bluesmen such as ISHMAN BRACEY and WALTER VINSON. McCoy moved to Memphis sometime in the mid-1920s and teamed up with MEMPHIS MINNIE in harmonica player JED DAVENPORT's Beale Street Jug Band. He and Minnie also worked as a duo. In 1929 Minnie and McCoy, who was calling himself Kansas Joe at the time, recorded for Columbia Records. The two musicians continued to perform together in Memphis and then Chicago and got involved romantically and married. They also recorded for the Vocalion label before they stopped performing together in 1934.

McCoy then went on to form a series of Chicago-based blues bands, which often included Charlie McCoy. In 1936 McCoy and his brother formed the Harlem Hamfats, a popular combo that mixed jazz and blues and worked regularly in Chicago. The group also recorded extensively for Decca; from 1936 to 1939 the label released some seventy-five Hamfat sides. After the Hamfats broke up in 1940, McCoy immediately formed Big Joe and His Washboard Band, which included brother Charlie on guitar, noted bass player Ransom Knowling, Robert Lee McCoy (no relation; later known as ROBERT NIGHTHAWK) on harmonica, and Amanda Sortier on washboard. The group recorded for the Okeh label.

McCoy's last band of note was Big Joe and His Rhythm, which recorded for the Bluebird label and played Chicago clubs up until the mid-'40s when the group dissolved. McCoy died in 1950.

Essential Listening:
Good Time Blues (Harmonicas, Kazoos, Washboards & Cow-Bells) (Various Artists)/Columbia–Legacy (CK 46780)
Memphis Minnie, Vol. 2: Early Recordings with "Kansas Joe" McCoy/Blues Classics (13)
Harlem Hamfats, 1936–1939/Document (DLP 547)

◄ MCCRACKLIN, JIMMY

(born August 13, 1921, Arkansas)

A major figure in California rhythm & blues in the post–World War II period, pianist Jimmy McCracklin has, over the years, recorded for a whole host of labels and has helped to define West Coast R&B with his smooth, fluid keyboards and his equally pleasing vocals. McCracklin recorded everything from traditional blues to thickly layered, big band rhythm & blues. Part of the reason why he has enjoyed such a long career as a recording artist stems from his ability to move from one style to the next with consistently convincing results.

McCracklin was born in Arkansas but raised in St. Louis. He lived there until he went into the navy during World War II. After the war, he settled in Los Angeles to work as a professional boxer. Calling himself Jimmy Mackey, McCracklin won nearly two dozen light-heavyweight bouts before retiring from the ring.

During this period, McCracklin also began playing the piano and started a second career in rhythm & blues. In 1945 he recorded with J.D. NICHOLSON for Globe Records and then for Excelsior. That same year McCracklin met Oakland record producer BOB GEDDINS with whom he would record on and off into the early 1960s. McCracklin recorded for Geddins's Cavatone label in 1947. Not content to stick with one label, McCracklin also cut sides for RPM/Modern, Trilon, Duke-Peacock, and Geddins's Down Town and Swingtime labels in the late 1940s and 1950s.

McCracklin's biggest hit, "The Walk," was released on the Checker (Chess) label in 1958. The record crossed over onto the pop charts, peaking at number 7, and getting McCracklin on Dick Clark's "American Bandstand" television show. McCracklin made it onto the pop charts a few more times in the early and mid-'60s, though none of the songs—"Just Got to Know," "Every Night, Every Day," "My Answer," and "Think"—matched the success of "The Walk."

McCracklin continued to perform and record into the 1980s, though by the end of the decade his output had decreased dramatically. Nonetheless, he remains one of the most prolific of all West Coast R&B artists.

Essential Listening:
Rockin' Man/Route 66 (KIX 29)
I'm Gonna Have My Fun/Route 66 (KIX 29)
You Deceived Me/Crown Prince (IG 405)
Same Lovin'/EveJim (2001)

◄ McCRAY, LARRY

(born April 5, 1960, Stephens, Ark.)

Singer-guitarist Larry McCray is a contemporary bluesman who blends soul, funk, rhythm & blues, and rock & roll with his traditional blues roots. *Ambition*, his 1990 debut album for the Point Blank–Charisma label, was originally released in England, where, in less than a year, it registered sales in the seventy-five thousand range. The disc's surprising success prompted the label to release *Ambition* in the U.S. the following year as part of Point Blank's maiden entry into the American blues market.

McCray was born in Arkansas, where his sister, Clara, his biggest influence, led her own blues band, Clara McCray & the Rockets. When McCray was twelve, he and his family moved to Michigan. At fifteen he began playing weddings and house parties in a band that included brothers Carl on bass and Steve on drums. During the recording of *Ambition*, McCray was still working on a General Motors assembly line. He continues to record and perform.

Essential Listening:
Ambition/Point Blank–Charisma (2-91388)

◄ MCDOWELL, MISSISSIPPI FRED

(born January 12, 1904, Rossville, Tenn.; died July 3, 1972, Memphis, Tenn.)

Mississippi Fred McDowell was one of the last great country bluesmen whose roughed-up bottleneck guitar style and coarsely textured vocals were extensively documented on record in the 1960s. Known more as a purveyor of the traditional Mississippi Delta blues sound rather than as a historically significant stylist, McDowell's guitar style can be traced back to the ground-breaking styles of CHARLEY PATTON and SON HOUSE, two of the Delta's earliest and most influential blues artists.

McDowell recorded regularly in the '60s and left his mark on blues-based rock artists like BONNIE RAITT and the ROLLING STONES. Raitt developed much of her slide guitar technique by listening to McDowell records. She even recorded some of his material in the 1970s. The Rolling Stones paid tribute to McDowell in 1971 with a potent version of his blues nugget "You Gotta Move" on their acclaimed *Sticky Fingers* album.

McDowell spent most of his life farming or playing blues. When not working in the fields, McDowell wandered the Delta, playing fish fries, dances, house parties, and juke joints. Folklorist ALAN LOMAX discovered McDowell in 1959 and was the first to record him. However, it wasn't until 1964 when Chris Strachwitz of Arhoolie Records traveled to McDowell's home in Como, Mississippi, and recorded him there that McDowell's career moved beyond playing for tips and spare change. Two mid-'60s Arhoolie albums, *Fred McDowell, Vol. 1* and *Vol. 2*, brought McDowell long-deserved attention. During the '60s he performed at many folk and blues festivals and appeared in such documentaries as *The Blues Maker* (1968), *Fred McDowell* (1969), and *Roots of American Music: Country Urban Music* (1971).

Though he scorned rock & roll—a favorite saying of his, "I don't play no rock and roll," was the title of a 1969 album he made for Capitol Records—McDowell was, nonetheless, a favorite among the blues-rock crowd as well as with traditional blues fans. McDowell died of cancer in 1972. He was inducted into the Blues Foundation's Hall of Fame in 1991.

Essential Listening:
Mississippi Fred McDowell/Flyright (CD 14)
Mississippi Delta Blues/Arhoolie (CD 304)
Fred McDowell and His Blues Boys/Arhoolie (1046)
Fred McDowell/Testament (2208)
Shake 'Em on Down/Tomato (269637-2)

◄ MCGHEE, BROWNIE

(born Walter McGhee, November 30, 1915, Knoxville, Tenn.)

Blues guitarist Brownie McGhee and harmonica player SONNY TERRY formed one of the longest and most popular duos in blues history. They performed and recorded together for nearly forty years and played a big part in exposing the Piedmont blues style to a white urban folk crowd in the late 1950s and early

1960s. In the process, they influenced an entire generation of folk and folk-blues artists.

McGhee was born and raised in Knoxville, Tennessee. He learned the guitar as a youth and, after dropping out of school in the late '20s, traveled with tent shows. Early on, McGhee was as much interested in gospel music as he was the blues, and in 1934 he joined the Golden Voices Gospel Quartet, a group with whom his father sang. By the late '30s, however, McGhee was back on the road, living the life of an itinerant bluesman.

McGhee, whose guitar style at the time was greatly influenced by that of BLIND BOY FULLER, eventually made it to Durham, North Carolina, where Fuller was based. In Durham, McGhee met Fuller and J.B. Long, the talent scout who was responsible for Fuller's recording success in the 1930s. Impressed with McGhee's blues style, Long arranged a Chicago recording session with him in 1940. His first record was a remake of Fuller's "Step It Up and Go" for the Okeh label. In 1941, Fuller, at age thirty-two, died suddenly of blood poisoning. In need of someone to fill Fuller's role as a recording artist, Long had McGhee use Fuller's guitar and cut a song McGhee wrote about his departed mentor called "The Death of Blind Boy Fuller." For a while, McGhee even went as Blind Boy Fuller #2.

It was at this time that McGhee left the South and moved to New York, where he teamed up with harp player Sonny Terry. They befriended LEADBELLY, who helped them secure performances at folk gatherings around the city. McGhee opened up Brownie McGhee's School of Blues in Harlem and gave blues guitar lessons. He also continued recording; he and Terry cut sides for Savoy and other labels in the '40s. The two also fell into a growing group of musicians that included REV. BLIND GARY DAVIS, Leadbelly, Woody Guthrie, Pete Seeger, and others who played clubs and coffeehouses and appealed to a white liberal audience.

By the late 1940s and through the 1950s, McGhee and Terry, together and as solo artists, were recording prolifically for numerous labels. McGhee used pseudonyms such as Spider Sam, Big Tom Collins, and Blind Boy Williams to avoid contract problems, and he didn't limit himself to just blues. McGhee also cut spirituals and gospel sides. Few if any country blues artists in the 1950s recorded more extensively than Brownie McGhee and Sonny Terry.

Not content with just being blues artists, McGhee and Terry also became actors, working in the Berkshires in Massachusetts and then in New York, appearing on Broadway in mid-'50s productions of Tennessee Williams's *Cat on a Hot Tin Roof* and Langston Hughes's *Simply Heaven*. In the early '60s, with country blues reaching more white audiences than ever before, McGhee and Terry played nearly every major folk and blues fest of note, plus dozens of colleges and most major cities where there were burgeoning blues scenes.

Despite years of performing, McGhee and Terry retained their original Piedmont blues style, which, in the early '60s, had become more popular than ever before with white audiences. The duo also toured Europe, appeared on national television and in blues documentaries, and continued to crisscross the U.S. right on into the mid-'70s when the McGhee-Terry partnership began to unravel. Sonny Terry died in 1986. Brownie McGhee has retired.

Essential Listening:
Brownie's Blues/Prestige-Bluesville (OBCCD 505-2)
Climbin' Up/Savoy (SJL 1137)
Brownie McGhee & Sonny Terry Sing/Smithsonian-Folkways (SF 40011)
Brownie McGhee, 1944–45/Travelin' Man (TMCD 04)

◄ MCGHEE, STICKS

(born Granville McGhee, March 23, 1918, Knoxville, Tenn.; died August 15, 1961, New York, N.Y.)

The brother of Brownie McGhee, guitarist-singer Sticks McGhee was best known for his 1949 R&B hit, "Drinking Wine, Spo-Dee-O-Dee, Drinking Wine."

McGhee was born and raised in Tennessee, where he learned how to play guitar. After serving in the army during World War II, McGhee moved to New York and met up with brother Brownie. The two often performed together in New York clubs; Sticks also led his own group, Sticks McGhee and His Buddies.

In 1949 McGhee signed a recording contract with Atlantic Records, which released "Drinking Wine, Spo-Dee-O-Dee, Drinking Wine." The song climbed to number 2 on the R&B charts. McGhee, however, was unable to match the success generated by his one and only hit. In the 1950s McGhee also recorded for the London, King, Red Robin, and Savoy labels. Toward the end of the decade, McGhee also occasionally worked with harmonica player SONNY TERRY, his brother's longtime partner. McGhee was diagnosed with cancer in 1960. He died a year later.

Essential Listening:
Drinkin' Wine Spo-Dee-O-Dee/Crown Prince (IG 401)

◄ MCMURRY, LILLIAN

(born December 30, 1921, Purvis, Miss.)

Lillian McMurry was the founder of Trumpet Records, an early-'50s label based out of Jackson, Mississippi, that produced some of the best recordings of SONNY BOY WILLIAMSON (Rice Miller) and other period bluesmen. From its inception in 1950 to its demise in 1955, Trumpet Records issued a number of records that faithfully reproduced a raw yet convincingly passionate blues sound that many other labels tried to imitate.

Before forming Trumpet, McMurry was the bookkeeper for her husband's furniture store. Excited by the music she heard from her black employees, she began selling records in the store. In late 1950 McMurry decided to record her own artists. Calling her label Trumpet, after the angel Gabriel's instrument, McMurry recorded gospel groups before recording harmonica player–singer Sonny Boy Williamson in 1951. Sonny Boy standards such as "Nine Below Zero," "Mighty Long Time," and "Cross My Heart" were all recorded for Trumpet. The slide guitarist ELMORE JAMES recorded "Dust My Broom," his trademark tune, for Trumpet. It became his and the label's biggest hit. Other blues artists that recorded for Trumpet included WILLIE LOVE, BIG JOE WILLIAMS, and

JERRY MCCAIN. McMurry got out of the record business after repeated attempts to collect money from distributors proved unsuccessful. She went back to working in her husband's furniture store. McMurry still resides in Jackson, Mississippi.

Essential Listening:

King Biscuit Time (Sonny Boy Williamson)/Arhoolie (CD 310)

◄ MCNEELY, BIG JAY

(born Cecil McNeely, April 29, 1927, Los Angeles, Calif.)

Big Jay McNeely was one of rhythm & blues' most important tenor saxophone stylists in the 1950s. His honking style, which was built around loud, distorted tones, helped bridge the gap between R&B and rock & roll in the latter's early years and was copied by many of his R&B sax contemporaries. McNeely was also known for his energetic live shows, which featured wild onstage histrionics and forays into the audience while playing his sax.

Born in Los Angeles, McNeely learned how to play the saxophone in school. In 1944 he formed his own band, the Earls of 44 (after one of his idols, jazz pianist Earl "Fatha" Hines) and began playing dances in Watts. Two years later he began his recording career, cutting swing sides for Exclusive Records. By the time he had switched to the Savoy label in 1948, McNeely had a new band, the Blue Jays, and a new sound that was steeped in rhythm & blues. His record "Deacon's Hop" made it to number 1 on the R&B charts in 1949, establishing McNeely as a major artist.

In the 1950s McNeely recorded for a slew of labels after his contract with Savoy expired, including Aladdin, Imperial, Federal, and Vee-Jay. In 1959 he recorded his biggest hit, "There Is Something on Your Mind," for the Swingin' label. The record, which featured the vocals of Little Sonny Warner, crossed over onto the pop charts, peaking at number 44.

McNeely was unable to match the success of "There Is Something on Your Mind" with later recordings; he eventually retired from recording and performing and took up religion. However, in 1983, McNeely was coaxed into a comeback. He formed his own record label, Big J, and released a live album, *Loose on Sunset*, that year. He also toured Europe, where his older recordings had been reissued and had generated interest in his honking sax style all over again. McNeely continues to perform.

Essential Listening:

Roadhouse Boogie/Saxophonograph (BP 505)

The Best of Big Jay McNeely, Vol. 2/Saxophonograph (BP 1300)

Loose on Sunset/Big J (101)

The Swingin' Cuts/Big J (103)

◄ MCSHANN, JAY

(born James McShann, January 12, 1916, Muskogee, Okla.)

In the late 1930s and early 1940s, Jay McShann led one of the better blues-based big bands. Only Count Basie's band outweighed McShann's in terms of full-bodied, chugging rhythms and freewheeling solos. With lead vocalists like WALTER BROWN and later JIMMY WITHERSPOON and saxophone players like Charlie Parker, McShann's band helped pave the way for the emergence of rhythm & blues immediately after World War II.

Born and raised in Oklahoma, McShann taught himself how to play piano. He moved to Kansas City in 1936 and played in jazz clubs and lounges. McShann enlarged the quartet he often performed with to seven pieces in 1938. A year later he built the band up to eleven musicians, which included a young Charlie Parker on saxophone. McShann's band became the most popular in Kansas City and in 1941 began recording for the Decca label.

Less than two weeks before the band's debut recording session, McShann discovered singer Walter Brown. He and Brown wrote the classic "Confessin' the Blues," which featured Brown on vocals. The McShann band was also known for "Hootie Blues," which included a dazzling sax solo by Parker. Unfortunately, World War II wreaked havoc on McShann's band; many of his musicians had been drafted and replacements were hard to find. McShann, too, was drafted in 1944. (For a while, Walter Brown led the band while McShann served in the armed forces.)

When the war ended, McShann put together a small, more R&B-bent band, which included singer Jimmy Witherspoon. The band recorded regularly, though by the mid-1950s rock & roll had all but sapped the market for McShann's swing-flavored blues and R&B. But McShann continued to work, mostly in the Midwest and on the West Coast. In the '70s he began making frequent trips to Europe, where he performed in small combo settings and recorded for the French Black and Blue label. Later in the decade he also began recording for the small Canadian label Sackville. In 1988 he was inducted into the Blues Foundation's Hall of Fame. Now in his late seventies, he still performs on occasion.

Essential Listening:
Jay McShann: Early Bird Charlie Parker (1941–43)/MCA (1338)
Confessin' the Blues/Affinity (AFF 66)
Goin' to Kansas City Blues/RCA (An1-1-1048[e])
Swingmatism/Sackville (3046)
Kansas City Hustle/Sackville (3021)
Blues from Kansas City: The Jay McShann Orchestra/Decca (GRD-614)

◄ MCTELL, BLIND WILLIE

(born May 5, 1901, Thompson, Ga.; died August 19, 1959, Milledgeville, Ga.)

Blind Willie McTell was the dean of the Atlanta blues school in the 1920s and 1930s. His impeccably fluid finger-picking on the twelve-string guitar (he also played six-string) helped define the rag-influenced Southeast and Piedmont guitar styles of the period. His softly stated, articulate vocals, which often made him sound like a white singer affecting a black vocal style, gave his broad repertoire a uniquely sensitive vitality.

McTell was a prolific recording artist; he recorded for many labels under a variety of pseudonyms from 1927 to 1956. His catalog includes not only blues but also rags, ballads, pop tunes, and folk numbers. McTell was, however, never much of a commercial success. Still, his influence on fellow Atlanta bluesmen and on white urban folkies and blues artists of the early '60s was profound. McTell's masterpiece, "Statesboro Blues," was recorded by the ALLMAN BROTHERS BAND in 1969 and became one of the group's trademark songs in concert.

Reports vary as to when McTell went blind. Some blues historians claim he was blind at birth; others insist he lost his sight during his teens. Whatever the truth, it is certain that by the time McTell began his recording career, he had been blind for a number of years and had attended three schools for the blind, where he learned to read braille.

McTell's mother taught him how to play guitar. When she died, McTell left home and joined up with traveling medicine shows and carnivals. McTell also performed with other Atlanta blues artists such as BUDDY MOSS and CURLEY WEAVER at house parties and fish fries, and had already developed a reputation around the city as a compelling guitarist when he cut his first records for Victor and Columbia in 1927 and 1928. From those early sessions came such McTell gems as "Statesboro Blues," "Mama, 'Tain't Long 'for' Day," and "Three Women Blues." From a 1929 session for Columbia came the McTell classic "Broke Down Engine Blues."

McTell recorded regularly through 1932; to skirt contractual obligations he often changed his name, but not his guitar or vocal styles. In 1935 McTell recorded in Chicago for Decca; in 1940 he recorded for JOHN LOMAX and the Library of Congress in Atlanta. When not recording or hoboing, McTell and longtime associate Curley Weaver played for tips and spare change on Atlanta's Decatur Street, a popular hangout for local bluesmen.

McTell resumed his recording career after World War II with Atlantic Records and Regal Records in 1949. However, he and his music failed to attract much attention, and he returned to Atlanta where he continued to sing on street corners. McTell's final recording session occurred in 1956; the songs he cut were eventually released on the Prestige-Bluesville label. McTell died in 1959. He was inducted into the Blues Foundation's Hall of Fame in 1981.

Essential Listening:

The Early Years (1927–1933)/Yazoo (CD 1005)

Blind Willie McTell—Complete Recorded Works, Vol. 1 (1927–31)/Document (DOCD 5006) (Austrian import)

Blind Willie McTell, (1927–1935)/Yazoo (1037)

Complete Library of Congress Recordings/RST (BDCD 6001)

Pig 'n' Whistle Red/Biograph (BCD 126 ADD)

◄ MELROSE, LESTER

(born 1891, Olney, Ill.; died April 12, 1968, Florida)

Lester Melrose was the main architect of the pre–World War II Chicago blues sound. A producer, talent scout, and music publisher, Melrose discovered and recorded nearly all of the era's most successful blues artists, including BIG BILL BROONZY, JOHN LEE "SONNY BOY" WILLIAMSON, WASHBOARD SAM, TAMPA RED, LONNIE JOHNSON, ARTHUR "BIG BOY" CRUDUP, BIG JOE WILLIAMS, and TOMMY MCCLENNAN, to name just some.

Although Melrose was responsible for recording the music of the greatest names in blues, his critics point to the overly familiar sound that was shared by so many of the records he made with Broonzy, Tampa Red, and the others. The sameness of "the Melrose sound" was due to his insistence that identical instrumentation—namely, guitar, bass, drums, piano, and harmonica or sax—be used again and again, except in unusual circumstances, no matter who the artist or the nature of the song.

Melrose also tended to use the same musicians as accompanists in his recording studio, further ensuring a recognizable sound. To Melrose's credit, many classic songs were recorded under his wing, and in his defense it can be pointed out that in the 1950s and 1960s, the Chess, Motown, and Stax/Volt labels used similar strategies to create their so-called "sounds."

Melrose got into the music business after World War I when he opened a Chicago music store with his brother, Walter. By 1926, Melrose was eager to make records rather than sell them. He sold his interest in the store to his brother and became a talent scout and producer. He found success early with Tampa Red and GEORGIA TOM DORSEY, who, as the Hokum Boys, recorded "It's Tight Like That." The record was a best-seller for Paramount and did much to create Melrose's career. The Depression dampened record production in the early 1930s, but by 1934, Melrose had forged associations with RCA (Bluebird) and Columbia and worked as a talent scout and producer until he retired in 1951. Melrose died in 1968.

◄ MEMPHIS JUG BAND, THE

The Memphis Jug Band was one of the most popular jug bands in Memphis during the jug band craze of the late 1920s and early 1930s. The group possessed a light, often sweet musical temperament that often sounded like the flip side of the deep country blues emanating out of the Mississippi Delta at the time. The band was founded in the Beale Street area of Memphis by guitarist and harmonica player WILL "Son" SHADE (aka Son Brimmer) in the mid-'20s. In 1927 Shade signed a recording contract with Victor Records, and with the Memphis Jug Band he cut nearly sixty sides for the label.

A number of Memphis street musicians passed through the band during its heyday, including CHARLIE BURSE, FURRY LEWIS, BIG WALTER "Shakey" HORTON, and CASEY BILL WELDON; its loosely constructed lineup was part of its inherent appeal. However, Shade was the group's guiding force. In fact, he played in various spin-offs of the original Memphis Jug Band right on up to his death in 1966.

Like Cannon's Jug Stompers, another popular Memphis-based jug band that also recorded in the late '20s and early '30s, the Memphis Jug Band's repertoire included a hodgepodge of blues, jazz, folk, rag, novelty, and pop songs, all colored with a minstrel and medicine show flair. In addition to the harmonica, Shade also used a kazoo to get his good-timey sound. Occasionally, Shade used local female singers such as Jennie Mae Clayton, Hattie Hart, or Minnie Wallace in the band.

Not only did jug bands like the Memphis Jug Band give the blues a lighter, more swinging dimension, but they also documented in song the street music of Memphis during the Depression and made certain that traditional blues didn't drown in its own melancholia.

Essential Listening:
The Memphis Jug Band/Yazoo (1067)

◄ MEMPHIS MINNIE

(born Lizzie Douglas, June 3, 1897, Algiers, La.; died August 6, 1973, Memphis, Tenn.)

Memphis Minnie ranks with MA RAINEY, BESSIE SMITH, and BIG MAMA THORNTON as one of the blues' most influential and historically significant female artists. While Rainey and Smith came out of the 1920s classic blues period, and Thornton out of the post–World War II urban blues era, Minnie's roots were in country blues, an idiom dominated by men. An able guitarist and an authoritative singer who packed her notes with punch and rough-edged passion, Minnie was also an excellent composer. Songs of hers such as "Bumble Bee," "Hoodoo Lady," and "I Want Something for You" are genuine blues classics. Minnie's command of the blues was such that her recording career spanned three decades and survived the numerous stylistic shifts that occurred within the blues. Along the way she influenced a number of prominent blues figures, from MUDDY WATERS on down, and almost single-handedly kept a female presence in what became an increasingly male form.

Minnie was born Lizzie Douglas in Louisiana. Before she turned ten, Minnie and her family had relocated to Wall, Mississippi, just south of Memphis. As a child she was called Kid Douglas and learned how to play the guitar and banjo. Sometime during her early teens she began playing and singing on Memphis street corners and eventually joined Ringling Brothers Circus and toured the South.

During the 1920s she settled into Memphis's Beale Street blues scene, where in 1929 she was discovered by a talent scout for Columbia Records. Accompanied by guitarist Kansas JOE MCCOY, her second husband (her first was the bluesman CASEY BILL WELDON), she recorded later that year under the name Memphis Minnie. Her first song, "Bumble Bee," was one of the most successful of the more than one hundred sides she recorded before retiring in the mid-1950s.

Minnie and Kansas Joe migrated to Chicago in 1930, where they quickly became part of the city's growing blues scene. Along with BIG BILL BROONZY, whom she reputedly beat in a "blues contest," and TAMPA RED, Minnie helped the country blues style ease into an urban setting. During the quarter century or so that she lived in Chicago, Minnie recorded for a number of labels, including Vocalion, Decca, and Bluebird, and with a number of bluesmen, most notably SUNNYLAND SLIM and LITTLE WALTER. For some of her sessions, Minnie employed a small combo; for others, she was accompanied by a second guitarist.

After her health began to fail in the mid-'50s, Minnie returned to Memphis and retired from performing and recording. She spent her twilight years in a nursing home, where she died of a stroke in 1973. Memphis Minnie was inducted into the Blues Foundation's Hall of Fame in 1980.

Essential Listening:
Hoodoo Lady (1933–1937)/Columbia (CK 46775)
Memphis Minnie, Vol. 1/Earl (BD 608)
Memphis Minnie, Vol. 2/Earl (BD 617)
Memphis Minnie, Vol. 1/Blues Classics (1)
Memphis Minnie, Vol. 2/Blues Classics (13)

◄ MEMPHIS SLIM

(aka Peter Chatman) (born John Chatman, September 3, 1915, Memphis, Tenn.; died February 24, 1988, Paris, France)

Memphis Slim was an important blues pianist and composer whose recordings in the 1940s helped connect the Chicago "Bluebird" sound of the 1930s with that of the early post–World War II period. His piano style was influenced by other great blues pianists such as ROOSEVELT SYKES and SPECKLED RED and included elements of boogie-woogie and traditional blues. Among Slim's most popular blues songs was the classic "Everyday (I Have the Blues)," which was a big hit for JOE WILLIAMS and the Count Basie Band in 1955.

As a youth growing up in Memphis, Slim hung out on Beale Street and occasionally worked its blues clubs, where he picked up valuable hints from other piano players. After roaming the South, Slim lived in Helena, Arkansas, before moving to Chicago in 1939. That same year he made his debut as a recording artist using the name of his father, Peter Chatman, and cutting some sides for the Okeh label. In 1940 he cut one of his trademark tunes, "Beer Drinking Woman" for Bluebird using his nickname, Memphis Slim. Later that year Slim teamed up with guitarist BIG BILL BROONZY after Broonzy's regular piano player, JOSH ALTHEIMER, had died. The two musicians played Chicago blues clubs and recorded together until 1944 when Slim branched off on his own and eventually formed the House Rockers, a seven-piece band that included a sax section. In 1946 Slim changed the name of the band to Memphis Slim and His Solid Band.

Slim recorded regularly during the late 1940s and 1950s for a number of labels, including Miracle, Chess, Vee-Jay, Bluesville, and Folkways. He also performed as a soloist and with such artists as WILLIE DIXON and SONNY BOY WILLIAMSON (Rice Miller). After a European tour with Dixon in 1960, Slim decided to leave Chicago and resettle there. In 1962 he moved to Paris, where he was able to record and perform regularly when other bluesmen back home were finding it increasingly difficult to secure steady work. Slim recorded for a variety of labels in the '60s, '70s and '80s and regularly toured Europe, where he was held in high esteem. When performing locally in Paris he'd show up at the club in a Rolls Royce. Before his death in 1988, the U.S. Senate honored him with the title of Ambassador-at-Large of Good Will while the French government bestowed on him the prestigious title of Commander of Arts and Letters. He was inducted into the Blues Foundation's Hall of Fame in 1989.

Essential Listening:

Memphis Slim, USA/Candid (9024)

Together Again One More Time/Antone's (ANT 003)

Tribute to Big Bill Broonzy, Leroy Carr, and Others/Candid (9023)

Life Is Like That/Charly (CD 249)

Memphis Slim Story/Esperance (ESPCD 1909)

Memphis Slim: The Real Folk Blues/Chess (9250)

Grinder Man Blues (with Little Brother Montgomery and Big Maceo)/RCA Heritage (2098-2-R)

Parisian Blues/Emarcy (834 658-2)

Steady Rolling Blues/Bluesville (BV 10751)

◄ MILBURN, AMOS

(born April 1, 1927, Houston, Tex.; died January 3, 1980, Houston, Tex.)

A rocking rhythm & blues pianist, singer, and bandleader in the late 1940s and early 1950s, Amos Milburn's records on the Aladdin label—especially those that dealt with alcohol consumption—were familiar visitors to the top of the R&B charts. "Bad Bad Whiskey" made it to number 1 in 1950, "Thinking and Drinking" to number 8 in 1952, "One Scotch, One Bourbon, One Beer" and "Let Me Go Home Whiskey" peaked at numbers 2 and 3, respectively, in 1953, and "Good Good Whiskey" went to number 5 in 1954. Milburn also recorded "Vicious Vicious Vodka" in 1954 and "Juice Juice" in 1956 to finish what must be the most complete set of drinking songs ever to appear in an R&B or rock & roll recording catalog.

Milburn was born in Houston and learned how to play piano by the time he was ten. In 1942, when he was fifteen years old, he lied about his age and enlisted in the navy, spending the war years in the Pacific theater. When he was discharged in 1945 Milburn returned to Houston, formed a band, and began playing the city's blues and jazz clubs. A year later he signed a recording contract with Aladdin Records and began cutting the lively jump blues songs that would lead straight to the birth of rock & roll. In 1948 he scored two number 1 hits, "Chicken Shack Boogie" and "Bewildered." The following year he registered another number 1 hit, "Roomin' House Boogie." Many of Milburn's best songs feature his boogie-woogie-influenced piano and saxophone riffs, played either by MAXWELL DAVIS or Don Wilkerson. Davis also arranged many of Milburn's hits.

In the early '50s Milburn continued to record regularly, preempting rock & roll with tunes such as "Let's Rock a While" in 1951 and "Rock, Rock, Rock"

in 1952. Unfortunately, Milburn was unable to make the leap into the more lucrative rock & roll market in the mid-'50s. He ended his association with Aladdin
in 1954, but continued to perform throughout the decade, often with CHARLES
BROWN and JOHNNY OTIS. In 1960 he had a brief relationship with King Records
and then with Motown, which released his album *Blues Boss*. Milburn spent his
remaining years as a performer doing one-nighters in lounges and bars. He suffered a series of strokes and the amputation of a leg before he died in 1980.

Essential Listening:
Amos Milburn: Blues & Boogie—His Greatest Hits/Sequel (NEX CD 132)
Amos Milburn and His Chicken Shackers/Route 66 (KIX 7)

◄ MILES, LIZZIE

*(born Elizabeth Landreaux, March 31, 1895, New Orleans, La.; died March
17, 1963, New Orleans, La.)*

Lizzie Miles was more a 1920s cabaret singer than a classic blueswoman. But
when she sang the blues, she sang them with conviction. A light-skinned Creole
who was born on Bourbon Street, Miles used her beauty and her big voice to
create a sophisticated, urbane style that was more suited for venues like the celebrated Cotton Club in Harlem than the tent shows of the South; though, in her
youth, she had worked Southern vaudeville shows and even joined up with a
circus. Miles sang pop ballads, vaudeville standards, and jazz-colored blues, both
in French and English. During her prime, she attracted the same kind of audience
that made EDITH WILSON, ALBERTA HUNTER, and LUCILLE HEGAMIN stars.

Miles began her career singing in front of New Orleans bands that included
such noted jazz musicians as King Oliver and Kid Ory. Eventually she left New
Orleans and moved to Chicago, then to New York, Paris, and back again to New
York, all the while working clubs and cabarets. She recorded for Okeh in 1921
and later did sessions for Emerson, Columbia, and Victor. Although her recording
catalog isn't large, songs such as "State Street Blues" demonstrate the vocal
dexterity she possessed.

In the late 1930s, Miles returned to New Orleans and retired. However, in the
1950s she resumed her career, performing and recording with the Bob Scobey
Band and appearing at the Monterey Jazz Festival in 1958. She retired a second
time in 1959. Miles died of a heart attack in 1963.

Essential Listening:
When Women Sing the Blues (Various Artists)/Blues Classics (26)
Super Sisters: Independent Women's Blues, Vol. 3 (Various Artists)/Rosetta (RR
1308)

◄ MILLER, JAY

(born May 5, 1922, Iopa, La.)

A producer and talent scout for Excello Records, Jay Miller was responsible
for bringing the sound of swamp blues to the blues scene in the 1950s and 1960s.
By recording artists such as SLIM HARPO, LIGHTNIN' SLIM, LONESOME SUNDOWN,

SILAS HOGAN, LAZY LESTER, and other mostly Louisiana bluesmen, Miller captured in the recording studio a "swampy" blues sound that featured raw, downhome blues with an accent on lazy rhythms, slippery guitar licks, and easy-flowing vocals.

Miller grew up on cowboy and country music. He learned how to play guitar as a child, and by the time he was in his late teens was playing in Louisiana country groups. Miller's career was cut short when he served in the armed forces during World War II. After his discharge he went into the electrical contracting business in Louisiana, but he eventually found his way back to music. He started the Fai Do Do label in the late 1940s and recorded mostly cajun and hillbilly artists. It wasn't until he met Ernie Young, the owner of the Nashville-based Excello Records, in 1955, that Miller began to make his mark in the blues. He began by leasing out sides he recorded with Lightnin' Slim; in short time he turned his Crowley, Louisiana, studio into a swamp blues center where songs such as Silas Hogan's "Everybody Needs Somebody," Lonesome Sundown's "My Home Is a Prison," and Slim Harpo's "Baby Scratch My Back," which made it to number 1 on the R&B charts and number 16 on the pop charts in 1966, put the Baton Rouge, Louisiana, area on the blues map.

Miller remained with Excello through most of the 1960s, until the sound of soul music eventually came to dominate black music tastes. Miller continued to work in music. He began Master Track Enterprises, which by 1993 included two twenty-four-track recording studios in Crowley. Artists who have recorded at Master Track include Paul Simon, John Fogerty, and Thomas Dolby.

Essential Listening:

Sound of the Swamp: The Best of Excello Records, Vol. 1 (Various Artists)/Rhino (R2-70896)

Southern Rhythm 'n' Rock: The Best of Excello Records, Vol. 2 (Various Artists)/ Rhino (R2-70897)

◄ MILLINDER, LUCKY

(born Lucius Millinder, August 8, 1900, Anniston, Ala.; died September 28, 1966, New York, N.Y.)

In the 1940s, the Lucky Millinder Orchestra provided a vital link between big band swing and rhythm & blues. Although Millinder didn't play an instrument and reputedly couldn't even read music, he nonetheless played a crucial role in the early development of jump blues. Smaller combos, such as ROY MILTON's Solid Senders, sought to incorporate Millinder's blues-based sense of swing into their own sound.

Millinder was born in Alabama but raised in Chicago. He got his start in music as an emcee. In 1934 Millinder took over the directorship of the Mills Blue Rhythm Band, one of the early black swing bands in the 1930s. Among those who performed with the band were trumpeter Red Allen, trombonist J.C. Higginbottom, clarinetist Buster Bailey, and saxophonist Tab Smith. Millinder worked with Bill Doggett's band in 1938 after the Blue Rhythm Band dissolved, and then formed the Lucky Millinder Orchestra in 1940. The orchestra became one of the most rhythmically exciting bands on the swing circuit.

The Millinder band was especially popular in Harlem as it gradually shifted away from swing and more toward early rhythm & blues. Among the orchestra's many noted members were Dizzy Gillespie and Bull Moose Jackson. Millinder eventually secured a recording contract with Decca; from 1942 to 1945 the orchestra landed four records at the top of the charts. One of the hits, "When the Lights Go on Again (All Over the World)" featured Gillespie on trumpet. Another one, "Who Threw the Whiskey in the Well," featured vocalist WYNONIE HARRIS.

Along with other black bands such as those led by Cab Calloway and Count Basie, the Millinder band paved the way for the R&B boom of the late 1940s. In 1949 Millinder scaled down his band in an attempt to cash in on the combo craze that was sweeping black music. Although the reduced Millinder band continued to record, the group could not match the success it enjoyed in the early and mid-1940s when it was a full-fledged orchestra. Millinder dissolved the band in 1952 and became a disc jockey. He died in 1966.

Essential Listening:
Shorty's Got to Go/Jukebox Lil (609)
Let It Roll Again/Jukebox Lil (613)

◄ MILTON, ROY

(born July 31, 1907, Wynnewood, Okla.; died September 18, 1983, Los Angeles, Calif.)

One of the early rhythm & blues pioneers, Roy Milton built the sound of his group, the Solid Senders, from the rich, horn-dominated sound of big band swing. Yet underneath his horn section (two saxophonists and a trumpet player) was a rocking, boogie-woogie rhythm section whose driving beat helped bring on rock & roll.

Milton was born and raised in Oklahoma and played in the brass section of his high school band before embarking on a career as a singer. He fronted some amateur bands in Tulsa before joining the Ernie Fields Orchestra in 1931. It was while Milton was with Fields that he began playing the drums after he had filled in for regular drummer Red Nicholson. Eager to front his own group, Milton left Fields in 1933 and moved to Los Angeles, where he eventually formed the Solid Senders, which included Camille Howard on piano and Milton on vocals and drums. Milton and his combo played scaled-down swing and prototype rhythm & blues up and down the West Coast in the 1930s and early 1940s. In 1945 Milton and the Solid Senders recorded for Lionel Hampton's Hamp-tone label and Milton's own Miltone label before signing with Juke Box, soon to be called Specialty. "R.M. Blues," one of the very first rhythm & blues hits, went all the way to number 2 on the charts in early 1946. The song not only established Milton and the Solid Senders as a recording unit, but also helped the fledgling Juke Box label achieve a firm footing in the music industry.

Milton and his Solid Senders recorded a string of hit songs that stretched all the way to 1953. Milton classics such as "Milton's Boogie," "Hop, Skip, and

Jump,'' ''Information Blues,'' and ''Best Wishes'' all made it into the top 10 of the R&B charts. But by 1954, interest in Milton's boogie brand of R&B began to wane; in its place came rock & roll. Although Milton and other late-'40s R&B artists such as AMOS MILBURN, WYNONIE HARRIS, and LOUIS JORDAN set the stage for rock with their chugging rhythms and driving backbeat, they made little progress in their attempt to cross over into the white pop market.

After leaving Specialty in 1954, Milton continued his recording career by making records for labels like King and Warwick. He and his band worked one-nighters in the late '50s and early '60s, but clearly Milton's heyday was behind him. Milton played with JOHNNY OTIS at the 1970 Monterey Jazz Festival, which enabled him to launch something of a comeback. Over the next few years, Milton occasionally performed with Otis and played solo dates in the U.S. and Europe. By the end of the '70s, however, Milton had all but retired from performing. He died in 1983.

Essential Listening:
Roy Milton & His Solid Senders/Specialty (SPCD 7004)
Grandfather of R&B/Jukebox Lil (600)
Roy Milton & His Solid Senders, Vol. 2: Groovy Blues/Specialty (SPCD 7024-2)

◄ MISSISSIPPI JOOK BAND, THE

Members: Roosevelt Graves (guitar); Uaroy Graves (tambourine); Cooney Vaughn (piano)

The Mississippi Jook Band was a rag- and boogie-influenced blues band that recorded in the mid-1930s for the American Record Company. The trio was made up of guitarist BLIND ROOSEVELT GRAVES, his one-eyed brother Uaroy on tambourine, and the much-admired pianist Cooney Vaughn. Before forming the Jook Band, Roosevelt Graves performed around southern Mississippi in the 1920s, occasionally with Uaroy. Vaughn played the area's juke joints, where he developed a reputation as a particularly skillful pianist who could play easy-flowing blues one moment and wailing boogie the next. The Graves brothers recorded both blues and gospel tunes for Paramount in 1929 before forming the Jook Band. Vaughn's only known recordings were made with the Jook Band.

Essential Listening:
Good Time Blues (*Harmonicas, Kazoos, Washboards & Cow-bells*) (Various Artists)/Columbia (CK 46780)

◄ MISSISSIPPI SHEIKS, THE

The Mississippi Sheiks was a loosely knit, good-time blues group that grew out of the Chatmon family band, one of the most popular of the Mississippi Delta–based string bands in the 1920s. Named after the Rudolph Valentino film *The Sheik* and based out of the Jackson area, the group's steadiest lineup, at least in terms of recording, was fiddle player Lonnie Chatmon and guitarist WALTER VINSON. On occasion, these two musicians would be joined by guitarists SAM CHATMON and BO CARTER (Armenter Chatmon). Sam Chatmon and Carter also had successful solo careers in the '30s. The Sheiks are best known for their song "Sitting on Top of the World," which they recorded in the 1930s. The blues standard was remade by HOWLIN' WOLF in 1957 and some ten years later by the blues-rock group CREAM, as well as by the Grateful Dead, Bob Dylan, and others.

The Sheiks began their recording career in 1930; it lasted five years and resulted in nearly eighty sides. Much of their catalog is a combination of rural string songs, bawdy blues, and dance numbers. Among their ribald classics are tunes such as "Bed Spring Poker" and "Driving That Thing," with their playful double entendre.

Essential Listening:
Raunchy Business: Hot Nuts & Lollypops (Various Artists)/Columbia (CK 46783)
Mississippi Sheiks, 1930–35/Document (595)
Stop and Listen/Yazoo (2006)

◄ MOLTON, FLORA

(born 1908, Louisa County, Va.; died May 31, 1990, Washington, D.C.)

Singer-guitarist Flora Molton was a Washington, D.C., street singer and a fixture in the city's blues and gospel scenes for nearly fifty years. Born in Virginia, Molton's earliest musical experiences were in the church. She learned to play the organ and the accordion before settling on the guitar, often playing it in the traditional bottleneck style.

Molton moved to Washington, D.C., in 1937, looking for work. Unable to get a job, she supported herself by singing and playing on the city's streets for spare change. Over the years Molton played with most of the members of the Washington, D.C., and Virginia blues scenes, including JOHN JACKSON, ARCHIE EDWARDS, PHIL WIGGINS, and JOHN CEPHAS. Molton also performed at the Smithsonian's Festival of American Folklife, the Philadelphia Folk Festival, and other regional fests, but she was best known as the last of a vanishing breed of D.C. street singers.

Molton recorded one album, *Molton's Truth Band*, for the L+R label. She released another, *I Want to Be Ready to Hear God When He Calls*, on her own Lively Stone label. Molton died in 1990.

Essential Listening:
Molton's Truth Band/L&R

◄ MONTGOMERY, LITTLE BROTHER

(born Eurreal Montgomery, April 18, 1906, Kentwood, La.; died September 6, 1985, Chicago, Ill.)

Little Brother Montgomery was one of the last of the original barrelhouse piano players. His versatility and deep understanding of the blues and blues-inflected music enabled him to perform and record for more than fifty years. Along the way, Montgomery played blues, jazz, and boogie-woogie at countless house-rent parties, club dates, and concerts, including Carnegie Hall (with Kid Ory's band in 1948), as well as in brothels, at dances, and in logging and lumber camps.

Thanks to a sharp memory, Montgomery provided blues historians and researchers with first-person accounts of barrelhouse culture and its related piano style near the end of his life.

Montgomery learned the rudiments of the piano by watching the players who performed in his father's barrelhouse on the grounds of the Kent Lumber Company in Kent, Louisiana. As a boy he was called "Little Brother Harper," though later the nickname was shortened to "Little Brother." According to Montgomery, he left home at age eleven and became an itinerant piano player, eventually performing with Clarence Desdunes and the Joyland Revelers and winding up in New Orleans and later Chicago. His recording career began in 1930 when he cut some sides with Paramount. Two of the songs he recorded for the label, "No Special Rider" and "Vicksburg Blues," became important songs in his repertoire.

Montgomery returned to the South and settled in Jackson, Mississippi, in the early 1930s. His recording career resumed in 1935 when he recorded for Bluebird. He cut twenty-two sides for the label, including his signature song, "Vicksburg Blues, No. 2," which has become a piano blues standard. Montgomery continued to record for other small "race" labels after he went back to Chicago in 1942. He was also in demand as a session piano player and accompanied blueswomen such as SIPPIE WALLACE, Minnie Hicks, and Irene Suggs in the recording studio.

For the next forty years Montgomery worked the Windy City's clubs and lounges when he wasn't touring or playing festivals or doing sessions for bluesmen such as OTIS RUSH and MAGIC SAM. After marrying Janet Floberg in 1967 (his second marriage), Montgomery formed his own label, FM (*F* for Floberg; *M* for Montgomery), and the two often recorded together in the living room of their home. Little Brother Montgomery last recorded in 1982; in all, he made some thirty albums in his career. He died in 1985.

Essential Listening:
Grinder Man Blues(Various Artists)/RCA Heritage (2098-2-R)
At Home/Earwig (4918)
Chicago—The Living Legends/Ace (CH 263)

◄ MOONEY, JOHN

(born April 3, 1955, East Orange, N.J.)

John Mooney is a neotraditionalist slide guitar player whose style is derivative of the harsh, slashing style of Mississippi Delta great SON HOUSE. Mooney was born in New Jersey and raised in Rochester, New York. He began playing House's rough-cut brand of country blues and slide guitar after meeting the legendary artist, who also lived in Rochester. For a while in the mid-'70s Mooney accompanied House in performance.

Mooney moved to New Orleans in 1976; a year later he signed a recording contract with the Blind Pig label and recorded his debut album, *Comin' Your Way*. Wanting to expand his blues sound, Mooney formed his Bluesiana band in 1983 and has toured extensively, opening shows for JOHNNY WINTER, BONNIE RAITT, ALBERT KING, CLARENCE "GATEMOUTH" BROWN, and others. Since then, Mooney has released three more albums, *Telephone King* on the Powerhouse label, *Late Last Night* on Bullseye Blues, and *Testimony* on Domino. In 1993 *Esquire* magazine called Mooney one of the best of the white blues-rock guitar stylists. Mooney also toured with Festival New Orleans that year, sharing the stage with BUCKWHEAT ZYDECO and other New Orleans acts. Mooney continues to record and perform.

Essential Listening:
Comin' Your Way/Blind Pig (BP 779)
Telephone King/Powerhouse (POW 4101)
Late Last Night/Bullseye Blues (BB 9505)
Testimony/Domino (DOMC 001)

◄ MOORE, ALEX

(born November 22, 1899, Dallas, Tex.; died January 20, 1989, Dallas, Tex.)

Alex Moore was a first-generation Dallas blues piano player whose style incorporated elements of ragtime and boogie-woogie. His career spanned some seven decades, though his recording catalog is relatively lean. In his later years Moore became one of the deans of Texas blues piano and provided a vital link with pre–World War II styles.

Moore, known as Whistlin' Alex, began his career in the 1920s playing Dallas house-rent parties and small clubs. He recorded some titles for the Columbia label when the company visited Dallas in 1929. Other sessions followed in 1937 with Decca and RPM/Kent in 1951. But mostly Moore was a live performer, playing Dallas nightclubs well into the 1950s. In 1960 he recorded for Arhoolie, which broadened his reputation beyond Texas. In 1969 he toured Europe with the American Folk Blues Festival package; Arhoolie released the album *Alex Moore—In Europe* shortly thereafter. Despite advancing age, Moore continued to work in Dallas into the 1980s In 1987 he received a Lifetime Achievement Award from the National Endowment for the Arts. The following year he recorded the album *Wiggle Tail* for Rounder Records. Moore died in 1989 at age eighty-nine.

Essential Listening:
Alex Moore/Arhoolie (1008)
Alex Moore—In Europe/Arhoolie (1048)
Wiggle Tail/Rounder (2091)

◄ MOORE, JOHNNY B.

(born January 24, 1950, Clarksdale, Miss.)

A blues guitarist in the style of B.B. KING, Johnny B. Moore played lead guitar in KOKO TAYLOR's Blues Machine in the '70s and early '80s before expanding his career to include session and sideman work and become a solo recording artist. His American debut album, *Hard Times*, was released in 1987 by the B.L.U.E.S. R&B label.

Moore grew up in the Mississippi Delta, where he sang in gospel groups and learned how to play the guitar. He moved to Chicago in 1964 and gradually worked his way into the city's blues scene. In the early '70s, Moore played weekend dates in small Chicago clubs and bars while keeping a day job. When Taylor offered him the lead guitar slot with the Blues Machine in 1975, Moore made music his main occupation.

Since then, Moore has performed extensively with Taylor and WILLIE DIXON until the latter's death in 1992. Frequent trips to Europe have enabled Moore to build a following there. He remains a part of the contemporary blues scene in Chicago.

Essential Listening:

Hard Times/B.L.U.E.S. R&B (3604)

◄ MORGAN, MIKE

(born November 30, 1959, Dallas, Tex.)

Mike Morgan is a Dallas-based guitarist who, with his band the Crawl, plays a brand of Texas blues that's ripe with rhythm & blues and traditional rock roots. On Morgan's first two albums, *Raw & Ready* (1990) and *Mighty Fine Dancin'* (1991), he explores a blues sound already cultivated by the likes of guitarist contemporaries ANSON FUNDERBURGH and RONNIE EARL.

Morgan was a motorcycle racer before he seriously took up the guitar. He lost his right eye in a motorcycle racing mishap and wears an eyepatch that has become something of a trademark. The Crawl has gone through numerous personnel changes since its inception in the mid-'80s; for a time its drummer was Uncle John Turner, who played with JOHNNY WINTER in the '60s.

In the early '90s, Morgan stopped touring with the Crawl, although he continued to record with the group. For *Full Moon Over Dallas*, the group's 1992 album, the band was called simply the Crawl, as opposed to Mike Morgan & the Crawl as on earlier recordings.

Essential Listening:

Raw & Ready/Black Top (BT 1051)

Mighty Fine Dancin'/Black Top (BT 1064)

Full Moon Over Dallas/Black Top (BT 1080)

◄ MOSS, BUDDY

(born Eugene Moss, January 26, 1914, Jewel, Ga.; died October 19, 1984)

Buddy Moss was a southeast harmonica player, singer, and guitarist whose popularity and recording output in the early 1930s were considerable. Not only did Moss record as a solo artist, but he was also a member of the Georgia Cotton Pickers and the Georgia Browns, two good-timey blues combos, and he frequently worked with guitarist CURLEY WEAVER as a performing duo. Along the way, Moss perfected the Piedmont blues style. Unfortunately, he was sent to prison in 1935, for allegedly murdering his wife, at the prime of his career. Moss's five-year stay behind bars effectively ended any chance he had to become as well known a Piedmont figure as, say, BLIND BOY FULLER. When he became a civilian again, his recording career was all but over.

Moss was born in Georgia into a sharecropping family. When not working the fields, Moss taught himself how to play blues harmonica. In 1928, he moved to the Atlanta area, where he occasionally played with both BARBECUE BOB (Robert Hicks), who taught him the rudiments of the guitar, and BLIND WILLIE MCTELL. In 1930 he recorded with the Georgia Cotton Pickers, a group that included Barbecue Bob and Curley Weaver. Moss's richly toned and tightly placed harmonica riffs gave their recordings color and presence. Moss supplied the same for the Georgia Browns, an offshoot of the Cotton Pickers in which Fred McMullen replaced Barbecue Bob on guitar and vocals.

Moss recorded regularly from 1933 to 1935, mostly as a solo artist for the American Record Company. In 1935 he was imprisoned. When he was paroled in late 1940, Moss resettled in Durham, North Carolina. In 1941, shortly after the death of noted Piedmont guitar player and recording artist Blind Boy Fuller, Moss went to New York to record with SONNY TERRY, BROWNIE MCGHEE, and other area bluesmen for the Okeh label. For Moss, little of note occurred from the session, and he spent the next ten years performing around North Carolina, often with Curley Weaver, before returning to Atlanta.

Moss was eventually rediscovered in 1965 at the height of the country blues revival. He occasionally performed at folk and blues fests, including the Newport Folk Festival in 1969 and the Atlanta Blues Festival in 1976, and did some recording in 1966 for the Biograph label. He died in 1984.

Essential Listening:

Good Time Blues (Harmonicas, Kazoos, Washboards & Cow-Bells)/Columbia (CK 46780)
Georgia Blues/Travelin' Man (800)
Buddy Moss, 1930–41/Travelin' Man (05)

◄ MOTEN, BENNIE

(born November 13, 1894, Kansas City, Mo.; died April 2, 1935, Kansas City, Mo.)

One of the great Kansas City bandleaders of the early 1930s, Bennie Moten, along with his Kansas City Orchestra, created a romping swing sound that kept a strong blues element in jazz, one that would later be explored more fully by the famous Count Basie band. Moten, an equally impressive pianist and composer, built his band with some of the best musicians of the day, including Basie on piano, singer JIMMY RUSHING, saxophonists Herschel Evans, Ben Webster, and Lester Young, trumpeter HOT LIPS PAGE, guitarist Eddie Durham, and even bass player WALTER PAGE, whose band the Blue Devils was once Moten's chief competition.

Moten began his career in the early 1920s leading a small combo and recording for the Okeh label. By the end of the decade Moten's group had grown to the size of a full-blown big band. Although the orchestra's popularity was confined primarily to the Midwest in the early '30s, the band was on the verge of becoming a major player in the swing era when Moten died in 1935. During a tonsillectomy his jugular vein was accidentally cut and the bandleader bled to death. He was forty-one years old.

Basie assumed control of Moten's band and shaped it into the Count Basie Orchestra, the best of the blues-based big bands of the swing era.

Essential Listening:
Bennie Moten, 1927–29/Classics (558)
Bennie Moten, 1930–32/Classics (591)

◄ MURPHY, MATT "GUITAR"

(born December 27, 1929, Sunflower, Miss.)

One of the blues' most respected sidemen, Matt "Guitar" Murphy has lent his beautifully inventive and crisp guitar work to a number of albums, including those made with MEMPHIS SLIM, JAMES COTTON, and the BLUES BROTHERS, among others. Murphy grew up in the Mississippi Delta but moved with his family to Memphis when he was three. Along with his brother Floyd, who also plays guitar, the Murphys worked their way into the city's vibrant blues scene in the early 1950s. Matt Murphy played guitar with HOWLIN' WOLF's band and, with JUNIOR PARKER, began the Blue Flames. Later, Floyd recorded with Parker and played on the latter's early-'50s Sun classic "Mystery Train."

Oddly, Matt Murphy recorded very little in the 1950s. He cut some sides with BOBBY "BLUE" BLAND, but it wasn't until Murphy joined Memphis Slim's band, the House Rockers, that his early guitar work was properly documented. Slim and the House Rockers recorded for the Vee-Jay and United Artists labels. Murphy continued his sideman and session work in the '60s and '70s with little fanfare. However, his part in the 1980 movie *The Blues Brothers* and his performance on the album *Briefcase Full of Blues* brought him much-earned exposure.

In 1985 Murphy teamed up with Memphis Slim again and recorded a live album, *Together Again One More Time*, at Antone's, the popular Austin, Texas, blues club. Two years later at Antone's, Murphy contributed to another live album, *James Cotton Live at Antone's Nightclub*. Finally, in 1990, with help from Floyd Murphy on second guitar, Matt recorded his first album, *Way Down South*, for the Antone's record label. Murphy continues to record and perform.

Essential Listening:
Together Again One More Time/Antone's (Ant CD 0305)
James Cotton Live at Antone's Nightclub/Antone's (Ant CD 007)
Way Down South/Antone's (Ant 0013)

◄ MUSSELWHITE, CHARLIE

(born January 31, 1944, Kosciusko, Miss.)

Harmonica player and vocalist Charlie Musselwhite was one of the first non-black blues artists to interpret the richly emotive harp styles of LITTLE WALTER, SONNY BOY WILLIAMSON (Rice Miller), and other great blues harp players. A Native American of Choctaw ancestry, Musselwhite, like PAUL BUTTERFIELD, proved that nonblack players could make a contribution to the form.

Musselwhite was born in Mississippi but grew up in Memphis, where he struck up friendships with WILL SHADE (aka Son Brimmer) of the MEMPHIS JUG BAND,

FURRY LEWIS, and other old-time bluesmen. By the time Musselwhite moved to Chicago in 1962, he had mastered the rudiments of both harp and guitar, thanks mostly to Shade, and was eager to learn the finer points of the blues. Musselwhite performed on Chicago's legendary Maxwell Street for tips with fellow bluesman JOHNNY YOUNG, and later worked his way into Chicago's black club scene, forging a working relationship with many of the city's bluesmen, including J.B. HUTTO and MIKE BLOOMFIELD. In 1966 Musselwhite signed a recording contract with Vanguard Records and released *Stand Back! Here Comes Charlie Musselwhite's Southside Blues Band*, one of the classic blues albums of the decade.

Throughout the late '60s and '70s Musselwhite recorded regularly and toured extensively. He cut three more albums for Vanguard, *Stone Blues* (1968) *Charlie Musselwhite* (1968), and *Tennessee Woman* (1969), plus a couple for Cherry Red Records, *Louisiana Fog* and *Blues from Chicago*, both in 1968, and performed at many of the period's biggest blues festivals, in the U.S. and abroad. In 1971 Musselwhite left Vanguard and signed with Arhoolie; he recorded two more acclaimed albums, *Takin' My Time* (1971) and *Goin' Back Down South* (1974), which artfully depict Musselwhite's by-now beautifully textured harp style.

Musselwhite also recorded for a number of other labels, including Paramount, Kicking Mule, and Capitol, though nearly all of these albums fell quickly into obscurity. He launched something of a comeback in 1990 when he signed with Alligator and recorded *Ace of Harps*, his best effort since his days as an Arhoolie artist. Musselwhite followed *Ace of Harps* with *Signature*, another acclaimed album on Alligator. Musselwhite continues to perform and record.

Essential Listening:
Stand Back! Here Comes Charlie Musselwhite's Southside Blues Band/Vanguard (VMD 79232)
Memphis Charlie/Arhoolie (303)
Ace of Harps/Alligator (4781)
Memphis, Tennessee/Mobile Fidelity Sound Lab (MFCD 775)
Signature/Alligator (AL 4801)

◄ MYERS, DAVID

(born October 30, 1926, Byhalia, Miss.)

The brother of harp player–guitarist LOUIS MYERS and an original member of seminal Chicago blues group the ACES, David Myers is one of the many unheralded architects of the city's post–World War II blues scene.

Myers was brought up in Mississippi, where he learned how to play guitar. In 1941 his family moved to Chicago. He and his brother began playing house-rent parties, eventually with harp player JUNIOR WELLS. In time the group became known as the Aces and, after bringing in drummer FRED BELOW, took its place as the leading electric blues band in Chicago, rivaled only by MUDDY WATERS's band. After Wells left the Aces to join the Waters band and harmonica player LITTLE WALTER began fronting the Aces, the group became known as the Jukes. Though the Myers brothers formed the nucleus of the band, it was Little Walter who grabbed the spotlight.

Myers left Little Walter in 1955 and joined his brother in a new band led by guitarist OTIS RUSH that also included drummer ODIE PAYNE, JR. In 1958 Myers switched from guitar to bass and became one of the first blues players to use an electric bass. Myers spent the rest of his career as a bass player in various incarnations of the Aces. He continues to work Chicago blues clubs as a solo guitarist and free-lance bassist.

Essential Listening:
The Best of Little Walter/MCA-Chess (CHD 9192)
The Best of Little Walter, Vol. Two/MCA-Chess (CHD 9292)
Kings of Chicago Blues, Vol. One/Vogue (LDM 3017)

◄ MYERS, LOUIS

(born September 18, 1929, Byhalia, Miss.)

A guitarist and harmonica player who has been part of Chicago's postwar blues scene since its inception, Louis Myers was an original member of the ACES, one of the city's first and most dynamic electric blues bands. The group also included older brother and fellow guitarist DAVID MYERS, plus harmonica player–singer JUNIOR WELLS and drummer FRED BELOW. When Wells left the Aces to join MUDDY WATERS's band, his place was taken by harp player–singer LITTLE WALTER Jacobs, who used Myers and the Aces on many of his now-legendary early Checker (Chess) recordings.

Myers was born in Mississippi but moved with his family to Chicago in 1941. He played house-rent parties in the mid-'40s with Othum Brown and BIG BOY SPIRES, then with his brother David before Junior Wells joined them. The trio began as the Little Boys, but by 1948 the Myers brothers and Wells were calling themselves the Three Deuces, then the Three Aces, followed by simply the Aces when drummer Fred Below joined the band in 1950. After Wells left to play with Muddy Waters, Little Walter came into the fold. Under Walter's leadership, Myers and the band often played as Little Walter & His Nightcats or Little Walter and His Jukes. But personality and musical differences prompted Myers to leave the band in 1954. Myers then teamed up with pianists OTIS SPANN and HENRY GRAY, guitarist OTIS RUSH (with whom he recorded on the Cobra label), plus other prominent Chicago bluesmen, such as guitarists EARL HOOKER and LUTHER TUCKER.

In the late 1950s and on through the 1960s, Myers worked extensively as a sideman in clubs and as a session musician in the recording studio. In 1971 he re-formed the Aces and recorded for the Black and Blue and Vogue labels. The Aces worked on and off during the '70s in Chicago and in Europe, where the group had developed a strong following. Myers recorded the album *I'm a Southern Man* for the Advent label in 1979. In the '80s he continued to play Chicago clubs and work as a session musician. Myers also made frequent appearances at the Chicago Blues Festival with different artists and put together still more reunions with the Aces. In 1991 he recorded the album *Tell My Story Movin'* for Earwig Records. Myers suffered a stroke shortly after the album's completion and he has since retired from touring.

Essential Listening:
The Best of Little Walter/MCA-Chess (CHC 9192)
The Best of Little Walter, Vol. Two/MCA-Chess (CHD 9292)
Kings of Chicago Blues, Vol. One/Vogue (LDM 3017)
I'm a Southern Man/Advent (2809)
Tell My Story Movin'/Earwig (4920)

◄ MYERS, SAM

(born February 19, 1936, Laurel, Miss.)

Singer, harmonica player, and drummer Sam Myers backed ELMORE JAMES in the 1950s and recorded for the Ace and Fury labels before forming his own band to work the chitlin' circuit in the 1960s and 1970s. Based in Jackson, Mississippi, Myers built his sound out of traditional Delta blues, but his harp style borrowed much from LITTLE WALTER. By the early 1980s, Myers's career had stalled; although he worked steadily in and around Jackson, he had been unable to break out beyond Mississippi.

That changed when contemporary blues guitarist ANSON FUNDERBURGH met Myers in 1986 and asked him to front his band, the Rockets. Since then, Myers has sung and played harp in the group, sharing the spotlight with Funderburgh and making the Rockets one of the most successful of the contemporary blues bands. In five years, from 1986 to 1991, Myers made four albums with Funderburgh and the Rockets: *My Love Is Here to Stay, Sins, Rack 'Em Up*, and *Tell Me What I Want To Hear*. In 1988 *Sins* won a W.C. HANDY Award for best blues recording of the year, while Funderburgh, Myers, and the Rockets also won best blues band that year. Myers, who has contributed original material to the Rockets' repertoire, continues to record and perform with the band.

Essential Listening:
(all with Anson Funderburgh and the Rockets):
My Love Is Here to Stay/Black Top (BT 1032)
Sins/Black Top (BT 1038)
Rack 'Em Up/Black Top (BT 1049)
Tell Me What I Want to Hear/Black Top (BT 1068)
Thru the Years: A Retrospective/Black Top (BT 1077)

N.

◄ NAFTALIN, MARK

(born August 2, 1944, Minneapolis, Minn.)

Blues keyboards player and songwriter Mark Naftalin was a member of the PAUL BUTTERFIELD Blues Band in the mid-1960s. Since then Naftalin has been a key figure in the San Francisco Bay Area blues scene, producing concerts, festivals, live radio broadcasts, and albums, as well as performing in area clubs.

Naftalin moved from Minneapolis to Chicago in 1961 to attend the University of Chicago. There he met harmonica player Paul Butterfield and guitarist ELVIN BISHOP. In 1965 he joined the Paul Butterfield Blues Band and recorded four albums with it, including the classic *East-West*. Naftalin left the Butterfield Band in 1968 and settled in San Francisco, where he played with ex-Butterfield guitarist MIKE BLOOMFIELD, often as Mike Bloomfield and Friends.

In 1979 Naftalin expanded his role in the Bay Area blues scene when he initiated "Mark Naftalin's Blue Monday Party," a weekly blues show that ran for nearly five years. From the Blue Monday Party came three television specials and more than eighty live radio broadcasts. Naftalin also hosted a weekly "Blues Power Hour" radio show on San Francisco's KALW-FM and led the Mark Naftalin Rhythm & Blues Revue, which at times featured guitarists LOWELL FULSON and LUTHER TUCKER. In 1981 Naftalin also began the annual Marin County Blues Festival, and in 1988 he started Winner Records, an independent blues label. Naftalin also continues to work as a blues musician in the Bay Area, often performing with guitarist RON THOMPSON.

Essential Listening:
The Paul Butterfield Blues Band/Elektra (7294-2)
East-West (The Paul Butterfield Blues Band)/Elektra (7315-2)

◄ NEAL, KENNY

(born October 14, 1957, Baton Rouge, La.)

The son of South Louisiana bluesman RAFUL NEAL, Kenny Neal began his career at age thirteen as the bass player in his father's back-up band. Since then, Neal, whose primary instruments are guitar and harmonica, has released a number of albums for Alligator Records and has starred in the black Broadway musical *Mule Bone*.

Neal's brand of blues leans heavily on funk rhythms and soul phrasings, and it's frequently punctuated with swamp blues guitar and harp licks. In addition to his father, Neal's influences include SLIM HARPO, who gave Neal his first harmonica, BUDDY GUY, with whom Neal played bass in the late '70s and Rudolph Richard, who played lead guitar in Slim Harpo's band. Prior to launching his solo career, Neal also performed in the Toronto-based Neal Brothers Blues Band, which included brothers Raful Jr., Noel, Larry, and Ronnie. In 1984, Neal returned to Baton Rouge and formed his own band. King Snake Records signed Neal in 1986, and the following year the label released his debut recording, *Bio on the Bayou*. The album was later re-mixed and rereleased by Alligator with a new title, *Big News from Baton Rouge!!*

Neal's career took a new direction when he agreed to play the part of Jim, a song and dance man, in the 1991 Broadway production of *Mule Bone*, the 1930 play written by African-American poet Langston Hughes and folklorist Zora Neal Hurston. In the musical, Neal performed songs composed by TAJ MAHAL. For his part, Neal won a Theatre World Award for the most outstanding new talent appearing in a Broadway or off-Broadway production in 1991. Neal continues to record and perform regularly in the U.S., Canada, and Europe.

Essential Listening:
Big News from Baton Rouge!!/Alligator (AL 4764)
Devil Child/Alligator (AL 4774)
Walking on Fire/Alligator (AL 4795)
Bayou Blood/Alligator (AL 4809)

◄ NEAL, RAFUL

(born June 6, 1936, Baton Rouge, La.)

A regionally popular, LITTLE WALTER–influenced harmonica player and vocalist from southern Louisiana, Raful Neal's first band, the Clouds, included BUDDY GUY on guitar. The band played Baton Rouge clubs and college fraternity parties. Neal began his recording career in 1958. His first single, a cover version of Polka Dot Slim's "Sunny Side of Love," came out on Don Robey's Houston-based Peacock label.

Neal, whose vocal style is steeped as much in rhythm & blues as soul and swamp blues, also recorded for a couple of small labels in the late '60s, namely, La Louisiane and Whit. However, he failed to attract serious attention outside Louisiana until 1987 when his version of the J.B. Lenoir tune "Man, Watch Your Woman," released on the Fantastic label, was nominated for a W.C. HANDY Award in the blues single of the year category. Neal's first album, *Louisiana Legend*, on King Snake/Fantastic followed.

Since then *Louisiana Legend* has been rereleased on Alligator Records. In 1991 Neal recorded a new album, *I Been Mistreated*, which includes a new version of "Man, Watch Your Woman," for Ichiban Records. Kenny Neal, a blues guitarist on the Alligator roster, is one of Raful Neal's ten offspring.

Essential Listening:
Louisiana Legend/Alligator (AL 4783)
I Been Mistreated/Ichiban (ICH 9004)

◄ NELSON, TRACY

(born December 27, 1944, French Camp, Calif.)

Tracy Nelson is a female blues and rhythm & blues singer who led the late '60s San Francisco band Mother Earth. Although some music historians have called Nelson a protegée of JANIS JOPLIN, the San Francisco scene's most famous female blues singer, Nelson did not rely on blues shouting, as Joplin did, but rather on soulful vocal strains.

Nelson was born in California but raised in Madison, Wisconsin, where, early on, she was exposed to folk and blues music. After entering the University of Wisconsin as a social work major in the early '60s, Nelson began singing in Madison coffeehouses and at fraternity parties with an R&B cover band called the Fabulous Imitators. She also frequently traveled to Chicago to listen to the blues. Around 1964 Nelson recorded a folk-blues album for Prestige titled *Deep Are the Roots*, which was produced by Sam Charters and recorded in Chicago. Two years later Nelson moved, first to Los Angeles and then to San Francisco, where she formed Mother Earth and performed at such noted rock venues as the Fillmore West and Avalon Ballroom. The band's first album, *Living with the Animals*, came out in 1969 on Mercury Records.

Later that year Nelson and Mother Earth resettled in Nashville, Tennessee. Although the band continued to produce albums, none of them fared as well, critically speaking, as *Living with the Animals*, and Nelson eventually parted company with Mother Earth. Nelson continued to record as a solo artist with CBS, Atlantic, MCA, and Flying Fish; most of her records were a blend of blues, country, and R&B. In 1993 Nelson recorded *In the Here and Now* for Rounder Records, her first true blues album since her debut nearly thirty years earlier. Nelson continues to record and perform.

Essential Listening:
In the Here and Now/Rounder (3123)

◄ NICHOLSON, J.D.

(born James David Nicholson, April 12, 1917, Monroe, La.; died July 25, 1991, Los Angeles, Calif.)

J.D. Nicholson was a fixture on the West Coast Blues scene, working as a bandleader, session pianist, and sideman for dozens of noted artists, including JIMMY MCCRACKLIN, BIG MAMA THORNTON, RAY AGEE, JOHNNY OTIS, and BIG JOE TURNER.

Born in Louisiana, where Memphis Slim allegedly taught him how to play piano, Nicholson moved to Los Angeles in 1926. By the early 1940s he was playing house-rent parties and small clubs in southern California, often with Jimmy McCracklin. In the 1950s, Nicholson's group, the Jivin' Fives, performed in L.A. clubs and toured the Southwest. When not on the road with his own band, Nicholson toured with many of the above-mentioned artists. He also recorded for a number of labels, including Globe, Modern, Liberty, and Hollywood.

Nicholson kept his career going in the 1960s by working one-nighters in and around California and by managing nightclubs. In the early '70s he joined the southern California blues band Bacon Fat, which featured harmonica players GEORGE "HARMONICA" SMITH and ROD PIAZZA. He later formed his own band, the Soulbenders, and continued performing until the late 1980s when old age and diabetes forced him to retire. He died in 1991.

Essential Listening:
Mr. Fulbright's Blues (Various Artists)/Pea-Vine (PCD 2008)

◄ NIGHTHAWK, ROBERT

(aka Robert Lee McCoy) (born Robert Lee McCullum, November 30, 1909, Helena, Ark.; died November 5, 1967, Helena, Ark.)

Robert Nighthawk was one of the great blues slide guitarists. His slashing slide style, which was deeply based in Delta blues, influenced ELMORE JAMES and EARL HOOKER, among other post–World War II guitarists, and kept alive the emotional richness and intensity so central to the country blues slide guitar tradition.

Nighthawk was born Robert Lee McCullum in 1909. Although he taught himself how to play harmonica, he didn't learn the basics of the guitar until his cousin, the blues guitarist HOUSTON STACKHOUSE, taught him how to play the instrument when Nighthawk was in his early twenties. Nighthawk then began playing juke joints and house parties in Arkansas and Mississippi, often with Stackhouse. Around 1935, Nighthawk moved to St. Louis after a scrape with the law and settled into the city's vibrant blues scene. Nighthawk's first recordings were made in 1937 for the Bluebird label, cutting sides both as a solo artist and as a sideman. Nighthawk played behind JOHN LEE "SONNY BOY" WILLIAMSON and SPECKLED RED among others and also recorded for Decca. One of his songs from this period, "Prowling Night-Hawk," led to his nom de blues.

Nighthawk was an inveterate roamer; he made trips to Chicago, but never stayed long enough to become a mainstay on the city's scene. He seemed more at home playing country jukes in the Delta and in his hometown of Helena. In 1943, he began appearing on Helena radio station KFFA, performing live over the airwaves and pushing Bright Star flour. Soon, Nighthawk became the chief competition of SONNY BOY WILLIAMSON (Rice Miller); Sonny Boy endorsed King Biscuit flour on the same station. Nighthawk also appeared on other Southern radio stations, including WROX out of Clarksdale, Mississippi, and WDIA out of Memphis.

Nighthawk's slide guitar style didn't mature until he came under the influence of TAMPA RED. Where Red's slide technique was often understated and mellow, Nighthawk's was more coarse and daring. Nighthawk used the slide to drive his brand of the blues rather than merely enhance it. MUDDY WATERS was impressed enough by Nighthawk's guitar work to help him secure a recording contract with Aristocrat (Chess) in 1948. Although he had something of a hit with "Black Angel Blues" in 1949, Nighthawk left the label the following year. In 1951 and 1952 he recorded for the United label, but widespread success eluded him.

Nighthawk spent the remainder of the 1950s and early 1960s rambling through the South, playing jukes and fish fries, with longer stops in Helena. He also traveled to and from Chicago. In 1964 he resumed his recording career with Decca, and a year later took Sonny Boy Williamson's place on KFFA's "King Biscuit Time," following the harmonica player's death. Nighthawk died in 1967. He was inducted into the Blues Foundation's Hall of Fame in 1983.

Essential Listening:

Bricks in My Pillow/Pearl (11)

Live on Maxwell Street, 1964/Rounder (2022)

Robert Nighthawk and Houston Stackhouse/Testament (2215)

Robert Lee McCoy (Robert Nighthawk)—Complete Recordings in Chronological Order, Vol. 1/Wolf (120)

Robert Lee McCoy (Robert Nighthawk)—Complete Recordings in Chronological Order, Vol. 2/Wolf (121)

Drop Down Mama (Various Artists)/MCA-Chess (CII 93002)

◄ NIGHTHAWKS, THE

Original members: Mark Wenner (harmonica, vocals), (born November 2, 1948, Washington, D.C.); Jimmy Thackery (guitar) (born May 19, 1953, Pittsburgh, Pa.); Jan Zukowski (bass) (born July 10, 1950, Washington, D.C.); Pete Ragusa (drums) (born March 8, 1949, Washington, D.C.)

Based out of Washington, D.C., the Nighthawks were formed in 1972 by harmonica player and vocalist Mark Wenner and guitarist JIMMY THACKERY at the tail end of the late-'60s blues boom. Since then, the band has gone on to become one of the East Coast's most consistently popular blues acts.

The Nighthawks played D.C. blues clubs with an initial repertoire of Chicago blues covers. By 1974 the band included drummer Pete Ragusa and bass player Jan Zukowski and began playing cities and college campuses from Florida to Maine. In addition to the band's own performances, the Nighthawks routinely backed up touring blues stars and played on albums by PINETOP PERKINS, LUTHER "GUITAR JR." JOHNSON, and members of the MUDDY WATERS Band.

In 1980 the Nighthawks signed with Mercury Records, which released the band's self-titled major label debut. In 1983 the band released *Ten Years Live*, a tenth-anniversary album that was later distributed by the Rounder/Varrick label. By the mid-'80s the Nighthawks were playing some three hundred dates per year and developing a national reputation. In 1985 Thackery left the Nighthawks; he was replaced by former Sea Level guitarist Jimmy Nalls and singer-saxophonist Jimmy Hall of Wet Willie. With Hall and Nalls at the helm, the Nighthawks toured Europe and increased fan support on the East Coast. In 1990 Nalls and Hall left the band. They were replaced by guitarist Danny Morris and keyboards player Mike Cowan. The following year, the Nighthawks signed with Powerhouse Records and released the album *Trouble*. In all the Nighthawks have recorded nearly twenty albums. The group continues to tour regularly.

Essential Listening:

Open All Night/Mobile Fidelity Sound Labs (MFCD 754)

Jacks and Kings/Adelphi (4120)

Ten Years Live/Varrick (001)

Live in Europe/Crosscut (CCD 11014)
Best of the Nighthawks/Genee (4120/25)
Trouble/Powerhouse (POW 4107)

◄ NIXON, HAMMIE

(born January 22, 1908, Brownsville, Tenn.; died August 17, 1984, Memphis, Tenn.)

A longtime companion of blues guitarist and singer SLEEPY JOHN ESTES, Hammie Nixon was an important figure in the development of the blues harmonica within a duo and band context. Unlike many other blues harp players who rose to stardom as singers and recording artists, Nixon remained a side musician and accompanist for nearly all of his career. Still, Nixon made his mark with carefully constructed harp phrases and delicate tonal shadings that embellished the country blues of Estes and most everyone else with whom Nixon played.

Nixon was born in Brownsville, Tennessee. He learned to play the harmonica by listening to harp great NOAH LEWIS of Cannon's Jug Stompers, who was also born and raised in Tennessee. Sometime in the mid-1920s, Nixon teamed up with Estes and mandolin player James "YANK" RACHELL. Together they played as a jug band—with Nixon on harp and jug—and became a popular attraction in Memphis.

Nixon spent much of the 1930s in Chicago; he accompanied Estes on many of his recordings for Champion and Decca in the mid-'30s and frequently worked as a sideman in the studio with other blues musicians, such as SON BONDS and Charlie Pickett. Nixon is also said to have influenced the harmonica style of JOHN LEE "SONNY BOY" WILLIAMSON, considered one of the greatest of the pre–World War II harmonica players.

Nixon moved back to Tennessee in the 1940s and remained there for much of the rest of his life. When Estes resumed his recording career in the early 1960s, Nixon played harp for him. Together the two bluesmen also performed around the U.S. and in Europe. After Estes's death in 1977, Nixon carried on as a solo artist and as a member of the Beale Street Jug Band. Nxion died in 1984.

Essential Listening:

Tappin' That Thing/High Water (1003)
I Ain't Gonna Be Worried No More (Sleepy John Estes)/Yazoo (2004)
The Legend of Sleepy John Estes (Sleepy John Estes)/Delmark (DD 603)
Brownsville Blues (Sleepy John Estes)/Delmark (DD 613)

◄ NIX, WILLIE

(aka the Memphis Blues Boy) (born Willie Nicks, August 6, 1922, Memphis, Tenn.; died July 9, 1991, Leland, Miss.)

A popular blues drummer and singer in Memphis in the late 1940s and early 1950s, Willie Nix recorded for Sun Records and was a member of the same Memphis/West Memphis crowd that spawned B.B. KING, JUNIOR PARKER, BOBBY "BLUE" BLAND, JOHNNY ACE, and others just after World War II.

Nix was born and raised in Memphis. As a youth he worked minstrel and medicine shows in the South, performing tap-dance routines. The rhythms he created would later show up in his drumming. When he returned to Memphis in the mid-1940s, Nix began playing with an assortment of bluesmen, including BIG WALTER HORTON, ROBERT JR. LOCKWOOD, and SONNY BOY WILLIAMSON (Rice Miller). Nix's popularity around Memphis increased after radio appearances on KWEM with the Three Aces, and then on WDIA with other Memphis blues artists.

Before recording for Sun in 1952 as the Memphis Blues Boy, Nix cut some sides for the RPM and Checker (Chess) labels. However, problems with the law (he allegedly committed murder) prompted him to leave Memphis for Chicago the following year, where he recorded for the Chance/Sabre label and worked into the city's burgeoning blues club scene. Nix remained in Chicago until 1958 when he returned to Memphis to serve a two-year prison sentence. For the rest of his life, Nix worked in and out of music, but he attracted little attention outside Memphis blues circles. He died in 1991.

Essential Listening:
Sun Records: The Blues Years (Various Artists)/Charly (105)

◄ NULISCH, DARRELL

(born September 14, 1952, Dallas, Tex.)

Singer and harmonica player Darrell Nulisch was a cofounder and front man of the group ANSON FUNDERBURGH and the Rockets, which was formed in 1978 in Texas.

Nulisch sang and played harp on two of the Rockets' albums, *Talk to You By Hand* and *She Knocks Me Out*, before leaving the group in 1985. He then spent a short time with MIKE MORGAN and the Crawl and nearly three years with RONNIE EARL and the Broadcasters, before forming Texas Heat in 1990, a group that includes ex–ROBERT CRAY drummer David Olson. A year later Nulisch and his band signed a recording contract with Black Top Records and released *Business as Usual*, the group's debut album. Nulisch and Texas Heat continue to record and perform.

Essential Listening:
Business as Usual/Black Top (BT 1070)
Thru the Years: A Retrospective (Anson Funderburgh and the Rockets)/Black Top
(BT 1077)

O.

◄ ODEN, ST. LOUIS JIMMY

(born James Oden, June 26, 1903, Nashville, Tenn.; died December 30, 1977, Chicago, Ill.)

A member of the St. Louis blues community in the 1920s (hence his nickname), pianist/songwriter Jimmy Oden was a familiar figure in Chicago blues circles in the early 1930s and '40s. More known for his composing skills than his piano-playing—his songs were recorded by everyone from MUDDY WATERS and LITTLE WALTER to JAMES COTTON and OTIS SPANN—Oden eventually faded from the Chicago blues scene in the late '60s.

Oden moved from Nashville, where he was born and raised, to St. Louis around 1917. During the 1920s he and fellow blues pianist ROOSEVELT SYKES played house parties in St. Louis, helping to make it one of the premiere cities in which to hear piano blues. In 1932 Oden and Sykes left St. Louis for Chicago; the two recorded for the Champion label and worked their way into the city's blues club scene. Oden spent the 1930s and 1940s performing with Sykes and other blues artists and recording for such labels as Bluebird, Columbia, and Bullet. His best known song, "Going Down Slow," was a hit for Bluebird in 1941. In 1949 Oden and Joe Brown began the J.O.B. label. Oden, however, did only one session for the label, and spent the 1950s recording for Savoy and Duke Records, among other labels, and touring with EDDIE BOYD, SUNNYLAND SLIM, and other Chicago bluesmen.

Oden continued to record into the '60s with still other labels, including Bluesville, Delmark, and Spivey, though his records were never big sellers. Failing health forced him to cut down on his performing, so that by 1970 Oden had retired from performing. He died in 1977.

Essential Listening:
St. Louis Jimmy Oden, 1932–48/Blues Documents (2058)
St. Louis Jimmy Oden, 1932–1938/Story of Blues (3508)

◄ ODOM, ANDREW

(aka B.B. Odom, Big Voice Odom)(born 1936, Denham Springs, La.; died December 23, 1991, Chicago, Ill.)

Andrew Odom was a gospel-influenced blues singer who worked with guitarists EARL HOOKER and later JIMMY DAWKINS before fronting the Canadian group the Gold Tops, and recording *Goin' to California*. The album was released post-humously in 1992; Odom died of a heart attack shortly after recording it.

Odom was born in Louisiana, where he sang in church choirs; he eventually moved to St. Louis in the mid-'50s, where he began his career as a blues vocalist. However, it wasn't until Odom moved to Chicago in 1960 and joined Earl Hooker's band that he began to gain notice in blues circles. Odom, whose gospel roots and riveting delivery led to frequent comparisons with BOBBY "BLUE" BLAND and B.B. KING (Odom began calling himself B.B. Odom in deference to King), stayed with Hooker until the guitarist's death in 1970. Odom then joined with Jimmy Dawkins and sang in his band for most of the 1970s. In the 1980s Odom performed in Chicago clubs, occasionally sitting in with BUDDY GUY, LITTLE MILTON, and MAGIC SLIM, and often fronting the Griff Band in the latter part of the decade. He also recorded for the French Isabel label. In 1990, Odom accepted an invitation to front the Gold Tops, a group that included guitarist Steve Katz, formerly of the BLUES PROJECT and Blood, Sweat and Tears. Odom and the band recorded *Goin' to California* for Flying Fish. He died after suffering a heart attack while driving to a Chicago club performance.

Essential Listening:
Goin' to California/Flying Fish (FF 70587)
Feel So Good/Evidence (ECD 26027-2)

◄ OTIS, JOHNNY

(born John Veliotes, December 28, 1921, Vallejo, Calif.)

Johnny Otis helped shape rhythm & blues in the late 1940s and played a key role in the music for the next thirty years. In his prime, Otis was a bandleader, musician, arranger, composer, producer, record company owner, talent scout, and R&B spokesman. He discovered ESTHER PHILLIPS and ETTA JAMES, to name just two major R&B artists. He wrote R&B classics like "Every Beat of My Heart" and "Willie and the Hand Jive." He produced the records of artists like JOHNNY ACE and BIG MAMA THORNTON. In short, few artists in rhythm & blues were involved in as many layers of the music as was Otis.

Though white, Otis grew up in a black Bay Area neighborhood and for his entire career maintained exceptionally close ties with the black community. Otis began as a swing band drummer; by 1945 he was leading his own big band. Although he had a hit with "Harlem Nocturne" that same year, Otis was wise enough to realize that the swing era was rapidly ending. He cut his band down to nine pieces in 1947 and it became a prototype for future R&B outfits with small horn sections. From 1950 to 1954, the Johnny Otis Orchestra was one of the top R&B bands in America. From 1950 to 1952 alone, Otis had eleven hits; three of them—"Double Crossing Blues," "Mistrustin' Blues," and "Cupid's Boogie"—made it to number 1 in 1950. Otis was also a popular performer; his revue, the Johnny Otis Rhythm & Blues Caravan, crisscrossed the country and showcased many R&B and early rock & roll artists.

In 1954, Otis became a disc jockey on Long Beach radio station KFOX and started Dig, a record company. He also began work with Etta James; the two of them wrote "Roll with Me, Henry," whose title was later changed to "The Wallflower." The song went to number 1 on the R&B charts and made James a star. Otis returned to the charts in 1958 with his song "Willie and the Hand Jive," which peaked at number 9 on the pop charts, and made it to number 5 on the R&B charts. Otis continued to record and tour in the 1960s and got deeply involved with the civil rights movement. In 1965 he wrote a book, *Listen to the Lambs*, which analyzed the Watts race riots of that year. During this time, Johnny's son, SHUGGIE OTIS, a young, talented blues-rock guitarist who had worked in his father's band since he was twelve, began his recording career. Johnny Otis's *Cold Shot* album in 1968 featured Shuggie on guitar.

Otis's career continued unabated into the 1980s; in 1982 he and Shuggie teamed up again to record *The New Johnny Otis Show (with Shuggie Otis)* for Alligator Records and toured regularly. Otis remains the dean of West Coast rhythm & blues; he still works as a disc jockey at KPFA in Berkeley, California, and performs at jazz and blues fests in the U.S. and Europe. In 1993 he released the album *Spirit of the Black Territory Bands* for the Arhoolie label. Otis lives on a farm in northern California.

Essential Listening:
The Capitol Years/Capitol (92858)
The Original Johnny Otis Show/Savoy (2230)
The Original Johnny Otis Show, Vol. 2/Savoy (2252)
The New Johnny Otis Show (with Shuggie Otis)/Alligator (4726)
Spirit of The Black Territory Bands/Arhoolie

◄ OTIS, SHUGGIE

(born John Otis, Jr., November 30, 1953, Los Angeles, Calif.)

The son of R&B bandleader JOHNNY OTIS, guitarist Shuggie Otis began playing blues and rhythm & blues when he was just twelve years old. Playing bass and lead guitar, Otis was the young darling of the West Coast blues scene in the 1960s. By the time he was in his midteens, Shuggie was performing in his father's band and doing session work in Los Angeles.

Otis's recording career began in 1968 when his father featured him on the album *Cold Shot*. His guitar work there led to a solo recording contract with Columbia (*Here Comes Shuggie Otis*) and projects with Al Kooper (*Kooper Session*) and Frank Zappa (*Hot Rats*). However, despite high expectations, Otis's career tailed off dramatically in the 1970s. Although he continued to record, his albums failed to make an impact in either rock or blues circles and Otis eventually faded from the scene. He resurfaced again in 1982 with the release of *The New Johnny Otis Show with Shuggie Otis*, recorded with his father for Alligator Records. Since then Otis has worked as a session musician and songwriter.

Essential Listening:
The New Johnny Otis Show (with Shuggie Otis)/Alligator (4726)

◄ OWENS, JACK

(born November 17, 1904, Bentonia, Miss.)

Singer-guitarist Jack Owens has recorded little, considering the number of years he's been playing the blues. Owens has been an important artist in the Mississippi blues scene, mainly because he carries on the Bentonia blues style, a haunting blues form with detailed guitar lines and wailing, falsetto-laced vocals made popular by SKIP JAMES in the early 1930s.

Born in Bentonia, Owens worked as a sharecropper and played house parties and area juke joints for years in virtual obscurity before being discovered by blues historian David Evans in 1966. Owens recorded for Evans in 1970 and since then has performed at numerous folk and blues fests, including the Chicago Blues Festival, usually with harmonica player Bud Spires, son of BIG BOY SPIRES. Owens was also featured in the Allen Lomax documentary *The Land Where the Blues Began*, a film about the origins of the blues. Despite his advanced age— Owens is in his late eighties—he continues to perform.

Essential Listening:

It Must Have Been the Devil/Testament (2222)

50 Years—Mississippi Blues in Bentonia (Various Artists)/Wolf
   Blues Jewels (WBJ 009)

P.

◄ PAGE, HOT LIPS

(born Oran Page, January 27, 1908, Dallas, Tex.; died November 5, 1954, New York, N.Y.)

Hot Lips Page, a trumpeter who worked with WALTER PAGE's Blue Devils, BENNIE MOTEN's orchestra, and Count Basie's band, along with leading his own band, was one of the early stars of jump blues. Often compared to LOUIS ARMSTRONG, mostly for his entertaining talents, Page played with flair and a tendency to fill his trumpet parts with strong blues tones and textures.

Early in his career Page worked with MA RAINEY, BESSIE SMITH, and other classic blues singers. In 1927 he joined Walter Page's Blue Devils, with whom he toured and recorded. By the early '30s he had jumped to Bennie Moten's band, where he played with Basie and other swing greats. After Moten's sudden death in 1935 (during a tonsillectomy), Page worked with Basie as a trumpeter and singer. Page eventually formed his own band and recorded for Decca in the late '30s.

During the war years Page worked regularly, touring and recording with the likes of Artie Shaw, Ben Webster, and other highly regarded jazzmen. By the late 1940s Page began crossing over into rhythm & blues, working with artists like WYNONIE HARRIS. Page continued to tour and record until his death in 1954.

Essential Listening:
Oran "Hot Lips" Page, 1942–1953/Foxy (9005/9006)

◄ PAGE, WALTER

(born February 9, 1900, Gellatin, Mo.; died December 20, 1957, New York, N.Y.)

Walter Page led one of the earliest and most influential blues-based swing bands, the Blue Devils. Also a highly regarded bass player, Page set new standards for the instrument during jazz's transition from Dixieland to swing.

Page began his career as a member of BENNIE MOTEN's orchestra in the early 1920s. In 1925 he formed the Blue Devils. Based out of Oklahoma City, the band quickly became one of the most popular of the "territory bands." Known for their hard blues swing, the Blue Devils included such luminaries as trumpeter HOT LIPS PAGE, alto saxophonist Buster Smith, tenor saxophonist Lester Young, pianist Count Basie, and singer JIMMY RUSHING. The band only recorded two pieces—"Blue Devil Blues" and "There's a Squabblin'"—before its top players left to join Moten's orchestra. Even Page rejoined Moten in 1931. After Moten's death in 1935, Page went on to play with the Basie band. He also worked with Billie Holiday and other jazz artists in the late 1940s and was an integral member of the club and recording scenes in New York before he died in 1957.

Essential Listening:

Count Basie: The Complete Decca Recordings/GRP-Decca (GRD-3-611)

Sweet and Low Blues—Big Bands and Territory Bands of the '20s (Various Artists)/New World (NW 256)

◄ PARKER, BOBBY

(born August 31, 1937, Lafayette, La.)

Guitarist and singer Bobby Parker recorded his first album, *Bent Out of Shape*, in 1993 for the Black Top label. Before that Parker, whose soulful, spicy guitar work has influenced LITTLE MILTON and Carlos Santana, among others, worked with BO DIDDLEY and PAUL "HUCKLEBUCK" WILLIAMS and played clubs in Washington, D.C., and Virginia.

Parker was born in Louisiana but moved to the West Coast at age six. In the early '50s he worked with the doo-wop group Otis Williams and the Charms and then played lead guitar in Bo Diddley's band. Parker began working with Hucklebuck Williams in 1958 and often performed with his band at the Apollo Theater in Harlem. During Parker's stint with Williams, he wrote and recorded "Blues Get Off My Shoulder" for the Vee-Jay label, but the record failed to make it onto the R&B charts.

Parker relocated to Washington, D.C., in 1961. Shortly thereafter he wrote and recorded "Watch Your Step," which was a regional hit for the V-Tone label. The song was later covered by the Spencer Davis Group, Dr. Feelgood, and Santana. In 1968 Parker toured England and recorded "It's Hard but It's Fair" for the Blue Horizon label. Parker spent the next two decades performing around Washington, D.C., and becoming a key figure in the city's blues scene. In 1993 he headlined the Jersey Shore Jazz & Blues Festival. He continues to record and perform.

Essential Listening:

Bent Out of Shape/Black Top (BT 1086)

◄ PARKER, JUNIOR

(aka Little Junior Parker) (born Herman Parker, Jr., March 27, 1932, West Memphis, Ark.; died November 18, 1971, Chicago, Ill.)

A talented singer whose smooth, honeyed voice was one of the best to come out of the late-1940s Memphis blues scene, Junior Parker was also a harmonica player, bandleader, and composer. His song "Mystery Train" was covered by Elvis Presley in 1954 during Presley's legendary Sun sessions. Parker's clipped, clean harp style owed much to that of SONNY BOY WILLIAMSON (Rice Miller), who reputedly taught him the finer points of the instrument. Yet it was Parker's vocals that made him an R&B star, on a par with his longtime friend BOBBY "BLUE" BLAND. Throughout the '50s and early '60s many of Parker's records made it onto the R&B charts, while his success leading the R&B tour package, Blues Consolidated, which frequently included Bland and BIG MAMA THORNTON, offered proof of his performing talents.

Parker began his career in Memphis while still a teen. He played harp with Sonny Boy Williamson before becoming a member of the original HOWLIN' WOLF band in 1949. Well known around Memphis, Parker sat in with the Beale Streeters, an informal group that included Bland, ROSCO GORDON, and JOHNNY ACE. In 1952 Parker formed his own band, the Blue Flames, and recorded some sides for the Modern label. His first recording success, however, was with Sun, for whom he recorded the countryish blues boogie "Feelin' Good" in 1953, followed by "Mystery Train." The former tune made it to number 5 on the R&B charts.

Coaxed by Texas producer DON ROBEY to record for his Duke label, Parker moved to Houston in 1954 and remained an important artist on the company's roster until 1958. During that time he toured with Blues Consolidated, one of the most popular R&B revues of the decade, and released such hits as "Barefoot Rock" and "Next Time You See Me." Parker continued to tour and record throughout the 1960s. The material he recorded for labels such as Mercury, Minit, United Artists, and Capitol was popular with longtime fans, but Parker never repeated the success he enjoyed in the 1950s. He died of a brain tumor in 1971.

Essential Listening:
Mystery Train (Junior Parker, James Cotton, Pat Hare)/Rounder (SS 38)
The Best of Little Junior Parker/MCA (27046)
Junior's Blues: The Duke Recordings, Vol. One/MCA-Duke (MCAD 10669)

◄ PATTON, CHARLEY

(born April 1891, Edwards, Miss.; died April 28, 1934, Indianola, Miss.)

Charley Patton was the first great Delta bluesman; from him flowed nearly all the elements that would comprise the region's blues style. Patton had a coarse, earthy voice that reflected hard times and hard living. His guitar style—percussive and raw—matched his vocal delivery. He often played slide guitar and gave that style a position of prominence in Delta blues. Patton's songs were filled with lyrics that dealt with more than mere narratives of love gone bad. Patton often injected a personal viewpoint into his music and explored issues like social mobility ("Pony Blues"), imprisonment ("High Sheriff Blues"), nature ("High Water Everywhere"), and mortality ("Oh Death") that went far beyond traditional male-female relationship themes.

Finally, Patton defined the life of a bluesman. He drank and smoked excessively. He reportedly had a total of eight wives. He was jailed at least once. He traveled extensively, never staying in one place for too long. He was superstitious and flirted with religion. He was cocky and often belligerent.

Patton's standing in blues history is immense; no country blues artist save BLIND LEMON JEFFERSON exerted more influence on the future of the form or on its succeeding generation of stylists than Patton. Everyone from SON HOUSE,

HOWLIN' WOLF, TOMMY JOHNSON, and ROBERT JOHNSON to MUDDY WATERS, JOHN LEE HOOKER, and ELMORE JAMES can trace their blues styles back to Patton.

In a sense, Charley Patton, in addition to being a bluesman of the highest caliber, might also have been the first rock & roller. Patton was far from passive when he performed in front of an audience. It was not uncommon for him to play the guitar between his knees or behind his back. He also played the instrument loud and rough. Patton jumped around and used the back of his guitar like a drum. He was a showman who made histrionics a part of the music. One can begin with Patton's protorock roots and see them extend through Howlin' Wolf, then into LITTLE RICHARD and James Brown, and finally into JIMI HENDRIX.

Little is known of Patton's early life. Some blues historians believe he was born in 1881; most likely he was born in 1891. When he was a child, his family moved from the Mississippi hill country to the Delta to work on the Dockery plantation. Here he came into contact with HENRY SLOAN, one of the earliest of the Delta bluesmen. Unfortunately, Sloan nor any of the Dockery plantation blues pioneers had the opportunity to record. But it is safe to assume that what eventually became Patton's blues style was shaped by what he heard these men play just after the turn of the century.

By 1915 or so Patton was well on his way to becoming one of the Delta's most popular bluesmen. He played picnics, parties, one-room juke joints, and levee camps, often with fellow guitarist and friend WILLIE BROWN. He hoboed around, gaining fame for his sharply delivered blues and his feisty personality. Patton finally got his chance to record in 1929 after he auditioned for Henry Speir, a white Jackson, Mississippi, music store owner. Speir contacted Paramount Records and set up a recording session for Patton in Richmond, Indiana. One of the first songs he recorded, "Pony Blues," became his first issued recording. It sold well, especially in the Delta region, and ultimately became a Patton trademark tune. In all, Patton recorded fourteen sides in Indiana before returning to Mississippi.

Patton's second recording session took place in Grafton, Wisconsin, at Paramount's home studio. Delta fiddler Henry "Son" Sims accompanied him on fiddle. The following year, 1930, Paramount issued thirteen Patton records, and Patton became a certified country blues star. He often performed with SON HOUSE, one of the guitarists who would take Patton's place in the Delta blues hierarchy after Patton's death four years later. Patton took House, along with Willie Brown and blues pianist Louise Johnson, with him to Grafton for his third recording session in mid-1930.

There would be one more recording session for Patton before he died. In early 1934, despite failing health, Patton and his wife, Bertha Lee, traveled to New York City to record for the American Record Company. This session is generally judged by blues historians to be his least fruitful, though one of the songs he cut, "Oh Death," was tragically prophetic. After the sessions, Patton and Bertha Lee returned to Mississippi. Just a few months later, Patton died of a heart condition. He was forty-three years old. Patton was inducted into the Blues Foundation's Hall of Fame in 1980.

Essential Listening:
Founder of the Delta Blues/Yazoo (1020)
King of the Delta Blues/Yazoo (2001)
Charley Patton: The Complete Recorded Works/Pea Vine (PCD 2255/6/7).

◄ PAYNE, JR., ODIE

(born August 27, 1926, Chicago, Ill.; died March 1, 1989, Chicago, Ill.)

Noted for his disciplined, well-placed beats and his sharp sense of time, Odie Payne, Jr., was a first-generation Chicago blues drummer who played behind dozens of postwar bluesmen, including many of those signed to Cobra and Chess Records. He learned the rudiments of drumming from bandleader Capt. Walter Dyett at Chicago's DuSable High School in the early 1940s. Payne was later drafted into the army, where he performed in the band. Upon his discharge, he joined the Army Reserves and became a member of the 354th Army Reserve Band and later the local National Guard band. In all, Payne spent more than twenty years playing drums and tuba in military bands.

Payne's first professional blues job was with TAMPA RED in 1949 with whom he performed regularly and recorded nearly forty sides. Later he performed with MEMPHIS MINNIE, MEMPHIS SLIM, ELMORE JAMES, and LITTLE WALTER, among others, and recorded with CHUCK BERRY, WILLIE DIXON, and even MUDDY WATERS. Payne's best work, however, was done backing up artists such as BUDDY GUY, MAGIC SAM, and OTIS RUSH in the early '60s, where his crisp accents and steady beat helped give new meaning to blues drumming. During the '60s he also recorded with JUNIOR WELLS and Magic Sam on the Delmark label.

Payne continued to perform in the '70s and '80s, often playing Chicago blues clubs as a free-lance drummer, with pianists SUNNYLAND SLIM, ERWIN HELFER, Little Brother Montgomery, and BLIND JOHN DAVIS. In 1988 Payne released his only solo album *No, What Did She Say?* on his son's (Odie Payne III) label, OPJ Records, shortly before Payne's death that year.

Essential Listening:
West Side Soul (Magic Sam)/Delmark (DD 615)
The Chess Box (Various Artists)/MCA-Chess

◄ PEG-LEG SAM

(born Arthur Jackson, December 18, 1911, Jonesville, S.C.; died October 27, 1977, Jonesville, S.C.)

A medicine-show musician, raconteur, and all-around entertainer, Peg-Leg Sam was a throwback to the days when songsters traveled the South with carnivals and vaudeville shows. He was also an imaginative and wonderfully colorful harmonica player who included blues in his varied repertoire. From the 1920s on, Sam, who got his nickname after a rail accident claimed part of his leg, worked first as a hoboing harp player and then as a member of various tent-show troupes.

Sam was traveling with the Chief Thunder Cloud Medicine Show in 1972 when he was discovered. That same year he recorded an album, *Medicine Show*

Man, for the Trix label, which exposed him to the folk and blues crowd and enabled him to work the festival circuit in the early and mid-'70s. Sam entertained audiences at the Philadelphia Folk Festival, the Atlanta Blues Festival, and the New Orleans Jazz & Heritage Festival among others, singing, playing his harp, dancing, and telling stories much the way tent-show performers would have done a half century earlier. Peg-Leg Sam died in 1977.

Essential Listening:
Medicine Show Man/Trix (3302)

◄ PEJOE, MORRIS

(born Morris Pejas, 1924, Palmetto, La.; died July 27, 1982, Detroit, Mich.)

Bluesman Morris Pejoe was a guitarist and singer who worked Chicago clubs in the '50s and recorded for a variety of labels. Pejoe's popularity, however, rarely spread much beyond the Windy City.

Pejoe was born in Louisiana, where he learned to play violin. In 1949 he moved to Beaumont, Texas, and was influenced by CLARENCE "GATEMOUTH" BROWN, who was one of the first artists to incorporate the violin into a blues context. By this time, however, Pejoe had also learned to play guitar, which became his main instrument. Two years later Pejoe moved to Chicago and began working with pianist HENRY GRAY. Pejoe recorded for Checker (Chess) in 1954 and later for Vee-Jay, Atomic-H, and other small labels, but none of his singles ever made the R&B charts.

As a featured club performer, Pejoe worked sparingly in the 1960s, which prompted his move to Detroit in the early '70s. He performed in Detroit blues clubs on occasion but was unable to muster much interest in his brand of blues outside the local scene. Pejoe died in 1982.

Essential Listening:
Wrapped in My Baby

◄ PERKINS, PINETOP

(born Joe Willie Perkins, July 7, 1913, Belzoni, Miss.)

A piano player from the Mississippi Delta, Pinetop Perkins played with such noted blues artists as ROBERT NIGHTHAWK and SONNY BOY WILLIAMSON (Rice Miller) before joining the MUDDY WATERS Band. Perkins, a disciple of PINE TOP SMITH (hence his nickname), built his style on rolling boogie-woogie patterns and neatly tailored backing riffs that made him one of the best of the modern blues pianists.

Perkins learned how to play guitar before piano. His first steady work was with blues pianist WILLIE LOVE in Leland, Mississippi. In 1943 when blues guitarist Robert Nighthawk heard Perkins and invited him to play in his band, Perkins was playing the piano. Perkins traveled with Nighthawk and played Delta jukes and parties before the two bluesmen wound up in Helena, Arkansas, in 1945. Nighthawk left his group and went to Chicago; rather than return to Mississippi, Perkins began backing Sonny Boy Williamson on his "King Biscuit Time" radio show on Helena's KFFA station and on swings through the Delta. Perkins eventually left Williamson and moved to Memphis in the late '40s, where he recorded his version of "Pinetop's Boogie," the classic Pine Top Smith song, for Sun Records in 1950. A year later Perkins resumed his relationship with Robert Nighthawk and headed to Chicago.

For the remainder of the 1950s and most of the 1960s, Perkins did session work and played with Nighthawk, EARL HOOKER, LITTLE MILTON, ALBERT KING, and others, splitting his time between Chicago and East St. Louis. Finally, in 1969, Muddy Waters asked Perkins to fill the void in his band left by the departure of OTIS SPANN. Perkins accepted the position and remained with Waters until 1980. During his twelve-year tenure with Waters, Perkins toured Europe and the U.S. and played on some of Waters's 1970s albums, including *King Bee*.

In 1980, Perkins and harp player JERRY PORTNOY, bassist Calvin Jones, and drummer Willie Smith left the Muddy Waters Band to form the LEGENDARY BLUES BAND. The band recorded two albums for Rounder Records, *Life of Ease* and *Red Hot 'n' Blue*, before Perkins, tired of constant touring, left the group. Although he considers himself retired, Perkins, now in his eighties, still performs.

Essential Listening:
Living Chicago Blues, Vol. 3/Alligator (AL 7703)
Life of Ease (with the Legendary Blues Band)/Rounder (2029)
Red Hot 'n' Blue (with the Legendary Blues Band)/Rounder (2035)
King Bee (with Muddy Waters)/Blue Sky (ZK 37064)
Boogie Woogie King/Evidence (ECD 26011-2)
On Top/Deluge (Del D 3002)
Portrait of a Delta Bluesman/Omega (OCD 3017)

◄ PETERSON, LUCKY

(born Judge Kenneth Peterson, December 13, 1964, Buffalo, N.Y.)

Lucky Peterson was a child blues prodigy. He learned how to play drums and organ by age three. By age five, he had recorded his first album, and in 1971 had a hit single. The song, a novelty number called "1,2,3,4," was produced by WILLIE DIXON and released by Today Records in 1968. The record led to national television appearances for young Peterson, including spots on "The Ed Sullivan Show" and "The Tonight Show."

Peterson's father, James, owned a popular blues club in Buffalo, New York, and was also a local blues singer. At his father's club, Peterson jammed with many established bluesmen. In the '70s and '80s Peterson played organ in the bands of LITTLE MILTON and BOBBY "BLUE" BLAND. By this time Peterson had also become an accomplished guitarist and had relocated to Florida, where he became a top studio musician for King Snake. He played on albums by KENNY NEAL (*Big News from Baton Rouge!!*) and RUFUS THOMAS (*That Woman Is Poison*), among others.

In 1989 Peterson cut *Lucky Strikes!* for Alligator Records and followed it up with *Triple Play* in 1990. Both records feature Peterson's keyboard and guitar talents along with his soul-flavored vocals. Peterson continues to record and perform.

Essential Listening:
Rough and Ready/King Snake (4031)
Lucky Strikes!/Alligator (AL 4770)
Triple Play/Alligator (AL 4789)

◄ PETWAY, ROBERT
(born, date and place unknown; died, date and place unknown)

A protégé and companion of bluesman TOMMY MCCLENNAN in the late 1920s
and 1930s, Mississippi Delta singer-guitarist Robert Petway possessed a blues
sound and style that was practically identical to that of his longtime friend and
partner. Although Petway recorded sparingly, he is best known for his memorable
rendition of "Catfish Blues." His recording remains the definitive version of the
traditional Delta blues song.

Almost nothing is known about the shy and reticent Petway. He grew up in
the Yazoo City area of Mississippi, where he befriended McClennan at an early
age. Both bluesmen were greatly influenced by Delta blues pioneer CHARLEY
PATTON. Petway and McClennan played house parties and jukes. They also traveled together and were living in the Greenwood, Mississippi, area when Mc-
Clennan went to Chicago to record for producer LESTER MELROSE and the Bluebird
label. Shortly thereafter, Petway, too, was signed to Bluebird, the only label he
ever recorded for during his short recording career. In 1941 and 1942, Petway
recorded fourteen sides in Chicago for Bluebird, including "Catfish Blues."
Eventually Petway disappeared from the scene. It's not known for certain if he
remained in Chicago or returned to the Mississippi Delta.
Essential Listening:
Robert Petway/Wolf (108)

◄ PHILLIPS, EARL
(born April 25, 1920, New York, N.Y.; died November 20, 1990, Chicago, Ill.)

Drummer Earl Phillips supplied the crunchy snare and the thumping bass that
together made up the heartbeat of most of HOWLIN' WOLF's great mid-'50s recordings. Songs such as "Smokestack Lightnin'," "Evil," and "Moanin' for My
Baby"—Wolf classics—demonstrate Phillips's drum style, which, although
rooted in jazz, was strongly flavored with rocking blues beats.

Born in Harlem in New York City, Phillips moved to Nashville, where he
learned to play drums in high school. While working on the railroad, he supplemented his income by giving drum lessons. Influenced by jazz drummer Chick
Webb, Phillips worked in a variety of swing bands in and around Nashville before
moving to Chicago in 1940. There he played with J.T. Brown, LITTLE WALTER,
and other Chicago bluesmen before MUDDY WATERS suggested in 1954 that he
team up with Howlin' Wolf. Phillips kept the beat for Howlin' Wolf throughout
much of the 1950s. Later, he made a number of records with JIMMY REED, BILLY
BOY ARNOLD, SNOOKY PRYOR, and EDDIE TAYLOR. Phillips died in 1990.

Essential Listening:
Howlin' Wolf (box set)/MCA-Chess (CHD3-9332)

◄ PHILLIPS, ESTHER

(aka Little Esther Phillips) (born Esther Mae Jones, December 23, 1935, Galveston, Tex.; died August 7, 1984, Carson, Calif.)

Esther Phillips was one of the great female rhythm & blues vocalists. Her style recalled the smooth fluidity of DINAH WASHINGTON, but it was her phrasing, which was astonishingly warm and tender, and the way she let feeling flow through the lyrics that made her such a compelling vocalist. Born in Texas, where she learned to sing in church, Phillips and her family moved to Los Angeles after World War II. A remarkably mature singer at age fourteen, she won an amateur talent contest in 1949 at a club owned by R&B bandleader JOHNNY OTIS. Impressed with her performance, Otis signed her to sing and record with his band. A few months later in 1950, Little Esther, as she was called, recorded "Double Crossing Blues" (Savoy) with the Otis Orchestra and became the youngest female vocalist to land a number 1 record on the R&B charts. She followed up her success with a duet with singer Mel Walker on "Mistrustin' Blues," which also went to number 1 that year, as did "Cupid's Boogie." Other Phillips records that made it onto the R&B charts in 1950 include "Misery" (number 9), "Deceivin' Blues" (number 4), "Wedding Boogie" (number 6), and "Faraway Blues" (number 6). Few female artists, R&B or otherwise, had ever enjoyed such incredible success in their debut year.

Phillips left Otis and the Savoy label at the end of 1950 and signed with Federal. But just as quickly as the hits had started, the hits stopped. Although she cut more than thirty sides for Federal, only one—"Ring-a-Ding-Doo"— charted; the song made it to number 8 in 1952. Not working with Otis was part of her problem; the other part was drugs. Phillips developed a growing heroin habit that prematurely ended her career before she had turned twenty.

Much to her credit, Phillips ultimately got well enough to launch a comeback in 1962. Now called Esther Phillips instead of Little Esther, she recorded a country tune, "Release Me," which went to number 1. Phillips had other hits in the '60s on the Atlantic label, but no more chart toppers, and she also waged another battle with heroin. Beating the drug a second time, she scored one of her greatest post-'50s vocal triumphs in 1972 with the song "Home Is Where the Hatred Is," a haunting account of drug use, penned by Gil Scott-Heron.

Phillips continued to record and perform throughout the '70s and early '80s. In 1983 she charted for the final time with "Turn Me Out," which only made it to number 83. A year later Phillips died of a liver ailment.

Essential Listening:
Little Esther Phillips: The Complete Savoy Recordings/Savoy Jazz (SLJ 2258)
The Johnny Otis Show: Live at Monterey!/Edsel (DED 266)

◄ PHILLIPS, SAM

(born January 5, 1923, Florence, Ala.)

Producer and record company owner Sam Phillips will always be best known for the discovery of Elvis Presley. Yet prior to Presley and the birth of rock & roll, Phillips played an important role in Memphis blues. In his Sun Studios, he recorded future blues greats B.B. KING and HOWLIN' WOLF, RUFUS THOMAS, JACKIE BRENSTON, ROSCO GORDON, and others. As a talent scout, record producer, and record company owner, Phillips was to Memphis blues what LEONARD AND PHIL CHESS were to Chicago blues.

Phillips hoped to study law but instead settled for a career in radio broadcasting and engineering. His first disc jockey job was in Muscle Shoals, Alabama. By 1945 he was in Memphis on WREC. Five years later Phillips opened up the Memphis Recording Service, a small recording studio on Union Avenue, and the short-lived Phillips Records with disc jockey friend Dewey Phillips (no relation). After one release, bluesman JOE HILL LOUIS's "Gotta Let You Go" backed with "Boogie in the Park," the label folded. Phillips then cultivated a relationship with the BIHARI BROTHERS, who were about to launch RPM, a subsidiary of Modern, their Los Angeles–based label. The Biharis hoped to build the new label's roster with down-home blues talent and forged an agreement with Phillips to record Memphis artists for RPM. One of the first bluesmen Phillips sent to RPM was B.B. King.

Phillips also set up an agreement with Chess Records similar to the one he had with RPM. In 1951, Phillips recorded "Rocket 88" by Jackie Brenston and leased it to Chess. Often called the first rock & roll record, "Rocket 88" went to the top of the R&B charts and forced Chess, RPM, and other labels take a serious interest in Memphis music.

Squabbles over talent acquisition with Chess and RPM led Phillips to rethink the idea of starting his own record company. In late 1951 he quit his disc jockey job at WREC. In 1952 he began Sun Records. Until the arrival of Elvis Presley and rock & roll two years later, Sun Records was largely a blues label. Although Phillips continued to make some blues records after Elvis had changed the course of popular music in 1954 and 1955, he mostly recorded country and rockabilly artists. Sun scored with records by Jerry Lee Lewis, Johnny Cash, Carl Perkins, and Roy Orbison in the mid- and late 1950s.

Phillips sold Sun Records in 1969. He was inducted into the Rock & Roll Hall of Fame in 1986.

Essential Listening:

Blue Flames: A Sun Blues Collection/Rhino–Sun (R2-70962)

◄ PIAZZA, ROD

(born December 18, 1947, Riverside, Calif.)

Rod Piazza began his career as a blues harmonica player in 1965 when he formed the Dirty Blues Band and recorded two albums for ABC/Bluesway: the group's self-titled debut in 1967 and *Stone Dirt* in 1968. A disciple of George

Smith, a chromatic harp player who was in the MUDDY WATERS Band in the 1950s, Piazza began performing with Smith in 1968 and worked with him on and off until Smith died in 1982. The duo formed their own band, Bacon Fat, and recorded a self-titled album for the Blue Horizon label in 1969.

During Piazza's apprenticeship with Smith, he also recorded the albums *Rod Piazza Blues Man* for the LMI label in 1973 and the *Chicago Flying Saucer Band* in 1979 for Gangster Records. In 1980 Piazza put together the Mighty Flyers, a band that includes his wife, Honey Alexander, on keyboards.

By the early 1980s, Piazza's reputation as a solid Chicago-style harp player enabled him to get frequent work as a session musician, backing up the likes of blues guitarists PEE WEE CRAYTON and JIMMIE ROGERS, plus rockers like Tommy Conwell & the Young Rumblers and the folk artist Michelle Shocked. Piazza also released two solo albums, *Harp Burn* (1986) and *So Glad to Have the Blues* (1988), and three albums with the Mighty Flyers from 1981 to 1989—*Radioactive Material* (1981), *File under Rock* (1984), and *From the Start to the Finish* (1985). In 1991, Piazza and the Mighty Flyers signed a recording contract with Black Top Records and released *Blues in the Dark*, which brought the group national exposure. Rod Piazza and the Mighty Flyers continue to record and perform.

Essential Listening:
Blues in the Dark/Black Top (BT 1062)
Alphabet Blues/Black Top (DT 1076)
The Essential Collection/Hightone (HCD 8041)
Harp Burn/Black Top (BT 1087)

◄ PICCOLO, GREG

(born May 10, 1951, Westerly, R.I.)

A tenor saxophonist and vocalist, Greg Piccolo has been a member of ROOM-FUL OF BLUES since 1970 and its leader since 1979 when he became the group's main singer. Roomful of Blues was one of the bands that spurred the '80s blues revival; members of the band, at one time or another, have included guitarists DUKE ROBILLARD and RONNIE EARL, keyboards players AL COPLEY and Ron Levy, and drummer Fran Christina.

Piccolo grew up in Rhode Island. In 1961, after hearing the sax break in Dion's "The Wanderer," he became interested in the instrument. Although he got his first saxophone at age thirteen, he didn't begin playing the instrument in earnest until he was nearly twenty years old, when he started to soak up the sax styles of Gene Ammons, Lester Young, and Coleman Hawkins. In 1990 he recorded a solo album, *Heavy Juice*, for the Black Top label, which paid tribute to these and other jazz and rhythm & blues saxophonists. Piccolo continues to perform with Roomful of Blues.

Essential Listening:
Heavy Juice/Black Top (BT 1061)
Hot Little Mama (Roomful of Blues)/Varrick (VR 021)
Dressed Up to Get Messed Up (Roomful of Blues)/(VR 018)
Live at Lupo's Heartbreak Hotel (Roomful of Blues)/Varrick (035)

◄ PITCHFORD, LONNIE

(born October 8, 1955, Lexington, Miss.)

A contemporary Mississippi Delta bluesman who has blended the traditional styles of ROBERT JOHNSON and ROBERT JR. LOCKWOOD with the more modern musings of B.B. KING and Z.Z. HILL, guitarist Lonnie Pitchford is also a master of the primitive, African-originated diddley-bow, a single-stringed instrument that paved the way for the bottleneck guitar technique so popular with Delta bluesmen.

Pitchford began his blues career playing the diddley-bow at family gatherings. Performances at Delta fish fries and area juke joints followed as did appearances at local folk and blues fests. Pitchford was featured in numerous blues documentaries, including Alan Lomax's *The Land Where the Blues Began* and *Deep Blues*.

In 1991, Pitchford performed at the Smithsonian Festival of American Folklife's tribute to Robert Johnson. A resulting live album, *Roots of Rhythm & Blues: A Tribute to the Robert Johnson Era*, was released in 1992 and was nominated for a Grammy Award. Pitchford continues to record and perform.

Essential Listening:

Roots of Rhythm & Blues: A Tribute to the Robert Johnson Era (Various Artists)/
   Columbia (CK 48584)

◄ PORTNOY, JERRY

(born November 25, 1943, Evanston, Ill.)

Before he formed his own group, the Streamliners, harmonica player–songwriter Jerry Portnoy toured and recorded with MUDDY WATERS, the LEGENDARY BLUES BAND, and RONNIE EARL and the Broadcasters. Portnoy replaced MOJO BUFORD in the Muddy Waters Band in 1974 and appeared on three Waters albums—*I'm Ready*, *Muddy "Mississippi" Waters Live*, and *King Bee*—before leaving the group in 1980 with pianist PINETOP PERKINS, drummer Willie Smith, and bass player Calvin Jones to form the Legendary Blues Band.

Portnoy stayed with the Legendary Blues Band until 1986, recording two albums, *Life of Ease* and *Red Hot & Blue*, with the group. After a short self-imposed sabbatical in the mid-'80s, Portnoy returned to the blues scene in 1987 and co-founded the group Ronnie Earl/Jerry Portnoy and the Broadcasters. Portnoy split with Earl and formed the Streamliners in 1989; two years later the group released its debut album, *Poison Kisses*, on the Modern Blues Recordings label. In 1991 and '93, Portnoy was a member of Eric Clapton's All-Star Blues Band. Portnoy remains active in the blues scene.

Essential Listening:

Life of Ease (with the Legendary Blues Band)/Rounder (2029)

Red Hot & Blue (with the Legendary Blues Band)/Rounder (2035)

Poison Kisses/Modern Blues Recordings (MBR 1202)

I'm Ready (Muddy Waters)/Blue Sky (ZK 34928)

Muddy "Mississippi" Waters (Muddy Waters)/Blue Sky (ZK 35712)

King Bee (Muddy Waters)/Blue Sky (ZK 37064)

◄ PRICE, LLOYD

(born March 9, 1932, New Orleans, La.)

Lloyd Price wrote and recorded "Lawdy Miss Clawdy," a song that not only kicked off his recording career but epitomized the New Orleans R&B sound of the early '50s. The song was produced by DAVE BARTHOLOMEW and featured FATS DOMINO on the piano; it went to number 1 on the charts in 1952 and became one of the year's best-selling singles.

Price ultimately had four more R&B hits for Specialty, which had released "Lawdy Miss Clawdy," before he was drafted in 1954. After his discharge two years later, Price signed with ABC/Paramount and began to veer away from true R&B. With the exception of "Stagger Lee" (a cleaned-up version of the old folk tune "Stag-o-Lee") which made it to number 1 in 1958, the majority of Price's postarmy hits were pop songs such as "Personality" and "I'm Gonna Get Married." Though Price continued to record throughout the '60s and early '70s, he spent much of his time running his two record companies, Double-L and Turntable. He continues to tour and perform in Louisiana.

Essential Listening:
Lawdy!/Specialty (SPCD 7010-2)

◄ PRICE, SAMMY

(born October 6, 1908, Honey Grove, Tex.; died April 15, 1992,
New York, N.Y.)

A blues pianist whose career began in the 1920s, Sammy Price was a solo artist, session musician, sideman, and bandleader who, over the years, performed with BIG JOE TURNER, GEORGIA WHITE, TRIXIE SMITH, COW COW DAVENPORT, JOHNNY TEMPLE, and many others and recorded a wide body of work. Although Price is known as a boogie-woogie pianist, having performed at Cafe Society, the trendy New York club, in the early 1940s, he was also adept when it came to blending elements of jazz into his blues repertoire. Many of his recordings with small groups were built on a jazz-blues foundation.

Born and raised in Texas, Price performed with the Alphonso Trent Band and other territory bands before moving to New York in the late 1930s. He found performance work in New York clubs and studio work with the Decca label, for whom he became a house pianist. Price also recorded and performed regularly with his own group, the Texas Bluesicians. By the 1950s Price had become a staple on the New York cabaret and club scene. He remained active as a performer into the 1980s, often performing in Europe. In 1990 his autobiography, *What Do They Want: A Jazz Autobiography*, was published by the University of Illinois Press. Price died in 1992.

Essential Listening:
Rockin' Boogie/Black and Blue (33.560)
Singing with Sammy/Blue Time (2002)
Sammy Price and His Bluesicians/Circle (LP 73)
Rib Joint/Savoy (4417)

Sweepin' the Blues Away, Vol. 2/Swingtime (1029)
Barrelhouse & Blues/Story of Blues (760159)

◄ Professor Longhair

*(born Henry Roeland "Roy" Byrd, December 19, 1918, Bogalusa, La.; died
January 30, 1980, New Orleans, La.)*

Professor Longhair was one of the pioneers of New Orleans rhythm & blues;
his "pupils" included FATS DOMINO, HUEY "PIANO" SMITH, ALLEN TOUSSAINT,
and DR. JOHN. Noted for an unorthodox, even eccentric, piano style that was
nothing less than a spicy rhythmic gumbo of blues, jazz, calypso, ragtime, and
zydeco, 'Fess, as he was called, played music that might have been a soundtrack
for a Crescent City documentary. In a word, Professor Longhair oozed New Orleans. One of the big reasons why he never became a major star during the 1950s,
like Domino and the other New Orleans pianists that followed him, was because
Longhair was reluctant to leave the city that gave his music its breadth and scope
in order to tour extensively and promote his records.

He was born Henry Roeland Byrd in Bogalusa, Louisiana, but he was raised
in New Orleans from the time he was an infant. Much of his youth was spent
hustling on New Orleans streets, working as a dancer and jack-of-all-trades entertainer. In addition to the piano, Longhair also learned how to play the drums
and guitar and in the early 1930s was in and out of local groups that played
house-rent parties and such. Longhair spent some time in the Civilian Conservation Corps in the late 1930s and then worked as a professional gambler before
going into the army during World War II. After being discharged in 1943, Longhair led a variety of groups that played New Orleans clubs, including the Mid-
Drifs, Professor Longhair and the Four Hairs, and Professor Longhair and His
Shuffling Hungarians. He made his recording debut with the latter group in 1949
on the Star Talent label. A year later he had a new group, the Blues Jumpers,
and a new record label, Mercury, which released "Baldhead," the one and only
Longhair song ever to make the R&B charts. It peaked at number 5.

Thereafter, Longhair recorded for Atlantic and Federal, and then a slew of
small labels such as Edd, Ron, Rip, and Watch, but never received much exposure
beyond New Orleans despite recording classics such as "Tipitina" (New Orleans's most famous R&B club would be named after the song), "Big Chief"
(the EARL KING song), and "Go to the Mardi Gras" (which has become an anthem
for Mardi Gras revelers). Longhair might not have been known much outside of
Louisiana, but in New Orleans his influence was substantial. With the exception
of bandleader and producer DAVE BARTHOLOMEW, and later on Allen Toussaint,
no single postwar artist had the impact on New Orleans R&B and blues that
Longhair did.

Even though Longhair was a New Orleans legend, by the mid-1960s he was
forced to support himself as a janitor. However, he was rediscovered in the early
'70s by an increasingly white audience taken with his rollicking R&B and thumping piano. Longhair performed at the New Orleans Jazz & Heritage Festival in
1971 and played every one thereafter until he died. During the 1970s he toured

Europe a few times and became a star there, and played U.S. festivals. He also resumed his recording career, cutting mostly live albums for Atlantic, Dancing Cat, and Krazy Krat. In 1979 he signed with Alligator Records and recorded the much-acclaimed *Crawfish Fiesta* album just prior to his death in 1980. Professor Longhair was inducted into the Blues Foundation's Hall of Fame in 1981.

Essential Listening:
New Orleans Piano/Atlantic (SD 7225)
Mardi Gras in New Orleans/Nighthawk (108)
Crawfish Fiesta/Alligator (4718)

◄ PRYOR, SNOOKY

(born James Edward Pryor, September 15, 1921, Lambert, Miss.)

Snooky Pryor was one of the early post–World War II Chicago harmonica players who helped make the instrument an integral part of modern blues. Influenced by JOHN LEE ''SONNY BOY'' WILLIAMSON, and later SONNY BOY WILLIAMSON (Rice Miller), Pryor recorded ''Telephone Blues,'' one of the first classic postwar Chicago blues songs. Other recordings he made with guitarist Moody Jones in the late 1940s are considered excellent examples of the early postwar Chicago blues style.

Pryor was born and raised in Mississippi, where as a child he learned the rudiments of the harmonica, later refining them by listening to the records of John Lee ''Sonny Boy'' Williamson. Like many other blues musicians in the mid- and late 1930s, Pryor hoboed through the South, playing juke joints and street corners for spare change. Pryor served in the army during World War II. After spending time in the Pacific theater, he returned to the States and was stationed at Fort Sheridan, just outside Chicago. On weekends Pryor often went into the city and jammed in clubs on the South Side. When he was discharged in 1945, he settled in Chicago and began working with HOMESICK JAMES, FLOYD JONES, and other bluesmen, first on Maxwell Street, and eventually in clubs.

Pryor began his recording career with Planet Records, which released ''Telephone Blues'' in 1948. He continued recording into the early 1950s for the J.O.B., Parrot, and Vee-Jay labels. Pryor also recorded regularly as a session musician and worked Chicago clubs in the 1950s and 1960s. However, by the 1970s Pryor had faded from the Chicago blues scene, performing only occasionally. He returned to the blues in the mid-'80s and signed a recording contract with Blind Pig Records. His first domestic album, *Snooky*, was released by the label in 1986.

Since then, Pryor has completed his comeback with such follow-up albums as *Too Cool to Move* for the Antone's label and *Back to the Country*, a project he did with JOHNNY SHINES in 1991 for Blind Pig. Pryor continues to record and perform.

Essential Listening:
Snooky/Blind Pig (BP 2387)
Too Cool to Move/Antone's (ANT 0017)
Back to the Country (with Johnny Shines)/Blind Pig (BP 74391)
Snooky Pryor/Paula (PCD 11)

R.

◄ RACHELL, YANK

(born James Rachell, March 16, 1910, Brownsville, Tenn.)

A longtime partner of blues guitarist and singer SLEEPY JOHN ESTES, Yank Rachell was one of just a handful of artists to play the mandolin in a blues setting. Born in Brownsville, Tennessee, Rachell supposedly traded one of his family's pigs for his first mandolin. As a teen he often worked Brownsville-area house parties and fish fries with Hambone Willie Newbern. Then in the early 1920s he met Estes and the two forged a friendship that lasted until Estes's death in 1977. In the late 1920s, Rachell, Estes, and Jab Jones formed the Three J's Jug Band and played Memphis clubs and street corners during the beginning of that city's jug band craze.

Rachell accompanied Estes when he recorded for the Victor label in 1929, but with the onset of the Depression, Rachell returned to Brownsville to farm, while Estes moved to Chicago. Rachell, however, did not abandon his blues career. During the 1930s he performed and recorded with JOHN LEE ''SONNY BOY'' WILLIAMSON, Dan Smith, and Elijah Jones, among others.

In 1958 Rachell moved to Indianapolis. After his wife died in 1961, he decided to resume performing and recording. He and Estes teamed up again and began playing coffeehouses and colleges as well as folk and blues fests in the '60s and through the early '70s. Rachell accompanied Estes in the recording studio and also made his own solo albums, including *Mandolin Blues* (Delmark) and *Blues Mandolin Man* (Blind Pig). When Estes passed on, Rachell all but retired. He did, however, perform at the 1993 Chicago Blues Festival as part of the special Delmark Records tribute.

Essential Listening:
James ''Yank'' Rachell, Volume 1/Wolf (WSE 106)
James ''Yank'' Rachell, Volume 2/Wolf (WSE 107)
Mandolin Blues/Delmark (606)
Blues Mandolin Man/Blind Pig (BP 1986)

◄ RADCLIFF, BOBBY

(born September 22, 1941, Washington, D.C.)

Bobby Radcliff is a New York–based blues guitarist whose style is a conglomeration of the styles of such great modern blues masters as MAGIC SAM, LOWELL FULSON, and BUDDY GUY. Radcliff grew up in Maryland, where he taught himself how to play guitar. At age seventeen he traveled to Chicago, in the hopes of meeting his idol, Magic Sam. He found Sam in Cooks County Hospital recuperating from a heart ailment. The two musicians became friends, and after his release from the hospital, Sam took Radcliff to some of the city's blues clubs, where he met bluesmen such as MAGIC SLIM, EDDY CLEARWATER, and OTIS RUSH.

Radcliff left Chicago intent on building his own career as a blues guitarist. He played blues clubs in the Washington, D.C., area and recorded an instantly ob-scure album, *Early in the Morning*, for A/OK Records and one single, "That's All I Need" backed with "It's Been a Long Long Day," for Aladdin in 1973.

Radcliff was finally discovered by fellow blues guitarist RONNIE EARL, who convinced Black Top's Hammond Scott to sign Radcliff to a recording contract. Radcliff's recording career began in earnest in 1988 when he completed the tracks that would make up his critically acclaimed album *Dresses Too Short*. A second Radcliff album, *Universal Blues*, came out in 1991. Radcliff continues to live in New York and performs regularly.

Essential Listening:
Dresses Too Short/Black Top (BT 1048)
Universal Blues/Black Top (BT 1067)
Black Top Blues-A-Rama, Vol. 3/Black Top (BT 1056)

◄ MA RAINEY

(born Gertrude Pridgett, April 26, 1886, Columbus, Ga.; died December 22, 1939, Columbus, Ga.)

Along with BESSIE SMITH, Gertrude "Ma" Rainey is regarded as the best of the 1920s classic blues singers. She was most likely the first woman to incorporate blues into minstrel and vaudeville stage shows, perhaps as early as 1902. Rainey is often called the Mother of the Blues since she inspired many of the female blues singers who followed her. Her influence was profound, despite the fact that before her recording debut she rarely performed outside the South.

Rainey's vocal delivery was closer to the raw, earthy blues style of Southern country blues artists than the more urbanized, cabaretlike presentation of the fe-male blues singers who began recording in the early '20s. On her best records Rainey sang with a rootsy, homespun authenticity. Thus, Rainey is the all-im-portant connection between male-dominated country blues and female-dominated urban blues in the 1920s.

Born Gertrude Pridgett into a family already experienced in down-home en-tertainment (both her parents were minstrel performers at one time), the young singer first appeared onstage in 1900. She became "Ma" Rainey after she married William "Pa" Rainey, a minstrel song and dance man, in 1904. The duo dubbed themselves "Rainey and Rainey (in some cases 'Ma' and 'Pa' Rainey), Assas-sinators of the Blues." They traveled the South, first with the Rabbit Foot Min-strels, where Rainey allegedly coached a young Bessie Smith, and later with Tolliver's Circus and Musical Extravaganza and other tent-show groups. In the '20s Rainey became a featured performer on the TOBA (Theater Owners' Book-ing Association) circuit.

Before signing a recording contract with Paramount Records in 1923, Rainey had almost a quarter century's worth of stagework to her credit. Paramount billed her signing this way: "Discovered at Last—'Mother of the Blues.' " The advertisement wasn't far off the mark. Rainey was thirty-eight years old when she began making records.

Rainey's recording career ended in 1928. During her six years of studio work she recorded some one hundred songs, including the classics "C.C. Rider" (aka "See See Rider") and "Jelly Bean Blues," the humorous "Ma Rainey's Black Bottom," and the deep blue "Bo Weavil Blues." In her career, Rainey was backed by such noted jazz musicians as cornet players LOUIS ARMSTRONG and Tommy Ladnier, pianists Fletcher Henderson and LOVIE AUSTIN, saxophonist Coleman Hawkins, and clarinetist Buster Bailey, as well as less noted members of her Georgia Band.

Not a singer blessed with conventional good looks—she was chubby-faced and stocky—Rainey nonetheless dressed the part of a blues queen. Her stage wardrobe consisted of lavishly sequined gowns, glittery headbands, and plenty of jewelry, including a necklace of gold coins. Offstage, Rainey was known to be sexually promiscuous.

Yet Rainey's popularity, especially with Southern audiences, came from her ability to write and sing songs steeped in country culture. Her songs dealt as much with the plights of sharecroppers and poor Southern blacks as with the pain of sexual mistreatment and infidelity.

Rainey's career dried up in the 1930s—as did the career of just about every other classic female blues singer of the previous decade. But her earnings were enough that she was able to retire from performing in 1933. Rainey returned to her hometown, Columbus, Georgia, where she died of a heart attack in 1939. Rainey was inducted into the Blues Foundation's Hall of Fame in 1983 and the Rock 'n' Roll Hall of Fame in 1990.

Essential Listening:
Ma Rainey's Black Bottom/Yazoo (1071)
The Immortal Ma Rainey/Milestone (2001)

◄ RAITT, BONNIE

(born November 8, 1949, Burbank, Calif.)

Bonnie Raitt began her career in the late '60s, singing and playing slide guitar like a Mississippi bluesman. However, she hardly had the upbringing of one. She was born and raised in Burbank, California; John Raitt, her father, was a Broadway singer and actor. After attending high school in Hollywood, Raitt enrolled at Radcliffe College in Massachusetts but quit school midway through to begin a career as a blues singer. Her ability to play slide guitar and her blues knowledge impressed the traditional blues artists she often performed with in Boston folk and blues clubs, and she was welcomed into true blues circles.

Raitt signed a recording contract with Warner Brothers Records and in 1971 released her highly praised self-titled debut album. She worked with SIPPIE WAL-

LACE, ARTHUR "BIG BOY" CRUDUP, and MISSISSIPPI FRED MCDOWELL, playing folk and blues fests and working the blues club circuit in the early and mid-'70s. Other albums—*Give It Up* in 1972, *Takin' My Time* in 1973, and *Streetlights* in 1974 —made her a cult favorite with the blues-rock crowd, though by this time her albums contained as much or more in the way of pop, rock, and folk than they did pure blues.

Raitt continued to make albums and tour, though her records sold less and less and her fan support dwindled. Then in 1989 she signed with Capitol Records. That year she released the album *Nick of Time* and pulled off one of the greatest career turnarounds in modern pop history. Not only did the album become her biggest-selling album ever, but because of it Raitt won six Grammy Awards. In 1992 her follow-up, *Luck of the Draw*, won four more. Though her albums are now stocked with pop songs, she still includes some blues numbers in live shows and remains an active supporter of the Rhythm & Blues Foundation.

Essential Listening:
Bonnie Raitt/Warner Bros. (1953)
Give It Up/Warner Bros. (2643)
Takin' My Time/Warner Bros. (2729)

◄ REED, A.C.

(born Aaron Corthen, May 9, 1926, Wardell, Mo.)

A.C. Reed is a Chicago-based saxophone player and songwriter who performed with EARL HOOKER, BUDDY GUY, ALBERT COLLINS, SON SEALS, and even the ROLLING STONES before he launched a solo career in 1982.

Reed, who took his stage name from close friend JIMMY REED, left Missouri, where he was born and raised, and came to Chicago in 1942. He worked in a foundry before studying at the Chicago Conservatory of Music for two years. Influenced by tenor saxophonists Gene Ammons and J.T. Brown, Reed added his melodic, R&B-colored sax style to the blues of WILLIE MABON and Earl Hooker, then to Dennis Binder's Rhythm & Blues All-Stars in the 1950s. In the early '60s, Reed cut singles for Age Records and other small labels, and had steady work as a session musician, backing many of Chicago's top-ranking blues artists in the recording studio.

Reed joined the Buddy Guy/JUNIOR WELLS band in 1967 and stayed in it for nearly a decade. Through Guy and Wells, Reed met the Rolling Stones, with whom he toured Europe. Reed also toured with Son Seals and Albert Collins's Icebreakers. In between tours he formed his own band, the Sparkplugs, and in 1980 he and the group recorded four tunes for Alligator Records' *Living Chicago Blues* series. Reed quit the Icebreakers in 1982 in order to record his debut solo album, *Take These Blues and Shove 'Em!* on the Ice Cube label. A single from the album, "I Am Fed Up This Music," was nominated for a W.C. HANDY Award for blues single of the year.

Reed's second album, *I'm in the Wrong Business*, was released by Alligator in 1987. Since then, Reed and his band have toured extensively.

Essential Listening:
Take These Blues and Shove 'Em!/Ice Cube (LP 1057)
I'm in the Wrong Business/Alligator (AL 4757)

◄ REED, DALTON

(born August 23, 1952, Cade, La.)

A soul-blues singer with roots firmly embedded in gospel music, Dalton Reed came onto the scene in 1992 with the release of his critically lauded debut album, *Louisiana Soul Man*, on the Bullseye Blues label.

As a child, Reed sang gospel. But after he learned to play the trumpet and joined his high school's marching band, he moved into rhythm & blues and soul. Reed worked in a few local bands before he formed his own group, Dalton Reed and the Musical Journey Band, and played bars in Louisiana, Texas, and Alabama. In 1986 he started his own label, Sweet Daddy Records, and released a single, "Givin' on in to Love." Reed and his brother Johnny then started a second label called Reed Brothers Records. In 1990 Dalton was discovered by Scott Billington of Bullseye Blues Records, who signed him to a recording contract. *Louisiana Soul Man* contained songs written by Doc Pomus and Delbert McClinton and brought back the sound of traditional Southern soul music, a form dormant since the 1960s. Reed continues to record and perform.

Essential Listening:
Louisiana Soul Man/Bullseye Blues (BB 9517)

◄ REED, JIMMY

(born Mathias James Reed, September 6, 1925, Dunleith, Miss.; died August 29, 1976, Oakland, Calif.)

Jimmy Reed was one of the most influential bluesmen of the post–World War II period. With a blues style that was rhythmically relaxed and uncommonly accessible, Reed sold more records in the 1950s and early 1960s than any other blues artist save B.B. KING. His "sweet" style of blues, rooted in traditional Delta groundwork, made its mark on listeners, both black and white, and had a profound effect on rock groups such as the ROLLING STONES and solo artists like Bob Dylan.

Where MUDDY WATERS and HOWLIN' WOLF confronted their listeners with gritty, urgent blues, Reed was more apt to stroke them with laid-back blues grooves that hit a responsive chord almost instantly. It's no surprise that Reed was able to cross over regularly onto the pop charts. With nonthreatening vocals, gentle harmonica riffs, and walking bass passages, Jimmy Reed and his blues were downright difficult not to like.

A big chunk of credit for Reed's success must go to guitarist EDDIE TAYLOR, his near-constant companion and the creator of the rhythms that fueled Reed's blues, and to Reed's wife, Mary Lee "Mama" Reed, who wrote many of his songs. Yet it was Reed who delivered the goods. It was he who set the feel of the songs and projected the warmth and the easy flow that made the Jimmy Reed repertoire so distinctive and popular.

Reed was born and raised in Mississippi, where he became boyhood friends with Eddie Taylor. It was Taylor who taught Reed the rudiments of the guitar. Reed moved to Chicago in 1943; shortly thereafter he was drafted and served in the navy until the end of World War II. After he was discharged, Reed returned to Chicago, but then moved to nearby Gary, Indiana. In 1949 he teamed up with old chum Taylor who had recently moved to Chicago, and the two began playing small clubs: Reed on guitar, harp, and vocals, and Taylor on guitar. Reed resettled in Chicago in 1953, and a recording session for the Chance label that year was followed by an audition with Chess, which the duo failed. Reed and Taylor next tried Vee-Jay Records. Recognizing the pair was an interesting alternative to the harsher blues acts that Chess was concerned with, Vee-Jay signed Reed.

Beginning in 1955, Jimmy Reed amassed an impressive string of hits that stretched into late 1961. It began with "You Don't Have to Go," continued with "Ain't That Lovin' You Baby," "You Got Me Dizzy," "Honest I Do," "Baby What Do You Want Me to Do," "Big Boss Man," and ended with "Bright Lights Big City." "Honest I Do" made it all the way to number 32 on the pop charts; "Baby What Do You Want Me to Do" peaked at number 37.

In the early '60s Reed played Carnegie Hall and the Apollo Theater and toured England, where he was a big star thanks to covers of his songs by the Stones. Although his tenure with Vee-Jay had ended by then, Reed continued to record. He cut sides for Exodus and ABC-Bluesway, though none of his records had come close to matching the critical and commercial success of his Vee-Jay output. In the 1970s Reed continued to tour and perform regularly, though his bouts with alcoholism began to take a toll on his music. Reed died in 1976. He was inducted into the Blues Foundation's Hall of Fame in 1980 and the Rock & Roll Hall of Fame in 1991.

Essential Listening:
The Best of Jimmy Reed/Vee-Jay (1039)
Upside Your Head/Charly (CD 61)
I'm the Man Down There/Charly (CRB 1028)
Ride 'Em on Down/Charly (CD 171)
Jimmy Reed/Paula (PCD 8)
Jimmy Reed at Carnegie Hall/Mobile Fidelity Sound Lab (MFSL 566)

◄ RHODES, SONNY

(born Clarence Smith, November 3, 1940, Smithville, Tex.)

Texas-born Sonny Rhodes has two trademarks: the tightly wrapped, CHUCK WILLIS–style turban he wears onstage, and the Hawaiian lap steel guitar he plays, which enables him to create a unique, piercing blues sound to go with his gruff vocals.

Influenced early on by the likes of T-BONE WALKER and PERCY MAYFIELD, Rhodes learned to play the guitar and bass before enlisting in the navy in 1957. After his tour of duty, he played bass for FREDDIE KING and ALBERT COLLINS. In 1963 Rhodes, like many other Texas bluesmen before him, moved to California in search of better recording opportunities. Eventually he settled in Oakland, where he forged a relationship with L.C. "Good Rockin' " ROBINSON, a fellow Texan who played the Hawaiian lap steel. Robinson taught Rhodes the basics of the instrument Rhodes had first heard bluesman HOP WILSON play back in Texas.

With the Hawaiian lap steel guitar his primary instrument, Rhodes recorded a few singles for Galaxy and other small labels, none of which attracted much notice. In Europe, he recorded a pair of albums in the late 1970s—*I Don't Want My Blues Colored Bright* and the live *In Europe*. In 1980 Rhodes cut the quirky *Forever and a Day* album; on it he was backed by the Paris National Symphony Orchestra. A self-released album, *Just Blues*, came out in 1985, followed by his debut for Ichiban Records, *Disciple of the Blues*, in 1991.

Rhodes spends most of his time touring, both in the States and in Europe, where he has a large following. He has headlined such fests as the Jersey Shore Jazz & Blues Festival and the San Francisco Blues Festival. He currently lives in New Jersey.

Essential Listening:
Disciple of the Blues/Ichiban (ICH 90002)

◄ RIDGLEY, TOMMY

(born October 30, 1925, Shrewesbury, La.)

New Orleans rhythm & blues vocalist Tommy Ridgley's career began when he won a talent contest in 1949 and was hired by DAVE BARTHOLOMEW to sing in front of his band. That same year Ridgley signed a recording contract with Imperial Records. His first record, "Shrewesbury Blues," was a regional hit and one of Imperial's initial successes. Ridgley recorded a number of other songs for Imperial before moving to Atlantic Records in 1953.

By the late 1950s, Ridgley had jumped with his band, the Untouchables, to Herald Records and continued to make regionally successful records, but none that dented the charts or introduced him to a national audience. Ridgley also recorded for Ric Records and a slew of other New Orleans labels in the '60s and '70s. He also performed regularly in the city's clubs and at the New Orleans Jazz & Heritage Festival. In 1992, Ridgley signed with the Modern Blues Recordings label and released *She Turns Me On*, an album of reinterpreted old songs and new songs. Ridgley continues to perform regularly in New Orleans.

Essential Listening:
The New Orleans King of the Stroll/Rounder (2079)
She Turns Me On/Modern Blues Recordings (MBCD 1203)

◄ ROBEY, DON

(born 1903, Houston, Tex.; died June 16, 1975, Houston, Tex.)

Don Robey was the kingpin of Texas blues and R&B in the 1950s and 1960s. Owner of the Duke, Peacock, Back Beat, and Songbird labels, plus the Buffalo Booking Agency and some Houston nightclubs, Robey ruled his rhythm & blues empire, often with an iron fist. More than one musician has claimed that Robey robbed his artists of royalty money and frequently took part of the publishing rights of songs he never wrote. (Robey often used the pseudonym Deadric Malone to take songwriter credit.) Yet Robey's "Duke-Peacock Sound," a combination of gospel-soaked vocal deliveries (courtesy of artists such as JOHNNY ACE, JUNIOR PARKER, BOBBY "BLUE" BLAND, and BIG MAMA THORNTON) and taut, brass-heavy arrangements from Joe Scott and bandleader Bill Harvey, made Houston-based rhythm & blues one of the most stylish sounds of the era.

Robey was born in Houston. Always interested in music, he began his career as a nightclub owner and as CLARENCE "GATEMOUTH" BROWN's manager in the late 1940s. Frustrated by the way Aladdin Records, the label Brown was recording for at the time, handled his client, Robey began his own record company. Calling the label Peacock, after the Houston nightclub he owned, Robey recorded Brown and a number of prominent gospel groups, including the Five Blind Boys of Mississippi and the Dixie Hummingbirds.

In 1952 Robey scored with his first hit single, "I'm Gonna Play the Honky Tonks" by Marie Adams. The record made it all the way up to number 3 on the R&B charts. Flushed with the song's success, Robey bought the Memphis R&B label Duke from WDIA disc jockey James Mattis, and in the process got the recording rights to Johnny Ace, JUNIOR PARKER, and Bobby "Blue" Bland.

Bland was Robey's most consistently successful artist. Beginning in 1957 with the song "Farther Up the Road," Bland registered three number 1 hits and a slew of top-10 entries for Robey's Duke label. Johnny Ace had two number 1s in the early 1950s and a third in 1955 ("Pledging My Love"), which was released after Ace's tragic death in late 1954.

Robey continued to turn out records until 1973, when he sold his labels to ABC-Dunhill. He died two years later.

Essential Listening:
Duke-Peacock's Greatest Hits/MCA-Duke-Peacock (MCAD-10666)
The Best of Duke-Peacock Blues/MCA-Duke-Peacock (MCAD-10667)

◄ ROBILLARD, DUKE

(born Michael Robillard, October 4, 1948, Woonsocket, R.I.)

Guitarist Duke Robillard was the founder of ROOMFUL OF BLUES, a New England rhythm & blues band that became a launching pad for many contemporary blues artists, including pianist AL COPLEY, sax player and singer GREG PICCOLO, guitarist RONNIE EARL, and Robillard himself. Robillard began the band in 1967 out of Westerly, Rhode Island.

In 1979, after countless one-nighters up and down the East Coast and two albums, Roomful's self-titled debut and *Let's Have a Party*, Robillard left the band and formed a new group, the Duke Robillard Band, which eventually became Duke Robillard & the Pleasure Kings. He and the Pleasure Kings recorded a couple of albums for Rounder Records in the 1980s: their self-titled debut and *Too Hot to Handle*. Robillard also worked for a brief time with singer Robert Gordon and then with the LEGENDARY BLUES BAND in 1979 and 1980, respectively. In 1990, Robillard replaced JIMMIE VAUGHAN as the lead guitarist in the FABULOUS THUNDERBIRDS, joining two other ex-Roomful musicians in the band, drummer Fran Christina and bass player Preston Hubbard. Robillard played on the T-Birds' 1991 album, *Walk That Walk, Talk That Talk*, and with his own band cut *Turn It Around* and *After Hours Swing Session* for Rounder. Robillard left the T-Birds in late 1992 and went back to leading his own band. On his albums, Robillard has experimented with various brands of blues, plus swing, jazz, and rock. He continues to record and perform, and remains one of contemporary blues' more inventive guitar stylists.

Essential Listening:
Duke Robillard & the Pleasure Kings/Rounder (3079)
Too Hot to Handle/Rounder (3082)
You Got Me/Rounder (3100)
Swing/Rounder (3102)
Turn It Around/Rounder (3116)
After Hours Swing Session/Rounder (3114)

◄ ROBINSON, FENTON

(born September 23, 1935, Greenwood, Miss.)

Despite an expressive and beautifully crafted guitar style, a compelling voice, and a penchant for writing songs that go well beyond conventional blues standards, stardom has eluded Fenton Robinson throughout most of his career. Robinson's elaborate chordal progressions on guitar recall the jazz-flavored work of T-BONE WALKER, his main influence, as well as that of B.B. KING. His soulful vocals and songwriting style cut a path that contemporary blues artists such as ROBERT CRAY have followed.

Born in Mississippi in 1935, Robinson moved to Memphis in 1953 and eventually recorded a number of singles with the Meteor and Duke labels. He relocated to Chicago in 1962 and performed with artists such as JUNIOR WELLS, OTIS RUSH, and SONNY BOY WILLIAMSON (Rice Miller). In 1967 he recorded the single "Somebody Loan Me a Dime" for the tiny Palos label. The song was later recorded by Boz Scaggs with guitar work by Duane Allman and became the flagship tune on Scaggs's 1969 self-titled debut album.

In 1974 Alligator Records released Robinson's debut album, the title track being "Somebody Loan Me a Dime," Robinson's signature tune. Although it received glowing reviews, including a five-star rating in the *New Rolling Stone Record Guide*, *Somebody Loan Me a Dime* generated only moderate sales for the new blues label. Alligator went on to release two other Robinson albums, *I Hear Some Blues Downstairs* in 1978 and *Night Flight* in 1984, which originally came out on the Dutch Black Magic label. Neither record generated much sales, but they were critically praised. Robinson continues to perform.

Essential Listening:
Somebody Loan Me a Dime/Alligator (AL 4705)
I Hear Some Blues Downstairs/Alligator (AL 4710)
Night Flight/Alligator (AL 4736)
Special Road/Evidence (ECD-26025-2)

◄ ROBINSON, L.C.

(born Louis Charles Robinson, May 15, 1915, Brenham, Tex.; died September 26, 1976, Berkeley, Calif.)

The brother-in-law of bottleneck guitarist-singer BLIND WILLIE JOHNSON, bluesman L.C. Robinson played a Hawaiian steel guitar and an electric fiddle. After leaving Texas, he became a popular member of the Bay Area music scene. Robinson grew up in Texas, where he heard both blues and western swing. Influenced by Leon McAuliffe, the steel guitarist in Bob Wills's Texas Playboys, Robinson played in bands with his brother, A.C. Robinson, in the Temple area of Texas in the mid-'30s. One band they were members of, the Three Hot Brown Boys, often played on KTEM radio.

In 1940, Robinson followed his brother to the West Coast and settled in San Francisco, where they re-formed the Three Hot Brown Boys and played Bay Area clubs and military bases during the war years. Later, the Robinsons changed the name of the group to the Combo Boys. Moving to Oakland after the war, Robinson played clubs and parties until around 1957 when he turned his attention to gospel music. Sometime in the mid-'60s he returned to the blues. He did some recording for the Liberty and World Pacific labels shortly thereafter but had little opportunity to record a full-length album. In 1971, he cut *Ups and Downs* for the Arhoolie label, an album on which Robinson was backed by MUDDY WATERS's band. Robinson occasionally to performed in the Bay Area until his fatal heart attack in 1976.

Essential Listening:
Ups and Downs/Arhoolie (1062)

◄ ROCKIN' DOPSIE

(born Alton Rubin, February 10, 1932, Carencro, La.; died August 26, 1993, Opelousas, La.)

Rockin' Dopsie (pronounced *Doop-sie*) began playing zydeco in the 1950s in rural Louisiana clubs. Like many other zydeco artists at the time, Dopsie soaked his zydeco with rhythm & blues. He remained a local artist until the late '60s when new interest in zydeco enabled him to make his first records with the Bon Temps and Blues Unlimited labels. Dopsie toured frequently, playing folk and blues festivals in the U.S. and doing dates in Europe in 1979, which led to a strong following abroad. Dopsie also signed a recording contract with Sonet Records of Sweden, which released his first albums: *Doing the Zydeco and Zy-De-Blue* in 1978, *Hold On* in 1979, *Big Bad Zydeco* in 1980, and *French Style* in 1982.

In the 1980s Dopsie and his group, the Twisters, capitalized on the wave of interest in roots music and, with the passing of zydeco king CLIFTON CHENIER in 1987, competed with BUCKWHEAT ZYDECO for the biggest share of the music's market. Dopsie had a cameo appearance on Paul Simon's *Graceland* album in 1986 and released a number of energetic, zydeco dance albums during the '80s, including *Rockin' Dopsie and the Twisters, Crowned Prince of Zydeco*, and *Sat-*

urday Night Zydeco! His last album, *Louisiana Music*, was recorded in 1991 and received a Grammy nomination. Doopsie died in 1993.

Essential Listening:
Rockin' Dopsie and the Twisters/Rounder (6012)
Crowned Prince of Zydeco/Maison de Soul (1020)
Saturday Night Zydeco!/Maison de Soul (014)
Louisiana Music/Atlantic

◄ ROCKIN' SIDNEY

(born Sidney Simien, April 9, 1938, Lebeau, La.)
Since the early 1950s, guitarist Rockin' Sidney had been delivering his zydeco-flavored brand of rhythm & blues to audiences in and around the Lake Charles area of Louisiana. Then, in 1986, Sidney hit paydirt with an energetic version of the zydeco standard "My Toot Toot," which made him, however briefly, a national star.

Sidney began working in Louisiana zydeco clubs when he was in his teens. In the mid-'50s he made some recordings for the Carl and Fame labels, none of which attracted much attention outside local circles. By the time he signed with Goldband Records in the mid-'60s, Sidney was wearing a turban a la CHUCK WILLIS and playing more R&B than zydeco. Sidney shifted musical gears in the mid-'70s, when, inspired by the work of CLIFTON CHENIER, he began balancing his live sets with zyedco. Sidney continued to perform in Louisiana until the mid-'80s and the fluke success of "My Toot Toot." After interest in the song waned, Sidney went back to doing mostly dates in his home state.

Essential Listening:
They Call Me Rockin'/JSP (CD 213)

◄ RODGERS, JIMMIE

(born September 8, 1897, Meridian, Miss.; died May 26, 1933, New York, N.Y.)
Though Jimmie Rodgers, the Singing Brakeman, was the father of country music, he was greatly influenced by the blues and incorporated a number of twelve-bar blues songs into his repertoire. Rodgers, who was born in Mississippi, worked on railroads with blacks, from whom he learned the blues. In 1924 he contacted tuberculosis and left his job as a brakeman to pursue a career as a singer. He began his recording career in 1927 with the Victor label and cut 110 sides before dying of tuberculosis in 1933.

Rodgers recorded such blues as "Long Tall Mama Blues," "TB Blues," and "Mississippi Delta Blues" and created thirteen "blue yodels" that featured a bluesy falsetto howl in a basic blues format. Rodgers's fame was such during the 1920s and the early years of the Depression that black blues artists were undoubtedly aware of Rodgers and his hillbilly-blues sound, though it's difficult to say what influence, if any, he had on them. Rodgers died when he was just thirty-five. In 1961, he was the first artist elected into the Country Music Hall of Fame.

Essential Listening:
First Sessions, 1927–28/Rounder (10561/2/4)
The Early Years, 1928–29/Rounder (10571/2/4)
America's Blue Yodeler, 1930–31/Rounder (10602/4)

◄ ROGERS, JIMMY

(born James Lane, June 3, 1924, Atlanta, Ga.)

Jimmy Rogers made his biggest mark on Chicago blues in the early 1950s when he was a member of the famed MUDDY WATERS Band. Rogers played second guitar behind Waters, whose slashing slide style was in sharp contrast to Rogers's more refined rhythms and chord passages and his walking bass notes. Together, however, these two guitar styles beautifully complemented each other and helped create what became known as the definitive Chicago blues sound.

Rogers was born in Atlanta, where he taught himself how to play blues harmonica. He learned to play guitar by listening to the records of BIG BILL BROONZY, MEMPHIS MINNIE, and other popular blues artists of the early 1930s, and to the radio—particularly KFFA out of Helena, Arkansas, which featured harp player SONNY BOY WILLIAMSON (Rice Miller) and his guitarist, JOE WILLIE WILKINS, each day at noon. By the time he was in his late teens, Rogers had made his way to Helena and West Memphis, where he occasionally played guitar with ROBERT JR. LOCKWOOD and ROBERT NIGHTHAWK. Rogers then accompanied SUNNYLAND SLIM to St. Louis and performed with him in St. Louis and East St. Louis clubs before heading to Chicago in 1941. Rogers played with a variety of bluesmen in Chicago, including Sunnyland Slim, BLUE SMITTY, and Memphis Minnie, before he teamed up with Waters in 1950. He also recorded for the Ora-Nelle label in 1947, but the material was not released.

Rogers played on many of Waters's legendary Chess tracks, including "Hoochie Coochie Man," "I Just Want to Make Love to You," "Mannish Boy," and "Rock Me." He also began his solo career while with Waters. In 1950 he used harp player LITTLE WALTER and bass player Big Crawford from the Waters band to cut "That's All Right" for Chess. Other sides he cut for Chess were often released under the name Jimmy Rogers and His Rocking Four.

Rogers left Muddy Waters in 1955; two years later he cut the only record of his to make the charts. "Walking By Myself," with Big Walter Horton on harp, made it to number 14 on the R&B charts in 1957. "Ludella" and "Sloppy Drunk" are other noted Rogers tunes from the '50s. For the remainder of the decade, Rogers worked as a sideman with HOWLIN' WOLF and with Sonny Boy Williamson (Rice Miller), and played Chicago clubs with his own band. By 1960, Rogers had retired from performing to raise his family and run a clothing store; he did no recording and played few performances of note for most of the '60s. That changed in 1971 when Rogers left the clothing business and became more active on the blues scene, often performing with JOHNNY LITTLEJOHN. He recorded his first solo album, *Gold Tailed Bird*, in 1973 for the Shelter label, with FREDDIE KING on second guitar. He also recorded with the Bob Riedy Blues Band, toured Europe with the American Folk Blues Festival and the Chicago Blues Festival packages, and regularly played Chicago clubs.

In the 1980s Rogers continued to tour and record. Two albums, *That's All Right* and *Sloppy Drunk*, came out on the French Black and Blue label. In 1990 he cut *Ludella*, one of his best solo efforts, with help from harmonica player and vocalist Kim Wilson, pianist PINETOP PERKINS, and guitarist HUBERT SUMLIN. Rogers continues to record and perform.

Essential Listening:
Chicago Bound/MCA-Chess (CHD 93000)
Muddy Waters: The Chess Box/MCA-Chess (CHD3-80002)
Ludella/Antone's (ANT 0012)
Chicago's Jimmy Rogers Sings the Blues/Shelter (SRZ 8016)

◄ ROGERS, ROY

(born July 28, 1950, Redding, Calif.)

Roy Rogers is a Bay Area slide guitarist whose neotraditional style is strongly reminiscent of the techniques of slide guitar players such as EARL HOOKER and ROBERT NIGHTHAWK. Rogers was also a member of the JOHN LEE HOOKER's Coast to Coast Band in the '80s and produced Hooker's two most commercially successful albums ever, *The Healer* and *Mr. Lucky*.

Rogers played in a number of bar bands around San Francisco until 1976 when he and harmonica player David Burgin cut an album, *A Foot in the Door*, for Waterhouse Records. In 1980 Rogers formed the Delta Rhythm Kings; two years later he also began working as the featured guitarist in the Coast to Coast Band. He stayed with Hooker and the band until 1986; that year Rogers's first solo album, the self-released *Chops Not Chaps*, was nominated for a W.C. HANDY Award. He recorded a second album, *Slidewinder*, in 1987, which was released on the Blind Pig label and featured a cameo appearance by Hooker.

Rogers's production work with Hooker on the song ''I'm in the Mood,'' on the album *The Healer*, earned him a Grammy nomination in 1990, while the *Mr. Lucky* album earned him a Grammy Award. Rogers continues to perform, produce records, and record, often with harmonica player Norton Buffalo.

Essential Listening:
Slidewinder/Blind Pig (BP 72687)
Blues on the Range/Blind Pig (BP 73589)
R&B (with Norton Buffalo)/Blind Pig (BP 74491)
Chops Not Chaps/Blind Pig (BP 74892)
Travelin' Tracks/Blind Pig (BP 5003)

◄ ROLAND, WALTER

(born, date unknown, Pratt City, Ala.; died, date and place unknown)

Walter Roland, who recorded from 1933 to 1935 was known as much for his piano accompaniment to blues singer LUCILLE BOGAN (aka Bessie Jackson) as he was for the sides he cut during his brief solo recording career. Roland's forte was his versatility. He was equally adept at slow, grinding blues as he was rag-flavored blues and boogie-woogie.

Almost nothing is known of Roland's life. He was popular in Birmingham, Alabama, blues circles in the 1920s and early 1930s and probably was a friend of fellow pianist JABO WILLIAMS. He also played guitar and sang and occasionally went by the name Alabama Sam. Where Roland derived his blues style from remains a mystery, as does what happened to him after 1935.

Essential Listening:

Piano Blues, Vol. 6/Magpie (4406)

Bessie Jackson and Walter Roland, 1927–1935/Yazoo (1017)

◄ ROLLING STONES, THE

Members: Mick Jagger (vocals) (born July 26, 1943, Dartford, England); Keith Richards (guitar) (born December 18, 1943, Dartford, England); Brian Jones (guitar) (born February 28, 1942, Cheltenham, England; died July 3, 1969, London, England); Charlie Watts (drums) (born June 2, 1941, Islington, London, England); Bill Wyman (bass) (born October 24, 1936, London, England)

One of the great rock groups of all time, the Rolling Stones began as a British rhythm & blues band whose members were all passionate blues fans. The Stones even took their name from a MUDDY WATERS song, "Rolling Stone." Despite a shift in musical direction away from R&B and Chicago blues just a few years after the group's inception in 1962, the Stones never completely abandoned their blues roots. Thirty years later they still pay tribute to the blues in their live shows and, occasionally, in the recording studio.

The group was an outgrowth of one of the first British blues bands, BLUES INCORPORATED, which, in the early '60s, included drummer Charlie Watts. Guitarist Brian Jones met vocalist Mick Jagger and guitarist Keith Richards during a Blues Incorporated jam at the Ealing Blues club in London. Shortly thereafter, Jones, Jagger, and Richards put together the Rolling Stones, with Dick Taylor on bass and Mick Avory on drums, and began playing another of London's R&B clubs, the Marquee. By early 1963, Bill Wyman had replaced Taylor and Charlie Watts had replaced the group's second drummer, Tony Chapman, and the Rolling Stones, as the world came to know them, was complete.

In the summer of 1963 the Stones played the National Jazz & Blues Festival, toured England with LITTLE RICHARD and BO DIDDLEY, and released their first single, a roughed-up version of CHUCK BERRY's "Come On." The following year the Stones released their debut album, *The Rolling Stones—England's Newest Hitmakers*. It contained interpretations of JIMMY REED's "Honest I Do," WILLIE DIXON's "I Just Want to Make Love to You," and Chuck Berry's "Carol."

Unlike other British rhythm & blues bands at the time, who borrowed extensively from black American artists but added little in the way of originality, the Stones put a nasty edge on their versions. Jagger's vocals, in particular, oozed with arrogance and sexual excitement, while the rest of the band built a backing sound that, when compared to the sound of the Beatles (their chief rivals), seemed almost obscene.

The Stones played America in 1964; for them, the highlight of the tour was their stop in Chicago where they met some of the blues musicians they had idolized, and recorded an EP, *5×5*, at the Chess Studios. For their second album, *12×5*, the Stones relied less on cover material, although there is a strong R&B feel to Jagger-Richards originals such as "Good Times, Bad Times," "Congratulations," and the instrumental "2120 South Michigan Avenue."

By the time of their third album, *Aftermath*, the first to be made up entirely of original material, the Stones had set aside their R&B interests and become a full-fledged rock band. Mid-'60s hit singles such as "Satisfaction," "19th Nervous Breakdown," and "Let's Spend the Night Together" were heavy-hitting rockers that served to solidify the band's reputation as rock's bad boys. That image was magnified when Brian Jones died mysteriously in his swimming pool in 1969. He was replaced by Mick Taylor, the former guitarist in JOHN MAYALL'S BLUESBREAKERS, reaffirming the band's connection to the blues.

But the rest of Rolling Stones' saga is really a rock & roll story. The group remained on the cutting edge of the music for years to come and forged a path many other bands would try to follow. In the '70s the Stones experimented with funk, reggae, and disco with varying degrees of success. As a way of keeping alive the blues link even when their music didn't, the Stones made it a point to use blues artists to open their concerts. Muddy Waters, B.B. KING, and IKE and Tina TURNER all played to large rock audiences, which increased their exposure in the white market and made the Stones look like keepers of the blues flame in the increasingly commercialized rock world.

In the '80s the Stones became more of a corporation than a rock band, but continued to tour and record nonetheless, holding on to the idea that they were still "the greatest rock & roll band in the world." Both Keith Richards and Mick Jagger initiated solo careers. The Rolling Stones were inducted into the Rock & Roll Hall of Fame in 1989.

Essential Listening:
The Rolling Stones—England's Newest Hitmakers/Decca (820 047-2)
12×5/Abkco (74022)
The Rolling Stones, Now/Abkco (74202)
The Rolling Stones Singles Collection—The London Years/Abkco (1218-2)

◄ ROOMFUL OF BLUES

Roomful of Blues began in 1967 as a Rhode Island–based bar band that played a potpourri of blues, jump blues, rhythm & blues, and jazz. Over the years, the band became a springboard for many of the white contemporary blues artists making records in the 1980s and 1990s. From the ranks of Roomful came pianists AL COPLEY and Ron Levy, guitarists DUKE ROBILLARD and RONNIE EARL, saxophonist GREG PICCOLO, drummer Fran Christina, and bass player Preston Hubbard. With the exception of Christina and Hubbard, both of whom are members of the

FABULOUS THUNDERBIRDS, all of the other musicians have gone on to enjoy solo careers with varying degrees of success.

Duke Robillard formed Roomful of Blues in Westerly, Rhode Island, with help from keyboards-playing friend Al Copley. Although the band went through regular personnel changes, its reputation as an exciting live act enabled it to enlarge its Boston and Rhode Island–area following into a regional following that included regular stops in New York and Washington, D.C. Roomful of Blues played shows with Count Basie and singer Helen Humes and secured a recording contract in 1977. The band's self-titled debut album came out on Island/Antilles Records, a label known more for reggae than blues. After its follow-up, *Let's Have a Party*, Robillard left the band to form Duke Robillard and the Pleasure Kings and was replaced by Earl. Singer LOU ANN BARTON joined the band for two years; she shared lead vocals with Piccolo. By this time the group had grown enough in stature with blues and R&B fans to tour nationally and back up big name blues acts, onstage and in the studio. The album *Eddie "Cleanhead" Vinson and Roomful of Blues* was released in 1982; *Blues Train*, with guest vocals from BIG JOE TURNER, came out a year later and was nominated for a Grammy.

In the mid-'80s, Roomful experienced two major personnel changes as Hubbard left to join the T-birds (and was replaced by Randy Simmons) and Copley left to pursue a solo career (and was replaced by Levy). Roomful's next albums came out on the Varrick label; *Dressed Up to Get Messed Up* and *Hot Little Mama!* both brought the band critical acclaim, while *Glazed*, which was recorded with New Orleans guitarist EARL KING, reaffirmed the band's legacy as the best back-up blues unit in America. A live recording, *Live at Lupo's Heartbreak Hotel*, was cut in Providence and demonstrated Roomful's aged-to-perfection bar-band blues sound. After a tour of Europe, Earl left the band in 1988 to devote full time to his side band, the Broadcasters. Roomful of Blues continues to perform and record, though it is now on its third generation of members.

Essential Listening:
Hot Little Mama!/Varrick (VR 021)
Dressed Up to Get Messed Up/Varrick (VR 018)
Live at Lupo's Heartbreak Hotel/Varrick (VR 035)

◄ RUSH, BOBBY

(born Emmett Ellis, Jr., November 10, 1940, Homer, La.)

Bobby Rush has built a career writing and singing funky blues, R&B, and mainstream soul songs that are popular with chitlin' circuit audiences in the South. The lyrics to his songs are often sexist or bawdy or both, yet they also reflect a particularly macho view of black Southern culture that few other artists have managed to get across as convincingly as Rush.

Rush grew up listening to blues records in Louisiana. In 1953, when he was in his early teens, he and his family moved to Chicago, where he eventually formed a band that, on occasion, included blues guitarists LUTHER ALLISON and FREDDIE KING. Brief recording stints with Jerry-O and ABC-Paramount followed. In 1971 Rush had his first hit. "Chicken Heads," released on the Galaxy label, broke into the R&B charts and has since become one of Rush's trademark tunes. In the '70s Rush also recorded for Warner Brothers, London Records, and Philadelphia International. However, it wasn't until he settled in Jackson, Mississippi, in 1983 and signed with LaJam Records that Rush found his biggest audience. Rush released five albums during the 1980s and became a top attraction in Southern clubs. In 1991 Rush switched to Urgent! Records, a subsidiary of Ichiban, and recorded *I Ain't Studdin' You*. A follow-up album, *Instant Replays: The Hits*, contained the best material from his LaJam catalog. Rush continues to record and perform regularly.

Essential Listening:
I Ain't Studdin' You/Urgent! (URG 4117)
Instant Replay: The Hits/Urgent! (URG 4125)

◄ RUSH, OTIS

(born April 29, 1934, Philadelphia, Miss.)

In the late 1950s and early 1960s, guitarist Otis Rush helped shape Chicago's West Side blues sound. Built on highly expressive guitar playing and an urban sensibility removed from the South Side's Delta-based blues sounds, the West Side blues school featured not only Rush but also MAGIC SAM and BUDDY GUY, two other premier blues guitarists.

Despite his contributions to Chicago blues, Rush has been, for the most part, underrecorded and underappreciated. Only among fellow blues musicians and serious fans does he remain a major blues figure, whose emotionally charged solos, achingly plaintive chord phrases, and careful attention to textural detail make him one of Chicago's greatest guitar stylists. Rush is also a stunning vocalist. His ability to equal with his singing what he achieves with his guitar playing has made his meager recording catalog that much more meaningful.

Rush's career has not been blessed with good fortune. Whether because of bad business deals or plain bad luck, Rush has been unable to fulfill his potential as a recording artist. Unfortunate past experiences led him to become increasingly frustrated with the record business in the '70s and '80s and particularly wary of recording contracts that bound him in any way. As a result, despite his veteran status in the blues community, new Rush recordings have been few and far between.

Rush was born and raised in Mississippi. As a youth he learned how to play the harmonica and the rudiments of guitar, though he played the instrument upside down and left-handed. Rush moved to Chicago in 1948; by 1954 he had begun to play the guitar in earnest, inspired first by the rugged Delta blues of MUDDY WATERS and HOWLIN' WOLF, and then by the recordings of B.B. and ALBERT KING. Rush gained enough respect in Chicago blues circles for composer and bass player WILLIE DIXON to help him secure a recording contract with Cobra Records in 1956. Rush's first single, a haunting, beautifully played rendition of Dixon's "I Can't Quit You, Baby," was the first single released by Cobra and its only R&B top-10 hit (the song reached number 9 on the charts). Rush continued to record for the short-lived Cobra label for the couple of years it was in existence. The tracks he recorded, especially "All Your Love," "Double Trouble," and "Groaning the Blues," defined his sound and the West Side blues sound. (Magic Sam also recorded for Cobra, while Guy recorded for Artistic, a subsidiary of Cobra.)

After Cobra's demise, Dixon took Rush to Chess. Though Rush was with the label from 1960 to 1962, it released only one of his singles, "So Many Roads, So Many Trains." The lack of attention at Chess prompted Rush to switch to the Duke label in 1962. He stayed with Duke until 1965; once again his total output amounted to one single, a tune called "Homework." Rush's future brightened some when five Rush tracks were included on the classic mid-'60s compilation *Chicago/The Blues/Today!* The album introduced Rush to white rock fans who had recently been exposed to electric blues. MIKE BLOOMFIELD of the PAUL BUTTERFIELD Blues Band was so moved by Rush's guitar work on the album and in the Chicago clubs he played that he convinced the band's manager, Albert Grossman, to represent Rush. Grossman, who also handled Bob Dylan and JANIS JOPLIN, got Rush a recording contract with Cotillion, the Atlantic Records subsidiary, in 1969. However, Rush's debut album, *Mourning for the Morning*, was a flop. Overproduced by Nick Gravenites and Bloomfield, who hoped to break Rush into the popular blues-rock field, the album failed to capture Rush's sparse, emotionally rich guitar style. Grossman tried Capitol Records next, and in 1971 Rush and Gravenites went back into the studio for Capitol and produced *Right Place, Wrong Time*, Rush's most inspired album. Incredibly, Capitol chose not to release it. In 1976, a tiny independent label, Bullfrog, purchased the album and released it, though by this time interest in the blues had receded to an all-time low and the album sold few copies.

Rush kept his career going by performing club dates and occasional festivals, but there were no major recording sessions. At one point in the early '80s, Rush actually quit playing his guitar and settled into retirement. He returned to performing in the mid-'80s. But for dates outside Chicago, Rush used pickup bands—a questionable comeback strategy at best. Even the blues revival of the 1980s and early 1990s failed to resuscitate his recording career, though Rush continues to perform.

Essential Listening:
Chicago Boss Guitars (Various Artists)/Paula (PCD 9)
Right Place, Wrong Time/Hightone (8007)
His Cobra Recordings, 1956–58/Paula (PCD 01)
Lost in the Blues/Alligator (ALCD 4797)
A Cold Day in Hell/Delmark (DD 638)

◄ RUSHING, JIMMY

(born August 26, 1903, Oklahoma City, Okla.; died June 8, 1972, New York, N.Y.)

Along with BIG JOE TURNER, Jimmy Rushing helped set the standards by which all other blues shouters would be judged. Rushing, a small, rotund man whose ability to sing over big bands was legendary, could also phrase his lyrics with great skill and incorporate much emotion in his delivery. From the late 1920s all the way up to 1950, Rushing and pianist-bandleader COUNT BASIE had a musical partnership that produced some of the very best big band blues of the pre- and postwar eras.

Rushing was born into a musical family in Oklahoma City. At an early age, he learned to play violin. He also studied music theory before he began playing piano. Rushing enrolled at Wilberforce University in Ohio but left school to go to California, where he occasionally performed with Jelly Roll Morton at house parties. Rushing returned to Oklahoma City in the mid-1920s; he then teamed up with WALTER PAGE's Kansas City band, the Blue Devils, and met Basie, the pianist in the band. Rushing recorded with the Blue Devils in 1929 on the Vocalion label. When the band dissolved in 1932, Rushing, Page, and Basie jumped to another Kansas City band, led by BENNIE MOTEN. When Moten died in 1935, Rushing and Page joined Basie's band. Basie's preference for blues and blues-flavored swing and Rushing's capacity to belt the blues with striking results helped make the band one of the very best of the swing era.

Rushing remained with Basie until Basie dissolved his band in 1950. Rushing retired to South Carolina but soon was back as a solo artist and leading his own combo. Basie and Rushing reunited at the 1957 Newport Jazz Festival. Though he continued to record and to perform in the U.S. and abroad, Rushing was never able to match the success he enjoyed with the Basie band. He died of cancer in 1972.

Essential Listening:
Blues I Love to Sing/Ace of Hearts (AH 119)
The Essential Jimmy Rushing/Vanguard (65-66)

S.

◄ SAFFIRE—THE UPPITY BLUES WOMEN

Original members: Anne Rabson (vocals, piano) (born April 12, 1945, New York, N.Y.); Gaye Adegbalola (vocals, guitar) (born March 21, 1944, Fredericksburg, Va.); Earlene Lewis (vocals, bass) (born January 31, 1945, Avenal, Calif.)

Saffire—The Uppity Blues Women recall the saucy salad days of 1920s female blues singers like SIPPIE WALLACE and IDA COX and return a unique feminine viewpoint to the blues. The group's repertoire is built upon layers of witty, often bawdy blues sarcasm, feminism, and an all-acoustic sound. Saffire's songs deal with topical subjects such as fading youth (''Middle-Aged Blues Boogie'') and materialism (''Even Yuppies Get the Blues''), along with time-honored blues topics such as sex (''One Good Man'') and drink (''Sloppy Drunk'').

Before forming Saffire in 1984, Adegbalola, a high school science teacher, and Rabson, a computer analyst, were both performing on weekends, first as solo acts and then as a duo in Fredericksburg, Virginia, blues clubs. Lewis, a real estate agent, was moonlighting in a bluegrass band. After joining forces the trio balanced day jobs and night gigs until 1988 when they turned Saffire into a full-time enterprise. The following year the group made a demo recording that led to a contract with Alligator Records. Saffire's self-titled debut album was released in 1990 and became one of the label's best-sellers that year. The band was nominated for five W.C. HANDY Awards. Adegbalola's ''Middle-Aged Boogie'' won a Handy for blues song of the year. Saffire's follow-up album, *Hot Flash*, was released in 1991 and was also well received. In 1992 during the recording of *Broadcasting*, Saffire's third album, Lewis left the group and was replaced by Andra Faye McIntosh. The trio continues to record and perform.

Essential Listening:
Saffire—The Uppity Blues Women/Alligator (AL 4780)
Hot Flash/Alligator (AL 4796)
Broadcasting/Alligator (AL 4811)

◄ SATAN & ADAM

(Satan, born Sterling Magee, May 20, 1936, Mt. Olive, Miss.; Adam Gussow, born April 3, 1958, Congers, N.Y.)

New York–based guitarist-singer-percussionist Satan (Sterling Magee) and harmonica player Adam (Gussow) began performing together on Harlem street corners in 1986 after a chance meeting and jam session. Their unique brand of blues is comprised of funk-flavored polyrhythms and unusual chordal structures that routinely defy conventional blues standards.

Before becoming a one-man-band street musician and then teaming with Gussow, Satan played behind KING CURTIS, BIG MAYBELLE, and ETTA JAMES, among other artists, while Gussow, a 1979 Princeton University graduate, was a busker in Paris and Amsterdam. Gussow also had a part in the road version of the Broadway musical *Big River* in 1987–88.

Satan simultaneously plays guitar and a homemade percussion setup consisting of a pair of hi-hat cymbals, tambourines, and a wooden sounding board, while Adam supplies color and lead passages with his harmonica. The two musicians had a cameo role in *Rattle & Hum*, the Irish rock group U2's concert film. Satan & Adam recorded their debut album, *Harlem Blues*, for the Flying Fish label in 1991 which was nominated for a W.C. HANDY Award for best traditional blues recording. Following the release of the album, the duo performed at the Chicago Blues Festival, the Newport Jazz Festival, and the Philadelphia River Blues Festival and toured Italy, Switzerland, and Finland. In 1993 Satan & Adam released *Mother Mojo*, also on flying fish. The pair continue to perform in New York City and blues clubs in the Eastern U.S.

Essential Listening:
Harlem Blues/Flying Fish (FF 70567)
Mother Mojo/Flying Fish (FF 70623)

◄ SAVOY BROWN

(Original members: Kim Simmonds (guitar) (born December 5, 1947, Newbridge, South Wales); John O'Leary (harmonica); Bryce Protius (vocals); Bob Hall (keyboards); Ray Chappell (bass); Leo Manning (drums)

Savoy Brown was part of the British blues-rock craze of the late 1960s. Led by guitarist Kim Simmonds, the group generated only moderate interest in England, unlike in the U.S., where it enjoyed a loyal following into the early '70s.

Formed in 1966, the band was originally called the Savoy Brown Blues Band and was modeled after a traditional Chicago blues band. That year Savoy Brown released its first single, "I Can't Quit You, Baby," on the tiny Purdah label. Shortly thereafter O'Leary left the group and was replaced by guitarist Martin Stone. Savoy Brown's debut album, *Shake Em Down*, came out in England only in 1967. After its release the band split up, with Simmonds retaining the rights to the Savoy Brown name and bringing in a new set of musicians. The new Savoy Brown included second guitarist "Lonesome" Dave Peverett, vocalist Chris Youlden, drummer Roger Earle, and bassist Rivers Jobe, who was eventually replaced by Tone Stevens.

Savoy Brown released its second album, *Getting to the Point*, in 1968 in England and in the U.S. The albums *Blue Matter* and *A Step Further* followed in 1969. Two more albums in 1970, *Raw Sienna* and *Lookin' In*, helped make Savoy Brown a popular touring band in the States. But after the latter album's release, Peverett, who had begun to assert himself as a lead guitarist and was capable of fronting his own band, left Savoy Brown, along with drummer Earle and bass player Stevens, to form Foghat.

Though Savoy Brown continued with yet another set of new musicians (still other personnel changes would follow throughout the '70s and '80s), the band became little more than a vehicle for the frenetic guitar work of Simmonds, the only original member of the band. Savoy Brown kept releasing albums; in 1988 it issued *Make Me Sweat* on GNP Crescendo. Simmonds and the latest version of Savoy Brown continue to perform.

Essential Listening:
The Savoy Brown Collection/Deram (844 328-2)

◄ SEALS, SON

(born Frank Seals, August 13, 1942, Osceola, Ark.)

Son Seals is one of the leading guitar stylists of Chicago's post-'60s blues generation. His penchant for piercing, razor-sharp notes recalls the guitar sounds of MAGIC SAM and ALBERT KING. A critics' favorite, Seals's recording catalog on Alligator Records contains some of the best blues guitar work heard in the 1970s. His landmark 1976 album, *Midnight Son*, was lauded by *Rolling Stone* as "one of the most significant blues albums of the decade."

As a child, Seals lived with his parents and twelve siblings in the back of an Osceola, Arkansas, juke joint his father operated. During the day, Seals would sneak onto the small stage and play the drums. During the evening, Seals listened to artists such as Albert King and ROBERT NIGHTHAWK perform at the juke. Along with Seals's father, King taught the younger Seals the rudiments of blues guitar. By the time Seals was seventeen, he had formed his own band, Son Seals and the Upsetters, and began playing Little Rock blues clubs, opening for blues artists such as B.B. KING and BOBBY "BLUE" BAND.

Before moving to Chicago in 1971, Seals first spent time playing second guitar behind EARL HOOKER, and then drums for Albert King. Upon arriving in Chicago, Seals played on occasion with HOUND DOG TAYLOR and the HouseRockers. He also performed regularly with his own band at the Expressway Lounge, which is where Alligator Records president BRUCE IGLAUER discovered him.

Seals's 1973 debut album, *The Son Seals Blues Band*, showcased his striking guitar talent and included the instrumental "Hot Sauce," which became one of his trademark tunes. For his follow-up album, *Midnight Son*, Seals abandoned his straight-ahead blues sound for one that featured blaring horns and rock rhythms. Seals's third album, *Live and Burning*, was recorded live at Chicago's Wise Fools Pub in 1978. Two more Alligator albums followed—*Chicago Fire* in 1980 and *Bad Axe* in 1984—before Seals left the label after a dispute with Iglauer (at the time his manager) concerning concert bookings. Seals re-signed with Alligator in 1991 and recorded *Living in the Danger Zone*, an album that featured more of his impressive guitar work. He continues to record and perform.

Essential Listening:
The Son Seals Blues Band/Alligator (AL 4703)
Midnight Son/Alligator (AL 4708)

Live and Burning/Alligator (AL 4712)
Chicago Fire/Alligator (AL 4720)
Bad Axe/Alligator (AL 4738)
Living in the Danger Zone/Alligator (AL 4798)

◄ SHADE, WILL

(aka Son Brimmer) (born February 5, 1898, Memphis, Tenn.; died September 18, 1966, Memphis, Tenn.)

Will Shade was one of the blues' earliest harmonica stylists. Born in Memphis, Shade learned how to play the guitar before he took up the harp. As a youth he played on the city's street corners, occasionally with bluesman FURRY LEWIS, and traveled with various medicine shows, during which time he learned to play the harp. When he returned to Memphis in the early '20s, Shade played bars on Beale Street as a solo performer. However, after hearing the Dixieland Jug Blowers, he formed his own group, the MEMPHIS JUG BAND, in 1927. The loosely composed group recorded extensively for the Victor label in the late '20s. Shade was also in demand as an accompanist and recorded and performed with other Memphis blues artists.

After the jug band craze began to wane, Shade and Memphis Jug Band guitarist CHARLIE BURSE played Memphis streets, parks, and juke joints, recording occasionally in the 1930s. A long recording hiatus followed, until 1956, when he and Burse were rediscovered and cut some sides for Folkways. By 1960, Shade had retired from performing. He died in 1966.

Essential Listening:
The Memphis Jug Band/Yazoo (1067)

◄ SHAKEY JAKE

(born James Harris, April 12, 1921, Earle, Ark.; died March 2, 1990, Forest City, Ark.)

Harmonica player Shakey Jake was a professional gambler turned bluesman who helped launch the career of his nephew, guitarist MAGIC SAM. Born in Arkansas, Jake taught himself how to play harmonica as a youth. After hoboing around the South and serving in the armed forces during World War II, Jake began sitting in with Chicago bluesmen in the city's bars and blues clubs and eventually formed his own band. One of Magic Sam's first professional stints was with Shakey Jake's band in the mid-1950s. Jake's debut recording for the Artistic label, "Call Me If You Need Me," featured Magic Sam's guitar work.

Jake continued to perform and record and act as Magic Sam's manager in the early '60s. He also recorded a pair of albums for Prestige-Bluesville in 1959 and 1960. Always eager to supplement his blues income with back-room dice games, Shakey Jake was one of the blues' more colorful characters. He toured Europe in 1962 with a blues package and often played Chicago clubs with Magic Sam before resettling in Los Angeles in the late '60s. In L.A. he started a short-lived blues club and label (Good Times) that began in 1977 and dissolved in 1982.

Jake also continued his own blues career, performing in and around Los Angeles until he moved to Arkansas around 1988. He died in 1990.

Essential Listening:
Further on Up the Road/World Pacific
The Devil's Harmonica/Polydor

◄ SHARIFF, OMAR

(born Dave Alexander, March 10, 1938, Shreveport, La.)

Omar Shariff, who made his earliest recordings using his birth name, Dave Alexander, is a Bay Area piano player whose style recalls elements of traditional boogie-woogie and the easy rhythmic flow of other West Coast blues pianists like CHARLES BROWN.

Born in Louisiana and raised in Marshall, Texas, Shariff taught himself how to play piano and began performing in local churches. He went into the navy in 1955; after his discharge in 1957, he moved to Oakland and worked as a sideman for L. C. ROBINSON, BIG MAMA THORNTON, LOWELL FULSON, and other California-based blues artists. In the early '70s Shariff recorded two albums as a solo artist for the Arhoolie label: *The Rattler* and *Dirt on the Ground*. In 1975 Shariff converted to Islam and changed his name. He performed only sporadically until 1992 when he launched something of a comeback with the release of his third album, *The Raven*.

Essential Listening:
The Rattler/Arhoolie (1067)
Dirt on the Ground/Arhoolie (1071)
The Raven/Arhoolie (365)

◄ SHAW, EDDIE

(born March 20, 1937, Stringtown, Miss.)

Eddie Shaw is one of the few saxophone players to have carved out a place in Chicago blues. Born in Mississippi, where he studied trombone and clarinet before switching to the saxophone, Shaw played in various jump-blues bands in the early '50s. In 1957, during a swing through Mississippi, MUDDY WATERS invited Shaw to join his road band. After moving to Chicago, Shaw became a popular saxophone sideman in the city's blues community, performing with Waters, as well as with HOWLIN' WOLF, MAGIC SAM, and OTIS RUSH. He and A.C. REED were the city's most popular blues saxophonists.

Shaw led the Wolf Gang, Howlin' Wolf's back-up band, from 1972 until Wolf's death in 1976, Shaw then took control over the group, renaming it Eddie Shaw and the Wolf Gang. A year later the band recorded the album *Have Blues, Will Travel* for the Simmons label. In 1975 Shaw also leased a popular West Side blues club, The 1815 Club, and renamed it Eddie's Place. The club became a popular hangout for local blues musicians.

Since then, Shaw has continued to record and perform; he cut *Movin' and Groovin' Man* for the French Isabel label in 1987 and *King of the Road* for

Rooster Blues in 1984. He also worked as a sideman with a number of Chicago blues bands. Shaw's son, EDDIE "VAAN" SHAW, JR., is a blues guitarist who frequently works with the Wolf Gang.

Essential Listening:

The Chicago Blues, Vol. 1 (Various Artists)/Alligator (7701)

King of the Road/Rooster Blues (7608)

In the Land of the Crossroads/Rooster Blues (R 72624)

Movin' and Groovin' Man/Evidence (ECD-26028-2)

◄ SHAW, JR., EDDIE "VAAN"

(born November 8, 1955, Greenville, Miss.)

Guitarist and singer Eddie "Vaan" Shaw, Jr., is the son of blues saxophonist EDDIE SHAW. Because his father was a fixture on the Chicago blues scene during the '70s—he was a member of HOWLIN' WOLF's band and a blues club owner —Shaw met many of the city's greatest blues musicians as a child. MAGIC SAM and HUBERT SUMLIN taught Shaw the basics of blues guitar. Shaw jammed with Sumlin and other bluesmen who frequented his father's West Side club, Eddie's Place (aka The 1815 Club), and played in the house band.

Shaw eventually became a member of his father's band, the Wolf Gang, made up of musicians that had backed Howlin' Wolf in the early and mid-'70s. Since then, Shaw has begun a solo career, though he also continues to work with his father. His album *Morning Rain* was released on the Wolf label in 1993.

Essential Listening:

King of the Road (Eddie Shaw)/Rooster Blues (7608)

Morning Rain/Wolf (120.872)

◄ SHAW, ROBERT

(born August 9, 1908, Stafford, Tex.)

Blues pianist Robert Shaw was a member of the so-called "Santa Fe Group," a collection of Texas barrelhouse piano players who worked the stops and work camps of the Santa Fe Railroad in the 1920s. Along with fellow pianists Edwin "Buster" Pickens and Son Becky, Shaw created a body of work that was lyrically and musically linked to railroad life and traditional Texas blues.

As a youth Shaw played house parties and jukes in Fort Bend County before becoming an itinerant bluesman who worked the Santa Fe railroad line. In the early '30s Shaw went to Oklahoma City and played in saloons and jukes. By the middle of the decade, Shaw was back in Texas, this time in Austin, where he semiretired from performing and opened up a grocery store.

Shaw was rediscovered in the 1960s; he recorded for the Almanac label in 1963 and began appearing at folk and blues festivals, including the Smithsonian's Festival of American Folklife. In the 1970s he played festivals in Europe and made some television appearances in the States before he eventually retired.

Essential Listening:

Robert Shaw: Texas Barrelhouse Piano/Arhoolie (377)

◄ SHIELDS, LONNIE

(born April 17, 1956, West Helena, Ark.)

Singer-guitarist Lonnie Shields is a contemporary Mississippi Delta area blues-man whose debut album, *Portrait*, was released on the Rooster Blues label in 1992. His intriguing blend of gospel, down-home blues, rhythm & blues, and soul makes Shields one of Mississippi's most promising young blues stars.

Shields grew up on gospel music in West Helena, Arkansas. After learning how to play the guitar, he played in local bands such as Shades of Black, doing mostly soul, funk, and R&B cover songs. Shields also sang gospel in West Helena before he joined the Unforgettable Blues Band and began playing the blues in Mississippi and Tennessee juke joints, often with drummer SAM CARR and har-monica player FRANK FROST of the JELLY ROLL KINGS.

In 1987 Shields began his recording career with Rooster Blues; the single "Cheatin' Woman" was a regional hit, which led to increased blues bookings and appearances at area blues festivals, such as the King Biscuit Festival in Ar-kansas and the Oxford, Mississippi, Folklife Festival. Interest in Shields has grown beyond the Delta with the release of *Portrait*. He continues to record and perform.

Essential Listening:
Portrait/Rooster Blues (R72626)

◄ SHINES, JOHNNY

(born April 15, 1915, Frayser, Tenn.; died April 20, 1992, Tuscaloosa, Ala.)

Guitarist and singer Johnny Shines was one of the last of the original Delta bluesmen who had traveled and performed with ROBERT JOHNSON and whose style, in large part, remained untouched by more modern blues sounds. Over the years Shines was repeatedly asked to tell Johnson stories, play Johnson songs, and work out on guitar what only Johnson himself was capable of playing. Some-what reluctantly, Shines and old friend and fellow bluesman ROBERT JR. LOCK-WOOD became the carriers of the Johnson legacy, often having their own contributions to country blues overlooked in the process.

Shines was born just outside of Memphis but raised in Arkansas. After learning how to play the guitar, he began performing in Arkansas jukes and playing for tips at Saturday night fish fries. He met Robert Johnson around 1934 and fre-quently traveled with him in the Delta region. He also accompanied Johnson up to Canada, where the two bluesmen performed gospel music on "The Elder Mo-ten Hour," a popular religious radio show. When Shines and Johnson returned from their trek up north, the two parted company. Shortly thereafter, Johnson was murdered in 1938. Shines had meanwhile gone to live in Memphis, where he played in W.C. HANDY Park and small clubs in the area.

Shines didn't stay long in Memphis; in 1941 he moved to Chicago where he hoped to find steady work. Shines played both Maxwell Street and local blues joints and in 1946 got his first chance to record, though the sides he cut for Okeh Records were not released until years later. In 1950 Shines recorded again, this time for Chess. Two years later he cut material for the J.O.B. label. Unfortunately, none of his blues sold well enough for either company to continue recording him. Shines continued to work, mostly as an accompanist, but since interest in the country Delta style was rapidly dwindling in favor of electric band blues, his career progressed little. By 1958, Shines was disgusted enough to sell his guitar and quit the blues.

Unable to turn his back entirely on the music, Shines kept in touch with the blues scene by photographing Chicago bluesmen and frequenting the city's blues clubs when not working his day job. Finally, in 1965, Shines resumed his blues career. He recorded tracks for Vanguard, and the company included some of them on their acclaimed *Chicago/The Blues/Today* compilation. The exposure Shines received from being on the album enabled him to continue recording. He cut sides for Testament and Blue Horizon and began to play folk and blues festivals.

In 1969, Shines relocated to Holt, Alabama, and spent the next decade touring practically nonstop, as if to make up for lost time. He performed in Europe and Japan, giving audiences authentic tastes of Delta blues and becoming one of the leading practitioners of the region's raw, earthy guitar form.

Shines was forced to cut down on his touring after he suffered a stroke in 1980; reduced dexterity of his fingers caused him to concentrate more on slide guitar. He continued to perform throughout the '80s and into the '90s, and to record, making some interesting albums with Rounder, Blind Pig, and other labels despite his limited ability on guitar. Shines died in 1992, the same year he was inducted into the Blues Foundation's Hall of Fame.

Essential Listening:
Dust My Broom: Johnny Shines and Robert Lockwood/Flyright (CD 10)
Standing at the Crossroads/Testament (2221)
Johnny Shines with Big Walter Hornton/Testament (2217)
Hey Ba-Ba-Re-Bop/Rounder (2020)
Robert Jr. Lockwood and Johnny Shines/Rounder (2023)
Mister Blues Is Back to Stay/Rounder (2026)
Johnny Shines/Hightone (HCD 8028)
Back to the Country (with Snooky Pryor)/Blind Pig (BP 74391)
Traditional Delta Blues/Biograph (BCD 121)

◄ SHORT, J.D.

(born December 26, 1902, Port Gibson, Miss.; died October 21, 1962, St. Louis, Mo.)

J.D. Short learned how to play and sing the blues in the Clarksdale region of the Mississippi Delta, mostly by listening to CHARLEY PATTON and other early Delta bluesmen. Though Short's Delta blues roots stayed with him his entire life, he is primarily known as a St. Louis blues artist. He moved there in 1923 and remained a member of the city's blues scene up until his death in 1962.

Short played guitar, piano, and harmonica and was also an engaging singer. His craggy vocal mannerisms had roots in traditional shouts and field hollers; yet it was the vibrato in his voice, the result of a nervous affliction that made his jaw quiver, which was responsible for the unique quality of his singing style.

Short made his first records for Paramount and Vocalion from 1930 to 1933 and spent the rest of the decade playing St. Louis house-rent parties and small clubs, occasionally with guitarist DAVID "HONEYBOY" EDWARDS, who allegedly was Short's cousin. Short was drafted into the army in 1942, but an injury sustained in basic training got him a medical discharge a year later. He returned to St. Louis, where he often performed with another cousin, guitarist BIG JOE WILLIAMS. Short also worked as a one-man band, playing bars and street corners. In 1958, he and Williams recorded the album *Stavin' Chain Blues* for the Delmark label. He also recorded for the Folkways label, shortly before suffering a fatal heart attack in 1962.

Essential Listening:
Legacy of the Blues, Vol. 8/GNP Crescendo (10018-2)
J.D. Short: 1930–33/Wolf (118)
Stavin' Chain Blues (with Big Joe Williams)/Delmark (DD 609)

◄ SIEGEL-SCHWALL BAND

Members. Jim Schwall (guitar) (born November 12, 1942, Evanston, Ill.); Mark "Corky" Siegel (vocals, piano, harmonica) (born October 24, 1943, Chicago, Ill.); Rollo Radford (bass) (born October 29, 1943, Chicago, Ill.); Sam Lay (drums) (born March 20, 1935, Birmingham, Ala.)

The Siegel-Schwall Band began in Chicago in the mid-1960s and was a contemporary of the PAUL BUTTERFIELD Blues Band. In 1965 Corky Siegel and Jim Schwall first played as a blues duo at the popular blues club Pepper's, before adding bass player Jos Davidson and drummer Russ Chadwick. When the Paul Butterfield Band ended its stay at another Chicago Club, Sir John's, the Siegel-Schwall Band took its slot. It was during the band's Sir John's stint that Vanguard Records offered the Siegel-Schwall Band a recording contract. Later in 1965, the band released its self-titled debut album. In all, the Siegel-Schwall Band made five albums for Vanguard.

In 1969 Chadwick and Davidson left the band and were replaced by bass player Rollo Radford and drummer SAM LAY. The Siegel-Schwall Band played the Fillmore West in San Francisco and numerous clubs and blues festivals throughout the U.S. In 1971 the group recorded *Three Pieces for Blues Band and Symphony Orchestra* with the San Francisco Symphony Orchestra, an album that married classical music and the blues with mixed results. That same year, the band began recording for Wooden Nickel, an RCA subsidiary. From 1971 to 1975 the Siegel-Schwall Band recorded another five albums before it dissolved.

The Siegel-Schwall Band re-formed in 1987 and recorded a live album, *The Siegel-Schwall Reunion Concert*, for Alligator Records. Since then, however, the band has been largely inactive, playing about a half dozen dates a year. Corky Siegel spends most of his time performing with his Chamber Blues group.

Essential Listening:
The Siegel-Schwall Reunion Concert/Alligator (AL 4760)
The Best of the Siegel-Schwall Band/Vanguard (79336)

◄ SIMS, FRANKIE LEE

(born April 30, 1917, New Orleans, La.; died May 10, 1970, Dallas, Tex.)

A first-cousin of LIGHTNIN' HOPKINS, Frankie Lee Sims was a post–World War II Texas blues guitarist who, instead of playing in a modern vein, opted for a more rugged traditional sound. Sims's guitar work was indeed jagged around the edges, and there was a roughed-up, almost rock & roll spirit to many of his songs that proved popular enough for him to perform regularly and record occasionally in the 1950s.

Sims's career began in Dallas after he was discharged from the marines in 1945. He first recorded for the Dallas-based Bluebonnet label in 1949. Sims played the city's blues clubs, often with fellow blues guitarist SMOKEY HOGG. In 1953 he recorded for the Specialty label; his one and only hit, "Lucy Mae," was released that year. He also recorded for Specialty in 1957 and for the Fire-Fury label in 1960, but little of note resulted from these sessions. The lack of attention prevented Sims from becoming a noted blues act. He continued working Dallas clubs until he eventually faded from the scene. He died in 1970.

Essential Listening:
Lucy Mae Blues/Specialty (2124)

◄ SINGER, HAL

(born Harold Singer, October 8, 1919, Tulsa, Okla.)

Saxophone player Hal Singer was one of the pioneers in developing the honking sax style that was popular in rhythm & blues in the late 1940s and 1950s as well as in early rock & roll. Growing up in Oklahoma, Singer played in a number of "territory" swing bands, including JAY MCSHANN's, before moving to New York in 1942. Based out of the Big Apple, Singer worked in the bands of Roy Eldridge, Earl Bostic, LUCKY MILLINDER, and Duke Ellington during the 1940s. While with the Ellington band, he signed a solo recording contract with the Savoy label and cut "Cornbread," which went to number 1 on the R&B charts in 1948.

Flushed with the success of "Cornbread," which became his signature song, Singer formed his own band and toured with it right on through the 1950s, playing as much rock & roll as rhythm & blues. When not on the road, Singer did session work for some of R&B's biggest names, including WYNONIE HARRIS, BIG MAYBELLE, Little Willie John, Little ESTHER PHILLIPS, JIMMY WITHERSPOON, and bluesmen T-BONE WALKER and LONNIE JOHNSON.

When interest in traditional rhythm & blues began to wane in the 1960s, thanks, in part, to the birth of soul music, Singer found new audiences in Europe. In 1965 he moved to Paris and has continued to tour and record there ever since. In 1990, Singer recorded the album *Royal Blue* with another American expatriate, pianist AL COPLEY.

Essential Listening:
The Roots of Rock 'n' Roll (Various Artists)/Savoy (SJL 2221)
Royal Blue (with Al Copley)/Black Top (BT 1054)

◄ SLOAN, HENRY

(born, date and place unknown; died, date and place unknown)

Henry Sloan was one of the very first bluesmen in the Mississippi Delta. Almost nothing is known of his life other than that he worked on the Dockery plantation—the same one that employed the father of blues legend CHARLEY PATTON. Sloan, a guitarist, became young Charley Patton's mentor.

Some blues historians believe Sloan might have been playing some form of primitive blues as early as the turn of the century. But since Sloan never recorded, there is no way of telling what his blues style sounded like or who, if anyone, he learned from.

Charley Patton undoubtedly learned from Sloan. He followed Sloan around, and when Patton was good enough on the guitar, he even played with Sloan on occasion. Sloan was some twenty years Patton's senior, so the relationship the two had was most likely the teacher-student kind. Sometime near the end of World War I Sloan was reported to have moved to Chicago. What he did there and when he died remains a mystery.

◄ SMALL, DRINK

(born January 28, 1933, Bishopville, S.C.)

Known as the Blues Doctor, guitarist Drink Small's trademarks are his gospel-influenced vocals and his vast repertoire, which includes elements of Piedmont, Delta, and soul-blues. It was gospel music rather than the blues that gave Small his first taste of success. In his early twenties, Small joined the South Carolina–based Spiritualaires as a singer and guitarist; the group recorded for Vee-Jay Records in the 1950s and became one of the top groups on the gospel circuit. In 1957, *Metron* magazine called Small gospel's best guitarist.

When the Spiritualaires broke up in 1959, Small switched musical gears and turned to the blues. That same year he recorded for Sharp Records and later released singles on his own Bishopville label, as well as on the Southland label. After performing in South Carolina blues clubs and on college campuses for nearly thirty years, Small released *The Blues Doctor: Live and Outrageous!* in 1988. The album was nominated for a W.C. HANDY Award in the category of best traditional blues recording. Ichiban Records then released Small's *The Blues Doctor* and a follow-up album, *Round Two*. Small tours regularly and is a member of the South Carolina Arts Commission.

Essential Listening:
The Blues Doctor/Ichiban (1062)
Round Two/Ichiban (9009)

◄ SMITH, BARKIN' BILL

(born August 18, 1928, Cleveland, Miss.)

Journeyman vocalist Bill Smith began his career singing spirituals and gospel tunes as a youth in Mississippi. Later, he learned how to sing the blues at house parties and barbecues, occasionally singing with TAMPA RED, ELMORE JAMES, and other bluesmen. In 1957, Smith moved to Chicago after brief stays in St. Louis and Detroit and began singing in blues clubs there. HOMESICK JAMES gave Smith his Barkin' Bill nickname on account of his loud baritone.

For a while in the 1970s Smith fronted his own band, the Playboys. But Smith had more success singing for bluesmen such as LONNIE BROOKS and SAM LAY than he did as a bandleader. In 1986 Smith met guitarist DAVE SPECTER when Specter signed on with Lay to tour Canada. Smith and Specter began a more permanent association in 1989 when Specter formed his group, the Bluebirds, with Smith as lead vocalist. They recorded their debut album, *Bluebird Blues*, for the Delmark label in 1991. Smith and Specter continue to perform.

Essential Listening:
Bluebird Blues/Delmark (DD 652)

◄ SMITH, BESSIE

(born April 15, 1894, Chattanooga, Tenn.; died September 26, 1937, Clarksdale, Miss.)

Bessie Smith was the greatest and most influential classic blues singer of the 1920s. Her full-bodied blues delivery coupled with a remarkable self-assuredness that worked its way in and around most every note she sang, plus her sharp sense of phrasing, enabled her to influence virtually every female blues singer who followed. During her heyday, she sold hundreds of thousands of records and earned upwards of $2000 per week, which was a queenly sum in the 1920s. She routinely played to packed houses in the South as well as the North and Midwest. By the time the decade had ended, Smith had become the most respected black singer in America and had recorded a catalog of blues that still stands as the yardstick by which all other female blues singers are measured.

For many blacks, Smith was more than just a blues singer. Thanks to an assertive personality and an emancipated, often excessive life-style that included much drinking, frequent fistfights, wild sexual encounters with both men and women, and little tolerance of people who aimed to exploit her, Smith became a black cultural symbol. To many blacks, her success represented a triumph over white domination in the entertainment business. She gave hope to oppressed black women and inspired countless other singers. Smith influenced everyone from Billie Holiday to Mahalia Jackson and JANIS JOPLIN. Although she died in 1937, still in the prime of her career, she left behind a legacy that is wonderfully rich and practically unparalleled. She ranks with the best artists the blues has ever produced.

Bessie Smith was born poor in Chattanooga, Tennessee, in 1894. Before she had reached womanhood, both her mother and father had died. She was raised by a sister, Viola, but it was Clarence, her oldest brother, who had the most influence on young Bessie. A natural showman, Clarence encouraged Bessie to learn how to sing and dance. After Clarence had joined a traveling vaudeville show, Smith and another brother, Andrew, began singing and dancing on Chattanooga street corners, earning pennies from passersby.

With the help of Clarence, who had arranged an audition with the same Moses Stokes Company for which he'd been working, Bessie began her professional career in 1912 as a dancer. Eventually Smith became a chorine and then a featured singer. Since MA RAINEY, the so-called Mother of the Blues, was also working for the Moses Stokes Company at the time Smith joined the troupe, many blues historians have theorized that Rainey taught Smith the basics of the blues and acted as her coach. The revisionist line of thinking, however, is that by the time she met Rainey, Smith was already familiar with the blues and had developed much of the vocal charisma that would later make her a great singer. Certainly it's safe to say that Rainey had at least some influence on Smith in those early days. Rainey was a powerful blues vocalist in her own right, and the two singers were known to be friends. Watching Rainey sing the blues with all the home-grown feeling that fueled her songs couldn't help but be appreciated by Bessie, who was, by now, in her late teens.

Smith was an established star with black audiences throughout the South by the time she moved to Philadelphia in 1921. Two more years would pass before she began her recording career, however. Shortly after moving to Philadelphia, Smith supposedly auditioned for Okeh and other record companies. Each time the talent scouts told her that her voice was "too rough" to record. Finally, Columbia Records' Frank Walker signed Smith to a recording contract and set her up in the studio on February 15, 1923. Nothing survives from Smith's very first recording date. However, on the following day, Smith, accompanied by Clarence Williams on piano, recorded "Gulf Coast Blues" and "Down Hearted Blues." The record sold more than 750,000 copies that year, making Smith a blues star on the same level as MAMIE SMITH (no relation), a vaudeville singer who had recorded the first blues song, "Crazy Blues," in 1920.

In all, Smith recorded at least 160 songs for Columbia from 1923 to 1933. Many of them, such as " 'Taint Nobody's Bizness If I Do," "Mama's Got the Blues," her self-penned "Back Water Blues," and "Poor Man's Blues," are certified blues classics. Not only do they illustrate Smith's firm vocal grasp of the blues and her ability to evoke deep, soulfully phrased feelings, but they also tell us much about black culture in the 1920s.

The lyrics to " 'Taint Nobody's Bizness If I Do" ("If I go to church on Sunday, / Then just shimmy down on Monday, / 'Tain't nobody's business if I do, do, do do") and Smith's vocal delivery of them reflected her boldness and self-determination, two traits much admired by her black fans. On "Mama's Got the Blues," Smith paid tribute to the virility of black men over "brown-skinned" ones. Smith wrote "Back Water Blues" after witnessing a flood destroy homes and property. "Poor Man's Blues" detailed the differences between the haves and have-nots in America in the 1920s. In the song Smith pleads to "Mister rich man" to give "the poor man a chance" and "help stop these hard, hard times."

Throughout the 1920s Smith recorded with a number of noted musicians, including pianists Fletcher Henderson and James P. Johnson, cornetist LOUIS ARMSTRONG, saxophonists Coleman Hawkins and Don Redman, and clarinetist Buster Bailey. Many of her early songs featured only a piano accompaniment, which allowed sole focus on Smith's vocal dexterity. Yet the songs Smith cut with Armstrong—among them a rendition of W.C. HANDY's "St. Louis Blues" and the ragtime gem "You've Been a Good Old Wagon"—featured the two most prominent black recording artists of the 1920s working off each other's talents and attested to the manner in which the best blues vocalists could sing against a jazz backdrop without losing the simplicity of their Southern blues roots.

In 1929 Smith recorded the haunting "Nobody Knows You When You're Down and Out," a tune blues historian William Barlow called Smith's "personal epitaph and a depression-era classic." Columbia dropped Smith from its roster in 1931, but she did record once more, this time in 1933, under the direction of talent scout John Hammond. One song that was recorded, "Gimmie a Pigfoot," included Benny Goodman on clarinet.

Smith continued to perform, mostly in the South, although the classic blues era was clearly over. Smith's rough-cut brand of the blues had succumbed to the polished, more mainstream sounds of swing. In 1935, while driving with friend and lover Richard Morgan through Clarksdale, Mississippi, their auto struck an oncoming truck. The crash mangled one of Smith's arms and she bled to death.

Bessie Smith was inducted into the Blues Foundation's Hall of Fame in 1980 and the Rock & Roll Hall of Fame in 1989.

Essential Listening:
The Complete Recordings of Bessie Smith, Vol. 1/Columbia (C2K 47091)
The Complete Recordings of Bessie Smith, Vol. 2/Columbia (C2K 47471)
The Complete Recordings of Bessie Smith, Vol. 3/Columbia (C2K 47474)
The Complete Recordings of Bessie Smith, Vol. 4/Columbia (C2K 52838)

◄ SMITH, BYTHER

(born April 17, 1932, Monticello, Miss.)

Guitarist-singer Byther Smith was a Chicago blues secret until the release of his debut album, *Housefire*, on the Bullseye Blues label in 1991. Smith's fiery guitar style is filled with OTIS RUSH–like passages that sting rather than soothe, and when coupled with his venom-tipped vocals, which often border on old-fashioned shouts, it's difficult to figure why Smith has languished in relative obscurity for most of his career.

A first cousin of J.B. LENOIR, Smith learned how to play the bass, drums, and harmonica before moving to Chicago in 1956. He learned the finer points of blues guitar from Lenoir and ROBERT JR. LOCKWOOD. But it wasn't until the early '60s that he began playing Chicago clubs. Smith scraped for work, occasionally backing SUNNYLAND SLIM, BIG MAMA THORNTON, and HOWLIN' WOLF. Steadier work came from Otis Rush, for whom he played rhythm guitar, and from JUNIOR WELLS, who had him substitute for BUDDY GUY. Smith released a couple of impressive singles, "Give Me My White Robe, Parts 1 and 2" and "Money Tree" backed with "So Unhappy" on the tiny BeBe label in the '70s. But with the release of *Housefire* for Bullseye, Smith began to get some of the recognition due him. He continues to record and perform.

Essential Listening:
Housefire/Bullseye Blues (BB 9503)

◄ SMITH, CLARA

(born 1895, Spartanburg, S.C.; died February 3, 1935, Detroit, Mich.)

Called Queen of the Moaners and the World's Greatest Moaner, vaudeville-blues vocalist Clara Smith possessed a voice that nearly rivaled Bessie Smith's (no relation). Smith began recording for Columbia in 1923; her first records were dragged-out, gloomy accounts of lost love and betrayal. Frequently backed by Fletcher Henderson on piano, Smith plodded her way through songs such as "Every Woman's Blues" and "Awful Moaning Blues," in the process creating sad portraits of a suffering, tragic heroine.

On later recordings in the 1920s, Smith refined her delivery somewhat so that her melancholia did not always get in the way of the songs she sang. Many of her best recordings were done from 1925 to 1928 and often included risqué sexual references. In all, she recorded some 125 songs, almost all of them for Columbia. Some of her records featured instrumental backing by such prominent jazz artists as cornetist LOUIS ARMSTRONG, saxophone player Coleman Hawkins, clarinetist Don Redman, and pianist James P. Johnson. Twice she recorded duets with Bessie Smith.

Little is known about Smith's early years, except that she worked the Southern vaudeville stops and ultimately became a popular performer on the TOBA (Theatre Owners' Booking Association) circuit. She moved to Harlem in 1923 and the following year opened up the Clara Smith Theatrical Club. When not recording or performing in New York cabarets and theaters, Smith frequently toured. Part of her popularity was due to her vocal versatility. In addition to singing the blues, Smith also incorporated vaudeville and pop numbers into her show, as well as comedy routines. Smith's last recordings were in 1932, although she continued to perform until suffering a fatal heart attack in Detroit in 1935.

Essential Listening:
Complete Recorded Works in Chronological Order, vols. 1–7/Document (566–572)

◄ SMITH, GEORGE "HARMONICA"

(born April 22, 1924, Helena, Ark.; died October 2, 1983, Los Angeles, Calif.)

A blues harmonica player best known as a member of the MUDDY WATERS Band, George Smith's career also included touring and recording stints with other noted blues artists such as OTIS SPANN, BIG MAMA THORNTON, and EDDIE TAYLOR. Smith was also a mainstay of the L.A. blues scene, often performing clubs and blues fests in Southern California. Smith was adept on both standard and chromatic harmonicas; his style owed a great deal to that of LITTLE WALTER.

Born in the blues-heavy town of Helena, Arkansas, Smith was raised in Cairo, Illinois. As a youth he worked at a variety of jobs, some with the federal government (Civilian Conservation Corps), and wandered the South, often playing his harmonica for tips on street corners. In 1951 he settled in Chicago; three years later he replaced Henry Strong, the harp player in Muddy Waters's band, who had been stabbed to death by a girlfriend. Smith only stayed with Waters for a year, and was replaced by JAMES COTTON. Throughout the '50s Smith split his time between Chicago and the West Coast and worked with Otis Spann, CHAMPION JACK DUPREE, OTIS RUSH, and other bluesmen. He also recorded on the Checker, R.P.M., and King labels, using monikers such as Little Walter Junior, the Harmonica King, and George Allen.

Smith teamed up with Waters again briefly in 1966 but remained with the band for just a few months. By the latter part of the decade Smith had moved to Los Angeles where he worked in the group Bacon Fat with harmonica player and student ROD PIAZZA. Smith continued to tour on and off with Waters in the '70s, along with Big Mama Thornton and another West Coast harmonica player and student, WILLIAM CLARKE. He died in 1983.

Essential Listening:
Oopin' Doopin' Doopin'/Ace (CH 60)
. . . of the Blues/Crosscut (1015)

◄ SMITH, HUEY "PIANO"

(born January 26, 1934, New Orleans, La.)

Rhythm & blues pianist Huey Smith was a popular New Orleans session musician and bandleader in the 1950s. His two hits, "Rocking Pneumonia and the Boogie-Woogie Flu" (1957) and "Don't You Just Know It" (1958), along with his rollicking live shows with his band, the Clowns, made him a favorite with rock & roll audiences.

Smith grew up on blues and gospel music in New Orleans. He began playing New Orleans clubs with GUITAR SLIM in 1950. Their professional relationship lasted until 1954, when RAY CHARLES replaced Smith and played on Slim's signature song, "The Things That I Used to Do." Smith worked for a time with EARL KING; he also did session work for LLOYD PRICE, LITTLE RICHARD, and SMILEY LEWIS.

In 1957 Smith formed the Clowns and hired Bobby Marchan to sing lead vocals. Buoyed by the success of "Rocking Pneumonia" and "Don't You Just Know It," Smith and the Clowns toured with R&B and rock & roll package shows in the late 1950s and continued recording for Ace Records until 1964. With interest fading in New Orleans rhythm & blues, Smith stopped touring and spent the rest of the '60s playing the city's clubs. By 1970 Smith had retired, though he attempted a couple of unsuccessful comebacks later in the decade.

Essential Listening:
Rocking Pneumonia and the Boogie-Woogie Flu/Ace (CH 69)

◀ SMITH, J.T. "FUNNY PAPA"

(aka J.T. Smith, Funny Paper Smith, the Howling Wolf) (born John T. Smith, c. 1885, Texas; died c. 1940)

A contemporary of BLIND LEMON JEFFERSON and DENNIS "LITTLE HAT" JONES, J.T. "Funny Papa" Smith helped forge the Texas blues guitar style of the late 1920s and 1930s. Smith's penchant for detailed melody lines and repetitive bass riffs enabled him to create a style that was not unlike the guitar work Jefferson displayed on his recordings in the mid- and late 1920s. He also had a surprisingly refined country blues vocal style. Smith's few Depression-era recordings give a good indication of prewar Texas blues.

Hardly anything is known about Smith's life. He was probably born in East Texas in or around 1885, lived for a time in Oklahoma, and, most likely, performed at the same area fairs, fish fries, dances, and picnics that other early Texas bluesmen did. Smith also accompanied blues singer TEXAS ALEXANDER on numerous occasions. As a featured artist, Smith recorded nearly twenty songs in 1930 and 1931, including his trademark tune, "Howling Wolf Blues, Parts One and Two." Probably because of a record company error, Smith's name was listed as "Funny Paper" instead of "Funny Papa" on his earliest records. And, in some parts, the name stuck.

Smith's career might have been more successful had he not murdered a man during a gambling fracas in the early '30s and been sent to prison. He did record some songs in 1935, but they were never released. Smith died around 1940.

Essential Listening:
Funny Papa Smith/The Original Howling Wolf/Yazoo (L 1031)

◀ SMITH, MAMIE

(born May 26, 1883, Cincinnati, Ohio; died October 30, 1946, New York, N.Y.)

Black vaudeville and cabaret singer Mamie Smith was the first vocalist to record a blues song. Her version of composer PERRY BRADFORD's "Crazy Blues," recorded for Okeh Records on August 10, 1920, was a national hit, reputedly selling some seventy-five thousand copies in the first month of its release and more than one million in the first year. The astounding success of "Crazy Blues" (backed by another Bradford tune, "It's Right Here for You") spurred other record companies to record blues songs for the previously untapped "race" market; no less than nine other record companies, including Black Swan, had recorded black female blues singers by the end of 1923. Although not a true blues singer, Smith nonetheless cut the path that other female blues vocalists such as BESSIE SMITH (no relation) would follow in the 1920s, and ushered in the era of the "classic" blues singer.

Information concerning Smith's early years is sketchy. It is known, however, that she danced for Tutt-Whitney's Smart Set Company as a teen and later worked as a singer in Harlem venues prior to 1920. Her first recordings, "That Thing Called Love" and "You Can't Keep a Good Man Down," were made in early

1920 after Bradford convinced Okeh Records executive Fred Hagar that blacks would buy recordings made by black singers. Sales estimates of the record ranged from fifty to a hundred thousand. Its success prompted Okeh to bring Smith back into the studio in August to record "Crazy Blues" and "It's Right Here for You."

Smith made a number of recordings for Okeh from 1920 to 1923 with her band the Jazz Hounds, led by cornetist Johnny Dunn and trombone player Dope Andrews. However, much of the material Smith recorded for Okeh and other record companies in the 1920s was closer to vaudeville than true blues.

Smith also set appearance standards for the blues divas that followed her. An attractive woman, Smith wore lavish costumes and fancy jewelry onstage. Her style was imitated by nearly every other black female blues singer in the 1920s.

Essential Listening:
Complete Recorded Works in Chronological Order, vols. 1–5/Document (551–555)

◄ SMITH, PINE TOP

(born Clarence Smith, January 11, 1904, Troy, Ala.; died March 15, 1929, Chicago, Ill.)

Pine Top Smith was a principal figure in the development of boogie-woogie piano in the 1920s. His song "Pine Top's Boogie" ranks as one of the most important pieces to come out of the era and has long since become a boogie-woogie standard. Smith influenced practically every noted boogie-woogie piano player that came after him, including ALBERT AMMONS, MEADE "LUX" LEWIS, and PETE JOHNSON.

Smith was born in Troy, Alabama, but grew up in Birmingham, where he taught himself how to play piano. He began performing in his midteens at house parties in Birmingham. But he soon moved to Pittsburgh, which led to work with MA RAINEY and with Butterbeans & Susie on the TOBA (Theater Owners' Booking Association) circuit. Smith was discovered by fellow boogie-woogie pianist COW COW DAVENPORT, who suggested he move to Chicago. Smith arrived in Chicago in 1928 and lived in the same apartment house that Albert Ammons and Meade "Lux" Lewis did. The three boogie-woogie pianists became friends and often jammed together.

Smith quickly worked his way into the city's house-rent party and club circuit and also began his recording career, cutting eight sides for Vocalion in 1928. Tragically, Smith's career and life came to a sudden end in 1929 when a bullet fired accidentally in a barroom fight struck him in the chest and killed him. At the time of his death, Smith was twenty-five years old.

Essential Listening:
Clarence "Pine Top" Smith/Romeo Nelson: Their Complete Recordings/Oldie Blues (2831)

◄ SMITH, TRIXIE

(born 1895, Atlanta, Ga.; died September 21, 1943, New York, N.Y.)

Trixie Smith is probably the least remembered of the four major female blues singers named Smith who recorded in the 1920s. (The other three were MAMIE SMITH, BESSIE SMITH, and CLARA SMITH, none of whom were related.) Unlike her namesakes, whose vocals were strong and supple, Smith's voice was thin, yet it had an affectionate quality.

Born and raised in Atlanta, Trixie Smith studied at Selma University before she decided on a singing career and moved to New York around 1915. She worked the TOBA (Theater Owners' Booking Association) circuit and performed in numerous New York vaudeville shows, ultimately becoming a featured vocalist. In 1921 Smith began recording for the Black Swan label. A live performance of one of her Black Swan songs, "Trixie's Blues," won her first place and a silver cup in a 1922 New York blues contest. She is most remembered for "Railroad Blues," a song that features one of Smith's most inspired vocal performances on record, and "The World Is Jazz Crazy and So Am I." Both songs feature LOUIS ARMSTRONG on cornet.

Although Smith did a bit of recording for Decca in 1938 and 1939, her recording career had effectively ended by 1926. Mostly she sustained herself by performing in cabaret revues, travelling musical shows, and taking small parts in theatrical productions. She died in 1943.

Essential Listening:
Trixie Smith, 1922–29/Blues Documents (2068)

◄ SMITH, WHISPERING

(born Moses Smith, January 25, 1932, Union Church, Miss.; died April 28, 1984, Baton Rouge, La.)

Swamp blues harmonica player and singer Whispering Smith was part of the Baton Rouge blues community in the 1950s and 1960s. Smith worked primarily with LIGHTNIN' SLIM and SILAS HOGAN; he also recorded on his own for the Excello and Arhoolie labels.

Before teaming up with Lightnin' Slim around 1960, Smith played the bars and juke joints in the Baton Rouge area. He began his recording career with Excello in 1963 but never registered any hits. Most of Smith's performance work was in Louisiana, though in the 1970s he toured Europe with the American Folk Blues Festival and the American Blues Legends. Smith continued his recording career through the '70s and appeared in the documentary *Blues Legends*, though he was never able to break out beyond being a regional artist. He died in 1984.

Essential Listening:
Louisiana Blues (Various Artists)/Arhoolie (1054)
Swamp Blues (Various Artists)/Excello (8015-8016)

◄ SMITTY, BLUE

(born Claude Smith, November 6, 1924, Marianna, Ark.)

Blues guitarist Blue Smitty was one of the many unsung musicians who had a small role in shaping the early post–World War II Chicago blues scene. Though he recorded little, Blue Smitty worked in a 1947 trio that included MUDDY WATERS and JIMMY ROGERS. He also had an influence on Waters as a guitar player, teaching him chords and single-string solos minus the bottleneck, Waters's preferred way of playing. Some blues historians consider Blue Smitty to be one of Chicago's earliest modern guitarists.

Claude Smith was born in Arkansas in 1924. He spent part of his childhood living with an aunt in Chicago, but by 1935 he had returned to Arkansas, where he learned to play the guitar and listened to SONNY BOY WILLIAMSON (Rice Miller) and ROBERT JR. LOCKWOOD play on KFFA's King Biscuit Flour Time. Smitty served in the armed forces during World War II. Upon his discharge in 1946, he returned to Chicago, where he met Waters. The following year, with Smitty and Waters on guitars and Rogers on harmonica, the trio began performing in small Chicago clubs.

In late 1947 Smitty moved to Harvey, Illinois, and formed his own band. In 1950 he moved to Joliet and began playing the blues joint Club 99. Two years later Smitty signed a recording contract with Chess and did one session, which resulted in the release of the single "Crying"/"Sad Story." Throughout the rest of the '50s and much of the '60s, Smitty continued to play clubs in and around Joliet, until he finally gave up music.

Essential Listening:

Drop Down Mama (Various Artists)/MCA-Chess (CH-93002)

◄ SMOTHERS, SMOKEY

(born Otis Smothers, March 21, 1929, Lexington, Miss.; died July 23, 1993, Chicago)

Smokey Smothers was a Chicago guitarist who, over the years, performed and recorded with many of the city's major bluesmen, including HOWLIN' WOLF, MUDDY WATERS, and LITTLE WALTER.

Smothers was born and raised in Mississippi and came to Chicago sometime in the mid-'40s. After playing street corners for spare change with BO DIDDLEY and other developing bluesmen, Smothers worked himself into the city's blues club scene in the mid-'50s, and remained there for the rest of his career. In the early '60s he recorded over a dozen sides for the King (Federal) label with Freddie King on second guitar. Smothers also recorded an album in 1986 called *Got My Eyes on You* for Red Beans, a small Chicago label, but it attracted little attention. With the exception of an occasional appearance at the Chicago Blues Festival, most of Smothers's work was in the city's small blues bars. His younger brother Abe "Little Smokey" Smothers is also a blues singer-guitarist.

Essential Listening:

Got My Eyes on You/Red Beans (009)

◄ Sons of Blues, The

The Sons of Blues began in the mid-'70s as a Chicago bar band. The group featured guitarist LURRIE BELL, whose father, CAREY BELL, is a noted Chicago harp player; bass player Freddie Dixon, son of legendary bass player and composer WILLIE DIXON; and harmonica player BILLY BRANCH. The band was included in two of Alligator Records' critically acclaimed anthologies, *Living Chicago Blues, Vol. 3* and *The New Bluebloods*, both of which documented up-and-coming and lesser-known Chicago blues artists and bands in the late '70s and '80s.

The Sons of Blues became an increasingly flexible outfit when Lurrie Bell began working with KOKO TAYLOR and both Dixon and Branch became frequent members of Willie Dixon's Chicago All-Stars. By 1982, Dixon and Bell left the Sons of Blues for good, leaving Branch to carry on. Branch then teamed up with bass player J.W. Williams, whose Chi-Town Hustlers was also a popular Chicago bar band. Also introduced into the Sons of Blues were guitarist Carl Weatherby and drummer Moses Rudes. This was the Sons of Blues personnel when it recorded its debut album, *Where's the Money*, for the Red Beans label, and the song "The Only Thing That Saved Me" for *The New Bluebloods* album in 1987. The Sons of Blues continues to perform in Chicago clubs.

Essential Listening:
Where's the Money/Red Beans (004)

◄ Spann, Otis

(born March 21, 1930, Jackson, Miss.; died April 25, 1970, Chicago, Ill.)

Best known as the pianist in the legendary MUDDY WATERS Band, Otis Spann was also a noted solo artist in the 1960s. His blend of traditional boogie-woogie bass figures and slow blues chord structures gave his piano style its emotional depth. In a band format, Spann was the ideal accompanist. He could melt into the rhythm section with full-bodied, but unobtrusive, riffs or could break out into the open with a powerful solo. Spann was also a convincing vocalist. His hazy voice seemed dulled by years of abuse, yet it contained the kind of blue tones that often took a song to a higher emotional plane.

Spann was mostly self-taught. After playing piano in his minister father's church in Mississippi, Spann split his time performing in juke joints and house parties with stints as a semipro football player and professional boxer. He went into the army in 1946. Upon being discharged in 1951, he settled in Chicago and began playing the city's blues clubs. In 1953 he joined the Muddy Waters band. Almost at once Spann's piano became an integral part of Waters's rocking blues sound and a mainstay in the band. In addition to recording with Waters, Spann also cut sides with HOWLIN' WOLF, LITTLE WALTER, and other Chess artists, becoming something of a house pianist at the label.

Spann began his solo career in 1960 when he cut *Otis Spann Is the Blues* accompanied by ROBERT JR. LOCKWOOD on guitar, though he continued to perform and record with Waters. Spann performed with the Waters Band at the now-legendary 1960 Newport Jazz Festival. The resulting live album, *Muddy Waters at Newport*, included "Goodbye Newport Blues," a song sung by Spann. The success of Spann's debut album enabled him to record extensively in the 1960s. He made records for a number of labels, including Testament, Fontana, Prestige, Storyville, Decca, Blue Horizon, and Vanguard. He often recorded using the Waters Band (*The Blues of Otis Spann*) or members of it (*The Blues Never Die* and *Otis Spann's Chicago Blues*). Spann also performed extensively in the '60s, touring Europe a number of times with and without the Waters Band and playing most major American blues festivals. In 1970, at the height of his career, Spann was diagnosed with cancer; he died that year at age forty. He was elected into the Blues Foundation's Hall of Fame in 1980.

Essential Listening:

Otis Spann's Chicago Blues/Testament (2211)
Otis Spann Is the Blues/Story of Blues (79001)
The Blues Never Die/Prestige (7719)
Otis Walking the Blues/Story of Blues (79025)
The Complete Candid Otis Spann/Lightnin' Hopkins Sessions/Mosaic (MD3-139)
Muddy Waters: The Chess Box/MCA-Chess (31268)
Muddy Waters At Newport/MCA-Chess (31269)

◀ SPECKLED RED

(born Rufus Perryman, October 23, 1892, Monroe, La.; died January 2, 1973, St. Louis, Mo.)

Boogie-woogie piano player Speckled Red was a familiar figure on the Memphis and St. Louis blues scenes in the 1930s. A black albino, he was born in Louisiana and later moved to Hampton, Georgia, where he learned the keyboard on a church organ. By the time he and his large family (he had fifteen siblings) relocated to Atlanta, Red was playing house-rent parties and juke joints.

In the mid-1920s Red moved to Detroit and played clubs and parties there until he worked his way back down South to Memphis where, in 1929, he made his first recordings. One of the sides the Brunswick label released, "The Dirty Dozens," became a hit. A year later Red recorded a sequel, "The Dirty Dozens No. 2," in Chicago. The only other recordings he made in the pre–World War II years were done in 1938 for Bluebird, but they attracted little attention.

Red moved to St. Louis and played small bars until he was rediscovered in 1954. Two years later he recorded for the Tone label and later toured the West Coast and Europe. He also recorded for Folkways in 1960. Shortly thereafter Red cut back on his performances due to advanced age. He died in 1973.

Essential Listening:

The Dirty Dozens/Delmark (DL 601)
Speckled Red (1929–1938)/Wolf (WSE 113)

◄ SPECTER, DAVE

(born May 21, 1963, Chicago, Ill.)

Dave Specter, a Chicago blues guitarist, released his debut album, *Bluebird Blues*, in 1991 on the Delmark label. The album featured vocalist BARKIN' BILL SMITH, with whom Specter has worked since 1989, and guest guitarist RONNIE EARL.

Before teaming up with Smith and forming his band, the Bluebirds, Specter worked with a number of Chicago bluesmen, including guitarists SON SEALS and HUBERT SUMLIN and drummer SAM LAY. It was during a Canadian tour with Lay in 1986 that Specter met Smith. Specter also logged time with the LEGENDARY BLUES BAND in the late 1980s before forming the Bluebirds. He continues to perform, mostly in Chicago.

Essential Listening:

Bluebird Blues/Delmark (DD 652)

◄ SPIRES, BIG BOY

(born Arthur Spires, October 1912, Yazoo City, Miss.; died 1990, Chicago, Ill.)

A Chicago blues guitarist and singer, Big Boy Spires came onto the city's blues scene after his move from Mississippi in 1943. Spires learned how to play some guitar in Mississippi. Upon arriving in Chicago, Spires played house-rent parties and clubs with artists like LOUIS MYERS and JUNIOR WELLS and eventually landed a recording contract with Checker, a subsidiary of the Chess label. "Murmur Low" and "One of These Days" are his best-known songs. Chess owner/producer Leonard Chess reputedly gave Spires his "Big Boy" nickname.

Spires formed his own group, the Rocket Four, in the early 1950s. The band's success in Chicago clubs led Spires to sign another recording contract, this time with the Chance label, though little came of it. Spires continued to perform in and around Chicago, though not on a steady basis, through the 1950s, '60s and '70s. He died in 1990. Spires's son, Bud Spires, is a blues harmonica player and singer who works with Mississippi bluesman Jack Owens.

Essential Listening:

Chicago Slickers, 1948–1953 (Various Artists)/Nighthawk (102)

Drop Down Mama (Various Artists)/MCA-Chess (CH 93002)

Wrapped in My Baby (Morris Pejoe, Big Boy Spires, and Willie Smith)/Pearl (PL-16)

◄ SPIVEY, VICTORIA

(born October 15, 1906, Houston, Tex.; died October 3, 1976, New York, N.Y.)

Victoria Spivey came from the same turn-of-the-century Texas blues mold that produced singer SIPPIE WALLACE (who, like Spivey, was born in Houston). Spivey was one of the few female blues vocalists of the 1920s to continue her career well beyond the classic blues era. In addition to being a stage performer and recording artist, Spivey was also a witty songwriter and a shrewd businesswoman.

Her keen grasp of the business end of the blues enabled her to keep touring and making records long after nearly all the other classic blues singers of the 1920s had faded from the scene.

As a blues singer, Spivey did not compare with the towering talent of BESSIE SMITH or Spivey's mentor, IDA COX; Spivey's voice might have lacked refinement and range, but her moaning wails and country blues phrasing not only reflected her Texas roots but also made her blues believable. Spivey wrote some of the more penetratingly direct blues songs of the classic blues era. "TB Blues" dealt with the rejection that tuberculosis victims faced in the '20s. "Dope Head Blues" might well have been the first blues song recorded about the dangers of cocaine, while "Organ Grinder Blues" dripped with eroticism.

Spivey began her career by singing and playing piano in Houston saloons and whorehouses. She recorded her first song, "Black Snake Blues," in 1926 for the Okeh label. Based out of Missouri in the late '20s, Spivey worked as a songwriter for the St. Louis Music Company and appeared in the all-black movie musical *Hallelujah!* In the 1930s she recorded for Victor, Vocalion, Decca, and Okeh and appeared as a featured performer in a number of musical shows, including the acclaimed *Hellzapoppin' Revue.* Spivey worked countless one-night stands, mostly in New York City, often working with dancer Billy Adams. In the 1950s, Spivey left show business, singing only in the church. But she came back to the blues in 1962 when she formed her own record company, Spivey Records, and resumed performing. Her timing was such that she was able to capitalize on the growing interest in blues and folk music. Spivey played major blues and folk festivals in the U.S. and Europe and recorded old-time classic blues singers such as LUCILLE HEGAMIN on her label. Spivey continued to perform until her death in 1976.

Essential Listening:
Victoria Spivey, 1926–1931/Document (590)

◄ STACKHOUSE, HOUSTON

(born September 28, 1910, Wesson, Miss.; died September 23, 1980, Helena, Ark.)

Not exactly a household name, even in blues circles, Houston Stackhouse was nonetheless an important guitar stylist and singer from Mississippi in the years just after World War II. He performed with harmonica ace SONNY BOY WILLIAMSON (Rice Miller) on the KFFA radio station out of Helena in the mid-'40s and was, at times, a member of his touring group. His crisp, snarling guitar sound helped give the Williamson band its hardened edge.

Stackhouse was a disciple of fellow Mississippi guitarist TOMMY JOHNSON. In the late '20s he performed with Johnson at Jackson-area parties and picnics, picking up many of Johnson's guitar traits. Stackhouse also played with ROBERT NIGHTHAWK, whom he reportedly taught to play the guitar. By the mid-1940s Stackhouse had gone to Helena, where he appeared with Williamson on the "King Biscuit Time" program the latter hosted every day at noon. From the daily performances on the radio evolved a band, the King Biscuit Entertainers, which included Stackhouse (and later JOE WILLIE WILKINS) on guitar, Sonny Boy Williamson on harp and vocals, PECK CURTIS on drums, and DUDLOW TAYLOR on piano.

In the 1950s, rather than migrate to Chicago, as many Delta musicians did in their search for increased opportunity, Stackhouse remained in Mississippi, working there and Arkansas, occasionally with Williamson and Peck Curtis and also with the Boyd Gilmore Trio. By the mid-'60s, Stackhouse had branched out to become a recording artist. He cut sides for the Testament and Flyright labels, which led to much-deserved exposure and frequent trips outside the Mississippi region to perform in festivals such as the Smithsonian Festival of American Folklife in Washington, D.C., and the Ann Arbor Blues Festival in Michigan.

In the '70s Stackhouse often performed with Joe Willie Wilkins's King Biscuit Boys in the U.S. and Europe. He died in 1980.

Essential Listening:
Houston Stackhouse, 1910–1980/Wolf (120 779)

◄ STOKES, FRANK

(born January 1, 1888, Whitehaven, Tenn.; died September 12, 1955, Memphis, Tenn.)

Frank Stokes was one of the early members of the Memphis blues scene. In the 1920s and 1930s, as a solo artist and as one half of the Beale Street Sheiks, Stokes became known for his rhythmic, minstrelesque blues songs. Together with other first-generation Memphis blues artists such as FURRY LEWIS, MEMPHIS MINNIE, and SLEEPY JOHN ESTES, Stokes provided the musical groundwork for what became one of the most active blues scenes of the pre–World War II and early postwar periods.

Stokes was born outside Memphis but raised in Mississippi. He traveled the South with tent shows and worked as a hoboing songster when he wasn't employed as a blacksmith. Sometime in the early 1920s, he began singing and playing on Memphis street corners and in local parks. Stokes was often accompanied by Dan Sane (or Sain), with whom he formed a duo, the Beale Street Sheiks. The group's sound, a combination of good-time and down-home blues, was essentially a throwback to earlier styles. From 1927 to 1929 the Sheiks recorded for the Paramount label, while Stokes cut some solo sides for Victor. In all, the Sheiks recorded some two dozen titles, and Stokes did another dozen on his own. With the arrival of the Depression and the decrease in recording opportunities, Stokes and Sane went back to playing street corners, occasional circuses, and traveling shows. Stokes gradually faded from the blues scene in the mid-1940s. He died in 1955.

Essential Listening:
The Beale Street Sheiks, 1927–1929/Document (DOCD 5012)
Creator of the Memphis Blues/Yazoo (1056)
Frank Stokes' Dream: The Memphis Blues, 1927–1931 (Various Artists)/Yazoo (1008)

◄ STREHLI, ANGELA

(born November 22, 1945, Lubbock, Tex.)

Singer Angela Strehli was one of the original members of the Austin, Texas, blues scene that began in the early 1970s. Along with STEVIE RAY and JIMMIE VAUGHAN, Kim Wilson, LOU ANN BARTON, and other noted Austin musicians, Strehli helped create a rock and rhythm & blues–influenced Austin sound that helped spur the blues revival of the 1980s.

Born and raised in Texas, Strehli learned to play harmonica and bass before she became a vocalist. She spent some time in California in the late 1960s but settled in Austin in 1970, where she sang in the bar band Southern Feeling. In 1975 Strehli quit performing on a regular basis and began working at a new Austin club, Antone's. She acted as stage manager and chief sound technician and often sat in with local bands.

In 1982 Strehli went back to singing full-time; she formed the Angela Strehli Band, which became one of Austin's most popular bar bands. In 1986 she recorded *Stranger Blues*, an EP that marked the debut of Antone's Records, a label that grew out of the club. A year later Antone's released *Soul Shake*, Strehli's first full-length album. In 1990, she relocated to the San Francisco Bay Area. That year she also recorded the album *Dreams Come True* with singers MARCIA BALL and Lou Ann Barton. Strehli continues to record and perform.

Essential Listening:

Soul Shake/Antone's (ANT 0006CD)

Dreams Come True (with Marcia Ball and Lou Ann Barton)/Antone's (ANT 0014)

◄ SUGAR BLUE

(born James Whiting, 1955, New York, N.Y.)

Sugar Blue is a melodramatic blues harmonica player whose style, a montage of sounds and whoops, was inspired by SONNY BOY WILLIAMSON (Rice Miller) and LITTLE WALTER Jacobs. Blue was born in Harlem into a musical family; he learned to play the harmonica in the mid-'60s by listening to Little Stevie Wonder and Bob Dylan albums. By the mid-'70s he was working as a sideman and appearing on albums by BROWNIE MCGHEE, VICTORIA SPIVEY, and ROOSEVELT SYKES.

Blue relocated to Paris in 1976; he played small clubs and street corners until he was discovered by the ROLLING STONES. Blue was invited to play harmonica on the Stones' 1978 hit "Miss You" and other tracks on the *Some Girls* album. Blue also appeared on the Stones' *Emotional Rescue* and *Tattoo You* albums and occasionally performed with the band in concert. During this time Blue also recorded two solo albums; *Cross Roads* and *Chicago to Paris* came out on the Blue Silver label in 1980 and 1982, respectively.

After the release of the latter album, Sugar Blue moved back to the U.S., settling in Chicago, where he began working with WILLIE DIXON's Chicago Blues All-Stars. In 1985 he won a Grammy Award with Dixon and the band for the album *Blues Explosion*, which was recorded live at the Montreux Jazz Festival.

In 1987 Blue appeared in the movie *Angel Heart* and contributed to the score; two years later he played on another Grammy-winning album, Willie Dixon's *Hidden Charms*, and appeared in concert with the Rolling Stones on their *Steel Wheels* tour. Blue continues to perform and record.

Essential Listening:
Cross Roads/Blue Silver
Chicago to Paris/Blue Silver
Some Girls (the Rolling Stones)/Columbia (CK 404 49)

◄ SUMLIN, HUBERT
(born November 16, 1931, Greenwood, Miss.)

For more than twenty years Hubert Sumlin played guitar in HOWLIN' WOLF's band. His terse, sharp-edged solos and scratchy tones became an integral part of Wolf's sound. Sumlin played on numerous Wolf classics, including "Spoonful," "I Ain't Superstitious," "Back Door Man," "Smokestack Lightnin'," and "The Red Rooster." Though not nearly as well known as other post–World War II Chicago guitarists, Sumlin has always been highly regarded in blues musicians' circles.

Sumlin was born in Mississippi but raised in Arkansas, just outside West Memphis. He learned to play the drums before he picked up a guitar. In 1954, after a brief stint with JAMES COTTON, Sumlin joined Howlin' Wolf's band and moved to Chicago. He toured with Wolf for two years before a personality clash led him to leave and join MUDDY WATERS's band. Sumlin toured with Waters for a year before returning to the Wolf fold, where he remained until Wolf's death in 1976.

Sumlin help lead the Wolf band for a while after Wolf's passing, but eventually branched out into a long-overdue solo career. He made an album called *Groove* with the French Black and Blue label, but it wasn't until the release of *Hubert Sumlin's Blues Party* in 1986 on the Black Top label that his solo career in the U.S. took shape. Sumlin continues to tour regularly.

Essential Listening:
Howlin' Wolf (box set)/MCA-Chess (CHD3-9332)
Hubert Sumlin's Blues Party/Black Top (BT 1036)

◄ SUNNYLAND SLIM
(born Albert Luandrew, September 5, 1907, Vance, Miss.)

Pianist Sunnyland Slim has had one of the longest blues careers and owns one of the biggest recording catalogs in all of blues. He began playing in the early 1920s and was still performing in the early '90s, appearing in 1991 at the Chicago Blues Festival. As to the number of recordings he has cut, either as featured artist or as sideman, a good estimate is somewhere around 250. He has probably recorded for two dozen labels using a variety of pseudonyms, including Delta Joe and Dr. Clayton's Buddy. Despite the large number of records he's made over the years Sunnyland never became a major recording artist in terms of gates or chart success. Some of his best work has been as an accompanist and a bandleader.

More important than Sunnyland Slim's longevity and extensive recording output is the legacy he embodies: he is the last of the original Delta blues piano players, a performer whose rugged sound and still-loud vocals recall the days when he banged the piano and shouted the blues in Mississippi juke joints.

Born and raised in Mississippi, Sunnyland taught himself how to play piano and began playing local jukes in the early 1920s. Eventually he left the Delta and briefly traveled around Arkansas and Tennessee before settling in Memphis sometime around 1925 or 1926. In 1928 he wrote "Sunnyland Train," which inspired his nickname. In Memphis he played Beale Street clubs as a solo artist and sideman.

Sunnyland moved to Chicago in the early '40s and worked with Jump Jackson's band and with new arrival MUDDY WATERS. It was Sunnyland who arranged for Waters's recording session with the Aristocrat label (later called Chess) in 1947. Sunnyland and bass player Big Crawford accompanied Waters at the session that produced "Gypsy Woman." A second session with Waters in 1948 resulted in "Good Looking Woman" and "Mean Disposition," both of which set the stage for Waters's recording of "I Can't Be Satisfied" and "I Feel Like Going Home," which as Aristocrat single 1306 helped ushered in the post–World War II Chicago blues scene.

By this time Sunnyland was not only recording extensively as an accompanist, but also as a solo artist. In the late 1940s and 1950s he recorded for more than a dozen different labels, including J.O.B., Regal/Mercury, and Apollo. He was also performing regularly in Chicago clubs with BIG BILL BROONZY, ROBERT JR. LOCKWOOD, BABY FACE LEROY, and others. The 1960s were no less busy. He toured Europe in 1963, which resulted in long-term relationships with audiences in England, Germany, Sweden, and Denmark, and near-annual tours there. He also recorded with J.B. HUTTO, BIG WALTER HORTON, JOHNNY SHINES, and others, on a wide variety of labels, including Delmark, Liberty, Storyville, and Spivey.

In the 1970s, Sunnyland began his own record label, Airways Records, and continued on at a pace that would have left bluesmen half his age gasping for air. More tours of Europe and more session work and performance dates with Chicago bluesmen continued right on through the 1980s. Recognized as the elder statesman of Chicago blues, Sunnyland and his All-Stars became favorites with Chicago Blues Festival crowds. Though he's well over eighty, Sunnyland Slim still does his part to keep the city's blues heritage bright.

Essential Listening:
Original J.O.B./Cobra Recordings/P-Vine (PCD 2164)
Sunnyland Slim/Flyright (566)
Chicago Blues Session/Southland (SCD 10)
Be Careful How You Vote/Earwig (4915)
Chicago Jump/Red Beans (007)

◄ SYKES, ROOSEVELT

(born January 31, 1906, Elmar, Ark.; died July 17, 1984, New Orleans, La.)

Roosevelt Sykes was one of the most important of the pre–World War II blues piano stylists. With a technique that emphasized intricate chord patterns and bass figures along with a crisp urban blues sensibility that would occasionally slip into the jazz realm, Sykes was a first-rate solo artist and a much-in-demand accompanist. He played major roles in both the St. Louis blues scene of the 1930s and the Chicago blues scene of the 1940s. Over a career that spanned just about a half century, he recorded regularly, performed extensively, and, in the process, helped elevate blues piano to a high art.

Sykes was born in Arkansas but grew up in St. Louis. He learned to play the organ in church and then used the skills to secure work as a barrelhouse piano player in the Helena, Arkansas, area, often working with fellow pianist Lee Green. Sometime in the late 1920s Sykes returned to St. Louis and used the city as a base while making regular trips to Memphis and Chicago. He first recorded in 1929. His version of the tune "Forty Four Blues," which he learned from Green, was released on the Okeh label and helped establish his reputation as a solid blues pianist.

Sykes spent the 1930s working St. Louis clubs as a solo artist or with other piano players such as ST. LOUIS JIMMY ODEN. He recorded for Victor and Decca and other small labels, often using a pseudonym (Dobby Bragg, Willie Kelly, or Easy Papa Johnson). He also did session work and played the part of a talent scout.

In 1941 Sykes went to Chicago, where he continued all the things he'd been doing in St. Louis. In addition, he frequently worked with MEMPHIS MINNIE, recorded with the Jump Jackson Band, and recorded on his own and as an accompanist for the Bluebird and Bullet labels. Nicknamed "the Honeydripper" for his way with women, Sykes named his band the Honeydrippers and toured the South regularly during and just after the war.

In 1954 when the Chicago blues scene began to favor the sound of the harder-edged electric blues bands, Sykes left the city and moved to New Orleans. He found work plentiful in the Crescent City and even played extended dates in St. Louis and Memphis, right on into the 1960s. The recording dates continued as well. In 1960 he cut sides for Decca and Prestige-Bluesville. In 1962 he recorded for Crown and in 1963 for Delmark. Sykes also began to tour Europe and the U.S., cashing in on the early-'60s blues revival.

Sykes continued a full slate of touring and recording through the '70s and early '80s. Although his dexterity had suffered somewhat, Sykes remained a convincing pianist to the very end of his career. He died in 1984.

Essential Listening:
The Country Blues Piano Ace/Yazoo (1033)
The Honeydripper, 1929–1941/Blues Documents (2013)
The Honeydripper, Vol. 2, 1936–1951/Blues Documents (2088)
In Europe/Delmark (616)
Raining in My Heart/Delmark (642)
Goldmine/Delmark (DD 616)
West Helena Blues (The Post-War Years, Vol. 2, 1945–1957)/Wolf (WBJ 005)

T ▶

◀ TAMPA RED

(born Hudson Whittaker or Woodbridge, c. 1904, Smithville, Ga.; died March 19, 1981, Chicago, Ill.)

Tampa Red was one of Chicago's earliest blues stars and most influential guitarists. Often called the Guitar Wizard, his slide-guitar and single-string solo style, while not typically rough or tormented like the style of some Mississippi Delta musicians, nonetheless inspired a number of other Chicago guitarists, namely, BIG BILL BROONZY and ROBERT NIGHTHAWK. Along with Broonzy, LONNIE JOHNSON, and SCRAPPER BLACKWELL, Tampa Red helped bridge the gap between country and urban blues in the 1930s and did much to integrate musicians coming to Chicago from down South into the city's blues scene.

Tampa Red was born in Georgia. The fact that he had red hair and was raised in Tampa, Florida, gave him his nickname. By the time he came to Chicago, sometime in the mid-1920s, he had already developed his slide-guitar technique. He played street corners for spare change and worked in some clubs, but it wasn't until he formed a partnership with pianist GEORGIA TOM DORSEY in 1928 that his career took shape. That same year the two musicians recorded "It's Tight Like That," a bouncy, bawdy blues, for the Paramount label. The record sold thousands of copies and initiated what became known as "the hokum sound," which featured light, airy melodies and sentimental or humorous lyrics. Georgia Tom and Tampa Red even went by the name the Hokum Boys. For the next couple of years, the duo performed extensively in Chicago and in Memphis and kept recording until Dorsey became disillusioned with the blues and turned to gospel music around 1930.

Tampa Red continued to perform and record, mostly for producer LESTER MELROSE and the Bluebird label. With piano-guitar duets still popular in the mid-'30s—thanks in large part to the records made by Scrapper Blackwell and LEROY CARR—Tampa Red teamed up with BIG MACEO Merriweather and continued what he began with Georgia Tom. Tampa also worked with Broonzy and other Chicago artists; his apartment became something of a hangout for bluesmen during the 1930s.

Although Tampa continued to record regularly in the mid-1940s and early 1950s, his kind of blues was soon overshadowed by the bigger-sounding electric blues bands. Tampa's increasing problem with alcohol also began to take its toll. Though he recorded two albums for Prestige-Bluesville in 1960, his best years were behind him and he retired from the blues scene. Tampa Red was inducted into the Blues Foundation's Hall of Fame in 1981. He died that same year.

Essential Listening:
The Guitar Wizard/Blues Classics (25)
Tampa Red, Vol. 2, 1929–1930/Blues Documents (2086)
Bottleneck Guitar, 1928–1937/Yazoo (1039)
Don't Tampa with the Blues/Prestige-Bluesville (OBCCD 516-2)
Tampa Red, 1928–1942/Story of Blues (3505)

◄ TAYLOR, DUDLOW

(born Robert Taylor, date and place unknown; died c. 1968)

Blues pianist Dudlow Taylor was an original member of the King Biscuit Entertainers, the group that performed with SONNY BOY WILLIAMSON (Rice Miller) on Helena radio station KFFA and in jukes around the city beginning in the early 1940s. Almost nothing is known about Taylor's personal life. Reputedly, he was born in Louisiana and came up to the Helena area as a youth. Taylor joined Williamson, guitarist ROBERT JR. LOCKWOOD, and drummer PECK CURTIS in the King Biscuit Entertainers in 1942. However, due to Taylor's limited capacity on the piano—he was not a schooled or technique player, though he apparently understood the natural nuances of the blues—Williamson and the others brought a second pianist, PINETOP PERKINS, into the group in 1943 to complement Taylor.

Unlike Perkins, Taylor remained with the King Biscuit Entertainers until the group's demise following the death of Williamson in 1965. Taylor died in the late '60s.

Essential Listening:
The Fifties: Juke Joint Blues (Various Artists)/Flair-Virgin (V2-86304)

◄ TAYLOR, EDDIE

(born January 29, 1923, Benoit, Miss.; died December 25, 1985)

Blues guitarist Eddie Taylor was the driving force behind most of JIMMY REED's great recordings in the 1950s. It was Taylor's intricate guitar work and his penchant for combining a down-home blues sensibility with a uniquely modern guitar sound that helped give Reed's blues such vitality. Although Taylor recorded on his own, his solo career was nearly always overshadowed by his connection to Reed.

Taylor was born and raised in Mississippi, where, as a child, he stood outside juke joints and listened to blues greats like CHARLEY PATTON and ROBERT JOHNSON. Taylor got his first guitar in 1936; after teaching himself how to play, he began to work fish fries and house parties in the Delta. Sometime around 1943, he moved to Memphis, where he played Beale Street amateur night shows and worked with JOE HILL LOUIS and other Memphis bluesmen. Taylor moved to Chicago in 1949 and played on Maxwell Street with musicians like FLOYD JONES and SNOOKY PRYOR before working himself into the city's blues club scene.

In 1953 Taylor began his partnership with Jimmy Reed, whom he had known back in the Delta as a child. Not only did Taylor play guitar in Reed's band, but he also taught Reed how to play guitar. Virtually every one of Reed's Vee-Jay classics has Taylor's guitar stamp on it.

In the mid-'50s Taylor branched out and began his solo recording career with Vee-Jay. Two of his 1955 records, "Big Town Playboy" and "Ride 'Em on Down," represent his best solo blues attempts. In addition to working with Reed, Taylor also logged time with MUDDY WATERS, JOHN LEE HOOKER, ELMORE JAMES, and other legendary blues artists, both in the 1950s and the 1960s.

Taylor continued his career as a much-in-demand side guitarist in the 1970s and early 1980s, working with HOMESICK JAMES, ROOSEVELT SYKES, JIMMY DAWK-INS, and others in the U.S. and in Europe. Taylor also continued his recording career, releasing albums on European labels like Wolf and domestic ones such as Antone's. Taylor died on Christmas Day in 1985. Two years later he was inducted into the Blues Foundation's Hall of Fame.

Essential Listening:
Still Not Ready for Eddie/Antone's (005)
Eddie Taylor and Jimmy Reed: Ride 'em on Down/Charly (171)

◄ TAYLOR, EVA

(born Irene Gibbons, June 22, 1895, St. Louis, Mo.; died October 31, 1977, Mineola, N.Y.)

Eva Taylor was a classic blues singer who recorded as early as 1922 and worked nightclubs and theaters on the East Coast, often appearing with her husband, pianist-arranger-producer CLARENCE WILLIAMS, throughout the 1920s and 1930s. Though her voice lacked the range and dynamics of more popular female blues singers like BESSIE SMITH, MA RAINEY, and IDA COX, Taylor enjoyed a long and prosperous career.

As a child, Taylor toured with vaudeville troupes, not only in the U.S. but also in Europe and the South Pacific. In the early 1920s she moved to New York City, where she became a popular club act, and married Williams. In 1922 Taylor recorded for the Black Swan label; later on, she cut sides for Okeh, Columbia, and Bluebird. Her repertoire was blues-based, but she also included jazz and pop pieces in her performances.

Taylor retired from show business in the early 1940s, though after the death of Williams in 1965, she went back to doing occasional concerts and club appearances until her death in 1977.

Essential Listening:
Eva Taylor and Clarence Williams/Retrieval (FJ 121)

◄ TAYLOR, HOUND DOG

(born Theodore Roosevelt Taylor, April 12, 1917, Natchez, Miss.; died December 17, 1975, Chicago, Ill.)

A riveting slide guitarist whose style recalled the slashing antics of ELMORE JAMES, Hound Dog Taylor was largely unknown outside of Chicago until he recorded his first album, the self-titled *Hound Dog Taylor and the HouseRockers*, in 1971. Taylor and his band—second guitarist Brewer Phillips and drummer Ted Harvey—had been playing the blues bars on Chicago's South Side when they were discovered by BRUCE IGLAUER of Alligator Records. Taylor was the first artist signed to the fledgling label.

Lacking any semblance of slickness, Taylor's brand of blues almost always included upbeat, rockin' rhythms and sexually charged slide-guitar work that cut through the rough interplay of Harvey and Phillips. Taylor's solos were remarkable for their raw intensity and coarse tones; it was not unusual for him to hit sour notes or play too loudly. But few blues guitarists played with as much emotional fervor. Taylor's long-standing Sunday afternoon sets at Florence's, a popular Chicago blues club, attracted the city's most noted bluesmen, who frequently sat in with the Houserockers.

Born and raised in Mississippi, Taylor didn't begin playing the guitar until he was twenty years old. After working Delta juke joints and house parties, he moved to Chicago in 1942. Taylor performed occasionally in South Side bars while holding a day job. By the late '50s, he had become a full-time musician. Taylor recorded one side for Firma Records and another for the Bea & Baby label in the early '60s, both of which went largely unnoticed. However, upon release of his Alligator debut in 1971, Taylor finally received the critical acclaim due him. In all, he recorded three albums for Alligator before succumbing to cancer in 1975. Taylor was inducted into the Blues Foundation's Hall of Fame in 1984.

Essential Listening:
Hound Dog Taylor and the HouseRockers/Alligator (AL 4701)
Natural Boogie/Alligator (AL 4704)
Beware of the Dog!/Alligator (AL 4707)
Genuine Houserocking Music/Alligator (AL 4727)

◄ TAYLOR, JOHNNIE

(born May 5, 1938, Crawfordsville, Ark.)

Rhythm & blues vocalist Johnnie Taylor (no relation to Little Johnny Taylor) began his career as a gospel and soul-blues singer before finding his niche in funk and black pop. Taylor is best known for his 1968 smash, "Who's Making Love," and his 1976 million-selling number 1 hit, "Disco Lady." Though both songs barely had a splash of blues in them, Taylor remained popular with black audiences, especially in the South, right on through the 1980s and early 1990s.

Taylor's bid for stardom occurred when he replaced his mentor, Sam Cooke, in the gospel group the Soul Stirrers in 1957. Taylor remained with the group until 1963, when he moved into soul-blues and rhythm & blues and signed a recording contract with Cooke's Sar label. When the label went bust two years later, Taylor went to Stax. He had nearly a half dozen minor hits before scoring big with "Who's Making Love," his first number 1 record.

By this time, Taylor had fully embraced soul music as his creative avenue, though he put his gospel vocal roots to good use in the process. From 1968 to 1971 he was a regular in the R&B top 10, getting his second number 1 hit with "Jody's Got Your Girl and Gone." Throughout the early and mid-'70s Taylor was particularly prolific, releasing singles for the Stax label at a feverish clip; three of them charted in 1971, as did another three in 1972. In 1973 Taylor got his third number 1 single, "I Believe In You (You Believe in Me)." But his biggest ever hit was "Disco Lady." Released just as the disco era was getting underway, the number 1 hit convinced Taylor to continue recording funk-flavored dance songs in the late '70s and early '80s. By the time he switched to the Malaco label in 1984, Taylor's career had cooled considerably, though he remains a top draw as a performer on the chitlin' circuit. Taylor continues to record for Malaco.

Essential Listening:
Raw Blues/Stax (SCD 8508-2)
This Is Your Night/Malaco (7421)
Wall to Wall/Malaco (7431)
Lover Boy/Malaco (7440)

◄ TAYLOR, KOKO

(born Cora Walton, September 28, 1935, Memphis, Tenn.)

With a voice that falls somewhere along the line of BIG MAMA THORNTON, Koko Taylor has been the undisputed Queen of the Blues since the mid-'70s when she first began recording for Alligator Records. Taylor's recording career actually began in the early '60s. She was discovered by WILLIE DIXON, who signed her to the Chess label. Dixon gave Taylor his song "Wang Dang Doodle" to record; together they made the blues classic into a million-selling single in 1966.

Taylor, the daughter of a Tennessee sharecropper, sang gospel and church songs before committing herself to the blues. In 1953 she moved to Chicago with her soon-to-be husband, Robert "Pops" Taylor. She found work as a domestic, but on weekends she and her husband frequented Chicago's blues clubs. Eventually Taylor began sitting in with HOWLIN' WOLF, MUDDY WATERS, BUDDY GUY, J.B. LENOIR, and other bluesmen. In addition to the success of "Wang Dang Doodle," Taylor's association with Dixon also resulted in two Chess albums, *Basic Soul* and *Koko Taylor*. Critically acclaimed sets at the Montreux Jazz Festival in Switzerland and the Ann Arbor Blues and Jazz Festival in Michigan in the early '70s, plus an appearance in the 1970 film *The Blues Is Alive and Well in Chicago*, led BRUCE IGLAUER to sign her to his Alligator label in 1974. Near-constant touring with her band, the Blues Machine, and a collection of Grammy-nominated albums that kept alive a female presence in blues prompted her fans and record company to crown Taylor Queen of the Blues.

By the end of the 1980s, Taylor had won ten W.C. HANDY Awards—more than any other blues artist. She performed at one of President George Bush's inaugural parties in 1989 and survived a near-fatal van crash (she suffered broken ribs, shoulder, and collarbone) that same year. In 1990, she appeared in the David Lynch film *Wild at Heart* and buried "Pops" Taylor, her husband-turned-manager and constant companion for thirty-seven years.

Taylor continues to record and tour regularly. In 1990 she released the album *Jump for Joy*, in which she veered away from her traditional Chicago blues-belting style in order to experiment with soul and more R&B-flavored material.

Essential Listening:
I Got What It Takes/Alligator (AL 4706)
The Earthshaker/Alligator (AL 4711)
From the Heart of a Woman/Alligator (AL 4724)
Queen of the Blues/Alligator (AL 4740)
Live from Chicago: An Audience with the Queen/Alligator (AL 4754)
Jump for Joy/Alligator (AL 4784)
What It Takes/The Chess Years/MCA-Chess (CHD 9328)

◄ TAYLOR, LITTLE JOHNNY
(born Johnny Young, February 11, 1943, Memphis, Tenn.)

Little Johnny Taylor (not to be confused with singer Johnnie Taylor) helped usher in the '60s soul-blues era with his signature song, "Part Time Love." The record reached the top of the R&B charts in 1963 and even made it into the top 20 on the pop charts. The song featured Taylor's expressive gospel intonations and sweaty bursts of pure passion on top of the same kind of blues base that other soul-blues artists like O.V. WRIGHT and OTIS CLAY built their careers on.

Taylor was born in Memphis, but his family moved to Los Angeles when he was still a child. His first musical experiences were in the church. By the time he was in his early teens, Taylor was singing in L.A. gospel groups. He toured and recorded with the Mighty Clouds of Joy and the Stars of Bethel in the mid-'50s, before switching to rhythm & blues and working with bandleader JOHNNY OTIS. Taylor's penchant for falsetto breaks in his songs and his gospel-drenched wails made him a favorite on the chitlin' circuit.

Taylor began his recording career in 1960 when he signed with the L.A.-based Swingin' label. But it wasn't until he jumped to Galaxy Records in 1963 that Taylor made it onto the charts. "You'll Need Another Favor" peaked at number 27. Its follow-up, "Part Time Love," established Taylor as a star. Though he was never able to match the success of "Part Time Love," Taylor returned to the charts in 1964 with "Since I Found a New Love" and in 1966 with "Zig Zag Lightning," though neither was a major hit.

Taylor left Galaxy in 1968 and signed with Ronn Records. Three years later, in 1971, he scored with "Everybody Knows About My Good Thing," which peaked at number 9. Taylor had a few more visits to the charts in the early '70s but then began to move away from his soul-blues stance, becoming more funk oriented. By the mid-1980s Taylor had returned somewhat to his original soul-blues style, though he never completely abandoned funk, and released albums such as *Stuck in the Mud* and *Ugly Man* on the Ichiban label. Taylor continues to record and perform.

Essential Listening:
Greatest Hits/Fantasy (4510)
Stuck in the Mud/Ichiban (1022)
Ugly Man/Ichiban (1042)

◄ TAYLOR, MELVIN

(born March 13, 1959, Jackson, Miss.)

A little-known Chicago guitarist and singer, Melvin Taylor has a blues style that is a rich, expressive synthesis of urban blues, jazz, and rhythm & blues.

Born in Mississippi, Taylor and his family moved to Chicago when he was three years old. As a youth, Taylor played drums and bass before settling on the guitar. By age fifteen he was playing in a local band, the Transistors. In the early '80s Taylor worked with the LEGENDARY BLUES BAND and toured Europe with it. He cut his debut album, *Melvin Taylor: Blues on the Run*, for the French-based Isabel label in 1981. Though the album was popular with European blues fans, it failed to catch on in the States. Taylor also led his own home grown Chicago bands, playing clubs and small blues bars. In 1984 he returned to Europe and recorded in Paris with pianist LUCKY PETERSON and other Chicago bluesmen. The material was later released in the U.S. on the Evidence label under the title *Plays the Blues for You* in 1993. Taylor continues to perform, mostly in and around Chicago and in Europe.

Essential Listening:
Plays the Blues for You/Evidence (ECD 26029-2)

◄ TAYLOR, MONTANA

(born Arthur Taylor, c. 1903, Butte, Mont.; died, date and place unknown)

Montana Taylor was one of Chicago's early boogie-woogie pianists. Born in Montana (hence his nickname) where his father ran a bar called the Silver City Club, Taylor moved with his family, first to Chicago and then to Indianapolis, when he was still a boy. He taught himself how to play the piano and by the early 1920s was playing Indianapolis speakeasies and house-rent parties.

In the late '20s Taylor relocated to Chicago, where there was more work. In 1929 he recorded a few sides for Vocalion, most notably "Detroit Rocks" and "Indiana Avenue Stomp." Both tunes featured a rollicking boogie-woogie style not unlike that of MEADE "LUX" LEWIS. During the Depression Taylor worked small clubs and bars. He had moved to Cleveland by the middle 1930s and played clubs and lounges there until he was rediscovered in 1946. That year he recorded with BERTHA "CHIPPIE" HILL and did some solo sides, including a remake of "Indiana Avenue Stomp." But after some performances with Hill, Taylor faded from the scene.

Essential Listening:
Vocalion: The Piano Blues, Vol. 3/Magpie (4403)

◄ TAYLOR, TED

(born Austin Taylor, February 16, 1934, Okmulgee, Okla.; died October 23, 1987, Lake Charles, La.)

Ted Taylor was a rhythm and blues singer and composer who effectively blended blues and gospel into his vocal and writing styles. Although he failed to gain major commercial success, a number of singles he cut in the 1950s and 1960s remain highly regarded among R&B and soul-blues fans.

Taylor was born in Oklahoma but got his start in Los Angeles as a teen when he began singing in such gospel groups as the Chosen Gospel Singers, the Spiritual Five, and the Zion Travelers. Eventually Taylor switched to rhythm & blues. He joined the Santa Monica Soul Seekers, which later became the Cadets/Jacks, and recorded with the group on the Modern label in the mid-1950s. Shortly thereafter, Taylor began a solo career, which led to records for the Ebb and Duke labels, among others, before signing with Okeh Records in 1962. Working with producer Carl Davis and then Billy Sherrill, Taylor released a batch of singles for Okeh, including a remake of "Be Ever Wonderful," a tune he had recorded for Duke. Taylor's first album, also called *Be Ever Wonderful*, was released by Okeh in 1963. His biggest hit, "Stay Away from My Baby," made it to number 14 on the R&B charts in 1965.

After his stint at Okeh, Taylor briefly recorded for Atco Records, with little success. He then began a long-term relationship with Ronn Records that lasted from 1966 until 1975. Taylor cut two dozen singles and four albums for Ronn and worked the chitlin' circuit in the South where he was a solid if not spectacular draw.

Taylor tried to crack the disco scene in the late '70s, after which he faded from visibility until the mid-'80s when he reemerged as a soul-blues singer. Taylor formed his own record company, Solpudgits, released a pair of blues albums, and was in the midst of a comeback when he was killed in an automobile accident in 1987.

Essential Listening:
Keep Walking On/Charly (1011)
Taylor Made/Paula (PCD 337)
Be Ever Wonderful/Laurie (LCD 6017)

◄ TEMPLE, JOHNNY

(born October 18, 1906, Canton, Miss.; died November 22, 1968, Jackson, Miss.)

Guitarist-singer Johnny Temple, a contemporary of TAMPA RED, BIG BILL BROONZY, and MEMPHIS MINNIE, was a popular Chicago-based blues recording artist in the 1930s. His most popular record, "Louise Louise Blues," was a hit in 1936.

Temple was born and raised in Mississippi. As a child he learned the rudiments of the guitar and mandolin and eventually began playing house parties and picnics. In the early 1930s, he moved to Chicago, where he quickly fell into the city's growing blues scene, often working with CHARLIE and JOE MCCOY in Chicago clubs. He began his recording career in 1935; with the release of ''Louise Louise Blues'' the following year on the Decca label, Temple grew popular enough to continue recording with various labels through most of the 1940s.

In the 1950s, Temple performed in Chicago clubs, often with BILLY BOY ARNOLD and BIG WALTER HORTON. But with Temple's '30s-style blues being overtaken by the more popular postwar modern blues, Temple returned to Mississippi in the mid-'50s. He continued to perform in and around Jackson but by the mid-'60s had faded from the scene. He died in 1968.

Essential Listening:
Johnny Temple, 1936–1940/Blues Documents (2067)
Johnny Temple, 1935–1939/Document (511)

◀ TEN YEARS AFTER

Original members: Alvin Lee (guitar, vocals) (born December 19, 1944, Nottingham, England); Leo Lyons (bass) (born November 30, 1944, Bedfordshire, England); Chick Churchill (keyboards) (born January 2, 1949, Flintshire, England); Ric Lee (drums) (born October 20, 1945, Staffordshire, England)

Ten Years After was a late-'60s British blues-rock band led by guitarist Alvin Lee. Originally called the Jaybirds, Ten Years After was formed in 1967 when Lee, whose trademark was sheer fret speed, and bassist Leo Lyons, with whom Lee had played in Germany, teamed up with drummer Ric Lee (no relation to Alvin) and keyboards player Chick Churchill. Signed to Deram, Decca's subsidiary label, Ten Years After recorded a self-titled debut album and a 1968 follow-up, *Undead*, recorded live at the Klooks Kleek Club in London. Its sound featured a combination of stiff British blues and jazz-influenced rock, with the spotlight on Lee's ambitiously quick guitar riffs. Lee and Ten Years After went from being an impressive but little-known blues-rock band to big stars, thanks to their rousing set at the Woodstock rock festival in 1969. Lee's lightning-quick guitar work on ''I'm Going Home'' made the performance one of the highlights of the Woodstock movie and soundtrack.

Though Ten Years After continued as a working unit until 1974—the band toured America twenty-eight times and released a collection of mostly unspectacular albums—the band's affinity for the blues all but disappeared. Lee began a solo career after the band's demise but was never quite able to capture the level of acclaim Ten Years After had once enjoyed. In 1989 the band reunited and recorded the album *About Time*, but it attracted little attention. Lee continues to perform and occasionally record.

Essential Listening:
The Essential Ten Years After/Chrysalis (F2-21857)
Cricklewood Green/Deram (18038)

◄ TERRY, SONNY

(born Saunders Terrell, October 24, 1911, Greensboro, N.C.; died March 12, 1986, New York, N.Y.)

Sonny Terry, one of the best harmonica players to come out of the southeast, was the longtime partner of guitarist BROWNIE MCGHEE. They made dozens of albums together in the post–World War II and modern periods and helped integrate blues into the New York folk scene in the 1940s and 1950s. As a harp stylist, Terry is best known for ''whoopin','' a method of playing that is built around high, shrill sounds.

Terry was born in North Carolina and was taught to play harmonica by his father. During his youth, he lost sight in both eyes in two separate accidents. Blind, he sought a career as a blues harmonica player and began traveling to Durham and Raleigh to perform on street corners. Sometime around 1934 he met BLIND BOY FULLER, one of the southeast's most popular blues guitarists and singers. Fuller encouraged Terry to come to Durham. After Terry moved there, the two bluesmen often performed together. Terry went with Fuller to New York in 1937 and accompanied him in the recording studio where they cut sides for Vocalion and American Record Company. The following year, 1938, Sonny Terry played John Hammond's legendary Spirituals to Swing concert in New York City.

After he returned to Durham, Terry met guitarist Brownie McGhee. The two performed together, but it wasn't until the death of Fuller in 1941 and McGhee's move to New York City a year later that the partnership became permanent.

Terry and McGhee found New York an ideal marketplace for blues. The two recorded together and, at times, as solo artists, and became friends with LEAD-BELLY, Woody Guthrie, Pete Seeger, and other folkies. In time Terry was also accompanying these new friends in the recording studio and on the concert stage. He also got involved in acting; in 1946 he had a part in the Broadway production of *Finian's Rainbow*, which had a run of more than one thousand performances. In the mid-'50s he returned to the Broadway stage, this time as a member of the cast of *Cat on a Hot Tin Roof*. McGhee was also in the show.

Terry and McGhee eventually began touring outside of New York, going as far north as Montreal. In the '50s they recorded for the Folkways, Fantasy, Savoy, and Old Town labels, among others. Terry and McGhee also recorded as accompanists. During all this recording Terry's harp style kept its southeastern blues edge; often it was difficult to tell that he'd been based in New York since the early '40s.

By recording so frequently, Terry became one of the best-known blues harp players among white audiences. However, for many black blues fans, Sonny Terry and Brownie McGhee had crossed over into the folk-blues realm. Some skeptics felt their music lacked the burning intensity of blues artists who played exclusively for black audiences.

Terry and McGhee benefitted from the folk-blues boom of the early '60s and became regular performers at major folk and blues festivals, including Newport. Terry also worked with Harry Belafonte and did Alka-Seltzer TV commercials. With McGhee, he toured Australia and Europe and continued to record.

Terry's schedule wasn't any less consuming in the '70s; trips to Europe, Australia, and New Zealand, appearances at the Philadelphia Folk Festival and Berkeley Blues Festival, and countless club dates kept him almost always on the road. In 1975 he found time to write *The Harp Styles of Sonny Terry*, which was published by Oak Publications. At around this time, the long partnership Terry enjoyed with McGhee dissolved, due mostly to personal squabbles. Terry recorded the album *Whoopin'* with JOHNNY WINTER and WILLIE DIXON for the Alligator label in the late '70s. Eventually Terry was forced to slow down. By the early '80s he performed less and less and had all but quit recording. He died in 1986, the same year he was inducted into the Blues Foundation's Hall of Fame.

Essential Listening:

Brownie McGhee & Sonny Terry Sing/Smithsonian/Folkways (SF 40011)
Sonny's Story/Original Blues Classics (OBC 503)
Sonny Is King/Original Blues Classics (OBC 521)
California Blues/Fantasy (24723)
The Folkways Years, 1941–1963/Smithsonian/Folkways (SF 40033)
Whoopin'/Alligator (AL 4734)

◄ THACKERY, JIMMY

(born May 19, 1953, Pittsburgh, Pa.)

Guitarist Jimmy Thackery was a founding member of the popular Washington, D.C., blues group the NIGHTHAWKS. Later he went on to front two other blues-based groups, the Assassins and the Drivers. Born in Pittsburgh and raised in Washington, D.C., Thackery learned how to play piano before guitar; he discovered the blues after attending a BUDDY GUY show as a teenager.

In 1972 Thackery and harmonica player Mark Wenner formed the Nighthawks, which became one of the most popular blues groups on the East Coast, playing clubs and college campuses from Maine to Florida. After doing some three hundred dates a year and recording more than a dozen albums with the Nighthawks over a thirteen-year stretch, Thackery quit the band in 1985 and formed the Assassins. Thackery's new group played as much rhythm & blues as straight blues. He cut three albums with the Assassins before the band dissolved in 1991. In its wake Thackery formed Jimmy Thackery and the Drivers, a trio that prominently featured Thackery's riveting guitar work. Signed to the Blind Pig label, the band released *Empty Arms Motel* in 1992. Thackery and the Drivers continue to record and perform.

Essential Listening:

Empty Arms Motel/Blind Pig (BPCD 5001)
Ten Years Live (the Nighthawks)/Varrick (001)
Open All Night (the Nighthawks)/Mobile Fidelity Sound Labs (MFCD 754)

◄ THOMAS, CHRIS

(born October 14, 1963, Baton Rouge, La.)

A contemporary blues-rock guitarist whose style is liberally splashed by the influences of JIMI HENDRIX and Prince, Chris Thomas is the son of TABBY THOMAS, a longtime Baton Rouge blues artist. Though Chris Thomas grew up surrounded by the blues—his father owned a popular Baton Rouge juke joint, Tabby's Blues Box—his main interest was blues-rock and reggae, especially that of Bob Marley.

Thomas played in Baton Rouge bars and made some early recordings in 1983. He accompanied his father on a European tour that year, which helped him turn toward the blues. He then released a single on his father's Blue Beat label. However, it was Arhoolie Records that released his first album, *The Beginning*, in 1986. Eager to expand his musical horizons, Thomas left Baton Rouge and moved to Austin, Texas, that same year. His reputation as a blazing lead guitarist prompted the Hightone label to sign Thomas to a recording contract. A subsequent deal with Sire Records meant his 1990 album, *Cry of the Prophets*, was released under a dual Sire/Hightone logo. Thomas's follow-up album, *Simple*, came out in 1993 and includes a version of the Bob Marley reggae classic "War." Thomas continues to tour and record. He lives in Copenhagen, Denmark.

Essential Listening:
The Beginning/Arhoolie (1096)
Cry of the Prophets/Sire/Hightone (26186)
Simple/Hightone (HCD 8043)

◄ THOMAS, GEORGE

(aka Clay Custer) (born c. 1885, Houston, Tex.; died 1930, Chicago, Ill.)

A pianist, composer, and music publisher, George Thomas was the eldest sibling of Houston's Thomas family, which included pianist-brother HERSAL THOMAS and classic blues singer SIPPIE WALLACE, their sister. Thomas was also one of the earliest boogie-woogie piano composers and soloists. The boogie-woogie bass line heard in at least three of his songs—"The New Orleans Hop Scop Blues" (published in 1916), "The Fives" (not the same tune JIMMY YANCEY later made famous) and "The Rocks" (recorded in 1923)—all preceded PINE TOP SMITH's famous boogie-woogie piece, "Pine Top's Boogie Woogie," the first major boogie-woogie record.

Thomas was born in Houston, where he learned how to play piano and worked in local theaters as a pit piano player. He met pianist-composer CLARENCE WILLIAMS in 1911; the two went into business together in New Orleans in 1914 when they started a music publishing company. The partnership lasted until Williams moved to Chicago in 1919. Thomas followed Williams to the Windy City in the early '20s. He recorded occasionally, played clubs, and established a music publishing firm of his own. He also provided a home there for Sippie Wallace and her husband, and Thomas's younger brother, Hersal. Thomas's daughter, Hociel, a blues singer, was working with Hersal when he died suddenly of food poisoning in 1926. George Thomas died in 1930 after injuries suffered in a streetcar accident.

Essential Listening:
The Piano Blues, Vol. 4: The Thomas Family/Magpie (PY 4404)

◄ THOMAS, HENRY "RAGTIME"

(born 1874, Big Sandy, Tex.; died 1930)

A Texas songster, Henry Thomas began recording when he was over fifty years old. He cut nearly two dozen sides from 1927 to 1929. This body of work reveals much about the songster tradition, which included black folksongs, jump-ups, rags, dance and novelty tunes, and early blues.

Thomas was born sometime in 1874 in or near Big Sandy, Texas. His share-cropper parents were former slaves. Self-taught on guitar and pan pipes (a home-made reed instrument that creates a high-pitched, whistling sound), Thomas left home as a youth to hobo through the South and scratch out a living as an itinerant street musician. Little is known about his life other than that he spent much of it hopping trains and entertaining passersby on street corners, in parks, and at train stations. Although Thomas spent most of his life in East Texas, he supposedly ventured to the Columbian Exposition in Chicago in 1893 and the World's Fair in St. Louis in 1904. All of his late-'20s recordings were made in Chicago.

Because Thomas was old enough to recall the years in the late 1800s when the earliest forms of the blues were taking shape, his recorded material is especially important to musicologists eager to trace the blues back to its conception.

Essential Listening:
Texas Worried Blues/Yazoo (1080/81)

◄ THOMAS, HERSAL

(born c. 1910, Houston, Tex.; died July 3, 1926, Detroit, Mich.)

Blues pianist Hersal Thomas was the younger brother of pianist-composer-publisher GEORGE THOMAS and classic blues singer SIPPIE WALLACE. Although he was just sixteen when he died, Thomas had already become one of Chicago's most popular blues pianists and had a considerable influence on more prominent boogie-woogie pianists like ALBERT AMMONS and Meade "Lux" Lewis.

Thomas was born in Houston and was inspired to learn to play the piano by older brother George, whose skills he shortly surpassed. By the time he was twelve Hersal was playing house parties and socials. Hersal backed up sister Sippie Wallace in New Orleans clubs until the two of them moved to Chicago in 1923 to live and work with George. In the three years that Hersal was in Chicago, he was a much-in-demand session musician and house-rent party performer.

In addition to recording with Wallace and his niece, Hociel Thomas (George's daughter), and working alongside jazz greats LOUIS ARMSTRONG and King Oliver, Hersal also recorded on his own. His two trademark tunes, "Suitcase Blues" and

"Hersal Blues," were recorded in 1925. In 1926, while working with Sippie Wallace in Detroit, Thomas died of food poisoning.

Essential Listening:
The Piano Blues, Vol. 4: The Thomas Family/Magpie (PY 4404)

◄ THOMAS, IRMA

(born February 18, 1941, Ponchatoula, La.)

A New Orleans rhythm & blues singer with a gruff, bluesy voice, Irma Thomas recorded a number of memorable singles in the early 1960s. The closest Thomas came to having a major hit was in 1964 with the song "Wish Someone Would Care." The tune, released on the Imperial label, made it to number 17 on the R&B charts.

Thomas was born in rural Louisiana and moved to New Orleans when she was a youth. She sang in church but after being discovered by bandleader TOMMY RIDGLEY began a career as a rhythm & blues singer in New Orleans clubs. Ridgley helped Thomas secure a recording contract with Ron Records in 1959; her first single, "Don't Mess with My Man," made it to number 22 on the charts. Thomas jumped to the Minit label, where she worked with ALLEN TOUSSAINT, then moved to Imperial and finally to Chess, with diminishing results.

Though Thomas was a New Orleans and chitlin' circuit favorite, national success eluded her. A move to California in the late '60s was fruitless. She returned to New Orleans in 1974 where she recorded for a number of labels, including Fungus and Maison de Soul. In the 1980s Thomas recorded a batch of albums for Rounder Records that proved her soulful, blues-based vocal style remained strong and convincing. She has also become a regular performer at the New Orleans Jazz & Heritage Festival. Thomas continues to perform.

Essential Listening:
Time Is on My Side/Kent (010)
The New Rules/Rounder (2046)
The Way I Feel/Rounder (2058)
Simply the Best: Live!/Rounder (2110)

◄ THOMAS, RAMBLIN'

(born Willard Thomas, c. 1902, Louisiana or Texas; died c. 1930s, Memphis, Tenn.)

Ramblin' Thomas was an early Texas guitarist and singer who recorded some eighteen sides for Paramount and Victor from 1928 to 1932. Self-taught on the guitar, Thomas was reportedly influenced by BLIND LEMON JEFFERSON, though it's difficult to tell from his recordings, some of which contain intriguing slide-guitar work. Thomas and his contemporaries—DENNIS "LITTLE HAT" JONES, OSCAR "BUDDY" WOODS, KING SOLOMON HILL, and J.T. "FUNNY PAPA" SMITH— provide a good indication of early Southwest (principally Texas) blues styles.

Very little is known about Thomas, other than that he scraped together a living by playing street corners in Shreveport and Dallas and working jukes as far north as Oklahoma.

Sometime after making his recordings, Thomas went to Memphis, where he is thought to have died in the 1930s. Ramblin' Thomas's brother, Jesse "Baby-face" Thomas, was also a blues guitarist, based mostly out of Oklahoma City and Shreveport, Louisiana, in the 1920s and 1930s.

Essential Listening:
Ramblin' Thomas/Matchbox (215)

◄ THOMAS, RUFUS

(born March 26, 1917, Cayce, Miss.)

Singer Rufus Thomas, a longtime member of the Memphis blues and R&B scenes, was the first Sun Records artist to have a national hit. Thomas scored with "Bear Cat" in 1953, which made it to number 3 on the R&B charts that year. The song was a response to the BIG MAMA THORNTON hit "Hound Dog." In the '60s and early '70s Thomas registered other hits for the Stax label, though the records were more soul than blues.

Thomas began his career as part of a comedy team with one of his high school teachers, Nat Williams. Their success encouraged Thomas to go on the road with tent shows, including the famous Rabbit Foot Minstrels, before returning to Memphis to work at the Palace Theater as an emcee and all-around entertainer.

Thomas's first recording session was for the Star Talent label in 1950. A year later he made some recordings for SAM PHILLIPS, who leased them to Chess. In 1953 Thomas signed with Phillips's Sun Records and recorded "Bear Cat." That same year he had a second hit, "Tiger Man (King of the Jungle)." During this time Thomas also began a long relationship with Memphis radio station WDIA, where he often worked as a disc jockey.

After a brief stay with Meteor Records in 1956, Thomas and his daughter Carla began recording for the Memphis-based Satellite label, which later changed its name to Stax. The two recorded "Cause I Love You," which became Satellite's first hit.

Rufus Thomas enjoyed considerable success with Stax in the early '60s when two of his records, "The Dog" and "Walking the Dog," were big hits, the latter crossing over into pop territory and going as high as number 10 on the charts. Buoyed by high record sales and increased exposure, Thomas toured with R&B and soul package shows in the U.S. and Europe throughout the decade.

In the early '70s Thomas had yet another round of recording success. One of the early explorers of Southern funk, Thomas recorded "Do the Funky Chicken," "(Do the) Push and Pull," and "The Breakdown" for Stax. All three records made it into the R&B top 5, with "Push and Pull" giving Thomas his first number 1 hit. Thomas continued with animal themes; in the early '70s he recorded "Do the Funky Penguin" and "The Funky Bird."

In 1972 Thomas performed at the Wattstax soul festival at the Los Angeles Coliseum. He continued to tour regularly, usually appearing onstage wearing hot pants, boots, and a cape. By the end of the decade, too old to be taken seriously as a disco act, Thomas reverted to rhythm & blues. He also continued to work as a disc jockey. In the '80s, he signed a recording contract with King Snake Records and cut the album *That Woman Is Poison!*, later rereleased by Alligator Records. Thomas continues to perform.

Essential Listening:
Blue Flames: A Sun Blues Collection/Rhino (Sun) (R2-70962)
The Complete Stax/Volt Singles: 1959–1968/Atlantic (7 82218-2)
That Woman Is Poison!/Alligator (AL 4769)

◄ THOMAS, SON

(born James Thomas, October 14, 1926, Eden, Miss.; died June 26, 1993, Greenville, Miss.)

Son Thomas was a little-known Delta blues guitarist and singer before being discovered in 1967 by blues researcher William Ferris, who wrote extensively about him in his book *Blues from the Delta*. Thomas later recorded, toured abroad, and became something of a Delta blues torchbearer. He was also a sculptor who used clay from the Mississippi hills and plaster of Paris to create his pieces. Some of Thomas's sculptures have been exhibited at Yale University and in Washington, D.C.

A lifelong resident of the Delta, Thomas learned to play blues guitar by listening to the radio. Once he was good enough to play in public, he'd accompany his Uncle Joe Cooper, a bluesman, at house parties and fish fries. By the time Ferris ran into him, Thomas was playing local jukes around his Leland, Mississippi, home. Shortly after meeting Ferris, Thomas made his first recordings and played the Memphis Blues Festival. In 1970 a documentary, *Delta Blues Singer: James "Sonny Ford" Thomas*, was made about his life and work. He also appeared in other documentaries, including *Give My Poor Heart Ease: Mississippi Delta Bluesmen* and *Mississippi Delta Blues*.

Thomas first toured Europe in 1981; he went back a half-dozen times more in the '80s and recorded the album *Good Morning School Girl* for the French Black and Blue label. A brain tumor operation and the resulting recuperation curtailed his overseas touring and recording in the early 1990s, though Thomas performed at the 1991 Delta Blues Festival in Greenville, Mississippi. He died of a heart attack in 1993.

Essential Listening:
Highway 61 Blues/Southern Culture (1701)
Son Down on the Delta/Flying High (6506)
Good Morning School Girl/Black and Blue (33.744)

◄ THOMAS, TABBY

(born Ernest Thomas, January 5, 1929, Baton Rouge, La.)

Tabby Thomas is as much a blues entrepreneur as a blues singer-guitarist-pianist. Though he was marginally successful as a recording artist in the 1950s and early 1960s—his biggest hit came in 1962 with "Voodoo Party" on the

Excello label—Thomas moved into the recording business and then the club business later in his career. In 1970 he began his own Baton Rouge–based record label, Blue Beat, followed by his own Baton Rouge blues club, Tabby's Blues Box and Heritage Hall, which, by the mid-1980s, had become the city's premier blues venue. Thomas has also maintained his career as a recording artist; in 1980 he recorded *25 Years with the Blues* for the Blues Unlimited label, followed by *Rocking with the Blues* on his own Blue Beat label, and *Blues Train* and *King of the Swamp Blues* on the Maison de Soul label.

Born in Baton Rouge, Thomas began his blues career in San Francisco after a stint in the army. A first-place showing in a talent contest there led him to record "Midnight Is Calling" for Hollywood Records. Eventually Thomas returned to Baton Rouge, where he formed Tabby Thomas and the Mellow, Mellow Men and began playing local clubs. In 1953 the outfit recorded two sides for the Jackson, Mississippi–based Delta label: "Thinking Blues" and "Church Members Ball." Other singles followed on the Feature, Zynn, Rocko, and Excello labels.

Thomas's career faded, however, in the mid-'60s, and he actually left the blues for a few years. He returned to the scene when he started Blue Beat. Since then, Thomas has been one of the main movers of the Baton Rouge blues scene. He continues to record and perform. Blues-rock guitarist-singer CHRIS THOMAS is his son.

Essential Listening:
25 Years with the Blues/Blues Unlimited (5007)
Rockin' with the Blues/Maison de Soul (1010)
Blues Train/Maison de Soul (1016)
King of the Swamp Blues/Maison de Soul (1026)

◄ THOMPSON, RON
(born July 5, 1953, Oakland, Calif.)

Guitarist and singer Ron Thompson was a member of JOHN LEE HOOKER's Coast-to-Coast Blues Band from 1975 to 1978 before forming his own group, the Resistors, which became one of northern California's most popular blues club bands. Thompson was born in Oakland. He began playing guitar at age eleven, and by the time he was in his late teens he was performing with Little Joe Blue and developing a slide guitar style that was heavily influenced by ELMORE JAMES.

Thompson worked Bay Area clubs as a solo and backing artist until he joined Hooker's band. In 1980 he started the Resistors and signed a recording contract with Takoma Records a year later. In 1983 he released his debut album, *Treat Her Like Gold*. Thompson was also performing with JIMMY MCCRACKLIN, BIG MAMA THORNTON, LOWELL FULSON, and ETTA JAMES. In 1987 Thompson released his second album, *Resister Twister*, on the Blind Pig label, followed by *Just Like a Devil*, a live recording for Winner Records that was nominated for a Bammie (Bay Area Music Award) in the category of best blues album. Thompson continues to record and perform.

Essential Listening:
Resister Twister/Blind Pig (BP 2487)
Just Like a Devil/Winner (D 444)

◄ THORNTON, BIG MAMA

(born Willie Mae Thornton, December 11, 1926, Montgomery, Ala.; died July 25, 1984, Los Angeles, Calif.)

Outside the blues community, Willie Mae "Big Mama" Thornton is best re-membered as the first artist to record "Hound Dog," the song Elvis Presley made into a million-selling rock & roll hit in 1956. Yet Thornton's contribution to blues and rhythm & blues extends well beyond her trademark tune. A rugged blues belter, Thornton was a direct descendant of such classic blues singers as MA RAINEY, BESSIE SMITH, and especially MEMPHIS MINNIE, the '30s blues woman whose style Thornton's most strongly resembled. Thornton is also the link be-tween these artists and the '60s blues-rock queen JANIS JOPLIN. Joplin recorded Thornton's classic "Ball n' Chain" and turned it into one of her most memorable songs.

Willie Mae Thornton was raised in a religious setting in Montgomery, Ala-bama; her father was a minister, and her mother was a church singer. Thornton's musical aspirations led her to leave home in 1941 when she was just fourteen and join the Georgia-based Hot Harlem Revue. Her seven-year tenure with the Revue gave her valuable singing and stage experience and enabled her to tour the South. In 1948 she settled in Houston, Texas, where she hoped to further her career as a singer. Thornton was also a self-taught drummer and harmonica player and frequently played both instruments onstage.

Thornton began her recording career in Houston, signing a contract with DON ROBEY and his Peacock label in 1951. While working with another Peacock artist, West Coast rhythm & blues bandleader JOHNNY OTIS, she recorded "Hound Dog," a song composers Jerry Leiber and Mike Stoller had given to her in Los Angeles. "Hound Dog" was released by Peacock in 1953 and soared to the number 1 slot on the R&B charts. Although Thornton became a star, she saw little of "Hound Dog's" profits. She continued to record for Peacock until 1957 and performed with R&B package tours that included JUNIOR PARKER and Little ESTHER PHILLIPS.

Despite her recording and touring success, Thornton's career began to fade in the late '50s and early '60s. To resuscitate it, she left Houston and relocated in the San Francisco Bay area, where she mostly played local blues clubs. In 1965 she performed with the American Folk Blues Festival package in Europe. While in England that year she recorded *Big Mama Thornton in Europe* and followed it up the next year in San Francisco with *Big Mama Thornton with the Chicago Blues Band*. Both albums came out on the Arhoolie label.

Thornton continued to record for Vanguard, Mercury, and other small labels in the '70s and to work the blues festival circuit until her death in 1984, the same year she was inducted into the Blues Foundation's Hall of Fame.

Essential Listening:
Ball n' Chain/Arhoolie (1039)
Big Mama Thornton with the Chicago Blues Band/Arhoolie (1032)
The Original Hound Dog/Ace (940)
Hound Dog: The Duke-Peacock Recordings/MCA-Duke-Peacock (MCAD 10668)

◄ THOROGOOD, GEORGE
(born, Wilmington, Del.)

Guitarist and singer George Thorogood came onto the scene in the late '70s with his roughly chiseled version of the Hank Williams proto-rock classic "Move It On Over." But it was Thorogood's raucous interpretation of the blues that established him in the early '80s—along with JOHNNY WINTER and STEVIE RAY VAUGHAN—as one of the torchbearers of contemporary blues-rock.

Thorogood was born and raised in Delaware, where he split his time between baseball and music. After hearing JOHN HAMMOND, JR., in concert in 1970, Thorogood moved to California to pursue a career as a blues guitarist. He found work opening shows for BONNIE RAITT and West Coast bluesmen but failed to land a recording contract. He returned to Delaware in 1973 and formed his group, the Delaware Destroyers. With a guitar sound that was firmly grounded in the styles of CHUCK BERRY and ELMORE JAMES, Thorogood played East Coast bars and developed a rabid following. His first record deal was with Rounder Records in 1978; incessant touring broadened his reputation as a fiery blues-rock performer. In 1980 Thorogood and his band went on their famous 50/50 Tour, playing all 50 states on 50 consecutive nights. They followed this feat with a series of acclaimed shows opening for the ROLLING STONES the following year. In 1985 Thorogood performed with ALBERT COLLINS at Live Aid. By the late '80s, Thorogood was able to fill midsized arenas as a headlining act. Thorogood continues to record and perform.

Essential Listening:
George Thorogood & the Destroyers/Rounder (3013)
Move It On Over/Rounder (3024)
More/Rounder (3045)
The Baddest of George Thorogood and the Destroyers/EMI (7 977182)

◄ TOUSSAINT, ALLEN
(born January 14, 1938, New Orleans, La.)

If DAVE BARTHOLOMEW was the architect of the New Orleans rhythm & blues sound in the 1950s, then fellow pianist-composer-singer-arranger-producer Allen Toussaint was the chief creator of the city's '60s sound. As Toussaint had apprenticed under Bartholomew, their dominance of New Orleans R&B, on into the 1970s, allowed for a smooth progression of ideas and sounds.

Born and raised in New Orleans, Toussaint was a member of the Flamingos before embarking on a career as a studio musician and arranger. Under Bartholomew's guidance, Toussaint worked with FATS DOMINO and other New Orleans

R&B artists before recording his debut solo album in 1958. Using the pseudonym Tousan, Toussaint cut *The Wild Sounds of New Orleans by Tousan* for the RCA label. Though the work gave a solid account of piano-fueled New Orleans R&B, Toussaint was unable to break nationally as a recording artist. In 1960 he began working for the Minit label and produced records by ERNIE K-DOE, CHRIS KENNER, LEE DORSEY, and Jessie Hill. From 1963 to 1965 Toussaint served time in the army; after his discharge he returned to record production and songwriting. Artists who have recorded Toussaint compositions include the ROLLING STONES, the YARDBIRDS, BONNIE RAITT, the Band, Little Feat, and Al Hirt. Hirt's version of Toussaint's "Java" made it to number 4 on the pop charts in 1964.

In the '70s and '80s Toussaint worked with such New Orleans artists as DR. JOHN, the Meters, and the Neville Brothers, often recording in his Sea Saint studio, which opened in 1972. Toussaint is still active in the New Orleans recording scene.

Essential Listening:
The Wild Sounds of New Orleans/Edsel (ED 275)

◀ TOWNSEND, HENRY

(born October 27, 1909, Shelby, Miss.)

Pianist and guitar player Henry Townsend was the central figure in the St. Louis blues scene in the 1920s and 1930s. Along with LONNIE JOHNSON, ROOSEVELT SYKES, PEETIE WHEATSTRAW, WALTER DAVIS, and BIG JOE WILLIAMS, Townsend helped make the city a blues center in the years before World War II.

Townsend came to St. Louis in the late teens. Playing guitar in open tunings, he recorded for Columbia and Paramount in 1929 and 1931, respectively. Townsend also learned to play piano by listening to ROOSEVELT SYKES; eventually he became proficient enough at the piano to perform with fellow blues pianists HENRY BROWN and Walter Davis, working juke joints and small clubs in and around St. Louis. Townsend also worked with Henry Spaulding and recorded for the Bluebird label in the late '30s. He became an in-demand session musician, recording with many top bluesmen of the time. Townsend continued to work with Walter Davis in St. Louis clubs through the 1940s and early '50s. But his recording career had dried up.

Townsend did some recording in 1960, but it wasn't until the end of the decade that he was able to breathe new life into his career. Recording for the Adelphi label, performing at folk and blues festivals, and playing clubs outside of St. Louis enabled him to launch something of a comeback. In 1979 he recorded *Mule*, a well-received album for Nighthawk that featured some of his best piano playing. He recorded for Wolf and Swingmaster in the early '80s and came to be regarded as a dean of St. Louis bluesmen. In 1984 he was the subject of a documentary, *That's The Way I Do It*, which aired on public television. Townsend still performs on occasion.

Essential Listening:
Henry Townsend and Henry Spaulding/Wolf (117)
Mule/Nighthawk (201)
St. Louis Blues, 1929–37/Wolf (WSE 110)

◄ TRI-SAX-UAL SOUL CHAMPS

*Members: Sil Austin (tenor saxophone) (born September 17, 1929); Grady
Jackson (alto saxophone); Mark Kazanoff (alto, tenor, baritone saxophones)*

A saxophone-centered studio band created by Black Top Records executive
Hammond Scott in 1989, the Tri-Sax-ual Soul Champs' *Go Girl!* album, recorded
in 1990 for Black Top, helped refocus attention on the saxophone as an integral
instrument in the development of urban blues, rhythm & blues, and rock & roll.

Sil Austin had worked with the Roy Eldridge Big Band, the Cootie Williams
Orchestra, and the TINY BRADSHAW Orchestra before forming his own group in
the mid-'50s and recording for Jubilee and Mercury. His 1956 R&B tune "Slow
Walk" was his biggest hit. As leader of the early-'50s house band at the Royal
Peacock, a popular blues and R&B nightclub in Atlanta, Grady Jackson backed
dozens of noted artists, including NAPPY BROWN, CLARENCE "GATEMOUTH"
BROWN, and ELMORE JAMES. When Jackson moved to Chicago in 1954 he played
with James, LITTLE WALTER, and BIG JOE TURNER before returning to Atlanta and
the Royal Peacock.

Mark Kazanoff is a noted Black Top session musician and a member of the
house band at Antone's, the famous Austin, Texas, blues club. Kazanoff has
backed EARL KING, Nappy Brown, RONNIE EARL, ANSON FUNDERBURGH, and numerous other contemporary blues artists.

Essential Listening:
Go Girl!/Black Top (BT 1059)

◄ TUCKER, BESSIE

(born, date and place unknown; died, date and place unknown)

Bessie Tucker was an East Texas classic blues singer whose primitive country
singing style was steeped in the folk and field holler vocal traditions. Though
petite, Tucker's voice was big and rough-hewn. Unfortunately, almost nothing is
known of her life, and she recorded little. A session in Memphis in 1928 for the
Victor label resulted in her signature song, "Penitentiary"—and according to
some reports Tucker might well have spent time in one.

Tucker disappeared from the recording scene in the 1930s. Reportedly she
remained in Texas.

Essential Listening:
Bessie Tucker and Ida May Mack: The Texas Moaners/Magpie (1815)

◄ TUCKER, LUTHER

(born January 20, 1936, Memphis, Tenn.; died June 18, 1993, San Francisco, Calif.)

Blues guitarist Luther Tucker was a noted session and side player in Chicago in the 1950s and 1960s. He was born in Memphis and moved to Chicago with his family at the end of World War II. Tucker first came onto the scene when he replaced DAVID MYERS in LITTLE WALTER's band, the Jukes, in 1955. He remained with Little Walter through most of the '50s, while his clipped, expressive guitar style later enabled him to secure additional work with MUDDY WATERS, SUNNY-LAND SLIM, SONNY BOY WILLIAMSON (Rice Miller), and HOWLIN' WOLF..

Tucker also logged time as a sideman with guitarist OTIS RUSH and harmonica player JAMES COTTON in the 1960s, recording with both artists. As work in Chicago blues clubs grew thin in the mid-'60s, Tucker relocated to the San Francisco area, where he played with JOHN LEE HOOKER, CHARLIE MUSSELWHITE, and other Bay Area blues artists. In the mid-'70s Tucker formed his own band, the Yellow Brick Road Club, and played San Francisco and Oakland blues clubs. Tucker remained a member of the Bay Area blues scene into the early '90s, playing clubs and festivals and occasionally recording as a sideman. He also made frequent trips to Austin, Texas, where he worked the city's blues clubs and did occasional studio work for the Antone's label. Tucker died of a heart attack in 1993.

◄ TURNER, BIG JOE

(born May 18, 1911, Kansas City, Mo.; died November 24, 1985, Inglewood, Calif.)

Big Joe Turner was one of the best blues shouters and a critical link between rhythm & blues and rock & roll. With a big, husky voice that he projected with amazing power and clarity, and a blues sensibility with which he sank into most every song he sang, Turner was a major figure in black music from the late 1930s until his death in 1985. He sang with some of the greatest bandleaders of the swing and R&B eras and made successful transitions from boogie-woogie to rhythm & blues to early rock & roll with remarkable ease.

Turner was born in Kansas City and learned to sing in church choirs and on street corners. In the 1930s, after the death of his father, Turner worked as a bartender and singer in Kansas City nightspots, often with pianist PETE JOHNSON. Turner also sang with Kansas City big bands led by BENNY MOTEN, Andy Kirk, and COUNT BASIE whenever they came home to play. Yet it was with boogie-woogie pianist Johnson that Turner was attracting the most attention. In 1938, talent scout John Hammond visited Kansas City looking for artists to perform at his Sprirituals to Swing concert later that year. He invited Turner and Johnson to come to New York. The duo appeared on Benny Goodman's Camel Caravan radio show and then performed on the Spirituals to Swing bill at Carnegie Hall. With Turner belting out the classic tune ''Roll 'Em Pete'' and Johnson hammering out its boogie-woogie rhythm, the two helped kick off a boogie-woogie craze that swept the country in the late '30s and early '40s.

Rather than return to Kansas City, Turner and Johnson set up residency at the Cafe Society, one of New York's premier jazz clubs, and, along with pianists MEADE "LUX" LEWIS and ALBERT AMMONS, became boogie-woogie kings. Turner had begun his recording career in 1938 when he cut sides for the Vocalion label. By the early '40s he was recording extensively for Decca, Okeh, and Vocalion. Turner also toured with Duke Ellington's Jump for Joy revue, worked with pianists Willie "The Lion" Smith and Art Tatum, and toured with Johnson and Ammons.

When interest in boogie-woogie began to wane, Turner shifted into rhythm & blues, working once again with Basie, as well as with R&B guitarists such as LOWELL FULSON and PEE WEE CRAYTON. In 1951 Turner signed a recording contract with Atlantic Records and cut a string of R&B classics that would lead the way straight into rock & roll. His most famous hit, "Shake, Rattle, and Roll," released in 1954, made it to number 1 and was covered shortly thereafter by Bill Haley and the Comets. But before "Shake" came the million-selling "Chains of Love," which reached the number 2 slot on the R&B charts and number 30 on the pop side, plus "Chill Is On," "Sweet Sixteen," "Don't You Cry," "TV Mama," and the number 1 smash, "Honey Hush." Turner's chart success continued after "Shake" with "Well All Right," "Flip Flop and Fly," "Hide and Seek," "The Chicken and the Hawk," "Morning, Noon, and Night," "Corrina Corrina," and "Lipstick Powder and Paint," adding up to a near domination of the R&B charts for Turner from 1951 to 1956.

Turner also was popular with young white audiences, who saw him as a father figure of rock & roll. He appeared in the movie *Shake, Rattle, and Rock* in 1957 and toured with Alan Freed's rock & roll package shows. Toward the end of the decade the rock & roll frenzy began to subside—Elvis Presley was drafted, LITTLE RICHARD turned to religion, Buddy Holly died in a plane crash, Jerry Lee Lewis married his cousin, severely damaging his career—and Turner went back to R&B. He resumed his partnership with Pete Johnson and toured Europe. He also performed at the Newport and Monterey Jazz Festivals, reestablishing himself with an audience that remembered him from before he became a rock & roller.

Turner spent the '60s performing regularly, both in the U.S. and abroad, and recording on occasion. In 1974, his connection to Kansas City was reaffirmed in the documentary *The Last of the Blue Devils*, which also featured Count Basie and JAY MCSHANN. Turner continued to record and perform into the '80s, and was inducted into the Blues Hall of Fame in 1983 and the Rock & Roll Hall of Fame in 1987. He suffered a fatal heart attack in 1985.

Essential Listening:
Greatest Hits/Atlantic (81752)
The Rhythm & Blues Years/Atlantic (781752-2)
Jumpin' the Blues/Arhoolie (2004)
The Boss of the Blues/Atlantic (8812)
I've Been to Kansas City, Vol. 1/MCA (42351)
Singing the Blues/Mobile Fidelity (MFCD 780)
Tell Me Pretty Baby/Arhoolie (333)
Texas Style/Evidence (ECD 26013-2)

◄ TURNER, IKE

(born November 5, 1931, Clarksdale, Miss.)

Though in recent years Ike Turner has been better known as the ex-husband of pop/R&B singer Tina Turner, he played a vital role in the early-'50s Memphis blues scene. As a bandleader, session musician, and talent scout, Turner worked with a number of great artists, including HOWLIN' WOLF, B.B. KING, JUNIOR PARKER, and JOHNNY ACE and played on "Rocket 88," the JACKIE BRENSTON single that many rock historians consider to be the first rock & roll record.

Turner was born and raised in Clarksdale, a center for Mississippi Delta blues. By the time he was in high school, he could play guitar and piano, and he performed with SONNY BOY WILLIAMSON (Rice Miller) and ROBERT NIGHTHAWK whenever they came to town. Turner formed the Kings of Rhythm while still in school. In 1951 he and the band, with his younger cousin, Jackie Brenston, went to Memphis and recorded "Rocket 88" for SAM PHILLIPS, who leased it to Chess. The song shot to number 1 on the R&B charts, making it one of the most successful records of the year.

Ambitious and eager to be a kingpin on the Memphis blues scene, Turner began working as a talent scout, sending acts to Sun, Chess, and RPM/Modern, before going to work full-time for the latter label. Turner also produced and played on many of the recording sessions of the acts he found, and continued working with the Dukes of Rhythm.

In 1954 Turner relocated to St. Louis where his band had become a top attraction. Two years later he met singer Annie Mae Bullock, whom he hired to sing with the Dukes of Rhythm. In 1958, Turner married Bullock, and she changed her name to Tina Turner. With Tina fronting the band, Turner altered the stage show to include sexy female back-up singers, the Ikettes, and developed a soul-pumping R&B sound that resulted in a number of early-'60s hits on the Sue label, including "A Fool in Love" (number 2 on the R&B charts in 1960) and "It's Gonna Work Out Fine" (number 2 in 1961). Turner also changed the name of the group to the Ike & Tina Turner Revue.

For the remainder of the decade and into the early '70s, the Ike & Tina Turner Revue was a major draw on the chitlin' circuit and up North, where they performed in black nightclubs. In 1966, they recorded with rock producer Phil Spector. The single "River Deep, Mountain High" contained Spector's "wall of sound" but bombed in the U.S. (In Europe it was greeted with more enthusiasm.) In 1969 the Turner Revue opened shows for the ROLLING STONES and in 1971 had a major pop hit with a riveting rendition of Creedence Clearwater Revival's "Proud Mary."

In 1974 the Ike & Tina Turner Revue came apart, and two years later the couple divorced. Ike's career and life began a downward spiral that led to drugs and prison, while Tina became one of the biggest female pop stars of the mid-'80s.

Ike Turner was inducted into the Rock & Roll Hall of Fame in 1991.

Essential Listening:
Sun: The Roots of Rock, Vol. 3 (The Delta Rhythm Kings)/Charly (CR 30103)
Ike Turner 1958/Paula (PCD 16)

◄ TURNER, TROY

(born August 25, Baton Rouge, La.)

Troy Turner is a blues-rock guitarist and singer whose biggest influences are JIMI HENDRIX and STEVIE RAY VAUGHAN. Born and raised in Baton Rouge, Louisiana, Turner's first musical experiences were in gospel. By the time he started high school, Turner had discovered both Hendrix and the blues. Inspired in part by bluesman KENNY NEAL and his father, RAFUL NEAL, both prominent members of the Baton Rouge blues scene, Turner formed a band, Third Gear, with Kenny Neal's younger brother, Darnell, in the mid-'80s. When Darnell left Third Gear to join his brother's group, Turner changed the name of his band to Troy Turner and Third Gear. The band played the Baton Rouge Blues Festival in 1988 and became regulars on Louisiana's swamp blues circuit. Turner was eventually offered a recording contract by King Snake Records and cut his debut album, *Teenage Blues in Baton Rouge*, in 1990.

Turner's second album, *Handful of Aces*, was recorded for the Ichiban label in 1992. On it, Turner further exhibited his fascination for Hendrix, filling many of the album's songs with wailing guitar solos. Turner continues to perform and record.

Essential Listening:
Teenage Blues in Baton Rouge/King Snake (KIN 4038)
Handful of Aces/Ichiban (ICH 9013)

V.

◄ VAN RONK, DAVE
(born June 30, 1936, Brooklyn, N.Y.)

A scraping, raspy-voiced singer and a guitarist heavily influenced by the southeastern blues school, Dave Van Ronk was a popular folk-blues artist in the early and mid-1960s and a leader of the Greenwich Village scene that included Bob Dylan, Phil Ochs, and Odetta. Van Ronk's original interests were in traditional jazz, country blues, and jug band music. He and blues historian Sam Charters formed the Ragtime Jug Stompers in 1963. But Van Ronk is best known for combining the earthy, narrative qualities of folk with down-home blues; his loud, domineering voice was often balanced by the delicacy of his Piedmont fingerpicking guitar style.

Always a traditionalist, Van Ronk eschewed the trappings of stardom by sticking to a repertoire and a performing style that serious folk and blues fans respected, but that had little crossover appeal. Unlike Dylan, who by the mid-'60s was discovered by rock fans and quickly turned into a major star, Van Ronk continued to work the coffeehouse and folk club circuit and the various folk festivals that had sprouted in the '60s. Along the way he recorded for a number of labels, including Folkways, Verve, Philo, and Fantasy. Van Ronk's bawdy, humorous songs and heartfelt commitment to roots music has enabled him to continue performing and occasionally recording.

Essential Listening:

The Folkways Years 1959–1961/Smithsonian Folkways (CD SF 40041)
Sunday Street/Philo (1036)
Somebody Else, Not Me/Philo (1065)

◄ VAUGHAN, JIMMIE
(born March 20, 1951, Dallas, Tex.)

Jimmie Vaughan, the older brother of STEVIE RAY VAUGHAN, was a key figure in the development of the Austin blues scene in the early '70s and a founder of the blues-based R&B band the FABULOUS THUNDERBIRDS. Known for his tasty guitar style, which embodies the dynamics and flair of FREDDIE KING and the deep blue tonal qualities of B.B. KING, Vaughan remains one of contemporary blues' more important stylists.

Vaughan was born and raised in Dallas. He spent much of his youth listening to blues on the radio and developing his talents on the guitar. After he formed a series of garage bands that failed to fit into the Dallas scene, Vaughan moved to Austin at age nineteen, where he apprenticed in obscure bar bands before forming the Storm in 1972. The Storm backed up visiting blues acts, including Freddie King, which enabled Vaughan to perfect his guitar by playing with many of his earliest influences.

Vaughan met Kim Wilson, a harmonica player from Minneapolis, in 1974. After Wilson had relocated to Austin, the two musicians, along with Keith Furguson on bass and Mike Buck on drums, formed the Fabulous Thunderbirds in 1975. After four years of playing small clubs and bars, the group signed a recording contract with Takoma Records and released its self-titled debut album. The Thunderbirds recorded four albums before *Tuff Enuff*, their fifth, broke them out nationally in 1986. The album featured Vaughan's stirring guitar work and helped him step out of the shadow of his brother, Stevie Ray, who had helped bring on the blues revival of the '80s with his invigorating blues-rock guitar work and such widely hailed albums as *Texas Flood* and *Couldn't Stand the Weather*.

Jimmie Vaughan remained with the Thunderbirds until 1989 when he left to pursue a solo career and make an album with Stevie Ray. In 1990 the two guitarists, going by the name the Vaughan Brothers, cut the album *Family Style* for Epic Records and planned to tour together. But just a few weeks before the album's release, Stevie Ray Vaughan was killed in a helicopter crash, less than a hour after sharing a stage with Jimmie. The tragic death of his brother devastated Jimmie Vaughan, forcing him to drop out of the recording and performing scenes.

Essential Listening:
Tuff Enuff/CBS (BFZ 40304)
The Fabulous Thunderbirds/Chrysalis (PV 41250)
The Essential Fabulous Thunderbirds/Chrysalis (F2-21851)
Family Style/Epic (ZK 46625)

◄ VAUGHAN, STEVIE RAY

(born October 3, 1954, Dallas, Tex.; died August 27, 1990, East Troy, Wis.)

No artist did more to energize the 1980s blues revival than Stevie Ray Vaughan. He was a guitar player whose style echoed the dazzling technique of JIMI HENDRIX as much as the virtuosity of blues greats from the Texas and Chicago schools. Vaughan ignited new interest in the blues at a time when longtime fans of the music were relying on old blues legends for their fix, and rock audiences had all but annulled the blues-rock marriage of the late '60s.

Vaughan cultivated a new passion for the blues mostly through his riveting live performances, which bristled with guitar power and blues excitement. By playing loud and paying his respects to Hendrix, Vaughan attracted rock listeners to his concerts. But his essential repertoire was the blues. His highly charged, emotionally expressive guitar solos gave the blues a brand-new vitality and reinvented the music in thoroughly modern terms.

Vaughan was born and raised in the Oak Cliff section of Dallas; from the start his main inspiration was his older brother, JIMMIE, who introduced him to both the guitar and the blues. As a youth in Dallas, Stevie Ray played in blues-rock bands such as the Chantones and the Blackbirds. But when brother Jimmie, who later would become the guitar player in the Austin-based rhythm & blues group the FABULOUS THUNDERBIRDS, left home in his teens to pursue a career in music, Stevie Ray was inspired to do the same. He quit high school at the end of his junior year and moved to Austin, where he joined the Cobras in 1975. Two years later he formed the Triple Threat Revue with blues-rock singer LOU ANN BARTON. The group played blues and R&B in Austin bars and roadhouses. In 1978 Triple Threat became Double Trouble. (Vaughan named his new group after the OTIS RUSH song by the same name.) Eventually the band would consist of bass player Tommy Shannon, who in the late '60s had played with JOHNNY WINTER, and drummer Chris Layton. Vaughan assumed all the guitar and vocal chores. Except for the addition of keyboards player Reese Wynans in 1985, the lineup remained constant until Vaughan's death in 1990.

Double Trouble quickly established itself as one of Austin's best bar bands. When manager Chesley Milliken gave friend Mick Jagger a videotape of one of Double Trouble's live performances, the ROLLING STONES singer was so impressed that he hired the band to play a private party in New York in 1982. That same year producer Jerry Wexler saw Double Trouble perform in Austin and was so moved by Vaughan's scintillating guitar work that he arranged for Double Trouble to play the 1982 Montreux Jazz Festival in Switzerland, reputedly marking the first time an unrecorded group or artist had played the prestigious fest. Rock singer David Bowie and folk-rock artist Jackson Browne were both in the Montreux audience the night Double Trouble performed. Equally impressed, Bowie hired Vaughan to play on his *Let's Dance* album, while Browne offered Vaughan and his band free recording time in his California studio. Shortly thereafter, legendary talent scout John Hammond, Sr., convinced Epic Records to sign Vaughan and Double Trouble to a recording contract. The band recorded its classic debut album, *Texas Flood*, in less than one week at Brown's Down Town studio in L.A. Critically acclaimed, the album showcased Vaughan's stunning guitar work and resurrected the blues at a time when the rest of pop music seemed infatuated with British-dominated techno dance-rock.

Texas Flood was nominated for two Grammys in 1984—best traditional blues recording and best rock instrumental (for the song "Rude Mood")—while the readers of *Guitar Player* magazine named *Texas Flood* blues album of the year and Vaughan best new talent and best electric blues player in 1983 and 1984. (Vaughan would also win the latter title in 1985, 1986, 1988, and 1989.)

Vaughan followed up *Texas Flood* with another acclaimed album, *Couldn't Stand the Weather*, which contained Vaughan's widely hailed interpretation of the Hendrix classic "Voodoo Chile (Slight Return)," in 1984, and *Soul to Soul*, an album on which Vaughan delved a bit into jazz and added the keyboards of Reese Wynans. During this time Vaughan was also pushing himself to the limit with drugs and alcohol; in 1986 he collapsed onstage in London. Vaughan then entered a rehabilitation clinic and kept a quiet profile until the release of *In Step* in 1989, his last official studio album, which included the song "Wall of Denial," a painful autobiographical account of his battle with drugs and alcohol.

Long overdue was a much-hoped-for album with brother Jimmie. In 1990, the Vaughan brothers recorded *Family Style*, a work that hinted of a new musical direction for Stevie Ray Vaughan and the possible partnership of the two musicians in future recording projects. Shortly before the release of *Family Style*, Vaughan performed with BUDDY GUY, ERIC CLAPTON, ROBERT CRAY, and brother Jimmie at an East Troy, Wisconsin, blues concert. Eager to get to Chicago, Vaughan hopped onto a helicopter immediately after the show. In dense fog, the copter crashed, killing everyone aboard. Vaughan was thirty-five years old. *Family Style* was released posthumously, as was *The Sky Is Crying*, a collection of previously unissued songs, and *In the Beginning*, a live recording from 1980.

Essential Listening:
Texas Flood/Epic (EK 38734)
Couldn't Stand the Weather/Epic (EK 39304)
Soul to Soul/Epic (EK 40036)
In Step/Epic (EK 45024)
The Vaughan Brothers/Family Style/Epic (EK 46225)
The Sky Is Crying/Epic (EK 47390)
In the Beginning/Epic (EK 53168)

◄ VAUGHN, JIMMY

(born March 20, 1925, Chicago, Ill.; died March 9, 1991, St. Louis, Mo.)

Rhythm & blues pianist and singer Jimmy Vaughn worked as a sideman and arranger with ALBERT KING and LITTLE MILTON in the 1950s and 1960s before moving to California and assuming the same jobs with BIG JOE TURNER, IKE TURNER, T-BONE WALKER, PHILLIP WALKER, and others in the 1960s and 1970s.

Vaughn was born in Chicago; when he was nine his family moved to Alton, Illinois. He learned to play piano and sing in the school chorus, and during his teens became interested in boogie-woogie piano styles, thanks, in part, to Tom "Barrelhouse Buck" McPharland, a popular local pianist who did some recording in the early 1930s. After a stint in the army during World War II, Vaughn began playing with local groups in St. Louis–area clubs. By the mid-'50s, Vaughn had joined blues guitarist Albert King's band as the piano player and arranger. In the early '60s Vaughn left King and began working with Little Milton before leaving the St. Louis area for the West Coast. Vaughn became greatly in demand as a musician, working with Ike and Tina Turner and other West Coast–based acts until the mid-1980s when he returned to Alton. In 1991 he recorded the album *Rockin' Eighty-Eights* with fellow St. Louis pianists JOHNNIE JOHNSON and CLAYTON LOVE for Modern Blues Recordings. Vaughn died of a stroke, shortly before the album's release.

Essential Listening:
Rockin' Eighty-Eights/Modern Blues Recordings (MBCD 1201)

◀ VAUGHN, MAURICE JOHN

(born Mary 10, 1952, Chicago, Ill.)

A Chicago blues guitarist, singer, and saxophone player, Maurice John Vaughn apprenticed with PHIL GUY and then A.C. REED before embarking on a solo career in 1984. Vaughn released his debut recording, *Generic Blues Album*, on his own Reecy label; Alligator reissued it in 1988.

Vaughn was born and raised in Chicago and spent his early years playing mostly saxophone in soul and rhythm & blues outfits such as the Chosen Few and the Gents of Soul. In the early '70s he taught himself how to play blues guitar. Vaughn then recorded and toured with Guy and performed with LUTHER ALLISON and SON SEALS before joining A.C. Reed's Sparkplugs. Vaughn played on Reed's *I'm in the Wrong Business* album for Alligator in 1984 and *I Got Money* for the French label Blue Phoenix. He also toured with Reed throughout much of the '80s. In 1987 Vaughn contributed a track to the Alligator compilation *The New Bluebloods: The Next Generation of Chicago Blues*, which led to Alligator's rerelease of the *Generic Blues Album* a year later. Vaughn remained active in Chicago's blues scene, though he didn't release a follow-up album until 1993 when Alligator issued *In the Shadow of the City*. Vaughn continues to perform.

Essential Listening:
Generic Blues Album/Alligator (ALCD 4763)
In the Shadow of the City/Alligator (ALCD 4813)

◀ VINSON, EDDIE "CLEANHEAD"

(born December 18, 1917, Houston, Tex.; died July 2, 1988, Los Angeles, Calif.)

A honking rhythm & blues alto saxophone player and a vocalist whose style was in the mold of the classic blues shouter, Eddie Vinson made his mark in the 1940s, first with Milt Larkin's band and then with the Cootie Williams Orchestra before embarking on a solo career. Nicknamed "Cleanhead" after a lye-laced straightener destroyed his hair, Vinson recorded extensively during his fifty-odd-year career and performed regularly in Europe and the U.S.

Vinson was born and raised in Houston. His parents, both pianists, introduced him to music at an early age. He began playing the saxophone in high school and joined Chester Boone's band, which included T-BONE WALKER on guitar, in 1935. A year later Vinson jumped to Milt Larkin's band and became part of one of the greatest saxophone sections in rhythm & blues. In addition to Vinson, the section included Arnett Cobb and Illinois Jacquet, both of whom went on to enjoy prestigious careers in R&B and jazz. Vinson stayed with Larkin until 1941. He then moved to New York and joined the Cootie Williams Orchestra, with which he remained through the mid-'40s, recording such classics as "Cherry Red" and touring with the big band. Vinson began his own band in 1945 and cut some of his best pieces, among them, "Kidney Stew" and "Cleanhead Blues."

After returning to Houston in 1954, Vinson worked the Southwest R&B circuit

and, for a brief period in 1957, played with the COUNT BASIE Band. In the early
'60s Vinson moved to Los Angeles and began working with the Johnny Otis
Revue. A 1970 appearance at the Monterey Jazz Festival with Otis spurred something of a comeback for Vinson. During the 1970s and early 1980s, Vinson
became a popular performer in Europe, where he also recorded regularly, specializing in an appealing jazz-blues hybrid style. Vinson also performed and made
records in the U.S. Recording for the Muse label, he cut an album with ROOMFUL
OF BLUES (*And a Roomful of Blues*) and made *Live at Sandy's*, a live recording
that featured the accompaniment of old friend Cobb and drummer Alan Dawson.
Vinson died in 1988.

Essential Listening:
Eddie "Cleanhead" Vinson/Delmark (631)
Back in Town/Charly (CD 50)
Mr. Cleanhead Steps Out/Saxophonograph (507)

◄ VINSON, MOSE

(born August 7, 1917, Holly Springs, Miss.)

An underrecorded and unheralded blues pianist whose retro style is rooted in
pre–World War II rag-flavored and boogie-woogie riffs, Mose Vinson has been
performing in Memphis clubs and churches since his arrival in the city in 1932.
Vinson learned how to play piano while growing up in the Mississippi Delta.
Most of his early musical experiences stemmed from the church, though by the
late 1920s he had moved into blues and jazz.

Vinson played house parties and juke joints in and around Memphis in the
1930s and 1940s. In the early '50s he did some session work for SAM PHILLIPS's
Memphis-based Sun label, playing on early sides cut by harmonica player JAMES
COTTON in 1954. Vinson spent the next thirty years or so performing only occasionally in Memphis clubs. In the early '80s he became associated with the
Center for Southern Folklore, which hired him to perform in schools and at special
cultural functions. Vinson continues to perform under the auspices of the Center.

Essential Listening:
Mystery Train (with Junior Parker, James Cotton, Pat Hare)/Rounder (CD SS 38)

◄ VINSON, WALTER

*(aka Walter Vincson) (born February 2, 1901, Bolton, Miss.; died April 22,
1975, Chicago, Ill.)*

A guitarist and singer, Walter Vinson was a member of the MISSISSIPPI SHEIKS
in the 1930s and a solo artist whose down-home style revealed much about early
Mississippi blues. As a youth, Vinson often performed with bluesmen such as
TOMMY JOHNSON, ISHMAN BRACEY, and CHARLIE MCCOY. Allegedly, Vinson was
an adopted son of the famed Chatmon family, whose band was one of the most
popular in Mississippi in the 1920s. Vinson and fiddle player Lonnie Chatmon
were the main members of the Sheiks in the early 1930s. Best known for their

songs "Sitting on Top of the World" and "Stop and Listen," the Sheiks played good-time and bawdy blues, dance numbers, and standards.

Vinson also recorded on his own in the 1930s with such labels as Paramount, Okeh, and Bluebird. In 1941 he relocated to Chicago, did his last recording session for Bluebird, and subsequently faded from the blues scene. In the 1960s, during the height of the folk-blues boom, Vinson made something of a comeback. He recorded for the Riverside label in 1961 and performed at festivals such as the Smithsonian's Festival of American Folklife (with Sam Chatman) during the '60s and early '70s. He entered a Chicago nursing home in 1972 and died three years later.

Essential Listening:

Rats Been on My Cheese/Agram (2003)

Charlie McCoy & Walter Vincson, 1928–1936/Earl Archives Blues Documents
    (BD 612)

The Mississippi Sheiks, 1930–35/Document (595)

Stop and Listen/Yazoo (2006)

W.

◄ WALKER, JIMMY

(born March 8, 1905, Memphis, Tenn.)

Jimmy Walker began his career as a boogie-influenced blues pianist and singer in Chicago in the 1930s when he worked clubs and house-rent parties with HOME-SICK JAMES and other blues guitarists. Walker continued as a member of the city's blues community throughout the 1940s; his role as a supporting musician grew larger in the 1950s when he worked with BIG JOE WILLIAMS, BILLY BOY ARNOLD, and ELMORE JAMES, though his popularity never expanded much beyond Chicago.

Walker's recording career began in 1964 when he recorded for the Testament label with fellow Chicago pianist ERWIN HELFER. The two continued a sporadic partnership throughout the '60s, culminating in 1973 with the recording of a piano duet album, *Blues and Boogie Woogie Piano, Duets and Solos*. Walker's first solo album, *Original Southside Blues Piano*, was cut ten years later, in 1983, for the Wolf label. Walker has continued to work clubs and occasional festivals.

Essential Listening:
Original South Side Blues Piano/Wolf (120-712)
Where's My Money? (The Sons of Blues)/Red Beans (RB 004)

◄ WALKER, JOE LOUIS

(born December 25, 1949, San Francisco, Calif.)

Blues guitarist and singer Joe Louis Walker emerged out of the San Francisco blues scene in the 1980s. Along with guitarist ROBERT CRAY, Walker helped keep a relatively youthful black presence in the decade's blues revival with a series of acclaimed albums on the Hightone label. Although he was born and raised in California, Walker's guitar style is derived from the styles of such Chicago stalwarts as OTIS RUSH, BUDDY GUY, and MAGIC SAM.

Walker started his career in the mid-'60s when he began playing San Francisco rock and blues clubs. In the late '60s he lived on and off with veteran bluesman MIKE BLOOMFIELD, who introduced Walker to many of the blues artists who came to the Bay Area to perform at the Fillmore West, the city's flagship rock theater, and the Matrix, a popular club. Walker often backed up such visiting blues guitarists as EARL HOOKER, Magic Sam, and LIGHTNIN' HOPKINS.

In late 1969, Walker moved to Vancouver, Canada, where he played in bar bands. Discouraged with his career as a blues artist, he went back to San Francisco in the early '70s and returned to school to get his high school diploma. He began singing with the Spiritual Corinthians, a gospel group, and performed with them at the New Orleans Jazz & Heritage Festival in 1985, the same year he graduated from City College of San Francisco. Walker rediscovered the blues in New Orleans and went on to tour Europe with a group called the Mississippi Delta Blues later that year. When he returned to the Bay Area, he started his own blues band.

In 1986, Walker signed a recording contract with Hightone Records and released his first album, *Cold Is the Night*. That record and two successive albums, *The Gift* (1988) and *Blue Soul* (1989), were widely hailed in U.S. blues circles. Trips to Europe made him a rising blues star overseas.

Walker's fourth album, *Live at Slim's, Vol. 1*, recorded in a Bay Area blues club in 1990, galvanized his reputation as a guitar stylist and performer. The album received enthusiastic reviews from *Rolling Stone* magazine and other major music periodicals, and Walker began playing major blues festivals and top blues clubs. Hightone released *Live at Slim's, Vol. 2* in 1992. Walker continues to record and perform.

Essential Listening:
Cold Is the Night/Hightone (8006)
The Gift/Hightone (8012)
Blue Soul/Hightone (8019)
Live at Slim's, Vol. 1/Hightone (8025)
Live at Slim's, Vol. 2/Hightone (8036)

◄ WALKER, JOHNNY "BIG MOOSE"

(born June 27, 1929, Greenville, Miss.)

Johnny "Big Moose" Walker, like SUNNYLAND SLIM, PINETOP PERKINS, and JIMMY WALKER (no relation), is one of the elder statesmen of Chicago piano blues. Born in Mississippi, Walker played piano at juke joints and house parties in and around Mississippi and southern Illinois with drummer KANSAS CITY RED and guitarist EARL HOOKER, before joining the army in 1953. After he was discharged in 1955, he played with LOWELL FULSON's band before moving to Chicago sometime around 1959.

In Chicago, Walker's stocky barrelhouse piano style was in much demand. He played behind many of Chicago's premier guitarists, including ELMORE JAMES, EARL HOOKER, MAGIC SAM, and OTIS RUSH, and was a fixture on the Chicago blues club scene. In the '70s, he again backed up Rush, along with guitarists SON SEALS, MIGHTY JOE YOUNG, JIMMY DAWKINS, and others.

Walker also had a solo recording career; in the '50s he cut sides for Modern and JOHNNY OTIS's Ultra label, while in the '60s he recorded for the Age label. Walker also played guitar on CURTIS JONES's Bluesville albums and toured as a bass player in MUDDY WATERS's band. In the late 1980s, failing health forced Walker to cut back on session and club work. In 1992 Walker suffered a stroke and retired from performing and recording.

Essential Listening:
Going Home Tomorrow/Isabel (900-52)

Blue Love/Red Beans (005)
Johnny "Big Moose" Walker/ABC-Bluesway (0036)

◄ WALKER, PHILLIP

(born February 11, 1937, Welsh, La.)

From 1955 to 1959 blues guitarist and singer Phillip Walker toured and recorded with zydeco king CLIFTON CHENIER's band and played behind the likes of ETTA JAMES, JIMMY REED, and LOWELL FULSON before moving to Los Angeles and becoming a part of the West Coast blues scene. Walker's exquisitely refined guitar style recalls the fluidity and jazz-flavored tones of both T-BONE WALKER (no relation) and B.B. KING. Although his albums have gone largely underappreciated, they contain some of the best West Coast blues guitar work of the post-1950s period.

Walker was born in Louisiana and grew up in Port Arthur, Texas. After his stint with Chenier, Walker worked for a short time with Memphis pianist and singer ROSCO GORDON before heading West. Walker performed regularly in blues and R&B clubs in southern California and cut his first records there for the Elko label. During the '60s Walker toured regularly with LITTLE RICHARD before forging a long-term partnership with producer Bruce Bromberg and songwriter Dennis Walker (no relation) in 1969. Four years later, in 1973, Walker signed a record deal with the Playboy label, which released a compilation of his best '60s singles, called *Bottom of the Top*. The album was poorly distributed and went largely unnoticed. Hightone Records rereleased *Bottom of the Top* in 1989.

After his relationship with Playboy dissolved, Walker went with Bromberg's Joilet label and in the mid-'70s recorded the album *Someday You'll Have These Blues*, which Alligator Records released in 1977. Although the recording received favorable reviews, it didn't sell well enough to warrant an Alligator follow-up. Hightone, however, rereleased this album in 1991. Walker worked the blues club and festival circuit in the 1980s. His first studio album for Hightone, called simply *Blues*, was produced by Bromberg and contained three songs by Dennis Walker. It was released in 1988. Walker continues to perform.

Essential Listening:
The Bottom of the Top/Hightone (8020)
Tough as I Want to Be/Rounder (2038)
Someday You'll Have These Blues/Hightone (8032)
Blues/Hightone (8013)

◄ WALKER, T-BONE

(born Aaron Thibeaux Walker, May 28, 1910, Linden, Tex.; died March 16, 1975, Los Angeles, Calif.)

Aaron T-Bone Walker was a creator of modern blues and a pioneer in the development of the electric guitar sound that shaped virtually all of popular music in the post–World War II period. Equally important, Walker was the quintessential blues guitarist. He influenced virtually every major post–World War II guitarist, including B.B. KING, JIMI HENDRIX, FREDDIE KING, ALBERT KING, BUDDY GUY, OTIS RUSH, ERIC CLAPTON, and STEVIE RAY VAUGHAN. No one has been able to match Walker's incredible command of tone and dynamics, his intricate jazz-flavored chording, or his ability to sustain excitement, both in what he played and how he played it. Walker was the master of the shuffle rhythm, and an incredibly effective soloist. Few guitarists, blues, rock, or otherwise, have played with more self-assurance and more presence, or have exhibited a more intimate understanding of how to elicit precisely phrased sounds from the instrument, than Walker.

From Walker, in fact, came the electric blues guitar style. He was the first blues artist to play the instrument, and the one who accomplished the most in exploring its wide range of possibilities. Walker was an expert in amplification. He also sounded as comfortable in the thick of a full orchestra as he did leading a small combo.

As if his exquisite guitar playing wasn't enough, Walker was also a first-class singer and entertainer. His full-bodied voice complemented his guitar playing. And like Delta bluesman CHARLEY PATTON before him, Walker often played guitar behind his back and neck and between his legs; he also did splits and twists. Undoubtedly he influenced CHUCK BERRY and Hendrix in the way they incorporated showmanship into their performance to heighten intensity and audience excitement.

With the possible exceptions of BLIND LEMON JEFFERSON, from whom Walker learned the basics of blues guitar, and LIGHTNIN' HOPKINS, Walker might well be the greatest blues artist to ever come out of Texas. Though he moved early on to the West Coast, the roots of his guitar style were in the Texas blues tradition, and two generations of Lone Star State guitarists have come of age paying tribute to him in some respect.

Walker was born in Linden, Texas, but his family moved to Dallas when he was two. Although he often sang with his stepfather, Marco Washington, Walker got a far better education in the blues from Jefferson, the creator of Texas blues. From about 1920 to 1923, Walker led Jefferson, a friend of the family, around the streets of Dallas, often holding Jefferson's tin can and collecting his tips. It was just after this time that Walker began to play guitar. Inspired by Jefferson and the music he heard around his house—both parents were musicians—Walker learned to play well enough to travel with the Dr. Breeding Medicine Show and various carnivals through Texas in the mid-1920s. Walker's reputation grew large enough so that in 1929 Columbia Records recorded him under the name Oak Cliff T-Bone. (Oak Cliff was the section of Dallas in which Walker lived.) He cut two songs: "Wichita Falls Blues" and "Trinity River Blues."

The following year Walker won a Dallas talent contest; the prize was a performance with Cab Calloway's big band. Walker played with other Texas bands after that, including the Lawson Brooks Band and the Count Biloski Band, before going to California in 1934. (Walker's departure from the Brooks band enabled his friend, Charlie Christian, to take his place. Christian became the first great electric guitar player in jazz.)

Walker spent most of the 1930s playing with small bands in and around Los Angeles. In 1935 or 1936 (accounts vary), Walker began experimenting with a prototype electric guitar and was one of the first guitarists anywhere to play the instrument in public. In 1935 jazz guitarist Eddie Durham played a nonelectric resonator guitar on the Jimmy Lunceford rendition of "Hittin' the Bottle"; three years later he recorded with the Kansas City Five and Six using an electric guitar. Christian and another jazz guitarist, Floyd Smith, would also record with an electric guitar before Walker got his chance in 1939.

That was the year Walker joined Les Hite's Cotton Club Orchestra and recorded the seminal "T-Bone Blues," one of the great modern blues classics. Walker sang on the record and Frank Palsey played guitar. The success of "T-Bone Blues" prompted Walker to leave Hite in 1941 and start his own band. He worked L.A. clubs with his combo and began recording for Capitol Records in 1942. He also did extended stays at the Rhumboogie Club in Chicago and recorded for the club's record label. In 1946 Walker returned to L.A. where he recorded a number of gems for the Black & White label, including the rollicking instrumental "T-Bone Jumps Again" and his signature song, "Call It Stormy Monday (But Tuesday Is Just as Bad)," which is generally considered to be one of the greatest blues songs of all time. At a session shortly after the one that produced "Stormy Monday," Walker cut "T-Bone Shuffle," which, like "Stormy Monday," has become an essential piece in every blues guitarist's repertoire.

Walker left Black & White Records in 1950 and signed with Imperial. In the five years he was with the label, Walker recorded slightly over fifty sides. None had the success of his late-'40s records with Black & White, though the guitarmanship heard on such songs as "I Walked Away" and "Cold Cold Feeling" revealed that Walker was certainly still capable of creating astonishing guitar passages.

Walker next moved to Atlantic Records, with whom he recorded until 1959. From this period came the flawless album *T-Bone Blues*, which ranks among the greatest modern blues albums. During this time Walker embarked on a touring strategy that had him playing in front of pickup bands rather than traveling with a band of his own. The quality of the bands was unpredictable, but his guitar work was just about always topnotch, despite growing health problems with ulcers and alcoholism.

Walker's sensitivity as a guitarist and his ability to entertain kept him a major touring attraction, though as a recording artist his best days were clearly behind him, both in creative output and sales. In 1962 Walker went to Europe with the American Folk Blues Festival package show, which enabled him to build a loyal following there. Walker would return to Europe a number of times in the next few years. At home, Walker played the Ann Arbor Blues Festival in 1969, the Berkeley Blues Festival in 1970, and venues such as Carnegie Hall and the Fillmore East in New York. He also continued to record; in 1970 he won a Grammy for his album *Good Feelin'*. But Walker's health problems entered a critical stage; his stomach problems and inability to quit drinking took their toll in the early

'70s. In 1974 he quit performing and recording after he suffered a stroke. In 1975 he died of bronchial pneumonia. Walker was inducted into the Blues Foundation's Hall of Fame in 1980 and the Rock & Roll Hall of Fame in 1987.

Essential Listening:
T-Bone Blues/Atlantic (8020-2)
The Complete Recordings of T-Bone Walker/Mosaic Records (MR6-130)
Low Down Blues/Charly (CD 7)
T-Bone Jumps Again/Charly (CRB 1019)
I Want a Little Girl/Delmark (DD 633)
The Complete Imperial Recordings, 1950–54/EMI (CDP 7-96737-2)

◄ WALKER, WILLIE

(aka Blind Willie Walker) (born 1896, South Carolina; died March 4, 1933, Greenville, S.C.)

Had Willie Walker recorded more extensively and lived longer, his reputation as a major Piedmont guitarist would doubtless have been even greater than it is. Walker's remarkably dexterous finger-picking technique and his stunning fluidity made him one of the region's premier stylists, along with BLIND BLAKE, BLIND BOY FULLER, and BLIND WILLIE MCTELL. Unfortunately, Walker recorded just four sides in his career, only two of which were ever released. He also died at age thirty-seven, a victim of the congenital syphilis that had caused his blindness at birth.

Walker was born somewhere in South Carolina. He began to develop his reputation as a rag-influenced blues guitarist after he moved to Greenville sometime around 1912. He got work playing in local string bands when not performing on street corners or in parks. He often worked with a second guitarist, Sam Brooks. Reputedly, a young JOSH WHITE led Walker around Greenville before White embarked on his own career as a blues artist.

Walker's one and only recording session occurred in Atlanta in 1930. The two songs that were released by the Columbia label—"South Columbia Rag" and "Dupree Blues"—are testament to Walker's guitar virtuosity. Walker died in 1933.

Essential Listening:
East Coast Blues, 1926–1935 (Various Artists)/Yazoo (1013)

◄ WALLACE, SIPPIE

(born Beulah Thomas, November 1, 1898, Houston, Tex.; died November 1, 1986)

Sippie Wallace, like fellow classic blues singer VICTORIA SPIVEY, was born in Texas and carried with her a tradition of Texas-styled blues that emphasized risqué lyrics and rough-cut, rural vocal phrasing rather than the sophisticated accents of the era's more cosmopolitan blues singers. Although her recording career stretched throughout most of the '20s, her best work was done from 1923 to 1927 when the likes of LOUIS ARMSTRONG, Johnny Dodds, Sidney Bechet, and CLARENCE WILLIAMS accompanied her in the recording studio.

Wallace was born Beulah Thomas in 1898 in Houston, an active blues town at the time. Though she learned the rudiments of singing and playing the piano in church, her older brother, GEORGE THOMAS, was probably the one who introduced her to the blues. Early on she began performing with her younger piano-playing brother, HERSAL THOMAS. By the time she was in her midteens, Wallace had left home for a career in show business. She performed with various Texas tent shows and built a solid following in Texas as a spirited blues singer. Wallace moved to New Orleans with brother Hersal in 1915; two years later she married Matt Wallace. After following her brothers to Chicago in 1923, Wallace worked her way into the city's bustling jazz scene. Her reputation as a hard-bottomed blues singer led to a recording contract with Okeh Records in 1923. Wallace's first recorded songs, "Shorty George" and "Up the Country Blues," the former written with her brother George, sold well enough to make Wallace a blues star in the early '20s.

Other successful recordings followed, including "Special Delivery Blues" (with Louis Armstrong on cornet), "Bedroom Blues" (written by George and Hersal Thomas), and the erotic blues "I'm a Mighty Tight Woman," which she recorded on two different occasions in the 1920s. From 1923 to 1927 Wallace recorded over forty sides for the Okeh label; nearly half of them were written by Wallace or Wallace and her brothers.

Wallace moved to Detroit in 1929 and faded from the recording scene in the early 1930s. Her husband Matt and brother George both died in 1936. (Younger brother Hersal had died of food poisoning in 1926 at age sixteen.) Grief-stricken with the passing of her brothers and husband, Wallace found religion; for some forty years she was a singer and organ player at the Leland Baptist Church in Detroit.

Aside from an occasional performance or recording date, Wallace did little in the blues until she launched a comeback in 1966 after her longtime friend Victoria Spivey coaxed her out of retirement and onto the folk and blues festival circuit. Around that time Wallace recorded an album of old blues standards with Spivey called simply *Sippie Wallace and Victoria Spivey*, which came out in 1970 on Spivey's own self-named label.

Wallace next recorded a new album of her old blues called *Sippie Wallace Sings the Blues* for the Storyville label in 1966. The album featured the keyboard work of ROOSEVELT SYKES and LITTLE BROTHER MONTGOMERY and included Wallace's signature song, "Women Be Wise, Don't Advertise Your Man." Supposedly the album helped inspire blues-pop singer BONNIE RAITT to take up the blues in the late '60s.

Wallace suffered a stroke in 1970 but managed to keep up her recording and performing career. Raitt helped Wallace land a recording contract with Atlantic Records in 1982. The resulting album, *Sippie*, featured Raitt's shimmering slide-guitar work and was nominated for a Grammy in 1983 in the traditional blues category. In 1984 the album won a W.C. HANDY Award for best blues album of the year. Sippie Wallace died at the age of eighty-eight in 1986.

Essential Listening:
Sippie Wallace, 1923–1929/Document (DLP 593)
Sippie Wallace, 1924–1927/Blues Documents (BD 2093)
Women Be Wise/Alligator (AL 4810)

◄ WALLACE, WESLEY

(born, date and place unknown; died, date and place unknown)

St. Louis pianist Wesley Wallace was an early boogie-woogie player whose fast-flowing style, with rolling bass lines and chattering melodies, made him highly respected in the 1920s. Unfortunately, virtually nothing is known of his personal life. Wallace might have been born in Illinois. He moved to St. Louis as a youth, where he played clubs and parties with the likes of JABO WILLIAMS, HENRY BROWN, ROOSEVELT SYKES, and LEROY CARR.

Wallace is best known for "No. 29," a recording he cut in 1930 for the Paramount label. The song, a talking narrative blues about a train trip from Nashville to New Orleans constructed over a repeating bass line, epitomizes the early St. Louis boogie-woogie piano style. A second Wallace recording, "Fanny Lee Blues," is also considered to be a major boogie-woogie work.

Essential Listening:
St. Louis Piano Blues, 1929–1934/Document (529)

◄ WALTON, MERCY DEE

(born August 30, 1915, Waco, Tex.; died December 2, 1962, Murphys, Calif.)

A Texas-born West Coast piano player who recorded during the 1950s for a variety of labels, Mercy Dee Walton was as comfortable playing hard blues as rhythm & blues. Although he learned to play piano as a youth and often performed at parties in and around Waco, Texas, his home, Walton's career as a blues artist didn't begin to take shape until he moved to the West Coast in 1938. For the next ten years or so Walton developed a following playing up and down the California coast. He began his recording career in 1949 when he cut four sides for the Spire label, which led to further sessions in the early '50s with Imperial and Specialty. Walton's best-known song, "One Room Country Shack," was recorded for Specialty in 1953 and later interpreted by jazz-blues pianist MOSE ALLISON.

In the mid-1950s Walton toyed with rock & roll and cut some sides for Flair. He also toured regularly with various rock & roll and rhythm & blues packages. In 1961 Walton resumed his recording career, this time with Arhoolie and Prestige-Bluesville. His recording comeback was short-lived, however. Walton died in 1962 of a cerebral hemorrhage. He was forty-seven years old.

Essential Listening:
Unfinished Boogie: Western Blues Piano, 1946–1952/Muskadine (104)
G.I. Fever/Crown Prince (IG 408)
Troublesome Mind/Arhoolie (369)

◄ WALTON, WADE

(born October 10, 1923, Lombardy, Miss.)

A harmonica- and guitar-playing barber who in his later years has acted as something of an ambassador of Mississippi Delta blues, Wade Walton runs a barbershop in Clarksdale, Mississippi, tells old blues stories, and occasionally performs for visiting blues fans. He is particularly known for playing the razor strop.

Walton learned how to play the harmonica and guitar at an early age and worked Delta juke joints and house parties before becoming a barber. He continued to play the blues, occasionally performing with IKE TURNER during the time Turner formed the Kings of Rhythm in the 1940s. Walton faded from the blues scene until the early 1960s when he recorded for the Arhoolie and Bluesville-Prestige labels. He also appeared in a number of blues documentaries, including *Blues Like Showers of Rain* (1970), *Mississippi Delta Blues* (1974), and *Mississippi Delta Bluesmen* (1975). Since then, Walton has continued to cut hair in Clarksdale; his barbershop has become something of a blues institution in the Delta.

Essential Listening:
I Have to Paint My Face (Various Artists)/Arhoolie (1005)

◄ WARD, ROBERT

(born October 15, 1938, Luthersville, Ga.)

For more than thirty years Robert Ward was an unsung guitarist whose distinctive vibrato-laden sound and soul-blues phrasing was appreciated by only a handful of serious blues and R&B record collectors. In 1990 Black Top Records' Hammond Scott found Ward living in Dry Branch, Georgia, and coaxed him out of retirement to record his first album, *Fear No Evil*. The work consisted of an original mix of blues, soul, and R&B, and was embellished with Ward's unique single-string guitar style and his warm Southern-soul vocals. The critically acclaimed album revitalized Ward's recording career and enabled him to begin performing regularly on the U.S. blues circuit.

Although he was born and raised in Georgia, Ward's career began in Dayton, Ohio, in 1960, the city he moved to after his discharge from the army. It was in Dayton that he formed the Ohio Untouchables, a bluesy R&B band that, in the '70s, became the Ohio Players—but long after Ward had left its fold in 1965. Though Ward played guitar on "I Found a Love," a 1962 hit single by the Detroit R&B group the Falcons, whose main singer was Wilson Pickett, Ward barely made a living as a musician. In the '60s, aside from cutting obscure singles that attracted little attention outside the Midwest, Ward also toured with Pickett. In the early '70s he did some session work for Motown, appearing on records by the Temptations and the Undisputed Truth. But around 1977, with the deaths of his wife and mother, Ward quit music and returned to Georgia. He remained in obscurity until the call from Black Top.

Ward is considered to be one of the more important blues-related finds of the late '80s and early '90s. His second album, *Rhythm of the People*, came out in 1993. Ward continues to record and perform.

Essential Listening:
Fear No Evil/Black Top (BT 1063)
Rhythm of the People/Black Top (BT 1088)

◄ WARREN, BABY BOY

(born Robert Warren, August 13, 1919, Lake Providence, La.; died July 1, 1977, Detroit, Mich.)

Along with JOHN LEE HOOKER, BOBO JENKINS, and EDDIE KIRKLAND, Robert "Baby Boy" Warren helped create Detroit's blues scene in the years immediately preceding World War II. Long after Hooker had become a national star and moved away, Warren remained active in Motown's blues circles, where he performed and occasionally recorded up until his death in 1977.

Warren was born in Louisiana and raised in Memphis. After an older brother taught him the basics of the blues guitar, he began playing for tips in parks and on street corners and spending time with HOWLIN' WOLF, ROBERT JR. LOCKWOOD, and other Memphis bluesmen. Spurred by the possibility of financial advancement, Warren moved to Detroit in the early '40s and got a job with General Motors. Building cars by day and playing blues at night, he eventually became one of Detroit's most popular blues entertainers though he was little known elsewhere. He began his recording career in 1949, cutting sides for the local Staff label. In the early 1950s he recorded for a number of other labels, including JVB and Cadet, and he often performed with SONNY BOY WILLIAMSON (Rice Miller) in Detroit blues clubs.

Warren continued to work for General Motors, which prevented widespread touring, though he did play a few dates in Europe in 1972. Warren died of a heart attack in 1977.

Essential Listening:
Detroit Blues: The Early 1950s/Blues Classics (12)

◄ WASHBOARD SAM

(born Robert Brown, July 15, 1910, Walnut Ridge, Ark.; died November 6, 1966, Chicago, Ill.)

Washboard Sam was the most popular of the blues-based washboard players of the 1930s and 1940s. His scratchy, percussive washboard sound enhanced the blues of BIG BILL BROONZY, BUKKA WHITE, JAZZ GILLUM, and other artists with whom he recorded. As good as Sam was on the washboard, he was also a prolific songwriter and a competent blues vocalist, both of which did much to insure his popularity.

Born Robert Brown, Washboard Sam was reputed to be the illegitimate son of Frank Broonzy, Big Bill Broonzy's father, making the two bluesmen half-brothers. Sam was raised in Arkansas and moved to Memphis in the 1920s to play his washboard on the city's street corners for tips. He did the same thing after he moved to Chicago in 1932. In 1935 he began recording for producer LESTER MELROSE and the Bluebird label. This led to further associations with other labels, such as Vocalion, Victor, Chess, and later Spivey, as well as numerous sessions with Broonzy and the other early Chicago artists mentioned above. Despite Sam's recording productivity and prewar popularity, he was unable to make the transition into postwar electric blues and he gradually faded from the blues scene in the mid-'50s. Sam died in 1966.

Essential Listening:
Big Bill Broonzy and Washboard Sam/Chess (MCA) (CHD 9251)
Washboard Sam/Blues Classics (10)

◄ WASHINGTON, DINAH

(born Ruth Lee Jones, August 29, 1924, Tuscaloosa, Ala.; died December 14, 1963, Detroit, Mich.)

From 1948 to 1961 singer Dinah Washington was one of rhythm & blues' most successful recording artists. Washington placed more than forty records on the R&B charts, including four number 1s (two of them duets with Brook Benton). Although she frequently crossed over into pop territory, Washington's gospel background and broad understanding of the blues gave many of her pop songs a bluesy sheen.

During her heyday, Washington was a major influence on other black female artists such as LAVERN BAKER, ETTA JAMES, RUTH BROWN, and ESTHER PHILLIPS. Her command of not only gospel, blues, and pop but also jazz made Washington one of the most versatile and expressive vocalists of the post–World War II period. The emotional depth of her style was such that critics often referred to the "cry" or "tear" in her voice. Though she died at age thirty-nine, Washington's vocal legacy ranks her with BESSIE SMITH, Billie Holiday, ESTHER PHILLIPS, and the other great blues-based black female vocalists.

Washington was born Ruth Lee Jones in Alabama but raised in Chicago. Early on she was attracted to music, particularly gospel, and sang in church choirs. In 1940 and 1941 she sang with the Sallie Martin Gospel Singers, but by this time Washington had become increasingly attracted to the secular sounds of blues and jazz. While working as a ladies' room attendant in a Chicago nightclub, Washington auditioned for agent Joe Glaser, who in turn recommended her to bandleader Lionel Hampton. She joined Hampton's band in 1943 and changed her name to Dinah Washington. She also made her recording debut in 1943; a session for the Keynote label resulted in "Evil Gal Blues" and "Salty Papa Blues," both of which illustrated her command of the jazz-flavored blues idiom.

Washington left Hampton in 1946 and began her solo career. She first recorded for the Apollo label, but in 1948 she joined the Mercury roster, where she remained until 1962. During her Mercury years, Washington scored with such classics as "Baby, Get Lost" in 1949, "Trouble in Mind" in 1952, "What a Diff'rence a Day Makes" in 1959, and two duets with Brook Benton in 1960: "Baby (You've Got What It Takes)" and "A Rockin' Good Way (To Mess Around and Fall in Love)."

In the last few years of her life, Washington had as much success in pop as she did in R&B. Beginning with "What a Diff'rence a Day Makes," Washington also attracted an increasingly large white audience. Unfortunately, Washington's private life was not as smoothly successful as her career. She was married seven times and struggled with a temper that, at times, was difficult for her to control.

Washington left Mercury in 1962 and signed with the Roulette label. But in 1963, at the peak of her career, Washington died of an accidental overdose of alcohol and either sleeping or diet pills. Thirty years later, in 1993, Washington was honored by the U.S. Postal Service with her name and likeness on a twenty-nine-cent stamp.

Essential Listening:
Dinah Washington Sings the Blues/Mercury (832 573-2)
Dinah Washington/Mercury (830 700-2)
The Bessie Smith Songbook/Polygram
Mellow Mama/Delmark (DD 451)
Dinah Washington's Greatest Hits/Mercury
Mellow Mama/Delmark (DD 451)
First Issue: The Dinah Washington Story/Mercury-Verve (514841)

◄ WASHINGTON, LEROY

(born, date and place unknown; died 1966, Oakdale, La.)

Louisiana guitarist and vocalist Leroy Washington recorded for the Excello label in the late 1950s. His best-known number, "Wild Cherry," was the first he cut for the label. Though it never made the R&B charts, the song was a regional hit that contained all the elements that comprised the Excello sound, namely, trebly, groove-laden guitar riffs and punchy swamp rock vocals.

Washington worked Louisiana clubs and dances in the '50s and '60s. After a performance in Oakdale in 1966, Washington suffered a fatal heart attack.

Essential Listening:
Leroy Washington/Flyright (574)

◄ WASHINGTON, TUTS

(born Isidore Washington, January 24, 1907, New Orleans, La.; died August 5, 1984, New Orleans, La.)

Piano player Tuts Washington had been a fixture on the New Orleans blues and boogie-woogie scene since the 1930s, performing in clubs with the likes of SMILEY LEWIS and Papa Celestin's Dixieland Band and at festivals, including the New Orleans Jazz & Heritage Fest. Along with CHAMPION JACK DUPREE and ARCHIBALD, Washington was part of the first generation of Crescent City blues-based piano players who influenced more-popular later players like JAMES BOOKER, HUEY "PIANO" SMITH, FATS DOMINO, ALLEN TOUSSAINT, and especially PROFESSOR LONGHAIR.

Washington's keyboard style was an eclectic mix of ragtime, jazz, and blues. Later on in the mid-'50s, when he began playing for tourists in the French Quarter, Washington added a pop sheen to his performances. Despite his popularity in New Orleans, Washington was never able to expand his career beyond the city. He recorded only one solo album—*New Orleans Piano Professor*—in 1983 for Rounder Records. Washington died during a performance at the New Orleans World's Fair a year later.

Essential Listening:
New Orleans Piano Professor/Rounder (11501)

◀ WASHINGTON, WALTER "WOLFMAN"

(born Edward Washington, December 20, 1943, New Orleans, La.)

Guitarist and charcoal-toned singer Walter "Wolfman" Washington was born and raised in New Orleans and grew up on gospel and church music. As a youth he sang in his mother's choir, but he eventually became enamored with blues and R&B. He broke into the New Orleans music scene playing behind singer JOHNNY ADAMS. In the early '60s Washington toured with LEE DORSEY and then with IRMA THOMAS before forming his own group, the All Fools Band, and working New Orleans clubs as a main act.

In the early '70s Washington toured Europe with a blues and R&B package show called A Taste of New Orleans. The exposure enabled him and his backing band, the Roadmasters, to tour Europe on their own in the late '70s. Washington began his recording career in 1981 with the release of *Rainin' in My Heart* on the tiny Hep Me label (the album was later rereleased on Maison de Soul). Washington switched to the Rounder label in 1985 and cut *Wolf Tracks*. Two other Rounder albums followed in the late '80s—*Out of the Dark* and *Wolf at the Door*. Washington moved to the Point Blank–Charisma label in 1991 and recorded the album *Sada*. Washington continues to record and perform regularly in New Orleans clubs.

Essential Listening:
Wolf Tracks/Rounder (20482/4)
Out of the Dark/Rounder (20682/4)
Wolf at the Door/Rounder (20982/4)
Sada/Point Blank–Charisma (91743-4)

◀ WATERS, ETHEL

(born October 31, 1896, Chester, Pa.; died September 1, 1977, Chatsworth, Calif.)

Ethel Waters had a long and distinguished career as a vocalist and actress, though the years she spent as a blues singer were limited to the early 1920s. With smooth, well-defined phrasing and a meticulous sense of timing, Waters's singing style rated with the best of the era's vocalists. Had she dedicated herself to solely singing the blues, Waters might well have been a great blues singer. But by the mid-'20s she began devoting most of her stage and recording time to vaudeville and pop tunes.

Waters arrived in New York in 1919 after spending time as a singer and dancer on the East Coast and Southern vaudeville circuit. Due to her slender appearance, she was billed as Sweet Mama Stringbean. In 1921 she cut two songs for Cardinal Records, "The New York Glide" and "At the New Jump Steady Ball." Later that year she became the first artist to release a blues record on the black-owned Black Swan label, recording "Down Home Blues" and "Oh Daddy" for the company. She went on to record for numerous other labels. In addition to making records, Waters frequently performed in New York, Philadelphia, and other cities with Fletcher Henderson's Jazz Masters in the Black Swan Troubadors troupe.

By the mid-'20s Waters had drifted from the blues and had become a successful pop singer. She easily adapted her suave and polished vocal style to sing breezy pop and show standards of the day. Waters performed in a number of revues, including *Africana, Paris Bound*, and *The Ethel Waters Broadway Revue*; she also added acting to her repertoire. In 1929 she landed her first role in a film called *On with the Show*. A year later she appeared in *Check and Double Check* with Amos 'n' Andy and Duke Ellington. Her performance in the film opened the door for roles in other '30s and '40s films, including *Pinky* in 1949, which won her an Oscar nomination for best supporting actress. In 1939 Waters became a Broadway star, appearing in *Mamba's Daughters* in a nonsinging, dramatic role. Her greatest theatrical achievement occurred in 1950 when she played a cook in the play *The Member of the Wedding* and won the New York Drama Critics Award for best actress.

Waters penned her best-selling autobiography, *His Eye Is on the Sparrow*, in 1951. She wrote a second autobiography, *To Me It's Wonderful*, in 1972. Waters also toured with evangelist Billy Graham from 1957 until her death in 1977.

Essential Listening:
Ethel Waters, 1938–40/Rosetta (1314)
Ethel Waters, 1924–28/Wolf (WJS 1009)

◄ WATERS, MUDDY

(born McKinley Morganfield, April 14, 1915, Rolling Fork, Miss.; died April 30, 1983, Chicago, Ill.)

Muddy Waters was the patriarch of post–World War II Chicago blues. A master artist who played slashing slide guitar and sang with the tough, sinewy view of a man who had seen his share of good and evil in life, Waters was also a compelling songwriter and song interpreter, a powerful stage performer and recording artist, and a superb bandleader. A list of those musicians who passed through his bands reads like a Who's Who of Chicago blues greats. Guitarists JIMMY ROGERS, PAT HARE, LUTHER TUCKER, and EARL HOOKER; harp players LITTLE WALTER, JUNIOR WELLS, BIG WALTER HORTON, JAMES COTTON, and CAREY BELL; bass player WILLIE DIXON; pianists MEMPHIS SLIM, OTIS SPANN, and PINETOP PERKINS; and drummers ELGIN EVANS, FRED BELOW, and FRANCIS CLAY are just some of the bluesmen who played in the Muddy Waters Band at one time or another. Many of these artists went on to lead prestigious blues bands of their own, or became highly respected sidemen, though none, save Little Walter, ever came close to attaining the success or building the legacy that Waters did.

The list of artists Waters influenced would go on almost indefinitely. Besides the entire generation of Chicago blues artists who came of age in the '50s and '60s, Waters also left his mark on dozens of British and American blues rockers. CHUCK BERRY, Bob Dylan, ERIC CLAPTON, JIMI HENDRIX, Jeff Beck, JOHNNY WINTER, STEVIE RAY VAUGHAN, ROBERT CRAY, and the ROLLING STONES (who named their group after one of Waters's songs) are just the tip of the iceberg.

The attraction of Waters's brand of blues is due to his brilliant blues artistry and his critical role in providing the link between deep Mississippi Delta blues and hard-edged, urban and electric Chicago blues; more than any other musician, Waters was responsible for the mesh between old and new blues in the early postwar period.

Waters also helped transform the blues guitar sound. Although other bluesmen had recorded with an electric guitar before Waters did, his importance as an innovative player is substantial. Waters's guitar work was raw and vital and executed with the same urgency as the blues of ROBERT JOHNSON and SON HOUSE, two of Waters's mentors.

Waters was a convincing blues dignitary; an impeccably sharp dresser and a man who, though uneducated, spoke about the blues with a simple eloquence, he helped cultivate for the blues a respect the music had never known before.

During the years 1951 to 1960, there wasn't a more compelling blues band anywhere than the Muddy Waters Blues Band. They juiced the music with a rocking backbeat and an unfiltered down-home intensity. Waters's blues possessed an honesty and emotional clarity. He saw the blues as a vehicle by which he could speak about human suffering, jubilation, and truth. For these reasons, he stands out as one of the greatest artists the blues has ever produced.

Waters was born into a Mississippi Delta sharecropping family in 1915. His mother died when he was three, and he was raised by his grandmother, who lived on Stovall's Plantation, just outside Clarksdale. Waters got his nickname as a child because he loved to play near a muddy creek. He learned how to sing out in the cotton fields, where, as a youth, he worked for fifty cents a day. When he was a young boy, perhaps seven or eight, Waters learned how to play the harmonica. He didn't learn how to play guitar until he was seventeen. Not long afterwards, he began to perform at house parties and fish fries with friends Scott Bohannon (or Bowhandle) and Henry "Son" Simms. Impressed by the deep blues sounds that Delta bluesman Son House drew from his guitar, Waters built his style from what he saw and heard House play. Later, Waters would also borrow guitar ideas from Robert Johnson.

Waters first recorded in 1941. He cut a number of songs for folklorist ALAN LOMAX, who was collecting songs for the Library of Congress. Two of them—"I Be's Troubled" and "Country Blues"—were released on a Library of Congress folk anthology album. A year later, when Lomax returned to the plantation, Waters recorded for him a second time.

Waters left the Mississippi Delta for Chicago in 1943. BIG BILL BROONZY helped him break into the city's thriving blues scene. For a while, Waters played acoustic guitar behind JOHN LEE "SONNY BOY" WILLIAMSON. But his reputation as a performer didn't take shape until 1944 when he began to play an electric guitar, teaming up with Jimmy Rogers on harp and Claude Smith on guitar, and then with EDDIE BOYD on piano (later joined by SUNNYLAND SLIM). Waters was still playing in a traditional Delta bottleneck style, but his sound was fatter and louder and far more moving than before.

Waters's first Chicago recordings, which were made in 1946 for producer LESTER MELROSE and Columbia Records, featured Waters with a five-piece band. These tracks weren't released until 1971. (Waters also allegedly recorded at least one song, "Mean Red Spider," using the pseudonym James "Sweet Lucy" Carter in 1946 or '47.) In 1947 Waters played guitar behind Sunnyland Slim on two Aristocrat sides, "Johnson Machine Gun" and "Fly Right Little Girl." Two other songs, "Gypsy Woman" and "Little Anna Mae," were recorded by Waters and bass player Big Crawford. Not impressed with the results, producer LEONARD CHESS nonetheless brought Waters and Crawford back into the recording studio in 1948, at which time the duo cut "I Can't Be Satisfied" and "Feel Like Going Home." The two songs were performed in a traditional Delta blues style, but Waters's shivering electric guitar gave them an exciting new edge. Chess released the songs as an Aristocrat single (number 1305). In less than a day, the record's entire stock had been sold.

The record's startling success prompted Chess to bring Waters back into the studio. Eager to stay with what worked, Chess insisted that the lineup—Waters on guitar and vocals and Crawford on bass—remain the same, even though at the time Waters was working regularly in Chicago clubs with a full band (featuring Jimmy Rogers on second guitar and harmonica and "Baby Face" Leroy Foster on drums and guitar. A little later Little Walter Jacobs joined the band on harmonica. Waters didn't get the opportunity to record with a band until 1950. By this time, his sound—harsh, heavy, and beat driven—was well in place, and blues history was made.

What followed in the years 1951 to 1960 was the greatest collection of electric blues recordings ever made. Waters originals like "Long Distance Call," "Mannish Boy," "Got My Mojo Working," "She Moves Me," and "She's Nineteen Years Old" were supplemented by the songs Willie Dixon had given to him: "Hoochie Coochie Man," "I Just Want to Make Love to You," and "I'm Ready," among others. These records defined the Chicago blues sound during its classic period. Though Waters had all but quit playing guitar at this point—his voice, thick and rough, gave the recordings and his live performances their incredible power.

Chess Records released Waters's debut album in 1958. Called *The Best of Muddy Waters*, it was a collection of his hit singles. That same year, Waters and his pianist, Otis Spann, toured England. The tour opened up a new audience for Waters abroad—and at home. White folk fans fascinated with the blues heard about Waters's triumph in England and sought out his records. For his next album Waters interpreted a collection of Big Bill Broonzy songs to take advantage of this new audience that seemed to prefer rural-flavored acoustic blues to the riveting electric style Waters had perfected in the '50s.

Yet it was Waters's electric band that transformed the Newport Folk Festival into a romping blues bash in 1960. Waters and his band were at their best as they worked their way through a feverish set on the Newport stage. Later that year

Chess released the live album *Muddy Waters at Newport*, and those new blues fans not at the fest found ample cause to seek out electric blues.

Yet Chess continued to push Waters as a folk-blues artist to capitalize on the continuing interest of white fans in down-home blues. The album *Folk Singer* was released in 1964. *The Real Folk Blues* and *More Real Folk Blues*, both of which contained old recordings, followed. To balance out Waters's catalog, Chess released the soulish *Muddy, Brass, and the Blues* in 1966, a deserved failure. A number of late-'60s and early-'70s albums, especially *Fathers and Sons, They Call Me Muddy Waters* (which won a Grammy for best ethnic/traditional recording in 1971), and *The London Muddy Waters Sessions* (which featured Waters jamming with English blues-rockers like RORY GALLAGHER) sold almost exclusively to white record buyers.

In the 1970s Waters toured almost constantly, playing all over the world. By 1977 he had ended his long-standing relationship with Chess and signed with CBS/Blue Sky. Collaborating with producer-guitarist Johnny Winter, Waters enjoyed a resurgence of his recording career with the album *Hard Again* in 1977, which won Waters his second Grammy and featured some of his most inspired studio work since the early '60s. The 1978 follow-up album, *I'm Ready*, was also a critical and commercial success; like its predecessor, *I'm Ready* featured reworkings of some of Waters's classic songs fueled with new energy and drive. A tour of the U.S. included a special performance at the White House for President Jimmy Carter and his staff, and a memorable rendition of "Mannish Boy" captured in the Band's farewell concert film, *The Last Waltz*.

Waters's final two albums, *Muddy "Mississippi" Waters Live* and *King Bee*, were also produced by Winter, whose devotion to Waters was unwavering. Waters and Winter often performed together in the early '80s, playing mostly to white blues and rock fans who often came to his shows to pay respect.

Waters died of a heart attack in his sleep in 1983 at age sixty-eight. He was inducted into the Blues Foundation's Hall of Fame in 1980 and the Rock & Roll Hall of Fame in 1987.

Essential Listening:
The Complete Plantation Recordings/MCA-Chess (CHD-9344)
Muddy Waters: The Chess Box/MCA-Chess (31268)
The Best of Muddy Waters/MCA-Chess (31268)
Muddy and the Wolf/MCA-Chess (9100)
Rolling Stone/MCA-Chess (9101)
Muddy Waters Sings Big Bill Broonzy/MCA-Chess (5907)
Muddy Waters at Newport/MCA-Chess (31269)
Rare and Unissued/MCA-Chess (9180)
Folksinger/MCA-Chess (9261)
The Real Folk Blues/MCA-Chess (9274)
More Real Folk Blues/MCA-Chess (9278)
Trouble No More/MCA-Chess (9291)
The London Muddy Waters Sessions/MCA-Chess (9298)
They Call Me Muddy Waters/MCA-Chess (9299)
Can't Get No Grindin'/MCA-Chess (9319)

Fathers and Sons/MCA-Chess (2-92522)
Muddy "Mississippi" Waters/CBS (PZ 35712)
Hard Again/CBS (PZ 34449)
King Bee/CBS (PZ 37064)
I'm Ready/CBS (PZ 34928)
Blues Sky/Epic Associated (ZK 46172)
Complete Muddy Waters/Charly (3)

◄ WATSON, JOHNNY "GUITAR"

(born February 3, 1935, Houston, Tex.)

Johnny "Guitar" Watson was part of the second generation of Texas-born blues guitarists who had been influenced by T-BONE WALKER and CLARENCE "GATEMOUTH" BROWN and had moved on to the West Coast in the 1950s. Watson grew up in Houston with ALBERT COLLINS and JOHNNY COPELAND. At age fifteen he left Houston for Los Angeles, where he worked with Chuck Higgins and his band the Mellowtones as a pianist.

By 1951 Watson was fronting his own band and playing guitar; two years later he signed a recording contract with the Federal label and billed himself as Young John Watson. Watson didn't adopt the "Guitar" nickname until he switched labels and moved over to Modern in 1955, at which time he worked with the MAXWELL DAVIS Orchestra and released one of his signature songs, "Those Lonely, Lonely Nights," which went to number 10 on the R&B charts in 1955.

Influenced by the stage antics and guitar acrobatics of GUITAR SLIM, Watson, who occasionally toured with Slim, developed a powerful live act, performing flashy moves such as playing guitar behind his back and wandering out into his audience in the midst of a solo. Later, JIMI HENDRIX would claim that Watson and Guitar Slim were two of his main influences.

In 1961 Watson went over to the King label; his single, "Cuttin' In," made it to number 6 on the R&B charts in 1962. He had two other records that charted in the '60s—"Mercy, Mercy, Mercy" (number 23) in 1967 and "Nobody" (number 40) in 1968—both of which he recorded with singer LARRY WILLIAMS.

Watson veered away from the blues in the 1970s and, ironically, enjoyed his greatest chart success. During a ten-year span that began in 1974, he experimented with funk, then disco, and landed fourteen singles on the charts, including his biggest hit, "A Real Mother for Ya," which made it to number 5 in 1977. Watson has since retired from performing.

Essential Listening:

Three Hours Past Midnight/Flair (2-91696)
The Gangster Is Back/Red Lightnin' (0013)

◄ WATTS, NOBLE

(aka the Thin Man) (born February 17, 1926, DeLand, Fla.)

Tenor saxophone player Noble Watts performed with numerous rhythm & blues and rock & roll artists in the 1950s, including PAUL "HUCKLEBUCK" WIL-

LIAMS, FATS DOMINO, CHUCK BERRY, Jerry Lee Lewis, and Buddy Holly. He also recorded on his own; in the mid-1950s, instrumentals such as "Hard Times" and "Jookin' " became Watts's signature pieces. Watts's saxophone style contained elements of jump blues and big band swing, while his penchant for honking made him a favorite with early rock & roll audiences.

Watts played the piano, violin, and trumpet before he settled on the tenor saxophone. While studying at Florida A&M University in the early 1940s, he played in the marching band with Julian "Cannonball" Adderly and his brother Nat, two sax-playing siblings who would make their mark in both jazz and rhythm & blues. After college, Watts worked with the Griffin Brothers, a touring R&B band that recorded for the Dot label in the late '40s, and then with the Paul "Hucklebuck" Williams Band in the 1950s. When the saxophone went out of style in pop music in the 1960s, Watts, like many of his contemporaries, faded from the scene. He worked for a while in the early 1970s as a member of the Apollo Theater house band in Harlem and played small clubs on the East Coast. Finally, in 1983, he returned to Florida, his home, signed a recording contract with King Snake Records, and began performing with label owner Bob Greenlee's R&B band the Midnight Creepers. In 1987, Watts recorded a comeback album, *The Return of the Thin Man*, on King Snake. It was rereleased on the Alligator label in 1990. In 1993 Wild Dog Records released Watts's *King of the Boogie Sax* album. Watts continues to record and perform.

Essential Listening:
The Return of the Thin Man/Alligator (AL 4785)
King of the Boogie Sax/Wild Dog (DOG 9102)

◄ WEAVER, CURLEY

(born James Weaver, March 25, 1906, Covington, Ga.; died September 20, 1962, Covington, Ga.)

A guitarist and singer, Curley Weaver was part of the Atlanta blues scene in the 1920s and 1930s. Weaver's contemporaries were BLIND WILLIE MCTELL, BUDDY MOSS, BARBECUE BOB, CHARLEY HICKS, and PEG LEG HOWELL; the close interaction among these artists did much to create the city's thriving blues scene during this period. Although Weaver recorded on his own, some of his best work was as an accompanist of artists such as Moss and McTell. Weaver was also a member of the Georgia Cotton Pickers and the Georgia Browns, two Atlanta-based groups that included, at one time or another, most of the above-mentioned bluesmen.

Weaver was born in rural Georgia; he came to Atlanta in 1925 with harmonica player Eddie Mapp. His boyhood friend Robert Hicks (Barbecue Bob) arranged a recording session for him in 1928 with Columbia Records, which resulted in the song "No No Blues," a local hit. The two friends also played together in the Georgia Cotton Pickers; Weaver played lead guitar, Hicks played rhythm, and Moss played harmonica. Although Weaver continued to record, he was never able to attain much commercial success. In the 1930s he often worked with guitarist Fred McMullen and McTell and the Georgia Browns, in the recording studio and on Atlanta street corners. Weaver's last recording session was with McTell in 1949 for the Regal label. In the 1950s Weaver began to lose his sight; he was completely blind by the time of his death in 1962.

Essential Listening:
Georgia Guitar Wizard/Blues Documents (2004)
Pig 'n' Whistle Red (Blind Willie McTell)/Biograph (BCD 126 ADD)

◄ WEBB, BOOGIE BILL

(born 1924, Jackson, Miss.; died August 23, 1990, New Orleans, La.)

Boogie Bill Webb was a New Orleans–based blues guitarist whose disregard for standard tunings, conventional chord changes, and consistent rhythms enabled him to create a chaotic, yet oddly compelling, sound. Webb was born in Mississippi but grew up in New Orleans. He learned the rudiments of the blues guitar as a child, picking up tips from Mississippi Delta bluesman TOMMY JOHNSON, a friend of his mother. Though Webb recorded four sides for Imperial Records in the early 1950s, he was never able to support himself solely with his music. Webb worked during the week and played the blues on weekends for most of his career.

In the late '60s Webb recorded for Arhoolie and a couple of tiny blues labels, but the results attracted little attention. It wasn't until his appearance at the New Orleans Jazz & Heritage Festival in 1984 that Webb's stature as a performer began to grow beyond local blues circles. Webb toured parts of the U.S. and Europe in the late '80s and released his first album, *Drinkin' and Stinkin'*, on the Flying Fish label in 1989. The album was well received, but Webb was unable to capitalize on it. He died in 1990 at age sixty-six.

Essential Listening:
Drinkin' and Stinkin'/Flying Fish (700506)

◄ WEBSTER, KATIE

(born Kathryn Thorne, January 9, 1939, Houston, Tex.)

A session pianist who played on more than five hundred singles in the '50s and '60s, Webster's career as a solo artist didn't take off until she signed with Alligator Records in 1988 and released her album *The Swamp Boogie Queen*. Her piano style is a mixture of traditional boogie-woogie and barrelhouse rhythms with robust elements of swamp blues, rhythm & blues, and gospel woven through her best work. Vocally, Webster recalls both old-time blues shouters and Southern church singers.

Webster did most of her session work for Excello and Goldband, who, between them, recorded the bulk of the region's best bluesmen, including SLIM HARPO, LIGHTNIN' SLIM, LONESOME SUNDOWN, Guitar, Jr. (LONNIE BROOKS), and LAZY LESTER. In 1962, when living in Lake Charles, Louisiana, Webster was discovered by soul singer Otis Redding; she toured with Redding on and off for two years and then became a regular member of his revue until his death in a 1967 plane crash. Fortunately for Webster, eight months pregnant at the time, she missed the fateful flight that killed not only Redding but four members of his back-up band, the Bar-Kays.

Following the tragic accident, Webster dropped out of music and moved to Oakland, California. She resumed her career in 1979 and recorded the album *Katie Webster Has the Blues* for Goldband, followed by *You Can Dig It* and *You Know That's Right*, the latter for the Arhoolie label. None of the records mustered much attention. In 1982, she toured Europe and garnered some acclaim, which led to festival and club dates in the U.S. In addition to *The Swamp Boogie Queen*, which included guest appearances by BONNIE RAITT, Kim Wilson of the FABU-LOUS THUNDERBIRDS, and ROBERT CRAY, Webster has also recorded the albums *Two-Fisted Mama!* and *No Foolin'* for Alligator. In 1993 Webster suffered a stroke which forced her to quit performing.

Essential Listening:
The Swamp Boogie Queen/Alligator (AL 4766)
Two-Fisted Mama!/Alligator (AL 4777)
No Foolin'/Alligator (AL 4803)

◄ WELDON, CASEY BILL

(born Will Weldon, July 10, 1909, Pine Bluff, Ark.; died, date and place unknown)

A slide guitarist and singer, Will Weldon was a member of the MEMPHIS JUG BAND in the 1920s. He later became a solo artist and recorded under the name Casey Bill Weldon. Not much is known about Weldon's early life. He probably got his start in music working the medicine shows that traveled throughout the South. In the early 1920s he began working on Memphis's Beale Street for spare change. During this time he met, worked with, and married MEMPHIS MINNIE, though by the late 1920s the relationship had ended. In 1927 Weldon recorded with the Memphis Jug Band; he also recorded some sides on his own for the Victor label.

Weldon eventually moved on to Chicago, where he changed his name to Casey Bill and altered his country blues–inflected singing and guitar style to one with a more urban slant. Weldon played a Hawaiian steel guitar and occasionally wrote topical songs like "WPA Blues" during the Depression. He recorded for Voca-lion and Bluebird from 1935 to 1937; he also played with BIG BILL BROONZY, Black Bob, and other early Chicago bluesmen. By the early 1940s, Weldon had faded from the city's blues scene. He reportedly went West and settled somewhere in California. One report had him in Detroit in the 1960s. Nothing is known about his death or final resting place.

Essential Listening:
Bottleneck Blues/Yazoo (1049)
Will Weldon/Earl (BD 605)
Master of the Steel Guitar/Old Tramp (1206)

◄ WELLINGTON, VALERIE

(born November 14, 1959, Chicago, Ill.; died January 4, 1993, Chicago, Ill.)

Blues singer Valerie Wellington began her career in Chicago blues clubs in the early 1980s. Before turning to the blues, Wellington sang soul and rhythm & blues with the Chi-Town Instamatics. She also studied classical music at the American Conservatory of Music from 1978 to 1981, where she majored in voice and piano. After being introduced to the classic blues of BESSIE SMITH and MA RAINEY, Wellington switched to the blues, forming a loose onstage partnership with BIG WALTER HORTON in 1982 and then becoming a solo artist. In 1983 Wellington recorded her debut album, *Million Dollar Secret*, for Rooster Blues Records. Backed by MAGIC SLIM & the Teardrops, the album featured Wellington's robust vocals and her strong stylistic connection with Smith and classic blues.

Wellington spent the rest of the 1980s making frequent trips to Europe and Japan and performing in Chicago clubs. During this time she also began a career in acting; she played Ma Rainey in the Chicago production of *The Little Dreamer* (*A Nite in the Life of Bessie Smith*) and BIG MAYBELLE in the movie *Great Balls of Fire*. Wellington died of a heart attack in 1993. She was just thirty-three years old.

Essential Listening:
Million Dollar Secret/Rooster Blues (R 72619)
Life in the Big City/GBW (GBW 002)

◄ WELLS, JUNIOR

(born Amos Blakemore, December 9, 1934, Memphis, Tenn.)

Junior Wells has been one of the principal blues harmonica stylists of Chicago's postwar era. Following in the footsteps of JOHN LEE "SONNY BOY" WILLIAMSON and especially LITTLE WALTER Jacobs, Wells helped define the Chicago blues harp sound in the 1950s, first with the ACES, then with MUDDY WATERS and BUDDY GUY, and finally as a solo artist. Since then, his sweeping harp solos, which often include articulate staccato wails and a sense of phrasing not unlike Little Walter, as well as his whiskey-soaked vocals, have made Wells one of the deans of Chicago blues.

Born and raised in Memphis, where he learned the rudiments of the blues harp from JUNIOR PARKER, Wells moved to Chicago in 1946 and fell in with LOUIS and DAVID MYERS. Calling themselves the Three Deuces, then the Three Aces, Wells and the Myers brothers played house-rent parties and occasional club dates in the late '40s. When they added drummer FRED BELOW in 1950 they became simply the Aces. Wells performed with the group—one of the best of Chicago's early postwar period—until 1952 when Muddy Waters asked him to take the place of Little Walter in his band. Ironically, Little Walter then took Wells's place in the Aces.

Wells's first stint with Waters lasted barely a year; in 1953 he was drafted. Not the army type, Wells went AWOL later that year and returned to Chicago to play with Waters and cut some sides for the States label. (The only song Wells recorded at the time with Waters was "Standing Around Crying" for Chess.) Wells eventually returned to military duty and was discharged in 1955. When he came back to Chicago, Wells worked for Waters for a short while, before re-forming a version of the Aces. Wells and his band worked Chicago clubs and frequently toured, playing black clubs in northern cities and the Southern blues circuit.

In 1958 Wells began playing with guitarist Buddy Guy, forging a loose part-nership that continued on and off for nearly two decades. Although Wells had been making records for the Profile and Chief labels and had backed up Guy for some of the material he cut for Chess in the early '60s, it wasn't until 1966, with the release of the album *Hoodoo Man Blues* (Delmark), that Wells became a major recording figure outside Chicago. A certified classic, the album featured Wells's scintillating harp and vocal work and Guy's backing guitar riffs and captured the vinegary blues of one of the most powerful Chicago bar bands of the '60s. The success of the Wells-Guy recording team on the Vanguard label continued with such Wells albums as *It's My Life, Baby!*, partly recorded live at Pepper's Lounge in Chicago, and *Coming at You.*

In 1970 Buddy Guy and Junior Wells toured Europe with the ROLLING STONES; two years later they released *Play the Blues*, an Atco album that featured cameos by ERIC CLAPTON, DR. JOHN, and the J. Geils Band. Another live Wells album, *Drinkin' TNT 'n' Smokin' Dynamite*, featured the Stones' Bill Wyman on bass. Through the rest of the '70s, Wells was a fixture on the Chicago club scene, often performing at the noted blues club Theresa's Lounge. During the '80s blues ren-aissance, Wells continued playing festivals and touring. In 1990 he recorded the album *Harp Attack!* with fellow blues harmonica players JAMES COTTON, CAREY BELL, and BILLY BRANCH. Wells continues to perform regularly.

Essential Listening:
Blues Hit Big Town/Delmark (DD 640)
Hoodoo Man Blues/Delmark (DD 612)
Messin with the Kid, 1957–1963/Paula (PCD 03)
Coming at You/Vanguard (VMD 79262)
It's My Life, Baby!/Vanguard (VMD 73120)
On Tap/Delmark (DD 635)
Harp Attack! (with James Cotton, Carey Bell, and Billy Branch)/Alligator (ALCD 4790)
Alone & Acoustic (with Buddy Guy)/Alligator (ALCD 4802)
Southside Blues Jam/Delmark (DD 628)
Drinkin' TNT 'n' Smokin' Dynamite (with Buddy Guy)/Blind Pig (BP 1182)

◄ WESTON, JOHN

(born December 12, 1927, Helena, Ark.)

Blues guitarist and singer John Weston is an Arkansas bluesman who played in relative obscurity for years before winning the Blues Foundation's amateur blues talent contest in 1989. Prior to that, Weston performed in local clubs in and around Helena, Arkansas, as well as outside Bubba's Blues Corner, the city's famous blues record store.

Weston was born and raised in Arkansas. He taught himself to play the guitar when he was thirty years old and learned the rudiments of the harmonica from WILLIE COBBS. Since winning the Lucille Award (named after B.B. KING's guitar and given to the winner of the annual amateur talent contest), Weston has performed at the Helena Blues Festival and occasionally toured outside Tennessee. In 1992 he recorded his debut album, *So Doggone Blue*, for the Fat Possum label. Weston continues to perform.

Essential Listening:
So Doggone Blue/Fat Possum (FP 1003)

◄ WHEATSTRAW, PEETIE

(born William Bunch, December 21, 1902, Ripley, Tenn.; died December 21, 1941, East St. Louis, Ill.)

One of the most popular blues recording artists of the 1930s, St. Louis pianist and singer Peetie Wheatstraw recorded more than 160 titles with a variety of guitar accompanists, including LONNIE JOHNSON, CHARLEY JORDAN, KOKOMO ARNOLD, and CHARLIE MCCOY. Wheatstraw was a less-than-compelling pianist, but his vocal style possessed wonderful range and color. He punctuated most of his songs with a falsetto "Ooh, well well" that became his trademark.

Little is known of Wheatstraw's early life until his arrival in East St. Louis, Illinois, sometime around 1929, which is when he apparently lifted the name Peetie Wheatstraw from a black folk tale. Inspired by the success that pianist LEROY CARR and guitarist SCRAPPER BLACKWELL enjoyed in Chicago at the time, Wheatstraw began a decade-long relationship with St. Louis's most noted blues guitarist, Lonnie Johnson, as well as with the other guitarists mentioned above.

Wheatstraw isn't looked upon as a particularly innovative recording artist; many blues critics consider his large output of material limited in the number of musical themes and ideas that it explores, most of them worked and reworked nearly to the point of exhaustion. It was Wheatstraw's vocal strength and bubbling self-confidence that enabled his records, released by such labels as Vocalion, Bluebird, and Decca, to sell through the 1930s. Wheatstraw was also a talented lyric writer. Many of his songs contain elaborate, clever phrases that, more often than not, focus on themes of sex, death, and the supernatural, often with the imperative that one should enjoy life to the fullest.

Wheatstraw was killed in an auto accident in 1941 at the height of his career. He was just thirty-nine years old.

Essential Listening:
The Devil's Son-in-Law, 1937–1941/Best of Blues (BOB 10)
Peetie Wheatstraw and Kokomo Arnold/Blues Classics (4)
The Devil's Son-in-Law/Blues Documents (2011)

◄ WHITE, ARTIE "BLUES BOY"

(born Vicksburg, Miss.)

Like many other blues singers, Artie White got his start in gospel. Born and raised in Mississippi, he was just twelve years old when he began singing with Vicksburg gospel group the Harps of David. He continued his gospel career in Chicago, where he moved in 1956, with the Full Gospel Wonders.

White became a blues singer in the early 1960s; he cut a number of singles for the PM, Gamma, and Altee labels, but they failed to attract much attention. He then bought Bootsy's Lounge and ran the Chicago club until he signed a recording contract with the Louisiana-based Ronn/Jewel label in 1985 and released his debut album, *Blues Boy.* Two years later, in 1987, White jumped to Ichiban Records where he recorded a flurry of albums, including *Tired of Sneaking Around*, which made it onto the R&B charts. With a style that is a mesh of soul, gospel, R&B, and blues, White continues to record and perform.

Essential Listening:
Nothing Takes the Place of You/Ichiban (ICH 1008)
Where It's At/Ichiban (ICH 1026)
Tired of Sneaking Around/Ichiban (ICH 1061)
Best of Artie White/Ichiban (ICH 1131)

◄ WHITE, BUKKA

(born Booker T. Washington White, November 12, 1909, Houston, Miss.; died February 26, 1977, Memphis, Tenn.)

Bukka White was a traditional Delta blues singer and slide guitarist whose coarse-cut vocals and jagged guitar riffs were often a study in blues primitivism. Despite the purity and rich expressiveness of his style, White never quite received the acclaim due him at the time he made the bulk of his recordings—from 1930 to 1940. But after his rediscovery in the early '60s, White's blues repertoire and indigenous Delta style were much better appreciated. Today, many blues historians consider his music nearly on a par with such early Delta blues greats as CHARLEY PATTON, TOMMY JOHNSON, and ROBERT JOHNSON.

White was born in the Mississippi hill country west of the blues-soaked Delta and learned to play guitar from his father, a railroad worker and part-time musician. By the time he reached adolescence, White had moved to the Delta, where he was exposed to the blues of Charley Patton, one of his main influences. White worked as a field hand, but he also played jukes and parties. Eventually he left the Delta and drifted about the South, playing for tips and spare change.

White's first recording session was in Memphis in 1930 for the Victor label. He recorded under the name Washington White and cut blues as well as religious numbers. Unable to make a living as a full-time musician, White played professional baseball in the Negro leagues and, for a spell, was also a professional fighter. In 1937 he reputedly shot a man and was arrested and sentenced to prison. White jumped bail that same year and ran to Chicago where he recorded two songs for Vocalion, including one of his most noted tunes, "Shake 'Em on

Down,'' before he was captured and sent to Parchman Farm, a notorious Mississippi prison.

White spent two years at Parchman; for most of his incarceration he provided musical entertainment for the inmates. He also recorded a couple of songs for ALAN LOMAX and the Library of Congress while at Parchman. Shortly after his release from prison in 1940, White resumed his recording career and cut some twelve songs for the Okeh and Vocalion labels, with accompaniment by WASHBOARD SAM.

With country blues growing out of favor in the 1940s, White found it increasingly difficult to continue his blues career. He eventually settled in Memphis, became a common laborer, and played only occasionally, until he was rediscovered by folk-blues guitarist John Fahey and blues aficionado Ed Dawson in 1963. Students at the University of California at Berkeley at the time, Fahey and Dawson recorded White in Memphis that year. That Bob Dylan had interpreted one of White's songs, ''Fixin' to Die Blues,'' on his self-titled debut album a year earlier only added to White's growing prestige as a classic country bluesman. A recording contract with Arhoolie Records followed, as did frequent performances on college campuses and in urban folk clubs. White played the Newport Folk Festival in 1966 and toured with the American Folk Blues Festival in England and Europe in 1967. In 1973 he performed at the New Orleans Jazz & Heritage Festival in New Orleans. White also recorded regularly in the '60s and '70s. *Big Daddy*, the album he recorded for Biograph in 1973, contains some of White's most inspired recorded performances. White died of cancer in 1977. He was inducted into the Blues Foundation's Hall of Fame in 1990.

Essential Listening:

Sky Songs/Arhoolie (CD 323)

The Complete Sessions, 1930–40/Travelin' Man (CD 03)

Big Daddy/Biograph (12049)

Three Shades of Blues (with Skip James and Blind Willie McTell)/Biograph (BCD 107)

Legacy of the Blues, Vol. 1/GNP Crescendo (10011)

◄ WHITE, GEORGIA

(born March 9, 1903, Sandersville, Ga.; died c. 1980)

Georgia White was a Chicago-based vocalist and piano player who began singing during the classic blues era, but was most popular in the mid- and late 1930s when she recorded for the Decca label.

Sometime in the early 1920s White moved to Chicago, where she sang and played piano in clubs and speakeasies. In 1930 she recorded with Jimmie Noone and his orchestra for the Vocalion label. It wasn't until 1935 that she began a solo recording career. Her 1936 recording of the classic ''Trouble in Mind'' became one of her signature songs. With a vocal style that could move freely from moaning classic blues to blues shouter and a piano style that incorporated many elements of boogie-woogie, White was one of Chicago's most popular club performers into the early 1940s.

White ended her recording tenure with Decca in 1941; she continued to play clubs well into the 1950s but eventually faded from the scene.

Essential Listening:
Georgia White Sings & Plays/Rosetta (RR 1307)

◄ WHITE, JOSH
(born February 11, 1914, Greenville, S.C.; died September 5, 1969, Manhasset, N.Y.)

Though born and raised in South Carolina, Josh White is best known as a New York folk-blues singer and guitarist who, along with LEADBELLY, SONNY TERRY, BROWNIE MCGHEE, and BIG BILL BROONZY, helped make blues a staple of American folk music. In addition to singing and playing a Piedmont brand of blues, complete with elaborate finger-picking techniques, White's repertoire also included spirituals and social-protest songs. A contemporary of folksinger Woody Guthrie, White's musical stance against racial prejudice and social injustice endeared him to members of both the Old and New Left movements in the '30s and '60s, respectively.

White began his association with the blues as a child when he earned money by leading blind blues singers such as Big Boy Arnold, WILLIE WALKER, and Joe Taggart around the Greenville-Spartanburg area of South Carolina. White debuted as a recording artist in 1928 when he went with Taggart to Chicago and accompanied him on guitar during sessions Taggart cut for the Paramount label. White first recorded as a solo artist in 1932 for the American Record Company. Early on, he used the pseudonyms Pinewood Tom, when he recorded blues, and Joshua White (the Singing Christian), when he recorded religious material.

White moved to New York in the early 1930s and remained there the rest of his life. He worked in a variety of settings: as the leader of the Josh White Singers and then of Josh White and his Carolinians; as a solo performer at New York house parties and small clubs; as an actor (he appeared in the shows *John Henry* and *The Man Who Went to War*, both with Paul Robeson, and had parts in such films as *Crimson Canary, To Hear Your Banjo Play*, and *The Walking Hills*); and as a performing colleague of Leadbelly and other black blues musicians who had relocated to New York in the 1930s and 1940s.

White's good looks and tidy blues style endeared him to white audiences. During the 1940s he performed for President Franklin Roosevelt and recorded for the Library of Congress. He toured Mexico in 1942 under the auspices of the U.S. State Department. White also recorded for a variety of other labels; his longest tenure, with Elektra, lasted from 1954 to 1962. In the late '50s and '60s, White became a fixture in the folk and country blues revival, playing folk and blues festivals and coffeehouses in the U.S. and Canada, as well as in England.

White died in 1969. His son, Josh White, Jr., is a folk-blues singer who often performs his father's songs.

Essential Listening:
Joshua White (1929–1941)/Document (DLP 597)
Joshua White, vol. 1/Earl Archives (BD 606)

Joshua White, vol. 2/Earl Archives (BD 619)
The Legendary Josh White/MCA (2-4170)

◄ WIGGINS, PHIL

(born May 8, 1954, Washington, D.C.)

One half of Cephas & Wiggins, a leading contemporary exponent of Piedmont blues, harmonica player Phil Wiggins began his association with guitarist and singer JOHN CEPHAS at the 1976 Festival of American Folklife in Washington, D.C., where the two jammed together. Prior to the fest, Wiggins had performed with some of the city's leading blues artists, including the locally noted slide guitarist and gospel singer FLORA MOLTON. Cephas had been playing house parties with WILBERT "BIG CHIEF" ELLIS, an old barrelhouse piano player, around Washington. After the festival, Cephas, Ellis, and Wiggins, along with bass player James Bellamy, formed the Barrelhouse Rockers. The group lasted one year; in 1977 Ellis died.

Cephas and Wiggins continued on as a duo, first playing in southeastern blues clubs, later at regional folk and blues fests, and then on national and international stages. In addition to playing most major fests in the U.S., they also toured Europe, Central and South America, Africa, Russia, China, and Australia during the 1980s, frequently under the auspices of the State Department. Their first two albums, *Living Country Blues, Vol. 1, Bowling Green John Cephas & Harmonica Phil Wiggins from Virginia, U.S.A.* and *Sweet Bitter Blues*, were released on the German L+R label in 1981 and 1983, respectively. Cephas & Wiggins's first U.S. release, *Dog Days of August* on the Flying Fish label, won a W.C. HANDY Award for the best traditional album of 1986, while the duo was named best blues entertainers of the year, an award that had previously gone to electric blues artists and bands. Cephas & Wiggins picked up another Handy award in 1990 for their follow-up album, *Guitar Man*. In 1992, Cephas & Wiggins released their third U.S. album, *Flip, Flop & Fly*. The duo continues to record and perform.

Essential Listening:

Dog Days of August/Flying Fish (FF 394)
Guitar Man/Flying Fish (FF 90470)
Flip, Flop & Fly/Flying Fish (FF 70580)

◄ WILKINS, JOE WILLIE

(born January 7, 1923, Davenport, Miss.; died March 28, 1979, Memphis, Tenn.)

Joe Willie Wilkins was a blues guitarist whose influence was far larger than his popularity as a recording artist. Primarily an accompanist, Wilkins played behind harp master SONNY BOY WILLIAMSON (Rice Miller) and was a member of the King Biscuit Entertainers, the group that made blues radio history in the 1940s with daily noontime broadcasts on KFFA out of Helena, Arkansas. With an altogether unique guitar style that was a blend of roughened Delta rhythms and searing single-string solos, Wilkins gave great guitar licks to most every blues artist he backed.

As a youth growing up in the Mississippi Delta, Wilkins learned how to play some harmonica, fiddle, and accordion before he settled on guitar. He played in small bands in the Clarksdale, Mississippi, area, but he was also a solo street corner musician, often going by the name Joe Willie, the Walkin' Seeburg (Seeburg manufactured jukeboxes). In the late 1930s Wilkins began traveling and performing with Sonny Boy Williamson and ROBERT JR. LOCKWOOD, the guitarist by whom Wilkins was much influenced. In 1941, after Williamson and Lockwood had signed on with KFFA and created "King Biscuit Time," the fifteen-minute dose of live blues that went out on the radio each midday, the two bluesmen assembled the King Biscuit Entertainers, a loosely organized band that included Wilkins and later HOUSTON STACKHOUSE on electric guitar as well as drummers PECK CURTIS and WILLIE NIX and piano players WILLIE LOVE, PINETOP PERKINS, and DUDLOW TAYLOR.

Wilkins often toured with Williamson in the late 1940s and played on many of Williamson's early recordings for the Trumpet label from 1951 to 1953. Wilkins even became the unofficial house guitarist at Trumpet. He later assumed a similar role for SAM PHILLIPS's Sun label in Memphis. Throughout the '50s and '60s, Wilkins, based out of Memphis, continued to work as a sideman. In the early '70s he formed Joe's King Biscuit Boys and worked clubs in and around Memphis. He died of a heart attack in 1979.

Essential Listening:
Joe Willie Wilkins & His King Biscuit Boys/Adamo (ADS 9507)

◄ WILKINS, ROBERT

(aka Rev. Robert Wilkins) (born January 16, 1896, Hernando, Miss.; died 1987)

A Mississippi-born guitarist and singer who later became a minister, Robert Wilkins was part of the Memphis blues scene in the 1920s. Wilkins wrote songs that contained personalized views of the world around him and irregular melodic structures that gave much of his material an unusual, intriguing edge. Wilkins was not, however, a rousing singer and his commercial success never matched his compositional talents.

Wilkins was taught to play guitar by his father. He moved to Memphis in 1915 and played street corners for tips before serving in the army during World War I. Upon his discharge, he returned to Memphis and resumed his role as a street musician until signing a recording contract with the Victor label in 1928. He also recorded for Brunswick in 1929 and 1930. Wilkins continued to perform in and around Memphis and had one more recording session in 1935, this time with Vocalion, before he quit the blues and began going to church. Eventually Wilkins became a minister in the Church of God in Christ.

Wilkins was rediscovered in the early 1960s at the height of the folk-blues boom. He recorded a bluesy gospel album, *Memphis Gospel Singer*, for the Piedmont label in 1964 and performed at the Newport Folk Festival that same year.

In 1968, the ROLLING STONES recorded a Wilkins song, "The Prodigal Son," which the group included on its album *Beggar's Banquet*. The original version of the song was called "That's No Way to Get Along" and was recorded by Wilkins during his blues days. The updated version contained lyrics that were more religious in nature. Wilkins continued to play an occasional folk or blues festival until his death in 1987. He was ninety-one years old.

Essential Listening:
The Original Rolling Stone/Yazoo (1077)
Robert Wilkins/Wolf (111)
Memphis Gospel Singer/OJL (8052)

◄ WILLIAMS, BIG JOE

(born October 16, 1903, Crawford, Miss.; died December 17, 1982,
Macon, Ga.)

Big Joe Williams, a Mississippi Delta blues guitarist and singer, began his recording career in the 1930s with the Bluebird label and continued making records and performing right up until his death in 1982. He was best known for his leathery vocals and the full-bodied sound of his nine-string guitar, both of which reflected a life of hoboing through the South, hopping freights, spending time in jail, playing juke joints, and maintaining a fiercely independent blues spirit. Williams was also a competent songwriter; he penned the blues classic "(Baby) Please Don't Go," which has been covered by countless blues and blues-rock artists.

Williams left Mississippi as a youth to travel through the South, playing levee and lumber camps. In the early 1920s he worked with the Birmingham Jug Band in the Rabbit Foot Minstrels revue and recorded with the group in 1930 for the Okeh label. Williams epitomized the traveling bluesman. He worked for spare change or food, he slept in railroad cars, and he wandered from town to town in the 1920s and early 1930s playing and singing CHARLEY PATTON–inspired country blues. After Williams wound up in St. Louis sometime in 1934, he performed with his cousin J.D. Short, a fellow blues musician, at house parties and clubs.

Through Short, Williams met record producer LESTER MELROSE of Bluebird Records, who signed him to a recording contract in 1935. For ten years Williams recorded for the label. "(Baby) Please Don't Go" was a hit in 1935; his 1941 version of "Crawlin' King Snake" was also a popular record. During this time Williams performed and recorded with a number of prominent bluesmen, including harmonica player JOHN LEE "SONNY BOY" WILLIAMSON, guitarists CHARLEY JORDAN and ROBERT NIGHTHAWK, and pianist PEETIE WHEATSTRAW.

Williams remained a noted blues artist in the 1950s and 1960s; his rough-and-tumble guitar style and rugged vocals became popular with folk-blues fans. His repertoire, which included blues and folk tunes learned in all his years of traveling, enabled him to continue recording at a time when the Chicago electric band sound dominated the blues. Williams cut material for the Trumpet, Cobra, Delmark, and Arhoolie labels and later for Testament and Bluesville, among others.

In the '60s Williams was a regular on the concert and coffeehouse circuits.

He toured Europe with the American Folk Blues Festival package in 1968 and 1972 and performed at such major U.S. festivals as the Ann Arbor Blues Festival in 1969 and the New Orleans Jazz & Heritage Festival in 1972. In 1974 he toured Japan. Despite his advancing age, Williams also managed to keep his recording career healthy. A number of Williams's albums were released on such labels as Storyville, Sonet, and Delmark in the late 1960s and 1970s. In addition, he appeared in blues documentaries like *The Devil's Music—A History of the Blues* (1976) and *Good Mornin' Blues* (1978). Through it all, Williams kept the Delta blues tradition alive and was one of the genre's most engaging performers. Williams died in 1982. Ten years later he was inducted into the Blues Foundation's Hall of Fame.

   Essential Listening:
Stavin' Chain Blues (with J.D. Short)/Delmark (DD 609)
Nine String Guitar Blues/Delmark (DD 627)
Blues on Highway 49/Delmark (DD 604)
Throw a Boogie Woogie (with Sonny Boy Williamson)/RCA (9599-2-R)
Shake Your Boogie/Arhoolie (CD 315)
Big Joe Williams, Vol. 1 (1935–41)/RST Blues Documents (BDCD 6003)
Big Joe Williams, Vol. 2 (1945–49)/RST Blues Documents (BDCD 6004)

◀ WILLIAMS, CLARENCE

(born October 8, 1898, Plaquemine, La.; died November 6, 1965, Queens, N.Y.)

   Clarence Williams was a blues composer as well as a pianist, record producer, arranger, and music publisher during the classic blues era. Along with fellow jack-of-all-trades talent PERRY BRADFORD, Williams helped the blues assume a legitimate status in popular music in the 1920s. He wrote songs for such blues singers as BESSIE SMITH and SARA MARTIN, and often worked with the comedic vaudeville act BUTTERBEANS & SUSIE. Included among Williams's most famous works are such songs as "Baby Won't You Please Come Home," "West End Blues," and "Gulf Coast Blues."

   Williams began his career in New Orleans, working in flophouses and minstrel shows as a singer and pianist. In the early 1920s he relocated to New York. From 1923 to 1928 he worked as a talent scout and session musician for Okeh Records. In addition to writing for Smith and other blues singers, Williams also recorded with jazzmen LOUIS ARMSTRONG, King Oliver, Coleman Hawkins, and Don Redman and had his own band, Clarence Williams and His Blue Five, which recorded in the mid-'20s. Later on, Williams headed other bands like the Stompers, Jazz Kings, and the Washboard Band.

   Williams continued writing songs and working in jazz and blues well into the 1940s. He faded from the scene after being hit by a taxi in New York in 1956 and eventually going blind. He died in 1965.

◄ WILLIAMS, JABO

(born Pratt City, Ala.; died, date and place unknown)

Jabo Williams was an early boogie-woogie piano player whose few recordings reveal a raw and wild style with rolling bass runs and rag-flavored right-hand riffs. Although Williams was born in Pratt City, Alabama, just outside of Birmingham, he is most closely associated with the St. Louis school of boogie-woogie pianists, since it was there that he became a popular club entertainer and recording artist.

Almost nothing else is known of Williams's life, other than the recordings he made for the Paramount label in the early 1930s. "Pratt City Blues" and "Jab's Blues" were his most noted Paramount sides. Williams ended his tenure with Paramount in 1932. After that, he vanished from the St. Louis blues scene.

Essential Listening:

Paramount, Vol. 2, 1927–32 (The Piano Blues) (Various Artists)/Magpie
(PYCD 05)

◄ WILLIAMS, JOE

(born Joseph Goreed, December 12, 1918, Cordele, Ga.)

Blues singer Joe Williams is best known for his work with the COUNT BASIE Band in the 1950s. Their version of the Memphis Slim classic "Everyday I Have the Blues" came from the album *Count Basie Swings, Joe Williams Sings*, one of the last great big band blues albums. Williams is also regarded as the last of the great big band blues singers.

Although born in Georgia, Williams and his family moved to Chicago when he was four years old. As a youth he sang gospel music in church choirs and with his group the Jubilee Boys. In the late '30s, Williams switched to jazz. He logged time with the bands of Les Hite, Coleman Hawkins, Jimmie Noone, and Lionel Hampton, as well as with boogie-woogie pianists ALBERT AMMONS and PETE JOHNSON. Williams began his recording career in 1946 when he cut sides with Red Saunders's band for the Okeh label. In the late '40s Williams continued his journeyman status with stints in bands led by Andy Kirk, Jay Burkhart, and Saunders, with whom he again recorded, this time as Jumpin Joe Williams. In 1952 Williams recorded his first version of "Everyday I Have the Blues." Backed by the King Kolax Orchestra, Williams's interpretation of the song made it to number 8 on the R&B charts.

Williams sang with the Count Basie Septet in 1950 and in 1954 joined Basie's new big band as a full-time member. From 1954 to 1961 the Basie-Williams bandleader-singer combination was the best in the big band blues idiom. During the '50s the group toured Europe and the U.S., made television appearances, played jazz festivals, and recorded regularly.

After Williams left Basie in 1961, he broadened his repertoire so that it included not only blues but also jazz and pop. Williams continued to tour and record regularly; he became a familiar face on television, appearing on such variety programs as "The Tonight Show," "Steve Allen," "Joey Bishop," "Merv Griffin,'' and ''Mike Douglas'' shows. A friend of Duke Ellington's, Williams sang at the Duke's funeral in 1974. He also resumed touring with the Basie band.

Williams continued to perform regularly at jazz festivals, both in the U.S. and abroad, as well as on the nightclub circuit. Although most of the post-Basie albums he recorded usually contained more jazz than blues, occasional works like *Me and the Blues* and *Nothin' but the Blues* proved that Williams had not lost touch with his early blues roots. Williams continues to perform and record.

Essential Listening:
Count Basie Swings, Joe Williams Sings/Verve
Me and the Blues/RCA
Nothin' but the Blues/Delos

◄ WILLIAMS, LARRY

(born May 10, 1935, New Orleans, La.; died January 2, 1980, Los Angeles, Calif.)

Larry Williams was a rhythm & blues singer and songwriter whose small string of late-'50s singles for the Specialty label made him a possible heir to the rock & roll throne vacated by LITTLE RICHARD after the latter's decision to leave pop music and become a minister. Williams began his career in 1954 as the pianist in LLOYD PRICE's band. In 1937 he signed a recording contract with Specialty and recorded a cover version of Price's ''Just Because'' that made it to number 11 on the R&B charts. Williams's self-penned follow-up record, ''Short Fat Fannie,'' went all the way to number 1 later that year. He also wrote and recorded ''Bony Moronie,'' which peaked at number 4. None of Williams's records charted in 1958, however, despite his writing and releasing the double-sided classic ''Dizzy Miss Lizzy'' and ''Slow Down.'' In 1959 Williams was arrested for drug possession. Convicted, he served time in jail, effectively ending any chance for major stardom.

In the mid-'60s Williams recorded for the Chess and Okeh labels. He often worked with JOHNNY ''GUITAR'' WATSON and toured England, where his reputation as an early rocker had not diminished—thanks to the Beatles, who covered ''Dizzy Miss Lizzy,'' ''Slow Down,'' and another Williams song, ''Bad Boy,'' and to the ROLLING STONES, who recorded a version of his ''She Said Yeah.''

Williams worked on and off as a producer in the early '70s with little success. He attempted a feeble comeback as a recording artist with the release of the disco-minded album *That Larry Williams* in 1978 for the Fantasy label. Not surprisingly, the album flopped. Two years later, at age forty-four, Williams committed suicide by shooting himself in the head in his L.A. home.

Essential Listening:
Here's Larry Williams/Specialty (SPCD 2109-2)
Bad Boy/Specialty (SPC 7002)
Unreleased Larry Williams/Specialty (SPCD 2158)

◄ WILLIAMS, LUCINDA

(born January 26, 1953, Lake Charles, La.)

No longer associated with the blues, Lucinda Williams nonetheless cut two acclaimed acoustic blues albums before moving into country music. *Ramblin'*, recorded in 1979, consisted of Williams's interpretations of chestnuts such as ROBERT JOHNSON's "Ramblin' on My Mind" and "Malted Milk Blues," and more traditional tunes like "You're Gonna Need that Pure Religion" and "Motherless Children." The 1980 *Happy Woman Blues* was made up of Williams originals.

Born in Louisiana, Williams began her career in the mid-'60s as a folkie inspired by Bob Dylan. By the early '70s she had begun to work significant amounts of blues into her repertoire. After moving to Houston in the late '70s, she played the same clubs as then–fellow folkies Nanci Griffith and Townes Van Zandt. Williams continued to be based out of Texas until 1984 when she moved to Los Angeles; four years later she cut her self-titled third album and had shifted her style into a more country vein. Williams continues to record and perform.

Essential Listening:
Ramblin'/Smithsonian/Folkways (CD SF 40042)
Happy Woman Blues/Smithsonian/Folkways (CD SF 40003)

◄ WILLIAMS, PAUL "HUCKLEBUCK"

(born July 13, 1915, Lewisburg, Tenn.)

Paul Williams, a honking saxophone player and bandleader, carved out a place in R&B history in 1949 with his number 1 hit record "The Hucklebuck," which stayed on the charts for thirty-two weeks, far longer than the typical R&B hit of the time. "The Hucklebuck" was actually Williams's rendition of the Charlie Parker tune "Now's the Time," which Parker cut for Savoy in 1945. Williams renamed the song after a popular late-'40s dance. "The Hucklebuck" became Williams's signature piece; its success prompted a sequel from Williams called "He Knows How to Hucklebuck," which reached number 13 on the charts in mid-1949.

Before "The Hucklebuck," Williams played in Clarence Dorsey's band. In 1947, after forming his own band, he signed a recording contract with the Savoy label and had a hit the following year with "35-30," which made it to number 8 on the charts. He scored with another hit, "Walkin' Around" (number 6), just prior to the release of "The Hucklebuck."

Williams spent the 1950s and the early 1960s as a session musician for Atlantic Records. He also directed the bands of James Brown and LLOYD PRICE before he faded from the R&B scene.

Essential Listening:
The Roots of Rock 'n' Roll (Various Artists)/Savoy (SJL 2221)

◄ WILLIAMS, ROBERT PETE

(born March 14, 1914, Zachary, La.; died December 31, 1980, Rosedale, La.)

The raw, unsettled country blues of Louisiana guitarist and singer Robert Pete Williams was highly original and emotionally striking. Illiterate and unschooled, Williams spent time at the Angola Prison Farm in the 1950s and is best known for his haunting prison songs. Most of them were steeped in an oddly metered, acoustic country style that depicted the hard life of incarceration and added up to some of the most penetrating blues ever recorded.

Born into a sharecropping family, Williams grew up in Zachary, a small hamlet outside of Baton Rouge. Not until he was twenty did he begin to play the blues. Williams made his first guitar out of a sugar box. He performed at Saturday night parties and fish fries but never made enough money to support himself and his family. His wife, envious of the attention given to Williams whenever he played, supposedly burned his guitar in a jealous rage. Williams nonetheless continued to perform in rural Louisiana juke joints until 1956 when, allegedly in self-defense, he shot and killed a man. He was convicted of murder, sentenced to life in prison, and sent to Angola. There, he recorded his famous prison blues songs—"Pardon Denied Again," "Angola Penitentiary Blues," "Prisoner's Talking Blues"—for folklorists Dr. Harry Oster and Richard Allen. Other songs from the recording sessions were later released on the Folk-Lyric and Arhoolie labels.

Thanks to Oster and Allen, who successfully pleaded for a pardon, Williams was released from Angola in 1959 after serving three and a half years. Due to strict parole regulations, Williams was unable to leave Louisiana until 1964, though his stirring blues had begun to attract considerable attention in blues circles outside of the state.

Williams's debut performance outside of Louisiana occurred at the famous 1964 Newport Folk Festival. The success of his set there enabled him to tour, often with MISSISSIPPI FRED MCDOWELL, and record throughout the remainder of the 1960s and most of the 1970s. In addition to Newport, Williams performed in Europe with the American Folk Blues Festival contingent in 1966 and 1972 and frequently played the New Orleans Jazz & Heritage Festival. Williams also recorded for a number of small labels, including Takoma, Fontana, and Storyville; releases from these companies further documented his rough-cut country blues. Williams died in 1980.

Essential Listening:
Angola's Prisoner's Blues/Arhoolie (2011)
Those Prison Blues/Arhoolie (2015)

◄ WILLIAMSON, JOHN LEE "SONNY BOY"

(aka Sonny Boy Williamson #1) (born March 30, 1914, Jackson, Tenn.; died June 1, 1948, Chicago, Ill.)

Perhaps more than any other blues harmonica player, John Lee "Sonny Boy" Williamson was responsible for the transition of the harp from a simple down-home instrument used mainly for novelty twists and light jug band riffs, to one that became an essential part of the early Chicago blues sound. The 1920s and 1930s had its share of innovative harp players; WILL SHADE, NOAH LEWIS, and HAMMIE NIXON—all early influences on Williamson—broke new ground by expanding the role of the instrument in country blues. Deford Bailey popularized the harmonica during his many performances on the Grand Ol' Opry radio program. But only Williamson was able to lift the blues harp onto a broader plane with his inventive phrasing and impeccably crisp, clean tones.

Williamson was also a talented vocalist, despite the handicap of a "slow tongue" that made some of his words slur. Williamson, however, cleverly worked his speech impediment into his singing style, so that its presence gave his voice an alluring drag. For the eleven years he was part of the Chicago blues scene, Williamson was one of its most popular and well-liked recording artists. Songs of his such as "Good Morning Little School Girl," "Sugar Mama Blues," "Early in the Morning," "Check Up on My Baby," and "Bluebird Blues" were all big hits for the Bluebird label in the 1930s and 1940s and had a major influence on the succeeding generation of blues harp players. Williamson's stature was such that Rice Miller, a great blues harmonica player who followed in his path, assumed Williamson's name as his own, presumably both to capitalize on Sonny Boy #1's fame and to carry on his legacy. Miller is often referred to as Sonny Boy Williamson #2.

John Lee Williamson was born in Jackson, Tennessee, where at an early age he taught himself how to play the harmonica. By the time he was in his midteens he was already a competent harp player. Williamson traveled with bluesmen like SLEEPY JOHN ESTES, YANK RACHELL, BIG JOE WILLIAMS, and ROBERT NIGHTHAWK during the Depression, earning the nickname "Sonny Boy" in the process. In 1937, at age twenty-three, Williamson settled in Chicago, where he quickly became in demand as a session player. That same year he was signed to the Bluebird label by famed producer LESTER MELROSE.

Williamson's early recordings harked back to the country blues harp style and blues sound he learned hoboing through the South in the early '30s. He often recorded with Big Joe Williams, who played a rough-edged nine-string acoustic guitar. Eventually Williamson transformed his singing and harp style to fit the small combo blues that Bluebird was regularly recording in Chicago during this time. In addition to Williams, Williamson also recorded and performed with guitarists such as TAMPA RED and BIG BILL BROONZY, as well as pianists like BLIND JOHN DAVIS, BIG MACEO, and EDDIE BOYD. By the outbreak of World War II, Williamson was a mainstay on the Chicago blues scene and unquestionably its most important and most popular harmonica player.

Tragically, at the height of his harp prowess and popularity, Williamson was murdered in 1948 as he walked home from a club date on Chicago's South Side. His death at age thirty-four was a major blow to the city's blues community. Williamson was inducted into the Blues Foundation's Hall of Fame in 1980.

Essential Listening:

Sonny Boy Williamson, Vol. 1 (1937–1938)/Document (DOCD 5055)
Sonny Boy Williamson, Vol. 2 (1938–1939)/Document (DOCD 5056)

Sonny Boy Williamson, Vol. 3 (1939–1941)/Document (DOCD 5057)
Sonny Boy Williamson, Vol. 4 (1941–1945)/Document (DOCD 5058)
Sonny Boy Williamson, Vol. 5 (1945–1947)/Document (DOCD 5059)
Throw a Boogie-Woogie (with Big Joe Williams)/RCA Heritage (9599-2)

◄ WILLIAMSON, SONNY BOY

(aka Rice Miller, Sonny Boy Williamson #2, Willie Williamson) (born Aleck Miller, 1910, Glendora, Miss.; died May 25, 1965, Helena, Ark.)

Sonny Boy Williamson was one of the most influential harmonica players in blues history, ranking with LITTLE WALTER Jacobs as the music's major post–World War II harp stylist. Aleck "Rice" Miller, believed to be his real name, or Sonny Boy Williamson #2, as he was often called, is not to be confused with John Lee "Sonny Boy" Williamson, who, in the 1930s and 1940s, was an important blues harmonica player in his own right and the first to use the "Sonny Boy" nickname.

Aside from being a harp player who helped set the course of modern blues, Sonny Boy Williamson #2 was also a legendary blues character whose colorful personality, unpredictable actions, and frequent stretching of the truth only served to enliven his blues with a rare, but warmly embraced, eccentricity.

Williamson's harp style included intricately woven phrasing, bold sonic textures, trills and vibrato, a wide range of dynamic passion, and a superb sense of timing. He was also an effective showman—he could, for instance, put the entire harp in his mouth and still draw notes. More important, his playing made the harp the center attraction, no matter how many other great blues musicians shared the stage with him. Yet Williamson was more than just a blues harp genius and potent performer; he was also a superb tunesmith. Many of his songs—"One Way Out," "Don't Start Me Talking," "Cross My Heart," "Eyesight to the Blind," "Mighty Long Time," "Help Me," and "Nine Below Zero"—are acknowledged classics and staples in any serious blues harmonica player's repertoire.

Williamson was also a convincing singer and the blues' first radio star. His daily performances on the Helena, Arkansas, radio station KFFA in the 1940s, which were heard throughout eastern Arkansas, western Tennessee, and the Mississippi Delta, not only made him a celebrity but also influenced an entire generation of blues musicians living in the region. Elements of Williamson's harmonica style can be heard in the styles of everyone from HOWLIN' WOLF, whom Williamson personally tutored, to MUDDY WATERS and JUNIOR WELLS and virtually all of the postwar Memphis blues school.

Despite his status, Williamson was an odd, elusive character. Worked into his wiry frame—he stood over six feet tall—was a complex web of personality traits that even his best friends found difficult to understand. He was a hothead who rarely turned from a fight. He was also a shrewd talker, a drinker, a liar, a loner, a gambler, a con man, and a ladies' man. To the end of his life he swore he was "the real Sonny Boy Williamson," though, in fact, John Lee Williamson had used the "Sonny Boy" tag years before Miller had adopted it as his own.

Because of his reluctance to talk about his early years when interviewed and his liberal interpretation of the truth when he did, Williamson's early biography remains muddy. Blues historians are reasonably certain he was born in 1910, although the years 1894, 1897, 1899, 1908, and 1909 have also been cited. Born and raised in Mississippi to sharecropping parents, Williamson taught himself how to play the harmonica and started performing in local jukes in the mid-1920s. By 1930 or so, Williamson began his wanderings through the South, playing in parks, on street corners, in lumber and levee camps, and at house parties and juke joints, occasionally in the company of other bluesmen such as ROBERT JR. LOCKWOOD, ROBERT JOHNSON, ELMORE JAMES, and Howlin' Wolf.

Although he was known in Delta blues circles thanks to his near-constant ramblings, it wasn't until Williamson and guitarist Lockwood began performing each day at noon on KFFA in 1941 that Williamson's reputation began to broaden. Called "King Biscuit Flour Time," the fifteen-minute radio program was sponsored by the Interstate Grocery Company and in its early days featured Williamson on harmonica and vocals and Lockwood on twelve-string guitar. In addition to playing a few blues numbers, Williamson chatted on the air and pushed King Biscuit flour. Although he was paid little for his services, Williamson was permitted to announce where he would be playing that evening. The advance advertising resulted in better pay from club owners and better tips than Williamson had received before becoming a radio personality.

Williamson and Lockwood were called the King Biscuit Entertainers and often did station-sponsored events off the air. Eventually the duo expanded into a full, though loosely organized, band with the addition of PECK CURTIS on drums and vocals, DUDLOW TAYLOR on piano, and later pianists PINETOP PERKINS and WILLIE LOVE and guitarist HOUSTON STACKHOUSE depending on who was available at the time. By the time he left the station in 1944 to go back on the road, Sonny Boy Williamson, the moniker Miller had begun using around the time he first performed on the air, had become a familiar name in many Southern black households. His face was even printed on the bags of King Biscuit corn meal to help sell the product.

After 1944 Williamson was no longer a daily personality on KFFA. Yet whenever he returned to Helena, which was often, he went back to the station and resumed his role as on-the-air performer and entertainer. Throughout the rest of the decade, Williamson performed in the Delta with guitarists Elmore James and JOE WILLIE WILKINS, pianist Willie Love, and drummer WILLIE NIX.

Despite his blues credentials and popularity, Williamson didn't begin his recording career until 1951 when he cut sides for Trumpet, the Jackson, Mississippi, label. Williamson's now-classic Trumpet tracks are raw and rough, especially when compared to his later recordings with Chess. Yet their coarse juke-joint swagger and brilliant harp work reveal much about Williamson's blues view and early performance style.

Williamson was based in the Memphis area until 1954 when he moved first to Detroit and then to Milwaukee and Cleveland. But he never severed his Southern roots, regularly returning to perform right to the very end of his career. After Trumpet had suspended operations in 1955, Williamson signed on with Checker, the Chess subsidiary label, with whom he recorded until the early '60s. Cutting sides with Chess session musicians like guitarists Lockwood and LUTHER TUCKER, pianists OTIS SPANN and LAFAYETTE LEAKE, bass player WILLIE DIXON, and drummer FRED BELOW, Williamson's sound became more tightly defined and assumed a greater sophistication than on the Trumpet sides.

Williamson continued to tour, working his way through St. Louis, Memphis, Helena, and the Delta, then back again to Chicago. In 1963 and 1964 he toured Europe as part of the American Folk Blues Festival package. He also performed and recorded with British blues-rock groups the ANIMALS and the YARDBIRDS (with ERIC CLAPTON on guitar), becoming as big a blues star in England as he was in the States.

Unfortunately, by this time Williamson's health had begun to deteriorate rapidly. In 1965 he returned to Helena and resumed, yet again, his appearances on KFFA's "King Biscuit Time." Shortly thereafter, he died. Williamson was inducted into the Blues Foundation's Hall of Fame in 1980.

Essential Listening:
King Biscuit Time/Arhoolie (310)
The Chess Years (box set)/Charly (CD 1)
One Way Out Blues/MCA-Chess (9116)
The Real Folk Blues/MCA Chess (9272)
More Real Folk Blues/MCA Chess (9277)
Bummer Road/MCA-Chess (324)
Sonny Boy Williamson and the Yardbirds: Live in London/Optimism
  (LR CD 2020)
Keep It to Ourselves/Alligator (4787)
Going in Your Direction/Alligator (2801)

◄ WILLIS, CHICK

(born September 24, 1934, Cabiness, Ga.)

Chick Willis is a Georgia blues singer-guitarist and a first cousin of '50s R&B artist CHUCK WILLIS. His style contains strains of funk and soul, though his forte is bawdy blues, as evidenced by his version of TAMPA RED's risqué hit "I Want to Play with Your Poodle" and his own "I Want a Big Fat Woman," both of which are found on Willis's *Now* album, released by Ichiban Records in 1989. The latter tune was nominated for a W.C. HANDY Award for top contemporary blues single that year.

Willis began his career in the early 1950s when he opened shows for Sam Cooke, BIG JOE TURNER, RAY CHARLES, and other blues and R&B acts. He also worked with Chuck Willis up until Chuck's death in 1958 and then began a long tenure as a chitlin' circuit performer. Although his recording debut was with the Ebb label in the 1950s, Willis didn't begin recording in earnest until he signed with Ichiban in 1989. Other Willis releases on the label include *Footprints in My Bed, Back to the Blues,* and *Holdin' Hands with the Blues.* Willis continues to tour regularly.

Essential Listening:
Now/Ichiban (ICH 1029)
Footprints in My Bed/Ichiban (ICH 1054)
Back to the Blues/Ichiban (ICH 1106)
Holdin' Hands with the Blues/Ichiban (ICH 1134)

◄ WILLIS, CHUCK

(born January 31, 1928, Atlanta, Ga.; died April 28, 1958, Atlanta, Ga.)

In 1957, R&B singer Chuck Willis had a number 1 R&B hit with his version of the blues standard "C.C. Rider." The record also crossed over onto the pop charts, peaking at number 12. Because of its stuttering Latin tempo, "C.C. Rider" helped popularize a dance called the Stroll that was built around a similar rhythm. Willis then began calling himself King of the Stroll and even the Sheik of the Stroll (Willis wore a turban onstage).

Willis began his recording career with Columbia/Okeh Records in 1951; during the five years he was with Okeh, he placed five releases on the R&B charts, including "My Story," which made it to number 2 in 1952. In 1956 Willis jumped to the Atlantic label. The success he enjoyed with "C.C. Rider" made him a major R&B attraction; however, a year after its release, Willis, age thirty, was killed in an auto crash. A posthumously released single, "What Am I Living For?" (with the Willis-penned "Hang Up My Rock and Roll Shoes" on the B-side), went to number 1 on the R&B charts and number 9 on the pop charts. Willis was the first cousin of Atlanta blues singer-guitarist CHICK WILLIS, with whom he often toured.

Essential Listening:
Be Good or Be Gone/Edsel (ED 159)

◄ WILSON, EDITH

(born Edith Goodall, September 2, 1896, Louisville, Ky.; died March 30, 1981, Chicago, Ill.)

Like many other female singers in the 1920s, Edith Wilson incorporated blues songs into a repertoire that was built mainly from cabaret and show tunes. Though she lacked the emotional depth that artists such as BESSIE SMITH and IDA COX brought to the classic blues form, Wilson helped introduce the blues to white audiences, both in the U.S. and Europe. The exposure she and other blues-flavored cabaret performers like her gave the music in nonblack markets enabled the genre to assume a stronger posture in pre–World War II pop music.

Edith Goodall was born in 1896 into a middle-class black family in Louisville, Kentucky. After deciding on a career in show business and marrying pianist Danny Wilson, she performed in Chicago, Washington, D.C., and New York before accepting a recording contract from Columbia Records in 1921. Backed by Johnny Dunn and the Original Jazz Hounds, Wilson cut "Nervous Blues," "Vampin' Liza Jane" and other songs, most of which were composed or arranged by PERRY BRADFORD. Rather than focus on recording, Wilson shifted her attention to performing, as comedy and histrionics increasingly became an integral part of her routine. By starring in such shows as *The Plantation Revue, Creole Follies*, and *Hot Chocolates*, Wilson cultivated a large following with white and upscale black audiences.

Although her relationship with Columbia Records ended in the mid-'20s, Wilson did cut a few more songs with different labels before effectively concluding her recording career in 1930. Throughout the '30s and '40s, she continued to perform in theaters and cabarets with big bands and revues and even appeared in a few films. Her most noted performing roles were on radio; Wilson played the part of Kingfish's mother-in-law on the "Amos and Andy" show, and shortly thereafter became the voice of Aunt Jemima for the Quaker Oats Company.

Wilson performed up until 1963 when she retired from the stage. However, a 1972 recording with Eubie Blake sparked a comeback that led to frequent folk and blues festival dates and an album for the Delmark label in 1976. One of her last noted performances was at the 1980 Newport Jazz Festival. She died a year later.

Essential Listening:
Edith Wilson, 1921–1922 with Johnny Dunn's Jazz Hounds/Fountain (FB 302)
He May Be Your Man/Delmark (637)

◄ WILSON, HOP

(born Harding Wilson, April 27, 1921, Grapeland, Tex.; died August 27, 1975, Houston, Tex.)

Hop Wilson played the electric Hawaiian steel slide guitar, giving his brand of blues an unusual countrified sound. Wilson influenced other Texas Hawaiian steel slide guitarists, namely L.C. "Good Rockin' " ROBINSON and SONNY RHODES, though his popularity as a recording artist and performer never went much beyond Houston, his hometown.

Influenced by BLIND LEMON JEFFERSON, Wilson learned how to play guitar and harmonica as a youth. In 1939 he got his first steel guitar and began working in Houston clubs and juke joints before serving in the army during World War II. Upon being discharged, he began in earnest his career as a blues artist, often performing with drummer Ivory Semien's band in the mid- and late 1950s. Around 1957 Wilson and Semien began recording for Goldband. When Semien began his own Ivory label in 1960, Wilson began recording for it. Wilson's final recordings were made in 1961, after which time he worked in and around Houston until his death in 1975.

Essential Listening:
Houston Ghetto Blues/P-Vine (1607)
Blues with Friends/Goldband (7781)

◄ WILSON, JIMMY

(born 1923, Houston, Tex.; died 1965, Dallas, Tex.)

Singer Jimmy Wilson is best known for his only hit, "Tin Pan Alley," a record that made it to number 10 on the R&B charts in 1953 and helped Bay Area producer, arranger, and record company owner BOB GEDDINS become established as a major West Coast blues figure. Geddins went on to record such artists as LOWELL FULSON, JIMMY MCCRACKLIN, RAY AGEE, JOHNNY FULLER, JUKE BOY BONNER, and MERCY DEE WALTON.

Wilson was born in Houston, where he was raised on gospel music. Intent on finding better recording and performing opportunities, he moved to the West Coast in 1947. His vocal style was ideally suited for slow, aching blues ballads in which he could best employ his gospel roots. After Wilson scored with "Tin Pan Alley," he released a few more singles but never again placed one in the charts, despite having one of the top voices in R&B and postwar blues. Wilson eventually returned to Texas; he died in Dallas in 1965.

Essential Listening:
Trouble in My House/Diving Duck (4305)

◄ WINTER, JOHNNY

(born February 23, 1944, Beaumont, Tex.)

In 1968 Johnny Winter, a young white blues guitarist and singer, at the time little known outside his home state of Texas, was suddenly hailed as America's answer to British blues-rock guitar giants ERIC CLAPTON, Jeff Beck, and Jimmy Page. Winter's self-titled debut album, released in 1969, contained powerful and authentic interpretations of Mississippi Delta and Chicago-style blues and cameos from WILLIE DIXON and BIG WALTER HORTON. The album helped introduce traditional blues forms to white hard rock audiences.

Because of his popularity with rock listeners, Winter soon abandoned his deep blues approach for one more steeped in blues-rock, and then moved on to hard rock. It wasn't until 1977 that Winter returned full-time to the blues. Since then, he's recorded a number of albums for a variety of labels, nearly all of which are guitar-drenched studies of the ongoing relationship between blues and rock.

Johnny Winter and his brother Edgar, both albinos, were brought up in Beaumont, Texas, a city known for its rich music scene. As a child, Johnny learned the rudiments of the ukulele before teaching himself guitar at age eleven. Around the same time, he began listening to swamp-blues artist CLARENCE GARLOW's local radio show, which inspired Winter to play the blues. At fourteen he fronted his own band, Johnny and the Jammers, which included Edgar on piano. The group cut a couple of records that were popular locally.

The Winter brothers continued to play in and around Beaumont until Johnny went to Chicago in 1963 in an attempt to work his way into the competitive blues scene there. Although he was unsuccessful and eventually went back to Texas, Winter met and played with other up-and-coming white blues players, namely guitarist MIKE BLOOMFIELD, who would become a guiding force in the PAUL BUTTERFIELD Blues Band and the ELECTRIC FLAG.

Upon returning to Texas, Winter put together a new band and played clubs throughout the South, performing not only blues but also top 40 and rock. In 1968, disgruntled with the way his career was going, Winter stripped away his pop repertoire to concentrate solely on the blues. He also visited England that year with the hopes of finding brighter recording and performing opportunities. While he was abroad, *Rolling Stone* magazine published an article about the Texas music scene that described Winter in glowing terms. The piece so impressed New York rock club owner Steve Paul that he flew to Texas, became Winter's manager, and flew Winter back to New York where he enjoyed a much-acclaimed stint at Paul's hip downtown Manhattan club, the Scene. Winter's success in New York attracted the interest of the major record companies. Columbia Records won a Winter bidding war and gave the guitarist one of the biggest advances in rock at that time, reputedly close to half a million dollars for several albums.

Winter's self-titled major label debut was released in late 1968 and was both a critical and commercial triumph. That summer he performed at many rock festivals, including Woodstock, and cultivated a large rock following. Winter's follow-up, *Second Winter*, contained both blues and rock. He then formed a new band, Johnny Winter And, that consisted of members of the rock group the McCoys, with Rick Derringer on second guitar. The band recorded two popular blues-flavored rock albums in 1971, *Johnny Winter And* and *Johnny Winter And Live*. But Winter's success had a down side. Near-constant touring and the pressures that came with rock stardom led Winter into a serious heroin habit. He temporarily retired in 1972 to kick his addiction and regain his health. He resumed recording in 1973 and released the album *Still Alive and Well* that year. The album showed that Winter had all but given up the blues for rock & roll. Two succeeding hard rock albums—*Saints and Sinners* and *John Dawson Winter III* —were released on Steve Paul's Blue Sky label.

After a lukewarm recording effort with brother Edgar called *Johnny and Edgar Winter: Together* and another live album, *Captured Live*, Winter finally returned to his blues roots. He recorded the album *Nothing but the Blues* with members of MUDDY WATERS's band. Two follow-up Winter albums on Blue Sky, *White, Hot and Blue* (1978) and *Raisin' Cain* (1980), lacked durable material, but work as producer for Muddy Waters won him high marks with blues fans. Winter produced four Muddy Waters albums for Blue Sky; two of them, *Hard Again* and *I'm Ready*, won Grammys and resuscitated Waters's fading career.

Due largely to shrinking interest in blues in the music industry and with mainstream record buyers, Winter went from 1980 to 1983 without a recording contract, though he continued to perform regularly. In 1983, an album called *Whoopin'* that Winter made with blues harp player SONNY TERRY, bassist Willie Dixon, and drummer Styve Homnick was released by Alligator Records and led to a contract with the Chicago-based blues label the following year. Winter's first Alligator release, *Guitar Slinger*, became the label's biggest-selling album up until that time. Follow-up albums *Serious Business* (1985) and *Third Degree* (1986) elaborated on the robust blues and blues-rock heard on *Guitar Slinger*. In 1986, Winter became the first white artist inducted into the Blues Foundation's Hall of Fame.

Winter left Alligator in 1988 and signed with MCA/Voyager. One rather nondescript album, *The Winter of '88*, resulted. In 1991 Winter moved to Point Blank–Charisma and released the albums *Let Me In*, which had a richer blues payload than its predecessor, and *Hey, Where's Your Brother*. Both albums were produced by Dick Shurman. Winter lives in New York City and continues to record and perform.

Essential Listening:

Raw to the Bone/Home Cooking

The Progressive Blues Experiment/CEMA Special Markets (57340-2)

The Johnny Winter Story/P-Vine (PCD 1611)

Johnny Winter/Columbia (CK 9826)

Second Winter/Columbia (CK 9947)

Nothin' but the Blues/Blue Sky (ZK 34813)

White, Hot, and Blue/Blue Sky

Guitar Slinger/Alligator (AL 4735)

Serious Business/Alligator (AL 4742)

Third Degree/Alligator (AL 4748)

Let Me In/Point Blank–Charisma (91744-2)

Scorchin' Blues/Columbia (CK/CT 52466)

Hey, Where's Your Brother/Point Blank–Charisma (86512)

◄ WITHERSPOON, JIMMY

(born August 8, 1923, Gurdon, Ark.)

Vocalist Jimmy Witherspoon came onto the blues scene in the mid-1940s when he replaced WALTER BROWN in JAY MCSHANN's big band. At the time, Witherspoon was a blues shouter, not unlike BIG JOE TURNER, his biggest influence. In the late '50s Witherspoon became more frequently associated with blues-flavored jazz; his rich, robust voice made the transition from blues and R&B to jazz with a deep blue tint a relatively easy process. Since then Witherspoon has blurred the line that exists between the two forms more than any other male vocalist.

Born in Arkansas, Witherspoon grew up on gospel; he began singing in the church choir when he was six years old. By the time he was in his midteens, Witherspoon had left Arkansas for California to search for brighter work opportunities. In 1941 he went into the merchant marine. While on leave in Calcutta, India, Witherspoon sat in with Teddy Weatherford's big band, proving to himself that he had what it took to become a professional blues singer. Upon his discharge from the service and return to California in 1944, Witherspoon was discovered by McShann in a small club. McShann hired him for his band, to take the lead vocal slot recently vacated by Brown. At first Witherspoon merely aped Brown's vocal style. But eventually he came into his own as a blues singer and helped keep McShann's band popular with audiences still hungry for big band blues.

Witherspoon left the McShann band in 1947, eager to start a solo career. In 1949, he cut a version of the old classic blues nugget ''Ain't Nobody's Business,'' originally recorded by BESSIE SMITH in 1922. Witherspoon's version, which featured a McShann-led backing band, came out on the Supreme label and made it all the way to the number 1 position on the R&B charts. The song remained on the charts an incredible thirty-four weeks, longer than any other previous R&B or blues record. Witherspoon's follow-up record, a rendition of the LEROY CARR tune "In the Evening When the Sun Goes Down," made it to number 5 on the charts that same year.

Witherspoon also recorded for Modern and other labels in the early '50s. But as the decade wore on and rock & roll had begun to make an impact on pop music, Witherspoon's popularity began to wane. Unable to make the transition into rock & roll, Witherspoon moved toward the jazzier side of blues. In 1959 he performed at the Monterey Jazz Festival. His acclaimed set there helped him revive his sagging career. For the next twenty-odd years Witherspoon recorded and performed with such jazz greats as Ben Webster, Coleman Hawkins, Roy Eldridge, Harry "Sweets" Edison, and Earl Hines, though Witherspoon was never able to recapture the kind of chart success he had in the late '40s.

In 1974 Witherspoon appeared in the film *The Black Godfather* and recorded for Capitol Records. A single, "Love Is a Five Letter Word," marked his return to the R&B charts, but the song peaked only at number 31, and Witherspoon was unable to sustain any serious comeback attempt, at least in terms of record sales. Through the remainder of the 1970s he performed occasionally at jazz festivals and played jazz venues in the U.S. and Europe.

Witherspoon was diagnosed with throat cancer in the early 1980s. Radiation treatments stifled the disease, and Witherspoon was able to resume his career, though his voice had lost some of its range and dynamics. Witherspoon continues to perform.

Essential Listening:
Hey Mr. Landlord, Jimmy Witherspoon with Jay McShann/Route 66 (KIX 31)
Goin' to Kansas City Blues, Jimmy Witherspoon with the Jay McShann Band/ RCA (An1-1-1048)
The 'Spoon Concerts/Fantasy (24701)
Baby, Baby, Baby/Original Blues Classics (527)
Evenin' Blues/Original Blues Classics (511)
Rockin' L.A./Fantasy (9660)
The Chess Years/MCA-Chess (CH 93003)
The Blues, the Whole Blues, and Nothing but the Blues/Indigo (IG 2001)

◄ WOODS, MITCH

(born April 3, 1951, Brooklyn, N.Y.)

Mitch Woods is a contemporary jump-blues pianist whose influences include LOUIS JORDAN, AMOS MILBURN, and ROY MILTON. Along with his band, the Rocket 88s, Woods carries on the vintage spunk and spirit of the best R&B bands of the late 1940s and early 1950s.

Woods moved from New York, where he had studied classical music and jazz, to San Francisco in 1970. He played Bay Area club dates as a solo artist and in a variety of groups until 1980 when he formed the Rocket 88s. Four years later, in 1984, Woods and his band recorded their debut album, *Steady Date*, for the Blind Pig label. Performances at numerous U.S. blues festivals and a tour of Europe in 1987 gave Woods and his band increased exposure. In 1988, Woods released his second Blind Pig album, *Mr. Boogie's Back in Town*, and followed it with regular touring in the U.S., Canada, and Europe. His third album, *Solid Gold Cadillac*, also on Blind Pig, came out in 1991 and featured cameo appearances by harp player CHARLIE MUSSELWHITE, guitarist RONNIE EARL, and the ROOMFUL OF BLUES horn section. Still based in the Bay Area, Woods continues to record and perform.

Essential Listening:
Steady Date/Blind Pig (BP 1784)
Mr. Boogie's Back in Town/Blind Pig (BP 2888)
Solid Gold Cadillac/Blind Pig (BP 74191)

◄ WOODS, OSCAR "BUDDY"

(aka the Lone Wolf) (born c. 1900, Shreveport, La.; died 1956, Shreveport, La.)

Slide guitarist and singer Oscar "Buddy" Woods was an important member of the early Shreveport, Louisiana, blues scene. It is believed that he was born around the turn of the century in Shreveport and that he worked private parties and social functions there in the 1920s. He first recorded with Ed Schaffer's Shreveport Home Wreckers in Memphis in 1930 on the Victor label. Two years later he recorded with the blues-influenced country singer Jimmie Davis (who later became governor of Louisiana) and again with Schaffer, this time billed as Eddie & Oscar. Both sessions were done for Victor.

Sometime in the mid-1930s Woods returned to the Shreveport area and resumed playing house parties and juke joints. He recorded sides with Decca and some other labels in the late 1930s with his combo the Wampus Cats. After doing a 1940 recording session for JOHN LOMAX and the Library of Congress, Woods faded from the blues scene. He reportedly died in Shreveport in 1956.

Essential Listening:
Complete Recordings, 1930–1938/Document (DLP 517)

◄ WRIGHT, BILLY

(born May 21, 1932, Atlanta, Ga.; died October 27, 1991, Atlanta, Ga.)

Billy Wright was a rhythm & blues singer whose outrageous stage costumes and effeminate facial makeup, along with his gospel-rooted shout-style vocals, were major influences on LITTLE RICHARD. Wright grew up on gospel, but by the time he was in his midteens, he was dancing in road shows. By the late 1940s he was also singing R&B, opening shows in Atlanta for many of the music's major acts, including WYNONIE HARRIS and PAUL "HUCKLEBUCK" WILLIAMS.

It was Williams who helped Wright secure a recording contract with Savoy Records in 1949. That year Wright recorded "Blues for My Baby," which made it to number 5 on the *Billboard* R&B charts. The song's success enabled Wright to tour the East Coast and South and play such venues as the Apollo Theater in New York. Wright's next single, "You Satisfy," also released in 1949, went to number 9 on the charts. He had two other hits in 1951—"Stacked Deck" (number 9) and "Hey Little Girl" (number 10)—before falling off the charts.

In the mid-'50s Wright recorded for Peacock Records, but unlike Little Richard, who had assumed much of his look and stage style, Wright was unable to cross over into rock & roll. Wright spent the rest of his career playing and working as an emcee in Atlanta clubs. He died in 1991.

Essential Listening:
The Prince of the Blues/Route 66 (KIX 13)
Going Down Slow/Savoy Jazz (SJL 1146)
Hey Baby, Don't You Want a Man Like Me?/Ace (CHA 193)

◄ WRIGHT, MARVA

(born March 20, 1948, New Orleans, La.)

New Orleans born and bred, blues vocalist Marva Wright began her career as a gospel singer, first with the St. John Baptist Youth Choir and then with such gospel outfits as the Geraldine Wright Christian Four Gospel Singers and Samuel Perfect & the Dimensions of Faith. Wright switched from gospel to rhythm & blues and jazz in 1986 before finally embracing the blues a year or so later. Working with a New Orleans bar band called Blues with a Feeling in the city's blues clubs, Wright established herself as a KOKO TAYLOR–influenced blues belter and often got session work backing up artists such as Joe Cocker, ALLEN TOUSSAINT, and the Neville Brothers.

In the late 1980s Wright began performing in Europe, often with other New Orleans blues and R&B artists such as WALTER "WOLFMAN" WASHINGTON and JOHNNY ADAMS. Wright's first album, *Heartbreakin' Woman*, was released on the Tipitina's label in 1990. It was awarded blues album of the year by the Louisiana Music Critics' Association. Wright is a regular performer in New Orleans clubs.

Essential Listening:
Heartbreakin' Woman/Tipitina's (1402)

◄ WRIGHT, O.V.

(born October 9, 1939, Leno, Tenn.; died November 16, 1980, Mobile, Ala.)

One of the great soul-blues singers, O.V. Wright was popular with black record buyers as a result of years of one-night stands on the chitlin' circuit. Wright built his vocal style from a strong gospel base and added to it strains of Memphis blues and charcoal soul tones. Although he never managed to cross over into more lucrative pop and mainstream blues territories, Wright exerted much influence on the vocal styles of ROBERT CRAY and other contemporary bluesmen.

Wright began his career as a Memphis gospel singer in the mid-1950s, working with such groups as the Sunset Travelers, the Spirit of Memphis Quartet, and the Highway QCs before launching a solo career and making the jump to soul-blues. Wright recorded "That's How Strong My Love Is" for the Goldwax label in 1964 (a song Otis Redding had a hit with shortly thereafter), before signing with Back Beat, a subsidiary of DON ROBEY's Duke-Peacock labels, the following year. It was with Back Beat that Wright had his biggest chart success. In 1965 "You're Gonna Make Me Cry" went to number 6 on the R&B charts, while "Eight Men,

Four Women'' peaked at number 4 in 1967. ''Ace of Spades'' made it to number 11 in 1970.

Wright continued to record for Back Beat into the early '70s, after which he moved to ABC Records for a brief spell following the sale of Duke-Peacock to ABC, and then onto the Hi label in 1976. A 1979 tour of Japan and the recording of a live album there seemed to open the door to greater success, but a year later Wright died suddenly of a heart attack. He was just forty-one years old.

Essential Listening:

Gone for Good/Charly (1050)

The Soul of O.V. Wright/MCA-Duke-Peacock (MCAD-10670)

Y ▶

◀ Yancey, Estelle "Mama"

(born January 1, 1896, Cairo, Ill.; died April 19, 1986, Chicago, Ill.)

Estelle "Mama" Yancey was the wife of blues pianist "Papa" JIMMY YANCEY. A blues vocalist, she often sang with her husband at informal get-togethers and house parties in the 1930s and 1940s and performed with him at Carnegie Hall in New York City in 1948. After her husband's death in 1951, Yancey occasionally recorded and performed with other pianists.

As a youth Yancey sang in church choirs and learned how to play the guitar. She married Jimmy Yancey in 1917. In addition to singing with her husband, Yancey also composed with him. In 1943 the Yanceys recorded for the Session label; they went back into the recording studio in 1951 to record the album *Pure Blues* for Atlantic Records. The session occurred just a few months before Jimmy Yancey's death that same year.

Yancey remained active in Chicago music circles up until the early 1980s. In 1961 she teamed up with pianist LITTLE BROTHER MONTGOMERY to record the album *South Side Blues* for the Riverside label, and in 1965 she recorded for Verve with pianist Art Hodes. Her final recording occurred in 1983 when she was 87 years old. She made the album *Maybe I'll Cry* with Chicago pianist ERWIN HELFER for the Red Beans label. Yancey died in 1986.

Essential Listening:
Jimmy & Mama Yancey: Chicago Piano, Vol. 1/Atlantic (7 82368-2)
South Side Blues/Riverside (RLP 9403)
Maybe I'll Cry/Red Beans (001)

◀ Yancey, Jimmy

(aka "Papa" Jimmy Yancey) (born February 20, 1898, Chicago, Ill.; died September 17, 1951, Chicago, Ill.)

Jimmy Yancey was a pioneering Chicago boogie-woogie pianist whose distinctive keyboard style was based on repeating bass figures—a staple of the boogie-woogie piano form—and often included stuttering, Latin-inspired bass riffs and restrained tempos that were frequently a notch or two below the quick pace of popular late-1930s players like MEADE "LUX" LEWIS, ALBERT AMMONS, and PETE JOHNSON. Despite limited club work and no recordings during the 1920s and nearly all of the 1930s, Yancey was nonetheless a highly influential figure in Chicago blues and jazz circles, regularly performing on the city's house-rent party circuit. He remained a popular draw at such gatherings until his death in 1951.

Yancey was born into a musical family in 1898. His father was a vaudeville entertainer, and his brother Alonzo was a ragtime pianist. Yancey began his career in entertainment as a young boy when he toured with his father as a tap dancer and singer. Before Yancey had turned sixteen, he had already crisscrossed America and Europe and had even performed for British royalty at Buckingham Palace. In 1915, with World War I underway and Vaudeville in steady decline, Yancey returned to Chicago, learned the rudiments of piano from his brother, and began playing parties and occasional clubs. Despite his success as a house party pianist, Yancey didn't make music his main occupation. He was also a groundskeeper at Comisky Park, home of the Chicago White Sox, a job he held for twenty-five years. Yancey is also said to have played semipro baseball with the Chicago All-Americans.

Yancey began his recording career in 1939 at the height of the boogie-woogie craze, though he had already been playing for two decades. His first recordings were done for the Solo Art label. He did other sessions in the 1940s and early 1950s for the Victor, Vocalion, Session, Paramount, and Atlantic labels. Piano pieces such as "Yancey Stomp," "State Street Special," and "35th and Dearborn" were Yancey's signature songs. In addition to solo recordings, he also cut sides with his wife, ESTELLE "MAMA" YANCEY, and fellow boogie-woogie pianist CRIPPLE CLARENCE LOFTON. In 1948 he and his wife performed at Carnegie Hall in New York. Three years later Yancey died of a diabetes-induced stroke in his Chicago home.

Yancey was inducted into the Rock & Roll Hall of Fame in 1986, acknowledging the importance his brand of boogie-woogie played in the birth of the music in the early 1950s.

Essential Listening:
Jimmy Yancey, Volume 1 (1939–40)/Document (DOCD 5041)
Jimmy Yancey, Volume 2 (1940–1943)/Document (DOCD 5042)
Jimmy Yancey, Volume 3 (1943–1950)/Document (DOCD 5043)
Jimmy and Mama Yancey: Chicago Piano, Vol. 1/Atlantic (82368)

◄ YARDBIRDS, THE

In the group's original early-'60s form, the Yardbirds was one of England's most compelling blues bands. By 1965 the group had shifted its focus away from straight blues and moved into progressive psychedelic rock, complete with unusual melodic structures, Indian raga influences, and inventive guitar work and guitar sounds. At their best, the Yardbirds led the way in the transition from imitative British blues to innovative British blues-rock in the mid-'60s. They also laid the foundation for what later would become blues-based heavy metal.

The Yardbirds' original members were Keith Relf, harmonica and vocals; Jim McCarty, drums; Paul Samwell-Smith, bass; Chris Dreja, rhythm guitar; and Anthony "Top" Topham, lead guitar. However, it was the band's post-Topham lead guitar lineup that gave the Yardbirds their biggest claim to fame. During the five years that the band existed, the Yardbirds featured England's three greatest blues-based rock guitarists: ERIC CLAPTON, Jeff Beck, and Jimmy Page.

In 1963, as the British blues boom was set to peak, Topham, Dreja, and McCarty joined forces with Relf and Samwell-Smith of the Metropolis Blues Quartet to form the Yardbirds. Shortly thereafter, original lead guitarist Topham chose art school over the band; he was replaced by Eric Clapton, who'd formerly played with the Roosters. Clapton increased the group's credibility, since his blues guitar chops, even back then, were impressive. As a result, the Yardbirds became protégés of the ROLLING STONES, at the time London's most popular blues and R&B band. The Yardbirds eventually succeeded the Stones as the top attraction at the Crawdaddy Club in London.

In 1964 the Yardbirds signed a recording contract with EMI's Columbia label. The band's first single was a remake of BILLY BOY ARNOLD's "I Wish You Would," issued that same year, followed by "Good Morning Little School Girl." That same year the Yardbirds released their debut British album, *Five Live Yardbirds*, recorded at the Marquee, another popular London club, and toured Europe with SONNY BOY WILLIAMSON (Rice Miller). A second live album, *Sonny Boy Williamson and the Yardbirds*, was released on the Fontana label in 1966.

Despite their original blues intentions, the Yardbirds, under the guidance of manager Giorgio Gomelsky, began to drift into rock and pop territories. In 1965, "For Your Love," a song penned by Graham Gouldman, later of the rock group 10cc, was recorded by the Yardbirds and made it into the top 10 in both England and the U.S., where their records were released on the Epic label. The group's commercial success and increasing interest in rock sounds prompted Clapton, a blues purist, to quit the Yardbirds in early 1965 and join JOHN MAYALL'S BLUES-BREAKERS. Clapton was replaced by Jeff Beck, formerly of the Tridents.

With Beck on lead guitar, the Yardbirds began their most musically adventurous period, and their blues roots were less prominent. Beck experimented with distortion and feedback and created wildly innovative guitar sounds in songs such as "Heart Full of Soul," "Shapes of Things," and "Over Under Sideways Down." Bassist Samwell-Smith played a key role in realizing these sounds in his role as the band's producer, a function that he performed on all of the Yardbirds' records until his exit from the group in the summer of 1966.

Despite the Yardbirds' critical acclaim, Beck's tenure with the band was short-lived. Illness and an inability to withstand the rigors of touring forced him to quit the group in late 1966, at which time Jimmy Page, who had joined the Yardbirds earlier that year, replacing Samwell-Smith on bass, switched to lead guitar. Page was replaced on bass by Chris Dreja. The Yardbirds stayed together another eighteen months or so, but the group's most fertile period was undoubtedly behind. When the group broke up in 1968 after an uneven string of singles, a disppointing album (*Little Games*), and a U.S. tour, Page formed the New Yardbirds. He asked Dreja to play bass in the band, but Dreja rejected the offer and began a career as a photographer. Page then brought in bass player John Paul Jones, drummer John Bonham, and singer Robert Plant and renamed the group

LED ZEPPELIN, which went on to become one of the most innovative blues-rock bands of the late '60s and the most popular heavy metal band of the '70s. The Yardbirds were inducted into the Rock & Roll Hall of Fame in 1992.

Essential Listening:

Five Live Yardbirds/Rhino (R2-70189)

The Yardbirds, Vol. 1: Smokestack Lightning (two-disc set)/CBS (A2K 48655)

The Yardbirds, Vol. 2: Blues, Backtracks, and Shapes of Things (two-disc set)/ CBS (A2K 48658)

Sonny Boy Williamson & the Yardbirds/Optimism Inc. (LR CD 2020)

◄ YOUNG, JOHNNY

(born January 1, 1918, Vicksburg, Miss.; died April 18, 1974, Chicago, Ill.)

A singer, guitarist, and mandolin player, Johnny Young was a regular member of the Chicago blues scene from the time of his arrival in the city in 1940 to his death there in 1974. Young never achieved the popularity enjoyed by many of the bluesmen with whom he performed. But his engaging mandolin and guitar work, along with his rugged vocals, made up a small but interesting part of the overall postwar Chicago blues sound.

A Mississippi native, Young was born in Vicksburg but raised in Rolling Fork. An uncle taught him the basics of the guitar and mandolin, and Young began working parties and dances as a teen. Like many other Delta bluesmen eager to improve their lot, Young migrated to Chicago, where he fell in with cousin Johnny Williams, plus MUDDY WATERS, HOWLIN' WOLF, and other transplanted blues artists, playing for tips along Chicago's Maxwell Street. Young recorded with Williams in 1947 for the Ora-Nelle label.

But Young worked in clubs and on street corners far more often than he did in recording studios. Throughout the 1950s Young was a regular performer in Chicago clubs. He resumed his recording career with Testament in 1963 and cut albums for the Arhoolie label in 1965 and 1967, using some of the best of Chicago's blues talent to accompany him—pianist OTIS SPANN and harp players JAMES COTTON and BIG WALTER HORTON, among others.

The release of albums such as *Johnny Young and His Chicago Blues Band* (Arhoolie) gave Young increased exposure outside Chicago blues circles, which led to appearances at blues festivals and concerts on college campuses. In 1969 Young began performing regularly with the Bob Riedy Chicago Blues Band. He also recorded for a variety of labels in the late '60s and early '70s, including Milestone, Vanguard, Blue Horizon, and Storyville. Young died of a heart attack in 1974.

Essential Listening:

Chicago Blues/Arhoolie (CD 325)

◄ YOUNG, MIGHTY JOE

(born Joseph Young, September 23, 1927, Shreveport, La.)

A journeyman guitarist who has performed in the bands of HOWLIN' WOLF, OTIS RUSH, JIMMY ROGERS, BILLY BOY ARNOLD, and numerous other blues artists, Mighty Joe Young also fronted his own bands and was a part of the Chicago club scene well into the 1980s. Although Young never became a major blues figure, his contributions to the blues as a sideman and a session player have made him a much-respected accompanist. Young ranks with fellow Chicago guitarist JIMMY DAWKINS as a purveyor of the West Side guitar style forged by the likes of Rush and MAGIC SAM in the late '50s and '60s.

Young was born in Louisiana but began his blues career in Milwaukee in the early 1950s. He moved to Chicago in 1956 and worked his way into the city's competitive club scene, often playing with Howlin' Wolf's band and harmonica player Billy Boy Arnold. When Jimmy Rogers left Muddy Waters to form his own band around 1958, he selected Young as the group's second guitarist. Young continued to perform regularly in Chicago clubs and occasionally tour throughout the '60s, '70s, and early '80s. He also recorded for labels such as Delmark, Ovation, and Sonet as a solo artist and backed up artists like Magic Sam, Dawkins, FENTON ROBINSON, and ALBERT KING in the recording studio. His group, Blues with a Touch of Soul, occasionally played behind KOKO TAYLOR. In 1986 Young had surgery for a pinched nerve in his neck. Complications from the operation forced him to take a two-year break from performing. By 1988, however, he resumed club work, performing primarily as a singer, since he has lost much of the feeling in his fingers.

Essential Listening:
Blues with a Touch of Soul/Delmark (629)
Bluesy Josephine/Black and Blue (59.521 2)
Legacy of the Blues, Vol. 4/GNP Crescendo (10014)

◄ YOUNG, ZORA

(born January 21, 1948, Prairie, Miss.)

A Chicago-based blues singer and songwriter, Zora Young incorporates everything from gospel and traditional blues to soul and rhythm & blues into her BIG MAYBELLE–esque vocal style.

Young was born and raised in Mississippi, where her stepfather was a preacher. As a youth, she sang gospel in church as well as on a local radio station, WROB, out of West Point, Mississippi. Young moved with her family in the mid-'50s to Chicago, where she continued to sing gospel. In 1971 Young began singing the blues; she often worked clubs on the Southern chitlin' circuit. Ten years later Young embarked on her first tour of Europe, where, in the '80s, she cultivated a strong club following. In the mid-'80s Young played the part of BESSIE SMITH in the stage tribute to the blues called *The Heart of the Blues*. She toured the U.S., Canada, and Japan with the troupe, which also included fellow Chicago blueswomen VALERIE WELLINGTON and Katherine Davis.

Young recorded her first album, *Stumbling Blocks and Stepping Stones*, on her own Black Lightning label in 1988. Her follow-up album, *Travelin' Light*, was recorded in 1991 with members of the LEGENDARY BLUES BAND. Young continues to perform regularly.

Essential Listening:

Stumbling Blocks and Stepping Stones/Black Lightning (007)
Travelin' Light/Deluge (Del 3003)

Z ▶

◀ ZZ TOP

Original members: Billy Gibbons (guitar); Dusty Hill (bass); Frank Beard (drums)

ZZ Top is very much a rock band in the way the group employs elaborate stage gimmicks and choreography to bolster its slick, MTV-directed image in concert and on video. But the trio—guitarist Billy Gibbons, bass player Dusty Hill, and drummer Frank Beard—often pays tribute to the blues, although buried under condensed layers of sound. Few rock bands play better boogie blues than ZZ Top, as the group invokes the drama and spirit of JOHN LEE HOOKER and other Mississippi Delta bluesmen in signature songs such as "Bluejean Blues," "LaGrange," "I'm Bad, I'm Nationwide," and "Tubesteak Boogie."

ZZ Top began in Texas in late 1969 when Gibbons, a member of the Moving Sidewalks, teamed up with Beard and Hill, formerly of an acid-rock soul band, the American Blues. Committed blues fans, the trio selected the name ZZ Top because it sounded something akin to B.B. KING. The group's first few albums were released on the London label and featured grinding blues and Texas power rock. Of them, *ZZ Top's First Album*, which was released in 1970, was the one that contained the group's most direct blues. But it was the 1975 album *Fandango*, with its hit song "Tush," that best exemplified how Top had built a Texas rock sound with a blues foundation.

ZZ Top found the most success, though, as a live act. Near-constant touring throughout the early and mid-'70s generated a large and loyal following. The band's now-legendary World Texas Tour of 1975 to 1976 included Texas livestock, snakes, and cacti as stage props. The band took a much-deserved break from touring in the late '70s. Then in 1979, ZZ Top released *Deguello*, the band's Warner Brothers debut. The 1983 album *Eliminator* elevated ZZ Top to superstar status and charted the course the group would follow for the rest of the decade: hard-driving, heavy-sounding rock with a blues tint, embellished with the now-familiar image of Gibbons, Hill, and Beard as self-styled definers of "cool." The trademark beards that Gibbons and Hill still wear, the ever-present sunglasses and baggy suits, their fascination with cars and Texas, and the detached macho flair of their music have enabled albums such as *Eliminator, Afterburner*, and *Recycler* to become huge sellers. The latter album contained the blues tribute song "My Head's in Mississippi," which sought to reaffirm the band's link with true blues.

Although ZZ Top long ago quit being a blues band in the traditional sense, the group's members have remained staunch supporters of the music. In 1989, when Gibbons, Hill, and Beard were given a piece of wood from the one-room shack that MUDDY WATERS once lived in just outside of Clarksdale, Mississippi, they had a guitar made from it called "The Muddywood," which toured the country and raised money for the Delta Blues Museum in Clarksdale. ZZ Top continues to tour and record and support the blues.

Essential Listening:

ZZ Top's First Album/Warner Bros. (2-3268)

Rio Grande Mud/Warner Bros. (2-3269)

Tres Hombres/Warner Bros. (2-3270)

Fandango!/Warner Bros. (2-3271)

Tejas/Warner Bros. (2-3272)

Greatest Hits/Warner Bros. (9 26846-2)

BIBLIOGRAPHY

Albertson, Chris. *Bessie*. New York: Stein & Day, 1972.

Antone, Susan. *The First Ten Years*. Austin: Antone's, 1985.

———. *Picture the Blues*. Austin: Antone's, 1986.

Baker, Houston A. *Blues, Ideology, and Afro-American Literature*. Chicago: The University of Chicago Press, 1984.

Bane, Michael. *White Boy Singin' the Blues*. New York: Penguin, 1982.

Barlow, William. *Looking Up at Down: The Emergence of Blues Culture*. Philadelphia: Temple University Press, 1989.

Bastin, Bruce. *Crying for the Carolines*. London: Studio Vista, 1971.

———. *Red River Blues: The Blues Tradition in the Southeast*. Urbana: University of Illinois Press, 1986.

Bradford, Perry. *Born with the Blues: His Own Story*. New York: Oak Publications, 1965.

Broven, John. *South to Louisiana: The Music of the Cajun Bayous*. Gretna: Pelican Publishing Co., 1983.

———. *Rhythm & Blues in New Orleans*. 1974. Gretna: Pelican Publishing Co., 1978.

Calt, Stephen, and Gayle Wardlow. *King of the Delta Blues* (The Life and Music of Charlie Patton). Newton, N.J.: Rock Chapel Press, 1988.

Charters, Samuel B. *The Country Blues*. 1959. New York: Da Capo, 1975.

———. *The Bluesmakers*. New York: DaCapo, 1991.

———. *The Legacy of the Blues* (Art and Lives of Twelve Great Bluesmen).

———. *Sweet as Showers of Rain*. New York: Oak Publications, 1973.

———. *The Roots of the Blues* (An African Search). 1981. New York: Da Capo, 1991.

Clarke, Donald, ed. *The Penguin Encyclopedia of Popular Music*. London: Viking, 1989.

Cone, James. *The Spirituals and the Blues: An Interpretation*. New York: Seabury Press, 1972.

Crowther, Bruce, and Mike Pinfold. *The Big Band Years*. New York: Facts on File, 1988.

Dahl, Linda. *Stormy Weather* (The Music and Lives of a Century of Jazzwomen). New York: Limelight Editions, 1989.

Dance, Helen Oakley. *Stormy Monday: The T-Bone Walker Story*. 1987. New York: Da Capo, 1990.

Dance, Stanley. *The World of Count Basie*. New York: Charles Scribner's Sons, 1980.

Dixon, Robert, and John Godrich. *Recording the Blues*. New York: Stein and Day, 1970.

Dixon, Willie (with Don Snowden). *I Am the Blues* (The Willie Dixon Story). New York: Da Capo, 1989.

Epstein, Dana. *Sinful Tunes and Spirituals: Black Folk Music to the Civil War*. Urbana: University of Illinois Press, 1977.

Escott, Colin (with Martin Hawkins). *Good Rockin' Tonight: Sun Records and the Birth of Rock 'n' Roll*. New York: St. Martin's Press, 1991.

Evans, David. *Big Road Blues* (Tradition and Creativity in the Folk Blues). 1982. New York: Da Capo.

————. *Tommy Johnson.* London: Studio Vista, 1971.

Fahey, John. *Charley Patton.* London: Studio Vista, 1970.

Ferris, William. *Blues from the Delta.* New York: Da Capo, 1978.

Finn, Julio. *The Bluesman* (The Musical Heritage of Black Men and Women in the Americas). New York: Interlink, 1992.

Friedwald, Will. *Jazz Singing* (America's Great Voices from Bessie Smith to Bebop and Beyond). New York: Charles Scribner's Sons, 1990.

Garon, Paul. *Blues and the Poetic Spirit.* New York: Da Capo Press, 1978.

————. *The Devil's Son-in-Law: The Story of Peetie Wheatstraw and His Songs.* London: Studio Vista, 1978.

Genovese, Eugene D. *Roll, Jordan, Roll: The World the Slaves Made.* New York: Pantheon Books, 1974.

Gert zur Heide, Karl. *Deep South Piano: The Story of Little Brother Montgomery.* London: Studio Vista, 1970.

Godrich, John, and Robert Dixon. *Blues and Gospel Records 1902–1942.* London: Storyville Publications, 1969.

Govenar, Alan. *The Early History of Rhythm & Blues.* Houston: Rice University Press, 1990.

————. *Meeting the Blues.* Dallas: Taylor Publishing Co., 1988.

Greenberg, Alan. *Love in Vain: the Life and Legend of Robert Johnson.* Garden City, N.Y.: Doubleday, 1983.

Groom, Bob. *The Blues Revival.* London: Studio Vista, 1971.

Guralnick, Peter. *Feel Like Going Home* (Portraits in Blues and Rock 'n' Roll). 1971. New York: First Perennial Library (Harper & Row), 1989.

————. *Lost Highway* (Journeys & Arrivals of American Musicians). Boston: David R. Godine, 1979.

————. *Sweet Soul Music* (Rhythm & Blues and the Southern Dream of Freedom). New York: Harper & Row, 1986.

————. *Nighthawk Blues.* New York: Thunder's Mouth Press, 1988.

————. *The Listener's Guide to the Blues.* New York: Facts on File, 1982.

————. *Searching for Robert Johnson.* New York: E.P. Dutton, 1989.

Hadley, Frank John. *The Grove Press Guide to the Blues on CD.* New York: Grove Press, 1993.

Handy, W.C. *Father of the Blues* (An Autobiography). 1941. New York: Da Capo, 1991.

————, ed. *Blues: An Anthology.* 1972. New York: Da Capo, 1990.

Hannusch, Jeff. *I Hear You Knockin'* (The Sound of New Orleans Rhythm and Blues). Ville Platte: Swallow Publications, 1985.

Harris, Sheldon. *Blues Who's Who.* New York: Da Capo, 1983.

Harrison, Daphne Duval. *Black Pearls: Blues Queens of the 1920s.* New Brunswick, N.J.: Rutgers University Press, 1988.

Herzhaft, Gerard. *Encyclopedia of the Blues.* Fayetteville: University of Arkansas Press, 1992.

Keil, Charles. *Urban Blues.* Chicago: University of Chicago Press, 1966.

Kienzle, Rich. *Great Guitarists* (The Most Influential Players in Blues, Country Music, Jazz and Rock). New York: Facts on File, 1985.

Leadbitter, Mike, ed. *Nothing But the Blues.* London: Hanover Books, 1971.

————. *Delta Country Blues.* Sussex: Blues Unlimited Publications, 1968.

————, and Neil Slaven. *Blues Records 1943–1966.* New York: Oak Publications, 1968.

Leib, Sandra. *Mother of the Blues* (A Study of Ma Rainey). Amherst: University of Massachusetts Press, 1981.

Leman, Nicholas. *The Promised Land* (The Great Black Migration and How It Changed America). New York: Vintage, 1991.

Lydon, Michael. *Boogie Lightning*. New York: Dial Press, 1974.

Lyons, Len, and Don Perlo. *Jazz Portraits* (The Lives and Music of the Jazz Masters). New York: William Morrow, 1989.

Marsh, Dave, and John Swenson. *The New Rolling Stone Record Guide*. New York: Random House/Rolling Stone Press, 1983.

McKee, Margaret, and Fred Chisenhall. *Beale Black and Blue: Life and Music on Black America's Main Street*. Baton Rouge: Louisiana State University Press, 1981.

Merrill, Hugh. *The Blues Route*. New York: William Morrow, 1990.

Miller, Jim, ed. *The Rolling Stone Illustrated History of Rock & Roll*. New York: Random House, 1980.

Mitchell, George. *Blow My Blues Away*. Baton Rouge: Louisiana State University Press, 1971.

Murray, Albert. *Stomping the Blues*. 1976. New York: Vintage, 1982.

Napier, Simon A., ed. *Back Woods Blues*. Sussex: Blues Unlimited Publications, 1968.

Neff, Robert, and Anthony Connor. *Blues*. Boston: David Godine, 1975.

Oakley, Giles. *The Devil's Music: A History of the Blues*. New York: Taplinger, 1977.

Obrecht, Jas, ed. *Blues Guitar* (The Men Who Made the Music). San Francisco: GPI Books, 1990.

Oliver, Paul. *Savannah Syncopators: African Retentions in the Blues*. New York: Stein & Day, 1970.

———. *The Story of the Blues*. Philadelphia. Chilton Book Co., 1969.

———. *The Blues Tradition*. New York: Oak Publications, 1970.

———. *Blues Off the Record: Thirty Years of Blues Commentary*. 1984. New York: Da Capo, 1988.

———. *The Meaning of the Blues*. New York: Collier Books, 1960.

———. *Songsters & Saints* (Vocal Traditions on Race Records). Cambridge: Cambridge University Press, 1984.

———. *Blues Fell This Morning* (Meaning in the Blues). Cambridge: Cambridge University Press, 1990.

———, ed. *The Blackwell Guide to Recorded Blues*. Cambridge: Blackwell Publishers, 1991.

———, Max Harrison and William Bolcom. *The New Grove Gospel, Blues and Jazz*. New York: W.W. Norton, 1986.

Olsson, Bengt. *Memphis Blues and Jug Bands*. London: Studio Vista, 1970.

Oster, Harry. *Living Country Blues*. Detroit: Folklore Associates, 1969.

Palmer, Robert. *Deep Blues* (A Musical and Cultural History of the Mississippi Delta). New York: Penguin, 1981.

Pareles, Jon, and Patricia Romanowski. *The Rolling Stone Encyclopedia of Rock & Roll*. New York: Summit, 1983.

Patoski, Joe Nick, and Bill Crawford. *Stevie Ray Vaughan: Caught in the Crossfire*. Boston: Little, Brown and Company, 1993.

Pearson, Barry Lee. *Sounds So Good to Me*. Philadelphia: University of Pennsylvania Press, 1984.

Pleasants, Henry. *The Great American Popular Singers*. New York: Simon & Schuster, 1974.

Quarles, Benjamin. *The Negro in the Making of America*. 1964. 3rd ed. New York: Collier Books, 1987.

Roberty, Marc. *Slowhand: The Life & Music of Eric Clapton*. New York: Harmony, 1991.

Rooney, James. *Bossmen: Bill Monroe and Muddy Waters*. 1971. Da Capo.

Rowe, Mike. *Chicago Blues* (The City and the Music). 1975. New York: Da Capo, 1981.

Russell, Ros. *Jazz Styles in Kansas City and the Southwest*. Berkeley: University of California Press, 1971.

Russell, Tony. *Blacks, Whites, and Blues*. London: Studio Vista, 1970.

Sackheim, Eric, ed. *The Blues Line: A Collection of Blues Lyrics*. New York: Schirmer Books, 1975.

Santelli, Robert. *Sixties Rock: A Listener's Guide*. Chicago: Contemporary, 1985.

Sawyer, Charles. *The Arrival of B.B. King*. New York: Da Capo.

Schuller, Gunther. *Early Jazz: Its Roots and Musical Development*. New York: Oxford University Press, 1968.

Scott, Frank. *The Down Home Guide to the Blues*. Chicago: a cappella books, 1991.

Shaw, Arnold. *Honkers and Shouters: The Golden Years of Rhythm and Blues*. New York: Macmillan Co., 1978.

————. *The Rockin' '50s* (The Decade That Transformed the Pop Music Scene). New York: Hawthorne Books, 1974.

————. *The World of Soul* (Black America's Contribution to the Pop Music Scene). New York: Cowles Book Co., 1970.

————. *Black Popular Music in America* (The Singers, Songwriters, and Musicians Who Pioneered the Sounds of American Music). New York: Schirmer, 1986.

Sidran, Ben. *Black Talk*. New York: Holt, Rinehart and Winston, 1971.

Silvester, Peter. *A Left Hand Like God* (A History of Boogie-Woogie Piano). New York: Da Capo, 1989.

Simon, George. *The Big Bands*. 1967. Rev. ed. New York: Macmillan Co., 1971.

Southern, Eileen. *The Music of Black Americans*. 1971. 2nd ed. New York: W.W. Norton & Company, 1983.

Stambler, Irwin. *Encyclopedia of Pop, Rock & Soul*. New York: St. Martin's Press, 1974.

Stewart-Baxter, Derrick. *Ma Rainey and the Classic Blues Singers*. New York: Stein and Day, 1970.

Taft, Michael. *Blues Lyric Poetry: A Concordance*. New York: Garland, 1984.

Titon, Jeff. *Early Downhome Blues: A Musical and Cultural Analysis*. Urbana: University of Illinois Press, 1977.

————. *Downhome Blues Lyrics* (An Anthology from the Post–World War II Era). Urbana: University of Illinois Press, 1990.

Tosches, Nick. *Unsung Heroes of Rock 'n' Roll*. New York: Charles Scribner's Sons, 1984.

Waters, Ethel. *To Me It's Wonderful*. New York: Harper & Row, 1979.

————, with Charles Samuels. *His Eye Is on the Sparrow*. Westport, Conn.: Greenwood Press, 1978.

Welding, Pete, and Toby Bryon, eds. *Bluesland* (Portraits of Twelve Major American Blues Masters). New York: Dutton, 1991.

Whitburn, Joel. *Joel Whitburn's Top R&B Singles 1942–1988*. Menomonee Falls, Wisc.: Record Research, 1988.

————. *The Billboard Book of Top 40 Hits, 1955 to Present*. New York: Billboard Publications, 1983.

White, Charles. *The Life and Times of Little Richard* (The Quasar of Rock). New York: Harmony Books, 1984.

Wilson, Charles Reagan, and William Ferris, eds. *Encyclopedia of Southern Culture*. Chapel Hill: University of North Carolina Press, 1989.

INDEX

FOR THE BEST IN PAPERBACKS, LOOK FOR THE 🐧

In every corner of the world, on every subject under the sun, Penguin represents quality and variety—the very best in publishing today.

For complete information about books available from Penguin—including Pelicans, Puffins, Peregrines, and Penguin Classics—and how to order them, write to us at the appropriate address below. Please note that for copyright reasons the selection of books varies from country to country.

In the United Kingdom: For a complete list of books available from Penguin in the U.K., please write to *Dept E.P., Penguin Books Ltd, Harmondsworth, Middlesex, UB7 0DA.*

In the United States: For a complete list of books available from Penguin in the U.S., please write to *Consumer Sales, Penguin USA, P.O. Box 999 — Dept. 17109, Bergenfield, New Jersey 07621-0120.* VISA and MasterCard holders call 1-800-253-6476 to order all Penguin titles.

In Canada: For a complete list of books available from Penguin in Canada, please write to *Penguin Books Canada Ltd, 10 Alcorn Avenue, Suite 300, Toronto, Ontario, Canada M4V 3B2.*

In Australia: For a complete list of books available from Penguin in Australia, please write to the *Marketing Department, Penguin Books Ltd, P.O. Box 257, Ringwood, Victoria 3134.*

In New Zealand: For a complete list of books available from Penguin in New Zealand, please write to the *Marketing Department, Penguin Books (NZ) Ltd, Private Bag, Takapuna, Auckland 9.*

In India: For a complete list of books available from Penguin, please write to *Penguin Overseas Ltd, 706 Eros Apartments, 56 Nehru Place, New Delhi, 110019.*

In Holland: For a complete list of books available from Penguin in Holland, please write to *Penguin Books Nederland B.V., Postbus 195, NL-1380AD Weesp, Netherlands.*

In Germany: For a complete list of books available from Penguin, please write to *Penguin Books Ltd, Friedrichstrasse 10-12, D-6000 Frankfurt Main 1, Federal Republic of Germany.*

In Spain: For a complete list of books available from Penguin in Spain, please write to *Longman, Penguin España, Calle San Nicolas 15, E-28013 Madrid, Spain.*

In Japan: For a complete list of books available from Penguin in Japan, please write to *Longman Penguin Japan Co Ltd, Yamaguchi Building, 2-12-9 Kanda Jimbocho, Chiyoda-Ku, Tokyo 101, Japan.*

FOR THE BEST IN PAPERBACKS, LOOK FOR THE 🐧

In every corner of the world, on every subject under the sun, Penguin represents quality and variety—the very best in publishing today.

For complete information about books available from Penguin—including Pelicans, Puffins, Peregrines, and Penguin Classics—and how to order them, write to us at the appropriate address below. Please note that for copyright reasons the selection of books varies from country to country.

In the United Kingdom: For a complete list of books available from Penguin in the U.K., please write to *Dept E.P., Penguin Books Ltd, Harmondsworth, Middlesex, UB7 0DA.*

In the United States: For a complete list of books available from Penguin in the U.S., please write to *Consumer Sales, Penguin USA, P.O. Box 999—Dept. 17109, Bergenfield, New Jersey 07621-0120.* VISA and MasterCard holders call 1-800-253-6476 to order all Penguin titles

In Canada: For a complete list of books available from Penguin in Canada, please write to *Penguin Books Canada Ltd, 10 Alcorn Avenue, Suite 300, Toronto, Ontario, Canada M4V 3B2.*

In Australia: For a complete list of books available from Penguin in Australia, please write to the *Marketing Department, Penguin Books Ltd, P.O. Box 257, Ringwood, Victoria 3134.*

In New Zealand: For a complete list of books available from Penguin in New Zealand, please write to the *Marketing Department, Penguin Books (NZ) Ltd, Private Bag, Takapuna, Auckland 9.*

In India: For a complete list of books available from Penguin, please write to *Penguin Overseas Ltd, 706 Eros Apartments, 56 Nehru Place, New Delhi. 110019.*

In Holland: For a complete list of books available from Penguin in Holland, please write to *Penguin Books Nederland B.V., Postbus 195, NL-1380AD Weesp, Netherlands.*

In Germany: For a complete list of books available from Penguin, please write to *Penguin Books Ltd, Friedrichstrasse 10-12, D-6000 Frankfurt Main 1, Federal Republic of Germany.*

In Spain: For a complete list of books available from Penguin in Spain, please write to *Longman, Penguin España, Calle San Nicolas 15, E-28013 Madrid, Spain.*

In Japan: For a complete list of books available from Penguin in Japan, please write to *Longman Penguin Japan Co Ltd, Yamaguchi Building, 2-12-9 Kanda Jimbocho, Chiyoda-Ku, Tokyo 101, Japan.*